STATUTORY INTERPRETATION
A PRACTICAL LAWYERING COURSE

Second Edition

■ ■ ■

Hillel Y. Levin
Associate Professor of Law
University of Georgia School of Law

AMERICAN CASEBOOK SERIES®

WEST
ACADEMIC
PUBLISHING

American Casebook Series is a trademark registered in the U.S. Patent and Trademark Office.

© 2014 LEG, Inc. d/b/a West Academic
© 2016 LEG, Inc. d/b/a West Academic
    444 Cedar Street, Suite 700
    St. Paul, MN 55101
    1-877-888-1330

West, West Academic Publishing, and West Academic are trademarks of West Publishing Corporation, used under license.

Printed in the United States of America

ISBN: 978-1-63460-519-9

To my family, who will never read this book;
and to my students, who might.

PREFACE

For several years, there have been clarion calls for changes within the law school classroom. Buzzwords like experiential learning, practical learning, skill building, problem solving, collaborative work, and others have been thrown around with increasing frequency. Many dedicated law school professors have been keenly interested in answering these calls but have not had teaching materials to work with. Some have developed their own materials, much to the benefit of their students. Unfortunately, traditional law school texts have been slow to incorporate such materials. This has left many professors with little guidance concerning how to successfully introduce such materials within the doctrinal classroom framework; and many teachers who have created their own materials have found students to be skeptical of materials from outside the primary text and unsure how they relate to the larger course structure and goals.

The central innovation of this book (I hope) is that it brings practical lawyering skills into the framework of the doctrinal classroom without casting off the many benefits of traditional law school pedagogy. It explains why students are asked to do some things that may be unfamiliar to them from their other law school courses, and it makes explicit the connections between the traditional doctrinal and case-based materials included, the new kinds of materials and exercises that are introduced, and the role of the attorney in the real world. In addition, it gives professors substantial freedom to work with these materials as they see fit.

I have developed these materials over the several years I have taught this course. I never expected that I would turn them into a book. Instead, I assumed that I would continue to incorporate them as supplementary to the traditional casebook I used and loved. However, student response to these supplements has been overwhelmingly positive, and many students and colleagues over the years have encouraged me to take this leap. My only real hope is that future students—mine and others'—might benefit in some way from this endeavor.

In addition to the usual edits, this second edition adds several recent Supreme Court cases, new exercises, and an extended discussion of the Rule Against Absurd Results.

HILLEL Y. LEVIN

March 2016

SUMMARY OF CONTENTS

TABLE OF CONTENTS

TABLE OF CASES

The principal cases are in bold type.

———

STATUTORY INTERPRETATION
A PRACTICAL LAWYERING COURSE

Second Edition

CHAPTER I

INTRODUCTION TO THE COURSE AND MATERIALS

▪ ▪ ▪

A. WHY STATUTORY INTERPRETATION IS CRITICAL AND DIFFICULT

Every attorney, no matter what area of specialization, confronts statutes on a regular basis. Most American state, federal, and local law begins with statutes, and many cases turn on questions of statutory interpretation. Everything from criminal law to environmental law, family law to tax law, corporate law to health care law, and pretty much everything else has been codified in statutes.

Strangely, until this point in your law school career, most of your courses have probably focused on judicial opinions as the primary source of American law and on the common-law approach as the central methodology for lawyers and judges. This coursebook is designed to give you a sophisticated understanding of how to work with statutes and to provide you with the practical lawyering tools and skills necessary to do so in practice.

In some ways, statutes as the source of law make the lawyer's job easier. After all, one reason to pass statutes is that they clarify the law in a way that cannot necessarily be accomplished by developing the law on a case-by-case basis, the way judges typically work.

Unfortunately—or fortunately, if you are trying to make a living as an attorney—statutes are often difficult to parse. There are many reasons for this. Statutes cover very complicated areas of the law and are sometimes written in highly technical language; they relate to each other and other legal sources in complex ways; they may be vague or ambiguous; they may leave certain questions unanswered; and social, technological, or other questions may arise that could never have been anticipated by the legislature that passed the statute. For all of these reasons (and others as well), statutory interpretation is a very challenging skill to master.

The following exercise may help you to understand why statutory interpretation can be difficult.

EXERCISE I.1

Consider the following very straightforward "statute":

"Food is prohibited in the classroom."

This statute seems clear enough. It obviously prohibits you from eating your peanut butter and jelly sandwich in the classroom. But suppose the following questions arise:

- Jessica wishes to know whether she may drink water.
- Damali wants to drink orange juice.
- Silvio wants to drink his yogurt smoothie.
- Turner wants to chew gum.
- Nirej likes to chew tobacco and spit into a small bucket he carries with him at all times.
- Kineisha wants to keep her peanut butter and jelly sandwich tucked away in her backpack to eat in the hall immediately after class.
- Sandra has a medical condition that requires her to eat at periodic intervals during the day, including during class.

How would you analyze these cases under the statute? What sources would you refer to? What is your gut instinct in all of these cases?

Come to class prepared to discuss your instincts and analysis.

B. GOALS OF THIS COURSE

This course is organized around four critical goals related to statutory interpretation:

- to become proficient at reading and understanding statutes;

- to gain a sophisticated understanding of the different theories of statutory interpretation;

- to master the practical tools of statutory interpretation; and

- to learn how to put these skills to use as an attorney.

What follows is a brief discussion of each of these goals.

1. BECOMING PROFICIENT AT READING STATUTES

Because statutes are such a central source of law, you must become proficient at reading them if you are going to succeed as an attorney. In this course, you will read a lot of statutes. In doing so, you will learn how they are organized, how to spot open questions, and how to read different statutory sections and different statutes together to understand the structure and substance of the law.

In addition, you will have an opportunity to edit statutes to improve them and, together with your classmates, to draft a statute. These role-playing exercises should help you to understand the difficulties inherent in writing and enacting statutes and give you additional insight in how to read them once they are written.

2. GAINING A SOPHISTICATED UNDERSTANDING OF THE DIFFERENT THEORIES OF STATUTORY INTERPRETATION

Different judges have different approaches to interpreting and applying statutes, just as they do with respect to interpreting the Constitution and other sources of law. This helps to explain why judges so frequently disagree about the meaning and application of statutory provisions.

A good portion of our semester will focus on the different approaches to resolving disagreements about statutory meaning and application. We will consider the claim to legitimacy of each approach, how each is applied as a practical matter, and how each relates to the other approaches.

To illustrate this, consider again the statute and questions in Exercise I.1. Some interpreters would try to read the statute as literally as possible to answer these questions. Others might focus on the intent of the person(s) who adopted the statute as the starting point for interpreting it. A third group might ask what the basic purpose of the statute is and interpret the statute to further that purpose. Another group might try to figure out how this statute fits in with the broader set of rules applicable to law students and to read the statute in a way that is consistent with that larger scheme. Still others might try to apply common sense to come up with a reading that seems most practical considering the circumstances.

Each of these approaches represents a different framework for resolving statutory questions, and judges adopting each of these approaches may come to different conclusions and have very different views of the appropriate role of the judge. In addition, these approaches lend themselves to different research sources, analytical methodologies, and types of argument.

Which general approach fits your intuition best? Why? How would you answer our questions using these different approaches? Where would you start your research under each approach? Do some of the approaches yield clearer answers than others? Do any of them yield clear answers to all of the questions?

We will explore these approaches in depth. We will consider questions like: What justifies each approach? What are the weaknesses of each approach? How is each approach used in practice by judges? Does a practicing lawyer need to adopt a consistent approach? How can a practicing lawyer make use of her knowledge and understanding of these theories of interpretation?

3.   MASTERING THE PRACTICAL TOOLS OF STATUTORY INTERPRETATION

Beyond the broad theoretical approaches to statutory interpretation, there are many practical tools of interpretation that you will have to master to become a successful lawyer. Some of these tools are referred to as "rules" and others as "canons." Some have complicated Latin names. Others don't really have names at all. But they are all really just types of arguments that lawyers and judges make about statutes.

Much of the course will focus on these tools of statutory interpretation. We will take them one-by-one, thinking about why each one is helpful, how each is used in practice, how to recognize each of them, how each relates to the others and to the theoretical approaches, how to deploy each tool individually and together with the others, and how to argue against each of them.

4. LEARNING HOW TO PUT THESE SKILLS TO USE AS AN ATTORNEY

In addition to being a doctrinal course, this is a practice-oriented and skills-focused class. By the time you leave this course, you should be able to read, understand, and analyze a statute; develop and make arguments and counterarguments about the statute's meaning and application; and draft a brief arguing that a court should adopt a particular reading of the statute. The course will also help you to develop broader practical lawyering skills like negotiation, drafting, advocacy, legal research, problem-solving, professionalism, collaborative lawyering, and developing client-centered strategy.

Students who have used these course materials often report that they make use of the tools of statutory interpretation in other classes, impressing their professors and classmates. Likewise, students frequently report that they use the interpretive and general lawyering skills they learn in this course in summer jobs, internships, clerkships, and other professional settings, impressing their supervisors and colleagues. Thus, this course may be understood as a combination of a traditional doctrinal law school class and a practical skills course.

C. COURSE MATERIALS AND APPROACH

In many ways this coursebook is similar to the casebooks you have used in most other law school courses. You will read a lot of judicial opinions, learn what the legal doctrine is and why, and think about what the law should be.

But unlike in other courses, the goal is not to learn a particular substantive area of the law (like contracts, environmental law, corporate law, and so on), but rather to master a particular skill set: how to interpret and apply statutes. In addition, given the practice-oriented focus of this course, some of the materials in this book may be new and different to you. For example, this book includes:

- Unedited and lightly edited judicial opinions. No one will edit cases for you when you are an attorney. You will have an advantage in practice if you learn how to identify and focus on the relevant and important parts of an opinion. As a consequence, some of the readings may be longer than those to which you are accustomed. But do not be daunted by the length of the cases. Just as when you are in practice you will know why you are reading a particular case, the cases in this book are preceded by a list of issues to focus on in your reading.

- Attorneys' briefs and other documents. Judges write judicial opinions (often with the substantial assistance of their clerks!). But it is quite unlikely that you will become a judge immediately upon graduating law school. More likely, you will be a practicing lawyer. Lawyers write briefs, memos, letters, and other documents. Therefore, it will be helpful for you to be familiar with the kinds of things lawyers produce in practice.

In addition, statutory interpretation and analysis is a fairly structured enterprise. Reading briefs will help you to internalize the typical way that lawyers think about questions of statutory interpretation.

Finally, reading the briefs will let you in on a very important secret: lawyers do much more work than judges. You will see that most judicial opinions crib from the briefs. This gives attorneys a tremendous amount of power. And, as a great philosopher once said, with great power comes great responsibility. In this case, the responsibility is to your client, and by carefully reading and analyzing lawyers' briefs, you will learn how lawyers make strategic choices to serve their clients' interests and to move the law forward.

- Exercises and simulations. These will help to put you in the position of real-life lawyers. Your professor may have you do some of these exercises in groups. This is because lawyering is a collaborative profession; in practice, you will often work with people on your "team"—and often with people on an opposing "team."

- Opportunities to develop arguments and to outline and draft a brief. By the time you finish this course, you should be able to draft a brief arguing a difficult question of statutory interpretation because you will get practice doing just that. Throughout the course, you will be given small problems of statutory interpretation. Most of these are based on real cases. We will spend a good deal of time in class developing arguments and counter-arguments for these cases. As the semester proceeds, you will begin to structure arguments into a coherent outline for a brief and, ultimately, to draft the argument section of a brief.

Many of the things you will do in this class will already be familiar to you from your law school experience, but some things will be different. For some of you, the differences will be a welcome change, but for others, they may take you out of your comfort zone. Whatever the case may be, keep in mind that these materials are designed to help you master the subject and to equip you with a critical skill set. If you approach the readings and assignments with this mindset, you will maximize the benefits that you gain from this course.

CHAPTER II

A CASE STUDY: THE CIVIL RIGHTS ACT OF 1964 AND THE AFFIRMATIVE ACTION QUESTION

■ ■ ■

We begin our study of statutory interpretation with a landmark piece of legislation—the Civil Rights Act of 1964—and a thorny question of statutory interpretation.

A. THE CIVIL RIGHTS ACT OF 1964: BRIEF HISTORY AND RELEVANT LANGUAGE

The Civil Rights Act of 1964 was a momentous piece of legislation. In the wake of President Kennedy's assassination, President Lyndon Johnson, together with key members of the House of Representatives and the Senate, mobilized public support and exerted pressure on Congress to adopt the most robust civil rights legislation yet enacted. Perhaps most controversial and consequential among its many provisions, the proposed Act would prohibit discrimination against Blacks (and ultimately, other groups as well) in the private sector.

The Act was bitterly opposed by many legislators and citizens. Some opponents couched their opposition in explicitly racist terms. Others expressed concerns about Title VII's potential intrusiveness on private businesses and the restrictions it places on business owners' ability to make business-minded decisions.

At times it appeared as though the Act would never pass both the House and the Senate as required to become law. However, through careful procedural maneuvering, and after a series of compromises to ameliorate the concerns of moderate fence-sitters, the Act was finally passed by both Houses of Congress and signed into law by the President. It was a major victory for reformers and civil rights advocates, and its repercussions are still felt today.

Title VII has generated a great deal of litigation. We will focus on the question of whether it prohibits private employers from adopting affirmative action programs. The relevant statutory text follows.

9

THE CIVIL RIGHTS ACT OF 1964

An Act to enforce the constitutional right to vote, to confer jurisdiction upon the district courts of the United States to provide injunctive relief against discrimination in public accommodations, to authorize the Attorney General to institute suits to protect constitutional rights in public facilities and public education, to extend the Commission on Civil Rights, to prevent discrimination in federally assisted programs, to establish a Commission on Equal Employment Opportunity, and for other purposes.

Be it enacted by the Senate and House of Representatives of the United States of America in Congress assembled, [t]hat this Act may be cited as the "Civil Rights Act of 1964."

Definitions

For the purposes of this subchapter—

(a) The term "person" includes one or more individuals, governments, governmental agencies, political subdivisions, labor unions, partnerships, associations, corporations, legal representatives, mutual companies, joint-stock companies, trusts, unincorporated organizations, trustees, trustees in cases under Title 11 [originally, bankruptcy], or receivers.

(b) The term "employer" means a person engaged in an industry affecting commerce who has fifteen or more employees for each working day in each of twenty or more calendar weeks in the current or preceding calendar year, and any agent of such a person. . . .

Unlawful Employment Practices, Section 703

(a) Employer practices

It shall be an unlawful employment practice for an employer—

(1) to fail or refuse to hire or to discharge any individual, or otherwise to discriminate against any individual with respect to his compensation, terms, conditions, or privileges of employment, because of such individual's race, color, religion, sex, or national origin; or

(2) to limit, segregate, or classify his employees or applicants for employment in any way which would deprive or tend to deprive any individual of employment opportunities or otherwise adversely affect his status as an employee, because of such individual's race, color, religion, sex, or national origin.

(b) Employment agency practices

It shall be an unlawful employment practice for an employment agency to fail or refuse to refer for employment, or otherwise to discriminate against, any individual because of his race, color, religion, sex, or national origin, or to classify or refer for employment any individual on the basis of his race, color, religion, sex, or national origin.

(c) Labor organization practices

It shall be an unlawful employment practice for a labor organization—

(1) to exclude or to expel from its membership, or otherwise to discriminate against, any individual because of his race, color, religion, sex, or national origin;

(2) to limit, segregate, or classify its membership or applicants for membership, or to classify or fail or refuse to refer for employment any individual, in any way which would deprive or tend to deprive any individual of employment opportunities, or would limit such employment opportunities or otherwise adversely affect his status as an employee or as an applicant for employment, because of such individual's race, color, religion, sex, or national origin; or

(3) to cause or attempt to cause an employer to discriminate against an individual in violation of this section.

(d) Training programs

It shall be an unlawful employment practice for any employer, labor organization, or joint labor-management committee controlling apprenticeship or other training or retraining, including on-the-job training programs to discriminate against any individual because of his race, color, religion, sex, or national origin in admission to, or employment in, any program established to provide apprenticeship or other training.

(e) Businesses or enterprises with personnel qualified on basis of religion, sex, or national origin; educational institutions with personnel of particular religion

Notwithstanding any other provision of this subchapter, (1) it shall not be an unlawful employment practice for an employer to hire and employ employees, for an employment agency to classify, or refer for employment any individual, for a labor organization to classify its membership or to classify or refer for

employment any individual, or for an employer, labor
organization, or joint labor-management committee controlling
apprenticeship or other training or retraining programs to admit
or employ any individual in any such program, on the basis of
his religion, sex, or national origin in those certain instances
where religion, sex, or national origin is a bona fide occupational
qualification reasonably necessary to the normal operation of
that particular business or enterprise, and (2) it shall not be an
unlawful employment practice for a school, college, university, or
other educational institution or institution of learning to hire
and employ employees of a particular religion if such school,
college, university, or other educational institution or institution
of learning is, in whole or in substantial part, owned, supported,
controlled, or managed by a particular religion or by a particular
religious corporation, association, or society, or if the curriculum
of such school, college, university, or other educational
institution or institution of learning is directed toward the
propagation of a particular religion.

(f) Members of Communist Party or Communist-action or Communistfront organizations

As used in this subchapter, the phrase "unlawful employment
practice" shall not be deemed to include any action or measure
taken by an employer, labor organization, joint labor-
management committee, or employment agency with respect to
an individual who is a member of the Communist Party of the
United States or of any other organization required to register as
a Communistaction or Communistfront organization by final
order of the Subversive Activities Control Board pursuant to the
Subversive Activities Control Act of 1950 [50 U.S.C. §§ 781 et
seq.].

(g) National security

Notwithstanding any other provision of this subchapter, it shall
not be an unlawful employment practice for an employer to fail
or refuse to hire and employ any individual for any position, for
an employer to discharge any individual from any position, or for
an employment agency to fail or refuse to refer any individual for
employment in any position, or for a labor organization to fail or
refuse to refer any individual for employment in any position,
if—

(1) the occupancy of such position, or access to the premises
in or upon which any part of the duties of such position is
performed or is to be performed, is subject to any
requirement imposed in the interest of the national security

of the United States under any security program in effect pursuant to or administered under any statute of the United States or any Executive order of the President; and

(2) such individual has not fulfilled or has ceased to fulfill that requirement.

(h) Seniority or merit system; quantity or quality of production; ability tests; compensation based on sex and authorized by minimum wage provisions

Notwithstanding any other provision of this subchapter, it shall not be an unlawful employment practice for an employer to apply different standards of compensation, or different terms, conditions, or privileges of employment pursuant to a bona fide seniority or merit system, or a system which measures earnings by quantity or quality of production or to employees who work in different locations, provided that such differences are not the result of an intention to discriminate because of race, color, religion, sex, or national origin, nor shall it be an unlawful employment practice for an employer to give and to act upon the results of any professionally developed ability test provided that such test, its administration or action upon the results is not designed, intended or used to discriminate because of race, color, religion, sex or national origin. It shall not be an unlawful employment practice under this subchapter for any employer to differentiate upon the basis of sex in determining the amount of the wages or compensation paid or to be paid to employees of such employer if such differentiation is authorized by the provisions of section 206(d) of Title 29 [section 6(d) of the Labor Standards Act of 1938, as amended].

(i) Businesses or enterprises extending preferential treatment to Indians

Nothing contained in this subchapter shall apply to any business or enterprise on or near an Indian reservation with respect to any publicly announced employment practice of such business or enterprise under which a preferential treatment is given to any individual because he is an Indian living on or near a reservation.

(j) Preferential treatment not to be granted on account of existing number or percentage imbalance

Nothing contained in this subchapter shall be interpreted to require any employer, employment agency, labor organization, or joint labor-management committee subject to this subchapter to grant preferential treatment to any individual or to any group because of the race, color, religion, sex, or national origin of such individual or group on account of an imbalance which may exist with respect to the total number or percentage of persons of any race, color, religion, sex, or national origin employed by any employer, referred or classified for employment by any employment agency or labor organization, admitted to membership or classified by any labor organization, or admitted to, or employed in, any apprenticeship or other training program, in comparison with the total number or percentage of persons of such race, color, religion, sex, or national origin in any community, State, section, or other area, or in the available work force in any community, State, section, or other area.

B. THE ORGANIZATIONAL STRUCTURE OF LEGISLATION

Becoming familiar with the typical organizational structure of statutes will help you to parse them. And, as we will soon see, the structure has implications for interpreting statutes as well. Statutes often begin with a broad statement of purpose, then provide definitions, and then provide the substantive provisions of the law. In the substantive provisions, statutes nearly always begin with the general rule and then identify exceptions, provisos, and caveats.

The Civil Rights Act of 1964 exemplifies this basic structure. It begins with a short declaration of purpose. It then provides definitions for important terms in the Act. Finally, it states the substantive provisions of the Act (in this case, section 703).

Now focus on section 703. It starts with the general rules that the Act adopts. In this case, section 703(a)—(d) provides the general rule that employers, employment agencies, and unions cannot discriminate against people on the basis of their race, color, religion, sex, or national origin.

After the general rule come some specified exceptions. Section 703(e)—(i) specifies particular activities that would *not* constitute unlawful employment practices, even though the activities may involve (or appear to involve) discrimination on the basis of race, color, religion, sex, or national origin. Finally, section 703(j) provides that the Act may not be interpreted to require anyone to provide preferential treatment to members of minority groups in order to balance out the workforce.

To be sure, there are variations on this organizational structure. For example, some statutes may not have a declaration of purpose. Others may begin with substantive provisions and then provide definitions. But the Civil Rights Act of 1964 is a good example of what is perhaps the most typical statutory structure. When you encounter statutes that differ from this structure, you should take a moment to orient yourself and identify the statute's different components. Again, these components are purpose, definitions, and substantive provisions, which, in turn, include general rules as well as exceptions, provisos, and caveats.

C. THE AFFIRMATIVE ACTION QUESTION

EXERCISE II.1

You are a lawyer who represents a private corporation. Your supervisor tells you that the business's management team is interested in diversifying and balancing its workforce. In particular, management wants to adopt an affirmative action program in order to increase the number of Black employees in supervisory positions. The team wants to do so in order to gain positive recognition for the corporation as an equal-opportunity employer and to prevent federal and state regulators from asserting that the corporation discriminates against Blacks due to the "poor diversity numbers" currently represented in the corporation's workforce.

In other words, the corporation wants to increase the number of Black employees in supervisory positions in order to avoid scrutiny (and, potentially, a lawsuit) for its previous employment practices. Those practices were race blind on their face, but they had the (possibly unintended) effect of largely excluding Blacks from such supervisory positions. Be aware that the Supreme Court has previously held that such a "disparate impact" (sometimes also called "disparate effects") argument could, in some circumstances, establish that a company violated the Civil Rights Act. Thus, minority groups and state and federal regulators could sometimes successfully sue a company for having "poor diversity numbers," even where the employment policies that produced those numbers were race blind and not necessarily intended to discriminate. Your client wishes to avoid such a lawsuit.

Based on the text of the statute and the brief information you received about its passage, generate as many statutory arguments as you can in favor of and against such affirmative action programs. Be prepared to defend the arguments and your conclusion.

In completing this assignment, put aside your own personal and political views about affirmative action policies and consider only the statute. You should focus on section 703(a)—(d) and (j), as well as on the word "discriminate" (which is undefined in the statute), your understanding of the purpose of the statute, the context in which the statute was enacted, and the statute's legislative history.

Apart from the written assignment, also consider your supervisor's question in light of the broad theoretical approaches we briefly touched on in reference to the "food is prohibited in the classroom" statute. What would a judge adopting each approach likely conclude? Which of the specific arguments you identified resonates most strongly with each approach?

D.   LAWYERING THE AFFIRMATIVE ACTION QUESTION

In a typical law school class you would proceed directly from the question to the Supreme Court's answer. This is not a typical law school class. Let's first consider some of the briefs in the case that presented this issue to the Supreme Court in order to reflect on the role of the lawyer and to learn how a brief concerning a question of statutory interpretation is constructed—and how judges come up with their analyses.

The briefs have been heavily edited because, at this point, the goal is mainly to familiarize you with their organizational structure and the strategic framing that the lawyers have adopted. Also, if they were not edited, you would spend a long time reading them, as they are extremely lengthy. In reading the briefs, focus on the following questions and issues:

- How are the briefs structured? What kinds of arguments appear first, second, and so on? Are the competing briefs mostly similar or mostly different in this regard?

- What would you say is the primary theme and strongest argument in each brief? How are those themes and arguments woven throughout the briefs? What are the major thematic disagreements between the two sides?

- What is the petitioner's reason for spending so much time on the legislative history? Why do you think the respondent spends less time on the legislative history?

- Which brief do you find most persuasive? Why?

- How many of the arguments made by the lawyers were you able to think of in advance?

Brief for Petitioner, United Steelworkers of America, AFL-CIO

. . . .

I. THE KAISER-USWA SELECTION PROGRAM DOES NOT VIOLATE TITLE VII.

This case turns entirely upon the proper construction of § 703 of Title VII, which must be drawn from the statutory language and the legislative history. Before turning to these materials, we pause to demonstrate that the question presented here is entirely open.

. . . .

a.   The Statutory Language

Section 703 of Title VII in its entirety "delineates which employment practices are illegal and thereby prohibited and which are not." *Franks v. Bowman Transportation Co.*, 424 U.S. 747, 758 (1976). The two subsections in point here are (d) and (j), which provide:

"(d) It shall be an unlawful employment practice for any employer, labor organization, or joint labor-management committee controlling apprenticeship or other training or retraining, including on-the-job training programs to discriminate against any individual because of his race, color, religion, sex, or national origin in admission to, or employment in, any program established to provide apprenticeship or other training."

"(j) Nothing contained in this title shall be interpreted to require any employer, employment agency, labor organization, or joint labor-management committee subject to this title to grant preferential treatment to any individual or to any group because of the race, color, religion, sex, or national origin of such individual or group on account of an imbalance which may exist with respect to the total number or percentage of persons of any race, color, religion, sex, or national origin employed by any employer, referred or classified for employment by any employment agency or labor organization, admitted to membership or classified by any labor organization, or admitted to, or employed in, any apprenticeship or other training program, in comparison with the total number or percentage of persons of such race, color, religion, sex, or national origin in any community, State, section, or other area, or in the available work force in any community, State, section, or other area."

Section 703(d) standing alone does little to advance the inquiry since its operative words are "discriminate against any individual . . . in admission to . . . any [training] program," and "[t]he concept of discrimination is susceptible to varying interpretations." But § 703(d) does not stand alone. And, §§ 703(d) and (j), read together, state that Title VII, in prohibiting discrimination, does not "require" an employer or union to grant a racial preference to eliminate a racial imbalance. This articulation of Title VII's basic norm—an articulation which was arrived at through a "meticulous" drafting process in which the drafters "tried to be mindful of every word, of every comma, and of the shading of every phrase"—strongly suggests that an employer or union is permitted to grant such a preference.

. . . .

b.   The 1964 Legislative History

1.   The Genesis of the House Bill

. . . .

2.   The Judiciary Committee Report

The Judiciary Committee's Report simply described the provisions of Title VII without elaboration, and thus contained no discussion of the bill's treatment of quotas. However, the opponents of the bill on the Committee, in their Minority Report, contended that the bill would empower the federal government to force employers and unions to adopt quotas to "racially balance" their workforces and memberships. The Minority's analysis began with this preliminary observation, which was italicized in the Report:

"Throughout this entire report the construction we have placed upon the provisions of the reported bill are based upon what we believe will be advanced by the administration, evidenced by numerous Executive orders, other administrative actions and statements of officials in the executive branch of the Federal Government. We do not mean to say that such construction is necessarily correct or that the powers granted are constitutional. Broad, obscure, and undefined wording is repeatedly used in the bill."

The Minority Report asserted that the Department of Labor had been demanding racial balancing in apprenticeship programs, and that "the administration intends to rely upon its own construction of 'discrimination' as including the lack of racial balance. . . ." The Minority Report then proceeded to list "examples" of the effects which passage of the bill would have:

"Under the power conferred by this bill, [the farmer] may be forced to hire according to race, to 'racially balance' those who work for him in every job classification or be in violation of Federal law."

. . . .

"[If a] union roster did not contain the names of the carpenters of the race needed to 'racially balance' the job, the union agent must, then, go into the street and recruit members of the stipulated race in sufficient number to comply with Federal orders, else his local could be held in violation of Federal law."

. . . .

"If [an employer's] firm is not 'racially balanced,' . . . he has no choice, he must employ the person of that race which, by ratio, is next up, even though he is certain in his own mind that the [person] he is not allowed to employ would be a superior employee."

. . . .

"If a job applicant can write and there is an opening and he is of the race called for to balance the makeup of the staff, that person must be employed in preference to someone of another race."

From the cited examples, the Minority Report drew these conclusions:

"That such mandatory provisions of law approach the ludicrous should be apparent. That this is, in fact, a not too subtle system of racism-in-reverse cannot be successfully denied."

These contentions in the Minority Report led the Republican sponsors of the bill on the Judiciary Committee, who were to play a critical role throughout the legislative process, to state the following in their "Additional Views":

"It must also be stressed that the [Equal Employment Opportunity] Commission must confine its activities to correcting abuse, not promoting equality with mathematical certainty. In this regard, nothing in the title permits a person to demand employment. Of greater importance, the Commission will only jeopardize its continued existence if it seeks to impose forced racial balance upon employers or labor unions. Similarly, management prerogatives and union freedoms are to be left undisturbed to the greatest extent possible. Internal affairs of employers and labor unions must not be interfered with except to the limited extent that correction is required in discrimination practices. Its primary task is to make certain that the channels of employment are open to persons regardless of their race and that jobs in companies or membership in unions are strictly filled on the basis of qualification."

3.   The House Floor Debate

When the bill reached the House floor, the opening speech in support of its passage was delivered by Representative Celler, the Chairman of the House Judiciary Committee. A portion of that speech was devoted to answering the "unfair and unreasonable criticism" which had been leveled at the bill:

"It has been claimed that the bill would deprive employers, workers, and union members of their right to be free to control their business affairs and their membership. Specifically, the charge has been made that the Equal Employment Opportunity Commission to be established by Title VII of the bill would have the power to prevent a business from employing and promoting the people it wished, and that a 'federal inspector' could order the hiring and promotion only of employees of certain races or religious groups. This description of the bill is entirely wrong. The Equal Employment Opportunity Commission would be empowered merely to investigate specific charges of discrimination and to attempt to mediate or conciliate the dispute. It would have no authority to issue any orders to anyone.

"In the event that wholly voluntary settlement proves to be impossible, the Commission could seek redress in the federal courts, but it would be required to prove in the court that the particular employer involved had in fact, discriminated against one or more of his employees because of race, religion or national origin. The employer would have ample opportunity to disprove any of the charges involved and would have the benefit of the protection of all the usual judicial procedures.

"No order could be entered against an employer except by a court, and after a full and fair hearing, and any such order would be subject to appeal as is true in all court cases.

"Even then, the court could not order that any preference be given to any particular race, religion or other group but would be limited to ordering an end to discrimination. The statement that a federal inspector could order the employment and promotion only of members of a specific racial or religious group is therefore patently erroneous. . . .

. . . .

"It is likewise not true that the Equal Employment Opportunity Commission would have power to rectify existing 'racial or religious imbalance' in employment by requiring the hiring of certain people without regard to their qualifications simply because they are of a given race or religion. Only actual discrimination could be stopped."

Representative Lindsay, one of the authors of the "Additional Views" in the Report, said:

"This legislation . . . does not, as has been suggested here—both on and off the floor—force acceptance of people in . . . jobs . . . because they are Negro. It does not impose quotas or any special privileges. . . . There is nothing whatever in this bill about racial balance as appears so frequently in the Minority Report of the Committee.

"What the bill does do is prohibit discrimination because of race or religion. . . .

"Everything in this proposed legislation has to do with providing a body of law which will surround and protect the individual from some power complex. This bill is designed for the protection of individuals. When an individual is wronged he can invoke the protection to himself. . . ."

Representative Minish, a supporter, added:

"Under Title VII, employment will be on the basis of merit, not race. This means that no quota system will be set up, no one will be forced to hire incompetent help because of race or religion, and no one will be given a vested right to demand employment for a certain job. The Title is designed to utilize to the fullest our potential work force, to permit every worker to hold the best job for which he is qualified. This can be done by removing the hurdles that have too long been placed in the path of minority groups who seek to realize their rights and to contribute to a full society."

A number of opponents then repeated the theme of the Minority Report, that Title VII would require employers and unions to engage in racial balancing. As Representative Alger put it, Title VII attempts to "enforce preferential treatment for the Negro by making jobs available to him for which he is not qualified because of injustices practiced upon his forebears."

Representative Healey, a supporter, replied:

"Opponents of the bill say that it sets up racial quotas for job[s]. . . . The bill does not do that. It simply requires . . . that industries involved in interstate commerce not deny a qualified person the right to work because of his race or religion."

Representatives Dowdy and Ashmore renewed the contention that Title VII would require racial balancing. Representative Goodell interjected:

"As I understand the gentleman's position, I do not think it can go unchallenged. There is nothing here as a matter of legislative history that would require racial balancing. . . . We are not talking about a union having to balance its membership or an employer having to balance the number of employees. There is no quota involved. It is a matter of an individual's rights having been violated, charges having been brought, investigation carried out and conciliation having been attempted and then proof in court that there was discrimination and denial of rights on the basis of race or color."

With no further discussions of quotas, the House passed the entire bill, including Title VII, and sent it to the Senate. Subsequently, the Republican sponsors in the House prepared a memorandum describing the bill as passed. In pertinent part, that memorandum stated:

"The Civil Rights Bill, as passed by the House, does not in any way require, reward, or encourage: (1) 'open occupancy' in private housing, (2) the transfer of students away from the neighborhood schools to create 'racial balance,' or (3) the imposition of racial quotas or preferences in either private or public employment of individuals.

. . . .

"But, Title VII does not permit the ordering of racial quotas in businesses or unions and does not permit interferences with seniority rights of employees or union members."

This memorandum drew two conclusions as to the meaning of Title VII: Title VII did not "permit" court-ordered quotas, and it did not "require, reward, or encourage" privately adopted quotas. No sponsor in the House had said anything inconsistent with either proposition. A copy of this memorandum was transmitted to Senator Kuchel, the Republican manager of the bill in the Senate, who introduced it at the close of his opening speech in support of the bill in the Senate.

4.   The Senate

The Senate, after lengthy debate, decided to take up the bill directly, without referring it to a Committee, and consequently there is no Committee Report in the Senate.

. . . .

During the 17-day debate over whether the bill should be sent to Committee, Senator Hill made a lengthy speech attacking Title VII. A major theme of that speech was that the bill would install quota systems throughout American employment. This theme was elaborated by Senator Robertson:

"An employer will not be free to make selection as to individuals he prefers to hire. This Title suggests that hiring should be done on some percentage basis in order that racial imbalance will be overcome. It is contemplated by this Title that the percentage of colored and white population in a community shall be in similar percentages in every business establishment that employs over 25 persons. Thus, if there were 10,000 colored persons in a city, and 15,000 whites, an employer with 25, would, in order to overcome racial imbalance, be required to have 10 colored personnel and 15 white. And if by chance that employer had 20 colored employees, he would have to fire 10 of them in order to rectify the situation. Of course, this works the other way around where whites would be fired. The impracticability and unworkability of this Title seems self-evident."

Senator Humphrey responded:

"The bill does not require that at all. If it did, I would vote against it. . . . [V]oluntary compliance procedures must be used. There is no percentage quota."

. . . .

On May 26, 1964, Senator Dirksen introduced the comprehensive "Dirksen-Mansfield" substitute for the House-passed bill, which left unchanged the basic prohibitory language of Title VII (§§ 703(a)–(d)), as well as the remedial provision (§ 706(g)), but which added several provisions (including § 703(j)) limiting or defining the scope of the substantive prohibitions. Senator Dirksen explained that the substitute "represents not merely weeks but months of labor":

"When I first looked at the House Bill, I saw in it some inequities and imperfections and technical errors which did not satisfy me."

. . . .

"As a result of the various conferences, and by the process of give and take, we have at long last fashioned what we think is a workable measure."

Senator Dirksen opined:

"I doubt very much whether in my whole legislative lifetime any measure has received so much meticulous attention. We have tried to be mindful of every word, of every comma, and of the shading of every phrase."

Senator Kuchel explained that the substitute was designed, *inter alia*, to recognize the respective "responsibilities" of the Federal Government, the States, and, in "this free land of ours," "the American citizen."

On June 1, Senators Mansfield, Dirksen, Miller, and Cooper engaged in a colloquy about the importance of establishing a legislative record explaining the meaning of the amendments accomplished by the substitute. As Senator Miller observed, while many Senators had received explanations in the respective Democratic and Republican caucuses, "that is not the point," as the courts would not have access to those caucuses in ascertaining the bill's meaning. What was needed were explanations on the record, "so that in future litigation—which is bound to occur—on this bill, a court will know what the intention of Congress was." Senator Dirksen announced that he was preparing a title-by-title explanation of the amendments. Senator Cooper noted that as Senator Dirksen was "the author in chief of most of the amendments," an explanation from him of their purpose "would provide a legislative interpretation."

On June 3, Senator Clark made a lengthy speech about the changes in Title VII, which he characterized as "perhaps more extensive" than any in the rest of the bill. He said that "the credit or the blame—whichever it may be" should go to Senator Dirksen, who was principally responsible for them. "[T]he imprint of the thinking of the Senator from Illinois [Mr. DIRKSEN], is on the substitute." Clark's "candid political judgment" was that "if we want any bill at all enacted, we must take the Dirksen amendment," for otherwise there were not enough votes to obtain cloture; but this was a conclusion "reached . . . reluctantly."

Senator Muskie characterized §§ 703(g) through (j) as "limit[ing] the term 'unlawful employment practice' by spelling out a number of situations that could not be considered unlawful."

On June 4, Senator Humphrey made one of the two major presentations explaining the purpose of the Dirksen-Mansfield substitute amendments. (The other was Senator Dirksen's written explanation the following day.) Senator Humphrey's full statement respecting § 703(j) was as follows:

"A new subsection 703(j) is added to deal with the problem of racial balance among employees. The proponents of the bill have carefully stated on numerous occasions that Title VII does not require an employer to achieve any sort of racial balance in his workforce by giving preferential treatment to any individual or group. Since doubts have persisted, subsection (j) is added to state this point expressly. This subsection does not represent any change in the substance of the title. It does state clearly and accurately what we have mentioned all along about the bill's intent and meaning."

Senator Dirksen's "explanation of the changes made in the substitute amendment" provided, as to § 703(j):

"New subsection (j) provides that this title does not require preferential treatment be given any individual or group on account of an imbalance which may exist with respect to the total number or percentage of persons of any race, color, religion, sex, or national origin employed, in comparison with the total number or percentage of such persons in that or any other area."

On June 9, the Senate took up Senator Ervin's amendment, which proposed to delete Title VII from the bill. Speaking in support of the amendment, Senator Sparkman predicted that Title VII would lead to imposed quotas despite "the so-called mitigating language" in the substitute (i.e. § 703(j)). Senator Clark spoke in opposition:

"This bill does not make anyone higher than anyone else. It establishes no quotas. It leaves an employer free to select whomever he wishes to employ. It enables the labor union to admit anyone it wishes to take in. It tells an employment agency that it can get a job for anyone for whom it wishes to get a job.

"All this is subject to one qualification, and that qualification is to state: 'In your activity as an employer, as a labor union, as an employment agency, you must not discriminate because of the color of a man's skin. You may not discriminate on the basis of race, color, religion, national origin or sex.'"

. . . .

5.   House Consideration of the Senate Amendments

As the Senate had substantially amended the bill passed by the House, it was necessary for the House to consider whether it would concur in the Senate's amendments. The House Judiciary Committee brought the bill to the floor of the House (without an explanatory report) with a recommendation that the House concur in the Senate's bill.

Three Republican members of the Judiciary Committee—all of whom had been signers of both the "Additional Views" in the Committee Report . . . and of the memorandum quoted . . . were the only Congressmen to refer to quotas during the House's debate on the Senate amendments. Representative Lindsay stated:

"[W]e wish to emphasize that this bill does not require quotas, racial balance, or any of the other things that the opponents have been saying about it."

Representative McCulloch, undertaking "to negate only a few of the most glaring inaccuracies that have had such wide dissemination," declared, *inter alia*:

"Third. The bill does not permit the Federal Government to interfere with the day-to-day operations of a business or labor organization.

"Fourth. The bill does not permit the Federal Government to require an employer or union to hire or accept for membership a quota of persons from a particular minority group.

"Fifth. The bill does not permit the Federal Government to destroy the job seniority rights of either union or non-union employees."

And, Representative MacGregor announced what we submit is the correct synthesis of all the legislative history:

"Important as the scope and extent of this bill is, it is also vitally important that all Americans understand what this bill does not cover.

"Your mail and mine, your contacts and mine with our constituents, indicates a great degree of misunderstanding about this bill. People complain about racial 'balancing' in the public schools, about open occupancy in housing, about preferential treatment or quotas in employment. There is a mistaken belief that Congress is legislating in these areas in this bill. When we drafted this bill we excluded these issues largely because the problems raised by these controversial questions are more properly handled at a governmental level closer to the American people and by communities and individuals themselves. The Senate has spelled out our intentions more specifically."

. . . .

c.   The Meaning of the 1964 Legislative History

First, the focus of the debate in Congress was not on whether employers and unions would be left free to adopt quotas, but whether under Title VII the Federal Government could require quotas. To this latter question, Congress' answer was unequivocal:

(a)   Quotas are not a remedy which courts may impose for proven discrimination under Title VII: Chairman Celler, one of the bill's managers in the House, the key Republican sponsors in the House, and Senators Humphrey and Kuchel, the co-managers in the Senate, made definitive statements to this effect, which were seconded by others, and never contradicted by any supporter of the bill. As Senator Humphrey explained, the last sentence of § 706(g)—authorizing hiring and promotion remedies only for the victims of discrimination—is the statutory provision which embodies the sponsors' intent in this respect.

(b)   An employer's or union's failure to adopt quotas to eliminate a racial imbalance is not itself "discrimination." The sponsors consistently contended that the bill as originally drafted made this clear, but in the face of continuing charges to the contrary Senator Dirksen's compromise bill—the means of securing the Republican votes necessary to break the filibuster—expressly so provided in § 703(j).

Second, the answer to the question whether employers and unions would be free to adopt quotas to eliminate a racial imbalance is not quite as certain, because a few liberal Senators who were principal sponsors of the bill made statements, prior to the adoption of § 703(j), signifying their belief that such quotas would constitute "discrimination." Nevertheless, the decisive weight of the evidence is that, as § 703(j) on its face suggests, Congress did not intend to make it unlawful for employers and unions to adopt quotas to eliminate a racial imbalance. The following considerations all support that ultimate conclusion:

(a)   Title VII was predicated solely on the Commerce Clause, and (in 1964) was addressed solely to the private sector. Congress understood, therefore, that it was writing on a clean slate. At the time the bill was being considered, under federal law employers and unions were free to select and assign employees to segregate or integrate their workforces; the Constitution, of course, is inapplicable to such private decisionmaking. It was for Congress to decide the extent of the intrusion which Title VII would make upon this existing entrepreneurial freedom.

(b) The dynamic in both Houses was that the bill would not pass without the support of legislators who were traditional "conservatives" in the sense that they opposed expansive governmental intrusion into the free enterprise system and free collective bargaining. These legislators, from the start, saw Title VII as containing the potential for far-reaching government dictation of day-to-day managerial and collective bargaining decisions. From the start, therefore, they announced that their support was conditioned upon acceptance of the principle that the bill would intrude upon private decision-making only to the extent necessary to address the evils at which the bill was aimed. As the Republican sponsors in the House declared, in their "Additional Views" accompanying the House Report reporting out the bill:

"[M]anagement prerogatives, and union freedoms are to be left undisturbed to the greatest extent possible. Internal affairs of employers and labor unions must not be interfered with except to the limited extent that correction is required in discriminatory practices."

This philosophy was repeatedly expressed by conservatives, and liberals invariably acknowledged that this was a basic principle underlying the bill.

(c) In the original House debate on Title VII, there is absolutely no indication that anyone thought Title VII would invalidate private decisions to eliminate racial imbalance in employment; and at the end of that debate, the Republican sponsors announced that under Title VII governmental imposition of quotas was forbidden, but private adoption was permissible (albeit not "rewarded" or "encouraged").

(d) The Senate debate divides into two parts: before § 703(j), and after. In the first period, a few liberal Senators expressed their view that Title VII reached all race-conscious selection decisions. None of these addressed a race-conscious program to integrate such as is here involved. Rather, in each instance, it was an expansion of an argument to show that Title VII does not require quotas. But their views do not express the will of Congress. For the conservative Republicans whose votes were critical to ending the filibuster redrafted the bill, added § 703(j), and in the words of Senator Dirksen, created a statute under which employers "do not have to" engage in racial balancing. From the date of § 703(j)'s introduction forward, not even the liberals suggested that Title VII forbade private decisions to eliminate racial imbalance.

(e) When the Senate bill returned to the House, its application to quotas was discussed only by the Republican sponsors, and they expressly stated that the bill neither required nor forbade racial balancing, but instead left the matter to private decision-making.

(f) Congress focused specifically on racial balancing in Title IV of the bill, and made a considered determination that the choice whether to engage in racial balancing to end *de facto* discrimination should be left to local decision-making. This choice was predicated upon an expressed deference to school board autonomy, quite similar to the deference expressed for "managerial prerogatives, and union freedom," and Congress recognized the analogy between its decision in the two titles.

. . . .

BRIEF OF RESPONDENT, BRIAN WEBER

I.   The Racial Quota Imposed by Kaiser and USWA Is Illegal Under
     Title VII Because It Discriminates Against Non-Minority Employees.

The 50 percent minority quota of Kaiser and USWA is an openly
discriminatory system of selection of applicants for on-the-job training
programs. The selection quota requires that minority employees be
favored over more senior white employees solely on the basis of race.
Under Title VII of the Civil Rights Act of 1964 and the authorities
interpreting this statute, the reverse racial quota is illegal.

A.   Race Discrimination Against Any Employee Is Prohibited Under
     Title VII, Whether or Not the Employee Is a Member of a
     Government-Recognized Minority Group.

Title VII of the Civil Rights Act of 1964 specifically prohibits
discrimination in employment against anyone on the basis of race.
Section 703(a) of Title VII prohibits an employer from discriminating
"against any individual with respect to his compensation, terms,
conditions, or privileges of employment, because of such individual's race,
color, religion, sex or national origin." Moreover, Section 703(d) prohibits
discrimination on grounds of race in the selection of applicants for
training programs. It states:

"It shall be an unlawful employment practice for any employer, labor
organization, or joint labor-management committee controlling
apprenticeship or other training or retraining, including on-the-job
training programs to discriminate against any individual because of his
race, color, religion, sex, or national origin in admission to, or
employment in, any program established to provide apprenticeship or
other training."

Section 703 makes no exception for discrimination against white
employees. In fact, the categorical prohibition of any racial discrimination
establishes that Title VII prohibits discrimination against white workers
as well as minority employees. Thus, the racial quota of Kaiser and
USWA violates the provisions of Title VII.

Our reading of Title VII is consistent with the decisions of this Court.
In *McDonald v. Santa Fe Trail Transportation Co.*, the Court ruled that
white persons may assert claims under Title VII and the same standards
that are used in cases brought by minority employees are applicable to
the claims of whites. The Court stated:

"Title VII of the Civil Rights Act of 1964 prohibits the discharge of
'any individual' because of 'such individual's race.' Its terms are not
limited to discrimination against members of any particular race. . . ."

"This conclusion is in accord with uncontradicted legislative history to the effect that Title VII was intended to "cover all white men and white women and all Americans," and create an 'obligation not to discriminate against whites.' We therefore hold today that Title VII prohibits racial discrimination against the white petitioners in this case upon the same standards as would be applicable were they Negroes and Jackson white."

The conclusion that whites are protected by Title VII is also supported by the decision of the Court in *Griggs v. Duke Power Co.* In *Griggs*, the Court held that tests administered to determine selection for employment that have a disproportionate adverse impact on minority applicants must be job related. In reviewing the purpose and intent of Congress in adopting Title VII, the Court stated:

"Congress did not intend by Title VII, however, to guarantee a job to every person regardless of qualifications. In short, the Act does not command that any person be hired simply because he was formerly the subject of discrimination, or because he is a member of a minority group. Discriminatory preference for any group, minority or majority, is precisely and only what Congress has proscribed. What is required by Congress is the removal of artificial, arbitrary, and unnecessary barriers to employment when the barriers operate invidiously to discriminate on the basis of racial or other impermissible classification."

Thus, the Court's holding establishes that Title VII outlaws preferences in favor of minority as well as non-minority employees.

In the decision last term in *City of Los Angeles, Department of Water and Power v. Manhart*, the Court in a sex discrimination case stated that Title VII was "designed to make race irrelevant in the employment market." The Court held that the policy of the statute requires a focus on fairness to individuals, not fairness to classes. In addition, the Court stated:

"The statute makes it unlawful 'to discriminate against any individual with respect to his compensation, terms, conditions or privileges of employment, because of such individual's race, color, religion, sex, or national origin.' The statute's focus on the individual is unambiguous. It precludes treatment of individuals as simply components of a racial, religious, sexual, or national class. . . ."

. . . .

The decisions of this Court establish the illegality of the racial selection criterion used for the craft training programs. The application of the racial quota creates a preference in favor of a minority worker, to the detriment of a white, each time a selection is made of a minority worker without the highest seniority status. The 50 percent quota creates two lines of seniority, one for the preferred minority workers and one for whites. For each person selected from the plant-wide seniority line for the training programs, a person must be selected from the seniority line of minority employees. Applying the "same standards as would be applicable" if separate seniority lines favoring whites had been created, the racial quota is illegal under Title VII.

Our interpretation of Title VII is also supported by the legislative history of the statute. This legislative history is reviewed exhaustively in the Brief of USWA and it is not necessary to present it in full in this brief. As USWA suggests, the legislative history demonstrates that the sponsors intended to prohibit any requirement of a preference to achieve a racial balance. In addition, this history establishes that Congress intended to prohibit preferences in favor of any race.

The intent of Congress concerning Title VII is demonstrated in the "Objections and Answers" submitted by Senator Joseph S. Clark, a floor manager of the bill. It states:

"Objection: The bill would require employers to establish quotas for nonwhites in proportion to the percentage of nonwhites in the labor market area.

"Answer: Quotas are themselves discriminatory."

The statement that "[q]uotas are themselves discriminatory" is supported by the observations of other sponsors of Title VII. In response to the claim that Title VII would allow the Commission to impose quotas, Senator Hubert S. Humphrey stated:

"[T]he very opposite is true. Title VII prohibits discrimination. In effect, it says that race, religion and national origin are not to be used as the basis for hiring and firing. . . ."

Senator Harrison A. Williams, Jr., another supporter of the bill, stated that "[t]hose opposed . . . should realize that to hire a Negro solely because he is a Negro is racial discrimination, just as much as a 'white only' employment policy." He added: "There is an absolute absence of discrimination for anyone; and there is an absolute prohibition against discrimination against anyone."

If any doubt as to the "color blind" meaning of Title VII could have existed, it should have been erased by the explanation of the bill submitted by Senator Humphrey, which had been approved by the bipartisan floor managers of the bill in both houses of Congress. It said:

"The title does not provide that any preferential treatment in employment shall be given to Negroes or any other persons or groups. It does not provide that any quota systems may be established to maintain racial balance in employment. In fact, the title would prohibit preferential treatment to any particular group, and any person, whether or not a member of any minority group, would be permitted to file a complaint of discriminatory employment practices. . . ."

Thus, no hidden meaning exists in the statute. The apparent intent to prohibit any race discrimination is supported by the legislative history.

. . . .

E. THE SUPREME COURT CONFRONTS THE AFFIRMATIVE ACTION QUESTION

UNITED STEELWORKERS V. WEBER

443 U.S. 193 (1979)

Now let's look at what the Supreme Court had to say in 1979, when it first considered the affirmative action question. In reading the majority, concurring, and dissenting opinions, focus on the following:

- Which theoretical approach to statutory interpretation seems to be most important to the author of each opinion? Try to identify the specific lines in each opinion where the author expresses his view of the judge's task in interpreting statutes.

- Identify all of the different kinds of arguments each author makes in support of his conclusion. How many of these arguments did you initially come up with when considering the question? How many of them come directly from the lawyers' briefs?

- How do the different Justices account for section 703(j) of the Act and the relationship between sections 703(a)–(d) and (j)?

- Do not get bogged down in the extensive legislative histories provided by Justices Brennan and Rehnquist. Instead, try to identify their dueling understandings of this legislative history. *Why* do they recite this extensive history? How does it relate to their votes in the case and how they understand the statute? In other words, what are they really arguing about?

- Which opinion do you find most persuasive? Why? After reading the opinions, have you changed your mind as to how you would have voted?

- Note that the statute was passed in 1964, but it was not until 1979 that the Supreme Court considered this question. What might account for this? Do you find it surprising?

MR. JUSTICE BRENNAN delivered the opinion of the Court.

Challenged here is the legality of an affirmative action plan—collectively bargained by an employer and a union—that reserves for black employees 50% of the openings in an in-plant craft-training program until the percentage of black craftworkers in the plant is commensurate with the percentage of blacks in the local labor force. The question for decision is whether Congress, in Title VII of the Civil Rights Act of 1964 . . . left employers and unions in the private sector free to take such race-conscious steps to eliminate manifest racial imbalances in traditionally segregated job categories. We hold that Title VII does not prohibit such race-conscious affirmative action plans.

I

In 1974, petitioner United Steelworkers of America (USWA) and petitioner Kaiser Aluminum & Chemical Corp. (Kaiser) entered into a master collective-bargaining agreement covering terms and conditions of employment at 15 Kaiser plants. The agreement contained, *inter alia*, an affirmative action plan designed to eliminate conspicuous racial imbalances in Kaiser's then almost exclusively white craftwork forces. Black crafthiring goals were set for each Kaiser plant equal to the percentage of blacks in the respective local labor forces. To enable plants to meet these goals, on-the-job training programs were established to teach unskilled production workers—black and white—the skills necessary to become craftworkers. The plan reserved for black employees 50% of the openings in these newly created in-plant training programs.

This case arose from the operation of the plan at Kaiser's plant in Gramercy, La. Until 1974, Kaiser hired as craftworkers for that plant only persons who had had prior craft experience. Because blacks had long been excluded from craft unions, few were able to present such credentials. As a consequence, prior to 1974 only 1.83% (5 out of 273) of the skilled craftworkers at the Gramercy plant were black, even though the work force in the Gramercy area was approximately 39% black.

Pursuant to the national agreement Kaiser altered its craft hiring practice in the Gramercy plant. Rather than hiring already trained outsiders, Kaiser established a training program to train its production workers to fill craft openings. Selection of craft trainees was made on the basis of seniority, with the proviso that at least 50% of the new trainees were to be black until the percentage of black skilled craftworkers in the Gramercy plant approximated the percentage of blacks in the local labor force.

During 1974, the first year of the operation of the Kaiser-USWA affirmative action plan, 13 craft trainees were selected from Gramercy's production work force. Of these, seven were black and six white. The most senior black selected into the program had less seniority than several white production workers whose bids for admission were rejected. Thereafter one of those white production workers, respondent Brain Weber (hereafter respondent), instituted this class action in the United States District Court for the Eastern District of Louisiana.

The complaint alleged that the filling of craft trainee positions at the Gramercy plant pursuant to the affirmative action program had resulted in junior black employees' receiving training in preference to senior white employees, thus discriminating against respondent and other similarly situated white employees in violation of §§ 703 (a) and (d) of Title VII. The District Court held that the plan violated Title VII, entered a judgment in favor of the plaintiff class, and granted a permanent injunction prohibiting Kaiser and the USWA "from denying plaintiffs, Brian F. Weber and all other members of the class, access to on-the-job training programs on the basis of race." A divided panel of the Court of Appeals for the Fifth Circuit affirmed, holding that all employment preferences based upon race, including those preferences incidental to bona fide affirmative action plans, violated Title VII's prohibition against racial discrimination in employment. . . .

We reverse.

II

We emphasize at the outset the narrowness of our inquiry. Since the Kaiser-USWA plan does not involve state action, this case does not present an alleged violation of the Equal Protection Clause of the Fourteenth Amendment. Further, since the Kaiser-USWA plan was adopted voluntarily, we are not concerned with what Title VII requires or with what a court might order to remedy a past proved violation of the Act. The only question before us is the narrow statutory issue of whether Title VII *forbids* private employers and unions from voluntarily agreeing upon bona fide affirmative action plans that accord racial preferences in the manner and for the purpose provided in the Kaiser-USWA plan. That question was expressly left open in *McDonald v. Santa Fe Trail Transp. Co.*, 427 U.S. 273, 281 n. 8 (1976), which held, in a case not involving affirmative action, that Title VII protects whites as well as blacks from certain forms of racial discrimination.

Respondent argues that Congress intended in Title VII to prohibit all race-conscious affirmative action plans. Respondent's argument rests upon a literal interpretation of §§ 703 (a) and (d) of the Act. Those sections make it unlawful to "discriminate . . . because of . . . race" in hiring and in the selection of apprentices for training programs. Since, the argument runs, *McDonald v. Santa Fe Trail Transp. Co., supra,* settled that Title VII forbids discrimination against whites as well as blacks, and since the Kaiser-USWA affirmative action plan operates to discriminate against white employees solely because they are white, it follows that the Kaiser-USWA plan violates Title VII.

Respondent's argument is not without force. But it overlooks the significance of the fact that the Kaiser-USWA plan is an affirmative action plan voluntarily adopted by private parties to eliminate traditional patterns of racial segregation. In this context respondent's reliance upon a literal construction of §§ 703 (a) and (d) and upon *McDonald* is misplaced. . . .

It is a "familiar rule, that a thing may be within the letter of the statute and yet not within the statute, because not within its spirit, nor within the intention of its makers." *Holy Trinity Church v. United States*, 143 U.S. 457, 459 (1892). The prohibition against racial discrimination in §§ 703 (a) and (d) of Title VII must therefore be read against the background of the legislative history of Title VII and the historical context from which the Act arose. . . . Examination of those sources makes clear that an interpretation of the sections that forbade all race-conscious affirmative action would "bring about an end completely at variance with the purpose of the statute" and must be rejected. . . .

Congress' primary concern in enacting the prohibition against racial discrimination in Title VII of the Civil Rights Act of 1964 was with "the plight of the Negro in our economy." 110 Cong. Rec. 6548 (1964) (remarks of Sen. Humphrey). Before 1964, blacks were largely relegated to "unskilled and semi-skilled jobs." *Ibid.* (remarks of Sen. Humphrey); *id.,* at 7204 (remarks of Sen. Clark); *id.,* at 7379–7380 (remarks of Sen. Kennedy). Because of automation the number of such jobs was rapidly decreasing. *See id.,* at 6548 (remarks of Sen. Humphrey); *id.,* at 7204 (remarks of Sen. Clark). As a consequence, "the relative position of the Negro worker [was] steadily worsening. In 1947 the nonwhite unemployment rate was only 64 percent higher than the white rate; in 1962 it was 124 percent higher." *Id.,* at 6547 (remarks of Sen. Humphrey). *See also id.,* at 7204 (remarks of Sen. Clark). Congress considered this a serious social problem.

As Senator Clark told the Senate:

"The rate of Negro unemployment has gone up consistently as compared with white unemployment for the past 15 years. This is a social malaise and a social situation which we should not tolerate. That is one of the principal reasons why the bill should pass." *Id.,* at 7220.

Congress feared that the goals of the Civil Rights Act—the integration of blacks into the mainstream of American society—could not be achieved unless this trend were reversed. And Congress recognized that that would not be possible unless blacks were able to secure jobs "which have a future." *Id.,* at 7204 (remarks of Sen. Clark). *See also id.,* at 7379–7380 (remarks of Sen. Kennedy).

As Senator Humphrey explained to the Senate:

"What good does it do a Negro to be able to eat in a fine restaurant if he cannot afford to pay the bill? What good does it do him to be accepted in a hotel that is too expensive for his modest income? How can a Negro child be motivated to take full advantage of integrated educational facilities if he has no hope of getting a job where he can use that education?" *Id.*, at 6547.

"Without a job, one cannot afford public convenience and accommodations. Income from employment may be necessary to further a man's education, or that of his children. If his children have no hope of getting a good job, what will motivate them to take advantage of educational opportunities?" *Id.*, at 6552.

These remarks echoed President Kennedy's original message to Congress upon the introduction of the Civil Rights Act in 1963. "There is little value in a Negro's obtaining the right to be admitted to hotels and restaurants if he has no cash in his pocket and no job." 109 Cong. Rec. 11159.

Accordingly, it was clear to Congress that "[t]he crux of the problem [was] to open employment opportunities for Negroes in occupations which have been traditionally closed to them," 110 Cong. Rec. 6548 (1964) (remarks of Sen. Humphrey), and it was to this problem that Title VII's prohibition against racial discrimination in employment was primarily addressed.

It plainly appears from the House Report accompanying the Civil Rights Act that Congress did not intend wholly to prohibit private and voluntary affirmative action efforts as one method of solving this problem. The Report provides:

"No bill can or should lay claim to eliminating all of the causes and consequences of racial and other types of discrimination against minorities. There is reason to believe, however, that national leadership provided by the enactment of Federal legislation dealing with the most troublesome problems *will create an atmosphere conducive to voluntary or local resolution of other forms of discrimination.*" H. R. Rep. No. 914, 88th Cong., 1st Sess., pt. 1, p. 18 (1963). (Emphasis supplied.)

Given this legislative history, we cannot agree with respondent that Congress intended to prohibit the private sector from taking effective steps to accomplish the goal that Congress designed Title VII to achieve. The very statutory words intended as a spur or catalyst to cause "employers and unions to self-examine and to self-evaluate their employment practices and to endeavor to eliminate, so far as possible, the last vestiges of an unfortunate and ignominious page in this country's history," . . . cannot be interpreted as an absolute prohibition against all private, voluntary, race-conscious affirmative action efforts to hasten the elimination of such vestiges. It would be ironic indeed if a law triggered by a Nation's concern over centuries of racial injustice and intended to improve the lot of those who had "been excluded from the American dream for so long," 110 Cong. Rec. 6552 (1964) (remarks of Sen. Humphrey), constituted the first legislative prohibition of all voluntary, private, race-conscious efforts to abolish traditional patterns of racial segregation and hierarchy.

Our conclusion is further reinforced by examination of the language and legislative history of § 703 (j) of Title VII. Opponents of Title VII raised two related arguments against the bill. First, they argued that the Act would be interpreted to require employers with racially imbalanced work forces to grant preferential treatment to racial minorities in order to integrate. Second, they argued that employers with racially imbalanced work forces would grant preferential treatment to racial minorities, even if not required to do so by the Act. *See* 110 Cong. Rec. 8618–8619 (1964) (remarks of Sen. Sparkman). Had Congress meant to prohibit all race-conscious affirmative action, as respondent urges, it easily could have answered both objections by providing that Title VII would not require or permit racially preferential integration efforts. But Congress did not choose such a course. Rather, Congress added § 703 (j) which addresses only the first objection. The section provides that nothing contained in Title VII "shall be interpreted to *require* any employer . . . to grant preferential treatment . . . to any group because of the race . . . of such . . . group on account of" a *de facto* racial imbalance in the employer's work force.

The section does not state that "nothing in Title VII shall be interpreted to *permit*" voluntary affirmative efforts to correct racial imbalances. The natural inference is that Congress chose not to forbid all voluntary race-conscious affirmative action.

The reasons for this choice are evident from the legislative record. Title VII could not have been enacted into law without substantial support from legislators in both Houses who traditionally resisted federal regulation of private business. Those legislators demanded as a price for their support that "management prerogatives, and union freedoms . . . be left undisturbed to the greatest extent possible." H. R. Rep. No. 914, 88th Cong., 1st Sess., pt. 2, p. 29 (1963). Section 703 (j) was proposed by Senator Dirksen to allay any fears that the Act might be interpreted in such a way as to upset this compromise. The section was designed to prevent 703 of Title VII from being interpreted in such a way as to lead to undue "Federal Government interference with private businesses because of some Federal employee's ideas about racial balance or racial imbalance." 110 Cong. Rec. 14314 (1964) (remarks of Sen. Miller). *See also id.*, at 9881 (remarks of [443 U.S. 193, 207] Sen. Allott); *id.*, at 10520 (remarks of Sen. Carlson) *id.*, at 11471 (remarks of Sen. Javits); *id.*, at 12817 (remarks of Sen. Dirksen).

Clearly, a prohibition against all voluntary, race-conscious, affirmative action efforts would disserve these ends. Such a prohibition would augment the powers of the Federal Government and diminish traditional management prerogatives while at the same time impeding attainment of the ultimate statutory goals. In view of this legislative history and in view of Congress' desire to avoid undue federal regulation of private businesses, use of the word "require" rather than the phrase "require or permit" in § 703 (j) fortifies the conclusion that Congress did not intend to limit traditional business freedom to such a degree as to prohibit all voluntary, race-conscious affirmative action.

We therefore hold that Title VII's prohibition in §§ 703 (a) and (d) against racial discrimination does not condemn all private, voluntary, race-conscious affirmative action plans.

. . . .

We conclude, therefore, that the adoption of the Kaiser-USWA plan for the Gramercy plant falls within the area of discretion left by Title VII to the private sector voluntarily to adopt affirmative action plans designed to eliminate conspicuous racial imbalance in traditionally segregated job categories. Accordingly, the judgment of the Court of Appeals for the Fifth Circuit is

Reversed.

MR. JUSTICE BLACKMUN, concurring.

While I share some of the misgivings expressed in MR. JUSTICE REHNQUIST'S dissent concerning the extent to which the legislative history of Title VII clearly supports the result the Court reaches today, I believe that additional considerations, practical and equitable, only partially perceived, if perceived at all, by the 88th Congress, support the conclusion reached by the Court today, and I therefore join its opinion as well as its judgment.

I

In his dissent from the decision of the United States Court of Appeals for the Fifth Circuit, Judge Wisdom pointed out that this litigation arises from a practical problem in the administration of Title VII. The broad prohibition against discrimination places the employer and the union on what he accurately described as a "high tightrope without a net beneath them." If Title VII is read literally, on the one hand they face liability for past discrimination against blacks, and on the other they face liability to whites for any voluntary preferences adopted to mitigate the effects of prior discrimination against blacks.

In this litigation, Kaiser denies prior discrimination but concedes that its past hiring practices may be subject to question. Although the labor force in the Gramercy area was approximately 39% black, Kaiser's work force was less than 15% black, and its craft work force was less than 2% black. Kaiser had made some effort to recruit black painters, carpenters, insulators, and other craftsmen, but it continued to insist that those hired have five years' prior industrial experience, a requirement that arguably was not sufficiently job related to justify under Title VII any discriminatory impact it may have had. The parties dispute the extent to which black craftsmen were available in the local labor market. They agree, however, that after critical reviews from the Office of Federal Contract Compliance, Kaiser and the Steelworkers established the training program in question here and modeled it along the lines of a Title VII consent decree later entered for the steel industry. Yet when they did this, respondent Weber sued, alleging that Title VII prohibited the program because it discriminated against him as a white person and it was not supported by a prior judicial finding of discrimination against blacks.

Respondent Weber's reading of Title VII, endorsed by the Court of Appeals, places voluntary compliance with Title VII in profound jeopardy. The only way for the employer and the union to keep their footing on the "tightrope" it creates would be to eschew all forms of voluntary affirmative action. Even a whisper of emphasis on minority recruiting would be forbidden. Because Congress intended to encourage private efforts to come into compliance with Title VII, *see Alexander v. Gardner-Denver Co.*, 415 U.S. 36, 44 (1974), Judge Wisdom concluded that employers and unions who had committed "arguable violations" of Title VII should be free to make reasonable responses without fear of liability to whites. Preferential hiring along the lines of the Kaiser program is a reasonable response for the employer, whether or not a court, on these facts, could order the same step as a remedy. The company is able to avoid identifying victims of past discrimination, and so avoids claims for backpay that would inevitably follow a response limited to such victims. If past victims should be benefited by the program, however, the company mitigates its liability to those persons.

Also, to the extent that Title VII liability is predicated on the "disparate effect" of an employer's past hiring practices, the program makes it less likely that such an effect could be demonstrated.

The "arguable violation" theory has a number of advantages. It responds to a practical problem in the administration of Title VII not anticipated by Congress. It draws predictability from the outline of present law and closely effectuates the purpose of the Act. Both Kaiser and the United States urge its adoption here. Because I agree that it is the soundest way to approach this case, my preference would be to resolve this litigation by applying it and holding that Kaiser's craft training program meets the requirement that voluntary affirmative action be a reasonable response to an "arguable violation" of Title VII.

II

The Court, however, declines to consider the narrow "arguable violation" approach and adheres instead to an interpretation of Title VII that permits affirmative action by an employer whenever the job category in question is "traditionally segregated." The sources cited suggest that the Court considers a job category to be "traditionally segregated" when there has been a societal history of purposeful exclusion of blacks from the job category, resulting in a persistent disparity between the proportion of blacks in the labor force and the proportion of blacks among those who hold jobs within the category.

"Traditionally segregated job categories," where they exist, sweep far more broadly than the class of "arguable violations" of Title VII. The Court's expansive approach is somewhat disturbing for me because, as MR. JUSTICE REHNQUIST points out, the Congress that passed Title VII probably thought it was adopting a principle of nondiscrimination that would apply to blacks and whites alike. While setting aside that principle can be justified where necessary to advance statutory policy by encouraging reasonable responses as a form of voluntary compliance that mitigates "arguable violations," discarding the principle of nondiscrimination where no countervailing statutory policy exists appears to be at odds with the bargain struck when Title VII was enacted.

A closer look at the problem, however, reveals that in each of the principal ways in which the Court's "traditionally segregated job categories" approach expands on the "arguable violations" theory, still other considerations point in favor of the broad standard adopted by the Court, and make it possible for me to conclude that the Court's reading of the statute is an acceptable one.

A

The first point at which the Court departs from the "arguable violations" approach is that it measures an individual employer's capacity for affirmative action solely in terms of a statistical disparity. The individual employer need not have engaged in discriminatory practices in the past. While, under Title VII, a mere disparity may provide the basis for a *prima facie* case against an employer, it would not conclusively prove a violation of the Act. As a practical matter, however, this difference may not be that great. While the "arguable violation" standard is conceptually satisfying in practice the emphasis would be on "arguable" rather than on "violation." The great difficulty in the District Court was that no one had any incentive to prove that Kaiser had violated the Act. Neither Kaiser nor the Steelworkers wanted to establish a past violation, nor did Weber. The blacks harmed had never sued and so had no established representative. The Equal Employment Opportunity Commission declined to intervene, and cannot be expected to intervene in every case of this nature. To make the "arguable violation" standard work, it would have to be set low enough to permit the employer to prove it without obligating himself to pay a damages award. The inevitable tendency would be to avoid hairsplitting litigation by simply concluding that a mere disparity between the racial composition of the employer's work force and the composition of the qualified local labor force would be an "arguable violation," even though actual liability could not be established on that basis alone.

B

The Court also departs from the "arguable violation" approach by permitting an employer to redress discrimination that lies wholly outside the bounds of Title VII. For example, Title VII provides no remedy for pre-Act discrimination; yet the purposeful discrimination that creates a "traditionally segregated job category" may have entirely predated the Act. More subtly, in assessing a *prima facie* case of Title VII liability, the composition of the employer's work force is compared to the composition of the pool of workers who meet valid job qualifications. When a "job category" is traditionally segregated, however, that pool will reflect the effects of segregation, and the Court's approach goes further and permits a comparison with the composition of the labor force as a whole, in which minorities are more heavily represented.

Strong considerations of equity support an interpretation of Title VII that would permit private affirmative action to reach where Title VII itself does not. The bargain struck in 1964 with the passage of Title VII guaranteed equal opportunity for white and black alike, but where Title VII provides no remedy for blacks, it should not be construed to foreclose private affirmative action from supplying relief. It seems unfair for respondent Weber to argue, as he does, that the asserted scarcity of black craftsmen in Louisiana, the product of historic discrimination, makes Kaiser's training program illegal because it ostensibly absolves Kaiser of all Title VII liability. Absent compelling evidence of legislative intent, I would not interpret Title VII itself as a means of "locking in" the effects of segregation for which Title VII provides no remedy. Such a construction, as the Court points out, would be "ironic," given the broad remedial purposes of Title VII.

. . . .

III

I also think it significant that, while the Court's opinion does not foreclose other forms of affirmative action, the Kaiser program it approves is a moderate one. The opinion notes that the program does not afford an absolute preference for blacks, and that it ends when the racial composition of Kaiser's craft work force matches the racial composition of the local population. It thus operates as a temporary tool for remedying past discrimination without attempting to "maintain" a previously achieved balance. Because the duration of the program is finite, it perhaps will end even before the "stage of maturity when action along this line is no longer necessary." And if the Court has misperceived the political will, it has the assurance that because the question is statutory Congress may set a different course if it so chooses.

MR. CHIEF JUSTICE BURGER, dissenting.

The Court reaches a result I would be inclined to vote for were I a Member of Congress considering a proposed amendment of Title VII. I cannot join the Court's judgment, however, because it is contrary to the explicit language of the statute and arrived at by means wholly incompatible with long-established principles of separation of powers. Under the guise of statutory "construction," the Court effectively rewrites Title VII to achieve what it regards as a desirable result. It "amends" the statute to do precisely what both its sponsors and its opponents agreed the statute was not intended to do.

When Congress enacted Title VII after long study and searching debate, it produced a statute of extraordinary clarity, which speaks directly to the issue we consider in this case. In § 703 (d) Congress provided:

"It shall be an unlawful employment practice for any employer, labor organization, or joint labor-management committee controlling apprenticeship or other training or retraining, including on-the-job training programs to discriminate against any individual because of his race, color, religion, sex, or national origin in admission to, or employment in, any program established to provide apprenticeship or other training."

Often we have difficulty interpreting statutes either because of imprecise drafting or because legislative compromises have produced genuine ambiguities. But here there is no lack of clarity, no ambiguity. The quota embodied in the collective-bargaining agreement between Kaiser and the Steelworkers unquestionably discriminates on the basis of race against individual employees seeking admission to on-the-job training programs. And, under the plain language of § 703 (d), that is "an unlawful employment practice."

Oddly, the Court seizes upon the very clarity of the statute almost as a justification for evading the unavoidable impact of its language. The Court blandly tells us that Congress could not really have meant what it said, for a "literal construction" would defeat the "purpose" of the statute—at least the congressional "purpose" as five Justices divine it today. But how are judges supposed to ascertain the purpose of a statute except through the words Congress used and the legislative history of the statute's evolution? One need not even resort to the legislative history to recognize what is apparent from the face of Title VII—that it is specious to suggest that § 703 (j) contains a negative pregnant that permits employers to do what §§ 703 (a) and (d) unambiguously and unequivocally forbid employers from doing.

Moreover, as MR. JUSTICE REHNQUIST'S opinion—which I join—conclusively demonstrates, the legislative history makes equally clear that the supporters and opponents of Title VII reached an agreement about the statute's intended effect. That agreement, expressed so clearly in the language of the statute that no one should doubt its meaning, forecloses the reading which the Court gives the statute today.

Arguably, Congress may not have gone far enough in correcting the effects of past discrimination when it enacted Title VII. The gross discrimination against minorities to which the Court adverts—particularly against Negroes in the building trades and craft unions—is one of the dark chapters in the otherwise great history of the American labor movement. And, I do not question the importance of encouraging voluntary compliance with the purposes and policies of Title VII. But that statute was conceived and enacted to make discrimination against any individual illegal, and I fail to see how "voluntary compliance" with the no-discrimination principle that is the heart and soul of Title VII as currently written will be achieved by permitting employers to discriminate against some individuals to give preferential treatment to others.

Until today, I had thought the Court was of the unanimous view that "[d]iscriminatory preference for any group, minority or majority, is precisely and only what Congress has proscribed" in Title VII. Had Congress intended otherwise, it very easily could have drafted language allowing what the Court permits today. Far from doing so, Congress expressly prohibited in §§ 703 (a) and (d) the very discrimination against Brian Weber which the Court today approves. If "affirmative action" programs such as the one presented in this case are to be permitted, it is for Congress, not this Court, to so direct.

It is often observed that hard cases make bad law. I suspect there is some truth to that adage, for the "hard" cases always tempt judges to exceed the limits of their authority, as the Court does today by totally rewriting a crucial part of Title VII to reach a "desirable" result. . . .

[B]eware the "good result," achieved by judicially unauthorized or intellectually dishonest means on the appealing notion that the desirable ends justify the improper judicial means. For there is always the danger that the seeds of precedent sown by good men for the best of motives will yield a rich harvest of unprincipled acts of others also aiming at "good ends."

MR. JUSTICE REHNQUIST, with whom THE CHIEF JUSTICE joins, dissenting.

In a very real sense, the Court's opinion is ahead of its time: it could more appropriately have been handed down five years from now, in 1984, a year coinciding with the title of a book from which the Court's opinion borrows, perhaps subconsciously, at least one idea. Orwell describes in his book a governmental official of Oceania, one of the three great world powers, denouncing the current enemy, Eurasia, to an assembled crowd:

"It was almost impossible to listen to him without being first convinced and then maddened. . . . The speech had been proceeding for perhaps twenty minutes when a messenger hurried onto the platform and a scrap of paper was slipped into the speaker's hand. He unrolled and read it without pausing in his speech. Nothing altered in his voice or manner, or in the content of what he was saying, but suddenly the names were different. Without words said, a wave of understanding rippled through the crowd. Oceania was at war with Eastasia! . . . The banners and posters with which the square was decorated were all wrong! . . . [T]he speaker had switched from one line to the other actually in mid-sentence, not only without a pause, but without even breaking the syntax." G. Orwell, Nineteen Eighty-Four 181–182 (1949).

Today's decision represents an equally dramatic and equally unremarked switch in this Court's interpretation of Title VII.

The operative sections of Title VII prohibit racial discrimination in employment *simpliciter*. Taken in its normal meaning, and as understood by all Members of Congress who spoke to the issue during the legislative debates, this language prohibits a covered employer from considering race when making an employment decision, whether the race be black or white. Several years ago, however, a United States District Court held that "the dismissal of white employees charged with misappropriating company property while not dismissing a similarly charged Negro employee does not raise a claim upon which Title VII relief may be granted." This Court unanimously reversed, concluding from the "uncontradicted legislative history" that "Title VII prohibits racial discrimination against the white petitioners in this case upon the same standards as would be applicable were they Negroes. . . ."

We have never wavered in our understanding that Title VII "prohibits *all* racial discrimination in employment, without exception for any group of particular employees." *Id.*, at 283 (emphasis in original). In *Griggs v. Duke Power Co.*, our first occasion to interpret Title VII, a unanimous Court observed that "[d]iscriminatory preference, for any group, minority or majority, is precisely and only what Congress has proscribed." And in our most recent discussion of the issue, we uttered words seemingly dispositive of this case: "It is clear beyond cavil that the obligation imposed by Title VII is to provide an equal opportunity for *each* applicant regardless of race, without regard to whether members of the applicant's race are already proportionately represented in the work force." *Furnco Construction Corp. v. Waters* . . . (emphasis in original).

Today, however, the Court behaves much like the Orwellian speaker earlier described, as if it had been handed a note indicating that Title VII would lead to a result unacceptable to the Court if interpreted here as it was in our prior decisions. Accordingly, without even a break in syntax, the Court rejects "a literal construction of § 703 (a)" in favor of newly discovered "legislative history," which leads it to a conclusion directly contrary to that compelled by the "uncontradicted legislative history" unearthed in *McDonald* and our other prior decisions. Now we are told that the legislative history of Title VII shows that employers are free to discriminate on the basis of race: an employer may, in the Court's words, "trammel the interests of the white employees" in favor of black employees in order to eliminate "racial imbalance." Our earlier interpretations of Title VII, like the banners and posters decorating the square in Oceania, were all wrong.

As if this were not enough to make a reasonable observer question this Court's adherence to the oft-stated principle that our duty is to construe rather than rewrite legislation, the Court also seizes upon § 703 (j) of Title VII as an independent, or at least partially independent, basis for its holding. Totally ignoring the wording of that section, which is obviously addressed to those charged with the responsibility of interpreting the law rather than those who are subject to its proscriptions, and totally ignoring the months of legislative debates preceding the section's introduction and passage, which demonstrate clearly that it was enacted to prevent precisely what occurred in this case, the Court infers from § 703 (j) that "Congress chose not to forbid all voluntary race-conscious affirmative action."

Thus, by a *tour de force* reminiscent not of jurists such as Hale, Holmes, and Hughes, but of escape artists such as Houdini, the Court eludes clear statutory language, "uncontradicted" legislative history, and uniform precedent in concluding that employers are, after all, permitted to consider race in making employment decisions. It may be that one or more of the principal sponsors of Title VII would have preferred to see a provision allowing preferential treatment of minorities written into the bill. Such a provision, however, would have to have been expressly or impliedly excepted from Title VII's explicit prohibition on all racial discrimination in employment. There is no such exception in the Act. And a reading of the legislative debates concerning Title VII, in which proponents and opponents alike uniformly denounced discrimination in favor of, as well as discrimination against, Negroes, demonstrates clearly that any legislator harboring an unspoken desire for such a provision could not possibly have succeeded in enacting it into law.

. . . .

II

Were Congress to act today specifically to prohibit the type of racial discrimination suffered by Weber, it would be hard pressed to draft language better tailored to the task than that found in § 703 (d) of Title VII:

"It shall be an unlawful employment practice for any employer, labor organization, or joint labor-management committee controlling apprenticeship or other training or retraining, including on-the-job training programs to discriminate against any individual because of his race, color, religion, sex, or national origin in admission to, or employment in, any program established to provide apprenticeship or other training."

Equally suited to the task would be § 703 (a) (2), which makes it unlawful for an employer to classify his employees "in any way which would deprive or tend to deprive any individual of employment opportunities or otherwise adversely affect his status as an employee, because of such individual's race, color, religion, sex, or national origin."

Entirely consistent with these two express prohibitions is the language of § 703 (j) of Title VII, which provides that the Act is not to be interpreted "to require any employer . . . to grant preferential treatment to any individual or to any group because of the race . . . of such individual or group" to correct a racial imbalance in the employer's work force. Seizing on the word "require," the Court infers that Congress must have intended to "permit" this type of racial discrimination. Not only is this reading of § 703 (j) outlandish in the light of the flat prohibitions of §§ 703 (a) and (d), but, as explained in Part III, it is also totally belied by the Act's legislative history.

Quite simply, Kaiser's racially discriminatory admission quota is flatly prohibited by the plain language of Title VII. This normally dispositive fact, however, gives the Court only momentary pause. An "interpretation" of the statute upholding Weber's claim would, according to the Court, " 'bring about an end completely at variance with the purpose of the statute.' " To support this conclusion, the Court calls upon the "spirit" of the Act, which it divines from passages in Title VII's legislative history indicating that enactment of the statute was prompted by Congress' desire " 'to open employment opportunities for Negroes in occupations which [had] been traditionally closed to them.' "

But the legislative history invoked by the Court to avoid the plain language of §§ 703 (a) and (d) simply misses the point. To be sure, the reality of employment discrimination against Negroes provided the primary impetus for passage of Title VII. But this fact by no means supports the proposition that Congress intended to leave employers free to discriminate against white persons. In most cases, "[l]egislative history . . . is more vague than the statute we are called upon to interpret." Here, however, the legislative history of Title VII is as clear as the language of §§ 703 (a) and (d), and it irrefutably demonstrates that Congress meant precisely what it said in §§ 703 (a) and (d)—that *no* racial discrimination in employment is permissible under Title VII, not even preferential treatment of minorities to correct racial imbalance.

III

In undertaking to review the legislative history of Title VII, I am mindful that the topic hardly makes for light reading, but I am also fearful that nothing short of a thorough examination of the congressional debates will fully expose the magnitude of the Court's misinterpretation of Congress' intent.

A

Introduced on the floor of the House of Representatives on June 20, 1963, the bill—H. R. 7152—that ultimately became the Civil Rights Act of 1964 contained no compulsory provisions directed at private discrimination in employment. The bill was promptly referred to the Committee on the Judiciary, where it was amended to include Title VII. With two exceptions, the bill reported by the House Judiciary Committee contained §§ 703 (a) and (d) as they were ultimately enacted. Amendments subsequently adopted on the House floor added 703's prohibition against sex discrimination and § 703 (d)'s coverage of "on-the-job training."

After noting that "[t]he purpose of [Title VII] is to eliminate . . . discrimination in employment based on race, color, religion, or national origin," the Judiciary Committee's Report simply paraphrased the provisions of Title VII without elaboration. H. R. Rep., pt. 1, p. 26. In a separate Minority Report, however, opponents of the measure on the Committee advanced a line of attack which was reiterated throughout the debates in both the House and Senate and which ultimately led to passage of § 703 (j). Noting that the word "discrimination" was nowhere defined in H. R. 7152, the Minority Report charged that the absence from Title VII of any reference to "racial imbalance" was a "public relations" ruse and that "the administration intends to rely upon its own construction of 'discrimination' as including the lack of racial balance. . . ." H. R. Rep., pt. 1, pp. 67–68. To demonstrate how the bill would operate in practice, the Minority Report posited a number of hypothetical employment situations, concluding in each example that the employer "*may be forced to hire according to race* to 'racially balance' those who work for him *in every job classification* or be in violation of Federal law." *Id.*, at 69 (emphasis in original).

When H. R. 7152 reached the House floor, the opening speech in support of its passage was delivered by Representative Celler, Chairman of the House Judiciary Committee and the Congressman responsible for introducing the legislation. A portion of that speech responded to criticism "seriously misrepresent[ing] what the bill would do and grossly distort[ing] its effects":

"[T]he charge has been made that the Equal Employment Opportunity Commission to be established by title VII of the bill would have the power to prevent a business from employing and promoting the people it wished, and that a 'Federal inspector' could then order the hiring and promotion only of employees of certain races or religious groups. This description of the bill is entirely wrong. . . .

"Even [a] court could not order that any preference be given to any particular race, religion or other group, but would be limited to ordering an end of discrimination. The statement that a Federal inspector could order the employment and promotion only of members of a specific racial or religious group is therefore patently erroneous.

" . . . The Bill would do no more than prevent . . . employers from discriminating against or *in favor* of workers because of their race, religion, or national origin.

"It is likewise not true that the Equal Employment Opportunity Commission would have power to rectify existing 'racial or religious imbalance' in employment by requiring the hiring of certain people without regard to their qualifications simply because they are of a given race or religion. Only actual discrimination could be stopped." 110 Cong. Rec. 1518 (1964) (emphasis added).

Representative Celler's construction of Title VII was repeated by several other supporters during the House debate.

Thus, the battle lines were drawn early in the legislative struggle over Title VII, with opponents of the measure charging that agencies of the Federal Government such as the Equal Employment Opportunity Commission (EEOC), by interpreting the word "discrimination" to mean the existence of "racial imbalance," would "require" employers to grant preferential treatment to minorities, and supporters responding that the EEOC would be granted no such power and that, indeed, Title VII prohibits discrimination "in favor of workers because of their race." Supporters of H. R. 7152 in the House ultimately prevailed by a vote of

290 to 130, and the measure was sent to the Senate to begin what became the longest debate in that body's history.

B

The Senate debate was broken into three phases: the debate on sending the bill to Committee, the general debate on the bill prior to invocation of cloture, and the debate following cloture.

1

When debate on the motion to refer the bill to Committee opened, opponents of Title VII in the Senate immediately echoed the fears expressed by their counterparts in the House, as is demonstrated by the following colloquy between Senators Hill and Ervin:

"Mr. ERVIN. I invite attention to . . . Section [703 (a)]. . . .

"I ask the Senator from Alabama if the Commission could not tell an employer that he had too few employees, that he had limited his employment, and enter an order, under [Section 703 (a)], requiring him to hire more persons, not because the employer thought he needed more persons, but because the Commission wanted to compel him to employ persons of a particular race.

"Mr. HILL. The Senator is correct. That power is written into the bill. The employer could be forced to hire additional persons. . . ." 110 Cong. Rec. 4764 (1964).

Senator Humphrey, perhaps the primary moving force behind H. R. 7152 in the Senate, was the first to state the proponents' understanding of Title VII. Responding to a political advertisement charging that federal agencies were at liberty to interpret the word "discrimination" in Title VII to require racial balance, Senator Humphrey stated: "[T]he meaning of racial or religious discrimination is perfectly clear. . . . [I]t means a distinction in treatment given to different individuals because of their different race, religion, or national origin." *Id.*, at 5423. Stressing that Title VII "does not limit the employer's freedom to hire, fire, promote or demote for any reasons—or no reasons—so long as his action is not based on race," Senator Humphrey further stated that "nothing in the bill would permit any official or court to require any employer or labor union to give preferential treatment to any minority group." *Ibid.*

After 17 days of debate, the Senate voted to take up the bill directly, without referring it to a committee. Consequently, there is no Committee Report in the Senate.

2

Formal debate on the merits of H. R. 7152 began on March 30, 1964. Supporters of the bill in the Senate had made elaborate preparations for this second round. Senator Humphrey, the majority whip, and Senator

Kuchel, the minority whip, were selected as the bipartisan floor managers on the entire civil rights bill. Responsibility for explaining and defending each important title of the bill was placed on bipartisan "captains." Senators Clark and Case were selected as the bipartisan captains responsible for Title VII. Vaas, Title VII: Legislative History, 7 B. C. Ind. & Com. L. Rev. 431, 444–445 (1966) (hereinafter Title VII: Legislative History).

In the opening speech of the formal Senate debate on the bill, Senator Humphrey addressed the main concern of Title VII's opponents, advising that not only does Title VII not require use of racial quotas, *it does not permit their use.* "The truth," stated the floor leader of the bill, "is that this title forbids discriminating against anyone on account of race. This is the simple and complete truth about title VII." 110 Cong. Rec. 6549 (1964). Senator Humphrey continued:

"Contrary to the allegations of some opponents of this title, there is nothing in it that will give any power to the Commission or to any court to require hiring, firing, or promotion of employees in order to meet a racial 'quota' or to achieve a certain racial balance.

"That bugaboo has been brought up a dozen times; but it is nonexistent. In fact, *the very opposite is true. Title VII prohibits discrimination.* In effect, it says that race, religion and national origin are not to be used as the basis for hiring and firing. Title VII is designed to encourage hiring on the basis of ability and qualifications, not race or religion." *Ibid.* (emphasis added).

At the close of his speech, Senator Humphrey returned briefly to the subject of employment quotas: "It is claimed that the bill would require racial quotas for all hiring, when in fact it provides that race shall not be a basis for making personnel decisions." *Id.*, at 6553.

Senator Kuchel delivered the second major speech in support of H. R. 7152. In addressing the concerns of the opposition, he observed that "[n]othing could be further from the truth" than the charge that "Federal inspectors" would be empowered under Title VII to dictate racial balance and preferential advancement of minorities. *Id.*, at 6563. Senator Kuchel emphasized that seniority rights would in no way be affected by Title VII: "Employers and labor organizations could not discriminate *in favor of or against* a person because of his race, his religion, or his national origin. In such matters . . . the bill now before us . . . is color-blind." *Id.*, at 6564 (emphasis added).

A few days later the Senate's attention focused exclusively on Title VII, as Senators Clark and Case rose to discuss the title of H. R. 7152 on which they shared floor "captain" responsibilities. In an interpretative memorandum submitted jointly to the Senate, Senators Clark and Case took pains to refute the opposition's charge that Title VII would result in preferential treatment of minorities. Their words were clear and unequivocal:

"There is no requirement in title VII that an employer maintain a racial balance in his work force. On the contrary, any deliberate attempt to maintain a racial balance, whatever such a balance may be, would involve a violation of title VII because maintaining such a balance would require an employer to hire or to refuse to hire on the basis of race. It must be emphasized that discrimination is prohibited as to any individual." *Id.*, at 7213.

Of particular relevance to the instant litigation were their observations regarding seniority rights. As if directing their comments at Brian Weber, the Senators said:

"Title VII would have no effect on established seniority rights. Its effect is prospective and not retrospective. Thus, for example, if a business has been discriminating in the past and as a result has an all-white working force, when the title comes into effect the employer's obligation would be simply to fill future vacancies on a nondiscriminatory basis. He would not be obliged—*or indeed permitted*—to fire whites in order to hire Negroes, *or to prefer Negroes for future vacancies, or, once Negroes are hired, to give them special seniority rights at the expense of the white workers hired earlier." Ibid.* (emphasis added).

Thus, with virtual clairvoyance the Senate's leading supporters of Title VII anticipated precisely the circumstances of this case and advised their colleagues that the type of minority preference employed by Kaiser would violate Title VII's ban on racial discrimination. To further accentuate the point, Senator Clark introduced another memorandum dealing with common criticisms of the bill, including the charge that racial quotas would be imposed under Title VII. The answer was simple and to the point: "Quotas are themselves discriminatory." *Id.*, at 7218.

Despite these clear statements from the bill's leading and most knowledgeable proponents, the fears of the opponents were not put to rest. Senator Robertson reiterated the view that "discrimination" could be interpreted by a federal "bureaucrat" to require hiring quotas. *Id.*, at 7418–7420. Senators Smathers and Sparkman, while conceding that Title VII does not in so many words require the use of hiring quotas, repeated the opposition's view that employers would be coerced to grant preferential hiring treatment to minorities by agencies of the Federal Government. Senator Williams was quick to respond:

"Those opposed to H. R. 7152 should realize that to hire a Negro solely because he is a Negro is racial discrimination, just as much as a 'white only' employment policy. Both forms of discrimination are prohibited by title VII of this bill. The language of that title simply states that race is not a qualification for employment. . . . Some people charge that H. R. 7152 favors the Negro, at the expense of the white majority. But how can the language of equality favor one race or one religion over another? Equality can have only one meaning, and that meaning is self-evident to reasonable men. Those who say that equality means favoritism do violence to common sense." *Id.*, at 8921.

Senator Williams concluded his remarks by noting that Title VII's only purpose is "the elimination of racial and religious discrimination in employment." *Ibid.* On May 25, Senator Humphrey again took the floor to defend the bill against "the well-financed drive by certain opponents to confuse and mislead the American people." *Id.*, at 11846. Turning once again to the issue of preferential treatment, Senator Humphrey remained faithful to the view that he had repeatedly expressed:

"The title does not provide that any preferential treatment in employment shall be given to Negroes or to any other persons or groups. It does not provide that any quota systems may be established to maintain racial balance in employment. In fact, *the title would prohibit preferential treatment for any particular group*, and any person, whether or not a member of any minority group, would be permitted to file a complaint of discriminatory employment practices." *Id.*, at 11848 (emphasis added).

While the debate in the Senate raged, a bipartisan coalition under the leadership of Senators Dirksen, Mansfield, Humphrey, and Kuchel was working with House leaders and representatives of the Johnson administration on a number of amendments to H. R. 7152 designed to enhance its prospects of passage. The so-called "Dirksen-Mansfield" amendment was introduced on May 26 by Senator Dirksen as a substitute for the entire House-passed bill. The substitute bill, which ultimately became law, left unchanged the basic prohibitory language of §§ 703 (a) and (d), as well as the remedial provisions in § 706 (g). It added, however, several provisions defining and clarifying the scope of Title VII's substantive prohibitions. One of those clarifying amendments, § 703 (j), was specifically directed at the opposition's concerns regarding racial balancing and preferential treatment of minorities, providing in pertinent part: "Nothing contained in [Title VII] shall be interpreted to require any employer . . . to grant preferential treatment to any individual or to any group because of the race . . . of such individual or group on account of" a racial imbalance in the employer's work force.

The Court draws from the language of § 703 (j) primary support for its conclusion that Title VII's blanket prohibition on racial discrimination in employment does not prohibit preferential treatment of blacks to correct racial imbalance. Alleging that opponents of Title VII had argued (1) that the Act would be interpreted to require employers with racially imbalanced work forces to grant preferential treatment to minorities and

(2) that "employers with racially imbalanced work forces would grant preferential treatment to racial minorities, even if not required to do so by the Act," the Court concludes that § 703 (j) is responsive only to the opponents' first objection and that Congress therefore must have intended to permit voluntary, private discrimination against whites in order to correct racial imbalance.

Contrary to the Court's analysis, the language of § 703 (j) is precisely tailored to the objection voiced time and again by Title VII's opponents. Not once during the 83 days of debate in the Senate did a speaker, proponent or opponent, suggest that the bill would allow employers *voluntarily* to prefer racial minorities over white persons. In light of Title VII's flat prohibition on discrimination "against any individual . . . because of such individual's race," such a contention would have been, in any event, too preposterous to warrant response. Indeed, speakers on both sides of the issue, as the legislative history makes clear, recognized that Title VII would tolerate no *voluntary* racial preference, whether in favor of blacks or whites. The complaint consistently voiced by the opponents was that Title VII, particularly the word "discrimination," would be *interpreted* by federal agencies such as the EEOC to *require* the correction of racial imbalance through the granting of preferential treatment to minorities. Verbal assurances that Title VII would not require—indeed, would not permit—preferential treatment of blacks having failed, supporters of H. R. 7152 responded by proposing an amendment carefully worded to meet, and put to rest, the opposition's charge. Indeed, unlike §§ 703 (a) and (d), which are by their terms directed at entities—*e. g.*, employers, labor unions—whose actions are restricted by Title VII's prohibitions, the language of § 703 (j) is specifically directed at entities—federal agencies and courts—charged with the responsibility of interpreting Title VII's provisions.

In light of the background and purpose of § 703 (j), the irony of invoking the section to justify the result in this case is obvious. The Court's frequent references to the "voluntary" nature of Kaiser's racially discriminatory admission quota bear no relationship to the facts of this case. Kaiser and the Steelworkers acted under pressure from an agency of the Federal Government, the Office of Federal Contract Compliance, which found that minorities were being "underutilized" at Kaiser's plants. *See* n. 2, *supra*. That is, Kaiser's work force was racially imbalanced. Bowing to that pressure, Kaiser instituted an admissions quota preferring blacks over whites, thus confirming that the fears of Title VII's opponents were well founded. Today, § 703 (j), adopted to allay those fears, is invoked by the Court to uphold imposition of a racial quota under the very circumstances that the section was intended to prevent.

Section 703 (j) apparently calmed the fears of most of the opponents; after its introduction, complaints concerning racial balance and preferential treatment died down considerably. Proponents of the bill, however, continued to reassure the opposition that its concerns were unfounded. In a lengthy defense of the entire civil rights bill, Senator Muskie emphasized that the opposition's "torrent of words . . . cannot obscure this basic, simple truth: Every American citizen has the right to equal treatment—not favored treatment, not complete individual equality—just equal treatment." 110 Cong. Rec. 12614 (1964).

With particular reference to Title VII, Senator Muskie noted that the measure "seeks to afford to all Americans equal opportunity in employment without discrimination. Not equal pay Not 'racial balance.' Only equal opportunity." *Id.*, at 12617.

Senator Saltonstall, Chairman of the Republican Conference of Senators participating in the drafting of the Dirksen-Mansfield amendment, spoke at length on the substitute bill. He advised the Senate that the Dirksen-Mansfield substitute, which included § 703 (j), "provides no preferential treatment for any group of citizens. In fact, *it specifically prohibits such treatment.*" 110 Cong. Rec. 12691 (1964) (emphasis added).

On June 9, Senator Ervin offered an amendment that would entirely delete Title VII from the bill. In answer to Senator Ervin's contention that Title VII "would make the members of a particular race special favorites of the laws," *id.*, at 13079, Senator Clark retorted:

"The bill does not make anyone higher than anyone else. It establishes no quotas. It leaves an employer free to select whomever he wishes to employ. . . .

"All this is subject to one qualification, and that qualification, is to state: 'In your activity as an employer . . . you must not discriminate because of the color of a man's skin. . . .'

"That is all this provision does. . . .

"It merely says, 'When you deal in interstate commerce, you must not discriminate on the basis of race. . . .'" *Id.*, at 13080.

The Ervin amendment was defeated, and the Senate turned its attention to an amendment proposed by Senator Cotton to limit application of Title VII to employers of at least 100 employees. During the course of the Senate's deliberations on the amendment, Senator Cotton had a revealing discussion with Senator Curtis, also an opponent of Title VII. Both men expressed dismay that Title VII would prohibit preferential hiring of "members of a minority race in order to enhance their opportunity":

"Mr. CURTIS. Is it not the opinion of the Senator that any individuals who provide jobs for a class of people who have perhaps not had sufficient opportunity for jobs should be commended rather than outlawed?

"Mr. COTTON. Indeed it is." *Id.*, at 13086.

Thus, in the only exchange on the Senate floor raising the possibility that an employer might wish to reserve jobs for minorities in order to assist them in overcoming their employment disadvantage, both speakers concluded that Title VII prohibits such, in the words of the Court, "voluntary, private, race-conscious efforts to abolish traditional patterns of racial segregation and hierarchy." Immediately after this discussion, both Senator Dirksen and Senator Humphrey took the floor in defense of the 25-employee limit contained in the Dirksen-Mansfield substitute bill, and neither Senator disputed the conclusions of Senators Cotton and Curtis. The Cotton amendment was defeated.

3

On June 10, the Senate, for the second time in its history, imposed cloture on its Members. The limited debate that followed centered on proposed amendments to the Dirksen-Mansfield substitute. Of some 24 proposed amendments, only 5 were adopted.

As the civil rights bill approached its final vote, several supporters rose to urge its passage. Senator Muskie adverted briefly to the issue of preferential treatment: "It has been said that the bill discriminates in favor of the Negro at the expense of the rest of us. It seeks to do nothing more than to lift the Negro from the status of inequality to one of *equality* of treatment." 110 Cong. Rec. 14328 (1964) (emphasis added). Senator Moss, in a speech delivered on the day that the civil rights bill was finally passed, had this to say about quotas:

"The bill does not accord to any citizen advantage or preference—it does not fix quotas of employment or school population—it does not force personal association. What it does is to prohibit public officials and those who invite the public generally to patronize their businesses or to apply for employment, to utilize the offensive, humiliating, and cruel practice of discrimination on the basis of race. In short, the bill does not accord special consideration; it establishes *equality*." *Id.*, at 14484 (emphasis added).

Later that day, June 19, the issue was put to a vote, and the Dirksen-Mansfield substitute bill was passed.

C

The Act's return engagement in the House was brief. The House Committee on Rules reported the Senate version without amendments on June 30, 1964. By a vote of 289 to 126, the House adopted H. Res. 789, thus agreeing to the Senate's amendments of H. R. 7152. Later that same day, July 2, the President signed the bill and the Civil Rights Act of 1964 became law.

IV

Reading the language of Title VII, as the Court purports to do, "against the background of [its] legislative history . . . and the historical context from which the Act arose," one is led inescapably to the conclusion that Congress fully understood what it was saying and meant precisely what it said. Opponents of the civil rights bill did not argue that employers would be permitted under Title VII voluntarily to grant preferential treatment to minorities to correct racial imbalance. The plain language of the statute too clearly prohibited such racial discrimination to admit of any doubt. They argued, tirelessly, that Title VII would be interpreted by federal agencies and their agents to require unwilling employers to racially balance their work forces by granting preferential treatment to minorities. Supporters of H. R. 7152 responded, equally tirelessly, that the Act would not be so interpreted because not only does it not require preferential treatment of minorities, it also does not *permit* preferential treatment of any race for any reason. It cannot be doubted that the proponents of Title VII understood the meaning of their words, for "[s]eldom has similar legislation been debated with greater consciousness of the need for 'legislative history,' or with greater care in the making thereof, to guide the courts in interpreting and applying the law." Title VII: Legislative History, at 444.

To put an end to the dispute, supporters of the civil rights bill drafted and introduced § 703 (j). Specifically addressed to the opposition's charge, § 703 (j) simply enjoins federal agencies and courts from interpreting Title VII to require an employer to prefer certain racial groups to correct imbalances in his work force. The section says nothing about voluntary preferential treatment of minorities because such racial discrimination is plainly proscribed by §§ 703 (a) and (d). Indeed, had Congress intended to except voluntary, race-conscious preferential treatment from the blanket prohibition of racial discrimination in §§ 703 (a) and (d), it surely could have drafted language better suited to the task than § 703 (j). It knew how. Section 703 (i) provides:

"Nothing contained in [Title VII] shall apply to any business or enterprise on or near an Indian reservation with respect to any publicly announced employment practice of such business or enterprise under which a preferential treatment is given to any individual because he is an Indian living on or near a reservation."

V

Our task in this case, like any other case involving the construction of a statute, is to give effect to the intent of Congress. To divine that intent, we traditionally look first to the words of the statute and, if they are unclear, then to the statute's legislative history. Finding the desired result hopelessly foreclosed by these conventional sources, the Court turns to a third source—the "spirit" of the Act. But close examination of what the Court proffers as the spirit of the Act reveals it as the spirit animating the present majority, not the 88th Congress. For if the spirit of the Act eludes the cold words of the statute itself, it rings out with unmistakable clarity in the words of the elected representatives who made the Act law. It is *equality*. Senator Dirksen, I think, captured that spirit in a speech delivered on the floor of the Senate just moments before the bill was passed:

" . . . [T]oday we come to grips finally with a bill that advances the enjoyment of living; but, more than that, it advances the equality of opportunity.

"I do not emphasize the word 'equality' standing by itself. It means equality of opportunity in the field of education. It means equality of opportunity in the field of employment. It means equality of opportunity in the field of participation in the affairs of government. . . .

"That is it.

"Equality of opportunity, if we are going to talk about conscience, is the mass conscience of mankind that speaks in every generation, and it will continue to speak long after we are dead and gone." 110 Cong. Rec. 14510 (1964).

There is perhaps no device more destructive to the notion of equality than the *numerus clausus*—the quota. Whether described as "benign discrimination" or "affirmative action," the racial quota is nonetheless a creator of castes, a two-edged sword that must demean one in order to prefer another. In passing Title VII, Congress outlawed *all* racial discrimination, recognizing that no discrimination based on race is benign, that no action disadvantaging a person because of his color is affirmative. With today's holding, the Court introduces into Title VII a tolerance for the very evil that the law was intended to eradicate, without offering even a clue as to what the limits on that tolerance may be. We are told simply that Kaiser's racially discriminatory admission quota "falls on the permissible side of the line." By going not merely *beyond*, but directly *against* Title VII's language and legislative history, the Court has sown the wind. Later courts will face the impossible task of reaping the whirlwind.

F. THE COURT REVISITS THE AFFIRMATIVE ACTION QUESTION

JOHNSON V. TRANSPORTATION AGENCY
480 U.S. 616 (1987)

In 1987, the Supreme Court had the opportunity to reconsider the *Weber* decision. As you read the following case, focus on the following questions and issues:

- Justice Brennan again writes the opinion for the majority. Unsurprisingly, he votes as he did in *Weber*. But how does he respond to Justice Scalia's dissent? Look closely at Footnote 7. What is his view concerning why judges should defer to precedent in statutory interpretation cases?

- How does Justice Stevens say he would have voted in *Weber*? How does he vote in *Johnson*? How does he reconcile this? What would the consequences be if the Court reversed *Weber*, according to Justice Stevens? What does this say about his approach to statutory interpretation and to precedent? How does it differ from Justice Brennan's? Justice Stevens seems to suggest that statutory meaning and application may change over time. What could possibly justify this?

- Suppose these cases presented a constitutional rather than statutory question. How much force would Justice Brennan's concern for precedent have? What about Justice Stevens's?

- Justice Scalia votes in Johnson as Justice Rehnquist did in *Weber*. But their opinions are very different in ways that reflect their different approaches to statutory interpretation. Can you articulate these differences?

- How does Justice Scalia respond to Justice Brennan's concern for precedent? How does he respond to Justice Stevens's? Does Justice Scalia care about precedent? If so, under what conditions? If not, why not?

- How would you have voted in *Weber*? How would you have voted in *Johnson*?

- For the most part, the Justices in both *Weber* and *Johnson* voted in ways that were consistent with their politics or party affiliations. Justice Brennan was a committed liberal. Justice Rehnquist was a staunch conservative, as is Justice Scalia. Do you think their opinions are guided by neutral application of the rules of statutory interpretation, or do their opinions merely serve as sophisticated rhetorical justifications for their political preferences? If the former, is the fact that their opinions in the case lined up nicely with their policy preferences just a happy coincidence? If the latter, what does this say about the project of statutory interpretation? Can judges ever separate their personal, political, and ideological preferences from their jobs as judges?

JUSTICE BRENNAN delivered the opinion of the Court.

Respondent, Transportation Agency of Santa Clara County, California, unilaterally promulgated an Affirmative Action Plan applicable, *inter alia*, to promotions of employees. In selecting applicants for the promotional position of road dispatcher, the Agency, pursuant to the Plan, passed over petitioner Paul Johnson, a male employee, and promoted a female employee applicant, Diane Joyce. The question for decision is whether in making the promotion the Agency impermissibly took into account the sex of the applicants in violation of Title VII of the Civil Rights Act of 1964. The District Court for the Northern District of California, in an action filed by petitioner following receipt of a right-to-sue letter from the Equal Employment Opportunity Commission (EEOC), held that respondent had violated Title VII. The Court of Appeals for the Ninth Circuit reversed. We granted certiorari. We affirm.

I

A

In December 1978, the Santa Clara County Transit District Board of Supervisors adopted an Affirmative Action Plan (Plan) for the County Transportation Agency. The Plan implemented a County Affirmative Action Plan, which had been adopted, declared the County, because "mere prohibition of discriminatory practices is not enough to remedy the effects of past practices and to permit attainment of an equitable representation of minorities, women and handicapped persons." Relevant to this case, the Agency Plan provides that, in making promotions to positions within a traditionally segregated job classification in which women have been significantly underrepresented, the Agency is authorized to consider as one factor the sex of a qualified applicant.

In reviewing the composition of its work force, the Agency noted in its Plan that women were represented in numbers far less than their proportion of the County labor force in both the Agency as a whole and in five of seven job categories. Specifically, while women constituted 36.4% of the area labor market, they composed only 22.4% of Agency employees. Furthermore, women working at the Agency were concentrated largely in EEOC job categories traditionally held by women: women made up 76% of Office and Clerical Workers, but only 7.1% of Agency Officials and Administrators, 8.6% of Professionals, 9.7% of Technicians, and 22% of Service and Maintenance Workers. As for the job classification relevant to this case, none of the 238 Skilled Craft Worker positions was held by a woman. The Plan noted that this underrepresentation of women in part reflected the fact that women had not traditionally been employed in these positions, and that they had not been strongly motivated to seek training or employment in them "because of the limited opportunities that have existed in the past for them to work in such classifications."

The Plan also observed that, while the proportion of ethnic minorities in the Agency as a whole exceeded the proportion of such minorities in the County work force, a smaller percentage of minority employees held management, professional, and technical positions.

The Agency stated that its Plan was intended to achieve "a statistically measurable yearly improvement in hiring, training and promotion of minorities and women throughout the Agency in all major job classifications where they are underrepresented." As a benchmark by which to evaluate progress, the Agency stated that its long-term goal was to attain a work force whose composition reflected the proportion of minorities and women in the area labor force. Thus, for the Skilled Craft category in which the road dispatcher position at issue here was classified, the Agency's aspiration was that eventually about 36% of the jobs would be occupied by women.

The Plan acknowledged that a number of factors might make it unrealistic to rely on the Agency's long-term goals in evaluating the Agency's progress in expanding job opportunities for minorities and women. Among the factors identified were low turnover rates in some classifications, the fact that some jobs involved heavy labor, the small number of positions within some job categories, the limited number of entry positions leading to the Technical and Skilled Craft classifications, and the limited number of minorities and women qualified for positions requiring specialized training and experience. As a result, the Plan counseled that short-range goals be established and annually adjusted to serve as the most realistic guide for actual employment decisions. Among the tasks identified as important in establishing such short-term goals was the acquisition of data "reflecting the ratio of minorities, women and handicapped persons who are working in the local area in major job classifications relating to those utilized by the County Administration," so as to determine the availability of members of such groups who "possess the desired qualifications or potential for placement." These data on qualified group members, along with predictions of position vacancies, were to serve as the basis for "realistic yearly employment goals for women, minorities and handicapped persons in each EEOC job category and major job classification."

The Agency's Plan thus set aside no specific number of positions for minorities or women, but authorized the consideration of ethnicity or sex as a factor when evaluating qualified candidates for jobs in which members of such groups were poorly represented. One such job was the road dispatcher position that is the subject of the dispute in this case.

B

On December 12, 1979, the Agency announced a vacancy for the promotional position of road dispatcher in the Agency's Roads Division.

Dispatchers assign road crews, equipment, and materials, and maintain records pertaining to road maintenance jobs. The position requires at minimum four years of dispatch or road maintenance work experience for Santa Clara County. The EEOC job classification scheme designates a road dispatcher as a Skilled Craft Worker.

Twelve County employees applied for the promotion, including Joyce and Johnson. Joyce had worked for the County since 1970, serving as an account clerk until 1975. She had applied for a road dispatcher position in 1974, but was deemed ineligible because she had not served as a road maintenance worker. In 1975, Joyce transferred from a senior account clerk position to a road maintenance worker position, becoming the first woman to fill such a job. During her four years in that position, she occasionally worked out of class as a road dispatcher.

Petitioner Johnson began with the County in 1967 as a road yard clerk, after private employment that included working as a supervisor and dispatcher. He had also unsuccessfully applied for the road dispatcher opening in 1974. In 1977, his clerical position was downgraded, and he sought and received a transfer to the position of road maintenance worker. He also occasionally worked out of class as a dispatcher while performing that job.

Nine of the applicants, including Joyce and Johnson, were deemed qualified for the job, and were interviewed by a two-person board. Seven of the applicants scored above 70 on this interview, which meant that they were certified as eligible for selection by the appointing authority. The scores awarded ranged from 70 to 80. Johnson was tied for second with a score of 75, while Joyce ranked next with a score of 73. A second interview was conducted by three Agency supervisors, who ultimately recommended that Johnson be promoted. Prior to the second interview, Joyce had contacted the County's Affirmative Action Office because she feared that her application might not receive disinterested review. The Office in turn contacted the Agency's Affirmative Action Coordinator, whom the Agency's Plan makes responsible for, *inter alia*, keeping the Director informed of opportunities for the Agency to accomplish its objectives under the Plan. At the time, the Agency employed no women in any Skilled Craft position, and had never employed a woman as a road dispatcher. The Coordinator recommended to the Director of the Agency, James Graebner, that Joyce be promoted.

Graebner, authorized to choose any of the seven persons deemed eligible, thus had the benefit of suggestions by the second interview panel and by the Agency Coordinator in arriving at his decision. After deliberation, Graebner concluded that the promotion should be given to Joyce. As he testified: "I tried to look at the whole picture, the combination of her qualifications and Mr. Johnson's qualifications, their test scores, their expertise, their background, affirmative action matters, things like that. . . . I believe it was a combination of all those."

The certification form naming Joyce as the person promoted to the dispatcher position stated that both she and Johnson were rated as well qualified for the job. The evaluation of Joyce read: "Well qualified by virtue of 18 years of past clerical experience including 3 1/2 years at West Yard plus almost 5 years as a [road maintenance worker]." The evaluation of Johnson was as follows: "Well qualified applicant; two years of [road maintenance worker] experience plus 11 years of Road Yard Clerk. Has had previous outside Dispatch experience but was 13 years ago." Graebner testified that he did not regard as significant the fact that Johnson scored 75 and Joyce 73 when interviewed by the two-person board.

Petitioner Johnson filed a complaint with the EEOC alleging that he had been denied promotion on the basis of sex in violation of Title VII. He received a right-to-sue letter from the EEOC on March 10, 1981, and on March 20, 1981, filed suit in the United States District Court for the Northern District of California. The District Court found that Johnson was more qualified for the dispatcher position than Joyce, and that the sex of Joyce was the "*determining factor* in her selection." The court acknowledged that, since the Agency justified its decision on the basis of its Affirmative Action Plan, the criteria announced in *Steelworkers v. Weber*, should be applied in evaluating the validity of the Plan. It then found the Agency's Plan invalid on the ground that the evidence did not satisfy *Weber's* criterion that the Plan be temporary. The Court of Appeals for the Ninth Circuit reversed, holding that the absence of an express termination date in the Plan was not dispositive, since the Plan repeatedly expressed its objective as the attainment, rather than the maintenance, of a work force mirroring the labor force in the County. The Court of Appeals added that the fact that the Plan established no fixed percentage of positions for minorities or women made it less essential that the Plan contain a relatively explicit deadline. The Court held further that the Agency's consideration of Joyce's sex in filling the road dispatcher position was lawful. The Agency Plan had been adopted, the court said, to address a conspicuous imbalance in the Agency's work force, and neither unnecessarily trammeled the rights of other employees, nor created an absolute bar to their advancement.

II

As a preliminary matter, we note that petitioner bears the burden of establishing the invalidity of the Agency's Plan. Only last Term, in *Wygant v. Jackson Board of Education*, we held that "[t]he ultimate burden remains with the employees to demonstrate the unconstitutionality of an affirmative-action program," and we see no basis for a different rule regarding a plan's alleged violation of Title VII. This case also fits readily within the analytical framework set forth in *McDonnell Douglas Corp. v. Green*. Once a plaintiff establishes a *prima facie* case that race or sex has been taken into account in an employer's employment decision, the burden shifts to the employer to articulate a nondiscriminatory rationale for its decision. The existence of an affirmative action plan provides such a rationale. If such a plan is articulated as the basis for the employer's decision, the burden shifts to the plaintiff to prove that the employer's justification is pretextual and the plan is invalid. As a practical matter, of course, an employer will generally seek to avoid a charge of pretext by presenting evidence in support of its plan. That does not mean, however, as petitioner suggests, that reliance on an affirmative action plan is to be treated as an affirmative defense requiring the employer to carry the burden of proving the validity of the plan. The burden of proving its invalidity remains on the plaintiff.

The assessment of the legality of the Agency Plan must be guided by our decision in *Weber*. In that case, the Court addressed the question whether the employer violated Title VII by adopting a voluntary affirmative action plan designed to "eliminate manifest racial imbalances in traditionally segregated job categories." The respondent employee in that case challenged the employer's denial of his application for a position in a newly established craft training program, contending that the employer's selection process impermissibly took into account the race of the applicants. The selection process was guided by an affirmative action plan, which provided that 50% of the new trainees were to be black until the percentage of black skilled craftworkers in the employer's plant approximated the percentage of blacks in the local labor force. Adoption of the plan had been prompted by the fact that only 5 of 273, or 1.83%, of skilled craftworkers at the plant were black, even though the work force in the area was approximately 39% black. Because of the historical exclusion of blacks from craft positions, the employer regarded its former policy of hiring trained outsiders as inadequate to redress the imbalance in its work force.

We upheld the employer's decision to select less senior black applicants over the white respondent, for we found that taking race into account was consistent with Title VII's objective of "break[ing] down old patterns of racial segregation and hierarchy." As we stated:

"It would be ironic indeed if a law triggered by a Nation's concern over centuries of racial injustice and intended to improve the lot of those who had 'been excluded from the American dream for so long' constituted the first legislative prohibition of all voluntary, private, race-conscious efforts to abolish traditional patterns of racial segregation and hierarchy." [Footnote 7]

We noted that the plan did not "unnecessarily trammel the interests of the white employees," since it did not require "the discharge of white workers and their replacement with new black hirees." Nor did the plan create "an absolute bar to the advancement of white employees," since half of those trained in the new program were to be white. Finally, we observed that the plan was a temporary measure, not designed to maintain racial balance, but to "eliminate a manifest racial imbalance." As JUSTICE BLACKMUN's concurrence made clear, *Weber* held that an employer seeking to justify the adoption of a plan need not point to its own prior discriminatory practices, nor even to evidence of an "arguable violation" on its part. Rather, it need point only to a "conspicuous . . . imbalance in traditionally segregated job categories." Our decision was grounded in the recognition that voluntary employer action can play a crucial role in furthering Title VII's purpose of eliminating the effects of discrimination in the workplace, and that Title VII should not be read to thwart such efforts.

In reviewing the employment decision at issue in this case, we must first examine whether that decision was made pursuant to a plan prompted by concerns similar to those of the employer in *Weber*. Next, we must determine whether the effect of the Plan on males and nonminorities is comparable to the effect of the plan in that case.

The first issue is therefore whether consideration of the sex of applicants for Skilled Craft jobs was justified by the existence of a "manifest imbalance" that reflected underrepresentation of women in "traditionally segregated job categories." In determining whether an imbalance exists that would justify taking sex or race into account, a comparison of the percentage of minorities or women in the employer's work force with the percentage in the area labor market or general population is appropriate in analyzing jobs that require no special expertise . . . , or training programs designed to provide expertise. . . . Where a job requires special training, however, the comparison should be with those in the labor force who possess the relevant qualifications. . . . The requirement that the "manifest imbalance" relate to a "traditionally segregated job category" provides assurance both that sex or race will be taken into account in a manner consistent with Title VII's purpose of eliminating the effects of employment discrimination, and that the interests of those employees not benefiting from the plan will not be unduly infringed.

. . . .

It is clear that the decision to hire Joyce was made pursuant to an Agency plan that directed that sex or race be taken into account for the purpose of remedying underrepresentation. The Agency Plan acknowledged the "limited opportunities that have existed in the past" for women to find employment in certain job classifications "where women have not been traditionally employed in significant numbers." As a result, observed the Plan, women were concentrated in traditionally female jobs in the Agency, and represented a lower percentage in other job classifications than would be expected if such traditional segregation had not occurred. Specifically, 9 of the 10 Para-Professionals and 110 of the 145 Office and Clerical Workers were women. By contrast, women were only 2 of the 28 Officials and Administrators, 5 of the 58 Professionals, 12 of the 124 Technicians, none of the Skilled Craft Workers, and 1—who was Joyce—of the 110 Road Maintenance Workers. The Plan sought to remedy these imbalances through "hiring, training and promotion of . . . women throughout the Agency in all major job classifications where they are underrepresented."

As an initial matter, the Agency adopted as a benchmark for measuring progress in eliminating underrepresentation the long-term goal of a work force that mirrored in its major job classifications the percentage of women in the area labor market. Even as it did so, however, the Agency acknowledged that such a figure could not by itself necessarily justify taking into account the sex of applicants for positions in all job categories. For positions requiring specialized training and experience, the Plan observed that the number of minorities and women "who possess the qualifications required for entry into such job classifications is limited." The Plan therefore directed that annual short-term goals be formulated that would provide a more realistic indication of the degree to which sex should be taken into account in filling particular positions. The Plan stressed that such goals "should not be construed as 'quotas' that must be met," but as reasonable aspirations in correcting the imbalance in the Agency's work force. These goals were to take into account factors such as "turnover, layoffs, lateral transfers, new job openings, retirements and availability of minorities, women and handicapped persons in the area work force who possess the desired qualifications or potential for placement." The Plan specifically directed that, in establishing such goals, the Agency work with the County Planning Department and other sources in attempting to compile data on the percentage of minorities and women in the local labor force that were actually working in the job classifications constituting the Agency work force. From the outset, therefore, the Plan sought annually to develop even more refined measures of the underrepresentation in each job category that required attention.

As the Agency Plan recognized, women were most egregiously underrepresented in the Skilled Craft job category, since none of the 238 positions was occupied by a woman. In mid-1980, when Joyce was selected for the road dispatcher position, the Agency was still in the process of refining its short-term goals for Skilled Craft Workers in accordance with the directive of the Plan. This process did not reach fruition until 1982, when the Agency established a short-term goal for that year of 3 women for the 55 expected openings in that job category—a modest goal of about 6% for that category.

We reject petitioner's argument that, since only the long-term goal was in place for Skilled Craft positions at the time of Joyce's promotion, it was inappropriate for the Director to take into account affirmative action considerations in filling the road dispatcher position. The Agency's Plan emphasized that the long-term goals were not to be taken as guides for actual hiring decisions, but that supervisors were to consider a host of practical factors in seeking to meet affirmative action objectives, including the fact that in some job categories women were not qualified in numbers comparable to their representation in the labor force.

By contrast, had the Plan simply calculated imbalances in all categories according to the proportion of women in the area labor pool, and then directed that hiring be governed solely by those figures, its validity fairly could be called into question. This is because analysis of a more specialized labor pool normally is necessary in determining underrepresentation in some positions. If a plan failed to take distinctions in qualifications into account in providing guidance for actual employment decisions, it would dictate mere blind hiring by the numbers, for it would hold supervisors to "achievement of a particular percentage of minority employment or membership . . . regardless of circumstances such as economic conditions or the number of available qualified minority applicants. . . ."

The Agency's Plan emphatically did not authorize such blind hiring. It expressly directed that numerous factors be taken into account in making hiring decisions, including specifically the qualifications of female applicants for particular jobs. Thus, despite the fact that no precise short-term goal was yet in place for the Skilled Craft category in mid-1980, the Agency's management nevertheless had been clearly instructed that they were not to hire solely by reference to statistics. The fact that only the long-term goal had been established for this category posed no danger that personnel decisions would be made by reflexive adherence to a numerical standard.

Furthermore, in considering the candidates for the road dispatcher position in 1980, the Agency hardly needed to rely on a refined short-term goal to realize that it had a significant problem of underrepresentation that required attention. Given the obvious imbalance in the Skilled Craft category, and given the Agency's commitment to eliminating such imbalances, it was plainly not unreasonable for the Agency to determine that it was appropriate to consider as one factor the sex of Ms. Joyce in making its decision. The promotion of Joyce thus satisfies the first requirement enunciated in *Weber*, since it was undertaken to further an affirmative action plan designed to eliminate Agency work force imbalances in traditionally segregated job categories.

We next consider whether the Agency Plan unnecessarily trammeled the rights of male employees or created an absolute bar to their advancement. In contrast to the plan in *Weber*, which provided that 50% of the positions in the craft training program were exclusively for blacks . . . the Plan sets aside no positions for women. The Plan expressly states that "[t]he 'goals' established for each Division should not be construed as 'quotas' that must be met." Rather, the Plan merely authorizes that consideration be given to affirmative action concerns when evaluating qualified applicants. As the Agency Director testified, the sex of Joyce was but one of numerous factors he took into account in arriving at his decision. . . . Similarly, the Agency Plan requires women to compete with all other qualified applicants. No persons are automatically excluded from consideration; all are able to have their qualifications weighed against those of other applicants.

In addition, petitioner had no absolute entitlement to the road dispatcher position. Seven of the applicants were classified as qualified and eligible, and the Agency Director was authorized to promote any of the seven. Thus, denial of the promotion unsettled no legitimate, firmly rooted expectation on the part of petitioner. Furthermore, while petitioner in this case was denied a promotion, he retained his employment with the Agency, at the same salary and with the same seniority, and remained eligible for other promotions.

Finally, the Agency's Plan was intended to *attain* a balanced work force, not to maintain one. The Plan contains 10 references to the Agency's desire to "attain" such a balance, but no reference whatsoever to a goal of maintaining it. The Director testified that, while the "broader goal" of affirmative action, defined as "the desire to hire, to promote, to give opportunity and training on an equitable, non-discriminatory basis," is something that is "a permanent part" of "the Agency's operating philosophy," that broader goal "is divorced, if you will, from specific numbers or percentages."

The Agency acknowledged the difficulties that it would confront in remedying the imbalance in its work force, and it anticipated only gradual increases in the representation of minorities and women. It is thus unsurprising that the Plan contains no explicit end date, for the Agency's flexible, case-by-case approach was not expected to yield success in a brief period of time. Express assurance that a program is only temporary may be necessary if the program actually sets aside positions according to specific numbers. This is necessary both to minimize the effect of the program on other employees, and to ensure that the plan's goals "[are] not being used simply to achieve and maintain ... balance, but rather as a benchmark against which" the employer may measure its progress in eliminating the underrepresentation of minorities and women. In this case, however, substantial evidence shows that the Agency has sought to take a moderate, gradual approach to eliminating the imbalance in its work force, one which establishes realistic guidance for employment decisions, and which visits minimal intrusion on the legitimate expectations of other employees. Given this fact, as well as the Agency's express commitment to "attain" a balanced work force, there is ample assurance that the Agency does not seek to use its Plan to maintain a permanent racial and sexual balance.

III

In evaluating the compliance of an affirmative action plan with Title VII's prohibition on discrimination, we must be mindful of "this Court's and Congress' consistent emphasis on 'the value of voluntary efforts to further the objectives of the law.'" The Agency in the case before us has undertaken such a voluntary effort, and has done so in full recognition of both the difficulties and the potential for intrusion on males and nonminorities. The Agency has identified a conspicuous imbalance in job categories traditionally segregated by race and sex. It has made clear from the outset, however, that employment decisions may not be justified solely by reference to this imbalance, but must rest on a multitude of practical, realistic factors. It has therefore committed itself to annual adjustment of goals so as to provide a reasonable guide for actual hiring and promotion decisions. The Agency earmarks no positions for anyone; sex is but one of several factors that may be taken into account in evaluating qualified applicants for a position. As both the Plan's language and its manner of operation attest, the Agency has no intention of establishing a work force whose permanent composition is dictated by rigid numerical standards.

We therefore hold that the Agency appropriately took into account as one factor the sex of Diane Joyce in determining that she should be promoted to the road dispatcher position. The decision to do so was made pursuant to an affirmative action plan that represents a moderate, flexible, case-by-case approach to effecting a gradual improvement in the representation of minorities and women in the Agency's work force. Such a plan is fully consistent with Title VII, for it embodies the contribution that voluntary employer action can make in eliminating the vestiges of discrimination in the workplace. Accordingly, the judgment of the Court of Appeals is

Affirmed.

. . . .

[Footnote 7] JUSTICE SCALIA's dissent maintains that *Weber's* conclusion that Title VII does not prohibit voluntary affirmative action programs "rewrote the statute it purported to construe." *Weber's* decisive rejection of the argument that the "plain language" of the statute prohibits affirmative action rested on (1) legislative history indicating Congress' clear intention that employers play a major role in eliminating the vestiges of discrimination, 443 U.S. at 201–204, and (2) the language and legislative history of § 703(j) of the statute, which reflect a strong desire to preserve managerial prerogatives so that they might be utilized for this purpose. *Id.*, at 204–207. As JUSTICE BLACKMUN said in his concurrence in *Weber*, "[I]f the Court has misperceived the political will, it has the assurance that because the question is statutory Congress may set a different course if it so chooses." *Id.* at 216. Congress has not amended the statute to reject our construction, nor have any such amendments even been proposed, and we therefore may assume that our interpretation was correct.

JUSTICE SCALIA's dissent faults the fact that we take note of the absence of congressional efforts to amend the statute to nullify *Weber*. It suggests that congressional inaction cannot be regarded as acquiescence under all circumstances, but then draws from that unexceptional point the conclusion that *any* reliance on congressional failure to act is necessarily a "canard." The fact that inaction may not always provide crystalline revelation, however, should not obscure the fact that it may be probative to varying degrees. *Weber*, for instance, was a widely publicized decision that addressed a prominent issue of public debate. Legislative inattention thus is not a plausible explanation for congressional inaction. Furthermore, Congress not only passed no contrary legislation in the wake of *Weber*, but not one legislator even proposed a bill to do so. The barriers of the legislative process therefore also seem a poor explanation for failure to act. By contrast, when Congress has been displeased with our interpretation of Title VII, it has not hesitated to amend the statute to tell us so. For instance, when Congress passed the Pregnancy Discrimination Act of 1978, 42 U.S.C. § 2000e(k), "it unambiguously expressed its disapproval of both the holding and the reasoning of the Court in [*General Electric Co. v. Gilbert*, 429 U.S. 125 (1976)]." *Newport News Shipbuilding & Dry Dock Co. v. EEOC*, 462 U.S. 669, 678 (1983). Surely, it is appropriate to find some probative value in such radically different congressional reactions to this Court's interpretations of the same statute.

As one scholar has put it, "When a court says to a legislature: 'You (or your predecessor) meant X,' it almost invites the legislature to answer: 'We did not.'" G. Calabresi, A Common Law for the Age of Statutes 31–32 (1982). Any belief in the notion of a dialogue between the judiciary and the legislature must acknowledge that on occasion an invitation declined is as significant as one accepted.

JUSTICE STEVENS, concurring.

While I join the Court's opinion, I write separately to explain my view of this case's position in our evolving antidiscrimination law and to emphasize that the opinion does not establish the permissible outer limits of voluntary programs undertaken by employers to benefit disadvantaged groups.

I

Antidiscrimination measures may benefit protected groups in two distinct ways. As a sword, such measures may confer benefits by specifying that a person's membership in a disadvantaged group must be a neutral, irrelevant factor in governmental or private decisionmaking or, alternatively, by compelling decisionmakers to give favorable consideration to disadvantaged group status. As a shield, an antidiscrimination statute can also help a member of a protected class by assuring decisionmakers in some instances that, when they elect for good reasons of their own to grant a preference of some sort to a minority citizen, they will not violate the law. The Court properly holds that the statutory shield allowed respondent to take Diane Joyce's sex into account in promoting her to the road dispatcher position.

Prior to 1978 the Court construed the Civil Rights Act of 1964 as an absolute blanket prohibition against discrimination which neither required nor permitted discriminatory preferences for any group, minority or majority. The Court unambiguously endorsed the neutral approach, first in the context of gender discrimination and then in the context of racial discrimination against a white person. As I explained in my separate opinion in *Regents of University of California v. Bakke*, and as the Court forcefully stated in *McDonald v. Santa Fe Trail Transportation Co.*, Congress intended " 'to eliminate all practices which operate to disadvantage the employment opportunities of any group protected by Title VII, including Caucasians.' " If the Court had adhered to that construction of the Act, petitioner would unquestionably prevail in this case. But it has not done so.

In the *Bakke* case in 1978 and again in *Steelworkers v. Weber*, a majority of the Court interpreted the antidiscriminatory strategy of the statute in a fundamentally different way. The Court held in the *Weber* case that an employer's program designed to increase the number of black craftworkers in an aluminum plant did not violate Title VII. It remains clear that the Act does not require any employer to grant preferential treatment on the basis of race or gender, but since 1978 the Court has unambiguously interpreted the statute to permit the voluntary adoption of special programs to benefit members of the minority groups for whose protection the statute was enacted. Neither the "same standards" language used in *McDonald*, nor the "color blind" rhetoric used by the Senators and Congressmen who enacted the bill, is now controlling. Thus, as was true in *Runyon v. McCrary*, the only problem for me is whether to adhere to an authoritative construction of the Act that is at odds with my understanding of the actual intent of the authors of the legislation. I conclude without hesitation that I must answer that question in the affirmative, just as I did in *Runyon*.

Bakke and *Weber* have been decided and are now an important part of the fabric of our law. This consideration is sufficiently compelling for me to adhere to the basic construction of this legislation that the Court adopted in *Bakke* and in *Weber*. There is an undoubted public interest in "stability and orderly development of the law."

The logic of antidiscrimination legislation requires that judicial constructions of Title VII leave "breathing room" for employer initiatives to benefit members of minority groups. If Title VII had never been enacted, a private employer would be free to hire members of minority groups for any reason that might seem sensible from a business or a social point of view. The Court's opinion in *Weber* reflects the same approach; the opinion relied heavily on legislative history indicating that Congress intended that traditional management prerogatives be left undisturbed to the greatest extent possible. As we observed last Term, " '[i]t would be ironic indeed if a law triggered by a Nation's concern over centuries of racial injustice and intended to improve the lot of those who had 'been excluded from the American dream for so long' constituted the first legislative prohibition of all voluntary, private, race-conscious efforts to abolish traditional patterns of racial segregation and hierarchy.' " In *Firefighters*, we again acknowledged Congress' concern in Title VII to avoid "undue federal interference with managerial discretion."

As construed in *Weber* and in *Firefighters*, the statute does not absolutely prohibit preferential hiring in favor of minorities; it was merely intended to protect historically disadvantaged groups against discrimination and not to hamper managerial efforts to benefit members of disadvantaged groups that are consistent with that paramount purpose. The preference granted by respondent in this case does not violate the statute as so construed; the record amply supports the conclusion that the challenged employment decision served the legitimate purpose of creating diversity in a category of employment that had been almost an exclusive province of males in the past. Respondent's voluntary decision is surely not prohibited by Title VII as construed in *Weber*.

II

Whether a voluntary decision of the kind made by respondent would ever be prohibited by Title VII is a question we need not answer until it is squarely presented. Given the interpretation of the statute the Court adopted in *Weber*, I see no reason why the employer has any duty, prior to granting a preference to a qualified minority employee, to determine whether his past conduct might constitute an arguable violation of Title VII. Indeed, in some instances the employer may find it more helpful to focus on the future. Instead of retroactively scrutinizing his own or society's possible exclusions of minorities in the past to determine the outer limits of a valid affirmative-action program—or indeed, any particular affirmative-action decision—in many cases the employer will find it more appropriate to consider other legitimate reasons to give preferences to members of underrepresented groups. Statutes enacted for the benefit of minority groups should not block these forward-looking considerations.

"Public and private employers might choose to implement affirmative action for many reasons other than to purge their own past sins of discrimination. The Jackson school board, for example, said it had done so in part to improve the quality of education in Jackson—whether by improving black students' performance or by dispelling for black and white students alike any idea that white supremacy governs our social institutions. Other employers might advance different forward-looking reasons for affirmative action: improving their services to black constituencies, averting racial tension over the allocation of jobs in a community, or increasing the diversity of a work force, to name but a few examples. Or they might adopt affirmative action simply to eliminate from their operations all *de facto* embodiment of a system of racial caste. All of these reasons aspire to a racially integrated future, but none reduces to 'racial balancing for its own sake.'"

The Court today does not foreclose other voluntary decisions based in part on a qualified employee's membership in a disadvantaged group. Accordingly, I concur.

[JUSTICE O'CONNOR'S concurrence and JUSTICE WHITE'S dissent have been omitted.]

JUSTICE SCALIA, dissenting.

With a clarity which, had it not proven so unavailing, one might well recommend as a model of statutory draftsmanship, Title VII of the Civil Rights Act of 1964 declares:

"It shall be an unlawful employment practice for an employer—

"(1) to fail or refuse to hire or to discharge any individual, or otherwise to discriminate against any individual with respect to his compensation, terms, conditions, or privileges of employment, because of such individual's race, color, religion, sex, or national origin; or

"(2) to limit, segregate, or classify his employees or applicants for employment in any way which would deprive or tend to deprive any individual of employment opportunities or otherwise adversely affect his status as an employee, because of such individual's race, color, religion, sex, or national origin."

The Court today completes the process of converting this from a guarantee that race or sex will *not* be the basis for employment determinations, to a guarantee that it often *will*. Ever so subtly, without even alluding to the last obstacles preserved by earlier opinions that we now push out of our path, we effectively replace the goal of a discrimination-free society with the quite incompatible goal of proportionate representation by race and by sex in the workplace. Part I of this dissent will describe the nature of the plan that the Court approves, and its effect upon this petitioner. Part II will discuss prior holdings that are tacitly overruled, and prior distinctions that are disregarded. Part III will describe the engine of discrimination we have finally completed.

I

On October 16, 1979, the County of Santa Clara adopted an Affirmative Action Program (County plan) which sought the "attainment of a County work force whose composition . . . includes women, disabled persons and ethnic minorities in a ratio in all job categories that reflects their distribution in the Santa Clara County area work force." In order to comply with the County plan and various requirements imposed by federal and state agencies, the Transportation Agency adopted, effective December 18, 1978, the Equal Employment Opportunity Affirmative Action Plan (Agency plan or plan) at issue here. Its stated long-range goal was the same as the County plan's: "to attain a work force whose composition in all job levels and major job classifications approximates the distribution of women, minority and handicapped persons in the Santa Clara County work force." The plan called for the establishment of a procedure by which Division Directors would review the ethnic and sexual composition of their work forces whenever they sought to fill a vacancy, which procedure was expected to include "a requirement that Division Directors indicate why they did *not* select minorities, women and handicapped persons if such persons were on the list of eligibles considered and if the Division had an underrepresentation of such persons in the job classification being filled." (emphasis in original).

Several salient features of the plan should be noted. Most importantly, the plan's purpose was assuredly not to remedy prior sex discrimination by the Agency. It could not have been, because there was no prior sex discrimination to remedy. The majority, in cataloging the Agency's alleged misdeeds, neglects to mention the District Court's finding that the Agency "has not discriminated in the past, and does not discriminate in the present against women in regard to employment opportunities in general and promotions in particular." This finding was not disturbed by the Ninth Circuit.

Not only was the plan not directed at the results of past sex discrimination by the Agency, but its objective was not to achieve the state of affairs that this Court has dubiously assumed would result from an absence of discrimination—an overall work force "more or less representative of the racial and ethnic composition of the population in the community." Rather, the oft-stated goal was to mirror the racial and sexual composition of the entire county labor force, not merely in the Agency work force as a whole, but in each and every individual job category at the Agency. In a discrimination-free world, it would obviously be a statistical oddity for every job category to match the racial and sexual composition of even that portion of the county work force *qualified* for that job; it would be utterly miraculous for each of them to match, as the plan expected, the composition of the *entire* work force. Quite obviously, the plan did not seek to replicate what a lack of discrimination would produce, but rather imposed racial and sexual tailoring that would, in defiance of normal expectations and laws of probability, give each protected racial and sexual group a governmentally determined "proper" proportion of each job category.

That the plan was not directed at remedying or eliminating the effects of past discrimination is most clearly illustrated by its description of what it regarded as the "Factors Hindering Goal Attainment"—*i.e.*, the existing impediments to the racially and sexually representative work force that it pursued. The plan noted that it would be "difficult" to attain its objective of across-the-board statistical parity in at least some job categories. . . .

Finally, the one message that the plan unmistakably communicated was that concrete results were expected, and supervisory personnel would be evaluated on the basis of the affirmative-action numbers they produced. The plan's implementation was expected to "result in a statistically measurable yearly improvement in the hiring, training and promotion of minorities, women and handicapped persons in the major job classifications utilized by the Agency where these groups are underrepresented." Its Preface declared that "[t]he degree to which each Agency Division *attains the Plan's objectives* will provide a direct measure of that Division Director's personal commitment to the EEO Policy," and the plan itself repeated that "[t]he degree to which each Division *attains the Agency Affirmative Action employment goals* will provide a measure of that Director's commitment and effectiveness in carrying out the Division's EEO Affirmative Action requirements." As noted earlier, supervisors were reminded of the need to give attention to affirmative action in every employment decision, and to explain their reasons for *failing* to hire women and minorities whenever there was an opportunity to do so.

The petitioner in the present case, Paul E. Johnson, had been an employee of the Agency since 1967, coming there from a private company where he had been a road dispatcher for 17 years. He had first applied for the position of Road Dispatcher at the Agency in 1974, coming in second. Several years later, after a reorganization resulted in a down-grading of his Road Yard Clerk II position, in which Johnson "could see no future," he requested and received a voluntary demotion from Road Yard Clerk II to Road Maintenance Worker, to increase his experience and thus improve his chances for future promotion. When the Road Dispatcher job next became vacant, in 1979, he was the leading candidate—and indeed was assigned to work out of class full time in the vacancy, from September 1979 until June 1980. There is no question why he did not get the job.

The fact of discrimination against Johnson is much clearer, and its degree more shocking, than the majority ... would suggest—largely because neither of them recites a single one of the District Court findings that govern this appeal, relying instead upon portions of the transcript which those findings implicitly rejected, and even upon a document (favorably comparing Joyce to Johnson) that was prepared *after* Joyce was selected. Worth mentioning, for example, is the trier of fact's determination that, if the Affirmative Action Coordinator had not intervened, "the decision as to whom to promote ... would have been made by [the Road Operations Division Director]," who had recommended that Johnson be appointed to the position. Likewise, the even more extraordinary findings that James Graebner, the Agency Director who made the appointment, "did not inspect the applications and related examination records of either [Paul Johnson] or Diane Joyce before making his decision," and indeed "did little or nothing to inquire into the results of the interview process and conclusions which [were] described as of critical importance to the selection process." In light of these determinations, it is impossible to believe (or to think that the District Court believed) Graebner's self-serving statements relied upon by the majority ..., such as the assertion that he "tried to look at the whole picture, the combination of [Joyce's] qualifications and Mr. Johnson's qualifications, their test scores, their expertise, their background, affirmative action matters, things like that." It was evidently enough for Graebner to know that both candidates (in the words of Johnson's counsel, to which Graebner assented) "met the M. Q.'s, the minimum. Both were minimally qualified." When asked whether he had "any basis," for determining whether one of the candidates was more qualified than the other, Graebner candidly answered, "No. . . . As I've said, they both appeared, and my conversations with people tended to corroborate, that they were both capable of performing the work."

After a 2-day trial, the District Court concluded that Diane Joyce's gender was *"the determining factor"* in her selection for the position. Specifically, it found that "[b]ased upon the examination results and the departmental interview, [Mr. Johnson] was more qualified for the position of Road Dispatcher than Diane Joyce"; that "[b]ut for [Mr. Johnson's] sex, male, he would have been promoted to the position of Road Dispatcher"; and that "[b]ut for Diane Joyce's sex, female, she would not have been appointed to the position. . . ." The Ninth Circuit did not reject these factual findings as clearly erroneous, nor could it have done so on the record before us. We are bound by those findings under Federal Rule of Civil Procedure 52(a).

II

The most significant proposition of law established by today's decision is that racial or sexual discrimination is permitted under Title VII when it is intended to overcome the effect, not of the employer's own discrimination, but of societal attitudes that have limited the entry of certain races, or of a particular sex, into certain jobs. Even if the societal attitudes in question consisted exclusively of conscious discrimination by other employers, this holding would contradict a decision of this Court rendered only last Term. . . .

Likewise on the assumption that the societal attitudes relied upon by the majority consist of conscious discrimination by employers, today's decision also disregards the limitations carefully expressed in last Term's opinions in *Sheet Metal Workers v. EEOC*. While those limitations were dicta, it is remarkable to see them so readily (and so silently) swept away. The question in *Sheet Metal Workers* was whether the remedial provision of Title VII empowers courts to order race-conscious relief for persons who were not identifiable victims of discrimination. Six Members of this Court concluded that it does, *under narrowly confined circumstances*. The plurality opinion for four Justices found that race-conscious relief could be ordered at least when "an employer or a labor union has engaged in persistent or egregious discrimination, or where necessary to dissipate the lingering effects of pervasive discrimination. . . ." There is no sensible basis for construing Title VII to permit employers to engage in race- or sex-conscious employment practices that courts would be forbidden from ordering them to engage in following a judicial finding of discrimination. As JUSTICE WHITE noted last Term:

"There is no statutory authority for concluding that if an employer desires to discriminate against a white applicant or employee on racial grounds he may do so without violating Title VII but may not be ordered to do so if he objects. In either case, the harm to the discriminatee is the same, and there is no justification for such conduct other than as a permissible remedy for prior racial discrimination practiced by the employer involved."

The Agency here was not seeking to remedy discrimination—much less "unusual" or "egregious" discrimination. *Firefighters*, like *Wygant*, is given only the most cursory consideration by the majority opinion.

In fact, however, today's decision goes well beyond merely allowing racial or sexual discrimination in order to eliminate the effects of prior societal *discrimination*. The majority opinion often uses the phrase "traditionally segregated job category" to describe the evil against which the plan is legitimately (according to the majority) directed. As originally used in *Steelworkers v. Weber*, that phrase described skilled jobs from which employers and unions had systematically and intentionally excluded black workers—traditionally segregated jobs, that is, in the sense of conscious, exclusionary discrimination. But that is assuredly not the sense in which the phrase is used here. It is absurd to think that the nationwide failure of road maintenance crews, for example, to achieve the Agency's ambition of 36.4% female representation is attributable primarily, if even substantially, to systematic exclusion of women eager to shoulder pick and shovel.

It is a "traditionally segregated job category" *not* in the *Weber* sense, but in the sense that, because of longstanding social attitudes, it has not been regarded *by women themselves* as desirable work. Or as the majority opinion puts the point, quoting approvingly the Court of Appeals: " 'A plethora of proof is hardly necessary to show that women are generally underrepresented in such positions and that strong social pressures weigh against their participation.' " Given this meaning of the phrase, it is patently false to say that "[t]he requirement that the 'manifest imbalance' relate to a 'traditionally segregated job category' provides assurance . . . that sex or race will be taken into account in a manner consistent with Title VII's purpose of eliminating the effects of employment discrimination." There are, of course, those who believe that the social attitudes which cause women themselves to avoid certain jobs and to favor others are as nefarious as conscious, exclusionary discrimination. Whether or not that is so (and there is assuredly no consensus on the point equivalent to our national consensus against intentional discrimination), the two phenomena are certainly distinct. And it is the alteration of social attitudes, rather than the elimination of discrimination, which today's decision approves as justification for state-enforced discrimination. This is an enormous expansion, undertaken without the slightest justification or analysis.

III

I have omitted from the foregoing discussion the most obvious respect in which today's decision o'erleaps, without analysis, a barrier that was thought still to be overcome. In *Weber*, this Court held that a private-sector, affirmative-action training program that overtly discriminated against white applicants did not violate Title VII. However, although the majority does not advert to the fact, until today the applicability of *Weber* to public employers remained an open question. In *Weber* itself, this Court has repeatedly emphasized that *Weber* involved only a private employer.... This distinction between public and private employers has several possible justifications. *Weber* rested in part on the assertion that the 88th Congress did not wish to intrude too deeply into private employment decisions. Whatever validity that assertion may have with respect to private employers (and I think it negligible), it has none with respect to public employers or to the 92d Congress that brought them within Title VII. Another reason for limiting *Weber* to private employers is that state agencies, unlike private actors, are subject to the Fourteenth Amendment. As noted earlier, it would be strange to construe Title VII to permit discrimination by public actors that the Constitution forbids.

In truth, however, the language of [the Act] draws no distinction between private and public employers, and the only good reason for creating such a distinction would be to limit the damage of *Weber*. It would be better, in my view, to acknowledge that case as fully applicable precedent, and to use the Fourteenth Amendment ramifications—which *Weber* did not address and which are implicated for the first time here—as the occasion for reconsidering and overruling it. It is well to keep in mind just how thoroughly *Weber* rewrote the statute it purported to construe. The language of that statute, as quoted at the outset of this dissent, is unambiguous: it is an unlawful employment practice "to fail or refuse to hire or to discharge any individual, or otherwise to discriminate against any individual with respect to his compensation, terms, conditions, or privileges of employment, because of such individual's race, color, religion, sex, or national origin." *Weber* disregarded the text of the statute, invoking instead its " 'spirit,' " and "practical and equitable [considerations] only partially perceived, if perceived at all, by the 88th Congress." It concluded, on the basis of these intangible guides, that Title VII's prohibition of intentional discrimination on the basis of race and sex does not prohibit intentional discrimination on the basis of race and sex, so long as it is "designed to break down old patterns of racial [or sexual] segregation and hierarchy," "does not unnecessarily trammel the interests of the white [or male] employees," "does not require the discharge of white [or male] workers and their replacement with new black [or female] hirees," "does [not] create an absolute bar to the advancement of white [or male] employees," and "is a temporary measure

... not intended to maintain racial [or sexual] balance, but simply to eliminate a manifest racial [or sexual] imbalance." In effect, *Weber* held that the legality of intentional discrimination by private employers against certain disfavored groups or individuals is to be judged not by Title VII but by a judicially crafted code of conduct, the contours of which are determined by no discernible standard, aside from (as the dissent convincingly demonstrated) the divination of congressional "purposes" belied by the face of the statute and by its legislative history. We have been recasting that self-promulgated code of conduct ever since—and what it has led us to today adds to the reasons for abandoning it.

The majority's response to this criticism of *Weber* asserts that, since "Congress has not amended the statute to reject our construction, . . . we . . . may assume that our interpretation was correct." This assumption, which frequently haunts our opinions, should be put to rest. It is based, to begin with, on the patently false premise that the correctness of statutory construction is to be measured by what the current Congress desires, rather than by what the law as enacted meant. To make matters worse, it assays the current Congress' desires *with respect to the particular provision in isolation,* rather than (the way the provision was originally enacted) as part of a total legislative package containing many *quids pro quo.* Whereas the statute as originally proposed may have presented to the enacting Congress a question such as "Should hospitals be required to provide medical care for indigent patients, with federal subsidies to offset the cost?," the question theoretically asked of the later Congress, in order to establish the "correctness" of a judicial interpretation that the statute provides no subsidies, is simply "Should the medical care that hospitals are required to provide for indigent patients be federally subsidized?" Hardly the same question—and many of those legislators who accepted the subsidy provisions in order to gain the votes necessary for enactment of the care requirement would not vote for the subsidy in isolation, now that an unsubsidized care requirement is, thanks to the judicial opinion, safely on the books.

But even accepting the flawed premise that the intent of the current Congress, with respect to the provision in isolation, is determinative, one must ignore rudimentary principles of political science to draw any conclusions regarding that intent from the failure to enact legislation. The "complicated check on legislation," erected by our Constitution creates an inertia that makes it impossible to assert with any degree of assurance that congressional failure to act represents (1) approval of the *status quo,* as opposed to (2) inability to agree upon how to alter the *status quo,* (3) unawareness of the *status quo,* (4) indifference to the *status quo,* or even (5) political cowardice. It is interesting to speculate on how the principle that congressional inaction proves judicial correctness would apply to another issue in the civil rights field, the liability of municipal corporations under § 1983. In 1961, we held that that statute did not reach municipalities. *See Monroe v. Pape.* Congress took no action to overturn our decision, but we ourselves did, in *Monell v. New York City Dept. of Social Services.* On the majority's logic, *Monell* was wrongly decided, since Congress' 17 years of silence established that *Monroe* had not "misperceived the political will," and one could therefore "assume that [*Monroe's*] interpretation was correct." On the other hand, nine years have now gone by since *Monell,* and Congress again has not amended § 1983. Should we now "assume that [*Monell's*] interpretation was correct"? Rather, I think we should admit that vindication by congressional inaction is a canard.

JUSTICE STEVENS' concurring opinion emphasizes the "undoubted public interest in 'stability and orderly development of the law'" that often requires adherence to an erroneous decision. As I have described above, however, today's decision is a demonstration not of stability and order but of the instability and unpredictable expansion which the substitution of judicial improvisation for statutory text has produced. For a number of reasons, *stare decisis* ought not to save *Weber.* First, this Court has applied the doctrine of *stare decisis* to civil rights statutes less rigorously than to other laws. Second, as JUSTICE STEVENS acknowledges in his concurrence, *Weber* was itself a dramatic departure from the Court's prior Title VII precedents, and can scarcely be said to be "so consistent with the warp and woof of civil rights law as to be beyond question." Third, *Weber* was decided a mere seven years ago, and has provided little guidance to persons seeking to conform their conduct to the law, beyond the proposition that Title VII does not mean what it says. Finally, "even under the most stringent test for the propriety of overruling a statutory decision . . . —'that it appear beyond doubt . . . that [the decision] misapprehended the meaning of the controlling provision,'" *Weber* should be overruled.

In addition to complying with the commands of the statute, abandoning *Weber* would have the desirable side effect of eliminating the requirement of willing suspension of disbelief that is currently a credential for reading our opinions in the affirmative-action field—from *Weber* itself, which demanded belief that the corporate employer adopted the affirmative-action program "voluntarily," rather than under practical compulsion from government contracting agencies; to *Bakke*, a Title VI case cited as authority by the majority here, which demanded belief that the University of California took race into account as merely one of the many diversities to which it felt it was educationally important to expose its medical students; to today's opinion, which—in the face of a plan obviously designed to force promoting officials to prefer candidates from the favored racial and sexual classes, warning them that their "personal commitment" will be determined by how successfully they "attain" certain numerical goals, and in the face of a particular promotion awarded to the less qualified applicant by an official who "did little or nothing" to inquire into sources "critical" to determining the final candidates' relative qualifications other than their sex—in the face of all this, demands belief that we are dealing here with no more than a program that "merely authorizes that consideration be given to affirmative action concerns when evaluating qualified applicants." Any line of decisions rooted so firmly in naivete must be wrong.

The majority emphasizes, as though it is meaningful, that *"No persons are automatically excluded from consideration; all are able to have their qualifications weighed against those of other applicants." Ibid.* One is reminded of the exchange from Shakespeare's King Henry the Fourth, Part I:

"GLENDOWER: I can call Spirits from the vasty Deep.

"HOTSPUR: Why, so can I, or so can any man. But will they come when you do call for them?"

Johnson was indeed entitled to have his qualifications weighed against those of other applicants—but more to the point, he was virtually assured that, after the weighing, if there was any minimally qualified applicant from one of the favored groups, he would be rejected.

Similarly hollow is the Court's assurance that we would strike this plan down if it "failed to take distinctions in qualifications into account," because that "would dictate mere blind hiring by the numbers." For what the Court means by "taking distinctions in qualifications into account" consists of no more than eliminating from the applicant pool those who are not even *minimally qualified* for the job. Once that has been done, once the promoting officer assures himself that all the candidates before him are "M. Q.'s" (minimally qualifieds), he can then ignore, as the Agency Director did here, how much better than minimally qualified some of the candidates may be, and can proceed to appoint from the pool solely on the basis of race or sex, until the affirmative-action "goals" have been reached. The requirement that the employer "take distinctions in qualifications into account" thus turns out to be an assurance, not that candidates' comparative merits will always be considered, but only that none of the successful candidates selected over the others solely on the basis of their race or sex will be utterly unqualified. That may be of great comfort to those concerned with American productivity; and it is undoubtedly effective in reducing the effect of affirmative-action discrimination upon those in the upper strata of society, who (unlike road maintenance workers, for example) compete for employment in professional and semiprofessional fields where, for many reasons, including most notably the effects of past discrimination, the numbers of "M. Q." applicants from the favored groups are substantially less. But I fail to see how it has any relevance to whether selecting among final candidates solely on the basis of race or sex is permissible under Title VII, which prohibits discrimination on the basis of race or sex.

Today's decision does more, however, than merely reaffirm *Weber*, and more than merely extend it to public actors. It is impossible not to be aware that the practical effect of our holding is to accomplish *de facto* what the law—in language even plainer than that ignored in *Weber*, *see* 42 U.S.C. § 2000e–2(j)—forbids anyone from accomplishing *de jure*: in many contexts it effectively *requires* employers, public as well as private, to engage in intentional discrimination on the basis of race or sex. This Court's prior interpretations of Title VII ... subject employers to a potential Title VII suit whenever there is a noticeable imbalance in the representation of minorities or women in the employer's work force. Even the employer who is confident of ultimately prevailing in such a suit must contemplate the expense and adverse publicity of a trial, because the extent of the imbalance, and the "job relatedness" of his selection criteria, are questions of fact to be explored through rebuttal and counterrebuttal of a *"prima facie* case" consisting of no more than the showing that the employer's selection process "selects those from the protected class at a 'significantly' lesser rate than their counterparts." If, however, employers are free to discriminate through affirmative action, without fear of "reverse discrimination" suits by their nonminority or male victims, they are offered a threshold defense against Title VII liability premised on numerical disparities. Thus, after today's decision the *failure* to engage in reverse discrimination is economic folly, and arguably a breach of duty to shareholders or taxpayers, wherever the cost of anticipated Title VII litigation exceeds the cost of hiring less capable (though still minimally capable) workers. (This situation is more likely to obtain, of course, with respect to the least skilled jobs—perversely creating an incentive to discriminate against precisely those members of the nonfavored groups *least* likely to have profited from societal discrimination in the past.) It is predictable, moreover, that this incentive will be greatly magnified by economic pressures brought to bear by government contracting agencies upon employers who refuse to discriminate in the fashion we have now approved. A statute designed to establish a color-blind and gender-blind workplace has thus been converted into a powerful engine of racism and sexism, not merely *permitting* intentional race- and sex-based discrimination, but often making it, through operation of the legal system, practically compelled.

It is unlikely that today's result will be displeasing to politically elected officials, to whom it provides the means of quickly accommodating the demands of organized groups to achieve concrete, numerical improvement in the economic status of particular constituencies. Nor will it displease the world of corporate and governmental employers (many of whom have filed briefs as *amici* in the present case, all on the side of Santa Clara) for whom the cost of hiring less qualified workers is often substantially less—and infinitely more predictable—than the cost of litigating Title VII cases and of seeking to convince federal agencies by nonnumerical means that no discrimination exists. In fact, the only losers in the process are the Johnsons of the country, for whom Title VII has been not merely repealed but actually inverted. The irony is that these individuals—predominantly unknown, unaffluent, unorganized—suffer this injustice at the hands of a Court fond of thinking itself the champion of the politically impotent. I dissent.

G. FURTHER EXPLORING THE ROLE OF PRECEDENT, "FIT," AND CHANGE IN STATUTORY MEANING AND APPLICATION OVER TIME

Central themes of *Johnson* are (1) whether and when judges should defer to precedent, even if the precedent was (in their opinion) wrongly decided, and (2) how *Weber* and *Johnson* fit into the larger tapestry of civil rights and discrimination law. Let's explore these concepts further in a different context: baseball.

FLOOD V. KUHN
407 U.S. 258 (1972)

As you read this case, focus on the following questions and issues:

- What is the "reserve clause?" Why is it a restraint on trade that is potentially at odds with the anti-trust laws?

- If Flood were a case of first impression, how would these Justices have voted?

- This case is touches on shifts in Commerce Clause doctrine between the 1920's and 1970's. As best you can explain, how did this doctrine change in the intervening years. More specifically, examine the views of Justice Holmes and explain what changed by 1970?

- How do the arguments in favor of retaining precedent compare in type and strength to the Justice Brennan's and Justice Stevens's different arguments for retaining *Weber* in *Johnson*?

- Many of the arguments in this case revolve around what exactly do we mean by stare *decisis* or "precedent." How many different interpretations of this doctrine can you find? Can you make out Justice Frankfurter's argument, (cited in the majority opinion) of how this opinion contradicts the doctrine of precedent?

- As a practical matter, what would happen if the baseball precedents upheld in *Flood* were instead overturned?

- According to the majority, the courts over the years have been preoccupied with the degree to which baseball is similar to other sports (like boxing, football, and basketball). Why does any of this matter?

- Each side in this case has an argument that the other side is acting like a legislature rather than like a court. What is the majority's claim against the Marshall dissent? How might the dissent(s) accuse the majority of the same?

- Take careful note of Justice Douglas's and Justice Marshall's dissenting opinions, both of which Justice Brennan joined. Is Justice Brennan consistent with his footnote 7 in *Johnson*? And how would Justices Marshall and Brennan mitigate the costs associated with overturning the precedents? Could this work in *Johnson*? Is it a good idea for courts to do this? Why or why not?

- How do you think Justice Scalia would have voted in *Flood* if he had been on the Court at the time? Why?

- Why do you think the opinion begins with an ode to baseball?

MR. JUSTICE BLACKMUN delivered the opinion of the Court.

For the third time in 50 years the Court is asked specifically to rule that professional baseball's reserve system is within the reach of the federal antitrust laws. Collateral issues of state law and of federal labor policy are also advanced.

I

The Game

It is a century and a quarter since the New York Nine defeated the Knickerbockers 23 to 1 on Hoboken's Elysian Fields June 19, 1846, with Alexander Jay Cartwright as the instigator and the umpire. The teams were amateur, but the contest marked a significant date in baseball's beginnings. That early game led ultimately to the development of professional baseball and its tightly organized structure.

The Cincinnati Red Stockings came into existence in 1869 upon an outpouring of local pride. With only one Cincinnatian on the payroll, this professional team traveled over 11,000 miles that summer, winning 56 games and tying one. Shortly thereafter, on St. Patrick's Day in 1871, the National Association of Professional Baseball Players was founded and the professional league was born.

The ensuing colorful days are well known. The ardent follower and the student of baseball know of General Abner Doubleday; the formation of the National League in 1876; Chicago's supremacy in the first year's competition under the leadership of Al Spalding and with Cap Anson at third base; the formation of the American Association and then of the Union Association in the 1880's; the introduction of Sunday baseball; interleague warfare with cut-rate admission prices and player raiding; the development of the reserve "clause"; the emergence in 1885 of the Brotherhood of Professional Ball Players, and in 1890 of the Players League; the appearance of the American League, or "junior circuit," in 1901, rising from the minor Western Association; the first World Series in 1903, disruption in 1904, and the Series' resumption in 1905; the short-lived Federal League on the majors' scene during World War I years; the troublesome and discouraging episode of the 1919 Series; the home run ball; the shifting of franchises; the expansion of the leagues; the installation in 1965 of the major league draft of potential new players; and the formation of the Major League Baseball Players Association in 1966.

Then there are the many names, celebrated for one reason or another, that have sparked the diamond and its environs and that have provided tinder for recaptured thrills, for reminiscence and comparisons, and for conversation and anticipation in-season and off-season: Ty Cobb, Babe Ruth, Tris Speaker, Walter Johnson, Henry Chadwick, Eddie

Collins, Lou Gehrig, Grover Cleveland Alexander, Rogers Hornsby, Harry Hooper, Goose Goslin, Jackie Robinson, Honus Wagner, Joe McCarthy, John McGraw, Deacon Phillippe, Rube Marquard, Christy Mathewson, Tommy Leach, Big Ed Delahanty, Davy Jones, Germany Schaefer, King Kelly, Big Dan Brouthers, Wahoo Sam Crawford, Wee Willie Keeler, Big Ed Walsh, Jimmy Austin, Fred Snodgrass, Satchel Paige, Hugh Jennings, Fred Merkle, Iron Man McGinnity, Three-Finger Brown, Harry and Stan Coveleski, Connie Mack, Al Bridwell, Red Ruffing, Amos Rusie, Cy Young, Smokey Joe Wood, Chief Meyers, Chief Bender, Bill Klem, Hans Lobert, Johnny Evers, Joe Tinker, Roy Campanella, Miller Huggins, Rube Bressler, Dazzy Vance, Edd Roush, Bill Wambsganss, Clark Griffith, Branch Rickey, Frank Chance, Cap Anson, Nap Lajoie, Sad Sam Jones, Bob O'Farrell, Lefty O'Doul, Bobby Veach, Willie Kamm, Heinie Groh, Lloyd and Paul Waner, Stuffy McInnis, Charles Comiskey, Roger Bresnahan, Bill Dickey, Zack Wheat, George Sisler, Charlie Gehringer, Eppa Rixey, Harry Heilmann, Fred Clarke, Dizzy Dean, Hank Greenberg, Pie Traynor, Rube Waddell, Bill Terry, Carl Hubbell, Old Hoss Radbourne, Moe Berg, Rabbit Maranville, Jimmie Foxx, Lefty Grove. The list seems endless.

And one recalls the appropriate reference to the "World Serious," attributed to Ring Lardner, Sr.; Ernest L. Thayer's "Casey at the Bat"; the ring of "Tinker to Evers to Chance"; and all the other happenings, habits, and superstitions about and around baseball that made it the "national pastime" or, depending upon the point of view, "the great American tragedy."

II

The Petitioner

The petitioner, Curtis Charles Flood, born in 1938, began his major league career in 1956 when he signed a contract with the Cincinnati Reds for a salary of $4,000 for the season. He had no attorney or agent to advise him on that occasion. He was traded to the St. Louis Cardinals before the 1958 season. Flood rose to fame as a center fielder with the Cardinals during the years 1958–1969. In those 12 seasons he compiled a batting average of .293. His best offensive season was 1967 when he achieved .335. He was .301 or better in six of the 12 St. Louis years. He participated in the 1964, 1967, and 1968 World Series. He played error-less ball in the field in 1966, and once enjoyed 223 consecutive errorless games. Flood has received seven Golden Glove Awards. He was co-captain of his team from 1965–1969. He ranks among the 10 major league outfielders possessing the highest lifetime fielding averages.

Flood's St. Louis compensation for the years shown was:

1961 $13,500 (including a bonus for signing) 1962 $16,000 1963 $17,500 1964 $23,000 1965 $35,000 1966 $45,000 1967 $50,000 1968 $72,000 1969 $90,000

These figures do not include any so-called fringe benefits or World Series shares.

But at the age of 31, in October 1969, Flood was traded to the Philadelphia Phillies of the National League in a multi-player transaction. He was not consulted about the trade. He was informed by telephone and received formal notice only after the deal had been consummated. In December he complained to the Commissioner of Baseball and asked that he be made a free agent and be placed at liberty to strike his own bargain with any other major league team. His request was denied.

Flood then instituted this antitrust suit in January 1970 in federal court for the Southern District of New York. The defendants (although not all were named in each cause of action) were the Commissioner of Baseball, the presidents of the two major leagues, and the 24 major league clubs. In general, the complaint charged violations of the federal antitrust laws and civil rights statutes, violation of state statutes and the common law, and the imposition of a form of peonage and involuntary servitude contrary to the Thirteenth Amendment and 42 U.S.C. § 1994, 18 U.S.C. § 1581, and 29 U.S.C. §§ 102 and 103. Petitioner sought declaratory and injunctive relief and treble damages.

Flood declined to play for Philadelphia in 1970, despite a $100,000 salary offer, and he sat out the year. After the season was concluded, Philadelphia sold its rights to Flood to the Washington Senators. Washington and the petitioner were able to come to terms for 1971 at a salary of $110,000. Flood started the season but, apparently because he was dissatisfied with his performance, he left the Washington club on April 27, early in the campaign. He has not played baseball since then.

III

The Present Litigation

Judge Cooper, in a detailed opinion, first denied a preliminary injunction, observing on the way:

"Baseball has been the national pastime for over one hundred years and enjoys a unique place in our American heritage. Major league professional baseball is avidly followed by millions of fans, looked upon with fervor and pride and provides a special source of inspiration and competitive team spirit especially for the young.

"Baseball's status in the life of the nation is so pervasive that it would not strain credulity to say the Court can take judicial notice that baseball is everybody's business. To put it mildly and with restraint, it would be unfortunate indeed if a fine sport and profession, which brings surcease from daily travail and an escape from the ordinary to most inhabitants of this land, were to suffer in the least because of undue concentration by any one or any group on commercial and profit considerations. The game is on higher ground; it behooves every one to keep it there."

Flood's application for an early trial was granted. The court next deferred until trial its decision on the defendants' motions to dismiss the primary causes of action, but granted a defense motion for summary judgment on an additional cause of action.

Trial to the court took place in May and June 1970. An extensive record was developed. In an ensuing opinion, Judge Cooper first noted that:

"Plaintiff's witnesses in the main concede that some form of reserve on players is a necessary element of the organization of baseball as a league sport, but contend that the present all-embracing system is needlessly restrictive and offer various alternatives which in their view might loosen the bonds without sacrifice to the game. . . .

. . . .

"Clearly the preponderance of credible proof does not favor elimination of the reserve clause. With the sole exception of plaintiff himself, it shows that even plaintiff's witnesses do not contend that it is wholly undesirable; in fact they regard substantial portions meritorious. . . ."

He then held that *Federal Baseball Club v. National League* (1922) and *Toolson v. New York Yankees, Inc.* (1953) were controlling; that it was not necessary to reach the issue whether exemption from the antitrust laws would result because aspects of baseball now are a subject of collective bargaining; that the plaintiff's state-law claims, those based on common law as well as on statute, were to be denied because baseball was not "a matter which admits of diversity of treatment"; that the involuntary servitude claim failed because of the absence of "the essential element of this cause of action, a showing of compulsory service"; and that judgment was to be entered for the defendants. Judge Cooper included a statement of personal conviction to the effect that "negotiations could produce an accommodation on the reserve system which would be eminently fair and equitable to all concerned" and that "the reserve clause can be fashioned so as to find acceptance by player and club."

On appeal, the Second Circuit felt "compelled to affirm." It regarded the issue of state law as one of first impression, but concluded that the Commerce Clause precluded its application. Judge Moore added a concurring opinion in which he predicted, with respect to the suggested overruling of *Federal Baseball* and *Toolson*, that "there is no likelihood that such an event will occur."

We granted certiorari in order to look once again at this troublesome and unusual situation.

IV

The Legal Background

A. *Federal Baseball Club v. National League* (1922) was a suit for treble damages instituted by a member of the Federal League (Baltimore) against the National and American Leagues and others. The plaintiff obtained a verdict in the trial court, but the Court of Appeals reversed. The main brief filed by the plaintiff with this Court discloses that it was strenuously argued, among other things, that the business in which the defendants were engaged was interstate commerce; that the interstate relationship among the several clubs, located as they were in different States, was predominant; that organized baseball represented an investment of colossal wealth; that it was an engagement in moneymaking; that gate receipts were divided by agreement between the home club and the visiting club; and that the business of baseball was to be distinguished from the mere playing of the game as a sport for physical exercise and diversion.

Mr. Justice Holmes, in speaking succinctly for a unanimous Court, said:

"The business is giving exhibitions of base ball, which are purely state affairs. . . . But the fact that in order to give the exhibitions the Leagues must induce free persons to cross state lines and must arrange and pay for their doing so is not enough to change the character of the business. . . . [T]he transport is a mere incident, not the essential thing. That to which it is incident, the exhibition, although made for money would not be called trade or commerce in the commonly accepted use of those words. As it is put by the defendants, personal effort, not related to production, is not a subject of commerce. That which in its consummation is not commerce does not become commerce among the States because the transportation that we have mentioned takes place. To repeat the illustrations given by the Court below, a firm of lawyers sending out a member to argue a case, or the Chautauqua lecture bureau sending out lecturers, does not engage in such commerce because the lawyer or lecturer goes to another State.

"If we are right the plaintiff's business is to be described in the same way and the restrictions by contract that prevented the plaintiff from getting players to break their bargains and the other conduct charged against the defendants were not an interference with commerce among the States."

The Court thus chose not to be persuaded by opposing examples proffered by the plaintiff, among them (a) Judge Learned Hand's decision on a demurrer to a Sherman Act complaint with respect to vaudeville entertainers traveling a theater circuit covering several States, *H. B. Marienelli, Ltd. v. United Booking Offices*; (b) the first Mr. Justice Harlan's opinion in *International Textbook Co. v. Pigg*, to the effect that correspondence courses pursued through the mail constituted commerce among the States; and (c) Mr. Justice Holmes' own opinion, for another unanimous Court, on demurrer in a Sherman Act case, relating to cattle shipment, the interstate movement of which was interrupted for the finding of purchasers at the stockyards, *Swift & Co. v. United States* (1905). The only earlier case the parties were able to locate where the question was raised whether organized baseball was within the Sherman Act was *American League Baseball Club v. Chase* (1914). That court had answered the question in the negative.

B.   *Federal Baseball* was cited a year later, and without disfavor, in another opinion by Mr. Justice Holmes for a unanimous Court. The complaint charged antitrust violations with respect to vaudeville bookings. It was held, however, that the claim was not frivolous and that the bill should not have been dismissed. *Hart v. B. F. Keith Vaudeville Exchange* (1923).

It has also been cited, not unfavorably, with respect to the practice of law, *United States v. South-Eastern Underwriters Assn.* (1944) (Stone, C. J., dissenting); with respect to out-of-state contractors, *United States v. Employing Plasterers Assn.* (1954) (Minton, J., dissenting); and upon a general comparison reference, *North American Co. v. SEC* (1946).

In the years that followed, baseball continued to be subject to intermittent antitrust attack. The courts, however, rejected these challenges on the authority of *Federal Baseball*. In some cases stress was laid, although unsuccessfully, on new factors such as the development of radio and television with their substantial additional revenues to baseball. For the most part, however, the Holmes opinion was generally and necessarily accepted as controlling authority. And in the 1952 Report of the Subcommittee on Study of Monopoly Power of the House Committee on the Judiciary, H. R. Rep. No. 2002, 82d Cong., 2d Sess., 229, it was said, in conclusion:

"On the other hand the overwhelming preponderance of the evidence established baseball's need for some sort of reserve clause. Baseball's history shows that chaotic conditions prevailed when there was no reserve clause. Experience points to no feasible substitute to protect the integrity of the game or to guarantee a comparatively even competitive struggle. The evidence adduced at the hearings would clearly not justify the enactment of legislation flatly condemning the reserve clause."

C. The Court granted certiorari (1953) in the *Toolson, Kowalski,* and *Corbett* cases . . . and, by a short *per curiam*, affirmed the judgments of the respective courts of appeals in those three cases. *Toolson v. New York Yankees, Inc.* (1953). *Federal Baseball* was cited as holding "that the business of providing public baseball games for profit between clubs of professional baseball players was not within the scope of the federal antitrust laws," and:

"Congress has had the ruling under consideration but has not seen fit to bring such business under these laws by legislation having prospective effect. The business has thus been left for thirty years to develop, on the understanding that it was not subject to existing antitrust legislation. The present cases ask us to overrule the prior decision and, with retrospective effect, hold the legislation applicable. We think that if there are evils in this field which now warrant application to it of the antitrust laws it should be by legislation. Without re-examination of the underlying issues, the judgments below are affirmed on the authority of *Federal Baseball Club of Baltimore v. National League of Professional Baseball Clubs*, so far as that decision determines that Congress had no intention of including the business of baseball within the scope of the federal antitrust laws."

This quotation reveals four reasons for the Court's affirmance of *Toolson* and its companion cases: (a) Congressional awareness for three decades of the Court's ruling in *Federal Baseball*, coupled with congressional inaction. (b) The fact that baseball was left alone to develop for that period upon the understanding that the reserve system was not subject to existing federal antitrust laws. (c) A reluctance to overrule *Federal Baseball* with consequent retroactive effect. (d) A professed desire that any needed remedy be provided by legislation rather than by court decree. The emphasis in *Toolson* was on the determination, attributed even to *Federal Baseball*, that Congress had no intention to include baseball within the reach of the federal antitrust laws. Two Justices dissented, stressing the factual aspects, revenue sources, and the absence of an express exemption of organized baseball from the Sherman Act. The 1952 congressional study was mentioned.

It is of interest to note that in *Toolson* the petitioner had argued flatly that *Federal Baseball* "is wrong and must be overruled," and that Thomas Reed Powell, a constitutional scholar of no small stature, urged, as counsel for an *amicus*, that "baseball is a unique enterprise," and that "unbridled competition as applied to baseball would not be in the public interest."

D. *United States v. Shubert* (1955) was a civil antitrust action against defendants engaged in the production of legitimate theatrical attractions throughout the United States and in operating theaters for the presentation of such attractions. The District Court had dismissed the complaint on the authority of *Federal Baseball* and *Toolson*. This Court reversed. Mr. Chief Justice Warren noted the Court's broad conception of "trade or commerce" in the antitrust statutes and the types of enterprises already held to be within the reach of that phrase. He stated that *Federal Baseball* and *Toolson* afforded no basis for a conclusion that businesses built around the performance of local exhibitions are exempt from the antitrust laws. He then went on to elucidate the holding in *Toolson* by meticulously spelling out the factors mentioned above:

"In *Federal Baseball*, the Court, speaking through Mr. Justice Holmes, was dealing with the business of baseball and nothing else. . . . The travel, the Court concluded, was 'a mere incident, not the essential thing.' . . .

. . . .

"In *Toolson*, where the issue was the same as in *Federal Baseball*, the Court was confronted with a unique combination of circumstances. For over 30 years there had stood a decision of this Court specifically fixing the status of the baseball business under the antitrust laws and more particularly the validity of the so-called 'reserve clause.' During this period, in reliance on the *Federal Baseball* precedent, the baseball business had grown and developed. . . . And Congress, although it had actively considered the ruling, had not seen fit to reject it by amendatory legislation. Against this background, the Court in *Toolson* was asked to overrule *Federal Baseball* on the ground that it was out of step with subsequent decisions reflecting present-day concepts of interstate commerce. The Court, in view of the circumstances of the case, declined to do so. But neither did the Court necessarily reaffirm all that was said in *Federal Baseball*. Instead, '[w]ithout re-examination of the underlying issues,' the Court adhered to *Federal Baseball* 'so far as that decision determines that Congress had no intention of including the business of baseball within the scope of the federal antitrust laws.' In short, *Toolson* was a narrow application of the rule of *stare decisis*.

" . . . If the *Toolson* holding is to be expanded—or contracted—the appropriate remedy lies with Congress."

E. *United States v. International Boxing Club* (1955) was a companion to *Shubert* and was decided the same day. This was a civil antitrust action against defendants engaged in the business of promoting professional championship boxing contests. Here again the District Court had dismissed the complaint in reliance upon *Federal Baseball* and *Toolson*. The Chief Justice observed that "if it were not for *Federal*

Baseball and *Toolson*, we think that it would be too clear for dispute that the Government's allegations bring the defendants within the scope of the Act." He pointed out that the defendants relied on the two baseball cases but also would have been content with a more restrictive interpretation of them than the *Shubert* defendants, for the boxing defendants argued that the cases immunized only businesses that involve exhibitions of an athletic nature. The Court accepted neither argument. It again noted that "*Toolson* neither overruled *Federal Baseball* nor necessarily reaffirmed all that was said in *Federal Baseball*." It stated:

"The controlling consideration in *Federal Baseball* and *Hart* was, instead, a very practical one—the degree of interstate activity involved in the particular business under review. It follows that *stare decisis* cannot help the defendants here; for, contrary to their argument, *Federal Baseball* did not hold that all businesses based on professional sports were outside the scope of the antitrust laws. The issue confronting us is, therefore, not whether a previously granted exemption should continue, but whether an exemption should be granted in the first instance. And that issue is for Congress to resolve, not this Court."

The Court noted the presence then in Congress of various bills forbidding the application of the antitrust laws to "organized professional sports enterprises"; the holding of extensive hearings on some of these; subcommittee opposition; a postponement recommendation as to baseball; and the fact that "Congress thus left intact the then-existing coverage of the antitrust laws." Mr. Justice Frankfurter, joined by Mr. Justice Minton, dissented. "It would baffle the subtlest ingenuity," he said, "to find a single differentiating factor between other sporting exhibitions . . . and baseball insofar as the conduct of the sport is relevant to the criteria or considerations by which the Sherman Law becomes applicable to a 'trade or commerce.' " He went on:

"The Court decided as it did in the *Toolson* case as an application of the doctrine of *stare decisis*. That doctrine is not, to be sure, an imprisonment of reason. But neither is it a whimsy. It can hardly be that this Court gave a preferred position to baseball because it is the great American sport. . . . If *stare decisis* be one aspect of law, as it is, to disregard it in identical situations is mere caprice.

"Congress, on the other hand, may yield to sentiment and be capricious, subject only to due process. . . .

"Between them, this case and *Shubert* illustrate that nice but rational distinctions are inevitable in adjudication. I agree with the Court's opinion in *Shubert* for precisely the reason that constrains me to dissent in this case."

Mr. Justice Minton also separately dissented on the ground that boxing is not trade or commerce. He added the comment that "Congress has not attempted" to control baseball and boxing. The two dissenting Justices, thus, did not call for the overruling of *Federal Baseball* and *Toolson*; they merely felt that boxing should be under the same umbrella of freedom as was baseball and, as Mr. Justice Frankfurter said, they could not exempt baseball "to the exclusion of every other sport different not one legal jot or tittle from it."

F.   The parade marched on. *Radovich v. National Football League* (1957) was a civil Clayton Act case testing the application of the antitrust laws to professional football. The District Court dismissed. The Ninth Circuit affirmed in part on the basis of *Federal Baseball* and *Toolson*. The court did not hesitate to "confess that the strength of the pull" of the baseball cases and of *International Boxing* "is about equal," but then observed that "[f]ootball is a team sport" and boxing an individual one.

This Court reversed with an opinion by Mr. Justice Clark. He said that the Court made its ruling in *Toolson* "because it was concluded that more harm would be done in overruling *Federal Baseball* than in upholding a ruling which at best was of dubious validity." He noted that Congress had not acted. He then said:

"All this, combined with the flood of litigation that would follow its repudiation, the harassment that would ensue, and the retroactive effect of such a decision, led the Court to the practical result that it should sustain the unequivocal line of authority reaching over many years.

"[S]ince *Toolson* and *Federal Baseball* are still cited as controlling authority in antitrust actions involving other fields of business, we now specifically limit the rule there established to the facts there involved, *i.e.*, the business of organized professional baseball. As long as the Congress continues to acquiesce we should adhere to—but not extend—the interpretation of the Act made in those cases. . . .

"If this ruling is unrealistic, inconsistent, or illogical, it is sufficient to answer, aside from the distinctions between the businesses, that were we considering the question of baseball for the first time upon a clean slate we would have no doubts. But *Federal Baseball* held the business of baseball outside the scope of the Act. No other business claiming the coverage of those cases has such an adjudication. We, therefore, conclude that the orderly way to eliminate error or discrimination, if any there be, is by legislation and not by court decision. Congressional processes are more accommodative, affording the whole industry hearings and an opportunity to assist in the formulation of new legislation. The resulting product is therefore more likely to protect the industry and the public alike. The whole scope of congressional action would be known long in advance and effective dates for the legislation could be set in the future without the injustices of retroactivity and surprise which might follow court action."

Mr. Justice Frankfurter dissented essentially for the reasons stated in his dissent in *International Boxing*. Mr. Justice Harlan, joined by MR. JUSTICE BRENNAN, also dissented because he, too, was "unable to distinguish football from baseball." Here again the dissenting Justices did not call for the overruling of the baseball decisions. They merely could not distinguish the two sports and, out of respect for *stare decisis*, voted to affirm.

G.   Finally, in *Haywood v. National Basketball Assn.* (1971), MR. JUSTICE DOUGLAS, in his capacity as Circuit Justice, reinstated a District Court's injunction *pendente lite* in favor of a professional basketball player and said, "Basketball . . . does not enjoy exemption from the antitrust laws."

H.   This series of decisions understandably spawned extensive commentary, some of it mildly critical and much of it not; nearly all of it looked to Congress for any remedy that might be deemed essential.

I.   Legislative proposals have been numerous and persistent. Since *Toolson* more than 50 bills have been introduced in Congress relative to the applicability or nonapplicability of the antitrust laws to baseball. A few of these passed one house or the other. Those that did would have expanded, not restricted, the reserve system's exemption to other professional league sports. And the Act of Sept. 30, 1961, and the merger addition thereto effected by the Act of Nov. 8, 1966, were also expansive rather than restrictive as to antitrust exemption.

V

In view of all this, it seems appropriate now to say that:

1.   Professional baseball is a business and it is engaged in interstate commerce.

2.   With its reserve system enjoying exemption from the federal antitrust laws, baseball is, in a very distinct sense, an exception and an anomaly. *Federal Baseball* and *Toolson* have become an aberration confined to baseball.

3.   Even though others might regard this as "unrealistic, inconsistent, or illogical," the aberration is an established one, and one that has been recognized not only in *Federal Baseball* and *Toolson*, but in *Shubert*, *International Boxing*, and *Radovich*, as well, a total of five consecutive cases in this Court. It is an aberration that has been with us now for half a century, one heretofore deemed fully entitled to the benefit of *stare decisis*, and one that has survived the Court's expanding concept of interstate commerce. It rests on a recognition and an acceptance of baseball's unique characteristics and needs.

4. Other professional sports operating interstate—football, boxing, basketball, and, presumably, hockey and golf—are not so exempt.

5. The advent of radio and television, with their consequent increased coverage and additional revenues, has not occasioned an overruling of *Federal Baseball* and *Toolson*.

6. The Court has emphasized that since 1922 baseball, with full and continuing congressional awareness, has been allowed to develop and to expand unhindered by federal legislative action. Remedial legislation has been introduced repeatedly in Congress but none has ever been enacted. The Court, accordingly, has concluded that Congress as yet has had no intention to subject baseball's reserve system to the reach of the antitrust statutes. This, obviously, has been deemed to be something other than mere congressional silence and passivity.

7. The Court has expressed concern about the confusion and the retroactivity problems that inevitably would result with a judicial overturning of *Federal Baseball*. It has voiced a preference that if any change is to be made, it come by legislative action that, by its nature, is only prospective in operation.

8. The Court noted in *Radovich* that the slate with respect to baseball is not clean. Indeed, it has not been clean for half a century.

This emphasis and this concern are still with us. We continue to be loath, 50 years after *Federal Baseball* and almost two decades after *Toolson*, to overturn those cases judicially when Congress, by its positive inaction, has allowed those decisions to stand for so long and, far beyond mere inference and implication, has clearly evinced a desire not to disapprove them legislatively.

Accordingly, we adhere once again to *Federal Baseball* and *Toolson* and to their application to professional baseball. We adhere also to *International Boxing* and *Radovich* and to their respective applications to professional boxing and professional football. If there is any inconsistency or illogic in all this, it is an inconsistency and illogic of long standing that is to be remedied by the Congress and not by this Court. If we were to act otherwise, we would be withdrawing from the conclusion as to congressional intent made in *Toolson* and from the concerns as to retrospectivity therein expressed. Under these circumstances, there is merit in consistency even though some might claim that beneath that consistency is a layer of inconsistency.

. . . .

We repeat for this case what was said in *Toolson*:

"Without re-examination of the underlying issues, the [judgment] below [is] affirmed on the authority of *Federal Baseball Club of Baltimore v. National League of Professional Baseball Clubs, supra*, so far as that decision determines that Congress had no intention of including the business of baseball within the scope of the federal antitrust laws."

And what the Court said in *Federal Baseball* in 1922 and what it said in *Toolson* in 1953, we say again here in 1972: the remedy, if any is indicated, is for congressional, and not judicial, action.

The judgment of the Court of Appeals is Affirmed.

MR. CHIEF JUSTICE BURGER, concurring.

I concur in all but Part I of the Court's opinion but, like MR. JUSTICE DOUGLAS, I have grave reservations as to the correctness of *Toolson v. New York Yankees, Inc.*; as he notes in his dissent, he joined that holding but has "lived to regret it." The error, if such it be, is one on which the affairs of a great many people have rested for a long time. Courts are not the forum in which this tangled web ought to be unsnarled. I agree with MR. JUSTICE DOUGLAS that congressional inaction is not a solid base, but the least undesirable course now is to let the matter rest with Congress; it is time the Congress acted to solve this problem.

MR. JUSTICE DOUGLAS, with whom MR. JUSTICE BRENNAN concurs, dissenting.

This Court's decision in *Federal Baseball Club v. National League*, made in 1922, is a derelict in the stream of the law that we, its creator, should remove. Only a romantic view of a rather dismal business account over the last 50 years would keep that derelict in midstream.

In 1922 the Court had a narrow, parochial view of commerce. With the demise of the old landmarks of that era, particularly *United States v. Knight Co., Hammer v. Dagenhart*, and *Paul v. Virginia*, the whole concept of commerce has changed.

Under the modern decisions ... the power of Congress was recognized as broad enough to reach all phases of the vast operations of our national industrial system. An industry so dependent on radio and television as is baseball and gleaning vast interstate revenues would be hard put today to say with the Court in the *Federal Baseball Club* case that baseball was only a local exhibition, not trade or commerce.

Baseball is today big business that is packaged with beer, with broadcasting, and with other industries. The beneficiaries of the *Federal Baseball Club* decision are not the Babe Ruths, Ty Cobbs, and Lou Gehrigs.

The owners, whose records many say reveal a proclivity for predatory practices, do not come to us with equities. The equities are with the victims of the reserve clause. I use the word "victims" in the Sherman Act sense, since a contract which forbids anyone to practice his calling is commonly called an unreasonable restraint of trade.

If congressional inaction is our guide, we should rely upon the fact that Congress has refused to enact bills broadly exempting professional sports from antitrust regulation. The only statutory exemption granted by Congress to professional sports concerns broadcasting rights. I would not ascribe a broader exemption through inaction than Congress has seen fit to grant explicitly. [Footnote 3]

There can be no doubt "that were we considering the question of baseball for the first time upon a clean slate" we would hold it to be subject to federal antitrust regulation. *Radovich v. National Football League*. The unbroken silence of Congress should not prevent us from correcting our own mistakes.

. . . .

[Footnote 3] The Court's reliance upon congressional inaction disregards the wisdom of *Helvering v. Hallock*, where we said:

"Nor does want of specific Congressional repudiations . . . serve as an implied instruction by Congress to us not to reconsider, in the light of new experience . . . those decisions. . . . It would require very persuasive circumstances enveloping Congressional silence to debar this Court from re-examining its own doctrines. . . . Various considerations of parliamentary tactics and strategy might be suggested as reasons for the inaction of . . . Congress, but they would only be sufficient to indicate that we walk on quicksand when we try to find in the absence of corrective legislation a controlling legal principle."

. . . .

MR. JUSTICE MARSHALL, with whom MR. JUSTICE BRENNAN joins, dissenting.

Petitioner was a major league baseball player from 1956, when he signed a contract with the Cincinnati Reds, until 1969, when his 12-year career with the St. Louis Cardinals, which had obtained him from the Reds, ended and he was traded to the Philadelphia Phillies. He had no notice that the Cardinals were contemplating a trade, no opportunity to indicate the teams with which he would prefer playing, and no desire to go to Philadelphia. After receiving formal notification of the trade, petitioner wrote to the Commissioner of Baseball protesting that he was not "a piece of property to be bought and sold irrespective of my wishes," and urging that he had the right to consider offers from other teams than the Phillies. He requested that the Commissioner inform all of the major league teams that he was available for the 1970 season. His request was denied, and petitioner was informed that he had no choice but to play for Philadelphia or not to play at all.

To non-athletes it might appear that petitioner was virtually enslaved by the owners of major league baseball clubs who bartered among themselves for his services. But, athletes know that it was not servitude that bound petitioner to the club owners; it was the reserve system. The essence of that system is that a player is bound to the club with which he first signs a contract for the rest of his playing days. He cannot escape from the club except by retiring, and he cannot prevent the club from assigning his contract to any other club.

Petitioner brought this action in the United States District Court for the Southern District of New York. He alleged, among other things, that the reserve system was an unreasonable restraint of trade in violation of federal antitrust laws. The District Court thought itself bound by prior decisions of this Court and found for the respondents after a full trial. The United States Court of Appeals for the Second Circuit affirmed. We granted certiorari . . . in order to take a further look at the precedents relied upon by the lower courts.

This is a difficult case because we are torn between the principle of *stare decisis* and the knowledge that the decisions in *Federal Baseball Club v. National League* and *Toolson v. New York Yankees, Inc.* are totally at odds with more recent and better reasoned cases.

In *Federal Baseball Club*, a team in the Federal League brought an antitrust action against the National and American Leagues and others. In his opinion for a unanimous Court, Mr. Justice Holmes wrote that the business being considered was "giving exhibitions of base ball, which are purely state affairs." Hence, the Court held that baseball was not within the purview of the antitrust laws. Thirty-one years later, the Court reaffirmed this decision, without reexamining it, in *Toolson*, a one-paragraph *per curiam* opinion. Like this case, *Toolson* involved an attack on the reserve system. The Court said:

"The business has . . . been left for thirty years to develop, on the understanding that it was not subject to existing antitrust legislation. The present cases ask us to overrule the prior decision and, with retrospective effect, hold the legislation applicable. We think that if there are evils in this field which now warrant application to it of the antitrust laws it should be by legislation."

Much more time has passed since *Toolson* and *Congress* has not acted. We must now decide whether to adhere to the reasoning of *Toolson*—i.e., to refuse to re-examine the underlying basis of *Federal Baseball Club*—or to proceed with a re-examination and let the chips fall where they may.

In his answer to petitioner's complaint, the Commissioner of Baseball "admits that under present concepts of interstate commerce defendants are engaged therein." There can be no doubt that the admission is warranted by today's reality. Since baseball is interstate commerce, if we re-examine baseball's antitrust exemption, the Court's decisions in *United States v. Shubert, United States v. International Boxing Club*, and *Radovich v. National Football League* require that we bring baseball within the coverage of the antitrust laws.

We have only recently had occasion to comment that:

"Antitrust laws in general, and the Sherman Act in particular, are the Magna Carta of free enterprise. They are as important to the preservation of economic freedom and our free-enterprise system as the Bill of Rights is to the protection of our fundamental personal freedoms. . . . Implicit in such freedom is the notion that it cannot be foreclosed with respect to one sector of the economy because certain private citizens or groups believe that such foreclosure might promote greater competition in a more important sector of the economy." *United States v. Topco Associates, Inc.*

The importance of the antitrust laws to every citizen must not be minimized. They are as important to baseball players as they are to football players, lawyers, doctors, or members of any other class of workers. Baseball players cannot be denied the benefits of competition merely because club owners view other economic interests as being more important, unless Congress says so.

Has Congress acquiesced in our decisions in *Federal Baseball Club* and *Toolson*? I think not. Had the Court been consistent and treated all sports in the same way baseball was treated, Congress might have become concerned enough to take action. But, the Court was inconsistent, and baseball was isolated and distinguished from all other sports. In *Toolson* the Court refused to act because Congress had been silent. But the Court may have read too much into this legislative inaction.

Americans love baseball as they love all sports. Perhaps we become so enamored of athletics that we assume that they are foremost in the minds of legislators as well as fans. We must not forget, however, that there are only some 600 major league baseball players. Whatever muscle they might have been able to muster by combining forces with other athletes has been greatly impaired by the manner in which this Court has isolated them. It is this Court that has made them impotent, and this Court should correct its error.

We do not lightly overrule our prior constructions of federal statutes, but when our errors deny substantial federal rights, like the right to compete freely and effectively to the best of one's ability as guaranteed by the antitrust laws, we must admit our error and correct it. We have done so before and we should do so again here. *See, e.g., Blonder-Tongue Laboratories, Inc. v. University of Illinois Foundation*; *Boys Markets, Inc. v. Retail Clerks Union.*

To the extent that there is concern over any reliance interests that club owners may assert, they can be satisfied by making our decision prospective only. Baseball should be covered by the antitrust laws beginning with this case and henceforth, unless Congress decides otherwise. [Footnote 5]

Accordingly, I would overrule *Federal Baseball Club* and *Toolson* and reverse the decision of the Court of Appeals.

. . . .

[Footnote 5] We said recently that "[i]n rare cases, decisions construing federal statutes might be denied full retroactive effect, as for instance where this Court overrules its own construction of a statute. . . ."

H. IS THE GROUND SHIFTING ON AFFIRMATIVE ACTION AGAIN?

In 2009 the Supreme Court had occasion once again to consider the legality of voluntary affirmative action programs.

Over the years however, the 1964 Civil Rights Act has been amended to include Sections (k) and (l), which codify as statute the results reached by several prior Supreme Court precedents, primarily *Griggs v. Duke Power Co.,* 401 U.S. 424, (1971), and *Albemarle Paper Co. v. Moody,* 422 U.S. 405 (1975). In terms of where they "fit" into the statute, they follow section (j) of the statute. Make sure to study them prior to reading the case.

(k) Burden of proof in disparate impact cases

(1)

(A) An unlawful employment practice based on disparate impact is established under this subchapter only if--

(i) a complaining party demonstrates that a respondent uses a particular employment practice that causes a disparate impact on the basis of race, color, religion, sex, or national origin and the respondent fails to demonstrate that the challenged practice is job related for the position in question and consistent with business necessity; or

(ii) the complaining party makes the demonstration described in subparagraph (C) with respect to an alternative employment practice and the respondent refuses to adopt such alternative employment practice.

(B)

(i) With respect to demonstrating that a particular employment practice causes a disparate Impact as described in subparagraph (A)(i), the complaining party shall demonstrate that each particular challenged employment practice causes a disparate impact, except that if the complaining party can demonstrate to the court that the elements of a respondent's decisionmaking process are not capable of separation for analysis, the decisionmaking process may be analyzed as one employment practice.

(ii) If the respondent demonstrates that a specific employment practice does not cause the disparate impact, the respondent shall not be required to demonstrate that such practice is required by business necessity.

(C) The demonstration referred to by subparagraph (A)(ii) shall be in accordance with the law as it existed on June 4, 1989, with respect to the concept of "alternative employment practice".

(2) A demonstration that an employment practice is required by business necessity may not be used as a defense against a claim of intentional discrimination under this subchapter.

(l) Prohibition of discriminatory use of test scores

It shall be an unlawful employment practice for a respondent, in connection with the selection or referral of applicants or candidates for employment or promotion, to adjust the scores of, use different cutoff scores for, or otherwise alter the results of, employment related tests on the basis of race, color, religion, sex, or national origin.

Now consider the following questions as you read the case.

As you read, try and typify the main form of statutory interpretation argument used by each of the Justices. Are there any 'moves' that we have not seen before?

- As this case is more recent, pay attention to who uses legislative history and how it is used.

- In terms of the statute, what is the plaintiff's central claim? What statutory authority does the City rely on in its defense?

- Justice Kennedy's opinion relates both Petitioners (plaintiff's) and Respondents (Defendant's) core statutory arguments. What reading of the statute does each side propose, and how does Kennedy's opinion thread the needle between them?

- Does the Court overturn *Weber* and *Johnson*? Or does the Court re-affirm these cases? Or does it do something else? To help you focus in on this question, assume you had two clients, one that wanted to institute a program very similar to the one approved of in *Weber*, and one with a program like the one in *Johnson*. How would you advise them? Most importantly, what legal and factual research would you like to perform?

- If you were concerned with the same issues as Stevens was in *Johnson*, how do you feel about this case? How does this case address the concerns about precedent? Can you see how Scalia is responding to the "reliance on precedent" line of argument developed by Stevens in *Johnson*?

- Can you think of other areas of the law in which the Court has moved the law incrementally rather than in wholesale steps?

- As you look at the dissent, do you see any statutory arguments used there that are absent in the other opinions?

RICCI V. DE STEFANO

557 U.S. 557, 129 S. Ct. 2658 (2009)

JUSTICE KENNEDY delivered the opinion of the Court.

In 2003, 118 New Haven firefighters took examinations to qualify for promotion to the rank of lieutenant or captain. The results would determine which firefighters would be considered for promotions during the next two years, and the order in which they would be considered. Many firefighters studied for months, at considerable personal and financial cost.

When the examination results showed that white candidates had outperformed minority candidates, the mayor and other local politicians opened a public debate that turned rancorous. Some firefighters argued the tests should be discarded because the results showed the tests to be discriminatory. They threatened a discrimination lawsuit if the City made promotions based on the tests. Other firefighters said the exams were neutral and fair. And they, in turn, threatened a discrimination lawsuit if the City, relying on the statistical racial disparity, ignored the test results and denied promotions to the candidates who had performed well. In the end the City took the side of those who protested the test results. It threw out the examinations.

The suit alleges that, by discarding the test results, the City and the named officials discriminated against the plaintiffs based on their race, in violation of both Title VII of the Civil Rights Act of 1964, 78 Stat. 253, as amended, 42 U.S.C. § 2000e. The City and the officials defended their actions, arguing that if they had certified the results, they could have faced liability under Title VII for adopting a practice that had a disparate impact on the minority firefighters. The District Court granted summary judgment for the defendants, and the Court of Appeals affirmed.

We conclude that race-based action like the City's in this case is impermissible under Title VII unless the employer can demonstrate a strong basis in evidence that, had it not taken the action, it would have been liable under the disparate-impact statute. The respondents, we further determine, cannot meet that threshold standard. As a result, the City's action in discarding the tests was a violation of Title VII.

I.

When the City of New Haven undertook to fill vacant lieutenant and captain positions in its fire department (Department), the promotion and hiring process was governed by the city charter, in addition to federal and state law. The charter establishes a merit system. That system requires the City to fill vacancies in the classified civil-service ranks with the most qualified individuals, as determined by job related examinations. Under the charter's "rule of three," the relevant hiring authority must fill each vacancy by choosing one candidate from the top three scorers on the list. To sit for the examinations, candidates for lieutenant needed 30 months' experience in the Department, a high-school diploma, and certain vocational training courses. Candidates for captain needed one year's service as a lieutenant in the Department, a high-school diploma, and certain vocational training courses.

After reviewing bids from various consultants, the City hired Industrial/Organizational Solutions, Inc. (IOS) to develop and administer the examinations. IOS began the test-design process by performing job analyses to identify the tasks, knowledge, skills, and abilities that are essential for the lieutenant and captain positions. IOS representatives interviewed incumbent captains and lieutenants and their supervisors. They rode with and observed other on-duty officers. At every stage of the job analyses, IOS, by deliberate choice, oversampled minority firefighters to ensure that the results—which IOS would use to develop the examinations—would not unintentionally favor white candidates.

For each test, IOS compiled a list of training manuals, Department procedures, and other materials to use as sources for the test questions. IOS presented the proposed sources to the New Haven fire chief and assistant fire chief for their approval. Then, using the approved sources, IOS drafted a multiple-choice test for each position. Each test had 100 questions, as required by CSB rules, and was written below a 10th-grade reading level. After IOS prepared the tests, the City opened a 3-month study period. It gave candidates a list that identified the source material for the questions, including the specific chapters from which the questions were taken.

Candidates took the examinations in November and December 2003. Seventy-seven candidates completed the lieutenant examination—43 whites, 19 blacks, and 15 Hispanics. Of those, 34 candidates passed—25 whites, 6 blacks, and 3 Hispanics. As the rule of three operated, this meant that the top 10 candidates were eligible for an immediate promotion to lieutenant. All 10 were white.

Forty-one candidates completed the captain examination—25 whites, 8 blacks, and 8 Hispanics. Of those, 22 candidates passed—16 whites, 3 blacks, and 3 Hispanics. *Ibid.* Seven captain positions were vacant at the time of the examination. Under the rule of three, 9 candidates were eligible for an immediate promotion to captain—7 whites and 2 Hispanics.

Based on the test results, the City officials expressed concern that the tests had discriminated against minority candidates.

The City's decision not to certify the examination results led to this lawsuit. The plaintiffs—who are the petitioners here—are 17 white firefighters and 1 Hispanic firefighter who passed the examinations but were denied a chance at promotions when the CSB refused to certify the test results. Petitioners filed suit, alleging that respondents, by arguing or voting against certifying the results, violated the disparate-treatment prohibition contained in Title VII of the Civil Rights Act of 1964.

The parties filed cross-motions for summary judgment. Respondents asserted they had a good-faith belief that they would have violated the disparate-impact prohibition in Title VII, § 2000e–2(k), had they certified the examination results. It follows, they maintained, that they cannot be held liable under Title VII's disparate-treatment provision for attempting to comply with Title VII's disparate-impact bar.

The District Court granted summary judgment for respondents. It ruled that respondents' "motivation to avoid making promotions based on a test with a racially disparate impact ... does not, as a matter of law, constitute discriminatory intent" under Title VII. The Court of Appeals affirmed in a one-paragraph, unpublished summary order; it later withdrew that order, issuing in its place a nearly identical, one-paragraph *per curiam* opinion adopting the District Court's reasoning.

II. A.

Title VII of the Civil Rights Act of 1964, 42 U.S.C. § 2000e *et seq.,* as amended, prohibits employment discrimination on the basis of race, color, religion, sex, or national origin. Title VII prohibits both intentional discrimination (known as "disparate treatment") as well as, in some cases, practices that are not intended to discriminate but in fact have a disproportionately adverse effect on minorities (known as "disparate impact").

As enacted in 1964, Title VII's principal nondiscrimination provision held employers liable only for disparate treatment. That section retains its original wording today. It makes it unlawful for an employer "to fail or refuse to hire or to discharge any individual, or otherwise to discriminate against any individual with respect to his compensation, terms, conditions, or privileges of employment, because of such individual's race, color, religion, sex, or national origin." § 2000e–2(a)(1). Disparate-treatment occurs where an employer has "treated [a] particular person less favorably than others because of" a protected trait." *Watson v. Fort Worth Bank & Trust,* 487 U.S. 977, 985–985 (1988). A disparate-treatment plaintiff must establish "that the defendant had a discriminatory intent or motive" for taking a job related action.

The Civil Rights Act of 1964 did not include an express prohibition on policies or practices that produce a disparate impact. But in *Griggs v. Duke Power Co.,* 401 U.S. 424, 91 S.Ct. 849, 28 L.Ed.2d 158 (1971), the Court interpreted the Act to prohibit, in some cases, employers' facially neutral practices that, in fact, are "discriminatory in operation." The *Griggs* Court stated that the "touchstone" for disparate-impact liability is the lack of "business necessity": "If an employment practice which operates to exclude [minorities] cannot be shown to be related to job performance, the practice is prohibited."

Twenty years after *Griggs,* the Civil Rights Act of 1991, 105 Stat. 1071, was enacted. The Act included a provision codifying the prohibition on disparate-impact discrimination. Under the disparate-impact statute, a plaintiff establishes a prima facie violation by showing that an employer uses "a particular employment practice that causes a disparate impact on the basis of race, color, religion, sex, or national origin." 42 U.S.C. § 2000e–2(k)(1)(A)(i). An employer may defend against liability by demonstrating that the practice is "job related for the position in question and consistent with business necessity." *Ibid.* Even if the employer meets that burden, however, a plaintiff may still succeed by showing that the employer refuses to adopt an available alternative employment practice that has less disparate impact and serves the employer's legitimate needs. §§ 2000e–2(k)(1)(A)(ii) and (C).

II. B.

Petitioners allege that when the CSB refused to certify the captain and lieutenant exam results based on the race of the successful candidates, it discriminated against them in violation of Title VII's disparate-treatment provision. The City counters that its decision was permissible because the tests "appear[ed] to violate Title VII's disparate-impact provisions."

Our analysis begins with this premise: The City's actions would violate the disparate-treatment prohibition of Title VII absent some valid defense. All the evidence demonstrates that the City chose not to certify the examination results because of the statistical disparity based on race—*i.e.,* how minority candidates had performed when compared to white candidates. As the District Court put it, the City rejected the test results because "too many whites and not enough minorities would be promoted were the lists to be certified." Respondents' own arguments show that the City's reasons for advocating non-certification were related to the racial distribution of the results. Without some other justification, this express, race-based decisionmaking violates Title VII's command that employers cannot take adverse employment actions because of an individual's race. See § 2000e–2(a)(1).

The District Court did not adhere to this principle, however. It held that respondents' "motivation to avoid making promotions based on a test with a racially disparate impact ... does not, as a matter of law, constitute discriminatory intent." And the Government makes a similar argument in this Court. It contends that the "structure of Title VII belies any claim that an employer's intent to comply with Title VII's disparate-impact provisions constitutes prohibited discrimination on the basis of race."

But both of those statements turn upon the City's objective—avoiding disparate-impact liability—while ignoring the City's conduct in the name of reaching that objective. Whatever the City's ultimate aim—however well intentioned or benevolent it might have seemed—the City made its employment decision because of race. The City rejected the test results solely because the higher scoring candidates were white. The question is not whether that conduct was discriminatory but whether the City had a lawful justification for its race-based action.

We consider, therefore, whether the purpose to avoid disparate-impact liability excuses what otherwise would be prohibited disparate-treatment discrimination. In providing this guidance our decision must be consistent with the important purpose of Title VII—that the workplace be an environment free of discrimination, where race is not a barrier to opportunity.

Petitioners take a strict approach, arguing that under Title VII, it cannot be permissible for an employer to take race-based adverse employment actions in order to avoid disparate-impact liability—even if the employer knows its practice violates the disparate-impact provision.

Petitioners would have us hold that, under Title VII, avoiding unintentional discrimination cannot justify intentional discrimination. That assertion, however, ignores the fact that, by codifying the disparate-impact provision in 1991, Congress has expressly prohibited both types of discrimination. We must interpret the statute to give effect to both provisions where possible.

Petitioners next suggest that an employer in fact must be in violation of the disparate-impact provision before it can use compliance as a defense in a disparate-treatment suit. Again, this is overly simplistic and too restrictive of Title VII's purpose. The rule petitioners offer would run counter to what we have recognized as Congress's intent that "voluntary compliance" be "the preferred means of achieving the objectives of Title VII." Forbidding employers to act unless they know, with certainty, that a practice violates the disparate-impact provision would bring compliance efforts to a near standstill. Even in the limited situations when this restricted standard could be met, employers likely would hesitate before taking voluntary action for fear of later being proven wrong in the course of litigation and then held to account for disparate treatment.

At the opposite end of the spectrum, respondents and the Government assert that an employer's good-faith belief that its actions are necessary to comply with Title VII's disparate-impact provision should be enough to justify race-conscious conduct. But the original, foundational prohibition of Title VII bars employers from taking adverse action "because of . . . race." § 2000e–2(a)(1). And when Congress codified the disparate-impact provision in 1991, it made no exception to disparate-treatment liability for actions taken in a good-faith effort to comply with the new, disparate-impact provision in subsection (k). Allowing employers to violate the disparate-treatment prohibition based on a mere good-faith fear of disparate-impact liability would encourage race-based action at the slightest hint of disparate impact. A minimal standard could cause employers to discard the results of lawful and beneficial promotional examinations even where there is little if any evidence of disparate-impact discrimination. That would amount to a *de facto* quota system, in which a "focus on statistics . . . could put undue pressure on employers to adopt inappropriate prophylactic measures." Even worse, an employer could discard test results (or other employment practices) with the intent of obtaining the employer's preferred racial balance. That operational principle could not be justified, for Title VII is express in disclaiming any interpretation of its requirements as calling for outright racial balancing. § 2000e–2(j).

The Court has held that certain government actions to remedy past racial discrimination—actions that are themselves based on race—are constitutional only where there is a " 'strong basis in evidence' " that the remedial actions were necessary. *Richmond v. J.A. Croson Co.,* 488 U.S. 469, 500, 109 S.Ct. 706, 102 L.Ed.2d 854 (1989). The plurality required a strong basis in evidence because "[e]videntiary support for the conclusion that remedial action is warranted becomes crucial when the remedial program is challenged in court by nonminority employees."

Congress has imposed liability on employers for unintentional discrimination in order to rid the workplace of "practices that are fair in form, but discriminatory in operation." But it has also prohibited employers from taking adverse employment actions "because of" race. § 2000e–2(a)(1). Applying the strong-basis-in-evidence standard to Title VII gives effect to both the disparate-treatment and disparate-impact provisions, allowing violations of one in the name of compliance with the other only in certain, narrow circumstances. The standard leaves ample room for employers' voluntary compliance efforts, which are essential to the statutory scheme and to Congress's efforts to eradicate workplace discrimination. And the standard appropriately constrains employers' discretion in making race-based decisions: It limits that discretion to cases in which there is a strong basis in evidence of disparate-impact liability, but it is not so restrictive that it allows employers to act only when there is a provable, actual violation.

Resolving the statutory conflict in this way allows the disparate-impact prohibition to work in a manner that is consistent with other provisions of Title VII, including the prohibition on adjusting employment-related test scores on the basis of race. See § 2000e–2(*l*).

Examinations like those administered by the City create legitimate expectations on the part of those who took the tests. As is the case with any promotion exam, some of the firefighters here invested substantial time, money, and personal commitment in preparing for the tests. Employment tests can be an important part of a neutral selection system that safeguards against the very racial animosities Title VII was intended to prevent. Here, however, the firefighters saw their efforts invalidated by the City in sole reliance upon race-based statistics.

If an employer cannot rescore a test based on the candidates' race, § 2000e–2(*l*), then it follows *a fortiori* that it may not take the greater step of discarding the test altogether to achieve a more desirable racial distribution of promotion-eligible candidates—absent a strong basis in evidence that the test was deficient and that discarding the results is necessary to avoid violating the disparate-impact provision. Restricting an employer's ability to discard test results (and thereby discriminate against qualified candidates on the basis of their race) also is in keeping with Title VII's express protection of bona fide promotional examinations. See § 2000e–2(h) ("[N]or shall it be an unlawful employment practice for an employer to give and to act upon the results of any professionally developed ability test provided that such test, its administration or action upon the results is not designed, intended or used to discriminate because of race")

For the foregoing reasons, we adopt the strong-basis-in-evidence standard as a matter of statutory construction to resolve any conflict between the disparate-treatment and disparate-impact provisions of Title VII. [In so holding, we do not] question an employer's affirmative efforts to ensure that all groups have a fair opportunity to apply for promotions and to participate in the process by which promotions will be made. But once that process has been established and employers have made clear their selection criteria, they may not then invalidate the test results, thus upsetting an employee's legitimate expectation not to be judged on the basis of race. Doing so, absent a strong basis in evidence of an impermissible disparate impact, amounts to the sort of racial preference that Congress has disclaimed, § 2000e–2(j), and is antithetical to the notion of a workplace where individuals are guaranteed equal opportunity regardless of race. We hold only that, under Title VII, before an employer can engage in intentional discrimination for the asserted purpose of avoiding or remedying an unintentional disparate impact, the employer must have a strong basis in evidence to believe it will be subject to disparate-impact liability if it fails to take the race-conscious, discriminatory action.

II. C.

The City argues that, even under the strong-basis-in-evidence standard, its decision to discard the examination results was permissible under Title VII. That is incorrect. Even if respondents were motivated as a subjective matter by a desire to avoid committing disparate-impact discrimination, the record makes clear there is no support for the conclusion that respondents had an objective, strong basis in evidence to find the tests inadequate, with some consequent disparate-impact liability in violation of Title VII.

On this basis, we conclude that petitioners have met their obligation to demonstrate that there is "no genuine issue as to any material fact" and that they are "entitled to judgment as a matter of law."

The racial adverse impact here was significant, and petitioners do not dispute that the City was faced with a prima facie case of disparate-impact liability. On the captain exam, the pass rate for white candidates was 64 percent but was 37.5 percent for both black and Hispanic candidates. On the lieutenant exam, the pass rate for white candidates was 58.1 percent; for black candidates, 31.6 percent; and for Hispanic candidates, 20 percent. The pass rates of minorities, which were approximately one-half the pass rates for white candidates, fall well below the 80-percent standard set by the EEOC to implement the disparate-impact provision of Title VII. Based on how the passing candidates ranked and an application of the "rule of three," certifying the examinations would have meant that the City could not have considered black candidates for any of the then-vacant lieutenant or captain positions.

Based on the degree of adverse impact reflected in the results, respondents were compelled to take a hard look at the examinations to determine whether certifying the results would have had an impermissible disparate impact. The problem for respondents is that a prima facie case of disparate-impact liability—essentially, a threshold showing of a significant statistical disparity, and nothing more—is far from a strong basis in evidence that the City would have been liable under Title VII had it certified the results. That is because the City could be liable for disparate-impact discrimination only if the examinations were not job related and consistent with business necessity, or if there existed an equally valid, less-discriminatory alternative that served the City's needs but that the City refused to adopt. § 2000e–2(k)(1)(A), (C). We conclude there is no strong basis in evidence to establish that the test was deficient in either of these respects.

II. C. 3.

The problem, of course, is that after the tests were completed, the raw racial results became the predominant rationale for the City's refusal to certify the results. The injury arises in part from the high, and justified, expectations of the candidates who had participated in the testing process on the terms the City had established for the promotional process. Many of the candidates had studied for months, at considerable personal and financial expense, and thus the injury caused by the City's reliance on raw racial statistics at the end of the process was all the more severe. Confronted with arguments both for and against certifying the test results—and threats of a lawsuit either way—the City was required to make a difficult inquiry. But its hearings produced no strong evidence of a disparate-impact violation, and the City was not entitled to disregard the tests based solely on the racial disparity in the results.

Our holding today clarifies how Title VII applies to resolve competing expectations under the disparate-treatment and disparate-impact provisions. If, after it certifies the test results, the City faces a disparate-impact suit, then in light of our holding today it should be clear that the City would avoid disparate-impact liability based on the strong basis in evidence that, had it not certified the results, it would have been subject to disparate-treatment liability.

Petitioners are entitled to summary judgment on their Title VII claim, and we therefore need not decide the underlying constitutional question. The judgment of the Court of Appeals is reversed, and the cases are remanded for further proceedings consistent with this opinion.

It is so ordered.

JUSTICE SCALIA, concurring.

I join the Court's opinion in full, but write separately to observe that its resolution of this dispute merely postpones the evil day on which the Court will have to confront the question: Whether, or to what extent, are the disparate-impact provisions of Title VII of the Civil Rights Act of 1964 consistent with the Constitution's guarantee of equal protection? The question is not an easy one.

The difficulty is this: Whether or not Title VII's disparate-treatment provisions forbid "remedial" race-based actions when a disparate-impact violation would *not* otherwise result—the question resolved by the Court today—it is clear that Title VII not only permits but affirmatively *requires* such actions when a disparate-impact violation *would* otherwise result. But if the Federal Government is prohibited from discriminating on the basis of race, then surely it is also prohibited from enacting laws mandating that third parties—*e.g.*, employers, whether private, State, or municipal—discriminate on the basis of race. As the facts of these cases illustrate, Title VII's disparate-impact provisions place a racial thumb on the scales, often requiring employers to evaluate the racial outcomes of their policies, and to make decisions based on (because of) those racial outcomes. That type of racial decisionmaking is, as the Court explains, discriminatory. To be sure, the disparate-impact laws do not mandate imposition of quotas, but it is not clear why that should provide a safe harbor. Would a private employer not be guilty of unlawful discrimination if he refrained from establishing a racial hiring quota but intentionally designed his hiring practices to achieve the same end? Surely he would. Intentional discrimination is still occurring, just one step up the chain. Government compulsion of such design would therefore seemingly violate equal protection principles. Nor would it matter that Title VII requires consideration of race on a wholesale, rather than retail, level. "[T]he Government must treat citizens as individuals, not as simply components of a racial, religious, sexual or national class."

It might be possible to defend the law by framing it as simply an evidentiary tool used to identify genuine, intentional discrimination—to "smoke out," as it were, disparate treatment. Disparate impact is sometimes (though not always, a signal of something illicit, so a regulator might allow statistical disparities to play some role in the evidentiary process. But arguably the disparate-impact provisions sweep too broadly to be fairly characterized in such a fashion—since they fail to provide an affirmative defense for good-faith (*i.e.*, nonracially motivated) conduct, or perhaps even for good faith plus hiring standards that are entirely reasonable. This is a question that this Court will have to consider in due course. It is one thing to free plaintiffs from proving an employer's illicit intent, but quite another to preclude the employer from proving that its motives were pure and its actions reasonable.

JUSTICE ALITO, with whom JUSTICE SCALIA and JUSTICE THOMAS join, concurring.

I join the Court's opinion in full. I write separately only because the dissent, while claiming that "[t]he Court's recitation of the facts leaves out important parts of the story," *post,* at 2690 (opinion of GINSBURG, J.), provides an incomplete description of the events that led to New Haven's decision to reject the results of its exam. The dissent's omissions are important because, when all of the evidence in the record is taken into account, it is clear that, even if the legal analysis in Parts II and III–A of the dissent were accepted, affirmance of the decision below is untenable.

I.

When an employer in a disparate-treatment case under Title VII of the Civil Rights Act of 1964 claims that an employment decision, such as the refusal to promote, was based on a legitimate reason, two questions—one objective and one subjective—must be decided. The first, objective question is whether the reason given by the employer is one that is legitimate under Title VII. If the reason provided by the employer is not legitimate on its face, the employer is liable. The second, subjective question concerns the employer's intent. If an employer offers a facially legitimate reason for its decision but it turns out that this explanation was just a pretext for discrimination, the employer is again liable.

The question on which the opinion of the Court and the dissenting opinion disagree concerns the objective component of the determination that must be made when an employer justifies an employment decision, like the one made in this litigation, on the ground that a contrary decision would have created a risk of disparate-impact liability. The Court holds—and I entirely agree—that concern about disparate-impact liability is a legitimate reason for a decision of the type involved here only if there was a "strong basis in evidence to find the tests inadequate." The Court ably demonstrates that in this litigation no reasonable jury could find that the city of New Haven (City) possessed such evidence and therefore summary judgment for petitioners is required. Because the Court correctly holds that respondents cannot satisfy this objective component, the Court has no need to discuss the question of the respondents' actual intent. As the Court puts it, "[e]ven if respondents were motivated as a subjective matter by a desire to avoid committing disparate-impact discrimination, the record makes clear there is no support for the conclusion that respondents had an objective, strong basis in evidence to find the tests inadequate."

According to the dissent, the objective component should be whether the evidence provided "good cause" for the decision, and the dissent argues—incorrectly, in my view—that no reasonable juror could fail to find that such evidence was present here. But even if the dissent were correct on this point, I assume that the dissent would not countenance summary judgment for respondents if respondents' professed concern about disparate-impact litigation was simply a pretext. Therefore, the decision below, which sustained the entry of summary judgment for respondents, cannot be affirmed unless no reasonable jury could find that the City's asserted reason for scrapping its test—concern about disparate-impact liability—was a pretext and that the City's real reason was illegitimate, namely, the desire to placate a politically important racial constituency.

JUSTICE GINSBURG, with whom JUSTICE STEVENS, JUSTICE SOUTER, and JUSTICE BREYER join, dissenting.

In assessing claims of race discrimination, "[c]ontext matters. In 1972, Congress extended Title VII of the Civil Rights Act of 1964 to cover public employment. At that time, municipal fire departments across the country, including New Haven's, pervasively discriminated against minorities. The extension of Title VII to cover jobs in firefighting effected no overnight change. It took decades of persistent effort, advanced by Title VII litigation, to open firefighting posts to members of racial minorities.

The white firefighters who scored high on New Haven's promotional exams understandably attract this Court's sympathy. But they had no vested right to promotion. Nor have other persons received promotions in preference to them. New Haven maintains that it refused to certify the test results because it believed, for good cause, that it would be vulnerable to a Title VII disparate-impact suit if it relied on those results. The Court today holds that New Haven has not demonstrated "a strong basis in evidence" for its plea. In so holding, the Court pretends that "[t]he City rejected the test results solely because the higher scoring candidates were white." That pretension, essential to the Court's disposition, ignores substantial evidence of multiple flaws in the tests New Haven used. The Court similarly fails to acknowledge the better tests used in other cities, which have yielded less racially skewed outcomes.

By order of this Court, New Haven, a city in which African-Americans and Hispanics account for nearly 60 percent of the population, must today be served—as it was in the days of undisguised discrimination—by a fire department in which members of racial and ethnic minorities are rarely seen in command positions. In arriving at its order, the Court barely acknowledges the pathmarking decision in *Griggs v. Duke Power Co.*, 401 U.S. 424, 91 S.Ct. 849, 28 L.Ed.2d 158 (1971), which explained the centrality of the disparate-impact concept to effective enforcement of Title VII. The Court's order and opinion, I anticipate, will not have staying power.

I. A.

The Court's recitation of the facts leaves out important parts of the story. Firefighting is a profession in which the legacy of racial discrimination casts an especially long shadow. In extending Title VII to state and local government employers in 1972, Congress took note of a U.S. Commission on Civil Rights (USCCR) report finding racial discrimination in municipal employment even "more pervasive than in the private sector." H.R.Rep. No. 92–238, p. 17 (1971). According to the report, overt racism was partly to blame, but so too was a failure on the part of municipal employers to apply merit-based employment principles. In making hiring and promotion decisions, public employers often "rel[ied] on criteria unrelated to job performance," including nepotism or political patronage. 118 Cong. Rec. 1817 (1972). Such flawed selection methods served to entrench preexisting racial hierarchies. The USCCR report singled out police and fire departments for having "[b]arriers to equal employment . . . greater . . . than in any other area of State or local government," with African-Americans "hold[ing] almost no positions in the officer ranks." *Ibid.* See also National Commission on Fire Prevention and Control, America Burning 5 (1973) ("Racial minorities are underrepresented in the fire departments in nearly every community in which they live.").

The city of New Haven (City) was no exception. In the early 1970's, African-Americans and Hispanics composed 30 percent of New Haven's population, but only 3.6 percent of the City's 502 firefighters. The racial disparity in the officer ranks was even more pronounced: "[O]f the 107 officers in the Department only one was black, and he held the lowest rank above private."

Following a lawsuit and settlement agreement, see *ibid.*, the City initiated efforts to increase minority representation in the New Haven Fire Department (Department). Those litigation-induced efforts produced some positive change. New Haven's population includes a greater proportion of minorities today than it did in the 1970's: Nearly 40 percent of the City's residents are African-American and more than 20 percent are Hispanic. Among entry-level firefighters, minorities are still underrepresented, but not starkly so. As of 2003, African-Americans and Hispanics constituted 30 percent and 16 percent of the City's firefighters, respectively. In supervisory positions, however, significant disparities remain. Overall, the senior officer ranks (captain and higher) are nine percent African-American and nine percent Hispanic. Only one of the Department's 21 fire captains is African-American. See App. in No. 06–4996–cv (CA2), p. A1588 (hereinafter CA2 App.). It is against this backdrop of entrenched inequality that the promotion process at issue in this litigation should be assessed.

II. B.

Haven, the record indicates, did not closely consider what sort of "practical" examination would "fairly measure the relative fitness and capacity of the applicants to discharge the duties" of a fire officer. Instead, the City simply adhered to the testing regime outlined in its two-decades-old contract with the local firefighters' union: a written exam, which would account for 60 percent of an applicant's total score, and an oral exam, which would account for the remaining 40 percent. The highest scoring African-American candidate ranked 13th; the top Hispanic candidate was 26th. As for the seven then-vacant captain positions, two Hispanic candidates would have been eligible, but no African-Americans. The highest scoring African-American candidate ranked 15th. These stark disparities, the Court acknowledges, sufficed to state a prima facie case under Title VII's disparate-impact provision. New Haven thus had cause for concern about the prospect of Title VII litigation and liability. City officials referred the matter to the New Haven Civil Service Board (CSB), the entity responsible for certifying the results of employment exams.

II. C.

Neither Congress' enactments nor this Court's Title VII precedents (including the now-discredited decision in *Wards Cove*) offer even a hint of "conflict" between an employer's obligations under the statute's disparate-treatment and disparate-impact provisions. Cf. *ante,* at 2673–2674. Standing on an equal footing, these twin pillars of Title VII advance the same objectives: ending workplace discrimination and promoting genuinely equal opportunity.

Yet the Court today sets at odds the statute's core directives. When an employer changes an employment practice in an effort to comply with Title VII's disparate-impact provision, the Court reasons, it acts "because of race"—something Title VII's disparate-treatment provision, see § 2000e–2(a)(1), generally forbids. This characterization of an employer's compliance-directed action shows little attention to Congress' design or to the *Griggs* line of cases Congress recognized as pathmarking. "[O]ur task in interpreting separate provisions of a single Act is to give the Act the most harmonious, comprehensive meaning possible in light of the legislative policy and purpose." A particular phrase need not "extend to the outer limits of its definitional possibilities" if an incongruity would result. Here, Title VII's disparate-treatment and disparate-impact proscriptions must be read as complementary.

In codifying the *Griggs* and *Albemarle* instructions, Congress declared unambiguously that selection criteria operating to the disadvantage of minority group members can be retained only if justified by business necessity. In keeping with Congress' design, employers who reject such criteria due to reasonable doubts about their reliability can hardly be held to have engaged in discrimination "because of" race. A reasonable endeavor to comply with the law and to ensure that qualified candidates of all races have a fair opportunity to compete is simply not what Congress meant to interdict. I would therefore hold that an employer who jettisons a selection device when its disproportionate racial impact becomes apparent does not violate Title VII's disparate-treatment bar automatically or at all, subject to this key condition: The employer must have good cause to believe the device would not withstand examination for business necessity. Cf. *Faragher v. Boca Raton,* 524 U.S. 775, 806, 118 S.Ct. 2275, 141 L.Ed.2d 662 (1998) (observing that it accords with "clear statutory policy" for employers "to prevent violations" and "make reasonable efforts to discharge their duty" under Title VII).

EEOC's interpretative guidelines are corroborative. "[B]y the enactment of title VII," the guidelines state, "Congress did not intend to expose those who comply with the Act to charges that they are violating the very statute they are seeking to implement." 29 CFR § 1608.1(a) (2008). Recognizing EEOC's "enforcement responsibility" under Title VII, we have previously accorded the Commission's position respectful consideration.

Our precedents defining the contours of Title VII's disparate-treatment prohibition further confirm the absence of any intra statutory discord. In *Johnson v. Transportation Agency, Santa Clara Cty.,* 480 U.S. 616, 107 S.Ct. 1442, 94 L.Ed.2d 615 (1987), we upheld a municipal employer's voluntary affirmative-action plan against a disparate-treatment challenge. Pursuant to the plan, the employer selected a woman for a road-dispatcher position, a job category traditionally regarded as "male." A male applicant who had a slightly higher interview score brought suit under Title VII. This Court rejected his claim and approved the plan, which allowed consideration of gender as "one of numerous factors." Such consideration, we said, is "fully consistent with Title VII" because plans of that order can aid "in eliminating the vestiges of discrimination in the workplace."

This litigation does not involve affirmative action. But if the voluntary affirmative action at issue in *Johnson* does not discriminate within the meaning of Title VII, neither does an employer's reasonable effort to comply with Title VII's disparate-impact provision by refraining from action of doubtful consistency with business necessity.

II. C. 3.

The Court's additional justifications for announcing a strong-basis-in-evidence standard are unimpressive. First, discarding the results of tests, the Court suggests, calls for a heightened standard because it "upset[s] an employee's legitimate expectation." This rationale puts the cart before the horse. The legitimacy of an employee's expectation depends on the legitimacy of the selection method. If an employer reasonably concludes that an exam fails to identify the most qualified individuals and needlessly shuts out a segment of the applicant pool, Title VII surely does not compel the employer to hire or promote based on the test, however unreliable it may be. Indeed, the statute's prime objective is to prevent exclusionary practices from "operat[ing] to 'freeze' the status quo."

Second, the Court suggests, anything less than a strong-basis-in-evidence standard risks creating "a *de facto* quota system, in which . . . an employer could discard test results . . . with the intent of obtaining the employer's preferred racial balance." Under a reasonableness standard, however, an employer could not cast aside a selection method based on a statistical disparity alone. The employer must have good cause to believe that the method screens out qualified applicants and would be difficult to justify as grounded in business necessity. Should an employer repeatedly reject test results, it would be fair, I agree, to infer that the employer is simply seeking a racially balanced outcome and is not genuinely endeavoring to comply with Title VII.

These cases present an unfortunate situation, one New Haven might well have avoided had it utilized a better selection process in the first place. But what this litigation/these cases do not present is race-based discrimination in violation of Title VII. I dissent from the Court's judgment, which rests on the false premise that respondents showed "a significant statistical disparity," but "nothing more."

CHAPTER III

PRODUCING LEGISLATION: EDITING, NEGOTIATING, AND DRAFTING STATUTES

■ ■ ■

Until this point, we have considered the role of courts and lawyers in interpreting statutes that have already been written. Of course, statutes do not produce themselves; someone has to write them.

The responsibility for writing and enacting statutes lies with the legislature. In reality, legislation is often written by staffers, interest groups, lobbyists, or others. But legislation does not become law until it is enacted by the legislature. Consequently, legal discourse typically assumes or speaks as though statutes were written by the legislature that enacted it.

This chapter consists of exercises designed to put you in the position of the legislature in drafting statutes. In addition, by the end of the chapter, you should have gained an understanding of some of the challenges imposed by the legislative process and the drafting process.

A. EDITING A STATUTE

EXERCISE III.1: CLARIFYING STATUTES

- Edit the Civil Rights Act of 1964 in a way that it now clearly prohibits voluntary affirmative action programs. Come up with at least two different ways to do so. Make as few changes to the text as possible. Note that Justices Rehnquist and Scalia claimed in *Weber* and *Johnson* that the statute was already as clear as possible. Do you agree?

- Edit the Civil Rights Act of 1964 in a way that it now clearly permits voluntary affirmative action programs. Come up with at least two different ways to do so. Make as few changes to the text as possible.

- Why do you think the statute was not written in any of the ways you identified? If you agree with Justice Rehnquist's dissent in *Weber*, why didn't Congress clarify the statute in the manner you suggested? If you agree with the majority in *Weber*, why wasn't the statute written as you suggested?

B.   THE CHALLENGES OF EVEN SIMPLE LEGISLATION

You have already discovered some of the challenges inherent in writing statutes. For example, regarding the Civil Rights Act, you saw that it was difficult for the requisite majorities in Congress to agree on anything from the broad scheme to the specific statutory language, that it was sometimes difficult for them to anticipate what questions might arise in the future under the statute, and that drafters and supporters of the bill had to make tradeoffs given the political and procedural constraints.

But the Civil Rights Act was a uniquely contentious and controversial piece of legislation. You may be wondering whether simpler and more run-of-the-mill legislation likewise generates similar drafting and interpretive challenges. The following exercise should help you to resolve that question.

EXERCISE III.2: THE CHALLENGES OF DRAFTING STATUTES

Read the following statute that was recently enacted in Georgia. After doing so, answer the following questions:

- Do you think this was an easy or difficult statute to enact? Why?

- Professor Lee commutes 70 miles to her office each day. She has loaded her iPhone with apps to help her make her commute time productive. Please advise her as to whether she may:

  o   Call a colleague to discuss a recent Supreme Court case.

  o   Call her assistant and dictate a letter of recommendation for a student.

  o   Use the iPhone's dictation app to dictate a letter of recommendation. Professor Lee will review the text when she gets to her office.

  o   Use the iPhone's dictation app to dictate a letter of recommendation and then send it automatically to her assistant for proofreading. To do so, she dictates the letter and then says "End letter. Email to Assistant." The letter is then sent automatically via email over AT&T's data network.

  o   Use the radio controls on her car stereo to locate and listen to the local NPR station.

  o   Use her iPhone NPR app to stream the NPR station from Houston, Texas.

  o   Fiddle with the iPod function on her iPhone to access her favorite playlist.

- Does your statutory analysis track with your intuition as to what the answers to these questions *should* be as a policy matter?

- Improve the statute by editing it. Why does the statute contain some ambiguities?

BE IT ENACTED BY THE GENERAL ASSEMBLY OF GEORGIA:

WHEREAS, the General Assembly finds that there has been a proliferation of cellular telephone use and that virtually every driver in Georgia now possesses such a device; and

WHEREAS, distractions caused by such devices, particularly the act of sending or reading text-based messages has resulted in numerous traffic accidents, injuries, and deaths throughout our state and nation; and

WHEREAS, young drivers are particularly susceptible to such distractions due to their inexperience and increased willingness to take risks while driving; and

WHEREAS, it is the responsibility of this body to take action to protect drivers from those who abuse their driving privilege by recklessly text messaging while driving.

SECTION 1.

This Act shall be known and may be cited as the "Caleb Sorohan Act for Saving Lives by Preventing Texting While Driving."

SECTION 2.

. . . .

SECTION 3.

Said title is further amended by revising Code Section 40–6–241, relating to drivers' exercise of due care and proper use of radios and mobile telephones, as follows:

"40–6–241.

A driver shall exercise due care in operating a motor vehicle on the highways of this state and shall not engage in any actions which shall distract such driver from the safe operation of such vehicle, provided that, except as prohibited by Code Section 40–6–241.1, the proper use of a radio, citizens band radio, mobile telephone, or amateur or ham radio shall not be a violation of this Code section."

SECTION 4.

Said title is further amended by inserting a new Code section to read as follows:

"40–6–241.1.

(a) As used in the Code section, the term 'wireless telecommunications device' means a cellular telephone, a text messaging device, a personal digital assistant, a standalone computer, or any other substantially similar wireless device that is used to initiate or receive a wireless communication with another person. It does not include citizens band radios, citizens band radio hybrids, commercial two-way radio communication devices, subscription-based emergency communications, in-vehicle security, navigation devices, and remote diagnostics systems, or amateur or ham radio devices.

(b)   No person who is 18 years of age or older or who has a Class C license shall operate a motor vehicle on any public road or highway of this state while using a wireless telecommunications device to write, send, or read any text-based communication, including but not limited to a text message, instant message, email, or Internet data.

(c)   The provisions of this Code section shall not apply to:

(1)   A person reporting a traffic accident, medical emergency, fire, serious road hazard, or a situation in which the person reasonably believes a person's health or safety is in immediate jeopardy;

(2)   A person reporting the perpetration or potential perpetration of a crime;

(3)   A public utility employee or contractor acting within the scope of his or her employment when responding to a public utility emergency;

(4)   A law enforcement officer, firefighter, emergency medical services personnel, ambulance driver, or other similarly employed public safety first responder during the performance of his or her official duties; or

(5)   A person engaging in wireless communication while in a motor vehicle which is lawfully parked.

(d)   Any conviction for a violation of the provisions of this Code section shall be a misdemeanor punishable by a fine of $150.00. The provisions of Chapter 11 of Title 17 and any other provision of law to the contrary notwithstanding, the costs of such prosecution shall not be taxed nor shall any additional penalty, fee, or surcharge to a fine for such offense be assessed against a person for conviction thereof. The court imposing such fine shall forward a record of the disposition to the Department of Driver Services. Any violation of this Code section shall constitute a separate offense."

SECTION 5.

. . . .

SECTION 6.

This Act shall become effective on July 1, 2010, and shall apply to offenses committed on or after such date.

SECTION 7.

All laws and parts of laws in conflict with this Act are repealed.

C. LEGISLATIVE RESEARCH AND DRAFTING

Legislators often adapt and adopt legislation from other jurisdictions rather than write laws from scratch. This requires them—or rather, their staffers or the lobbyists and other drafters they turn to for assistance—to be able to research, analyze, synthesize, edit, and improve on legislation from other jurisdictions or model statutes. They also need to think strategically about the likelihood that the statutes will pass and the relevant concerns and constituencies they should consider.

EXERCISE III.3: RESEARCHING AND ADAPTING LEGISLATION AND DEVELOPING LEGISLATIVE STRATEGY

Some Georgia state legislators are interested in adopting new legislation to explicitly allow for the testing of driverless cars on Georgia roads. These legislators task you, a legislative aide, with answering the following questions:

- What other states have adopted such statutes?

- What do these other statutes provide? Are they substantively the same? Different?

- What potential problems and questions does the legislation need to consider and address?

- What interest groups should these legislators work with? Who is likely to support the legislation? Who is likely to oppose it?

- Provide a proposed statute.

D. LEGISLATIVE PROCEDURE, NEGOTIATION, AND DRAFTING

One reason that drafting a statute is difficult is that legislators must work within certain procedural constraints. Another difficulty is that legislators must work collaboratively with people who have different policy views in order to form necessary coalitions. The following exercise will give you the opportunity to negotiate and draft a simple statute. Consider whether there are any issues worth finessing as you draft the statute.

EXERCISE III.4

Background

The current policy in the law library is that students may eat whatever they like and are responsible for cleaning up after themselves. Recently, however, the school's administration has received complaints about this policy. The administration takes these complaints seriously and is considering a policy change.

This has become a hot-button issue for all of the various stakeholders in the law school. In an attempt to settle the issue in a community-building, consensus-driven way, the Dean has decided to put together a task force representing all of the interest groups. The 22-member task force is charged with drafting a new set of rules concerning food in the library.

The Dean is inclined to favor of some kind of new restrictions. As she wrote in her charge to the committee, "The status quo is unacceptable. We cannot have garbage strewn throughout the library, and we cannot have student and library property destroyed by spills." That said, she is also inclined to accept whatever the task force approves by a simple majority vote. However, she has said that if any proposal can get at least 15 out of 22 votes, she will almost certainly adopt it, and the closer to unanimous the task force is, the happier she will be.

In order to encourage the task force to reach a resolution, the Dean has declared that if the task force fails to do so, she will unilaterally draft rules that she guarantees will satisfy no one.

The Task Force

The task force consists of 22 members, each with one vote. The members are divided among six factions:

Students:

The students collectively have 10 members on the task force, and therefore 10 votes in total. They were elected in a special election as representatives of the student body for this particular issue. However, they are split into three factions.

Student Faction 1. This group has seven members (and thus seven votes). This group was elected on a platform of adamant opposition to restrictions on food in the library. They believe that students are adults, and further that, because of the demands of law school, it would be punitive to prohibit students from eating in the library where they spend so much time. They have no objection to requiring students to clean up after themselves or to reasonable punishment of those who do not adequately do so.

Student Faction 2. This group has two members (and thus two votes) and was elected on a platform of favoring prohibitions on food in the library. This group represents students who find the food in the library to be extremely distracting. Some students have complained about being disturbed by noises from others eating; others have sat down in spots in the library only to find out afterwards that they sat in leftovers that other students failed to clean up; and one student had her computer destroyed when another student accidentally spilled coffee on it. One member of this faction also hopes to serve as elected president or vice president of the student council next year.

Student Faction 3. This group has one member (and thus one vote). She doesn't care about any general policies concerning food in the library, but she represents students with diabetes and other medical conditions that sometimes require them to eat throughout the day. These students believe strongly that if there are new restrictions on food in the library, those with medical conditions should be exempted from the restrictions. This member of the task force (and the students she represents) have argued that such an exemption would be required by law, and further, that if the law school does not adopt such an exemption, these students would file a lawsuit.

Librarians:

The librarians have five members (and thus five votes) on the task force. They are united in their adamant opposition to food in the library for students. They are tired of reminding students, often in vain, to clean up after themselves, and they are upset by spills that damage library property (such as computers, books, and furniture). They frequently bring up the problem the library had five years ago with rats being attracted to the library by all of the crumbs. But they are equally adamant that librarians should be permitted to have food in the library. After all, they say, "We work here. Where else are we going to eat? Besides, we are permanent employees, so we are good stewards of the library. We clean up after ourselves because we work together—no one wants to be the outcast who doesn't clean up!—and we have a responsibility to our workplace that we take seriously. Librarians haven't been the problem; students have."

Faculty:

The faculty faction has four members (and thus four votes) on the task force. They are somewhat opposed to regulating food in the library for ideological reasons. They believe that students are adults who should be treated as such. To them, this means that students should be allowed to eat in the library. They have suggested that students bothered by the noise can wear earplugs or find someplace else to work. On the other hand, if students do not clean up after themselves, or if they ruin library property or the property of others, they must pay the consequences. At the same time, however, they view the librarians as their colleagues and therefore are predisposed in favor of supporting the librarians. Moreover, faculty members have an interest in remaining on good terms with the librarians because both groups are long-term stakeholders in the institution, and, further, faculty members sometimes turn to librarians for assistance on research projects. Thus, the faculty members on the task force are torn between their ideological views and their personal relationships, and they are open to persuasion.

Alumni:

The alumni have three members on the task force (and thus three votes). Like the faculty, they are torn and persuadable. They view their allegiance as towards the law school as a lasting institution. For this reason, and because they are involved in fundraising for the school, they are somewhat in favor of increased regulations because they are concerned that potential donors given tours of the law school would be put off by the sight of garbage strewn about the library. On the other hand, they are nostalgic about their own days as students, and they fondly recall their days studying for exams in the library with friends, bonding over bags of Doritos and cans of warm Red Bull or Tab (depending on their graduation years), and they hope that current and future students will have similar experiences.

Your Assignments

You will work in groups of six people each. Each group must negotiate and attempt to agree upon and draft a new Food in the Library Policy. Each person will represent one of the six factions listed above. (In the event that a group has seven students, the seventh student should work on a team with one of the other members of the group.)

Each small group must produce a single document that includes the following:

- A statute that the group adopted, if the group was able to vote one through, together with the vote tally; or, in the alternative, an explanation of how close the group came to reaching a majority or super-majority and why it was unable to do so. (Recall that the various factions have differing numbers of votes.) The format of the statute is listed below.

- A legislative history that briefly describes the process the group designed and followed in the deliberations and any information that would be useful for the Dean and others to have in the future. For example, were competing statutes drafted and voted upon? Who took the lead in negotiations? Were negotiations formal or informal? How did they proceed? How long did it take to reach an agreement? Were agreements reached with the whole working group present, or in private conversations? How should ambiguities be resolved? What were the hangups and how were they resolved? This should be no longer than three pages (and may certainly be shorter!).

- A short statement by each student answering the following questions: Which faction did you represent, how did you vote, and why did you vote for or against the proposed rules? How did you contribute to the final statute, and how were your constituents served by the vote and participation in the process? Finally, did any of the issues we have discussed relating to how statutes should be, and are, interpreted influence you in any way? If so, how? Each student's explanation should be no longer than two pages (and may certainly be shorter!).

You will be evaluated on how well each person served his or her faction's and constituent's interests and how well the final statute is drafted. Of course, you may best serve your faction's and constituent's interests by voting against the proposed rules, but remember that the Dean would really like to see as much consensus as possible—and everyone's interests will suffer if the Dean ends up writing her own rules.

Format of the Statute:

The legislation you draft must follow the following format:

- The Act must have a Title.
- Section (a) of the Act must describe the purpose(s) of the Act.
- Section (b) of the Act must define any terms that require definition.
- Section (c) of the Act must lay out the substantive provisions of the Act.
- Section (d) of the Act must state how, and by whom, the substantive provisions will be enforced and what the penalties for noncompliance are.

Posting and Reading the Statutes:

After turning in your statute and materials, you must post your statutes and legislative history (but not each individual student's report) on the class webpage. You must read several of the statutes and legislative histories written by other groups. In reviewing these materials and reflecting on your own drafting experience, consider and be prepared to discuss in class:

- What was the most difficult aspect of agreeing to and drafting your statute?
- How are the other statutes similar to and different from yours? Why are they different? Were they different in their entire

approach to the problem or in their details? Did you consider these alternative approaches? If so, why did you reject them? If not, why not?

- How did the procedural rules you were required to follow help to shape your statute? What incentives did they create? Which faction(s) wielded the most power and why? What would have happened if only a simple majority were required to pass the statute? What would have happened if you had more time? What would have happened if the Dean did not express a clear and strong desire that some new statute be adopted?

- In light of your experience drafting statutes, in your view, what should judges do when they encounter ambiguities with the statute?

CHAPTER IV

THE THEORIES OF STATUTORY INTERPRETATION

■ ■ ■

By this point, you should recognize that there are several different approaches to statutory interpretation. In this chapter, we will consider them in greater depth. What are their claims to legitimacy? What are their strengths and weaknesses? How do lawyers and judges use them in actual cases?

At the outset, you should be aware that most judges and lawyers make use of several different theories of interpretation. In other words, there are very few judges (and no successful lawyers) who dogmatically adhere to any one particular approach in all cases. However, it is certainly the case that some judges are more closely associated with, and prefer to adopt, one approach or another.

This chapter begins with an overview of the various theoretical approaches to interpretation. It then offers several cases in which the approaches are applied. The chapter concludes with an exercise designed to help concretize your understanding of the approaches and to consider how lawyers can make use of these approaches to further the interests of their clients.

A. OVERVIEW OF THE THEORIES OF INTERPRETATION

This introduction offers a basic overview of the approaches to statutory interpretation. For students interested in considering the different approaches in greater depth, suggested articles and books are included at the end of the section. Your instructor may assign some of these readings.

1. INTENTIONALISM

Until relatively recently, legislative intent has been the touchstone of statutory interpretation. The language of intentionalism continues to appear in judicial literature. Intentionalists base their approach on the proposition that a statute becomes a law because of the enacting legislature, and therefore a judge interpreting the statute, acting as an agent of the legislature, should seek to implement the will of the legislature by gleaning the enacting legislature's intent. Because words are imperfect vehicles for conveying meaning, it may be necessary to look beyond the language of the statute in order to understand what the legislature meant by its words. Thus, intentionalists pay careful attention to legislative context and history to determine what the legislature had in mind.

This approach reflects our natural tendencies when faced with an authoritative instruction. For example, if a parent instructs an older child to "pick up" a younger child, the older child will have to interpret the command. On the one hand, it could mean that the older child must physically lift the younger child into the air; on the other hand, it could mean that the older child should go to where the younger child is and escort her home. The plain language of the instruction could support either interpretation, and the older child's job would be to determine which one the parent intended. Context would be of much use, of course, but if the older child overheard the parents' discussion that led to the issuance of the command, he would draw reasonable inferences from that discussion as well.

The inquiry into legislative intent is dominated by researching the context and legislative history to determine what the legislature had in mind. In the ideal case, when a court is confronted with a difficult question of statutory interpretation, researching the legislative history would reveal that the legislature considered the very question at issue and clearly resolved it. Practically, though, the search for such golden nuggets rarely produces anything authoritative. In most cases, therefore, intentionalists seek evidence of either the legislature's general intent (whether the legislature intended for the statute to be broadly or narrowly interpreted, for example) or its reconstructed or imagined intent (what would the legislature have agreed upon, had it considered this particular question?).

Think back to the *Weber* case. Justice Rehnquist's dissenting opinion is an excellent example of intentionalism. Recall that Justice Brennan, too, mounted an intentionalist argument, mustering as much legislative history as he could. This reflects the primacy of the intentionalist model across the ideological spectrum. Do you think that their opinions are best understood as making claims concerning the legislature's actual, general, or reconstructed/imagined intent?

Intentionalists maintain that by requiring courts to implement the meaning intended by the original Congress, judges act as honest agents of the legislature and are prevented from considering any other factors in deciding upon a course of action. For example, the older child in the hypothetical described above may not ask whether it is a good idea to pick the younger child up at all, or whether lifting or escorting, respectively, would be better for the younger child's psyche or safety. Rather, he must simply try to fulfill what he understands to be the directive. Similarly, under the intentionalist approach, the judicial interpreter has no business asking which potential meaning of a statute would be better; instead, her job is only to determine what the legislature meant. If the legislature determines that the court has misperceived its intent, or that its intent yielded undesirable results, then the legislature is free to clarify.

Over the past three decades, intentionalism has come under sustained attack by scholars and some influential judges. First, critics of intentionalism argue that legislative history is not a legitimate source of statutory meaning. As Judge Alex Kozinski succinctly put it, "[t]he two Houses and the President agree on the text of statutes, not on [legislative history captured in] committee reports or floor statements. To give substantive effect to this flotsam and jetsam of the legislative process is to short-circuit the constitutional scheme for making law." Further, critics maintain that there is no such thing as legislative intent; the legislature is a collective body that does not have a collective mind. That is, individual legislators may have intentions, but the legislature as a whole does not.

Opponents of intentionalism also maintain that reliance on legislative history encourages bad behavior on the part of legislators. After all, if legislators know that courts will scour the legislative history to give a statute effect, the legislators can avoid the political risk inherent in producing clear statutory directives on controversial issues. Instead, they can simply insert clues and hints throughout the legislative history in the hopes that courts will seize on them and interpret the statute accordingly. In other words, even without cobbling together a majority to enact a particular legislative faction's preferences, the faction may be able to achieve the same result by pushing in its preferred direction in the legislative history. This undercuts intentionalism's claim to democratic and constitutional legitimacy and incentivizes legislatures to generate statutes that are unclear, to delegate difficult and contested policy questions to courts, and to engage in gamesmanship in the production of the legislative record.

These problems, in turn, undermine intentionalists' claim that their approach serves to constrain judges. Because legislators attempt to direct statutory interpretation by inserting various comments in the legislative record, the record is often littered with vague and/or contradictory statements that yield no authoritative answer to specific questions of statutory interpretation. This, coupled with the fact that the legislative history rarely, if ever, contains a golden nugget that directly resolves a difficult question of statutory interpretation, ultimately allows, and even requires, a judge to pick and choose legislative history that reflects her values and supports her preferred result. As Judge Leventhal famously put it, relying on legislative history is akin to "looking over a crowd of people and picking out your friends." Thus, according to the textualists' critique, intentionalism offers little to constrain judges, who may simply cloak their own preferences in the language and rhetoric of legislative intent.

Although intentionalist rhetoric continues to be employed by judges in some cases, and judges continue to look to legislative history for guidance in interpreting statutes, it is fair to say that intentionalism's grip on interpretation has declined in recent years as a result of these critiques, and its dominance has been challenged and somewhat displaced by textualism.

2. TEXTUALISM

Textualists begin with the same core proposition that intentionalists do, namely that a statute's authority comes from its enactment as law and, thus, that a statute's meaning does not change over time. However, textualists fiercely reject the notion that judges should seek to determine legislative intent. Consequently, textualists reject most use of legislative history in statutory interpretation. Instead, textualists argue that only the text of the statute itself has the force of law, and the job of the judge is to determine how the average member of the enacting legislature would have understood the text.

To determine the appropriate textualist reading of a statute, textualists seek to apply the "plain meaning" of the statute, often using what are known as the textual canons of interpretation (covered in the next chapter). For textualists, words are to be understood according to their plain meaning, which can be gleaned, as appropriate, from customary usage or dictionaries, or, where relevant, by reference to well-developed technical or legal meanings.

Textualists also stress that the structure of the statute and the statute's relationship with related statutes provides substantial guidance as to the appropriate interpretation or application. Thus, where the plain language of the statute is amenable to multiple possible meanings, textualists maintain that the judge should apply the one that is most coherent with the statutory scheme as a whole and with the larger statutory landscape at the time the statute was enacted. This requires the judge to adopt a fiction—a "benign fiction," according to Justice Scalia (the most famous textualist), but a fiction nonetheless—that legislators mean to, and have sufficient knowledge and information to, pass statutes that are internally coherent and consistent with the larger body of contemporaneous law.

Like intentionalists, textualists argue that their approach both has democratic legitimacy, because only the text of the statute itself has the force of law, and serves to constrain judges from imposing their own values on the law, because judges must simply put themselves in the place of the average legislator at the time of enactment and ask how that person would understand the statutory provision. And, like intentionalists, textualists argue that the address for any grievances with the result of a particular case is the legislature, rather than the courts. Recall Justice Scalia's dissent in *Johnson* as an example of textualism.

Despite its emerging dominance, textualism has also been subject to substantial criticism. First, critics argue textualism constrains little more than does intentionalism. Statutes are the product of legislative compromise, and the legislature sometimes declines to resolve a particular question because it could not achieve a majority if it did. Therefore, judges who insist that there is a textualist answer to every question are seeking a phantom. Moreover, because statutory ambiguity can be a result of the absence of legislative agreement, textualist judges inevitably fill such legislative gaps with their own values or assumptions, even as they stridently disclaim doing so.

Opponents of textualism also take aim at its claim to democratic legitimacy. Specifically (and this critique applies equally to intentionalism), critics argue that textualism depends on an unrealistic account of the democratic process. Public choice theory suggests, and the evidence bears out, that statutes are difficult to enact, amend, or repeal. In other words, even where the majority of the population (and the legislature) supports updating the law, it is unlikely that the law will be updated. Therefore, textualists' "solution" to the problem of undesirable results—"take it to the legislature"—is no solution at all.

Further, some argue that textualism sometimes leads to manifestly unjust results. If your boss tells you to drop everything and come to her office immediately, should you literally drop everything? What if you are holding her baby?

Finally, some opponents of textualism and intentionalism argue that the law-generating process involves a great deal more than the actions of legislatures. Statutory meaning and application accrues over time, as subsequent legislatures, judges, and administrative agencies all interpose related rules and meanings on existing statutory schemes. Therefore, these critics assert that textualists and intentionalists are wrong— descriptively and normatively—to assert that statutory meaning is to be found only with the enacting legislature.

Textualism has emerged as a powerful force, rhetorically at least. As we will see, however, few judges are *only* textualists. Recall Justice Scalia's opinion in *Johnson*. He did not completely dismiss precedent as a potential source of statutory meaning and application, did he? How can this be reconciled with textualist theory?

3.   PURPOSIVISM

A third dominant approach to statutory interpretation is known as purposivism. Purposivism is often associated with a broader school of legal thought known as Legal Process theory, developed by famous legal scholars Henry Hart, Albert Sacks, Lon Fuller, Herbert Wechsler, and others. In the statutory interpretation context, purposivists maintain that the role of the judge is to understand the fundamental purpose of the statute in question, and to interpret and apply it in particular cases in a manner that faithfully advances that purpose. Most purposivists would agree, however, that where the plain text of a statute prohibits such a reading of the statute, the judge should not violate the statute's plain text.

Although Justice Brennan's opinion in *Weber* is couched as intentionalist, it may best be defended on purposivist grounds. That is, Justice Brennan believed that the primary purpose of Title VII was to give minorities job opportunities that they did not previously have while intruding as little as possible on the prerogatives of private business owners; these purposes are served by reading the statute to allow employers to adopt voluntary affirmative action programs. Justice Rehnquist might argue that the purpose of the statute is to mandate colorblindness in employment; as such, affirmative action programs would interfere with that purpose.

This disagreement highlights some of the central problems with purposivism. A statute may have more than one purpose. Indeed, it is possible that many legislators believed that Title VII would promote *both* equal employment for minorities *and* colorblindness. They may not have anticipated the conflict between the two. Alternatively, it is possible that different legislators had different goals. So who is to say which of those goals should triumph when they come into conflict?

Further, because a statute's purposes may conflict or be unclear, a judge may resolve ambiguities or doubts in a manner that is consistent with his own policy preferences. Thus, it may come as no surprise that Justice Brennan, a political liberal, read Title VII in a manner that permitted affirmative action, whereas Justice Rehnquist, a political conservative, read the same statute to prohibit affirmative action.

Purposivism remains a touchstone to interpretation among judges, but almost no judicial opinion relies entirely on purposivism, and, as in Justice Brennan's opinion in *Weber*, the purposivist approach is often cloaked with intentionalist or textualist rhetoric.

4.   PRAGMATISM

Pragmatism is an approach to interpretation that is most closely associated with the broader Legal Realist school of thought. Judge Richard Posner, an influential appellate court judge and legal scholar, has been the most articulate proponent of pragmatism in recent years.

Judge Posner argues that the object of statutory interpretation is to produce the best results for society through a process he calls practical reasoning. Unfortunately, practical reasoning cannot be translated into a clear methodology. Instead, it requires judges to consider, on a case-by-case basis, the text of the statute, its history and purpose, the coherence of the legal system, the relationship between old statutes and present realities, common sense, the practical consequences of different rulings, custom, experience, intuition, and so forth.

Pragmatism in statutory interpretation is justified on the basis of three primary claims. First, Congress cannot reasonably and does not actually expect that its statutes will govern every situation that arises. Congress has neither the time nor the expertise to resolve every future question that may arise under the statutory regime it enacts. Relatedly, because legislators often cannot agree amongst themselves on how to resolve the most difficult questions, they may leave statutory gaps that leave such questions unresolved or addressed in only vague language in order to allow them to pass a bill. As a result, Congress effectively delegates the resolution of unforeseen or vaguely addressed issues to the courts.

Second, pragmatists maintain that judges are institutionally well-situated to resolve questions of statutory interpretation and application in a sensible way. Judges have a broader understanding and command of the law than most legislators, and therefore can bring a measure of coherence to the law. Moreover, the judiciary is relatively stable over time—both in an absolute sense and as compared with the legislature—and thus brings stability and predictability to the law. Finally, judges deal with issues on a case-by-case basis, which allows them to consider how the law affects real people rather than the abstract and hypothetical circumstances often anticipated by the legislature.

Third, pragmatists point out that legislation is exceedingly difficult to enact, amend, or repeal. As a result, as society changes and as more and more law is produced, old laws remain on the books. At times, newer laws and older laws will be in tension with each other, and at other times, older laws will be profoundly anachronistic. In his seminal work, *A Common Law for the Age of Statutes*, Judge Guido Calebresi famously argued on this basis for allowing judges to expressly abrogate even unambiguous statutes that they deemed anachronistic, much as judges may be empowered to do when considering common law principles. Most modern pragmatists do not extend the theory this far, but they do rely on the same political reality that statutes are difficult to change as circumstances and the surrounding body of the law change. In such cases, pragmatists typically suggest that where statutes are internally ambiguous, or where old and new statutes sit together uneasily, judges should use their practical reasoning to introduce coherence into the law.

Pragmatism rejects the notion that statutory meaning is always fixed at enactment. Instead, it encourages judges to consider modern realities and the practical consequences of their rulings, which implicitly suggests that as realities change, so may the interpretation or proper application of the statute. Further, pragmatism asserts that the law is meant to solve problems and must make sense. As such, judges should do what makes the most sense in any given case, at least where the statute's text is not entirely clear. Thus, the original legislature's intent or likely understanding of the statute is of minimal importance. Pragmatists further argue that all judges must make policy choices, so they ought to be honest about it rather than cloak it in the formal language of intentionalism, textualism, or purposivism.

Justice Blackmun's concurring opinion in *Weber*—which essentially casts aside the statute's text in favor of "practical and equitable" considerations—is an unusually candid example of pragmatic thinking on the Supreme Court.

This approach to statutory interpretation is subject to frequent attacks by intentionalists and textualists for reasons that should be obvious. First, critics take aim at the political legitimacy of pragmatism, suggesting that there is no constitutional basis for shifting statutory meaning over time. Likewise, critics maintain that whatever the failures and limitations of the political branches, there is no constitutional and democratically legitimate basis for taking the lawmaking authority away from the legislature and handing it to unelected, unaccountable judges. (Note that some states elect their judges who hold retention elections. Should judges in such states perhaps be freer to apply pragmatism?) Further, although legislation may be difficult to pass, amend, or fix, critics say that it does not follow that judges are empowered to effectively make law by judicial fiat. In addition, critics doubt that judges are in any position to determine what makes for good policy or that the case-by-case nature of the judicial process lends itself to doing so. Finally, opponents of pragmatism maintain that this approach lends itself to unpredictable results, which itself represents a threat to justice and the rule of law.

Some would argue that all judges are, to a greater or lesser degree, pragmatic, but very few will admit to it. As such, it is the rare judicial opinion that is explicitly couched as pragmatic, but pragmatic arguments may sometimes be implicit.

5. DYNAMIC STATUTORY INTERPRETATION

Dynamic statutory interpretation was first developed by Bill Eskridge, one of the leading scholars of statutory interpretation of the past three decades. Like the pragmatists, Professor Eskridge maintains that a statute's meaning and proper application may change over time. The three theoretical pillars of pragmatism—congressional delegation to judges, the relative ability of judges to bring coherence and stability to the law, and the problems associated with the difficulty of enacting, amending, and repealing statutes—feature prominently in his work.

Professor Eskridge's primary additional insight is that statutory meaning develops (and should develop) over time in a way that is responsive to the changing preferences of the political branches. That is, statutes gain or change meaning based on the changing values and preferences of the legislative and executive branches as a result of either shifting political majorities (for example, new parties or factions attain power) or shifts in preferences that apply across parties (for example, a general consensus emerges among all or most officials, regardless of party affiliation, that *de jure* discrimination on the basis of race is repugnant). Such shifts are expressed in new legislation that may coexist uneasily with old legislation, new regulations, and new legislative priorities and agendas. This process of meaning-generation, in turn, provides democratic legitimacy to statutes that could not presently be enacted when those old statutes are viewed and interpreted in light of the new preferences.

Therefore, according to Eskridge, the preferences of contemporary legislators and administrative officials, together with the other considerations identified by the pragmatists, are to be taken into account by the judge engaging in statutory interpretation and application. Naturally, because legislative and administrative preferences may change over time, so too may statutory meaning and application.

Professor Eskridge's approach is both descriptive and prescriptive; that is, he maintains that judges both *do* and *should* employ dynamic statutory interpretation. However, few judges admit to being engaged in dynamic interpretation. Professor Eskridge suggests that *Weber* is an example of dynamism. Although the question presented in the case is perhaps questionable or indeterminate from an intentionalist or textualist standpoint, it is likely true that the majority of the legislature and the relevant administrative agency at the time *Weber* was decided probably supported the result.

The critiques that apply to pragmatism apply with equal force to dynamic statutory interpretation. In addition, critics question whether judges can possibly identify current preferences of policymakers in the majority of cases, even if those preferences were a legitimate source of statutory meaning. That is, just as the enacting legislature is a pluralistic body to which individual preferences and views cannot be imputed, so too is the contemporary legislature—and that does not even take into account dynamic statutory interpretation's additional focus on the preferences of contemporary administrative officials. Indeed, trying to identify the preferences of contemporary officials may be even more problematic than trying to identify the preferences of the enacting legislature. After all, the enacting legislature at least passed relevant legislation and produced related legislative history that can provide guidance as to legislators' preferences; the preferences of contemporary lawmakers, by contrast, may prove far more difficult to predict, given that they may well have not produced any related legislation at all.

Finally, critics of both pragmatism and dynamic statutory interpretation argue that these approaches offer no real methodology to judges engaging with statutory interpretation and application. As a result, judges may operate without constraint, potentially substituting their own preferences for those of the legislature, using a grab bag of tools and arguments to produce unpredictable results that may destabilize the law.

6. CONTEMPORARY MEANING AND EXPECTATIONS

An additional approach to, or theme within, statutory interpretation is what Professor Hillel Y. Levin refers to as the contemporary meaning and expectations approach. As with pragmatism and dynamism, Professor Levin argues that statutory meaning and application may legitimately change over time. However, he suggests that any such changes cannot be justified by either practical considerations or the contemporary preferences of the legislature and executive. Instead, he suggests that the lodestar for statutory interpretation must be what those regulated by the statute reasonably understand it to require. Otherwise, the court will undermine their legitimate expectations and reliance interests and destabilize the law and the institutions and practices that society has developed.

Levin suggests that the argument between Justices Stevens and Scalia in *Johnson* concerning the value of the *Weber* precedent reflects this approach. What they are really arguing about is whether *Weber* was reasonably understood by employers and the public as permitting all voluntary affirmative action programs, or whether it represents an outlier that could not have been reasonably be relied on for the proposition that the defendant in *Johnson* asserted. Levin also suggests that the *Flood v. Kuhn* case demonstrates a similar concern for public meaning and reliance expectations developed as a result of judicial precedent.

Finally, Levin points to a series of specific doctrines of statutory interpretation that implicitly resonate with the contemporary meaning and expectations approach, offers a sustained theoretical defense of the approach, and develops a methodology for judges to apply it. Levin maintains that though his approach shares much with pragmatism and dynamic statutory interpretation, it operates to constrain judges to a greater degree and is more predictable because it prizes and promotes stability in the law.

Of course, Levin's approach is subject to substantial criticism. As with pragmatism and dynamic statutory interpretation, its constitutional and democratic legitimacy is contestable. Further, it may be extremely difficult to identify a single "public meaning" of a statute or to assess its "reasonableness." Although the contemporary meaning and expectations approach may accurately capture some judicial decisions and doctrines, it is not likely to be explicitly adopted by judges.

EXERCISE IV.1

Read the famous law review article, The Case of the Speluncean Explorers, which can be found at 112 Harv. L. Rev. 1851 (1999). Consider the following questions:

- Which opinion represents which theory (or theories) of interpretation?

- Which opinion best represents you own view of how this "case" should be decided? That is, which would you join? Alternatively, how would you write an opinion in the case?

- What is your sense of how the Supreme Court would resolve this "case" today?

- Which opinion do you think Lon Fuller, the author of the article, would have joined?

7. FURTHER READINGS

There is a wealth of material on the theories of statutory interpretation. Those interested in the topic should consider the following (brief and woefully incomplete!) list of articles and books, in no particular order, for further study:

- ANTONIN SCALIA & BRYAN A. GARNER, READING LAW: THE INTERPRETATION OF LEGAL TEXTS (2012). This book discusses and defends textualism.

- Richard A. Posner, *The Incoherence of Antonin Scalia*, NEW REPUBLIC, Sept. 13, 2012, *available at* http://www.newrepublic.com/ article/magazine/books-and-arts/106441/scalia-garner-reading-the-law-textual-originalism#. This article is a review of Reading Law and a defense of pragmatism. Posner and Garner engaged in an extended exchange on legal blogs following the publication of this (scathing) review.

- Frank H. Easterbrook, *What Does Legislative History Tell Us?*, 66 CHI.-KENT L. REV. 441 (1990). Judge Easterbrook, a leading proponent of textualism, assesses and critiques the use of legislative history. Judge Easterbrook has written many other worthwhile articles on statutory interpretation.

- Alex Kozinski, *Should Reading Legislative History Be an Impeachable Offense?*, 31 SUFFOLK U. L. REV. 807 (1998). In this article, Judge Kozinski, another committed textualist, criticizes the use of legislative history in statutory interpretation.

- Stanley Fish, *There Is No Textualist Position*, 42 SAN DIEGO L. REV. 629 (2005). In this article, Professor Fish argues against the textualist approach.

- Gerald C. MacCallum, Jr., *Legislative Intent*, 75 YALE L.J. 754 (1966). In this article, Professor MacCallum carefully assesses judicial appeals to legislative intent.

- RICHARD A. POSNER, HOW JUDGES THINK (2008). This book develops Judge Posner's theory of pragmatism and his view concerning the proper role of the judge.

- GUIDO CALABRESI, A COMMON LAW FOR THE AGE OF STATUTES (1982). This book explores the role of the judge in interpreting statutes, offering a sophisticated, though highly contested, pragmatic approach.

- WILLIAM N. ESKRIDGE, JR., DYNAMIC STATUTORY INTERPRETATION (1994). This book offers an extended explanation and discussion of Eskridge's theory of dynamic statutory interpretation. Professor Eskridge also helpfully reviews and assesses the dominant approaches to statutory interpretation. A shorter account can be found in his article, *Dynamic Statutory Interpretation*, 135 U. PA. L. REV. 1479 (1987). Professor Eskridge, one of the leading thinkers on statutory interpretation, has written many other worthwhile articles and books.

- HENRY M. HART, JR. & ALBERT M. SACKS, THE LEGAL PROCESS: BASIC PROBLEMS IN THE MAKING AND APPLICATION OF LAW (William N. Eskridge, Jr. & Philip P. Frickey, eds., Foundation Press 1994). This is the leading set of materials for the Legal Process school of thought and is the touchstone for purposivism in statutory interpretation.

- David L. Shapiro, *Continuity and Change in Statutory Interpretation*, 67 N.Y.U. L. REV. 921, 942 (1992). In this article, Professor Shapiro makes the case that several doctrines and tools of statutory interpretation serve to stabilize the law and allow for incremental change over time.

- FRANK B. CROSS, THE THEORY AND PRACTICE OF STATUTORY INTERPRETATION (2009). This book reviews the dominant approaches to statutory interpretation and uses an empirical methodology to assess their use by judges.

- Hillel Y. Levin, *Contemporary Meaning and Expectations in Statutory Interpretation*, 2012 U. ILL. L. REV. 1103 (2012). This article develops Levin's contemporary meaning and expectations approach to interpretation.

- Aaron-Andrew P. Bruhl & Ethan J. Leib, *Elected Judges and Statutory Interpretation*, 79 U. CHI. L. REV. 1215 (2012). In this article, Professors Bruhl and Leib consider whether elected judges should approach statutory interpretation differently from appointed judges. Can you anticipate reasons why they should or should not?

- Abbe R. Gluck & Lisa Schultz Bressman, *Statutory Interpretation from the Inside-an Empirical Study of Congressional Drafting, Delegation, and the Canons: Part I*, 65 Stan. L. Rev. 901 (2013), and Lisa Schultz Bressman & Abbe R. Gluck, *Statutory Interpretation from the Inside: An Empirical Study of Congressional Drafting, Delegation and the Canons: Part II*, 66 Stan. L. Rev. 725 (2014). In these Articles, Gluck and Bressman empirically review the realities of legislative drafting and consider their implications on theoretical and practical debates in the field.

B. THE THEORIES OF INTERPRETATION IN ACTION

Now that you have a basic understanding of the dominant approaches to statutory interpretation, you are prepared to thoughtfully consider their use in some leading cases of statutory interpretation.

HOLY TRINITY CHURCH V. UNITED STATES
143 U.S. 457 (1892)

As you read the following case, focus on these issues:

- What is the difficulty with reading the statute?

- Which theory of interpretation does the opinion adopt?

- Identify all possible arguments *against* the Court's opinion.

- Why do you think the Court focuses so much on this country's Christian heritage?

- How would a textualist like Justice Scalia have voted? How would an opinion by Justice Scalia read?

- How would you have voted in this case? Why?

MR. JUSTICE BREWER delivered the opinion of the Court.

Plaintiff in error is a corporation duly organized and incorporated as a religious society under the laws of the state of New York. E. Walpole Warren was, prior to September, 1887, an alien residing in England. In that month the plaintiff in error made a contract with him, by which he was to remove to the city of New York, and enter into its service as rector and pastor; and, in pursuance of such contract, Warren did so remove and enter upon such service. It is claimed by the United States that this contract on the part of the plaintiff in error was forbidden by [statute]; and an action was commenced to recover the penalty prescribed by that act. The circuit court held that the contract was within the prohibition of the statute, and rendered judgment accordingly, and the single question presented for our determination is whether it erred in that conclusion.

The first section describes the act forbidden, and is in these words:

"Be it enacted by the senate and house of representatives of the United States of America, in congress assembled, that from and after the passage of this act it shall be unlawful for any person, company, partnership, or corporation, in any manner whatsoever, to prepay the transportation, or in any way assist or encourage the importation or migration, of any alien or aliens, any foreigner or foreigners, into the United States, its territories, or the District of Columbia, under contract or agreement, parol or special, express or implied, made previous to the importation or migration of such alien or aliens, foreigner or foreigners, to perform labor or service of any kind in the United States, its territories, or the District of Columbia."

It must be conceded that the act of the corporation is within the letter of this section, for the relation of rector to his church is one of service, and implies labor on the one side with compensation on the other. Not only are the general words "labor" and "service" both used, but also, as it were to guard against any narrow interpretation and emphasize a breadth of meaning, to them is added "of any kind"; and, further . . . the fifth section, which makes specific exceptions, among them professional actors, artists, lecturers, singers, and domestic servants, strengthens the idea that every other kind of labor and service was intended to be reached by the first section.

While there is great force to this reasoning, we cannot think congress intended to denounce with penalties a transaction like that in the present case. It is a familiar rule that a thing may be within the letter of the statute and yet not within the statute, because not within its spirit nor within the intention of its makers. This has been often asserted, and the Reports are full of cases illustrating its application. This is not the substitution of the will of the judge for that of the legislator; for frequently words of general meaning are used in a statute, words broad enough to include an act in question, and yet a consideration of the whole legislation, or of the circumstances surrounding its enactment, or of the absurd results which follow from giving such broad meaning to the words, makes it unreasonable to believe that the legislator intended to include the particular act. . . .

. . . .

The common sense of man approves the judgment mentioned by Puffendorf, that the Bolognian law which enacted "that whoever drew blood in the streets should be punished with the utmost severity," did not extend to the surgeon who opened the vein of a person that fell down in the street in a fit. The same common sense accepts the ruling . . . that [a statute, which enacts that] a prisoner who breaks prison shall be guilty of felony, does not extend to a prisoner who breaks out when the prison is on fire, "for he is not to be hanged because he would not stay to be burnt."

. . . .

Among other things which may be considered in determining the intent of the legislature is the title of the act. We do not mean that it may be used to add to or take from the body of the statute, but it may help to interpret its meaning.

. . . .

Now, the title of this act is, "An act to prohibit the importation and migration of foreigners and aliens under contract or agreement to perform labor in the United States, its territories, and the District of Columbia." Obviously the thought expressed in this reaches only to the work of the manual laborer, as distinguished from that of the professional man. No one reading such a title would suppose that congress had in its mind any purpose of staying the coming into this country of ministers of the gospel, or, indeed, of any class whose toil is that of the brain. The common understanding of the terms "labor" and "laborers" does not include preaching and preachers, and it is to be assumed that words and phrases are used in their ordinary meaning. So whatever of light is thrown upon the statute by the language of the title indicates an exclusion from its penal provisions of all contracts for the employment of ministers, rectors, and pastors.

Again, another guide to the meaning of a statute is found in the evil which it is designed to remedy; and for this the court properly looks at contemporaneous events, the situation as it existed, and as it was pressed upon the attention of the legislative body. "The motives and history of the act are matters of common knowledge. It had become the practice for large capitalists in this country to contract with their agents abroad for the shipment of great numbers of an ignorant and servile class of foreign laborers, under contracts by which the employer agreed, upon the one hand, to prepay their passage, while, upon the other hand, the laborers agreed to work after their arrival for a certain time at a low rate of wages. The effect of this was to break down the labor market, and to reduce other laborers engaged in like occupations to the level of the assisted immigrant. The evil finally became so flagrant that an appeal was made to congress for relief by the passage of the act in question, the design of which was to raise the standard of foreign immigrants, and to discountenance the migration of those who had not sufficient means in their own hands, or those of their friends, to pay their passage."

It appears, also, from the petitions, and in the testimony presented before the committees of congress, that it was this cheap, unskilled labor which was making the trouble, and the influx of which congress sought to prevent. It was never suggested that we had in this country a surplus of brain toilers, and, least of all, that the market for the services of Christian ministers was depressed by foreign competition. Those were matters to which the attention of congress, or of the people, was not directed. So far, then, as the evil which was sought to be remedied interprets the statute, it also guides to an exclusion of this contract from the penalties of the act.

A singular circumstance, throwing light upon the intent of congress, is found in this extract from the report of the senate committee on education and labor, recommending the passage of the bill: "The general facts and considerations which induce the committee to recommend the passage of this bill are set forth in the report of the committee of the house. The committee report the bill back without amendment, although there are certain features thereof which might well be changed or modified, in the hope that the bill may not fail of passage during the present session. Especially would the committee have otherwise recommended amendments, substituting for the expression, "labor and service," whenever it occurs in the body of the bill, the words "manual labor" or "manual service," as sufficiently broad to accomplish the purposes of the bill, and that such amendments would remove objections which a sharp and perhaps unfriendly criticism may urge to the proposed legislation. The committee, however, believing that the bill in its present form will be construed as including only those whose labor or service is manual in character, and being very desirous that the bill become a law before the adjournment, have reported the bill without change."

And, referring back to the report of the committee of the house, there appears this language: "It seeks to restrain and prohibit the immigration or importation of laborers who would have never seen our shores but for the inducements and allurements of men whose only object is to obtain labor at the lowest possible rate, regardless of the social and material well-being of our own citizens, and regardless of the evil consequences which result to American laborers from such immigration. This class of

encourages legislature to be lazy

immigrants care nothing about our institutions, and in many instances never even heard of them. They are men whose passage is paid by the importers. They come here under contract to labor for a certain number of years. They are ignorant of our social condition, and, that they may remain so, they are isolated and prevented from coming into contact with Americans. They are generally from the lowest social stratum, and live upon the coarsest food, and in hovels of a character before unknown to American workmen. They, as a rule, do not become citizens, and are certainly not a desirable acquisition to the body politic. The inevitable tendency of their presence among us is to degrade American labor, and to reduce it to the level of the imported pauper labor."

We find, therefore, that the title of the act, the evil which was intended to be remedied, the circumstances surrounding the appeal to congress, the reports of the committee of each house, all concur in affirming that the intent of congress was simply to stay the influx of this cheap, unskilled labor.

But, beyond all these matters, no purpose of action against religion can be imputed to any legislation, state or national, because this is a religious people. This is historically true. From the discovery of this continent to the present hour, there is a single voice making this affirmation. The commission to Christopher Columbus, prior to his sail westward, is from "Ferdinand and Isabella, by the grace of God, king and queen of Castile," etc., and recites that "it is hoped that by God's assistance some of the continents and islands in the ocean will be discovered," etc. The first colonial grant, that made to Sir Walter Raleigh in 1584, was from "Elizabeth, by the grace of God, of England, Fraunce and Ireland, queene, defender of the faith," etc.; and the grant authorizing him to enact statutes of the government of the proposed colony provided that "they be not against the true Christian faith nowe professed in the Church of England." The first charter of Virginia, granted by King James I. in 1606, after reciting the application of certain parties for a charter, commenced the grant in these words: "We, greatly commending, and graciously accepting of, their Desires for the Furtherance of so noble a Work, which may, by the Providence of Almighty God, hereafter tend to the Glory of his Divine Majesty, in propagating of Christian Religion to such People, as yet live in Darkness and miserable Ignorance of the true Knowledge and Worship of God, and may in time bring the Infidels and Savages, living in those parts, to human Civility, and to a settled and quiet Government; DO, by these our Letters-Patents, graciously accept of, and agree to, their humble and well-intended Desires."

Language of similar import may be found in the subsequent charters of that colony, from the same king, in 1609 and 1611; and the same is true of the various charters granted to the other colonies. In language more or less emphatic is the establishment of the Christian religion declared to be one of the purposes of the grant. The celebrated compact made by the pilgrims in the Mayflower, 1620, recites: "Having undertaken for the Glory of God, and Advancement of the Christian Faith, and the Honour of our King and Country, a Voyage to plant the first Colony in the northern Parts of Virginia; Do by these Presents, solemnly and mutually, in the Presence of God and one another, covenant and combine ourselves together into a civil Body Politick, for our better Ordering and Preservation, and Furtherance of the Ends aforesaid."

The fundamental orders of Connecticut, under which a provisional government was instituted in 1638–39, commence with this declaration: "Forasmuch as it hath pleased the Allmighty God by the wise disposition of his diuyne pruidence so to Order and dispose of things that we the Inhabitants and Residents of Windsor, Hartford, and Wethersfield are now cohabiting and dwelling in and vppon the River of Conectecotte and the Lands thereunto adioyneing; And well knowing where a people are gathered togather the word of God requires that to mayntayne the peace and vnion of such a people there should be an orderly and decent Gouerment established according to God, to order and dispose of the affayres of the people at all seasons as occation shall require; doe therefore assotiate and conioyne our selues to be as one Publike State or Comonwelth; and doe, for our selues and our Successors and such as shall be adioyned to vs att any tyme hereafter, enter into Combination and Confederation togather, to mayntayne and presearue the liberty and purity of the gospell of our Lord Jesus wch we now p^rfesse, as also the disciplyne of the Churches, wch according to the truth of the said gospell is now practised amongst vs."

In the charter of privileges granted by William Penn to the province of Pennsylvania, in 1701, it is recited: "Because no People can be truly happy, though under the greatest Enjoyment of Civil Liberties, if abridged of the Freedom of their Consciences, as to their Religious Profession and Worship; And Almighty God being the only Lord of Conscience, Father of Lights and Spirits; and the Author as well as Object of all divine Knowledge, Faith, and Worship, who only doth enlighten the Minds, and persuade and convince the Understandings of People, I do hereby grant and declare," etc.

Coming nearer to the present time, the declaration of independence recognizes the presence of the Divine in human affairs in these words: "We hold these truths to be self-evident, that all men are created equal, that they are endowed by their Creator with certain unalienable Rights, that among these are Life, Liberty, and the pursuit of Happiness." "We, therefore, the Representatives of the united States of America, in General Congress, Assembled, appealing to the Supreme Judge of the world for the rectitude of our intentions, do, in the Name and by Authority of the good People of these Colonies, solemnly publish and declare," etc.; "And for the support of this Declaration, with a firm reliance on the Protection of Divine Providence, we mutually pledge to each other our Lives, our Fortunes, and our sacred Honor."

If we examine the constitutions of the various states, we find in them a constant recognition of religious obligations. Every constitution of every one of the 44 states contains language which, either directly or by clear implication, recognizes a profound reverence for religion, and an assumption that its influence in all human affairs is essential to the well-being of the community. This recognition may be in the preamble, such as is found in the constitution of Illinois: "We, the people of the state of Illinois, grateful to Almighty God for the civil, political, and religious liberty which He hath so long permitted us to enjoy, and looking to Him for a blessing upon our endeavors to secure and transmit the same unimpaired to succeeding generations," etc.

It may be only in the familiar requisition that all officers shall take an oath closing with the declaration, "so help me God." It may be in clauses like that of the constitution of Indiana, art. 11, § 4: "The manner of administering an oath or affirmation shall be such as is most consistent with the conscience of the deponent, and shall be esteemed the most solemn appeal to God." Or in provisions such as are found in articles 36 and 37 of the declaration of rights of the constitution of Maryland: "That, as it is the duty of every man to worship God in such manner as he thinks most acceptable to Him, all persons are equally entitled to protection in their religious liberty: wherefore, no person ought, by any law, to be molested in his person or estate on account of his religious persuasion or profession, or for his religious practice, unless, under the color of religion, he shall disturb the good order, peace, or safety of the state, or shall infringe the laws of morality, or injure others in their natural, civil, or religious rights; nor ought any person to be compelled to frequent or maintain or contribute, unless on contract, to maintain any place of worship or any ministry; nor shall any person, otherwise competent, be deemed incompetent as a witness or juror on account of his religious belief: provided, he believes in the existence of God, and that, under his dispensation, such person will be held morally accountable for his acts, and be rewarded or punished therefor, either in this world or the world to come. That no religious test ought ever to be required as a qualification for any office of profit or trust in this state, other than a declaration of belief in the existence of God; nor shall the legislature prescribe any other oath of office than the oath prescribed by this constitution." Or like that in articles 2 and 3 of part 1 of the constitution of Massachusetts: "It is the right as well as the duty of all men in society publicly, and at stated seasons, to worship the Supreme Being, the great Creator and Preserver of the universe. * * * As the happiness of a people and the good order and preservation of civil government essentially depend upon piety, religion, and morality, and as these cannot be generally diffused through a community but by the institution of the public worship of God and of public instructions in piety, religion, and morality: Therefore, to promote their happiness, and to secure the good order and preservation of their government, the people of this commonwealth have a right to invest their legislature with power to authorize and require, and the legislature shall, from time to time, authorize and require, the several towns, parishes, precincts, and other bodies politic or religious societies to make suitable provision, at their own expense, for the institution of the public worship of God and for the support and maintenance of public Protestant teachers of piety, religion, and morality, in all cases where such provision shall not be made voluntarily." Or, as in sections 5 and 14 of article 7 of the constitution of Mississippi: "No person who denies the being of a God, or a future state of rewards and punishments, shall hold any office in the civil de partment of this state. * * * Religion morality, and knowledge being necessary to good government, the preservation of liberty, and the happiness of mankind, schools, and the means of education, shall forever be encouraged in this state." Or by article 22 of the constitution of Delaware, which required all officers, besides an oath of allegiance, to make and subscribe the following declaration: "I, A. B., do profess faith in God the Father, and in Jesus Christ His only Son, and in the Holy Ghost, one God, blessed for evermore; and I do acknowledge the Holy Scriptures of the Old and New Testament to be given by divine inspiration."

Even the constitution of the United States, which is supposed to have little touch upon the private life of the individual, contains in the first amendment a declaration common to the constitutions of all the states, as follows: "Congress shall make no law respecting an establishment of religion, or prohibiting the free exercise thereof," etc.,—and also provides in article 1, § 7, (a provision common to many constitutions,) that the executive shall have 10 days (Sundays excepted) within which to determine whether he will approve or veto a bill.

There is no dissonance in these declarations. There is a universal language pervading them all, having one meaning. They affirm and reaffirm that this is a religious nation. These are not individual sayings, declarations of private persons. They are organic utterances. They speak the voice of the entire people. While because of a general recognition of this truth the question has seldom been presented to the courts, yet we find that in *Updegraph v. Com.*, it was decided that, "Christianity, general Christianity, is, and always has been, a part of the common law of Pennsylvania; . . . not Christianity with an established church and tithes and spiritual courts, but Christianity with liberty of conscience to all men." And in *People v. Ruggles*, Chancellor KENT, the great commentator on American law, speaking as chief justice of the supreme court of New York, said: "The people of this state, in common with the people of this country, profess the general doctrines of Christianity as the rule of their faith and practice; and to scandalize the author of these doctrines is not only, in a religious point of view, extremely impious, but, even in respect to the obligations due to society, is a gross violation of decency and good order. The free, equal, and undisturbed enjoyment of religious opinion, whatever it may be, and free and decent discussions on any religious subject, is granted and secured; but to revile, with malicious and blasphemous contempt, the religion professed by almost the whole community is an abuse of that right. Nor are we bound by any expressions in the constitution, as some have strangely supposed, either not to punish at all, or to punish indiscriminately the like attacks upon the religion of Mahomet or of the Grand Lama; and for this plain reason, that the case assumes that we are a Christian people, and the morality of the country is deeply ingrafted upon Christianity, and not upon the doctrines or worship of those impostors." And in the famous case of *Vidal v. Girard's Ex'rs*, this court, while sustaining the will of Mr. Girard, with its provision for the creation of a college into which no minister should be permitted to enter, observed: "It is also said, and truly, that the Christian religion is a part of the common law of Pennsylvania."

If we pass beyond these matters to a view of American life, as expressed by its laws, its business, its customs, and its society, we find every where a clear recognition of the same truth. Among other matters note the following: The form of oath universally prevailing, concluding with an appeal to the Almighty; the custom of opening sessions of all deliberative bodies and most conventions with prayer; the prefatory words of all wills, "In the name of God, amen"; the laws respecting the observance of the Sabbath, with the general cessation of all secular business, and the closing of courts, legislatures, and other similar public assemblies on that day; the churches and church organizations which abound in every city, town, and hamlet; the multitude of charitable organizations existing every where under Christian auspices; the gigantic missionary associations, with general support, and aiming to establish Christian missions in every quarter of the globe. These, and many other matters which might be noticed, add a volume of unofficial declarations to the mass of organic utterances that this is a Christian nation. In the face of all these, shall it be believed that a congress of the United States intended to make it a misdemeanor for a church of this country to contract for the services of a Christian minister residing in another nation?

Suppose, in the congress that passed this act, some member had offered a bill which in terms declared that, if any Roman Catholic church in this country should contract with Cardinal Manning to come to this country, and enter into its service as pastor and priest, or any Episcopal church should enter into a like contract with Canon Farrar, or any Baptist church should make similar arrangements with Rev. Mr. Spurgeon, or any Jewish synagogue with some eminent rabbi, such contract should be adjudged unlawful and void, and the church making it be subject to prosecution and punishment. Can it be believed that it would have received a minute of approving thought or a single vote? Yet it is contended that such was, in effect, the meaning of this statute. The construction invoked cannot be accepted as correct. It is a case where there was presented a definite evil, in view of which the legislature used general terms with the purpose of reaching all phases of that evil; and thereafter, unexpectedly, it is developed that the general language thus employed is broad enough to reach cases and acts which the whole history and life of the country affirm could not have been intentionally legislated against. It is the duty of the courts, under those circumstances, to say that, however broad the language of the statute may be, the act, although within the letter, is not within the intention of the legislature, and therefore cannot be within the statute.

The judgment will be reversed, and the case remanded for further proceedings in accordance with this opinion.

UNITED STATES V. LOCKE
471 U.S. 84 (1985)

As you read this case, focus on these issues:

- What is the ambiguity or difficulty in the statute?

- How would you characterize each of the opinions in terms of the theories of statutory interpretation?

- Identify specific arguments in the opinions that resonate with textualist, intentionalist, pragmatic, and other theories of interpretation.

- How would a textualist like Justice Scalia have voted? How would an opinion by Justice Scalia read?

- Which opinion do you agree with, if any, and why?

- According to each of the Justices, what should a reasonable claim holder have done in this case?

JUSTICE MARSHALL delivered the opinion of the Court.

The primary question presented by this appeal is whether the Constitution prevents Congress from providing that holders of unpatented mining claims who fail to comply with the annual filing requirements of the Federal Land Policy and Management Act of 1976 (FLPMA) shall forfeit their claims.

I

From the enactment of the general mining laws in the 19th century until 1976, those who sought to make their living by locating and developing minerals on federal lands were virtually unconstrained by the fetters of federal control. The general mining laws, still in effect today, allow United States citizens to go onto unappropriated, unreserved public land to prospect for and develop certain minerals. "Discovery" of a mineral deposit, followed by the minimal procedures required to formally "locate" the deposit, gives an individual the right of exclusive possession of the land for mining purposes; as long as $100 of assessment work is performed annually, the individual may continue to extract and sell minerals from the claim without paying any royalty to the United States. For a nominal sum, and after certain statutory conditions are fulfilled, an individual may patent the claim, thereby purchasing from the Federal Government the land and minerals and obtaining ultimate title to them. Patenting, however, is not required, and an unpatented mining claim remains a fully recognized possessory interest.

By the 1960's, it had become clear that this 19th-century laissez-faire regime had created virtual chaos with respect to the public lands. In 1975, it was estimated that more than 6 million unpatented mining claims existed on public lands other than the national forests; in addition, more than half the land in the National Forest System was thought to be covered by such claims. Many of these claims had been dormant for decades, and many were invalid for other reasons, but in the absence of a federal recording system, no simple way existed for determining which public lands were subject to mining locations, and whether those locations were valid or invalid. As a result, federal land managers had to proceed slowly and cautiously in taking any action affecting federal land lest the federal property rights of claimants be unlawfully disturbed. Each time the Bureau of Land Management (BLM) proposed a sale or other conveyance of federal land, a title search in the county recorder's office was necessary; if an outstanding mining claim was found, no matter how stale or apparently abandoned, formal administrative adjudication was required to determine the validity of the claim.

After more than a decade of studying this problem in the context of a broader inquiry into the proper management of the public lands in the modern era, Congress in 1976 enacted the FLPMA (codified at 43 U.S.C.

§ 1701 *et seq.*). Section 314 of the Act establishes a federal recording system that is designed both to rid federal lands of stale mining claims and to provide federal land managers with up-to-date information that allows them to make informed land management decisions. For claims located before FLPMA's enactment, the federal recording system imposes two general requirements. First, the claims must initially be registered with the BLM by filing, within three years of FLPMA's enactment, a copy of the official record of the notice or certificate of location. Second, in the year of the initial recording, and "prior to December 31" of every year after that, the claimant must file with state officials and with BLM a notice of intention to hold the claim, an affidavit of assessment work performed on the claim, or a detailed reporting form. Section 314(c) of the Act provides that failure to comply with either of these requirements "shall be deemed conclusively to constitute an abandonment of the mining claim . . . by the owner."

The second of these requirements—the annual filing obligation—has created the dispute underlying this appeal. Appellees, four individuals engaged "in the business of operating mining properties in Nevada," purchased in 1960 and 1966 10 unpatented mining claims on public lands near Ely, Nevada. These claims were major sources of gravel and building material: the claims are valued at several million dollars, and, in the 1979–1980 assessment year alone, appellees' gross income totaled more than $1 million. Throughout the period during which they owned the claims, appellees complied with annual state-law filing and assessment work requirements. In addition, appellees satisfied FLPMA's initial recording requirement by properly filing with BLM a notice of location, thereby putting their claims on record for purposes of FLPMA.

At the end of 1980, however, appellees failed to meet on time their first annual obligation to file with the Federal Government. After allegedly receiving misleading information from a BLM employee, appellees waited until December 31 to submit to BLM the annual notice of intent to hold or proof of assessment work performed required under § 314(a) of FLPMA. As noted above, that section requires these documents to be filed annually "prior to December 31." Had appellees checked, they further would have discovered that BLM regulations made quite clear that claimants were required to make the annual filings in the proper BLM office "on or before December 30 of each calendar year." Thus, appellees' filing was one day too late.

This fact was brought painfully home to appellees when they received a letter from the BLM Nevada State Office informing them that their claims had been declared abandoned and void due to their tardy filing. In many cases, loss of a claim in this way would have minimal practical effect; the claimant could simply locate the same claim again and then rerecord it with BLM. In this case, however, relocation of appellees' claims, which were initially located by appellees' predecessors in 1952 and 1954, was prohibited by the Common Varieties Act of 1955, 30 U.S.C. § 611; that Act prospectively barred location of the sort of minerals yielded by appellees' claims. Appellees' mineral deposits thus escheated to the Government.

After losing an administrative appeal, appellees filed the present action in the United States District Court for the District of Nevada. Their complaint alleged, *inter alia,* that § 314(c) effected an unconstitutional taking of their property without just compensation and denied them due process. On summary judgment, the District Court held that § 314(c) did indeed deprive appellees of the process to which they were constitutionally due. The District Court reasoned that § 314(c) created an impermissible irrebuttable presumption that claimants who failed to make a timely filing intended to abandon their claims. Rather than relying on this presumption, the Government was obliged, in the District Court's view, to provide individualized notice to claimants that their claims were in danger of being lost, followed by a post-filing-deadline hearing at which the claimants could demonstrate that they had not, in fact, abandoned a claim. Alternatively, the District Court held that the 1-day late filing "substantially complied" with the Act and regulations.

Because a District Court had held an Act of Congress unconstitutional in a civil suit to which the United States was a party, we noted probable jurisdiction under 28 U.S.C. § 1252. We now reverse.

II

Appeal under 28 U.S.C. § 1252 brings before this Court not merely the constitutional question decided below, but the entire case. The entire case includes nonconstitutional questions actually decided by the lower court as well as nonconstitutional grounds presented to, but not passed on, by the lower court. These principles are important aids in the prudential exercise of our appellate jurisdiction, for when a case arrives here by appeal under 28 U.S.C. § 1252, this Court will not pass on the constitutionality of an Act of Congress if a construction of the Act is fairly possible, or some other nonconstitutional ground fairly available, by which the constitutional question can be avoided. Thus, we turn first to the nonconstitutional questions pressed below.

III

A

Before the District Court, appellees asserted that the § 314(a) requirement of a filing "prior to December 31 of each year" should be construed to require a filing "on or before December 31." Thus, appellees argued, their December 31 filing had in fact complied with the statute, and the BLM had acted ultra vires in voiding their claims.

Although the District Court did not address this argument, the argument raises a question sufficiently legal in nature that we choose to address it even in the absence of lower court analysis. It is clear to us that the plain language of the statute simply cannot sustain the gloss appellees would put on it. . . . While we will not allow a literal reading of a statute to produce a result "demonstrably at odds with the intentions of its drafters," with respect to filing deadlines a literal reading of Congress' words is generally the only proper reading of those words. To attempt to decide whether some date other than the one set out in the statute is the date actually "intended" by Congress is to set sail on an aimless journey, for the purpose of a filing deadline would be just as well served by nearly any date a court might choose as by the date Congress has in fact set out in the statute. "Actual purpose is sometimes unknown," and such is the case with filing deadlines; as might be expected, nothing in the legislative history suggests why Congress chose December 30 over December 31, or over September 1 (the end of the assessment year for mining claims), as the last day on which the required filings could be made. But "[d]eadlines are inherently arbitrary," while fixed dates "are often essential to accomplish necessary results." Faced with the inherent arbitrariness of filing deadlines, we must, at least in a civil case, apply by its terms the date fixed by the statute.

Moreover, BLM regulations have made absolutely clear since the enactment of FLPMA that "prior to December 31" means what it says. As the current version of the filing regulations states:

"The owner of an unpatented mining claim located on Federal lands . . . shall have filed or caused to have been filed *on or before December 30* of each calendar year . . . evidence of annual assessment work performed during the previous assessment year or a notice of intention to hold the mining claim."

Leading mining treatises similarly inform claimants that "[i]t is important to note that the filing of a notice of intention or evidence of assessment work must be done *prior* to December 31 of each year, *i.e.,* on or before December 30." If appellees, who were businessmen involved in the running of a major mining operation for more than 20 years, had any questions about whether a December 31 filing complied with the statute, it was incumbent upon them, as it is upon other businessmen, to have checked the regulations or to have consulted an attorney for legal advice. Pursuit of either of these courses, rather than the submission of a last-minute filing, would surely have led appellees to the conclusion that December 30 was the last day on which they could file safely.

In so saying, we are not insensitive to the problems posed by congressional reliance on the words "prior to December 31." But the fact that Congress might have acted with greater clarity or foresight does not give courts a *carte blanche* to redraft statutes in an effort to achieve that which Congress is perceived to have failed to do. "There is a basic difference between filling a gap left by Congress' silence and rewriting rules that Congress has affirmatively and specifically enacted." Nor is the Judiciary licensed to attempt to soften the clear import of Congress' chosen words whenever a court believes those words lead to a harsh result. On the contrary, deference to the supremacy of the Legislature, as well as recognition that Congressmen typically vote on the language of a bill, generally requires us to assume that "the legislative purpose is expressed by the ordinary meaning of the words used." "Going behind the plain language of a statute in search of a possibly contrary congressional intent is 'a step to be taken cautiously' even under the best of circumstances." When even after taking this step nothing in the legislative history remotely suggests a congressional intent contrary to Congress' chosen words, and neither appellees nor the dissenters have pointed to anything that so suggests, any further steps take the courts out of the realm of interpretation and place them in the domain of legislation. The phrase "prior to" may be clumsy, but its meaning is clear. Under these circumstances, we are obligated to apply the "prior to December 31" language by its terms.

The agency's regulations clarify and confirm the import of the statutory language by making clear that the annual filings must be made on or before December 30. These regulations provide a conclusive answer to appellees' claim, for where the language of a filing deadline is plain and the agency's construction completely consistent with that language, the agency's construction simply cannot be found "sufficiently unreasonable" as to be unacceptable.

We cannot press statutory construction "to the point of disingenuous evasion" even to avoid a constitutional question. We therefore hold that BLM did not act ultra vires in concluding that appellees' filing was untimely.

. . . .

JUSTICE O'CONNOR, concurring.

. . . I share many of the concerns expressed in the dissenting opinions of Justice POWELL and Justice STEVENS. If the facts are as alleged by appellees, allowing the BLM to extinguish active mining claims that appellees have owned and worked for more than 20 years would seem both unfair and inconsistent with the purposes underlying FLPMA.

The Government has not disputed that appellees sought in good faith to comply with the statutory deadline. Appellees contend that in order to meet the requirements of § 314, they contacted the BLM and were informed by agency personnel that they could file the required materials on December 31, 1980. Appellees apparently relied on this advice and hand-delivered the appropriate documents to the local BLM office on that date. The BLM accepted the documents for filing, but some three months later sent appellees a notice stating that their mining claims were "abandoned and void" because the filing was made on, rather than prior to, December 31, 1980. Although BLM regulations clarify the filing deadlines contained in § 314, the existence of those regulations does not imply that appellees were unjustified in their confusion concerning the deadlines or in their reliance on the advice provided by BLM's local office. The BLM itself in 1978 issued an explanatory pamphlet stating that the annual filings were to be made "on or before December 31" of each year. Moreover, the BLM evidently has come to understand the need to clarify the nature of the annual filing requirement, because it now sends reminder notices every year to holders of recorded mining claims warning them that the deadline is approaching and that filings must be made on or before December 30.

The unusual facts alleged by appellees suggest that the BLM's actions might estop the Government from relying on § 314(c) to obliterate a property interest that has provided a family's livelihood for decades. The Court properly notes that the estoppel issue was not addressed by the District Court and will be open on remand. In this regard, I merely note that in my view our previous decisions do not preclude application of estoppel in this context. In *Heckler v. Community Health Services of Crawford County, Inc.*, we expressly declined to adopt "a flat rule that estoppel may not in any circumstances run against the Government." Such a rule was unnecessary to the decision in that case, and we noted our reluctance to hold that "there are *no cases* in which the public interest in ensuring that the Government can enforce the law free from estoppel might be outweighed by the countervailing interest of citizens in some minimum standard of decency, honor, and reliability in their dealings with their Government."

Although "it is well settled that the Government may not be estopped on the same terms as any other litigant," we have never held that the Government can extinguish a vested property interest that has been legally held and actively maintained for more than 20 years merely because the private owners relied on advice from agency personnel concerning a poorly worded statutory deadline and consequently missed a filing deadline by one day. Thus, if the District Court ultimately determines that appellees reasonably relied on communications from the BLM in making their annual filing on December 31, 1980, our previous decisions would not necessarily bar application of the doctrine of equitable estoppel. Accordingly, the fact that the Court reverses the decision of the District Court does not establish that appellees must ultimately forfeit their mining claims.

JUSTICE POWELL, dissenting.

I agree with much of Justice STEVENS' dissent. I write separately only because under the special circumstances of this case I do not believe it necessary to decide what Congress actually intended. Even if the Court is correct in believing that Congress intended to require filings on or before the next-to-the-last day of the year, rather than, more reasonably, by the end of the calendar year itself, the statutory deadline is too uncertain to satisfy constitutional requirements. It simply fails to give property holders clear and definite notice of what they must do to protect their existing property interests.

. . . .

Justice STEVENS correctly points to a number of circumstances that cast doubt both on the care with which Congress drafted § 314 and on its meaning. Specifically, he notes that (i) the section does not clearly describe *what* must be filed, let alone *when* it must be filed; (ii) BLM's rewording of the deadline in its implementing regulations indicates that the BLM itself considered the statutory deadline confusing; (iii) lest there be any doubt that the BLM recognized this possible confusion, even it had described the section in a pamphlet distributed to miners in 1978 as requiring filing *"on or before December 31"*; (iv) BLM, charged with enforcing the section, has interpreted it quite flexibly; and (v) irrationally requiring property holders to file by one day before the end of the year, rather than by the end of the year itself, creates "a trap for the unwary." As Justice STEVENS also states, these facts, particularly the last, suggest not only that Congress drafted § 314 inartfully but also that Congress may actually have intended to require filing "on or before," not "prior to," December 31. This is certainly the more reasonable interpretation of congressional intent and is consistent with all the policies of the Act.

I do not believe, however, that given the special circumstances of this case we need determine what Congress actually intended. As the Court today recognizes, the Takings Clause imposes some limitations on the Government's power to impose forfeitures. In *Texaco, Inc. v. Short*, we identified one of the most important of these limitations when we stated that "the State has the power to condition the permanent retention of [a] property right on the performance of *reasonable conditions*. . . ." Furthermore, conditions, like those here, imposed after a property interest is created must also meet due process standards. These standards require, among other things, that there be no question as to what actions an individual must take to protect his interests. Together the Takings and Due Process Clauses prevent the Government from depriving an individual of property rights arbitrarily.

In the present case there is no claim that a yearly filing requirement is itself unreasonable. Rather, the claim arises from the fact that the language "prior to December 31" creates uncertainty as to when an otherwise reasonable filing period ends. Given the natural tendency to interpret this phrase as "by the end of the calendar year," rather than "on or before the next-to-the-last day of the calendar year," I believe this uncertainty violated the standard of certainty and definiteness that the Constitution requires. The statement in at least one of the Government's own publications that filing was required "on or before December 31" supports this conclusion. Terminating a property interest because a property holder reasonably believed that under the statute he had an additional day to satisfy any filing requirements is no less arbitrary than terminating it for failure to satisfy these same conditions in an unreasonable amount of time. Although the latter may rest on impossibility, the former rests on good-faith performance a day late of what easily could have been performed the day before. Neither serves a purpose other than forcing an arbitrary forfeiture of property rights to the State.

I believe the Constitution requires that the law inform the property holder with more certainty and definiteness than did § 314 when he must fulfill any recording requirements imposed after a property interest is created. Given the statutory uncertainty here, I would find a forfeiture imposed for filing on December 31 to be invalid.

I accordingly dissent.

JUSTICE STEVENS, with whom JUSTICE BRENNAN joins, dissenting.

The Court's opinion is contrary to the intent of Congress, engages in unnecessary constitutional adjudication, and unjustly creates a trap for unwary property owners. First, the choice of the language "prior to December 31" when read in context in 43 U.S.C. § 1744(a) is, at least, ambiguous, and, at best, "the consequence of a legislative *accident,* perhaps caused by nothing more than the unfortunate fact that Congress is too busy to do all of its work as carefully as it should." In my view, Congress actually intended to authorize an annual filing at any time prior to the close of business on December 31st, that is, prior to the end of the calendar year to which the filing pertains. Second, even if Congress irrationally intended that the applicable deadline for a calendar year should end *one day before* the end of the calendar year that has been recognized since the amendment of the Julian Calendar in 8 B.C., it is clear that appellees have substantially complied with the requirements of the statute, in large part because the Bureau of Land Management has issued interpreting regulations that recognize substantial compliance. Further, the Court today violates not only the long-followed principle that a court should "not pass on the constitutionality of an Act of Congress if a construction of the statute is fairly possible by which the question may be avoided," but also the principle that a court should "not decide a constitutional question if there is some other ground upon which to dispose of the case."

I

Congress enacted § 314 of the Federal Land Policy and Management Act to establish for federal land planners and managers a federal recording system designed to cope with the problem of stale claims, and to provide "an easy way of discovering which Federal lands are subject to either valid or invalid mining claim locations." I submit that the appellees' actions in this case did not diminish the importance of these congressional purposes; to the contrary, their actions were entirely consistent with the statutory purposes, despite the confusion created by the "inartful draftsmanship" of the statutory language.

A careful reading of § 314 discloses at least three respects in which its text cannot possibly reflect the actual intent of Congress. First, the description of what must be filed in the initial filing and subsequent annual filings is quite obviously garbled. Read literally, § 314(a)(2) seems to require that a notice of intent to hold the claim and an affidavit of assessment work performed on the claim must be filed "on a detailed report provided by § 28–1 of Title 30." One must substitute the word "or" for the word "on" to make any sense at all out of this provision. This error should cause us to pause before concluding that Congress commanded blind allegiance to the remainder of the literal text of § 314.

Second, the express language of the statute is unambiguous in describing the place where the second annual filing shall be made. If the statute is read inflexibly, the owner must "file in the office of the Bureau" the required documents. Yet the regulations that the Bureau itself has drafted, quite reasonably, construe the statute to allow filing in a mailbox, provided that the document is actually received by the Bureau prior to the close of business on January 19 of the year following the year in which the statute requires the filing to be made. A notice mailed on December 30, 1982, and received by the Bureau on January 19, 1983, was filed "in the office of the Bureau" during 1982 within the meaning of the statute, but one that is hand-delivered to the office on December 31, 1982, cannot be accepted as a 1982 "filing."

The Court finds comfort in the fact that the implementing regulations have eliminated the risk of injustice. But if one must rely on those regulations, it should be apparent that the meaning of the statute itself is not all that obvious. To begin with, the regulations do not use the language "prior to December 31"; instead, they use "on or before December 30 of each year." The Bureau's drafting of the regulations using this latter phrase indicates that the meaning of the statute itself is not quite as "plain" as the Court assumes; if the language were plain, it is doubtful that the Bureau would have found it necessary to change the language at all. Moreover, the Bureau, under the aegis of the Department of the Interior, once issued a pamphlet entitled "Staking a Mining Claim on Federal Lands" that contained the following information:

"Owners of claims or sites located on or before Oct. 21, 1976, have until Oct. 22, 1979, to file evidence of assessment work performed the preceding year or to file a notice of intent to hold the claim or site. Once the claim or site is recorded with BLM, *these documents must be filed on or before December 31 of each subsequent year.*"

"Plain language" indeed.

. . . .

In light of the foregoing, I cannot believe that Congress intended the words "prior to December 31 of each year" to be given the literal reading the Court adopts today. The statutory scheme requires periodic filings on a calendar-year basis. The end of the calendar year is, of course, correctly described either as "prior to the close of business on December 31," or "on or before December 31," but it is surely understandable that the author of § 314 might inadvertently use the words "prior to December 31" when he meant to refer to the end of the calendar year. As the facts of this case demonstrate, the scrivener's error is one that can be made in good faith. The risk of such an error is, of course, the greatest when the reference is to the end of the calendar year. That it was in fact an error seems rather clear to me because no one has suggested any rational basis for omitting just one day from the period in which an annual filing may be made, and I would not presume that Congress deliberately created a trap for the unwary by such an omission.

It would be fully consistent with the intent of Congress to treat any filing received during the 1980 calendar year as a timely filing for that year. Such an interpretation certainly does not interfere with Congress' intent to establish a federal recording system designed to cope with the problem of stale mining claims on federal lands. The system is established, and apparently, functioning. Moreover, the claims here were *active;* the Bureau was well aware that the appellees intended to hold and to operate their claims.

. . . .

Appellants acknowledge that "[i]t may well be that Congress wished to require filing by the end of the calendar year and that the earlier deadline resulted from careless draftmanship." I have no doubt that Congress would have chosen to adopt a construction of the statute that filing take place by the end of the calendar year if its attention had been focused on this precise issue. . . .

CHISOM V. ROEMER

501 U.S. 380 (1991)

As you consider the following case, focus on these issues:

- What theories of interpretation are represented?

- Identify all of the textual arguments made by the majority and dissent. How do the Justices respond to one another?

- What non-textualist arguments are made? What theories do they resonate with?

- One major point of disagreement is the meaning of the word "representatives." Do you agree with Justice Scalia's emphatic argument that elected judges would not naturally be thought of as representatives?

- What do you think of the argument between Justices Stevens and Scalia about the meaning of the word "and?"

- What is "the dog that didn't bark" argument that Justice Scalia refers to? How does Justice Stevens deploy the argument? Do you agree with him that this provides evidence as to Congress's likely intent?

- Do you think Congress carefully considered the question of whether section 2 should apply to judicial elections? If so, what do you think it probably intended? If not, then which Justice has the better argument?

- Can you think of any reason that Congress would not have wanted section 2 to apply to judicial elections?

- Which opinion do you agree with? Why?

JUSTICE STEVENS delivered the opinion of the Court.

. . . .

In 1982, Congress amended § 2 of the Voting Rights Act to make clear that certain practices and procedures that *result* in the denial or abridgment of the right to vote are forbidden even though the absence of proof of discriminatory intent protects them from constitutional challenge. The question presented by these cases is whether this "results test" protects the right to vote in state judicial elections. We hold that . . . judicial elections are embraced within that coverage.

I

Petitioners . . . brought this action against the Governor and other state officials (respondents) to challenge the method of electing justices of the Louisiana Supreme Court from the New Orleans area. . . .

The Louisiana Supreme Court consists of seven justices, five of whom are elected from five single-member Supreme Court Districts, and two of whom are elected from one multi-member Supreme Court District. Each of the seven members of the court must be a resident of the district from which he or she is elected and must have resided there for at least two years prior to election. Each of the justices on the Louisiana Supreme Court serves a term of 10 years. The one multi-member district, the First Supreme Court District, consists of the parishes of Orleans, St. Bernard, Plaquemines, and Jefferson. Orleans Parish contains about half of the population of the First Supreme Court District and about half of the registered voters in that district. More than one-half of the registered voters of Orleans Parish are black, whereas more than three-fourths of the registered voters in the other three parishes are white.

Petitioners allege that "the present method of electing two Justices to the Louisiana Supreme Court at-large from the New Orleans area impermissibly dilutes minority voting strength" in violation of § 2 of the Voting Rights Act. . . .

II

. . . [T]his case presents us solely with a question of statutory construction. That question involves only the scope of the coverage of § 2 of the Voting Rights Act as amended in 1982. . . .

III

The text of § 2 of the Voting Rights Act as originally enacted read as follows:

"SEC. 2. No voting qualification or prerequisite to voting, or standard, practice, or procedure shall be imposed or applied by any State or political subdivision to deny or abridge the right of any citizen of the United States to vote on account of race or color."

The terms "vote" and "voting" were defined elsewhere in the Act to include "all action necessary to make a vote effective *in any primary, special, or general election.*" § 14(c)(1). The statute further defined vote and voting as "votes cast with respect to candidates for public or party office and propositions for which votes are received in an election."

At the time of the passage of the Voting Rights Act of 1965, § 2, unlike other provisions of the Act, did not provoke significant debate in Congress because it was viewed largely as a restatement of the Fifteenth Amendment. . . . This Court took a similar view of § 2 in *Mobile v. Bolden*. There, we recognized that the coverage provided by § 2 was unquestionably coextensive with the coverage provided by the Fifteenth Amendment; the provision simply elaborated upon the Fifteenth Amendment. Section 2 protected the right to vote, and it did so without making any distinctions or imposing any limitations as to which elections would fall within its purview. As Attorney General Katzenbach made clear during his testimony before the House, "[e]very election in which registered electors are permitted to vote would be covered" under § 2.

The 1965 Act made it unlawful "to deny or abridge" the right to vote "on account of race or color." Congress amended § 2 in 1975 by expanding the original prohibition against discrimination "on account of race or color" to include non-English-speaking groups. It did this by replacing "race or color" with "race or color, or in contravention of the guarantees set forth in section 4(f)(2)" of the Act. The 1982 amendment further expanded the protection afforded by § 2.

Justice Stewart's opinion for the plurality in *Mobile v. Bolden*, which held that there was no violation of either the Fifteenth Amendment or § 2 of the Voting Rights Act absent proof of intentional discrimination, served as the impetus for the 1982 amendment. One year after the decision in *Mobile*, Chairman Rodino of the House Judiciary Committee introduced a bill to extend the Voting Rights Act and its bilingual requirements, and to amend § 2 by striking out "to deny or abridge" and substituting "in a manner which *results* in a denial or abridgment of." The "results" test proposed by Chairman Rodino was incorporated . . . into the 1982 amendment to § 2, and is now the focal point of this litigation.

Under the amended statute, proof of intent is no longer required to prove a § 2 violation. Now plaintiffs can prevail under § 2 by demonstrating that a challenged election practice has resulted in the denial or abridgment of the right to vote based on color or race. Congress not only incorporated the results test in the paragraph that formerly constituted the entire § 2, but also designated that paragraph as subsection (a) and added a new subsection (b) to make clear that an application of the results test requires an inquiry into "the totality of the circumstances." The full text of § 2 as amended in 1982 reads as follows:

"SEC. 2. (a) No voting qualification or prerequisite to voting or standard, practice, or procedure shall be imposed or applied by any State or political subdivision in a manner which results in a denial or abridgement of the right of any citizen of the United States to vote on account of race or color, or in contravention of the guarantees set forth in section 4(f)(2), as provided in subsection (b).

"(b) A violation of subsection (a) is established if, based on the totality of circumstances, it is shown that the political processes leading to nomination or election in the State or political subdivision are not equally open to participation by members of a class of citizens protected by subsection (a) in that its members have less opportunity than other members of the electorate to participate in the political process and to elect representatives of their choice. The extent to which members of a protected class have been elected to office in the State or political subdivision is one circumstance which may be considered: *Provided,* That nothing in this section establishes a right to have members of a protected class elected in numbers equal to their proportion in the population."

The two purposes of the amendment are apparent from its text. Section (a) adopts a results test, thus providing that proof of discriminatory intent is no longer necessary to establish *any* violation of the section. Section (b) provides guidance about how the results test is to be applied.

Respondents contend ... that Congress' choice of the word "representatives" in the phrase "have less opportunity than other members of the electorate to participate in the political process and to elect representatives of their choice" in section (b) is evidence of congressional intent to exclude vote dilution claims involving judicial elections from the coverage of § 2. We reject that construction because we are convinced that if Congress had such an intent, Congress would have made it explicit in the statute, or at least some of the Members would have identified or mentioned it at some point in the unusually extensive legislative history of the 1982 amendment. . . .

IV

The [respondents argue that] § 2 provides two distinct types of protection for minority voters—it protects their opportunity "to participate in the political process" and their opportunity "to elect representatives of their choice." Although the majority interpreted "representatives" as a word of limitation, it assumed that the word eliminated judicial elections only from the latter protection, without affecting the former. In other words, a standard, practice, or procedure in a judicial election, such as a limit on the times that polls are open, which has a disparate impact on black voters' opportunity to cast their ballots under § 2, may be challenged even if a different practice that merely affects their opportunity to elect representatives of their choice to a judicial office may not. This reading of § 2, however, is foreclosed by the statutory text and by our prior cases.

Any abridgment of the opportunity of members of a protected class to participate in the political process inevitably impairs their ability to influence the outcome of an election. As the statute is written, however, the inability to elect representatives of their choice is not sufficient to establish a violation unless, under the totality of the circumstances, it can also be said that the members of the protected class have less opportunity to participate in the political process. The statute does not create two separate and distinct rights. Subsection (a) covers every application of a qualification, standard, practice, or procedure that results in a denial or abridgment of *"the right"* to vote. The singular form is also used in subsection (b) when referring to an injury to members of the protected class who have less "opportunity" than others "to participate in the political process *and* to elect representatives of their choice." It would distort the plain meaning of the sentence to substitute the word "or" for the word "and." Such radical surgery would be required to separate the opportunity to participate from the opportunity to elect.

. . . .

The results test mandated by the 1982 amendment is applicable to all claims arising under § 2. If the word "representatives" did place a limit on the coverage of the Act for judicial elections, it would exclude all claims involving such elections from the protection of § 2. For all such claims must allege an abridgment of the opportunity to participate in the political process *and* to elect representatives of one's choice. . . .

V

[R]espondents . . . place their principal reliance on Congress' use of the word "representatives" instead of "legislators" in the phrase "to participate in the political process and to elect representatives of their choice." When Congress borrowed the phrase from [our earlier opinions], it replaced "legislators" with "representatives." This substitution indicates, at the very least, that Congress intended the amendment to cover more than legislative elections. Respondents argue . . . that the term "representatives" was used to extend § 2 coverage to executive officials, but not to judges. We think, however, that the better reading of the word "representatives" describes the winners of representative, popular elections. If executive officers, such as prosecutors, sheriffs, state attorneys general, and state treasurers, can be considered "representatives" simply because they are chosen by popular election, then the same reasoning should apply to elected judges.

Respondents suggest that if Congress had intended to have the statute's prohibition against vote dilution apply to the election of judges, it would have used the word "candidates" instead of "representatives." But that confuses the ordinary meaning of the words. The word "representative" refers to someone who has prevailed in a popular election, whereas the word "candidate" refers to someone who is seeking an office. Thus, a candidate is nominated, not elected. When Congress used "candidate" in other parts of the statute, it did so precisely because it was referring to people who were aspirants for an office. . . .

[O]f course . . . "judges need not be elected at all," and . . . ideally public opinion should be irrelevant to the judge's role because the judge is often called upon to disregard, or even to defy, popular sentiment. The Framers of the Constitution had a similar understanding of the judicial role, and as a consequence, they established that Article III judges would be appointed, rather than elected, and would be sheltered from public opinion by receiving life tenure and salary protection. . . .

The fundamental tension between the ideal character of the judicial office and the real world of electoral politics cannot be resolved by crediting judges with total indifference to the popular will while simultaneously requiring them to run for elected office. When each of several members of a court must be a resident of a separate district, and must be elected by the voters of that district, it seems both reasonable and realistic to characterize the winners as representatives of that district. Indeed, at one time the Louisiana Bar Association characterized the members of the Louisiana Supreme Court as representatives for that reason: "Each justice and judge now in office shall be considered as a representative of the judicial district within which is situated the parish of his residence at the time of his election. . . ."

The close connection between §§ 2 and 5 further undermines respondents' view that judicial elections should not be covered under § 2. Section 5 requires certain States to submit changes in their voting procedures to the District Court of the District of Columbia or to the Attorney General for preclearance. Section 5 uses language similar to that of § 2 in defining prohibited practices: "any voting qualification or prerequisite to voting, or standard, practice, or procedure with respect to voting." This Court has already held that § 5 applies to judicial elections. If § 2 did not apply to judicial elections, a State covered by § 5 would be precluded from implementing a new voting procedure having discriminatory effects with respect to judicial elections, whereas a similarly discriminatory system already in place could not be challenged under § 2. It is unlikely that Congress intended such an anomalous result.

. . . .

The judgment of the Court of Appeals is reversed, and the cases are remanded for further proceedings consistent with this opinion.

It is so ordered.

JUSTICE SCALIA, with whom THE CHIEF JUSTICE and JUSTICE KENNEDY join, dissenting.

Section 2 of the Voting Rights Act of 1965 is not some all-purpose weapon for well-intentioned judges to wield as they please in the battle against discrimination. It is a statute. I thought we had adopted a regular method for interpreting the meaning of language in a statute: first, find the ordinary meaning of the language in its textual context; and second, using established canons of construction, ask whether there is any clear indication that some permissible meaning other than the ordinary one applies. If not—and especially if a good reason for the ordinary meaning appears plain—we apply that ordinary meaning.

Today, however, the Court adopts a method quite out of accord with that usual practice. It begins not with what the statute says, but with an expectation about what the statute must mean absent particular phenomena ("[*W*]*e are convinced* that if Congress had . . . an intent [to exclude judges] Congress would have made it explicit in the statute, or at least some of the Members would have identified or mentioned it at some point in the unusually extensive legislative history"); and the Court then interprets the words of the statute to fulfill its expectation. Finding nothing in the legislative history affirming that judges were excluded from the coverage of § 2, the Court gives the phrase "to elect representatives" the quite extraordinary meaning that covers the election of judges.

As method, this is just backwards, and however much we may be attracted by the result it produces in a particular case, we should in every case resist it. Our job begins with a text that Congress has passed and the President has signed. We are to read the words of that text as any ordinary Member of Congress would have read them and apply the meaning so determined. In my view, that reading reveals that § 2 extends to vote dilution claims for the elections of representatives only, and judges are not representatives.

I

As the Court suggests, the 1982 amendments to the Voting Rights Act were adopted in response to our decision in *Mobile v. Bolden*, which had held that the scope of the original Voting Rights Act was coextensive with the Fifteenth Amendment, and thus proscribed intentional discrimination only. I agree with the Court that that original legislation, directed toward intentional discrimination, applied to all elections, for it clearly said so:

"No voting qualification or prerequisite to voting, or standard, practice, or procedure shall be imposed or applied by any State or political subdivision to deny or abridge the right of any citizen of the United States to vote on account of race or color."

The 1982 amendments, however, radically transformed the Act. As currently written, the statute proscribes intentional discrimination only if it has a discriminatory effect, but proscribes practices with discriminatory effect whether or not intentional. This new "results" criterion provides a powerful, albeit sometimes blunt, weapon with which to attack even the most subtle forms of discrimination. The question we confront here is how broadly the new remedy applies. The foundation of the Court's analysis, the itinerary for its journey in the wrong direction, is the following statement: "It is difficult to believe that Congress, in an express effort to broaden the protection afforded by the Voting Rights Act, withdrew, without comment, an important category of elections from that protection." There are two things wrong with this. First is the notion that Congress cannot be credited with having achieved anything of major importance by simply saying it, in ordinary language, in the text of a statute, "without comment" in the legislative history. As the Court colorfully puts it, if the dog of legislative history has not barked nothing of great significance can have transpired. Apart from the questionable wisdom of assuming that dogs will bark when something important is happening, we have forcefully and explicitly rejected the Conan Doyle approach to statutory construction in the past. We are here to apply the statute, not legislative history, and certainly not the absence of legislative history. Statutes are the law though sleeping dogs lie.

The more important error in the Court's starting point, however, is the assumption that the effect of excluding judges from the revised § 2 would be to "withdr[aw] ... an important category of elections from [the] protection [of the Voting Rights Act]." There is absolutely no question here of *withdrawing* protection. Since the pre-1982 content of § 2 was coextensive with the Fifteenth Amendment, the entirety of that protection subsisted in the Constitution, and could be enforced through the other provisions of the Voting Rights Act. Nothing was lost from the prior coverage; *all* of the new "results" protection was an add-on. The issue is not, therefore, as the Court would have it, whether Congress has cut back on the coverage of the Voting Rights Act; the issue is how far it has extended it. Thus, even if a court's expectations were a proper basis for interpreting the text of a statute, while there would be reason to expect that Congress was not "withdrawing" protection, there is no particular reason to expect that the supplemental protection it provided was any more extensive than the text of the statute said.

What it said, with respect to establishing a violation of the amended § 2, is the following:

"... A violation ... is established if ... it is shown that the political processes leading to nomination or election ... are not equally open to participation by members of a [protected] class ... in that its members have less opportunity than other members of the electorate *to participate in the political process* and *to elect representatives of their choice.*"

Though this text nowhere speaks of "vote dilution," [we have elsewhere] understood it to proscribe practices which produce that result, identifying as the statutory basis for a dilution claim the second of the two phrases highlighted above—"to elect representatives of their choice." Under this interpretation, the other highlighted phrase—"to participate in the political process"—is left for other, *nondilution* § 2 violations. If, for example, a county permitted voter registration for only three hours one day a week, and that made it more difficult for blacks to register than whites, blacks would have less opportunity *"to participate* in the political process" than whites, and § 2 would therefore be violated—even if the number of potential black voters was so small that they would on no hypothesis be able *to elect* their own candidate.

The Court, however, now rejects [that] reading of the statute, and asserts that before a violation of § 2 can be made out, *both* conditions of § 2(b) must be met. As the Court explains,

"As the statute is written, ... the inability to elect representatives of their choice is not sufficient to establish a violation unless, under the totality of the circumstances, it can also be said that the members of the protected class have less opportunity to participate in the political process. The statute does not create two separate and distinct rights. . . . It would distort the plain meaning of the sentence to substitute the word 'or' for the word 'and.' Such radical surgery would be required to separate the opportunity to participate from the opportunity to elect."

This is unquestionably wrong. If both conditions must be violated before there is any § 2 violation, then minorities who form such a small part of the electorate in a particular jurisdiction that they could on no conceivable basis "elect representatives of their choice" would be entirely without § 2 protection. Since, as the Court's analysis suggests, the "results" test of § 2 judges a violation of the "to elect" provision on the basis of whether the practice in question prevents actual election, then a protected class that with or without the practice will be unable to elect its candidate can be denied equal opportunity "to participate in the political process" with impunity. The Court feels compelled to reach this implausible conclusion of a "singular right" because the "to participate" clause and the "to elect" clause are joined by the conjunction "and." It is unclear to me why the rules of English usage require that conclusion here, any more than they do in the case of the First Amendment—which reads "Congress shall make no law . . . abridging . . . the right of the people peaceably to assemble, and to petition the Government for a redress of grievances." This has not generally been thought to protect the right peaceably to assemble only when the purpose of the assembly is to petition the Government for a redress of grievances. So also here, one is deprived of an equal "opportunity . . . to participate . . . and to elect" if *either* the opportunity to participate *or* the opportunity to elect is unequal. The point is in any event not central to the present case—and it is sad to see the Court repudiate *Thornburg*, create such mischief in the application of § 2, and even cast doubt upon the First Amendment, merely to deprive the State of the argument that elections for judges *remain* covered by § 2 *even though* they are not subject to vote dilution claims.

The Court, petitioners, and petitioners' *amici* have labored mightily to establish that there is *a* meaning of "representatives" that would include judges, and no doubt there is. But our job is not to scavenge the world of English usage to discover whether there is any possible meaning of "representatives" which suits our preconception that the statute includes judges; our job is to determine whether the *ordinary* meaning includes them, and if it does not, to ask whether there is any solid indication in the text or structure of the statute that something other than ordinary meaning was intended.

There is little doubt that the ordinary meaning of "representatives" does not include judges, see Webster's Second New International Dictionary 2114 (1950). The Court's feeble argument to the contrary is that "representatives" means those who "are chosen by popular election." On that hypothesis, the fan-elected members of the baseball all-star teams are "representatives"—hardly a common, if even a permissible, usage. Surely the word "representative" connotes one who is not only *elected by* the people, but who also, at a minimum, *acts on behalf of* the people. Judges do that in a sense—but not in the ordinary sense. As the captions of the pleadings in some States still display, it is the prosecutor who represents "the People"; the judge represents the Law—which often requires him to rule against the People. It is precisely because we do not *ordinarily* conceive of judges as representatives that we held judges not within the Fourteenth Amendment's requirement of "one person, one vote." The point is not that a State could not make judges in some senses representative, or that all judges must be conceived of in the Article III mold, but rather, that giving "representatives" its ordinary meaning, the ordinary speaker in 1982 would not have applied the word to judges. It remains only to ask whether there is good indication that ordinary meaning does not apply.

. . . .

[I]n my view the ordinary meaning of "representatives" gives clear purpose to congressional action that otherwise would seem pointless. As an initial matter, it is evident that Congress paid particular attention to the scope of elections covered by the "to elect" language. As the Court suggests, that language for the most part tracked this Court's [earlier] opinions ... but the word "legislators" was not copied. Significantly, it was replaced not with the more general term "candidates" used repeatedly elsewhere in the Act, but with the term "representatives," which appears nowhere else in the Act (except as a proper noun referring to Members of the federal lower House, or designees of the Attorney General). The normal meaning of this term is broader than "legislators" (it includes, for example, school boards and city councils as well as senators and representatives) but narrower than "candidates."

The Court says that the seemingly significant refusal to use the term "candidate" and selection of the distinctive term "representative" are really inconsequential, because "candidate" could not have been used. According to the Court, since "candidate" refers to one who has been nominated but *not yet* elected, the phrase "to elect candidates" would be a contradiction in terms. The only flaw in this argument is that it is not true, as repeated usage of the formulation "to elect candidates" by this Court itself amply demonstrates. ... And the phrase is used in the complaint of the minority plaintiffs in the other § 2 case decided today. In other words, far from being an impermissible choice, "candidates" would have been the natural choice, even if it had not been used repeatedly elsewhere in the statute. It is quite absurd to think that Congress went out of its way to replace that term with "representatives," in order to convey what "candidates" naturally suggests (viz., coverage of *all* elections) and what "representatives" naturally does not.

. . . .

Finally, the Court suggests that there is something "anomalous" about extending coverage under § 5 of the Voting Rights Act to the election of judges, while not extending coverage under § 2 to the same elections. This simply misconceives the different roles of § 2 and § 5. The latter requires certain jurisdictions to preclear changes in election methods before those changes are implemented; it is a means of assuring in advance the absence of all electoral illegality, not only that which violates the Voting Rights Act but that which violates the Constitution as well. In my view, judges *are* within the scope of § 2 for nondilution claims, and thus for those claims, § 5 preclearance would enforce the Voting Rights Act with respect to judges. Moreover, intentional discrimination in the election of judges, whatever its form, is constitutionally prohibited, and the preclearance provision of § 5 gives the Government a method by which to prevent that. The scheme makes entire sense without the need to bring judges within the "to elect" provision.

All this is enough to convince me that there is sense to the ordinary meaning of "representative" in § 2(b)—that there is reason to Congress' choice—and since there is, then, under our normal presumption, that ordinary meaning prevails. I would read § 2 as extending vote dilution claims to elections for "representatives," but not to elections for judges. For other claims under § 2, however—those resting on the "to participate in the political process" provision rather than the "to elect" provision—no similar restriction would apply. Since the claims here are exclusively claims of dilution, I would affirm the judgment of the Fifth Circuit.

* * *

As I said at the outset, these cases are about method. The Court transforms the meaning of § 2, not because the ordinary meaning is irrational, or inconsistent with other parts of the statute, but because it does not fit the Court's conception of what Congress must have had in mind. When we adopt a method that psychoanalyzes Congress rather than reads its laws, when we employ a tinkerer's toolbox, we do great harm. Not only do we reach the wrong result with respect to the statute at hand, but we poison the well of future legislation, depriving legislators of the assurance that ordinary terms, used in an ordinary context, will be given a predictable meaning. Our highest responsibility in the field of statutory construction is to read the laws in a consistent way, giving Congress a sure means by which it may work the people's will. We have ignored that responsibility today. I respectfully dissent.

UNITED STATES V. MARSHALL

908 F.2d 1312 (7th Cir. 1990)

As you read this case, consider the following issues:

- Which theories of interpretation are represented?

- If Judge Posner, the avatar of pragmatism, relied purely on pragmatism in his opinion, how would it read? What other kinds of arguments does he make? Why?

- Who do you think has the best textualist interpretation? Why?

- Whose opinion do you agree with? Why?

- What do you think Congress actually intended? How would you have voted if you were considering this statute in Congress?

- What are the benefits of Judge Posner's pragmatic approach? What are its costs?

EASTERBROOK, CIRCUIT JUDGE.

Two cases consolidated for decision in banc present ... questions concerning the application and constitutionality of the statute and sentencing guidelines that govern sales of lysergic acid diethylamide (LSD).

Stanley J. Marshall was convicted after a bench trial and sentenced to 20 years' imprisonment for conspiring to distribute, and distributing, more than ten grams of LSD, enough for 11,751 doses. Patrick Brumm, Richard L. Chapman, and John M. Schoenecker were convicted by a jury of selling ten sheets (1,000 doses) of paper containing LSD. Because the total weight of the paper and LSD was 5.7 grams, a five-year mandatory minimum applied. The district court sentenced Brumm to 60 months (the minimum), Schoenecker to 63 months, and Chapman to 96 months' imprisonment. . . .

[We must resolve w]hether 21 U.S.C. § 841(b)(1)(A)(v) and (B)(v), which set mandatory minimum terms of imprisonment—five years for selling more than one gram of a "mixture or substance containing a detectable amount" of LSD, ten years for more than ten grams—exclude the weight of a carrier medium. . . .

I

According to the Sentencing Commission, the LSD in an average dose weighs 0.05 milligrams. Twenty thousand pure doses are a gram. But 0.05 mg is almost invisible, so LSD is distributed to retail customers in a carrier. Pure LSD is dissolved in a solvent such as alcohol and sprayed on paper or gelatin; alternatively the paper may be dipped in the solution. After the solvent evaporates, the paper or gel is cut into one-dose squares and sold by the square. Users swallow the squares or may drop them into a beverage, releasing the drug. Although the gelatin and paper are light, they weigh much more than the drug. Marshall's 11,751 doses weighed 113.32 grams; the LSD accounted for only 670.72 mg of this, not enough to activate the five-year mandatory minimum sentence, let alone the ten-year minimum. The ten sheets of blotter paper carrying the 1,000 doses Chapman and confederates sold weighed 5.7 grams; the LSD in the paper did not approach the one-gram threshold for a mandatory minimum sentence. This disparity between the weight of the pure LSD and the weight of LSD-plus-carrier underlies the defendants' arguments.

A

If the carrier counts in the weight of the "mixture or substance containing a detectable amount" of LSD, some odd things may happen. Weight in the hands of distributors may exceed that of manufacturers and wholesalers. Big fish then could receive paltry sentences or small fish draconian ones. Someone who sold 19,999 doses of pure LSD (at 0.05 mg per dose) would escape the five-year mandatory minimum of § 841(b)(1)(B)(v) and be covered by § 841(b)(1)(C), which lacks a minimum term and has a maximum of "only" 20 years. Someone who sold a single hit of LSD dissolved in a tumbler of orange juice could be exposed to a ten-year mandatory minimum. Retailers could fall in or out of the mandatory terms depending not on the number of doses but on the medium: sugar cubes weigh more than paper, which weighs more than gelatin. One way to eliminate the possibility of such consequences is to say that the carrier is not a "mixture or substance containing a detectable amount" of the drug. Defendants ask us to do this.

. . . .

B

It is not possible to construe the words of § 841 to make the penalty turn on the net weight of the drug rather than the gross weight of carrier and drug. The statute speaks of "mixture or substance containing a detectable amount" of a drug. "Detectable amount" is the opposite of "pure"; the point of the statute is that the "mixture" is not to be converted to an equivalent amount of pure drug.

The structure of the statute reinforces this conclusion. The 10-year minimum applies to any person who possesses, with intent to distribute, "100 grams or more of phencyclidine (PCP) or 1 kilogram or more of a mixture or substance containing a detectable amount of phencyclidine (PCP)", § 841(b)(1)(A)(iv). Congress distinguished the pure drug from a "mixture or substance containing a detectable amount of" it. All drugs other than PCP are governed exclusively by the "mixture or substance" language. Even brute force cannot turn that language into a reference to pure LSD. Congress used the same "mixture or substance" language to describe heroin, cocaine, amphetamines, and many other drugs that are sold after being cut—sometimes as much as LSD. There is no sound basis on which to treat the words "substance or mixture containing a detectable amount of", repeated verbatim for every drug mentioned in § 841 except PCP, as *different* things for LSD and cocaine although the language is identical, while treating the "mixture or substance" language as meaning the *same* as the reference to pure PCP in 21 U.S.C. § 841(b)(1)(A)(iv) and (B)(iv).

Although the "mixture or substance" language shows that the statute cannot be limited to pure LSD, it does not necessarily follow that blotter paper *is* a "mixture or substance containing" LSD. That phrase cannot include all "carriers." One gram of crystalline LSD in a heavy glass bottle is still only one gram of "statutory LSD." So is a gram of LSD being "carried" in a Boeing 747. How much mingling of the drug with something else is essential to form a "mixture or substance"? The legislative history is silent, but ordinary usage is indicative.

"Substance" may well refer to a chemical compound, or perhaps to a drug in a solvent. LSD does not react chemically with sugar, blotter paper, or gelatin, and none of these is a solvent. "Mixture" is more inclusive. Cocaine often is mixed with mannitol, quinine, or lactose. These white powders do not react, but it is common ground that a cocaine-mannitol mixture is a statutory "mixture."

LSD and blotter paper are not commingled in the same way as cocaine and lactose. What is the nature of their association? The possibility most favorable to defendants is that LSD sits on blotter paper as oil floats on water. Immiscible substances may fall outside the statutory definition of "mixture." The possibility does not assist defendants—not on this record, anyway. LSD is applied to paper in a solvent; after the solvent evaporates, a tiny quantity of LSD remains. Because the fibers absorb the alcohol, the LSD solidifies inside the paper rather than on it. You cannot pick a grain of LSD off the surface of the paper. Ordinary parlance calls the paper containing tiny crystals of LSD a mixture.

. . . .

CUMMINGS, CIRCUIT JUDGES, with whom BAUER, CHIEF JUDGES, and WOOD, JR., CUDAHY, and POSNER, CIRCUIT JUDGES, join, dissenting:

[The majority mistakenly assumes] that the words "mixture or substance" are not ambiguous and are not therefore susceptible of interpretation by the courts. . . .

Six courts, including the district court in *Marshall*, have explicitly considered whether the carrier in an LSD case is a mixture or substance within the meaning of 21 U.S.C. § 841. Five of these courts have concluded that the blotter paper is a "mixture or substance" within the meaning of the statute. These courts rely primarily on the 1986 amendments to Section 841, which altered the references to various drugs, including LSD, by adding the words "mixture or substance containing a detectable amount of [the drug in question]." . . .

The sixth court, the United States District Court for the District of Columbia, held that blotter paper was not a mixture or substance within the meaning of the statute. The court relied not only on ordinary dictionary definitions of the words mixture and substance but also on a November 30, 1988, Sentencing Commission publication, entitled "Questions Most Frequently Asked About the Sentencing Guidelines," which states that the Commission has not taken a position on whether the blotter paper should be weighed. The conclusion that the Commission has not yet resolved this question is further supported by a Sentencing Commission Notice issued on March 3, 1989, which requested public comments on whether the Commission should exclude the weight of the carrier for sentencing purposes in LSD cases.

The [*United States v.*] *Healy* court also stated that Congress could have intended the words "mixture or substance" to refer to the liquid in which the pure LSD is dissolved. Finally, the *Healy* court relied on a Guidelines table designed to provide a sentencing court with an equivalent weight for sentencing purposes in cases in which the number of doses distributed is known but the actual weight is unknown. The table provides that a dose of LSD weighs .05 milligrams. This weight closely approximates the weight of one dose of LSD without blotter paper, but is not an accurate reflection of one dose with blotter paper.

The court in *Healy* did not refer to the legislative history of the statute to support the proposition that Congress did not intend the weight of the carrier to be included in LSD cases. This is not surprising since the only reference to LSD in the debates preceding the passage of the 1986 amendments to Section 841 was a passing reference that does not address quantities or weights of drugs. . . .

Two subsequent pieces of legislative history, however, do shed some light on this question. In a letter to Senator Joseph R. Biden, Jr., dated April 26, 1989, the Chairman of the Sentencing Commission, William W. Wilkens, Jr., noted the ambiguity in the statute as it is currently written:

"With respect to LSD, it is unclear whether Congress intended the carrier to be considered as a packaging material, or, since it is commonly consumed along with the illicit drug, as a dilutant ingredient in the drug mixture. The Commission suggests that Congress may wish to further consider the LSD carrier issue in order to clarify legislative intent as to whether the weight of the carrier should or should not be considered in determining the quantity of LSD mixture for punishment purposes."

Presumably acting in response to this query, Senator Biden added to the Congressional Record for October 5, 1989, an analysis of one of a series of technical corrections to 21 U.S.C. § 841 that were under consideration by the Senate that day. This analysis states that the purpose of the particular correction at issue was to remove an unintended "inequity" from Section 841 caused by the decisions of some courts to include the weight of the blotter paper for sentencing purposes in LSD cases. According to Senator Biden, the correction "remedie[d] this inequity by removing the weight of the carrier from the calculation of the weight of the mixture or substance." . . . The amended bill was passed by a unanimous vote of the Senate and is currently pending before the House.

Comments in more recent issues of the Congressional Record indicate that S. 1711 is not expected to pass the House of Representatives. In the meantime, however, a second attempt to clarify Congress' intent in amending 21 U.S.C. § 841 to include the words mixture or substance has now been introduced in the Senate. On April 18, 1990, Senator Kennedy introduced an amendment to S. 1970 (a bill establishing constitutional procedures for the imposition of the death penalty) seeking to clarify the language of 21 U.S.C. § 841. That amendment, Amendment No. 1716, states:

"Section 841(b)(1) of title 21, United States Code, is amended by inserting the following new subsection at the end thereof:

"(E) In determining the weight of a 'mixture or substance' under this section, the court shall not include the weight of the carrier upon which the controlled substance is placed, or by which it is transported."

To be sure there are difficulties inherent in relying heavily on this subsequent legislative history. The first is that these initiatives to clarify the manner in which 21 U.S.C. § 841 and the sentencing guidelines treat LSD offenders may never be enacted. The second is that a given amendment may be viewed not as a clarification of Congress' original intent, but as the expression of an entirely new intent. At the very least, however, this subsequent legislative history, coupled with the fact that the Sentencing Commission has yet to resolve its position on the matter, refutes the proposition that the language of the statute and the Guidelines "couldn't be clearer."

It was established at oral argument that when illegal drugs are sold in capsules, the weight of the capsule is not included in calculating the total weight of the drugs for charging or sentencing purposes. Capsules are made of gelatin, Webster's Medical Desk Dictionary 97 (1986); Dorland's Illustrated Medical Dictionary 226 (23d ed. 1957), and yet their weight is not included. But the majority holds that when LSD is sold on gelatin the weight of the gelatin is included. Thus, apparently some gelatin is part of a "mixture or substance" and some is not. Does the determination depend on the shape into which the gelatin has been formed or on some other criterion? Would the gelatin be a part of the mixture or substance in an LSD case if a defendant sprayed an LSD-alcohol solution into a capsule, but not if a grain of LSD were placed into the capsule with a tweezers? It is not enough to say that "ordinary usage" precludes including the weight of a heavy glass bottle or a Boeing 747. The words "mixture or substance" are ambiguous, and a construction of those words that can avoid invalidation on constitutional grounds is therefore appropriate. . . .

As the government has conceded, however, LSD is not sold by weight, but by dose. A given number of doses will fetch a given price in the market. Neither the price of those doses nor the number of purchasers of those doses will increase because the LSD is sold on blotter paper instead of in its granular or liquid form. Thus a dealer selling LSD that weighs more because he has chosen to sell the drug on blotter paper will not be a more significant market participant than one who has chosen to sell the same number of doses in granular or liquid form. In fact, it is more likely that those individuals in possession of LSD in its granular or liquid form will be the major actors in any given LSD-trafficking network. They are the individuals who will have either manufactured the drug or acquired it in order to apply it to a chosen carrier medium to facilitate eventual distribution. But under the current statutory scheme, and at a weight per dose of .05 milligrams, such a major dealer would be able to possess up to 20,000 doses of LSD in granular form without subjecting himself to the mandatory five-year minimum penalty of 21 U.S.C. § 841(b)(1)(A)(v). A statute that produces such a result and yet purports to punish major participants more severely cannot survive even the limited scrutiny of rational basis review. . . .

The majority has decided that ambiguous language is clear and that rational basis review is toothless. I therefore respectfully dissent.

POSNER, CIRCUIT JUDGE, joined by BAUER, CHIEF JUDGE, and CUMMINGS, WOOD, JR., and CUDAHY, CIRCUIT JUDGES, dissenting.

In each of these cases consolidated for decision en banc . . . , the district court sentenced sellers of LSD in accordance with an interpretation of 21 U.S.C. § 841 that is plausible but that makes the punishment scheme for LSD irrational. It has been assumed that an irrational federal sentencing scheme denies the equal protection of the laws and therefore violates the due process clause of the Fifth Amendment. The assumption is proper, and in order to avoid having to strike down the statute we are entitled to adopt a reasonable interpretation that cures the constitutional infirmity, even if that interpretation might not be our first choice were there no such infirmity.

The statute fixes the minimum and maximum punishments with respect to each illegal drug on the basis of the weight of the "mixture or substance containing a detectable amount of" the drug. Examples are five years minimum and twenty years maximum for selling a hundred grams of a "mixture or substance containing a detectable amount of" heroin and ten years minimum and forty years maximum for selling a kilogram of such a mixture or substance. The corresponding weights for LSD are one gram and ten grams. The quoted words are critical. Drugs are usually consumed, and therefore often sold, in a diluted form, and the adoption by Congress of the "mixture or substance" method of grading punishment reflected a conscious decision to mete out heavy punishment to large retail dealers, who are likely to possess "substantial street quantities," which is to say quantities of the diluted drug ready for sale. That decision is well within Congress's constitutional authority even though it may sometimes result in less severe punishment for possessing a purer, and therefore a lighter, form of the illegal drug than a heavier but much less potent form.

. . . .

Based as it is on weight, the system I have described works well for drugs that are sold by weight; and ordinarily the weight quoted to the buyer is the weight of the dilute form, although of course price will vary with purity. The dilute form is the product, and it is as natural to punish its purveyors according to the weight of the product as it is to punish moonshiners by the weight or volume of the moonshine they sell rather than by the weight of the alcohol contained in it. . . .

LSD, however, is sold to the consumer by the dose; it is not cut, diluted, or mixed with something else. Moreover, it is incredibly light. An average dose of LSD weighs .05 milligrams, which is less than two millionths of an ounce. To ingest something that small requires swallowing something much larger. Pure LSD in granular form is first diluted by being dissolved, usually in alcohol, and then a quantity of the solution containing one dose of LSD is sprayed or eyedropped on a sugar cube, or on a cube of gelatin, or, as in the cases before us, on an inch-square section of "blotter" paper. (LSD blotter paper, which is sold typically in sheets ten inches square containing a hundred sections each with one dose of LSD on it, is considerably thinner than the paper used to blot ink but much heavier than the LSD itself.) After the solution is applied to the carrier medium, the alcohol or other solvent evaporates, leaving an invisible (and undiluted) spot of pure LSD on the cube or blotter paper. The consumer drops the cube or the piece of paper into a glass of water, or orange juice, or some other beverage, causing the LSD to dissolve in the beverage, which is then drunk. This is not dilution. It is still one dose that is being imbibed. Two quarts of a 50-proof alcoholic beverage are more than one quart of a 100-proof beverage, though the total alcoholic content is the same. But a quart of orange juice containing one dose of LSD is not more, in any relevant sense, than a pint of juice containing the same one dose, and it would be loony to punish the purveyor of the quart more heavily than the purveyor of the pint. It would be like basing the punishment for selling cocaine on the combined weight of the cocaine and of the vehicle (plane, boat, automobile, or whatever) used to transport it or the syringe used to inject it or the pipe used to smoke it. The blotter paper, sugar cubes, etc. are the vehicles for conveying LSD to the consumer.

The weight of the carrier is vastly greater than that of the LSD, as well as irrelevant to its potency. There is no comparable disparity between the pure and the mixed form (if that is how we should regard LSD on blotter paper or other carrier medium) with respect to the other drugs in section 841, with the illuminating exception of PCP. There Congress specified alternative weights, for the drug itself and for the substance or mixture containing the drug. For example, the five-year minimum sentence for a seller of PCP requires the sale of either ten grams of the drug itself or one hundred grams of a substance or mixture containing the drug.

Ten sheets of blotter paper, containing a thousand doses of LSD, weigh almost six grams. The LSD itself weighs less than a hundredth as much. If the thousand doses are on gelatin cubes instead of sheets of blotter paper, the total weight is less, but it is still more than two grams, which is forty times the weight of the LSD. In both cases, if the carrier plus the LSD constitutes the relevant "substance or mixture" (the crucial "if" in this case), the dealer is subject to the minimum mandatory sentence of five years. One of the defendants before us (Marshall) sold almost 12,000 doses of LSD on blotter paper. This subjected him to the ten-year minimum, and the Guidelines then took over and pushed him up to twenty years. Since it takes 20,000 doses of LSD to equal a gram, Marshall would not have been subject to even the five-year mandatory minimum had he sold the LSD in its pure form. And a dealer who sold fifteen times the number of doses as Marshall—180,000—would not be subject to the ten-year mandatory minimum sentence if he sold the drug in its pure form, because 180,000 doses is only nine grams.

At the other extreme, if Marshall were not a dealer at all but dropped a square of blotter paper containing a single dose of LSD into a glass of orange juice and sold it to a friend at cost (perhaps 35 cents), he would be subject to the ten-year minimum. The juice with LSD dissolved in it would be the statutory mixture or substance containing a detectable amount of the illegal drug and it would weigh more than ten grams (one ounce is about 35 grams, and the orange juice in a glass of orange juice weighs several ounces). So a person who sold one dose of LSD might be subject to the ten-year mandatory minimum sentence while a dealer who sold 199,999 doses in pure form would be subject only to the five-year minimum. Defendant Dean sold 198 doses, crowded onto one sheet of blotter paper: this subjected him to the five-year mandatory minimum, too, since the ensemble weighed slightly more than a gram.

There are no reported orange juice cases; for that matter there are no reported *federal* cases in which the carrier is a sugar cube rather than a gelatin cube, although sugar cubes are said to be a common LSD carrier, and in two state cases defendants have been prosecuted for unlawful possession of one and of six LSD-laced sugar cubes, respectively. A sugar cube weighs more than two grams, so a seller of a mere six sugar cubes laced with LSD—six doses—would, if prosecuted federally, have bought himself the mandatory minimum ten-year sentence.

All this seems crazy but we must consider whether Congress might have had a reason for wanting to key the severity of punishment for selling LSD to the weight of the carrier rather than to the number of doses or to some reasonable proxy for dosage (as weight is, for many drugs). The only one suggested is that it might be costly to determine the weight of the LSD in the blotter paper, sugar cube, etc., because it is so light! That merely underscores the irrationality of basing the punishment for selling this drug on weight rather than on dosage. But in fact the weight is reported in every case I have seen, so apparently it can be determined readily enough; it *has* to be determined in any event, to permit a purity adjustment under the Guidelines. If the weight of the LSD is difficult to determine, the difficulty is easily overcome by basing punishment on the number of doses, which makes much more sense in any event. To base punishment on the weight of the carrier medium makes about as much sense as basing punishment on the weight of the defendant.

A person who sells LSD on blotter paper is not a worse criminal than one who sells the same number of doses on gelatin cubes, but he is subject to a heavier punishment. A person who sells five doses of LSD on sugar cubes is not a worse person than a manufacturer of LSD who is caught with 19,999 doses in pure form, but the former is subject to a ten-year mandatory minimum no-parole sentence while the latter is not even subject to the five-year minimum. If defendant Chapman, who received five years for selling a thousand doses of LSD on blotter paper, had sold the same number of doses in pure form, his Guidelines sentence would have been fourteen months. And defendant Marshall's sentence for selling almost 12,000 doses would have been four years rather than twenty. . . .

This is a quilt the pattern whereof no one has been able to discern. The legislative history is silent, and since even the Justice Department cannot explain the why of the punishment scheme that it is defending, the most plausible inference is that Congress simply did not realize how LSD is sold. The inference is reinforced by the statutory treatment of PCP.

. . . .

Differences in the severity of punishment are determined by differences in the weight of the carrier medium, even though that weight is completely irrelevant to culpability. . . .

That irrationality is magnified when we compare the sentences for people who sell other drugs prohibited by 21 U.S.C. § 841. Marshall, remember, sold fewer than 12,000 doses and was sentenced to twenty years. Twelve thousand doses sounds like a lot, but to receive a comparable sentence for selling heroin Marshall would have had to sell ten kilograms, which would yield between one and two million doses. To receive a comparable sentence for selling cocaine he would have had to sell fifty kilograms, which would yield anywhere from 325,000 to five million doses. While the corresponding weight is lower for crack—half a kilogram—this still translates into 50,000 doses.

LSD is a potentially dangerous drug, especially for psychotics (whom it can drive to suicide). But many things are dangerous for psychotics. No one believes that LSD is a more dangerous drug than heroin or cocaine (particularly crack cocaine). The general view is that it is *much* less dangerous. There is no indication that Congress believes it to be more dangerous, or more difficult to control. The heavy sentences that the law commands for minor traffickers in LSD are the inadvertent result of the interaction among a statutory procedure for measuring weight, adopted without understanding how LSD is sold; a decision to specify harsh mandatory minimum sentences for drug traffickers, based on the weight of the drug sold; and a decision (gratuitous and unreflective, as far as I can see) by the framers of the Guidelines to key punishment to the statutory measure of weight, thereby amplifying Congress's initial error and ensuring that the big dealer who makes or ships the pure drug will indeed receive a shorter sentence than the small dealer who handles the stuff in its street form. As the wholesale value of LSD may be as little as 35 cents a dose, a seller of five sugar cubes could be subject to a mandatory minimum prison term of ten years for selling $2 worth of illegal drugs. Dean received six years (no parole, remember) for selling $73 worth. The irrationality is quite bad enough if we confine our attention to LSD sold on blotter paper, since the weight of blotter paper varies considerably, making punishment turn on a factor that has no relation to the dosages or market values of LSD.

Well, what if anything can we judges do about this mess? The answer lies in the shadow of a jurisprudential disagreement that is not less important by virtue of being unavowed by most judges. It is the disagreement between the severely positivistic view that the content of law is exhausted in clear, explicit, and definite enactments by or under express delegation from legislatures, and the natural lawyer's or legal pragmatist's view that the practice of interpretation and the general terms of the Constitution (such as "equal protection of the laws") authorize judges to enrich positive law with the moral values and practical concerns of civilized society. Judges who in other respects have seemed quite similar, such as Holmes and Cardozo, have taken opposite sides of this issue. Neither approach is entirely satisfactory. The first buys political neutrality and a type of objectivity at the price of substantive injustice, while the second buys justice in the individual case at the price of considerable uncertainty and, not infrequently, judicial willfulness. It is no wonder that our legal system oscillates between the approaches. The positivist view, applied unflinchingly to this case, commands the affirmance of prison sentences that are exceptionally harsh by the standards of the modern Western world, dictated by an accidental, unintended scheme of punishment nevertheless implied by the words (taken one by one) of the relevant enactments. The natural law or pragmatist view leads to a freer interpretation, one influenced by norms of equal treatment; and let us explore the interpretive possibilities here. One is to interpret "mixture or substance containing a detectable amount of [LSD]" to exclude the carrier medium—the blotter paper, sugar or gelatin cubes, and orange juice or other beverage. That is the course we rejected in *United States v. Rose*, as have the other circuits. I wrote *Rose*, but I am no longer confident that its literal interpretation of the statute, under which the blotter paper, cubes, etc. are "substances" that "contain" LSD, is inevitable. The blotter paper, etc. are better viewed, I now think, as carriers, like the package in which a kilo of cocaine comes wrapped or the bottle in which a fifth of liquor is sold.

Interpreted to exclude the carrier, the punishment schedule for LSD would make perfectly good sense; it would not warp the statutory design. The comparison with heroin and cocaine is again illuminating. The statute imposes the five-year mandatory minimum sentence on anyone who sells a substance or mixture containing a hundred grams of heroin, equal to 10,000 to 20,000 doses. One gram of pure LSD, which also would trigger the five-year minimum, yields 20,000 doses. The comparable figures for cocaine are 3250 to 50,000 doses, placing LSD in about the middle. So Congress may have wanted to base punishment for the sale of LSD on the weight of the pure drug after all, using one and ten grams of the pure drug to trigger the five-year and ten-year minima (and corresponding maxima—twenty years and forty years). This interpretation leaves "substance or mixture containing" without a referent, so far as LSD is concerned. But we must remember that Congress used the identical term in each subsection that specifies the quantity of a drug that subjects the seller to the designated minimum and maximum punishments. In thus automatically including the same term in each subsection, Congress did not necessarily affirm that, for each and every drug covered by the statute, a substance or mixture containing the drug *must* be found.

The flexible interpretation that I am proposing is decisively strengthened by the constitutional objection to basing punishment of LSD offenders on the weight of the carrier medium rather than on the weight of the LSD. Courts often do interpretive handsprings to avoid having even to *decide* a constitutional question. In doing so they expand, very questionably in my view, the effective scope of the Constitution, creating a constitutional penumbra in which statutes wither, shrink, are deformed. A better case for flexible interpretation is presented when the alternative is to nullify Congress's action: when in other words there is not merely a constitutional question about, but a constitutional barrier to, the statute when interpreted literally. This is such a case.

. . . .

The point is not that the judicial imagination can conjure up anomalous applications of the statute. A statute is not irrational because its draftsmen lacked omniscience. The point is that graduating punishment to the weight of the carrier medium produces, in the case of LSD, a systematically, unavoidably bizarre schedule of punishments that no one is able to justify. I would give respectful consideration to *any* rationale for the schedule advanced by the legislators, the framers of the Guidelines, or the Department of Justice. None has been advanced. . . .

Our choice is between ruling that the provisions of section 841 regarding LSD are irrational, hence unconstitutional, and therefore there is no punishment for dealing in LSD—Congress must go back to the drawing boards, and all LSD cases in the pipeline must be dismissed—and ruling that, to preserve so much of the statute as can constitutionally be preserved, the statutory expression "substance or mixture containing a detectable amount of [LSD]" excludes the carrier medium. Given *this* choice, we can be reasonably certain that Congress would have preferred the second course; and this consideration carries the argument for a flexible interpretation over the top.

. . . .

The literal interpretation adopted by the majority is not inevitable. All interpretation is contextual. The words of the statute—interpreted against a background that includes a constitutional norm of equal treatment, a (closely related) constitutional commitment to rationality, an evident failure by both Congress and the Sentencing Commission to consider how LSD is actually produced, distributed, and sold, and an equally evident failure by the same two bodies to consider the interaction between heavy mandatory minimum sentences and the Sentencing Guidelines—will bear an interpretation that distinguishes between the carrier vehicle of the illegal drug and the substance or mixture containing a detectable amount of the drug. The punishment of the crack dealer is not determined by the weight of the glass tube in which he sells the crack; we should not lightly attribute to Congress a purpose of punishing the dealer in LSD according to the weight of the LSD carrier. We should not make Congress's handiwork an embarrassment to the members of Congress and to us.

MATTER OF JACOB
86 N.Y.2d 651 (N.Y. 1995)

As you read the following case, focus on these issues:

- In what way is the statute ambiguous?

- How do sections 110 and 117 of the statute interact when read together? If these sections were read literally, or in their most natural way, what would have to happen in order for appellants to become adoptive parents?

- How does the majority read section 117? Why?

- The majority references legislative intent and purpose. Do you think the majority's opinion is best understood as intentionalist or purposivist, or something else? How would you characterize each of the opinions in terms of the theories of statutory interpretation?

- Identify specific arguments in the opinions that resonate with textualist, intentionalist, pragmatic, and other theories of interpretation.

- Which opinion do you agree with, if any, and why?

- What do you think motivated the majority in this case?

- What do you think the legislature would do in response to the majority's opinion?

CHIEF JUDGE KAYE.

Under the New York adoption statute, a single person can adopt a child (Domestic Relations Law § 110). Equally clear is the right of a single homosexual to adopt. These appeals call upon us to decide if the unmarried partner of a child's biological mother, whether heterosexual or homosexual, who is raising the child together with the biological parent, can become the child's second parent by means of adoption.

Because the two adoptions sought—one by an unmarried heterosexual couple, the other by the lesbian partner of the child's mother—are fully consistent with the adoption statute, we answer this question in the affirmative. To rule otherwise would mean that the thousands of New York children actually being raised in homes headed by two unmarried persons could have only one legal parent, not the two who want them.

THE ADOPTIONS SOUGHT

In *Matter of Jacob*, Roseanne M. A. and Jacob's biological father (from whom she is divorced) separated prior to the child's birth and Roseanne M. A. was awarded sole custody. Jacob was a year old when Stephen T. K. began living with him and his mother in early 1991. . . . Jacob's biological father consented to the adoption.

Though acknowledging that "the granting of an adoption in this matter may be beneficial to Jacob," Family Court dismissed the petition for lack of standing on the ground that Domestic Relations Law § 110 does not authorize adoptions by an unmarried couple. The Appellate Division affirmed, two Justices dissenting, and an appeal to this Court was taken as of right.

In *Matter of Dana*, appellants are G. M. and her lesbian partner, P. I., who have lived together in what is described as a long and close relationship for the past 19 years. . . . In 1989, the two women decided that P. I. would have a child they would raise together. P. I. was artificially inseminated by an anonymous donor, and on June 6, 1990, she gave birth to Dana. G. M. and P. I. have shared parenting responsibilities since Dana's birth and have arranged their separate work schedules around her needs. With P. I.'s consent, G. M. filed a petition to adopt Dana in April 1993.

In the court-ordered report recommending that G. M. be permitted to adopt, the disinterested investigator described Dana as an attractive, sturdy and articulate little girl with a "rich family life," which includes frequent visits with G. M.'s three grown children from a previous marriage "who all love Dana and accept her as their baby sister." Noting that G. M. "only has the best interest of Dana in mind," the report concluded that she "provides her with a family structure in which to grow and flourish."

As in *Matter of Jacob*, Family Court, while conceding the favorable results of the home study and "in no way disparaging the ability of [G. M.] to be a good, nurturing and loving parent," . . . held that the adoption was further prohibited by Domestic Relations Law § 117 which it interpreted to require the automatic termination of P. I.'s relationship with Dana upon an adoption by G. M. Despite its conclusion that G. M. had standing to adopt, the Appellate Division nevertheless affirmed on the ground that Domestic Relations Law § 117 prohibits the adoption. We granted leave to appeal.

Limiting our analysis, as did the courts below, to the preserved statutory interpretation issues, we conclude that appellants have standing to adopt under Domestic Relations Law § 110 and are not foreclosed from doing so by Domestic Relations Law § 117. . . .

THE CONTEXT OF OUR STATUTORY ANALYSIS

Two basic themes of overarching significance set the context of our statutory analysis.

First and foremost, since adoption in this State is "solely the creature of . . . statute," the adoption statute must be strictly construed. What is to be construed strictly and applied rigorously in this sensitive area of the law, however, is legislative purpose as well as legislative language. Thus, the adoption statute must be applied in harmony with the humanitarian principle that adoption is a means of securing the best possible home for a child.

Ten years ago, in *Matter of Robert Paul P.*, we refused to allow the adoption of a 50-year-old man by his 57-year-old homosexual partner even though the statutory language permitted the adoption. Our refusal in *Robert Paul P.* rested solely on the fact that the adult adoption sought in that case would have been "wholly inconsistent with the underlying public policy of providing a parent-child relationship for the welfare of the child."

The very next year, in *Matter of Best*, we again chose not to construe the words of the adoption statute strictly, declining to permit an adopted child to inherit under the will of his biological grandmother because "[p]owerful policy considerations militate against construing a class gift to include a child adopted out of the family." One commentator has characterized our decision in *Best* as "in defiance of . . . the text of the Domestic Relations Law . . . yet in accordance with current societal views of adoption and the adoptive relationship."

What *Matter of Robert Paul P.* and *Matter of Best* underscore is that in strictly construing the adoption statute, our primary loyalty must be to the statute's legislative purpose—the child's best interest. "The adoptive family arises out of the State's concern for the best interest of the child."

This profound concern for the child's welfare is reflected in the statutory language itself: when "satisfied that the best interests of the . . . child will be promoted thereby," a court *"shall* make an order approving the adoption."

This policy would certainly be advanced in situations like those presented here by allowing the two adults who actually function as a child's parents to become the child's legal parents. The advantages which would result from such an adoption include Social Security and life insurance benefits in the event of a parent's death or disability, the right to sue for the wrongful death of a parent, the right to inherit under rules of intestacy and eligibility for coverage under both parents' health insurance policies. In addition, granting a second parent adoption further ensures that two adults are legally entitled to make medical decisions for the child in case of emergency and are under a legal obligation for the child's economic support.

Even more important, however, is the emotional security of knowing that in the event of the biological parent's death or disability, the other parent will have presumptive custody, and the children's relationship with their parents, siblings and other relatives will continue should the coparents separate. . . .

A second, related point of overriding significance is that the various sections comprising New York's adoption statute today represent a complex and not entirely reconcilable patchwork. Amended innumerable times since its passage in 1873, the adoption statute was last consolidated nearly 60 years ago, in 1938. Thus, after decades of piecemeal amendment upon amendment, the statute today contains language from the 1870's alongside language from the 1990's.

Though courts surely must, and do, strive to give effect to every word of a statute, our analysis must recognize the difficulty—perhaps unique difficulty—of such an endeavor here. With its long, tortuous history, New York's adoption statute today is a far cry from a "methodical[ ] and meticulous[ ]" expression of legislative judgment. That the questions posed by these appeals are not readily answerable by reference to the words of a particular section of the law, but instead require the traditional and often close and difficult task of statutory interpretation is evident even in the length of today's opinions—whichever result is reached.

Against this backdrop, we turn to the particular provisions at issue.

DOMESTIC RELATIONS LAW § 110

Despite ambiguity in other sections, one thing is clear: section 110 allows appellants to become adoptive parents. Domestic Relations Law § 110, entitled "Who May Adopt," provides that an "adult unmarried person or an adult husband and his adult wife together may adopt another person." Under this language, both appellant G. M. in *Matter of Dana* and appellant Stephen T. K. in *Matter of Jacob*, as adult unmarried persons, have standing to adopt and appellants are correct that the Court's analysis of section 110 could appropriately end here.

Endowing the word "together" as used in section 110 with the overpowering significance of enforcing a policy in favor of marriage (as the dissent does) would require us to rewrite the statute. The statute uses the word "together" only to describe married persons and thus does not preclude an unmarried person in a relationship with another unmarried person from adopting. Rather, by insisting on the joint consent of the married persons, the statutory term "together" simply insures that one spouse cannot adopt a child without the other spouse's knowledge or over the other's objection. Since each of the biological mothers here is not only aware of these proceedings, but has expressly consented to the adoptions, section 110 poses no statutory impediment.

The conclusion that appellants have standing to adopt is also supported by the history of section 110. The pattern of amendments since the end of World War II evidences a successive expansion of the categories of persons entitled to adopt regardless of their marital status or sexual orientation. The language in section 110 permitting adoptions by "an adult or minor husband and his adult or minor wife together," for example, is the result of 1951 legislation intended to enlarge the class of potential adoptive parents to include minors. The sponsors of the bill, passed during the Korean War, were concerned that the child of a young father drafted into the military would be unable to take his father's surname.

Another illustration of such expansion is the 1984 amendment increasing the number of potential adoptive parents by permitting adoption by adults not yet divorced but living apart from their spouses pursuant to separation agreements. Supporting that amendment was New York's "strong policy of assuring that as many children as possible are adopted into suitable family situations." As explained, . . . "the marital status of a person should have no predetermined effect on the ability of that person to provide appropriate care to an adopted child."

Consistent with this trend, the latest amendment to Domestic Relations Law § 110 further increased the number of potential adoptive parents by permitting adoptions by nondivorced adults who have lived apart from their spouses for 18 months.

These amendments reflect some of the fundamental changes that have taken place in the makeup of the family. Today, for example, at least 1.2 of the 3.5 million American households which consist of an unmarried adult couple have children under 15 years old, more than a six-fold increase from 1970. Yet further recognition of this transformation is evidenced by the fact that unlike the States of New Hampshire and Florida, New York does not prohibit adoption by homosexuals. Indeed, as noted earlier, an administrative regulation is in place in this State forbidding the denial of an agency adoption based solely on the petitioner's sexual orientation,

A reading of section 110 granting appellants, as unmarried second parents, standing to adopt is therefore consistent with the words of the statute as well as the spirit behind the modern-day amendments: encouraging the adoption of as many children as possible regardless of the sexual orientation or marital status of the individuals seeking to adopt them.

DOMESTIC RELATIONS LAW § 117

Appellants having standing to adopt pursuant to Domestic Relations Law § 110, the other statutory obstacle relied upon by the lower courts in denying the petitions is the provision that "[a]fter the making of an order of adoption the natural parents of the adoptive child shall be relieved of all parental duties toward and of all responsibilities for and shall have no rights over such adoptive child or to his property by descent or succession." Literal application of this language would effectively prevent these adoptions since it would require the termination of the biological mothers' rights upon adoption thereby placing appellants in the "Catch-22" of having to choose one of two coparents as the child's only legal parent.

As outlined below, however, neither the language nor policy underlying section 117 dictates that result.

[Section 117] speaks principally of estate law. Words such as "succession," "inheritance," "decedent," "instrument" and "will" permeate the statute. Read contextually, it is clear that the Legislature's chief concern in section 117 was the resolution of property disputes upon the death of an adoptive parent or child. . . . Thus, from the very beginning of what is now section 117, both the scholarly commentary about the section and its dozen or so amendments have centered on issues of property rights and inheritance.

. . . .

Moving beyond the language and history of section 117 itself, our reading of the statute is further supported by recent amendments to other sections of the adoption law which provide elaborate procedural mechanisms for regulating the relationships between the child, the child's (soon-to-be former) biological parents and the persons who will become the child's parents upon adoption.

In the context of agency adoptions, Social Services Law § 383–c, enacted in 1990, provides that biological parents willing to give their child up for adoption must execute a written instrument, known as a "surrender," stating "in conspicuous bold print on the first page" that "the parent is giving up all rights to have custody, visit with, write to or learn about the child, forever."

The second category of adoption—private placement—is also regulated by a newly revised statute requiring the execution of a written "consent" stating that "no action . . . may be maintained . . . for the custody of the child." In fact, the procedure mandated by Domestic Relations Law § 115–b closely parallels that of Social Services Law § 383–c. Both statutes, for example, require biological parents to execute a document that effectively terminates parental rights. Both provisions require a Judge or Surrogate (if the document is executed in court) to inform the biological parents of the consequences of their act, and advise them of their right to be represented by counsel. More importantly, both statutes provide generally that the biological parents' "surrender" or "consent" may be revoked within 45 days, and that an adoption proceeding may not be commenced until after the expiration of that period (Social Services Law § 383–c[8][b]; Domestic Relations Law § 115–b[4][d]). Thus, by the time the adoptive parents become the child's legal parents, the biological parents have already formally agreed to relinquish their relationship with the child.

The procedural safeguards contained in Social Services Law § 383–c and Domestic Relations Law § 115–b—safeguards that reflect modern sensitivities as to the level of procedural protection required for waiver of parental rights—further indicate that section 117 does not invariably mandate termination in all circumstances. Under the language of section 117 alone, a biological mother's rights could theoretically be severed unilaterally, without notice as to the consequences or other procedural protections. Though arguably adequate in 1938 when the statute was enacted, such a summary procedure would be unlikely to pass muster today.

The above-described amendments to Social Services Law § 383–c and Domestic Relations Law § 115–b suggest that the Legislature in recent years has devised statutory vehicles other than section 117 to carefully regulate and restrict parental rights during the adoption process, again militating against a rigid application of subdivision (1)(a).

. . . .

Finally, even though the language of section 117 still has the effect of terminating a biological parent's rights in the majority of adoptions between strangers—where there is a need to prevent unwanted intrusion by the child's former biological relatives to promote the stability of the new adoptive family—the cases before us are entirely different. As we recognized in *Matter of Seaman*, "complete severance of the natural relationship [is] not necessary when the adopted person remain[s] within the natural family unit as a result of an intrafamily adoption."

One example of an adoption where the Legislature has explicitly acknowledged that termination is unwarranted is when the child, with the consent of the biological parent, is adopted by a "stepparent." A second, implicit exception occurs in the adoptions by teenage fathers authorized by the 1951 amendment to section 110. Since minor fathers adopting their own biological children are not "stepparents" under the language of Domestic Relations Law § 117(1)(d), they would be prohibited from adopting were section 117's termination language to be mandatory in all cases. The seemingly automatic cut-off language of section 117 could not have been intended to bar these adoptions, however, since they are precisely what the Legislature sought to encourage in the first place.

. . . .

Given the above, it is plain that an interpretation of section 117 that would limit the number of beneficial intrafamily adoptions cannot be reconciled with the legislative intent to authorize open adoptions and adoptions by minors. The coexistence of the statute's seemingly automatic termination language along with these more recent enactments creates a statutory puzzle not susceptible of ready resolution.

One conclusion that can be drawn, however, is that section 117 does not invariably require termination in the situation where the biological parent, having consented to the adoption, has agreed to retain parental rights and to raise the child together with the second parent. Despite their varying factual circumstances, each of the adoptions described above—stepparent adoptions, adoptions by minor fathers and open adoptions—share such an agreement as a common denominator. Because the facts of the cases before us are directly analogous to these three situations, the half-century-old termination language of section 117 should not be read to preclude the adoptions here. Phrased slightly differently, "the desire for consistency in the law should not of itself sever the bonds between the child and the natural relatives."

"Where the language of a statute is susceptible of two constructions, the courts will adopt that which avoids injustice, hardship, constitutional doubts or other objectionable results." Given that section 117 is open to two differing interpretations as to whether it automatically terminates parental rights in all cases, a construction of the section that would deny children like Jacob and Dana the opportunity of having their two de facto parents become their legal parents, based solely on their biological mother's sexual orientation or marital status, would not only be unjust under the circumstances, but also might raise constitutional concerns in light of the adoption statute's historically consistent purpose—the best interests of the child.

. . . .

CONCLUSION

To be sure, the Legislature that last codified section 117 in 1938 may never have envisioned families that "include . . . two adult lifetime partners whose relationship is . . . characterized by an emotional and financial commitment and interdependence." Nonetheless, it is clear that section 117, designed as a shield to protect new adoptive families, was never intended as a sword to prohibit otherwise beneficial intrafamily adoptions by second parents.

BELLACOSA, J., Dissenting.

JUDGES SIMONS, TITONE and I respectfully dissent and vote to affirm in each case.

These appeals share a statutory construction issue under New York's adoption laws. While the results reached by the majority are intended to have a benevolent effect on the individuals involved in these two cases, the means to those ends transform the legislative adoption charter governing countless other individuals. Additionally, the dispositional methodology transcends institutional limitations on this Court's proper exercise of its authority, fixed by internal discipline and by the external distribution of powers among the branches of government.

The majority minimizes the at-will relationships of the appellants couples who would be combined biological-adoptive parents in each case, but the significant statutory and legally central relevancy is inescapable. Unlike married and single parent households, each couple here cohabits only day-to-day, no matter the depth or length of their voluntary arrangements. Their relationships lack legal permanency and the State has not endowed them with the benefits and enforceable protections that flow from relationships recognized under color of law. Nowhere do statutes, or any case law previously, recognize de facto, functional or second parent adoptions in joint circumstances as presented here.

Specifically, in the respective cases, the availability of adoption is implicated because of the operation-of-law consequences under Domestic Relations Law § 117 based on: (1) the relationship of the biological parent and the putative adoptive child if a *male and female unmarried cohabiting couple,* one of whom is the biological mother of the child, *jointly petitions* to adopt the five-year-old child; and (2) the relationship of the biological parent and her child if the *lesbian partner* of the biological mother *petitions alone* to adopt the five-year-old child. Neither case presents an issue of ineligibility because of sexual orientation or of discrimination against adoption on that basis, despite the majority's evocations in that regard.

. . . .

Although adoption has been practiced since ancient times, the authorization for this unique relationship derives solely from legislation. It has no common-law roots or evolution. Therefore, our Court has approved the proposition that the statutory adoption charter exclusively controls.

The judicial role is most sensitive, but no case has ever recognized a judicially created right of adoption. This restraint is especially pertinent when the Legislature has expressly enacted a plenary, detailed legislative plan. The majority acknowledges New York's unique legislative developments and the several major cases in which adoptions have been disallowed that together document these juridically limiting principles, yet the majority's ruling and result paradoxically turn away from those consistent guideposts.

. . . .

A transcendent societal goal in the field of domestic relations is to stabilize family relationships, particularly parent-child bonds. That State interest promotes permanency planning and provides protection for an adopted child's legally secure familial placement. Therefore, statutory authorizations should not be substantively transformed under the guise of interpretation, and all facets of the adoption statutes should be harmonized.

Notably, too, for contextual understanding of these cases, New York State has long refused to recognize common-law marriages (*see,* Domestic Relations Law § 11). It also does not recognize or authorize gay or lesbian marriages, though efforts to secure such legislation have been pursued (*see,* 1995 Assembly Bill A–648; 1994 Assembly Bill A–10508).

I.

Domestic Relations Law § 110, entitled "Who May Adopt," provides at its outset that *"[a]n adult unmarried person or an adult husband and his adult wife together* may adopt another person." Married aspirants are directed to apply "together," i.e., jointly, as spouses, except under circumstances not applicable in these cases.

In *Dana,* appellant G. M. asserts that she may petition as "[a]n adult unmarried person," without regard to the legal consequences of other related provisions of the adoption charter. She petitioned individually and qualifies under section 110, irrespective of her sexual orientation. The *Dana* case, therefore, is not a case involving the right of homosexuals to adopt, nor, self-evidently, is the *Jacob* case.

. . . .

The statutory language and its history instructively reveal no legislative intent or hint to extend the right and responsibility of adoption to cohabiting unmarried adults. The opposite obtains, notably in the *Jacob* case, in the direct contraindication of Domestic Relations Law § 11 expressing the State's long-standing public policy refusal to recognize at-will common-law relationships as marriages. Confusion is thus sown by the holdings today by blurring plain meaning words and clear lines between relationships that are legally recognized and those that are not. Under the newly fashioned theory rooted in ambiguity, any number of people who choose to live together—even those who may not cohabit—could be allowed to adopt a child together. The result in these cases and *reductio ad absurdum* illustrations flowing from appellants' theorem—that singular may mean plural and vice versa under a general axiom of statutory construction inapplicable in the face of specificity—are far beyond any discernible legislative intent of New York lawmakers. Marriages and single parent households are not, after all, mere social conventions generally or with respect to adoption circumstances; they enjoy legal recognition and special protections for empirically proper social reasons and public policies.

. . . .

The words chosen by the Legislature demonstrate its conclusion that a stable familial entity is provided by either a one-parent family or a two-parent family when the concentric interrelationships enjoy a legal bond. The statute demonstrates that the Legislature, by express will and words, concluded that households that lack legally recognized bonds suffer a relatively greater risk to the stability needed for adopted children and families, because individuals can walk out of these relationships with impunity and unknown legal consequences.

Next, the Legislature specified the exceptions in section 110 permitting a married individual to petition for adoption without consent of the other spouse. . . . The failure of the Legislature to provide for the circumstances of these two cases examined in the light of successive particularized legislative amendatory actions, is yet another cogent refutation of the uniquely judicial authorization of adoption, unfurled today under the twin banners of statutory interpretation and ambiguity.

. . . .

As former Chief Judge Breitel noted in another connection, the "judicial process is not permitted to rove generally over the scene of human affairs. Instead, it must be used, on pain of violating the proprieties, within the framework of a highly disciplined special system of legal rules characteristic of the legal order." The rulings today constitute a rejection of such wise admonitions about appropriate limitations on the judicial process and power.

. . . .

II.

A key societal concern in adoption proceedings is, we all agree, the best interests of children. The judicial power to grant an adoption cannot be exercised, however, by simply intoning the phrase "the best interests of the adoptive child" as part of the analysis to determine qualification for adoption. That approach bypasses crucial, threshold steps and begs inescapably interwoven questions that must be considered and answered at the outset of the purely statutory construction issue in these cases. Before a court can arrive at the ultimate conclusion that an adoption is in the best interests of a child therefore, it is first obliged to discern whether the particular application is legislatively authorized. Reversing the analysis erects the building before the foundation is in place.

. . . .

III.

A principal factor in these cases must also ultimately include consideration of the inexorable operation-of-law consequences that flow from section 117, a distinctive feature of New York's adoption laws. Specifically, courts are statutorily mandated to apply Domestic Relations Law § 110 together with the interconnected features of § 117.

Domestic Relations Law § 117 provides: "After the making of an order of adoption the natural parents of the adoptive child *shall be relieved of all parental duties toward and of all responsibilities for and* shall have no rights over such adoptive child *or* to his [or her] property by descent or succession." The plain and overarching language and punctuation of section 117 cannot be judicially blinked, repealed or rendered obsolete by interpretation.

Section 117 says that it severs all facets of a biological parent's conjunctively listed relationships upon adoption of the child. This Court has recognized that "[t]he purpose of the section . . . was to define the relation, after adoption, of the child to its natural parents and to its adopting parents, together in their reciprocal rights, duties and privileges." That is a critically extant, interpretive proposition from this Court and not some merely atavistic utterance.

. . . .

Appellants in both cases nevertheless propose the theory that section 117 is meant to apply only to inheritance succession of property rights after adoption and should have no effect on the wider expanse and array of rights and responsibilities of a biological parent with an adoptive child.

The language of section 117 reveals, however, that the biological parents'
duties, responsibilities and rights with respect to the adoptive child are
separate and distinct from, and more comprehensive than, a single,
narrow category of inheritance rights. The use of the disjunctive "or"
before the phrase, "property by descent or succession," cannot be
discounted or avoided; it denotes the important and elemental legislative
demarcation. These observations are not some syntactical or grammatical
exercise. Indeed, syntax and grammar are necessary tools of precise
expression, acceptable norms of interpretation and reasonably uniform
understanding and, when coupled with disciplined, thorough statutory
construction principles, they bear legitimately and cogently on sound and
supportable legal analysis.

. . . .

The majority states that "from the very beginning of what is now section
117, both the scholarly commentary about the section and its dozen or so
amendments have centered on issues of property rights and inheritance."
This statement sidesteps and subordinates the original and still operative
language of section 117 itself: "The parents of an adopted child are, from
the time of the adoption, *relieved from all parental duties* toward, and of
all responsibility for, the child so adopted, and have no rights over it."
Inheritance was not mentioned and the comprehensive sweep of the
statute could not be plainer. . . .

The rationale of these cases is likely to engender significant legal
uncertainty and practical problems between biological and adoptive
parents. Conflicts concerning the upbringing of children, for example,
with respect to visitation rights, schooling, medical care, religious
preference and training and the like, may ensue. Such a net of foreseeable
and unseen sequelae is hardly conducive to the settled, permanent, new
home environment and set of relationships directed by section 117.

A careful examination of the Legislature's unaltered intent based on the
entire history of the statute reveals the original purpose of section 117
was to enfold adoptees within the exclusive embrace of their new families
and to sever all relational aspects with the former family. . . .

C. HOW LAWYERS USE THE THEORIES OF INTERPRETATION

As a lawyer, would you describe yourself as a textualist or a pragmatist? Perhaps a dynamist? Or maybe a purposivist?

Trick question! As a lawyer, you need to be fluent in all of these modes of interpretation without being wedded to any of them. After all, most lawyers can't really say to a client, "Well, I'd love to take your case, but I can't because I'm a textualist, and your case would have to be argued from a purposivist position." Likewise, no lawyer would dare say to a judge, "Your Honor, you seem to be asking a question about legislative intent, but frankly, you really aren't allowed to consider that material, so I'm going to decline to answer the question."

Does this mean that the theories of interpretation are irrelevant to lawyers and are only of interest to certain judges and academics? Hardly. Understanding these theories of interpretation can help you to be a better lawyer. Can you think of some ways you could make use of your knowledge and mastery of these materials?

D. EXERCISE: REVIEWING, MASTERING, AND USING THE THEORIES OF INTERPRETATION

EXERCISE IV.2

The United States excludes (that is, prohibits) certain non-citizens from entering the country under the Immigration and Nationality Act. In 1950, the Senate Judiciary Committee issued a report analyzing the existing immigration system and proposing a comprehensive rewriting of the Act. One of its recommendations was to amend the bill's text to specifically exclude "homosexuals and other sex perverts" from entry into the country.

When the bill came up in the Senate the next year, the proposed exclusion ground did not specifically exclude homosexuals. Instead, it excluded "aliens afflicted with psychopathic personality, epilepsy, or a mental defect." This language was ultimately adopted in 1952 and was added to the list of reasons for exclusion in the statute.

The Senate Report explained that "the Public Health Service has advised that the provision for the exclusion of aliens afflicted with psychopathic personality or a mental defect . . . is sufficiently broad to provide for the exclusion of homosexuals and sex perverts." Further, at the time, the American Psychiatric Association's Diagnostic and Statistical Manual: Mental Disorders identified homosexuality as a mental disorder, and specifically as a "sociopathic personality disorder." Finally, homosexuality was widely considered a mental defect in American society.

In 2006, Charles Bertis, a native of Canada, wishes to enter the United States. Bertis was travelling with his American husband, Marcus Tillery. (Same-sex marriage is lawful in Canada.) Immigration officials refused to allow Bertis into the country, pursuant to this provision of the Immigration and Nationality Act, on the grounds that he is homosexual.

Analyze this case according to the various theories of interpretation you have explored. Consider:

- What are the relevant considerations for each theoretical approach? What additional research might you want to do for each?

- How do you think a judge applying each theoretical approach would decide this case? What would the judge find most persuasive according to each theoretical approach? Do all of the approaches point to a clear answer?

- How would you vote as a judge? Why?

- How would you structure a brief for each side as a lawyer?

- Suppose this case arose not in 2006, but in 2015, after the Supreme Court recognized same-sex marriage as a constitutional right. Would your opinion as to the correct result change?

CHAPTER V

THE PRACTICAL TOOLS OF STATUTORY INTERPRETATION

■ ■ ■

Now that you understand the different approaches to statutory interpretation we are ready to identify and evaluate the specific tools that judges and lawyer use to interpret statutes. In some cases, these tools are referred to as "doctrines," in others, as "rules," and in others, as "canons." There is no important distinction among these terms.

This chapter begins with an introductory exercise. It then divides the different tools among sections. Each tool is illustrated with a brief case summary labeled "Example" in boldface type, and sometimes with longer edited or unedited cases. In between each section are edited or unedited cases that demonstrate how judges put different kinds of arguments together. Finally, sprinkled throughout the chapter are various exercises designed to help test your understanding of the different tools and to give you practice in deploying them.

A. AN INTRODUCTORY EXERCISE

EXERCISE V.1

This exercise is adapted and modified from a 1958 debate between Lon Fuller and H.L.A. Hart, two leading philosophers, in the pages of the Harvard Law Review. The hypothetical case they discuss is perhaps the most famous hypothetical in all of legal literature.

A recently enacted statute reads as follows:

"Section 1. The Council finds that vehicles create safety problems when they are operated in Central Park.

"Section 2. No vehicles of any kind shall be allowed in Central Park. Any person who brings or drives a vehicle into Central Park shall be guilty of a misdemeanor, which may be punished by a fine not exceeding $500 or by a two-day incarceration in the municipal jail, or both.

"Section 3. Notwithstanding Section 2, bicycles shall be permitted in Central Park, so long as they are being pushed or carried and not ridden."

Barney Fife made the following arrests for violations of the statute:

211

1.   Omar and Sura Khalifa were arrested for bringing a manual wheelchair into the park. Omar was sitting in the wheelchair due to his having sustained injuries in Operation Iraqi Freedom, during which he served in the 82nd Airborne. His daughter, Sura, was pushing the wheelchair.

2.   Crystal Jackson was arrested for operating her electric wheelchair in the park. Crystal uses the wheelchair due to a degenerative muscle condition in her legs. The wheelchair was paid for by Medicare.

3.   Nirej Viswanathan was arrested for operating an automobile in the park. The automobile was an ambulance, and Viswanathan is an EMT who responded to an emergency call. The shortest way for him to get to the site of the emergency was through the park. Viswanathan and several doctors will testify that had Viswanathan arrived at the scene any later, the patient would have died.

4.   Angel Estevez, age 7, was arrested for riding a waveboard in the park.

Your assignments:

- If you represented the defendants in each of these cases, what arguments would you make on their behalf? Would you advise them to take a plea deal? What additional sources and information would you want to research?

- If you were the prosecutor in each case, what arguments would you make? Would you advise the government to offer a plea deal? What additional sources and information would you want to research?

- Suppose that section 1 of the statute instead read, "The Council finds that vehicles cause noise pollution and detract from pedestrians' enjoyment of the park." Would you argue your cases any differently?

EXERCISE V.2

Courts across the country are sometimes faced with cases presenting facts similar to the famous Vehicles in the Park hypothetical. When they decide such cases, law nerds all around the country rejoice. A case from Georgia raised the following question: Is a riding lawnmower a "motor vehicle" under a statute addressing theft of a motor vehicle?

Based on the following materials, how should this case be decided?

The Statute at Issue: Punishment for Theft

OCGA § 16–8–12 (a)(5)—

(A) If the property which was the subject of the theft was a motor vehicle or was a motor vehicle part or component which exceeded $100.00 in value [the offender shall be punished] by imprisonment for not less than one nor more than ten years or, in the discretion of the trial judge, as for a misdemeanor; provided, however, that any person who is convicted of a second or subsequent offense under this paragraph shall be punished by imprisonment for not less than one year nor more than 20 years.

General Principles of Interpretation: Title 1 of the GA Code

OCGA § 1–3–1(b)—

"In all interpretations of statutes, the ordinary signification shall be applied to all words, except words of art or words connected with a particular trade or subject matter, which shall have the signification attached to them by experts in such trade or with reference to such subject matter.

The "Chop Shop Act"

OSGA § 16–8–80–86—

"Motor vehicle" includes every device in, upon, or by which any person or property is or may be transported or drawn upon a highway which is self-propelled or which may be connected to and towed by a self-propelled device and also includes any and all other land based devices which are self-propelled but which are not designed for use upon a highway, including, but not limited to, farm machinery and construction equipment

Car-Jacking Statute

OCGA § 16–5–44.1—

"Motor vehicle" means any vehicle which is self-propelled.

Forfeiture of Motor Vehicles Statute

OCGA §§ 16–6–13.2—

"Motor vehicle" or "vehicle": Any motor vehicle as defined in Code Section 40–1–1 (Definitions from traffic code)

Motor Vehicles and Traffic Law: Title 40

§ 40–1–1. Definitions—

As used in this title:

(33) "Motor vehicle" means every vehicle which is self-propelled other than an electric personal assistive mobility device (EPAMD).

(59) "Special mobile equipment" means every vehicle not designed or used primarily for the transportation of persons or property and only incidentally operated or moved over a highway, including but not limited to: ditch-digging apparatus, well-boring apparatus, and road construction and maintenance machinery such as asphalt spreaders, bituminous mixers, bucket loaders, tractors other than truck tractors, ditchers, leveling graders, finishing machines, motor graders, road rollers, scarifiers, earth-moving carryalls and scrapers, power shovels and drag lines, and self-propelled cranes and earth-moving equipment.

Interpretive Presumptions of Which to be Aware

- All statutes are presumed to be enacted with full knowledge of existing law and their meaning and effect is to be determined with reference to the constitution as well as other statutes and decisions of the courts.

- The fundamental rules of statutory construction that require us to construe the statute according to its terms, to give words their plain and ordinary meaning, and to avoid a construction that makes some language mere surplusage.

- Criminal statute must be construed strictly against criminal liability and, if it is susceptible to more than one reasonable interpretation, the interpretation most favorable to the party facing criminal liability must be adopted. [Note: this is typically referred to as the Rule of Lenity.]

- A statute is enacted by the legislature with full knowledge of the existing condition of the law. It is therefore construed in connection and in harmony with the existing law, and as a part of a general and uniform system of jurisprudence.

- The legislature's last expression on a subject controls.

HARRIS V. STATE

286 Ga. 245 (Ga. Sup. Ct. 2009)

Here is how the Georgia Supreme Court resolved this issue. As you read the case, consider these questions:

- Would you typically refer to a ride-on lawnmower as a vehicle? What about as a motor vehicle?

- Who do you think has the better argument, the majority or the dissent? Why?

- Which theories of interpretation do the majority and dissent appear to be using?

- Identify the different kinds of arguments made by each side. There are textual arguments related to specific words, structural arguments about how laws fit together, and more.

- What role does the majority say the rule of lenity should play in deciding this and other cases? Why do you think the dissent rejects the rule of lenity?

NAHMIAS, JUSTICE.

We granted certiorari to decide whether the Court of Appeals erred in concluding that a riding lawnmower is a "motor vehicle" as that term is used in the statute punishing theft of a motor vehicle, OCGA § 16–8–12(a)(5)(A). We hold that the Court of Appeals did err and that appellant's conviction for theft of a motor vehicle should be reversed and the case remanded for resentencing.

1.   Franklin Lloyd Harris and two associates stole a Toro riding lawnmower worth more than $500 from outside a Home Depot in Dalton, Georgia. They loaded the lawnmower into the back of a van and drove it to Athens, Tennessee, where they sold it. Police later identified Harris as one of the thieves, and he was charged with and convicted by a jury of theft of a motor vehicle (Count 1) and felony theft by taking (Count 2). The trial court merged Count 2 into Count 1 and sentenced Harris, who had three prior felony convictions, to the statutory maximum of ten years in prison. See OCGA § 17–10–7.

At the close of the State's case at trial and in a motion for new trial, Harris argued that a riding lawnmower does not qualify as a "motor vehicle" under OCGA § 16–8–12(a)(5)(A), but the trial court rejected that argument. The Court of Appeals affirmed the convictions, also holding, among other things, that a riding lawnmower is a "motor vehicle" under that statute. Only that issue is raised on certiorari before this Court.

2.   OCGA §§ 16–8–2 through 16–8–9 set forth a series of theft-related criminal offenses including theft by taking, which prohibits "unlawfully tak [ing] . . . any property of another with the intention of depriving him of the property," OCGA § 16–8–2. OCGA § 16–8–12 then establishes different punishment ranges for different varieties of theft. "If the property which was the subject of the theft exceeded $500.00 in value," the penalty is "imprisonment for not less than one nor more than ten years or, in the discretion of the trial judge, as for a misdemeanor." OCGA § 16–8–12(a)(1). This was the "felony theft by taking" offense of which Harris was convicted in Count 2.

OCGA § 16–8–12(a)(5) provides, in relevant part and with emphasis supplied, as follows:

> (A) The provisions of paragraph (1) of this subsection notwithstanding, if the property which was the subject of the theft was a *motor vehicle* or was a *motor vehicle* part or component which exceeded $100.00 in value . . . , by imprisonment for not less than one nor more than ten years or, in the discretion of the trial judge, as for a misdemeanor; provided, however, that any person who is convicted of a second or subsequent offense under this paragraph shall be punished by imprisonment for not less than one year nor more than 20 years.

(B) Subsequent offenses committed under this paragraph, including those which may have been committed after prior felony convictions unrelated to this paragraph, shall be punished as provided in Code Section 17–10–7.

This is the "motor vehicle theft" of which Harris was convicted in Count 1. It applies only if the stolen property was a "motor vehicle" or a "motor vehicle part or component which exceeded $100.00 in value," although the penalty differs from that for felony theft by taking only for repeat violators or for thefts of motor vehicles or parts worth between $100 and $500.

3.   In deciding whether the riding lawnmower that Harris stole is such a "motor vehicle," we begin with the ordinary meaning of that phrase, which is not a term of art or a technical term. See OCGA § 1–3–1(b) ("In all interpretations of statutes, the ordinary signification shall be applied to all words, except words of art or words connected with a particular trade or subject matter, which shall have the signification attached to them by experts in such trade or with reference to such subject matter."). A riding lawnmower capable of carrying a person is certainly a "vehicle," in the broad sense in which that single word is commonly used. See Webster's New World College Dictionary (2005 ed.) (Webster's Dictionary) (defining "vehicle" to include "any device or contrivance for carrying or conveying persons or objects, esp. over land or in space, as an automobile, bicycle, sled, or spacecraft"). A riding lawnmower is also a "vehicle with a motor," as are a huge range of mechanized vehicles from children's battery-powered mini-cars to mopeds, automobiles, trucks, trains, ships, and space shuttles. If an expansive phrase such as "a vehicle with a motor" were used in OCGA § 16–8–12(a)(5)(A), as occurs in a few other places in the Code, see, e.g., OCGA § 16–5–44.1(a)(2) (" '[m]otor vehicle' means any vehicle which is self-propelled"), this would be an easy case.

But the two-word phrase used in OCGA § 16–8–12(a)(5)(A)—"motor vehicle"—has a narrower connotation. A "motor vehicle" is commonly understood to mean a self-propelled vehicle with wheels that is designed to be used, or is ordinarily used, to transport people or property on roads. That is the dictionary definition of the term. See Webster's Dictionary (defining "motor vehicle" as "a vehicle on wheels, having its own motor and not running in rails or tracks, *for use on streets or highways; esp., an automobile, truck, or bus*" (emphasis supplied)). Not surprisingly, that is also how a large number of Georgia statutes specifically define the term, although the precise wording of the various iterations may differ.

By this ordinary meaning, a riding lawnmower is *not* a "motor vehicle." To be sure, a riding lawnmower is *capable* of transporting people or property and of driving on the street for short stretches, but that is not what the machine is designed for or how it is normally used—there being little grass to mow on streets, and there being faster and less noisy ways of moving people and property around. The parties have identified only one other court that has considered whether a riding lawnmower qualifies as a "motor vehicle" in the theft context, and that court reached the same conclusion. . . .

4.   Looking beyond the specific provision at issue to the statutory scheme as a whole only confirms this interpretation. The General Assembly did not specifically define the term "motor vehicle" in the theft article or the criminal title of the Georgia Code or in the few general definitions in OCGA § 1–3–3. The term "motor vehicle" is used hundreds of times in many contexts throughout the Code, often without definition; where a specific definition is provided, as noted previously, it usually, although not invariably, corresponds to the term's ordinary meaning.

The entire Title 40 of the Code is labeled "Motor Vehicles and Traffic," and it includes at its outset a set of detailed definitions for many vehicle-related terms. Although those definitions are introduced with the phrase "[a]s used in this title," they are the formulations to which both parties direct our attention, to which the Court of Appeals has cited in interpreting the theft article, and to which some sections of the Criminal Code that use the term "motor vehicle" expressly refer for a definition, see, e.g., OCGA §§ 16–6–13.2 (provision on forfeiture of motor vehicles used in pimping and pandering, defining " '[m]otor vehicle' or 'vehicle' " as "any motor vehicle as defined in Code Section 40–1–1"); 16–9–70 (same, in provision on criminal use of an article with an altered identification mark). It is therefore worth some analysis of the definitions in Title 40.

Reflecting the word's ordinary meaning, Title 40 defines "vehicle" very broadly, to mean "every device in, upon, or by which any person or property *is or may be transported or drawn upon a highway,* excepting devices used exclusively upon stationary rails or tracks." OCGA § 40–1–1(75) (emphasis supplied). Although Harris argues to the contrary, a riding lawnmower is a "vehicle" by this definition, as most people have at some time seen a riding lawnmower transporting a person upon a highway, if only to get the device around a barrier or from one side of the street to another. Title 40 then appears to define "[m]otor vehicle" broadly, to mean "every vehicle which is self-propelled other than an electric personal assistive mobility device (EPAMD)." OCGA § 40–1–1(33). Reading that provision in isolation, as the State urges us to do, a riding lawnmower would be a "motor vehicle," as it is a "vehicle which is self-propelled" (and is not an EPAMD), or, to use the similar phrase discussed previously, it is a "vehicle with a motor."

However, if we are to look to OCGA § 40–1–1 for guidance, then we should read all of the definitions contained in that section together, and a set of vehicles that would otherwise qualify as "motor vehicles" is carved out of that category, leaving the term with its more natural connotation:

" 'Special mobile equipment' means every vehicle not designed or used *primarily* for the transportation of persons or property and only *incidentally* operated or moved over a highway, including but not limited to: ditch-digging apparatus, well-boring apparatus, and road construction and maintenance machinery such as asphalt spreaders, bituminous mixers, bucket loaders, *tractors other than truck tractors,* ditchers, leveling graders, finishing machines, motor graders, road rollers, scarifiers, earth-moving carryalls and scrapers, power shovels and drag lines, and self-propelled cranes and earth-moving equipment. The term does not include house trailers, dump trucks, truck mounted transit mixers, cranes or shovels, or other vehicles *designed for* the transportation of persons or property to which machinery has been attached."

OCGA § 40–1–1(59) (emphasis supplied).

With this definition, the General Assembly recognized that some "vehicles which are self-propelled" are not designed for or ordinarily used to transport persons or property and are not ordinarily used on the road—even if such vehicles are able to do so or are used incidentally to do so. A riding lawnmower fits easily within this definition, as a riding lawnmower is closely akin to a "tractor" with a mowing attachment; moreover, like much of the construction equipment listed in OCGA § 40–1–1(59), riding lawnmowers are used primarily to work along and around highways, not to move people or goods on highways. Accordingly, if in interpreting OCGA § 16–8–12 we look to OCGA § 40–1–1, the definition there that most closely applies to riding lawnmowers is "special mobile equipment" rather than simply "motor vehicle."

This understanding of the interaction between the term "motor vehicle" as used in OCGA § 16–8–12 and the definitions in OCGA § 40–1–1 is bolstered by the "Chop Shop" Act, OCGA §§ 16–8–80 through 16–8–86, which is also part of Chapter 8 of the Criminal Code. In the Chop Shop Act's definitions section, OCGA § 16–8–82(2), the General Assembly again used the term "motor vehicle," but needed to define it specifically to reach some items that would otherwise be excluded from the ordinary meaning of that term and would be "special mobile equipment" under OCGA § 40–1–1. The definition of "motor vehicle" therefore begins in a way that mirrors the definitions of "vehicle" and "motor vehicle" in OCGA § 40–1–1(75) and (33), but then it *adds* language to include the type of construction, farm, and other machinery—like riding lawnmowers—that otherwise would be excluded from coverage by the ordinary meaning of "motor vehicle" and the definition of "special mobile equipment":

" 'Motor vehicle' includes every device in, upon, or by which any person or property is or may be transported or drawn upon a highway [cf. OCGA § 40–1–1(75)] which is self-propelled or which may be connected to and towed by a self-propelled device [cf. OCGA § 40–1–1(33)] *and also includes any and all other land based devices which are self-propelled but which are not designed for use upon a highway, including, but not limited to, farm machinery and construction equipment* [cf. OCGA § 40–1–1(59)]."

OCGA § 16–8–82(2) (emphasis and bracketed material supplied).

These legislative distinctions also make some sense. What most distinguishes the theft of a "motor vehicle" from the theft of other property is not its value or its ability to be easily escaped *with*, as many items are more valuable or more easily loaded into the back of a van and driven away. What makes motor vehicles, as that term is properly understood, most worthy of specialized treatment is that they are an unusual type of personal property which, once stolen, can be readily escaped *in*. A thief can steal and escape quickly in an automobile, a motorcycle, a truck, or even a four-wheeler, but not on a riding lawnmower, asphalt spreader, or skid steer. The Chop Shop Act, which is of more recent vintage, is more focused on the marketability of already-stolen vehicles and their parts, which may include vehicles of large value (like construction and farm equipment) even if those vehicles are more difficult to steal in the first place.

Similarly, in another provision of the Criminal Code, motor vehicle hijacking (commonly referred to as "carjacking"), where the ability to easily escape in a stolen vehicle might otherwise reinforce the ordinary meaning of "motor vehicle," the General Assembly again found it necessary to *expressly* define the term to be broader and to convey the intent to cover *all* vehicles with a motor. See OCGA § 16–5–44.1(a)(2) ("As used in this Code section: . . . 'motor vehicle' means any vehicle which is self-propelled.").

5.   The dissenting opinion would interpret a riding lawnmower to be a "motor vehicle," as that term is used in the motor vehicle theft statute, because a riding lawnmower comes within the specific definitions of "motor vehicle" used in the chop shop and carjacking statutes, which are also theft-related offenses in Title 16, and because, the dissent argues, criminal theft statutes are designed to "protect individuals from having their personal property *taken*." This analysis is misguided, however, in several ways.

First and most fundamentally, the dissent entirely ignores the ordinary meaning of the term "motor vehicle," a term the General Assembly elected not to define in some other way in OCGA § 16–8–12(a)(5)(A) or in the theft article or the criminal title generally. It also disregards the definitions of the term predominantly employed throughout the Code, including but by no means limited to in Title 40, that confirm the ordinary meaning of the term.

Second, it is illogical to conclude that a term used in OCGA § 16–8–12(a)(5)(A) without specific definition must be interpreted more broadly because of two different and more expansive definitions of the same term used in two other statutes that were enacted some time later. Indeed, if the term "motor vehicle" as used in *any* criminal theft statute clearly means "any vehicle which is self-propelled," it would have been unnecessary for the General Assembly to specifically define the term in that way in the later-enacted carjacking statute—or to define the term in yet another way in the Chop Shop Act. The dissent does not explain which of those two definitions is the one supposedly applicable to OCGA § 16–8–12(a)(5)(A). Moreover, its view that the term *already meant* what the General Assembly later used many words to define would render those many words surplusage, in violation of another fundamental canon of statutory construction. . . .

Finally, saying that the criminal theft statutes are designed to protect individuals from having their personal property taken provides little support to the argument that a riding lawnmower is a "motor vehicle" for purposes of the motor vehicle theft provision. Under the theft by taking statute, OCGA § 16–8–2, and other general criminal theft statutes, it is a crime to steal a riding lawnmower or any other personal property. The penalty provisions in OCGA § 16–8–12 and the substantive and penalty provisions of the more specific statutes in the theft article obviously apply to more limited sets of situations and items, and they should not be read to reach beyond what their text says.

. . . .

7. It might be contended that the answer to the question presented is not crystal clear, as suggested by the length of this opinion. But to the extent that, after applying the usual tools of statutory construction, it is uncertain or ambiguous whether OCGA § 16–8–12(a)(5)(A) applies to a riding lawnmower, the rule of lenity would require us to give the benefit of that doubt to the accused.

The General Assembly may of course expressly define "motor vehicle" more broadly, but we are not at liberty to do so. For these reasons, we hold that a riding lawnmower is not a "motor vehicle" as that term is used in the motor vehicle theft statute.

. . . .

All the Justices concur, except THOMPSON, HINES, and MELTON, JJ., who dissent.

MELTON, JUSTICE, dissenting.

This case involves the crime of theft. In the context of *theft* within Title 16 of the Georgia Code, the legislature has specifically defined the term "motor vehicle" broadly enough to encompass a riding lawnmower. The majority, however, erroneously relies on inapplicable "motor vehicle" definitions that apply to the *use* of a vehicle on the roads, as opposed to the *theft* of a vehicle, in order to reach its intended conclusion that a riding lawnmower is not a "motor vehicle" for purposes of sentencing for theft. I therefore must respectfully dissent from the majority's erroneous conclusion that a riding lawnmower is not a "motor vehicle" for purposes of sentencing pursuant to OCGA § 16–8–12(a)(5)(A).

OCGA § 16–8–12(a)(5)(A) provides that

"if the property which was the subject of [a] *theft* was a motor vehicle or was a motor vehicle part or component which exceeded $100.00 in value . . . , [the thief shall be punished] by imprisonment for not less than one nor more than ten years or, in the discretion of the trial judge, as for a misdemeanor; provided, however, that any person who is convicted of a second or subsequent offense under this paragraph shall be punished by imprisonment for not less than one year nor more than 20 years."

(Emphasis supplied.)

Although the term "motor vehicle" is not defined in OCGA § 16–8–12(a)(5)(A), "[i]n construing [this] statute, the cardinal rule is to glean the intent of the legislature." In order to do this, we must presume that the statute was enacted by the legislature with full knowledge of the existing condition of the law and with reference to it. It is therefore to be construed in connection and *in harmony with* the existing law, and as a part of a general and uniform system of jurisprudence, and its meaning and effect is to be determined in connection, not only with the common law and the constitution, but also with reference to other statutes and the decisions of the courts.

Accordingly, because the statute at issue here deals with the punishment relating to the theft of a motor vehicle, our task in this case is to determine the consistent intent of the legislature as it relates to the definition of the term "motor vehicle" in the context of criminal theft. In this regard, the legislature has made clear elsewhere in Title 16 that, when a "motor vehicle or motor vehicle part known to be *illegally obtained by theft*" is taken to a "chop shop" in order to be sold or disposed of, a "motor vehicle" would consist of

"every device in, upon, or by which any person or property is or may be transported or drawn upon a highway which is self-propelled or which may be connected to and towed by a self-propelled device and also includes *any and all other land based devices which are self-propelled but which are not designed for use upon a highway, including, but not limited to, farm machinery and construction equipment.*"

(Emphasis supplied.) OCGA § 16–8–82(2). This definition of "motor vehicle" is obviously broad enough to encompass a riding lawnmower. Thus, if a riding lawnmower were stolen and taken to a "chop shop," it would be a "motor vehicle" for purposes of its theft and storage or dismantling at a chop shop.

Under the majority's analysis, however, a riding lawnmower would not be a "motor vehicle" if simply stolen, but would magically transform into a "motor vehicle" once taken to a chop shop for dismantling or sale. Similarly, an engine worth over $100 that was stolen from a riding lawnmower would not become a "motor vehicle part" until it was taken to a chop shop. Far from construing OCGA § 16–8–12(a)(5)(A) "in harmony with" existing pronouncements by the legislature, the majority has interpreted the statute in a manner that creates conflict and leads to an absurd result. As such, the majority's interpretation cannot stand.

OCGA § 16–5–44.1 provides even more evidence that the majority's interpretation of the term "motor vehicle" runs directly contrary to the intent of the legislature. Indeed, when a person, "while in possession of a firearm or weapon obtains a motor vehicle from the person or presence of another by force and violence[,]" that person commits the offense of hijacking a "motor vehicle." OCGA § 16–5–44.1(b). "Motor vehicle" is broadly defined here as "any vehicle which is self-propelled." OCGA § 16–5–44.1(a)(2). Again, in the context of a vehicle being stolen, the legislature has made clear that the definition of "motor vehicle" would encompass a riding lawnmower. Yet, the majority would cite this statute to reach exactly the opposite result.

Moreover, the majority directly violates well-established rules of statutory construction when it contends that it is "illogical" to consider the definitions of "motor vehicle" from the "later enacted" hijacking and chop shop statutes when trying to discern the definition of "motor vehicle" in the context of theft. "Indeed, the courts are not only to be guided by the General Assembly's last expression on a subject, but *the latest declaration controls*." Thus, again, these latest declarations from the legislature on the definition of "motor vehicle" in the context of theft only further support the notion that the legislature clearly intended to treat a riding lawnmower as a "motor vehicle" for purposes of theft. The majority, however, would interpret these latest and controlling definitions of the term "motor vehicle" in a manner that would reach a result that is directly contrary to the legislature's expressed intent.

The problems with the majority arise from its reliance on Title 40 of the Georgia Code, as opposed to the aforementioned Georgia criminal statutes dealing directly with the theft of motor vehicles, in its attempt to glean the legislature's intent with respect to the definition of the term "motor vehicle" in the context of motor vehicle theft. Title 40 has no applicability here, as the Code sections therein relating to "Motor Vehicles and Traffic" are designed to protect the public by regulating the *use* of vehicles on the road. They are not designed to protect individuals from having their personal property *taken,* as the criminal theft statutes are specifically designed to do. Indeed, our focus in this case is not on the thief's potential ability to drive away in a stolen car as the majority contends, but on the thief's act of stealing the property of another. The legislature has specifically included a broad definition of "motor vehicle" in the criminal theft context in order to accomplish the ends or protecting individuals from having their personal property stolen.

. . . .

Consistent with the Court of Appeals' conclusion, but contrary to the Court of Appeals' and the majority's analysis, the legislature has made clear that, in the context of criminal theft, a riding lawnmower is in fact a "motor vehicle." I would therefore affirm the judgment of the Court of Appeals, but only by following the clear intent of the legislature that both the majority and the Court of Appeals have ignored.

. . . .

B. ARGUMENTS FROM LEGAL TEXTS: THE TEXTUAL TOOLS OF INTERPRETATION

1. THE TEXT OF THE STATUTE AT ISSUE

The first place to look when considering how to interpret and apply a statute is, not surprisingly, to the text of the statute itself. This is not only true according to self-described textualists; everyone agrees that we must begin with the text. Indeed, nearly all judges agree that if the text is unambiguous, the inquiry goes not further.

The courts have developed many tools—remember, these are often referred to as "rules," "doctrines," or "canons"—for interpreting statutes that focus on the statutory text. We consider the most important of these textual tools in this subsection.

There are three critical things to keep in mind when trying to understand and apply these rules. The first is that the terms "rule" and "doctrine" are used loosely. These are not like many rules in sports, where if you know the relevant rule for a particular scenario, you can conclusively apply it and move on (for example, if a batter hits a baseball over the wall in the outfield in between the foul poles and no defender catches the ball, it is a home run). In the statutory interpretation context, individual rules will rarely be dispositive; no single rule of statutory interpretation is absolute. Indeed, sometimes two rules may apply and lead to diametrically opposed results. When different tools point to different outcomes, judges will try to identify the most cogent and coherent arguments, often falling back on theories of interpretation or substantive values. It is therefore the job of the interpreter—in your case, the lawyer—to generate an understanding of the statute or an argument about its meaning using all of the textual tools of interpretation (and other kinds of tools besides, which we will consider later).

One problem with this is that the more flexibility we allow in applying the tools, the more difficult the job of statutory drafting and interpretation becomes. Can you see why this is the case? Which theories of interpretation do you think tend to treat these rules as more "rule-like"? Which do you think allow for greater flexibility?

The second critical point to remember is that while these rules may sound complicated—some have fancy Latin names that are difficult to pronounce—they usually capture and reflect our normal intuitions about how to understand everyday language. Try to match the rules identified below with your intuitions. This may help you to understand, remember, and correctly apply them in the future.

Third, as you consider the rules identified below, notice the order in which they are presented. Rules that relate to the meaning of individual words or terms are discussed first, then those that relate to the surrounding words and syntax, then those that relate to the larger statutory scheme, and finally those that relate to other legal texts.

When confronted with a question of statutory interpretation, it is useful to think in this order. Imagine that you are looking at the ambiguous statute through a microscope. Look through the most powerful lens first, the one that zooms all the way in on the relevant words in question. Next, zoom out a bit and look at the immediate context in which the words appear. Next, zoom out further to look at the entire statute. Last, zoom out still further to look at other legal texts that may bear on the meaning of the ambiguous statute in question. (As we will see later, you will continue to zoom out even beyond legal texts, but for now we are considering only textual arguments.) The best legal arguments are those that operate at all, or at least multiple, levels of focus. This is also usually the order in which briefs and judicial opinions are written—think back to the lawnmower case.

(A) The Meaning of Words

Very often, a statute's ambiguity is due to a question about the definition of a single word or term in the statute. For example, in the "No Vehicles" hypothetical, one thing we really want to know is, what is the meaning of "vehicle" as used in this statute? In Title VII of the Civil Rights Act, how is "discriminate" used?

Of course, if the statute itself defines a word, that definition—even if odd or counterintuitive—trumps any alternative definition. But when important words are undefined in the statute or the statutory definition is inconclusive, courts have adopted several rules of interpretation.

• Ordinary Meaning

The first rule is that words are to be understood according to their ordinary meaning. This is based on the assumption (and perhaps the hope and admonition) that legislators use words in their typical way.

Example. In *Shlahtichman v. 1–800 Contacts, Inc.*, 615 F.3d 794 (7th Cir. 2012), the Seventh Circuit held that a statute limiting the credit card information that companies could "print" on receipts did not apply to online receipts sent by email because the term "print" ordinarily implies something that is recorded in tangible form on paper.

Of course, the ordinary meaning rule has limits. Sometimes different people use the same words in different ways, so any word may have more than one ordinary meaning. Indeed, often the source of ambiguity in a statute is that the ordinary meaning is itself contested. For example, for some people, the ordinary meaning of the word "shoe" would include a sandal, whereas for others, it does not.

Similarly, the ordinary meaning of words or phrases may depend on context. Thus, for instance, a request that you "pick up my daughter" may mean "physically lift my daughter" or "retrieve my daughter." The phrase "pick up" would mean something different to you if the daughter were sitting in a puddle than if she were off at daycare.

For these reasons, the ordinary meaning rule alone will not always resolve even those statutory ambiguities that relate to the meaning of simple words or phrases.

- Dictionary Meaning

Judges often resort to dictionaries to understand the meaning of statutory terms.

Example. In *United States v. Costello*, 666 F.3d 1040 (7th Cir. 2012), which you will read later in this chapter, the court consulted the dictionary to determine whether an American woman who allowed her Mexican boyfriend (who was in the country illegally) to live with her had "harbored" him.

Judges often maintain that the most relevant dictionaries are those that were current as of the time that the statute was written—because these reflect then-prevalent usage—but courts have not developed any hard-and-fast rules concerning which dictionaries are canonical, and they will often cite to dictionaries that were not contemporaneous to the statute's passage.

Sometimes judges will look to dictionaries as repositories of ordinary meaning. This makes some sense. After all, dictionaries are written to reflect or prescribe how words are used in society, so they may be viewed as capturing the ordinary meaning. Therefore, it can be helpful to think of dictionaries as potential sources for an ordinary meaning argument.

In other cases, however, a dictionary definition may be pitted against the judge's intuition concerning a term's ordinary meaning. For instance, the dictionary definition of the word "vehicle" may be "a thing used to convey people or goods," and thus include skateboards, tricycles, shopping carts, and even a prosthetic leg. However, most people probably do not typically think of these as vehicles. In such cases, a judge may have to choose between what she perceives to be the ordinary meaning and the dictionary meaning.

Although it is obvious why judges would look to dictionaries, the practice is not without controversy and limitation. Some judges (usually in dissenting opinions) and scholars maintain that it is too easy to cherry-pick favorable definitions. After all, there are multiple dictionaries to choose from, and even a single entry in a dictionary may offer several alternative definitions. A judge who selects a single definition from among several possibilities as *the* authoritative definition may thus be cloaking her preferences in neutral-sounding terms.

For these reasons, while dictionaries are certainly useful resources, lawyers and judges rarely rely on them alone, particularly where both sides to a case can muster arguments based on the dictionary or ordinary meaning. Judges often caution that they will not adhere slavishly to dictionary definitions. Dictionaries simply serve as tools to be used in the service of a larger, well-crafted argument.

• Legal Meaning

Some words and phrases are legal terms of art or have acquired an established legal meaning through longstanding use at common law or in other legal contexts. Sometimes these legal definitions are consistent with ordinary usage and dictionary definitions, but sometimes they differ in important ways. The courts typically (but not always) hold that a term's established legal meaning trumps the ordinary or dictionary meaning.

Example. In *Gilbert v. United States*, 370 U.S. 650 (1962), the Court referred to the common law meaning of the term "forgery" to determine the meaning of the term as used in a statute. The Court held that a person who endorses a check made out to another by falsely claiming that he is an agent of the payee is not guilty of forgery. The person made a false claim, but he did not "forge" anything under the legal meaning of that term.

Note that courts sometime deviate from this rule if the judges have reason to believe that the legislature did not intend or understand that the traditional legal meaning would control.

Example. The traditional legal meaning of the word "person" typically includes corporations and other entities (though not a sovereign). Therefore, courts generally read the word "person" in a statute to apply to artificial persons. However, in *Rowland v. California Men's Colony*, 506 U.S. 194 (1993), the Court held that only a natural person could file for *in forma pauperis* status in court under a statute allowing some "persons" to proceed in that manner. Likewise, in *FCC v. AT&T*, 131 S. Ct. 1177 (2011), the Court held that the statutory term "personal privacy" only applied to natural persons; that is, corporations and other entities do not have "personal privacy."

The reasoning behind what we can call the legal meaning rule is that Congress is said to be aware of legal meaning and therefore uses terms consistently with their legal meaning unless it expressly states otherwise. It is likely a fiction that legislators know what a statutory term's common law or legal meaning is (indeed, they may not even know that the term actually appears in the statute). Can you articulate some alternative reasons why this rule may nevertheless make sense?

• Technical Meaning

Finally, courts will sometimes consider a term's technical meaning, especially if the statute is directed to a particular and specialized audience or subject matter. However, this rule is not often applied.

Example. In *Nix v. Hedden*, 149 U.S. 304 (1893), a very famous and fun old case, the Court considered whether a tomato was a fruit or a vegetable for the purposes of a statute imposing a higher tariff on vegetables. The Court considered the technical meaning of the word "fruit," which botanists tell us includes tomatoes, but held that because people ordinarily include tomatoes among vegetables, the higher tariff applied. This brings to mind the old distinction between knowledge and wisdom: knowledge is knowing that a tomato is a fruit; wisdom is knowing not to put a tomato in your fruit salad.

(B) The Meaning of Words from Their Immediate Context

For reasons we have discussed, sometimes the meaning and proper application of a statutory term will remain in doubt even after resorting to the sources of definitions discussed above. To develop an understanding of the questionable term, courts will also consider the immediate context in which the term appears.

Once again, this reflects the normal human intuition that we can understand words from their context. If someone asks you to "pick up my daughter from daycare," you immediately understand that he is not asking you to physically lift her off of the ground, but rather to retrieve her from a particular place. Focusing too much on the specific words "pick up" would not have helped you at all, but by zooming out with the proverbial microscope to the surrounding words they become quite clear and unambiguous.

In this subsection we consider several rules of interpretation that relate to the immediate context in which an ambiguous term appears.

• The Rule Against Surplusage

Simply stated, the rule against surplusage is that every word and provision in a statute must be given effect. That is, every word and provision adds something new and is not merely duplicative or redundant of things that already appear in the statute.

Question: In the previous sentence, did every term add something new, or is the word "redundant," well, redundant? If you believe that it is redundant, then does the rule against surplusage actually reflect normal human language and intuition? Is this rule consistent with the general principle that the textual rules of interpretation reflect the normal practices of language comprehension? If not, then why do you think judges adopt this rule? And do you see why some commentators and judges are skeptical of the rule?

Example. In *Gregory v. Dillards*, 494 F.3d 694 (8th Cir. 2007) (rev'd *en banc* on other grounds, 565 F.3d 464 (2009), the court held that a state statute prohibiting discrimination in "any place of public accommodation" applied to retail establishments. The court reasoned that although retailers were not listed among the examples of "public accommodations," the phrase preceding the examples, "including, but not limited to," would be rendered surplusage if it did not apply to retailers.

As usual, the rule against surplusage is not always dispositive. Judges recognize that legislation sometimes includes redundant words and thus that some terms cannot be given independent meaning. In addition, when applying the rule against surplusage would violate the plain meaning rule, the court will be especially hesitant to do so.

- *Noscitur a Sociis*

The Latin phrase *noscitur a sociis* means "it is known by its associates." According to this rule, sometimes referred to as the "birds of a feather flock together" rule of interpretation, an ambiguous word in a list may be understood by reference to the words around it. As is typical of these rules, *noscitur a sociis* is consistent with the ordinary manner in which we interpret language. If I say, "I need to buy glasses," I could mean drinking glasses or eyeglasses. However, if I say, "I need to buy glasses, plates, bowls, and silverware," you would intuitively apply *noscitur a sociis* to determine that I am referring to drinking glasses.

This rule is particularly applicable to statutes that include lists in which most of the terms are clear but one is ambiguous. Therefore, it is often implicated in statutes governing tariffs and other taxes.

Example. In *Jewelpak v. United States*, 131 F. Supp. 2d 100 (C.I.T. 2002), the judge considered whether presentation boxes used to ship, store, and display items of jewelry should be classified for the purposes of assessing tariffs as "jewelry boxes," as the government maintained, or as "packaging," as the importer maintained. The court first noted that either classification could apply to the boxes at issue. In the face of this apparent ambiguity, the court looked to the surrounding words in the statute for guidance. The items listed along with jewelry box included suitcases, briefcases, cigarette cases, and musical instrument cases, among others. From this, the judge concluded that the relevant question is whether the boxes at issue are suitable for reuse and long term use, which was the common thread linking all of the items.

Note that this rule may sometimes be in tension with the rule against surplusage. This is because *noscitur a sociis* tends to limit the meaning of ambiguous terms (because they must share something in common with the surrounding terms), whereas the rule against surplusage tends to be more expansive (because the ambiguous term should not be so similar to the surrounding terms as to be redundant).

Example. Consider again *Gregory v. Dillards*, the example used above to illustrate the rule against surplusage. The relevant statute prohibited discrimination by "places of public accommodation," which was defined as "all places or businesses holding out to the general public, goods, services, privileges, facilities, advantages or accommodations . . . or such public places providing food, shelter, recreation and amusement. . . ." Can you articulate an argument using *noscitur a sociis* that retailers are *not* covered? Hint: Begin by identifying the ambiguous term in the definition that could arguably apply to retailers.

- *Ejusdem Generis*

Ejusdem generis is a close cousin to *noscitur a sociis*. Under *ejusdem generis*, generic or "catch-all" terms appearing at the end of a list (or sometimes at the beginning) are to be understood by reference to the specific terms in the list. Again, this reflects everyday intuition. If a farmer asks his employee to "bring in the horses, sheep, cattle, and other animals," the employee would immediately understand that the farmer is referring to the livestock on the farm rather than to the flock of wild geese that are meandering around the property. Likewise, he would not think to herd in all of the butterflies, even though butterflies are certainly "animals."

Example. In *Economy Cover Corp. v. United States*, 411 F. Supp. 783 (Cust. Ct. 1976), the United States Customs Court considered whether certain protective suit covers should be classified as "like furnishings" for the purpose of taxation. The relevant statutory provision applied the tax to "[c]urtains and drapes . . . ; napkins, table covers, mats, scarves, runners, doilies, centerpieces, antimacassars, and furniture slipcovers; and like furnishings. . . ." The court applied *ejusdem generis* and concluded that the commonality between the listed items is that they are all used to ornamentally or functionally enhance or protect the home or articles that are used in a home, and that suit covers do not share this quality.

Example. In *Keenan v. Bowers*, 91 F. Supp. 771 (E.D.S.C. 1950), the court considered whether a diamond ring that had been accidentally flushed down the toilet could be deducted from taxes as a "casualty." The relevant statute allowed for a deduction if the loss of property "arises from fires, storms, shipwrecks, or other casualty, or from theft." The court acknowledged that, in the abstract, the term "casualty" *could* apply to flushing the ring down the toilet. However, in applying *ejusdem generis*, the judge held that to qualify as a "casualty" within the meaning of the statute, there must be a sudden or destructive force that led to the loss.

In his estimation, accidentally flushing a ring down the toilet is not similar in kind to a loss due to fire, storm, or shipwreck.

The difference between *noscitur a sociis* and *ejusdem generis* is quite simple, though even judges sometimes confuse the two. The former applies when the ambiguous term is a specific one, like "glasses." The latter applies when the ambiguous term is a generic one, like "other animals."

As with *noscitur a sociis*, *ejusdem generis* favors narrow interpretations of ambiguous terms, so it is also sometimes in tension with the more expansive rule against surplusage. It is easy to see why if you return to the example of our farmer. *Ejusdem generis* made us think that he intended for the employee to bring in other livestock. But what if there are no other farm animals on the farm? The rule against surplusage would tell the employee that the farmer must mean *something* by the phrase "and other animals." He probably still does not mean the wild geese and butterflies, but maybe he is referring to the pet dog and cat, which probably do not share the quality of "livestockness" with the enumerated animals but do share the quality of living on the farm or of being domesticated.

Example. Consider yet again *Gregory v. Dillards*. After providing the basic definition of "places of public accommodation," the statute offers several examples that would qualify. It introduces these examples by stating "including but not limited to" and then lists several categories of places that qualify, such as hotels, restaurants, gas stations, theaters, and several others. None of the examples listed seems especially similar to retailers. Can you identify an argument using *ejusdem generis* (or something similar to it) that retailers are not covered? Hint: "Including but not limited to" is similar to a catch-all phrase like "and other places."

In general, the trick when arguing a case that implicates *ejusdem generis* is to come up with an alternative commonality among the specific words from that offered by your opponent. Depending on which side you are arguing, you will want to come up with a narrower or broader commonality. Can you come up with two alternative meanings of the phrase "including but not limited to" based on *ejusdem generis*, one that applies to retailers and one that does not? This trick also works for *noscitur a sociis*.

- *Expressio Unius est Exclusio Alterius*

This rule of interpretation, basically translated as "the expression of one thing excludes the alternatives," is essentially an argument from negative implication. If I specify that you may drink water in class, you might reasonably conclude that I am not giving you permission to drink soda or eat spaghetti and meatballs. The rule is commonly used in statutory interpretation under the assumption that the legislature considered its words carefully, and in choosing to state one thing, it deliberately intended to exclude things that are unstated.

Example. A state constitution provided that superior court judges must be elected by both branches of the legislature. The legislature passed a statute allowing the governor to appoint a temporary superior court judge. In *State ex rel. M'Cready v. Hunt*, 2 Hill 1 (S.C. Ct. App. 1834), the court declared the statute unconstitutional, reasoning that because the constitution provided for one specific way to appoint judges, no alternative method could be adopted.

Although this rule is used fairly often, it is also rejected by courts in at least as many cases. After all, if I tell my daughter that she may not eat the candy bar on the counter, she would not reasonably conclude that she may eat the one in the cabinet. Likewise, a sign that says "please do not pee in the pool" does not tacitly give permission to have a bowel movement in the pool. In determining whether to apply *expressio unius*, courts may consider whether there is reason to believe that the legislature considered and rejected alternatives, as well as whether the legislature meant for the statute to cover all situations.

Example. In *Abdullah v. American Airlines, Inc.*, 969 F. Supp. 337 (D. Virgin Islands 1997), the court considered whether the Federal Aviation Act, governing aviation safety, preempted state aviation safety laws. The plaintiff argued from *expressio unius* that state laws were not preempted because a separate statute, the Airline Deregulation Act, stated specifically that federal laws governing aviation rates, routes, and services preempted state laws, but it did not say anything about state aviation safety laws being preempted. The court rejected this application of *expressio unius* because there was no evidence that Congress meant for the Airline Deregulation Act, which was focused on rate, route, and services deregulation, to have any bearing on the Federal Aviation Act.

The upshot from all of this is that it is necessary to apply this rule with care and, as always, not to rely on it alone.

*   Syntactic and Semantic Rules

Syntax and semantics can also serve as contextual guides to statutory meaning and application.

First, the grammar canon provides that statutory terms should be understood in a manner consistent with proper English grammar. That is, we should assume that legislators are literate, and thus that legislation includes proper grammar rather than grammatical mistakes. For example, courts assume that there is subject-verb agreement, noun-pronoun agreement, male-female pronoun consistency (though courts nearly always apply the word "he" in statutes to both sexes), and a meaningful distinction between the words "and" and "or."

Second, with some exceptions, courts typically distinguish between the words "may," which is permissive, and "shall," which is mandatory.

Third, the word "including" is generally interpreted to introduce a list of examples. Therefore, the list that follows is not exclusive.

Fourth, courts usually apply the last-antecedent rule, which states that qualifying words or phrases refer only to the last antecedent in the sentence. For example, if a local ordinance prohibits cutting down "old growth trees and pine trees with landscape significance," then *all* old growth trees are off-limits, whether or not they have landscape significance. The term "landscape significance" only modifies the last antecedent, namely pine trees. How would you rewrite the ordinance in such a way as to apply the "landscape significance" qualifier to both kinds of trees?

However, courts sometimes apply the series qualifier rule, which would lead to the opposite result. Under this rule, a qualifying phrase at the end of a list qualifies *all* items in the list.

How should courts choose whether to apply the last-antecedent rule or the series qualifier rule in any given case?

(C) The Broader Statutory Context: The Whole Act Rule

Thus far, we have focused on ambiguous words themselves and the immediate statutory context in which they appear. It is now time to zoom out a bit more with our microscope and consider how the entire statutory text in which the ambiguous words appear can help to resolve questions of statutory interpretation. Under the Whole Act Rule, a statute as a whole should be assumed to be coherent and consistent.

This rule is often defended on the grounds that the legislature enacts the statute as a whole and therefore means for it to be internally coherent. As we have seen, however, the legislature is often less than completely careful with its language, and the more complex a statute is, the messier and less consistent it is likely to be. After all, different provisions are drafted and inserted into a bill by different people, sometimes with different agendas, and at different times. Courts nevertheless apply the Whole Act Rule where possible; that is, when they can make sense of a statutory provision in a way that renders the statute consistent, they will do so. Can you defend this? Also, how should courts treat statutory provisions within the same statute that are enacted at different times, as when a statute is amended at a later time?

There are several different applications of the broad Whole Act Rule.

• The Rules of Consistent Usage and Meaningful Variation

Courts typically assume that a statutory term has the same meaning everywhere it is used within a statute. Therefore, if a word can be understood based on its context in one provision, that same meaning applies when the term is used in a different provision. As usual, this presumption is rebuttable based on context. (Consider: The United States Constitution uses the word "state" in four different, inconsistent ways.)

Example. In *B.A.A. v. Chief Medical Officer*, 421 N.W.2d 118 (Iowa 1988), the Iowa Supreme Court held that because a finding of "serious mental impairment" in one statutory provision required a showing of dangerousness, the use of the same term in a different provision of the same statute also required a showing of dangerousness.

Courts also assume the reverse. That is, when a statute uses different terms, the presumption is that the terms mean different things. Otherwise, the legislature would have used the same term.

Example. In *Mississippi Poultry Association v. Madigan*, 31 F.3d 293 (5th Cir. 1994), the statute at issue contained two provisions regarding the safety requirements governing the sale of poultry. One provision provided that foreign poultry products imported into the United States had to have been processed in facilities under conditions that were the "the same as" the conditions imposed by federal law for similar poultry products produced in the United States. Elsewhere, the statute provided that states may impose their own requirements on poultry products that are produced and will only be sold within the state, so long as the state's requirements are "at least equal to" federal standards. Because the statute used two different terms—"the same as" and "at least equal to"—to describe the standards for *foreign* producers and *state* producers, the relevant administrative agency was not permitted to interpret the "same as" language to mean "at least equal to." In other words, these two phrases had to have different substantive meanings.

- The Rule Against Surplusage (Again)

You were previously introduced to the rule against surplusage. In that earlier discussion, we considered the rule as it applied within the immediate context surrounding an ambiguous term. The rule also applies in the broader statutory context, that is, across provisions within a single statute. Stated simply, if one reading of an ambiguous term would render something else in the statute meaningless, that reading should be rejected.

Example. Consider again the *Mississippi Poultry* case. The court held that if the administrative agency only held poultry products produced in foreign countries to the "at least equal to" standard, the language "the same as" and the provision in which it appeared would effectively be surplusage.

- Exceptions and Provisos

Exceptions and provisos are to be interpreted narrowly.

Example. In Wisconsin, employees may not file personal injury lawsuits against coworkers for injuries sustained on the job. Instead, their only recourse is through the workers' compensation system. However, the statute provided an exception that allowed an injured employee to file a suit against a "coemployee for negligent operation of a motor vehicle." In *McNeil v. Hansen*, 2007 WI 56 (2007), the court considered whether a coworker who turned the key on a non-working car that was being repaired and caused injury to the plaintiff had "operated" a motor vehicle. The court concluded that because the general statutory scheme disfavored lawsuits against coworkers, the term "operation of a motor vehicle" must be interpreted narrowly. Consequently, it did not apply under these facts, and the plaintiff could not proceed against his coworker.

- Titles and Headings

Courts may look to titles and headings in statutes as sources of statutory meaning unless the statute explicitly provides otherwise.

Example. In *INS v. National Center for Immigrants' Rights*, 502 U.S. 183 (1991), a regulation provided that certain excludable aliens who had been arrested could be released pending a determination of deportability on a bond containing a "condition barring employment." Because the title of the regulation referred to a "condition against unauthorized employment," the Supreme Court concluded that the term "barring employment" did not prohibit those aliens who were *authorized* to work from seeking employment during release. (Note that this example comes from an administrative regulation rather than a statute, but the type of argument is the same in both contexts.)

Most courts would agree, however, that if a title or heading irreconcilably conflicts with the plain language of the statute, the plain language controls.

- Prefatory Materials

Prefatory materials, which include preambles, congressional findings, and purpose clauses, may be used to interpret an ambiguous statutory term.

Example. In *Sutton v. United Airlines, Inc.*, 527 U.S. 471 (1999), the Supreme Court found significance in a preamble to the Americans with Disabilities Act. The preamble stated that 43 million Americans had disabilities. Because many more millions suffer from poor vision, the Supreme Court concluded that myopia (nearsightedness) did not constitute a disability under the statute.

(D) Exercise: Interpreting a Statute Based on Its Text

Before moving beyond the statutory text at issue, let's consider a relatively straightforward case. As you will see, despite the case's banality (there's nothing exciting here like affirmative action!), it demonstrates that even the most boring and apparently simple cases can implicate several interpretive tools.

For the purposes of this exercise, you are a law clerk to a judge. The judge hands you a case and says, "This case is about boots and shoes. Please make sense of it."

The relevant statute places a special tariff on the importation of "[f]ootwear with outer soles made of rubber, plastics, leather or composition leather and uppers of textile materials." The statute further states that this tariff applies to "footwear of the slip-on type, that is held to the foot without the use of laces or buckles or other fasteners." Other sections of this statute apply different tariffs to "tennis shoes, basketball shoes, gym shoes, and golf shoes." Still other sections refer to "ski boots and snowboard boots."

An importer imports UGG Classic Crochet boots into the United States for sale. The government and the importer agree that UGG Classic Crochet boots are sold as boots, that they must be pulled on with the hands, that they extend above the ankle, and that they have no laces, buckles, or other fasteners.

The government maintains that these boots are subject to this tariff. However, the importer argues that term "footwear of the slip-on type" does not apply to the UGG Classic Crochet boots because they must be pulled on and thus are not of the "slip-on type."

In support of his arguments the importer asserts that the footwear industry does not consider any boots, and especially those that must be pulled on, to be of the "slip-on type." He also points to The Complete Footwear Dictionary (yes, this exists), which provides that a slip-on is "a plain but dressy pump without lacings or other fastenings, worn by either men or women. Any shoe without fastenings."

An alternative industry dictionary, The Dictionary of Shoe Industry Terminology (yes, this one exists too!), defines a slip-on as "any shoe into which the wearer merely slips the foot, held without benefit of lacing, buckles or other fastening." Finally, the Webster's Dictionary states that a slip-on is "an article of clothing that is easily slipped on or off, and may include a glove or shoe without fastening; or a garment (as a girdle) that one steps into and pulls up."

Based on this information and any other information relevant to the rules we have identified, identify all possible arguments for the government and the importer. Then decide which side should win and outline the opinion for the judge.

2.   INTERPRETATION IN LIGHT OF OTHER STATUTES

Thus far, we have considered only *intra*-textual sources of statutory meaning—that is, the words that appear in the text of the statute at issue. Not all cases presenting questions of statutory interpretation can be resolved intra-textually. The next step, therefore, is to zoom out even further and consider evidence from other statutory texts.

(A) Related Statutes

As we have previously seen, one source of meaning of ambiguous terms is the common law. Likewise, we have learned from the consistent usage rule that a single term used in multiple places within a statute should be interpreted to mean the same thing in each place.

There is an extended (and weaker) version of these rules that provides that terms used in common across different statutes should be interpreted in the same manner. This presumption can be further broken down into two different rules: the *in pari materia* rule and the borrowed statute rule.

First, the *in pari materia* rule applies when multiple statutes use identical terms or deal with related issues. In such a case, the courts typically presume that a single statutory term has the same meaning across statutes.

Thus, if an ambiguous term appears in one statute, its meaning may be clarified by reference to another statute. The context of the second statute may make it clear what the term means there. Alternatively, the courts may have already ruled as to the meaning of the term in the second statute. Either way, we may presumptively apply that interpretation to the ambiguous term at issue. More broadly stated, the *in pari materia* rule provides that related statutes should be read in harmony with one another. The more closely related the statutes are, the more strongly this presumption applies.

Example. In *R. v. Arthur*, 1 Q.B. 810 (1968), a British court considered the meaning of the word "person" in relation to an arson statute. The statute defined "aggravated arson" as an arson committed when a "person" was inside the dwelling. The defendant argued that he had not committed aggravated arson under the statute because the only person in the building was himself, and the law meant "other person." The court agreed because another statute using the term "person," the Offenses Against the Person Act, did not apply to self-mutilation or suicide.

The borrowed statute rule applies when a later statute is modeled on an earlier statute or on a similar statute from another jurisdiction. In such a case, a court will look to any authoritative judicial interpretations from the earlier-enacted legislation to interpret the later-enacted legislation. Note that the borrowed statute rule is relatively weaker than the *in pari materia* rule; that is, if the court believes that the court in the jurisdiction from which the statute was adopted was simply mistaken, it may easily reject that interpretation.

Example. In *Pope v. Brock*, 912 So. 2d 935 (Miss. 2005), the Mississippi Supreme Court followed the California Supreme Court's interpretation of a statute concerning the tolling of a statute of limitations because it was clear that the Mississippi statute was modeled on the California statute.

The traditional justification for these rules is that the legislature chooses its language carefully and is aware of the surrounding body of law when it enacts legislation. Thus, it uses a single term across legislation in the same manner. Likewise, if a legislature borrowed the language for a statute from a different jurisdiction, we assume that it was aware of and approved of the interpreting decisions from the courts in the other jurisdiction.

This intent-based claim is subject to critique. After all, it can hardly be the case that legislators are aware of terminology used in hundreds of other statutes or that they necessarily consider the judicial opinions from other jurisdictions prior to passing a statute.

Even more problematic, the *in pari materia* rule applies even where the second statute is enacted or interpreted *after* the passage of legislation at issue. How can a later-enacted or later-interpreted statute tell us anything about what the previous statute meant?

Do any of the theories of interpretation offer an alternative justification for these rules?

(B) Statutory Development

Courts will often compare a statute to its predecessor statute. If the legislature reenacted the predecessor statute without changing it, courts assume that it meant to reaffirm the previous decisions of the courts interpreting the statute. More importantly, if the legislature made substantive changes to the language of the statute, courts generally understand the changes to be significant.

Note, however, that courts will sometimes look to the legislative history (discussed below) of the new provision to determine whether the legislature's decision to change the language was purposeful. If the change in the language would effect a substantial change to the larger body of the law, but if no one in the legislature indicated such, then the court may be hesitant to read the new statute as effecting such a momentous change. Why do you suppose this is so?

In other words, courts apply the rules of consistent usage and meaningful variation as between predecessor and amended statutes, but they do so with somewhat less consistency. Why do you think that's the case?

(C) Conflicts Between Specific and General Statutes

Typically, if a specific statutory provision irreconcilably conflicts with a general statutory provision, the specific provision controls; that is, the specific provision is understood to be an exception to the general rule. The reason for this is that the specific provision represents the legislature's most careful consideration of the issue in question.

Example. In *State v. Kalvig*, 296 Minn. 395 (1973), the Supreme Court of Minnesota considered two criminal statutes that conflicted with respect to a single defendant. One statute specifically made welfare fraud a misdemeanor, while the other, which applied more broadly to theft crimes, could also have applied to the defendant, but made the alleged acts felonious. The Court held that the defendant could be charged only with a misdemeanor because the specific statute trumped the more general one.

(D) Conflicts Between Earlier- and Later-Enacted Statutes

When a later-enacted statute conflicts with an earlier-enacted statute, the more recent statute controls. The reason for this is that the more recent statute reflects the legislature's most recent decision on the issue.

Example. In *In re Estate of Winn*, 214 Ariz. 149 (2007), the Arizona Supreme Court considered a conflict between a specific provision of the Adult Protective Services Act (APSA) and a more general provision in the Arizona probate code. The court held that the APSA provision governed because it was the more recently enacted of the statutes.

This case also implicated the rule concerning specific vs. general provisions. Thus, the court held that while the probate code provision generally applied to all estates, the APSA provision controlled—it was more specific to the circumstance at hand because it applied to the administration of the estates of a specific group of people, namely incapacitated or vulnerable adults.

(E) No Repeals by Implication

Courts also maintain that later statutes cannot repeal earlier statutes merely by implication. If the legislature means to repeal an earlier-enacted statute or provision, it must do so explicitly.

There are several possible justifications for this rule. First, legislatures might be assumed to be aware of already-existing statutes, and if they intended to repeal them, they would have said so. Second, although we may not be able to assume that legislatures are *actually* aware of already-existing legislation, this rule helps to discipline them by giving them an incentive to be as clear and careful as possible (because if they mean to repeal the earlier statute but do not explicitly say so, courts will not step in to fix their mess). Third, we have an interest in clarity and stability in the law, and if legislation can easily be repealed merely by implication, then there would always be doubts about the continued viability of previous legislation anytime the legislature addresses the same subject in newer legislation. Can you match each of these justifications with a different theory of interpretation?

Example. In *United States v. Lahey Clinic Hospital*, 399 F.3d 1 (1st Cir. 2005), the court rejected an argument that certain provisions of the Medicare Act providing for an administrative process through which the government could assert that Medicare had overpaid a provider of health services impliedly repealed a federal statute giving the federal courts jurisdiction over lawsuits brought by the government.

You should immediately see the potential tension between this rule and the rule that more recent statutes trump earlier statutes. One way to resolve this tension in some cases is to restate the rule as follows: repeals by implication are strongly disfavored, but a statute or provision that directly contradicts an earlier-enacted statute or provision does serve as a repeal.

Example. In the Medicare Act case, the court was able to reconcile the Medicare Act provision with the statute providing for jurisdiction in federal courts. Namely, the two provisions simply allowed for two different means of redress.

Example. In contrast, in *Washington v. State*, 30 P.3d 1134 (Nev. 2001), the court confronted an odd problem: one statute classified a particular crime as a felony, but a more recent statute classified the same crime as a misdemeanor. The court held that the more recent statute effectively repealed the earlier statute—even though the later statute did not so state explicitly—because there was no way whatsoever to reconcile the two.

In other cases, the tension among various rules is resolved if the court can identify the later-enacted statute as providing merely an exception to the general rule adopted in the earlier statute. This conforms to our ordinary understanding of how people speak. For instance, if the general rule in my house is that my children may eat only in the kitchen, but in one particular case I allow them to eat in the family room, it would be unreasonable to conclude that I meant to repeal the general rule altogether. Rather, they should understand the new rule—allowing them to eat under some specific circumstances in the family room—as a narrow exception.

Now consider *Zedalis v. Foster*, 343 So. 2d 849 (Fla. 2d DCA 1976). The court was confronted with a conflict between a 1949 statute, which provided that notice prior to certain public meetings for a specific county be published for two consecutive weeks, and a 1955 statute, which applied statewide and required only a single published notice for such meetings. In this case, three different rules were implicated: no implied repeals; later statutes govern; and more specific statutes govern. Articulate how these were implicated. How do you think the court should have ruled in the case?

3. THE RULE AGAINST ABSURD RESULTS

There is one final rule that we must consider. In itself, it is not a textual rule of interpretation, but it is the standard argument against the application of any of the textual rules of interpretation, particularly when all else fails. This is the rule against absurd results. Under this rule, no statute will be read in a way that no rational person could possibly approve of.

This rule is highly controversial, not so much because any courts reject altogether it, but because there is substantial disagreement as to what constitutes an absurdity. It is most successfully used in cases of true ambiguity. That is, where two different interpretations are plausible, the court will reject the interpretation that leads to absurd results. It also applies to so-called scrivener's errors, where the legislature plainly misspelled or simply used the wrong term in a legislative pronouncement.

Example. In *Amalgamated Transit Union Local 1309 v. Laidlaw Transit Service, Inc.*, 435 F.3d 1140 (9th Cir. 2006), the court considered a statute that required that an application for appeal be filed "not less than 7 days" after the entry of the underlying order. Plainly, the statute meant "not more than 7 days" (what would the result be if the court construed the statute strictly?) and the Ninth Circuit so held.

Lawyers sometimes try to use the rule against absurd results when they have few other arguments available to them as a means of arguing that the result of a case represents terrible policy choices on the part of the legislature. Lawyers nearly always lose these cases. Why?

GRIFFIN V. OCEANIC CONTRACTORS, INC.
458 U.S. 564 (1982)

As you read the following case concerning the Rule Against Absurd Results, consider the following questions:

- What makes the results of the plain language arguably absurd? Do you agree that this is an absurd result?

- According to Justice Rehnquist, what is the job of the Court? How might Justice Scalia reframe this?

- What evidence does Justice Rehnquist muster that supports the plain language interpretation?

- Justice Rehnquist's opinion favors "the little guy." The dissent by Justice Stevens, which you do not have, favors the corporation. What do you make of that? What does it say about statutory interpretation and politics on the bench?

- According to Justice Rehnquist, when does the Rule Against Absurd Results apply? Why doesn't it apply in this case? Would he support its application in the *Amalgamated Transit* case briefly discussed above?

What theory or theories of interpretation are most consistent with the Rule Against Absurd Results? Why does the Court seem to want to narrow the application of this rule?

JUSTICE REHNQUIST delivered the opinion of the Court.

This case concerns the application of 46 U.S.C. § 596, which requires certain masters and vessel owners to pay seamen promptly after their discharge and authorizes seamen to recover double wages for each day that payment is delayed without sufficient cause. The question is whether the district courts, in the exercise of discretion, may limit the period during which this wage penalty is assessed, or whether imposition of the penalty is mandatory for each day that payment is withheld in violation of the statute.

I

On February 18, 1976, petitioner signed an employment contract with respondent in New Orleans, agreeing to work as a senior pipeline welder on board vessels operated by respondent in the North Sea. The contract specified that petitioner's employment would extend "until December 15, 1976 or until Oceanic's 1976 pipeline committal in the North Sea is fulfilled, whichever shall occur first." The contract also provided that respondent would pay for transportation to and from the worksite, but that if petitioner quit the job prior to its termination date, or if his services were terminated for cause, he would be charged with the cost of transportation back to the United States. Respondent reserved the right to withhold $137.50 from each of petitioner's first four paychecks "as a cash deposit for the payment of your return transportation in the event you should become obligated for its payment." On March 6, 1976, petitioner flew from the United States to Antwerp, Belgium, where he reported to work at respondent's vessel, the "Lay Barge 27," berthed in the Antwerp harbor for repairs.

On April 1, 1976, petitioner suffered an injury while working on the deck of the vessel readying it for sea. Two days later he underwent emergency surgery in Antwerp. On April 5, petitioner was discharged from the hospital and went to respondent's Antwerp office, where he spoke with Jesse Williams, the welding superintendent, and provided a physician's statement that he was not fit for duty. Williams refused to acknowledge that petitioner's injury was work-related and denied that respondent was liable for medical and hospital expenses, maintenance, or unearned wages. Williams also refused to furnish transportation back to the United States, and continued to retain $412.50 in earned wages that had been deducted from petitioner's first three paychecks for that purpose. Petitioner returned to his home in Houston, Tex., the next day at his own expense. He was examined there by a physician who determined that he would be able to resume work on May 3, 1976. On May 5, petitioner began working as a welder for another company operating in the North Sea.

In 1978 he brought suit against respondent under the Jones Act, and under general maritime law, seeking damages for respondent's failure to pay maintenance, cure, unearned wages, repatriation expenses, and the value of certain personal effects lost on board respondent's vessel. Petitioner also sought penalty wages under Rev.Stat. § 4529, as amended, 46 U.S.C. § 596, for respondent's failure to pay over the $412.50 in earned wages allegedly due upon discharge. The District Court found for petitioner and awarded damages totalling $23,670.40.

Several findings made by that court are particularly relevant to this appeal. First, the court found that petitioner's injury was proximately caused by an unseaworthy condition of respondent's vessel. Second, the court found that petitioner was discharged from respondent's employ on the day of the injury, and that the termination of his employment was caused solely by that injury. Third, it found that respondent's failure to pay petitioner the $412.50 in earned wages was "without sufficient cause." Finally, the court found that petitioner had exercised due diligence in attempting to collect those wages.

In assessing penalty wages under 46 U.S.C. § 596, the court held that "[t]he period during which the penalty runs is to be determined by the sound discretion of the district court and depends on the equities of the case." It determined that the appropriate period for imposition of the penalty was from the date of discharge, April 1, 1976, through the date of petitioner's reemployment, May 5, 1976, a period of 34 days. Applying the statute, it computed a penalty of $6,881.60. Petitioner appealed the award of damages as inadequate.

The Court of Appeals for the Fifth Circuit affirmed. That court concluded, *inter alia*, that the District Court had not erred in limiting assessment of the penalty provided by 46 U.S.C. § 596 to the period beginning April 1 and ending May 5. The court recognized that the statute required payment of a penalty for each day during which wages were withheld until the date they were actually paid, which in this case did not occur until September 17, 1980, when respondent satisfied the judgment of the District Court. Nevertheless, the court believed itself bound by prior decisions within the Circuit, which left calculation of the penalty period to the sound discretion of the district courts. It concluded that the District Court in this case had not abused its discretion by assessing a penalty only for the period during which petitioner was unemployed.

We granted certiorari to resolve a conflict among the Circuits regarding the proper application of the wage penalty statute. We reverse the judgment of the Court of Appeals as to that issue.

II

A

The language of the statute first obligates the master or owner of any vessel making coasting or foreign voyages to pay every seaman the balance of his unpaid wages within specified periods after his discharge. It then provides:

> "Every master or owner who refuses or neglects to make payment in the manner hereinbefore mentioned without sufficient cause shall pay to the seaman a sum equal to two days' pay for each and every day during which payment is delayed beyond the respective periods. . . ."

The statute in straightforward terms provides for the payment of double wages, depending upon the satisfaction of two conditions. First, the master or owner must have refused or failed to pay the seaman his wages within the periods specified. Second, this failure or refusal must be "without sufficient cause." Once these conditions are satisfied, however, the unadorned language of the statute dictates that the master or owner "*shall pay* to the seaman" the sums specified "*for each and every day* during which payment is delayed." The words chosen by Congress, given their plain meaning, leave no room for the exercise of discretion either in deciding whether to exact payment or in choosing the period of days by which the payment is to be calculated. . . . Our task is to give effect to the will of Congress, and where its will has been expressed in reasonably plain terms, "that language must ordinarily be regarded as conclusive."

The District Court found that respondent had refused to pay petitioner the balance of his earned wages promptly after discharge, and that its refusal was "without sufficient cause." Respondent challenges neither of these findings. Although the two statutory conditions were satisfied, however, the District Court obviously did not assess double wages "for each and every day" during which payment was delayed, but instead limited the assessment to the period of petitioner's unemployment. Nothing in the language of the statute vests the courts with the discretion to set such a limitation.

B

Nevertheless, respondent urges that the legislative purpose of the statute is best served by construing it to permit some choice in determining the length of the penalty period. In respondent's view, the purpose of the statute is essentially remedial and compensatory, and thus it should not be interpreted literally to produce a monetary award that is so far in excess of any equitable remedy as to be punitive.

Respondent, however, is unable to support this view of legislative purpose by reference to the terms of the statute. "There is, of course, no more persuasive evidence of the purpose of a statute than the words by which the legislature undertook to give expression to its wishes." Nevertheless, in rare cases the literal application of a statute will produce a result demonstrably at odds with the intentions of its drafters, and those intentions must be controlling. We have reserved "some 'scope for adopting a restricted rather than a literal or usual meaning of its words where acceptance of that meaning . . . would thwart the obvious purpose of the statute.'" This, however, is not the exceptional case.

As the Court [has] recognized . . . the "evident purpose" of the statute is "to secure prompt payment of seamen's wages . . . and thus to protect them from the harsh consequences of arbitrary and unscrupulous action of their employers, to which, as a class, they are peculiarly exposed." This was to be accomplished "by the imposition of a liability which is not exclusively compensatory, but designed to prevent, by its coercive effect, arbitrary refusals to pay wages, and to induce prompt payment when payment is possible." Thus, although the sure purpose of the statute is remedial, Congress has chosen to secure that purpose through the use of potentially punitive sanctions designed to deter negligent or arbitrary delays in payment.

The legislative history of the statute leaves little if any doubt that this understanding is correct. The law owes its origins to the Act of July 20, 1790, passed by the First Congress. Although the statute as originally enacted gave every seaman the right to collect the wages due under his contract "as soon as the voyage is ended," it did not provide for the recovery of additional sums to encourage compliance. Such a provision was added by the Shipping Commissioners Act of 1872, which provided for the payment of "a sum not exceeding the amount of two days' pay for each of the days, not exceeding ten days, during which payment is delayed." The Act of 1872 obviously established a ceiling of 10 days on the period during which the penalty could be assessed and, by use of the words "not exceeding," left the courts with discretion to choose an appropriate penalty within that period.

Congress amended the law again in 1898. As amended, it read in relevant part:

> "Every master or owner who refuses or neglects to make payment in manner hereinbefore mentioned without sufficient cause shall pay to the seaman a sum equal to one day's pay for each and every day during which payment is delayed beyond the respective periods."

The amending legislation thus effected two changes: first, it removed the discretion theretofore existing by which courts might award less than an amount calculated on the basis of each day during which payment was delayed, and, second, it removed the 10-day ceiling which theretofore limited the number of days upon which an award might be calculated. The accompanying Committee Reports identify the purpose of the legislation as "the amelioration of the condition of the American seamen," and characterize the amended wage penalty in particular as "designed to secure the promptest possible payment of wages." H.R.Rep.No.1657, 55th Cong., 2d Sess., 2, 3 (1898). Nothing in the legislative history of the 1898 Act suggests that Congress intended to do anything other than what the Act's enacted language plainly demonstrates: to strengthen the deterrent effect of the statute by removing the courts' latitude in assessing the wage penalty.

The statute was amended for the last time in 1915 to increase further the severity of the penalty by doubling the wages due for each day during which payment of earned wages was delayed. There is no suggestion in the Committee Reports or in the floor debates that, in so doing, Congress intended to reinvest the courts with the discretion it had removed in the Act of 1898. Resort to the legislative history, therefore, merely confirms that Congress intended the statute to mean exactly what its plain language says.

III

Respondent argues, however, that a literal construction of the statute in this case would produce an absurd and unjust result which Congress could not have intended. The District Court found that the daily wage to be used in computing the penalty was $101.20. If the statute is applied literally, petitioner would receive twice this amount for each day after his discharge until September 17, 1980, when respondent satisfied the District Court's judgment. Petitioner would receive over $300,000 simply because respondent improperly withheld $412.50 in wages. In respondent's view, Congress could not have intended seamen to receive windfalls of this nature without regard to the equities of the case.

It is true that interpretations of a statute which would produce absurd results are to be avoided if alternative interpretations consistent with the legislative purpose are available. In refusing to nullify statutes, however hard or unexpected the particular effect, this Court has said:

> "Laws enacted with good intention, when put to the test, frequently, and to the surprise of the law maker himself, turn out to be mischievous, absurd or otherwise objectionable. But in such case the remedy lies with the law making authority, and not with the courts."

It is highly probable that respondent is correct in its contention that a recovery in excess of $300,000 in this case greatly exceeds any actual injury suffered by petitioner as a result of respondent's delay in paying his wages. But this Court has previously recognized that awards made under this statute were not intended to be merely compensatory:

"We think the use of this language indicates a purpose to protect seamen from delayed payments of wages by the imposition of a liability which is not exclusively compensatory, but designed to prevent, by its coercive effect, arbitrary refusals to pay wages, and to induce prompt payment when payment is possible."

It is in the nature of punitive remedies to authorize awards that may be out of proportion to actual injury; such remedies typically are established to deter particular conduct, and the legislature not infrequently finds that harsh consequences must be visited upon those whose conduct it would deter. . . . It is enough that Congress intended that the language it enacted would be applied as we have applied it. The remedy for any dissatisfaction with the results in particular cases lies with Congress and not with this Court. Congress may amend the statute; we may not.

. . . .

Now read Thorpe v. Borough of Thorpe, 770 F.3d 255 (2014). As you do so, consider the following questions:

- On what basis does the Third Circuit find for the defendant?

- How does the Third Circuit deploy the Rule Against Absurd Results? Why would the plaintiff's interpretation be "absurd," according to the court? Do you agree?

- Does the opinion seem consistent with the Supreme Court's decision in *Griffin*?

After having read the Third Circuit's decision, read the following amicus brief filed in support of the plaintiffs' motion for certiorari. As you do, consider the following questions:

- How is this brief structured? Why does it deviate from the typical approach to statutory interpretation?

- Should the Rule Against Absurd Results be abandoned?

- Do you agree with the authors of the brief that the Third Circuit erred?

- The Supreme Court ultimately rejected the motion for certiorari. Why do you think it did so?

SAC AND FOX NATION OF OKLAHOMA, ET AL., PETITIONERS, v. BOROUGH OF JIM THORPE, ET AL., RESPONDENTS

Supreme Court of the United States
2015 WL 4086911 (U.S.)

On Petition for a Writ of Certiorari to the United States Court of Appeals for the Third Circuit

Brief of Amici Curiae Scholars of Statutory Interpretation and Native American Law in Support of Petitioners

INTEREST OF *AMICI CURIAE*

Amici are professors at law schools across the country. Some amici teach courses, lecture widely, conduct research, and publish extensively in the field of statutory interpretation and related subjects. Their interest is in preserving the integrity of the judiciary and the judicial role as it relates to statutory interpretation. Other amici are experts in the field of Native American law who are deeply familiar with the statute at issue and its importance to Native American tribes. This brief draws on amici's extensive research and expertise in the fields of statutory interpretation and Native American law.

While amici may disagree regarding many statutory interpretation issues, they all agree that the Third Circuit's opinion in this case significantly deviates from this Court's precedents, reflects confusion as to the proper application of the canons of interpretation (specifically the absurdity doctrine), encourages other courts to similarly misuse those canons, and raises separation-of-powers questions. Amici believe that in this case, the Third Circuit's misapplication of the absurdity canon requires that certiorari be granted and the lower court's decision reversed.

SUMMARY OF ARGUMENT

The Third Circuit candidly acknowledged that under the plain language of the Native American Graves and Repatriation Act ("NAGPRA"), 25 U.S.C. §§ 3001–3013, the Borough of Jim Thorpe qualifies as a "museum." Under section 7 of the Act, where a "museum" holds the human remains of a Native American, the Native American descendants can demand the return of the remains for proper handling and burial on ancestral lands. 25 U.S.C. § 3005 *et seq.* Section 2 of the Act, in turn, defines "museum" to mean "any institution or State or local government agency . . . that receives Federal funds and has possession of, or control over, Native American cultural items." 25 U.S.C. § 3001(8).

As the court recognized, "the Borough has 'possession of, or control over,' Jim Thorpe's remains"; "he is of Native American descent"; and "the

Borough received federal funds after the enactment of NAGPRA."
Consequently—and as the Third Circuit acknowledged—NAGPRA's plain
language requires the return of Jim Thorpe's remains to his lineal
descendants for burial on his ancestral lands. *See* 25 U.S.C. § 3005(a)(1)
(requiring that, upon the request of a known lineal descendant of the
Native American, a museum "shall expeditiously return [Native
American human] remains and associated funerary objects").

Nevertheless, in an application of the so-called "absurdity doctrine," the
court nullified the statute's plain language on the ground that applying
the provision as written would lead to purportedly absurd results. The
Third Circuit's reasoning and conclusion misuse the absurdity doctrine.
Rather than identifying any absurdity, the opinion below simply amounts
to a disagreement with the wisdom of the policy choices reflected in the
statutory text. Further, it reflects abiding confusion about how and when
to apply the absurdity doctrine and, in turn, invites other lower courts to
similarly misapply the canon.

This Court should grant the petition for certiorari and reverse the
decision below.

ARGUMENT

I.   The Opinion Below Misuses the Absurdity Doctrine.

The familiar cardinal rule of statutory interpretation is that the plain
meaning of statutory language controls. *See, e.g., BedRoc Ltd., LLC v.
United States,* 541 U.S. 176, 183 (2004) ("[O]ur inquiry begins with the
statutory text, and ends there as well if the text is unambiguous."); *Blue
Chip Stamps v. Manor Drug Stores,* 421 U.S. 723, 756 (1975) ("The
starting point in every case involving construction of a statute is the
language itself."). Where a provision's plain meaning or its proper
application is unclear, this Court considers various canons and
presumptions to assist in resolving the ambiguity. *Corley v. United
States,* 556 U.S. 303, 325 (2009) ("Canons of interpretation are quite often
useful . . . when statutory language is ambiguous." (internal quotation
marks omitted)).

One such rule is that, where statutory language is ambiguous, the Court
prefers an interpretation that avoids absurd results over one that leads to
absurdity. *See Griffin v. Oceanic Contractors, Inc.,* 458 U.S. 564, 575
(1982) ("[I]nterpretations of a statute which would produce absurd results
are to be avoided if alternative interpretations consistent with the
legislative purpose are available."); *Commissioner v. Brown,* 380 U.S. 563,
571 (1965) ("[T]he courts, in interpreting a statute, have some 'scope for
adopting a restricted rather than a literal or usual meaning of its words
where acceptance of that meaning would lead to absurd results . . . or
would thwart the obvious purpose of the statute." (internal quotation

marks omitted; alteration in original)). This is the typical use of the absurdity doctrine.

The Third Circuit, however, did not deploy the absurdity doctrine in this common and benign manner. Instead, it invoked a more far-reaching form of the canon: in the rarest of circumstances, the unambiguous *plain language* of a statute may be nullified when it would lead to an absurd result. *See Griffin,* 458 U.S. at 571 ("[I]n rare cases the literal application of a statute will produce a result demonstrably at odds with the intentions of its drafters, and those intentions must be controlling."). The justifications for and boundaries of this use of the canon are controversial and subject to substantial judicial and scholarly debate. *See, e.g., Zuni Pub. Sch. Dist. No. 89 v. Dep't of Educ.,* 550 U.S. 81, 105 (2007) (Stevens, J., concurring) ("[A] judicial decision that departs from statutory text may represent 'policy-driven interpretation.'" (citation omitted)); *Dodd v. United States,* 545 U.S. 353, 359 (2005) ("Although we recognize the potential for harsh results in some cases, we are not free to rewrite the statute that Congress has enacted."); *see also* John F. Manning, *The Absurdity Doctrine,* 116 Harv. L. Rev. 2387 (2003) (discussing and critiquing justifications for the absurdity doctrine); Linda D. Jellum, *Why Specific Absurdity Undermines Textualism,* 76 Brook. L. Rev. 917 (2011) (same); Veronica M. Dougherty, *Absurdity and the Limits of Literalism: Defining the Absurd Result Principle in Statutory Interpretation,* 44 Am. U. L. Rev. 127 (1994) (same).

Despite such debates, there is widespread agreement that nullifying a statute's plain language under the absurdity doctrine raises serious constitutional separation-of-powers questions and, consequently, is appropriate only in the most extraordinary circumstances. *See, e.g., Fla. Dep't of Rev. v. Piccadilly Cafeterias, Inc.,* 554 U.S. 33, 52 (2008) ("[W]e reiterate that it is not for us to substitute our view of . . . policy for the legislation which has been passed by Congress." (internal quotation marks omitted; alteration in original)); *Crooks v. Harrelson,* 282 U.S. 55, 60 (1930) ("[A]n application of the [absurdity] principle so nearly approaches the boundary between the exercise of the judicial power and that of the legislative power as to call rather for great caution and circumspection in order to avoid usurpation of the latter."). In particular, the absurdity doctrine must never be used to substitute a court's policy preferences for those expressed by the legislature in the language of the statute. *See Dodd,* 545 U.S. at 359 ("[W]hen the statute's language is plain, the sole function of the courts—at least where the disposition required by the text is not absurd—is to enforce it according to its terms." (quotation marks omitted)); *Commissioner v. Asphalt Prods. Co.,* 482 U.S. 117, 121 (1987) ("Judicial perception that a particular result would be unreasonable may enter into the construction of ambiguous provisions, but cannot justify disregard of what Congress has plainly and intentionally provided."); *Tenn. Valley Auth. v. Hill,* 437 U.S. 153, 196 (1978) ("It is not our province to rectify policy or political judgments by the Legislative Branch, however egregiously they may disserve the public interest.").

Consistent with these principles, this Court has invoked the absurdity doctrine to nullify a statute's unambiguous plain language in only the narrowest circumstances. Appropriate circumstances may include where: (1) a provision's plain language is in tension with the overall structure of the statute;[3] (2) the plain language raises constitutional questions;[4] (3) the plain language flatly contradicts the legislature's express purpose and intent in enacting the law;[5] or (4) the plain language leads to a manifestly irrational result that would be "so monstrous, that all mankind would, without hesitation," reject it.[6]

The first three justifications for nullifying a statute's plain language due to absurdity are not relevant in this case. The decision below cites no tension within the law, raises no constitutional objection to the plain language, and cites no evidence of legislative intent contradicting the result that flows from applying the statute's plain meaning.[7]

While the court below did not say so explicitly, its invocation of the absurdity doctrine resonates, at best, with the fourth—and most controversial and limited—circumstance in which the canon might apply. That is, the court evidently concluded that applying the plain meaning of "museum" to the Borough is irrational. But this Court has repeatedly warned against the danger of judges deeming statutory schemes "irrational" simply because the policies seem misconceived. *See, e.g., United States v. Gonzales,* 520 U.S. 1, 10 (1997) ("Given [a] clear

---

[3]   *Clinton v. City of New York,* 524 U.S. 417, 429 n.14 (1998) (finding an absurd result where "the structure of [the statute]" precluded applying the plain language); *Green v. Bock Laundry Mach. Co.,* 490 U.S. 504, 528 (1989) (Scalia, J., concurring) (confronting "absurd" statute and arguing that the proper interpretation is one that is "most compatible with the surrounding body of law into which the provision must be integrated").

[4]   *Green,* 490 U.S. at 527-28 (Scalia, J., concurring) (confronting statute which, if interpreted literally, produced an absurd, and perhaps unconstitutional, result).

[5]   *Pub. Citizen v. U.S. Dep't of Justice,* 491 U.S. 440, 454-67 (1989) (applying the absurdity doctrine where an exhaustive review of legislative history demonstrated that the words chosen by Congress did not reflect legislative intent); *United States v. Ron Pair Enters., Inc.,* 489 U.S. 235, 242-43 (1989) (recognizing the legitimacy of applying the absurdity doctrine in the "rare case [in which] the literal application of a statute would produce a result demonstrably at odds with the intentions of its drafters," but declining to apply the principle to the statute at issue because strict application of the plain meaning would not truly "contravene the intent of the framers of the Code" (alteration in original)).

[6]   *Sturges v. Crowninshield,* 17 U.S. (4 Wheat.) 122, 202-03 (1819).

[7]   Although the court claimed that a literal reading of "museum" would contradict legislative intent, Pet. App. 17a-19a, the evidence it cited suggested—at most—only that circumstances like these were not encompassed by Congress's *central* purpose in enacting the statute. The court cited nothing in the legislative history or statutory text showing that Congress wished to *preclude* repatriation of human remains where the original burial was in accordance with the wishes of the next-of-kin, or where there may be competing claims among family members.

legislative directive, it is not for the courts to carve out statutory exceptions based on judicial perceptions of good . . . policy."); *Chisom v. Roemer,* 501 U.S. 380, 417 (1991) (Scalia, J., dissenting) ("When we adopt a method that psychoanalyzes Congress rather than reads its laws, when we employ a tinkerer's toolbox, we do great harm.").

In order to limit the potential for this sort of abuse, this Court has tightly circumscribed the circumstances in which the plain meaning of a statute may be absurd on the ground of irrationality: it must be "so bizarre that Congress could not have intended it," *Demarest v. Manspeaker,* 498 U.S. 184, 190–91 (1991) (internal quotation marks omitted), or "so gross as to shock the general moral or common sense." *Crooks,* 282 U.S. at 60; *see also Small v. United States,* 544 U.S. 385, 404 (2005) ("We should employ [the absurdity doctrine] only 'where the result of applying the plain language would be, in a genuine sense, absurd, *i.e.,* where it is quite impossible that Congress could have intended the result . . . and where the alleged absurdity is so clear as to be obvious to most anyone.'" (citation omitted; alteration in original)). In most cases, even strange or troubling results will not meet this standard. For example, in *Barnhart v. Sigmon Coal Co.,* the Court refused to apply the absurdity doctrine even where the plain meaning led to manifestly counterintuitive results. 534 U.S. 438, 459 (2002); *see also Hallstrom v. Tillamook Cnty.,* 493 U.S. 20, 30 (1989) (similar); *Locke v. United States,* 471 U.S. 84, 93–96 (1985) (similar).

The Third Circuit's decision ignores these admonitions and takes the concept of irrationality far beyond what this Court has countenanced. The Third Circuit identified two supposed irrationalities: first, that the plain language would require repatriation even where the original burial was "in accordance with the wishes of the decedent's next-of-kin"; and second, that NAGPRA would be used "to settle familial disputes within Native American families."

But this case is not one of the rare instances in which the absurdity doctrine may legitimately be used to nullify a statute's plain language. To the contrary, the plain language here is entirely rational, harmonious with NAGPRA's structure, and consistent with Congress's purposes for enacting it. The court might have considered Congress's policy choices, reflected in the statute's plain language, to be distasteful, overbroad, or ill-conceived; but none of these characteristics rises to the level of irrationality necessary to justify nullifying NAGPRA's plain language. *See Locke,* 471 U.S. at 95 ("[T]he fact that Congress might have acted with greater clarity or foresight does not give courts a *carte blanche* to redraft statutes in an effort to achieve that which Congress is perceived to have failed to do.").

A. NAGPRA's Plain Language Applies Even Where the Original Burial Was in Accordance with the Wishes of the Decedent's Next-of-Kin.

The court below made much of the fact that Thorpe's burial in the Borough was in accordance with the wishes of his next-of-kin, and thus presumably lawful at the time. In light of this, the court concluded that applying NAGPRA in such cases would be absurd. The court cited no language in the legislative history to affirmatively support this assertion. Instead, it relied on its own apparent discomfort with the repatriation requirement where the initial interment was lawful. But NAGPRA's text and structure make clear that human remains must be repatriated even where, as here, the agency or museum lawfully obtained them.[8]

Two categories of objects are subject to NAGPRA: (1) human remains and associated funerary objects; and (2) unassociated funerary objects, sacred objects, and objects of cultural patrimony. *See* 25 U.S.C. § 3001(3) (defining "cultural items"). NAGPRA recognizes that an agency or museum may have a right of possession to either type of item. It defines a "right of possession" as "possession obtained with the voluntary consent of an individual or group that had authority of alienation." *Id.* § 3001(13). For human remains and associated funerary objects, a right of possession exists where the object was "obtained with full knowledge and consent of the next of kin." *Id.* With respect to an unassociated funerary object, sacred object, or object of cultural patrimony, a right of possession exists where the object was obtained "from an Indian tribe or Native Hawaiian organization with the voluntary consent of an individual or group with authority to alienate such object." *Id.*

It is uncontested that the Borough has a right of possession to Jim Thorpe's remains, as they were given to the Borough by Thorpe's lawful next-of-kin. *Id.* Such a right of possession, however, does not free the Borough from its obligations under NAGPRA. The statute explicitly

---

[8]   That Jim Thorpe's remains were buried rather than publicly displayed is irrelevant. Whether the remains were actually displayed in a glass case or, as here, interred underground as part of a shrine does not determine an entity's status as a museum. First, the statute defines what it means to be a "museum," and that definition is paramount. *See Burgess v. United States,* 553 U.S. 124, 130 (2008) ("When a statute includes an explicit definition, we must follow that definition" (quotation marks omitted)). Nothing in the statutory definition of "museum" suggests that a distinction between interment and display of human remains is relevant.

Second, even the plain or dictionary meaning of the word "museum" easily encompasses Jim Thorpe's mausoleum. *See The Compact Oxford-English Dictionary* 1136 (2d ed. 1991) ("2.a. A building or portion of a building used as a repository for the preservation and exhibition of objects illustrative of antiques, natural history, fine and industrial art, or some particular branch of any of these subjects, either generally or with reference to a definite region or period. Also applied to the collection of objects itself."). Jim Thorpe's gravesite was designed to bring in curious tourists and provide them with information and entertainment. In fact, the towns of Mauch Chunk and East Mauch Chunk believed that Thorpe's body could be used to generate revenue, and, once the towns combined, the Borough built an above-ground mausoleum to attract visitors. Pet. at 10. The gravesite therefore easily falls within the dictionary meaning of "museum," even though Jim Thorpe's remains are interred rather than displayed there.

provides that a right of possession in Native American cultural items confers benefits that differ depending on the object's category.[9] Under section 7, if the agency or museum can "prove that it has a right of possession" to "unassociated funerary objects, sacred objects, and objects of cultural patrimony," then it may retain them and need not return them to the claimant—in other words, they are exempt from the repatriation requirement. 25 U.S.C. § 3005(c).

But NAGPRA does not extend this exemption to human remains or associated funerary objects. *See NAGPRA Regs.,* 60 Fed. Reg. 62,134, 62,153 (Dec. 4, 1995) ("The right of possession basis for retaining cultural items in an existing collection does not apply to human remains or associated funerary objects, only to unassociated funerary objects, sacred objects, and objects of cultural patrimony."). Instead, it provides that an agency or museum holding a right of possession to such objects merely escapes criminal prosecution for illegal trafficking. 18 U.S.C. § 1170. That is, unlike in cases where the museum had no right of possession to the human remains, it will not be subject to criminal penalties. Yet the repatriation requirement still obligates the museum to return this category of objects to lawful claimants.

Thus, Congress recognized that an agency or museum might have initially obtained human remains through lawful means, and it provided certain benefits to possessors in those circumstances. But, as the plain language of NAGPRA makes clear, Congress decided to treat human remains and associated funerary objects differently from other kinds of objects, by requiring that they be returned to lineal descendants or other enumerated claimants.[10] Thus, how an entity initially obtained human remains has no bearing on its obligation to return them.

It is easy to imagine rational reasons why Congress may have chosen to draw this distinction. First, it could have concluded that human remains and associated funerary objects are qualitatively different from other kinds of cultural items and bear more importance to tribes. This would justify NAGPRA's different treatment of the two categories of objects.

Second, Congress could have drawn this distinction because of differences in the property status of the two categories of objects. With respect to repatriation, Congress initially made no distinction between human remains and associated funerary objects, on the one hand, and other

---

[9] The Third Circuit appears to have overlooked or ignored the different treatment of the two categories of objects. *See* Pet. App. 22a (discussing § 3001(13), which defines "right of possession" to include human remains, but failing to mention 18 U.S.C. § 1170, which provides that a museum with a "right of possession" to human remains merely is immune from criminal liability). *See also infra* Part II.A.

[10] *Compare* 25 U.S.C. § 3005(c), *with* 18 U.S.C. § 1170.

cultural objects, on the other.[11] By the time the statute was enacted, however, it provided for the two categories of objects to be treated differently when the museum or agency had a right of possession.[12] Congress may have made this distinction due to a concern that, where a right of possession to non-human remains existed, the repatriation requirement could implicate the Takings Clause. But that concern did not apply in the case of human remains. *See NAGPRA Regs.,* 60 Fed. Reg. at 62,153 ("American law generally recognizes that human remains can not [sic] be 'owned.' "); *cf.* H.R. Rep. No. 101–877, at 14–15, 25–29 (1990), *as reprinted in* 1990 U.S.C.C.A.N. 4367, 4373–74, 4384–88 (noting that definition of "right of possession" was amended "to meet the concerns of the Justice Department about the possibility of a 5th amendment taking of the private property of museums through the application of the terms of the Act").

B. NAGPRA Explicitly Anticipates and Provides Guidance for Resolving Familial Disputes.

The Third Circuit also identified a second purportedly absurd result of applying the plain language: NAGPRA would be used to resolve disputes within Native American families as to the proper treatment of ancestral remains. As the court put it, NAGPRA was not intended "to settle [such] familial disputes within Native American families."

This, too, misuses and unduly expands the absurdity doctrine. Congress well understood that NAGPRA could give rise to family disputes. First, simply as a matter of logic, *any* scheme that (like NAGPRA) gives remote descendants the opportunity to make claims on ancestral remains and other objects invariably invites competing claims. After all, different descendants might have different views on the matter.

Second, even a cursory review of NAGPRA's language reveals that Congress explicitly anticipated family disputes. Section 7 provides that if there are "competing claims" concerning an object, then "the agency or museum may retain [the] item" until the dispute is resolved. 25 U.S.C. § 3005(e). Moreover, the statute provides a mechanism for resolving familial disputes over an item's disposition. Section 8 directs the Secretary of the Interior to establish a review committee that is tasked with "monitor[ing] and review[ing] the implementation of the ... repatriation activities required [by NAGPRA]." *Id.* § 3006(a). Most notably, subsection 8(c)(4) charges the review committee with "facilitating the resolution of any disputes among Indian tribes, Native Hawaiian organizations, *or lineal descendants* and Federal agencies or museums relating to the return of such items. . . ." *Id.* § 3006(c)(4) (emphasis

---

[11] As introduced on July 10, 1990, NAGPRA's repatriation requirement made no distinction between the two categories of objects. *See* H.R. 5237, 101st Cong. § 6(a) (as introduced in the House, July 10, 1990).

[12] *See* 25 U.S.C. § 3005(c).

added). To resolve disputes, the review committee is directed to compile a report and recommendations for proper handling of such disputed items. *Id.* § 3006(c)(9), (e). And if resolution cannot be achieved through this administrative process, NAGPRA grants federal district courts ultimate enforcement authority. *Id.* § 3013. In a district court proceeding under this section, the review committee's report and recommendation are admissible evidence. *Id.* § 3006(d).

Although NAGPRA does not mandate exhaustion of this administrative process prior to initiating suit in a district court, the fact that Congress created this detailed process demonstrates that it fully expected that there could be competing claimants. That manifest expectation defeats any notion that the possibility of intra-familial disputes justifies application of the absurdity doctrine. Of course, a disinterested observer might question the wisdom of the mechanism Congress devised for resolving such disputes. But given that Congress explicitly incorporated that mechanism into the statutory scheme, there is no legitimate basis for applying the absurdity doctrine on the ground that the statute's plain meaning would implicate intra-familial disputes.

C. The Opinion Below Would Not Eliminate the Supposed Absurdities.

Even assuming that the result of applying the plain language might be irrational for the reasons given by the Third Circuit, the decision below would not eliminate these absurdities—a fact that only underscores the extent to which the court's decision untethers the absurdity doctrine from its proper moorings.

Suppose that the next-of-kin of a Native American had given that person's remains to an entity that is a "real" museum in the eyes of the Third Circuit, and that certain lineal descendants then made a claim for repatriation. Just as in the present case, the museum would hold a right of possession, and a dispute could arise among the family members. That is, these supposed absurdities could occur in even the most run-of-the-mill cases that come within NAGPRA's scope. Nullifying NAGPRA's plain language to negate the Borough's status as a museum therefore does nothing at all to address the Third Circuit's concerns, as there is no connection between its reasoning (that the statute may give rise to absurd results) and its ultimate holding (that the Borough is not a "museum" as defined in section 2 of NAGPRA). This logical disconnect between the Third Circuit's reasoning and its holding thoroughly undermines the decision below.

In sum, applying the plain language in this case leads to no absurdities at all, but only to results that are fully anticipated by, consistent with, and provided for in the statutory scheme.

II. The Opinion Below Distorts Other Well-Established Canons of Statutory Construction.

In the course of misapplying the absurdity doctrine, the Third Circuit's opinion flouts other established canons of statutory interpretation, each of which would demand an outcome different from the one the court reached. These canons reflect the importance of judicial restraint and respect for statutory text and separation of powers where, as here, the statute's language is clear and consistent with legislative purposes.

A. The *Expressio Unius* Canon Requires the Opposite Result.

The familiar *expressio unius* canon of construction strongly supports the Petitioners. This canon dictates that "[w]hen Congress includes particular language in one section of a statute but omits it in another section of the same Act . . . it is generally presumed that Congress acts intentionally and purposely in the disparate inclusion or exclusion." *Clay v. United States,* 537 U.S. 522, 528 (2003) (internal quotation marks omitted). In other words, the canon reflects "the common sense language rule that the expression of one thing suggests the exclusion of another thing." Jacob Scott, *Codified Canons and the Common Law of Interpretation,* 98 Geo. L.J. 341, 351 (2010).

In NAGPRA, Congress expressly provided that in certain enumerated circumstances, a "right of possession" negates the obligation to repatriate cultural items. Yet this carve-out is limited to "Native American unassociated funerary objects, sacred objects or objects of cultural patrimony." 25 U.S.C. § 3005(c). *See supra* Part I.A. The existence of retention provisions applicable to certain cultural items—and not others—establishes that Congress knew how to preserve a museum's ability to retain human remains rightfully in its possession, yet chose not to do so. *See Hardt v. Reliance Standard Life Ins. Co.,* 560 U.S. 242, 252 (2010). Indeed, Congress considered—but rejected—a provision that would have treated human remains like other cultural objects for purposes of repatriation. *See* H.R. 5237, 101st Cong. § 6(c) (as introduced in the House, July 10, 1990).

In circumstances such as these, the *expressio unius* canon applies with full force, and precludes a court from reading into the statute what Congress declined to include. *See, e.g., Clay,* 537 U.S. at 528; *Russello v. United States,* 464 U.S. 16, 23 (1983).

B. The Opinion Below Violates the Canon That Exceptions Are to Be Narrowly Construed.

Further, the opinion below disregards the principle that, where "a general statement of policy is qualified by an exception" the court "usually read[s] the exception narrowly in order to preserve the primary operation of the provision." *Commissioner v. Clark,* 489 U.S. 726, 739 (1989). As this

Court has explained, "[t]o extend an exemption to other than those plainly and unmistakably within its terms and spirit is to abuse the interpretative process and to frustrate the announced will of the people." *A.H. Phillips Inc. v. Walling,* 324 U.S. 490, 493 (1945).

Regrettably, the effect of the Third Circuit's decision was to do just that. Congress provided a right-of-possession exception to the general policy of repatriation of cultural items. It limited that exception, however, to encompass only unassociated funerary objects, sacred objects or objects of cultural patrimony. *See supra* Part I.A. By effectively expanding that exception to include human remains, the Third Circuit's opinion gives it a scope far beyond what Congress intended—and, indeed, a scope so broad as to encompass *all* cultural items. Had Congress desired such an outcome, it would have permitted any museum or agency with a right of possession to avoid repatriation without regard to the type of cultural item at issue. But that is not what Congress did.

Congress' varied approach to different types of cultural items when crafting exceptions to the repatriation requirement is easily explained. *See supra* Part I.A. Accordingly, the statute's express treatment of human remains is properly viewed as a deliberate policy decision by the legislature, rather than an oversight to be remedied by the courts. *See Mobil Oil Corp. v. Higginbotham,* 436 U.S. 618, 625 (1978) ("There is a basic difference between filling a gap left by Congress' silence and rewriting rules that Congress has affirmatively and specifically enacted.").

CONCLUSION

Contrary to the opinion of the Third Circuit, applying the plain language of NAGPRA would not produce an absurd result. In fact, the return of Jim Thorpe's remains to his ancestral lands would be fully consistent with the statutory scheme and with Congress's goals. Judges are entitled to question the wisdom of a statute and the policy choices it reflects, but they may not nullify the statute's plain language on this basis. This Court should grant the petition and reverse the decision below.

4. THE TEXTUAL TOOLS IN ACTION

The textual rules of interpretation are the touchstone of statutory interpretation. Opinions and lawyers' briefs nearly always begin with the textual rules, and cases often are decided on these grounds alone. However, as we have already seen, these rules cannot generally be used in isolation because they are too often inconclusive individually. Instead, lawyers must build their cases by referencing multiple textual rules (and other rules that we will study in the coming sections as well). The following cases, presented in ascending order of complexity and sophistication, demonstrate how the textual tools (and others) are used together by judges.

CASHMAN v. DOLCE INTERNATIONAL/HARTFORD, INC.

225 F.R.D. 73 (D. Conn. 2004)

This case is a district court opinion that references several of the textual tools of interpretation (among others) to determine whether a state is permitted to sue under a statute.

As you read the opinion, consider the following:

- Identify all of the textual arguments the judge makes and the possible counterarguments.

- Notice that the textual arguments depend on a substantive presumption lurking in the background. Can you identify it? Why do you think this presumption exists? Where does it come from? We will consider such presumptions later in this chapter.

- Notice how the opinion moves from the most text-based arguments to the broadest structural arguments. This reflects the "microscope" approach previously introduced in this chapter. To an even greater degree than the Supreme Court opinions you typically read, this is how lawyers' briefs and lower court opinions are written.

- The judge musters several textual and structural arguments, a background presumption, and legislative history in his decision. But he also identifies a policy rationale supporting his decision. What is that rationale? Do you buy it? Why doesn't he just stick with the textual and structural arguments, given how strong they are?

- The State Plaintiffs have at least one textual argument in their favor. Can you identify it? Why does the judge reject it? What other arguments would you make if you were the State Plaintiffs?

- How does a district court opinion read differently from an appellate court opinion?

- Notice the long string cites with parentheticals that the judge uses to buttress his legal arguments. (Several of them have been edited out because of their length, but you should get the flavor from what is included.) These are even longer and more extensive than what one would typically see in an appellate court opinion, but they are fairly typical of carefully written district court opinions. Why do you think that's the case? What does it mean for a practicing attorney?

KRAVITZ, DISTRICT JUDGE.

. . . .

Plaintiffs claim that Defendants' actions violated the Worker Adjustment and Retraining Notification Act (WARN Act).

Defendants have moved to dismiss this action, claiming that [some] Plaintiffs lack standing to bring an action under the WARN Act. . . .

I.

The Court recognizes that on a motion to dismiss it must accept as true all of the factual allegations contained in the Amended Complaint and the exhibits attached to it, and must draw all reasonable inferences in favor of Plaintiffs. That said, the underlying facts in this case are not in serious dispute.

Defendant OLY owned the Hastings Hotel & Conference Center ("Hotel & Conference Center") in Hartford, Connecticut. Defendant Dolce managed the Hotel & Conference Center, but did not own it. On or about December 30, 2003, OLY informed Dolce of OLY's likely bankruptcy filing and of its intention to close the Hotel & Conference Center. On December 30, 2003, Dolce gave written notice to the rapid response unit of the Connecticut Department of Labor, to Mayor Perez, and to 117 Dolce employees including Ms. Lee, advising them of the impending bankruptcy of the hotel owners and of the permanent layoff of all Dolce employees at the Hotel & Conference Center, effective December 30, 2003. The notice . . . stated that it was "provided pursuant to [the WARN Act], which requires employers to give notice to employees who will lose their jobs in certain layoffs or workplace closings."

Plaintiffs allege that Defendants violated the notice provisions of the WARN Act by failing to provide the Connecticut Department of Labor, the City of Hartford, and the Hotel & Conference Center's employees with 60 days advance written notice of their termination. In their motion to dismiss, Defendants assert that the [Connecticut Department of Labor, henceforth referred to as the] State Plaintiffs have no standing to sue under the WARN Act. . . .

II.

The WARN Act prohibits employers of 100 or more employees from ordering "a plant closing or mass layoff until the end of a 60-day period after the employer serves written notice of such an order." Employers are supposed to give the required written notice to the following: to each representative of affected employees as of the time of the notice or, if there is no such representative, to each affected employee; to the State or entity designated by the State to carry out rapid response activities; and to the chief elected official of the local governmental unit within which such closing or layoff is to occur.

Failure to provide a WARN Act notice subjects an employer to potential civil liability and civil penalties. Employers are potentially liable to each aggrieved employee . . . for back pay and for benefits under an employee benefit plan . . . all calculated for the period of violation of the WARN Act up to a maximum of 60 days. An employer who violates the notice provisions "with respect to a unit of local government" is also "subject to a civil penalty of not more than $500 for each day of such violation." These specific monetary remedies are the exclusive remedies for violating the WARN Act; no other remedies are possible. In particular, the Act states that "a Federal court shall not have authority to enjoin a plant closing or mass layoff."

A.

The principal issue raised by Defendants' motion to dismiss requires the Court to decide who can sue to enforce the provisions of the WARN Act; that is, who has standing to enforce the WARN Act. Section 2104(a)(5) of the Act provides as follows:

"A person seeking to enforce such liability, including a representative of employees or a unit of local government aggrieved under [§ 2104(a)(1) or § 2104(a)(3)], may sue either for such person or for other persons similarly situated, or both, in any district court of the United States for any district in which the violation is alleged to have occurred, or in which the employer transacts business."

There is no dispute that "[a]ggrieved employees" such as Ms. Lee have standing to sue under the WARN Act because they are "person[s] seeking to enforce" the liability provisions in § 2104(a)(1) of the Act to recover back pay and benefits for the time period when notice of an impending layoff or termination was owed, but not given. Similarly, there is no question that aggrieved "unit[s] of local government" such as the City Plaintiffs have standing to enforce the liability provisions in § 2104(a)(3) of the Act, which permit recovery of civil penalties of $500 per day of missed notice. Furthermore, the Supreme Court has held that § 2104(a)(5)'s express reference to "a representative of employees" specifically abrogated otherwise applicable associational standing limitations and manifested Congress' intention to grant unions standing to sue on behalf of their members for damages to which the members are entitled under § 2104(a)(1).

The question posed in this case is whether Congress also granted the State Labor Department and its Commissioner standing to sue the Defendants under the WARN Act. Examining the language, structure, and legislative history (or lack thereof) of the WARN Act, the Court concludes that Congress did not confer standing on the State Plaintiffs to sue to enforce the WARN Act.

1.   The Statutory Language. When examining a statute, courts must begin—and often must end—with the language of the statute itself. *See Leocal v. Ashcroft,* 543 U.S. 1, ___, 125 S.Ct. 377, 382, 160 L.Ed.2d 271 (2004) ("Our analysis begins with the language of the statute."); *Hughes Aircraft Co. v. Jacobson,* 525 U.S. 432, 438, 119 S.Ct. 755, 142 L.Ed.2d 881 (1999) ("As in any case of statutory construction, our analysis begins with 'the language of the statute.' And where the statutory language provides a clear answer, it ends there as well.") (quoting *Estate of Cowart v. Nicklos Drilling Co.,* 505 U.S. 469, 475, 112 S.Ct. 2589, 120 L.Ed.2d 379 (1992)); *United States v. Gayle,* 342 F.3d 89, 92 (2d Cir. 2003) ("Statutory construction begins with the plain text and, if that text is unambiguous, it usually ends there as well.").

On its face, the text of § 2104(a)(5) grants standing to "person[s]" and explicitly defines the term "person" to include a "representative of employees or a unit of local government." Therefore, the clear, unambiguous and plain text of the WARN Act contemplates three—and only three—categories of plaintiffs who have standing to enforce the WARN Act: "persons," "representatives of employees," and "units of local government."

The State Plaintiffs do not argue that a State should be considered a "unit of local government" under the WARN Act. And for good reason, since the Act explicitly defines a "unit of local government" as "any general purpose *political subdivision of a State* which has the power to levy taxes and spend funds, as well as general corporate and police powers." A state cannot be a political subdivision of itself, and the State Plaintiffs do not contend otherwise.

The State Plaintiffs also cannot argue that they are a "representative of employees," because that phrase is specifically defined by the WARN Act as "an exclusive representative of employees within the meaning of section 159(a) or 158(f) of this title [the National Labor Relations Act] or section 152 of Title 45 [the Railway Labor Act]." Because the WARN Act limits the term "representative of employees" to its most common (and common sense) usage in the employment context—namely labor unions— the State Plaintiffs cannot be considered "a representative of employees" under the Act. Once again, the State Plaintiffs do not contend otherwise, and the State Plaintiffs explicitly represented to the Court at oral argument that they were suing directly under § 2104(a)(5) in their own right and not as *parens patriae* on behalf of the employees.

Finally, all parties would agree that the term "person" most naturally refers to laid-off employees like Ms. Lee, who claim to have been injured as a result of a failure by the employer to comply with the WARN Act.

Indeed, there can be no dispute that the primary purpose of the WARN Act as a whole is to protect workers, and the primary purpose of § 2104(a)(5) in particular is to penalize employers who fail to comply with the Act and ensure that aggrieved employees are able to recover back pay and benefits. Nevertheless, in their quest to obtain standing to enforce the WARN Act, the State Plaintiffs seek to shoe-horn themselves into the term "person," a word that simply does not fit them.

To begin with, the text of the WARN Act must be read and interpreted in the context of the general presumption that when Congress uses the term "person" in a federal statute, it does not intend to include a sovereign such as the State of Connecticut, unless there is good reason to believe otherwise. Numerous courts have recognized that "[i]t is a longstanding interpretive presumption that 'person' does not include the sovereign." *Vermont Agency of Natural Resources v. United States ex rel. Stevens,* 529 U.S. 765, 780, 120 S.Ct. 1858, 146 L.Ed.2d 836 (2000); *see, e.g., Will v. Michigan Dep't of State Police,* 491 U.S. 58, 64, 109 S.Ct. 2304, 105 L.Ed.2d 45 (1989) ("[I]n common usage, the term 'person' does not include the sovereign, [and] statutes employing the [word] are ordinarily construed to exclude it."); *United States v. United Mine Workers,* 330 U.S. 258, 275, 67 S.Ct. 677, 91 L.Ed.884 (1947) ("In common usage, that term [person] does not include the sovereign, and statutes employing it will ordinarily not be construed to do so."); *United States v. Errol D., Jr.,* 292 F.3d 1159, 1163 (9th Cir. 2002) ("[A]lthough it is possible that Congress intended 'person' to be construed broadly . . . such speculation cannot by itself suffice to overcome this longstanding presumption."); *United States ex rel. Long v. SCS Business & Technical Institute, Inc.,* 173 F.3d 870, 874 (D.C. Cir. 1999) ("[I]f the . . . rule has any meaning at all, it must create at minimum a default rule; states are excluded from the term person absent an affirmative contrary showing."); *United States v. Streater,* No. 3:97CR232 (EBB), 1999 WL 66534, at *2 (D.Conn. Jan. 19, 1999) ("It is a canon of statutory construction that the general words of a statute do not include the government . . . unless the text of the statute expressly includes the government."); *see also* 1 U.S.C. § 1 (default definition of "person" in the Dictionary Act does not include the government). *Cf. United States v. Ekanem,* 383 F.3d 40, 43 (2d Cir. 2004) (concluding from the context of the Mandatory Victims Restitution Act of 1996, 18 U.S.C. § 3663A, that the term "victim" is not "limited by the default definition of 'person' in the Dictionary Act but instead includes the Government.").

Ordinarily, therefore, when Congress decides to include states within the term "person," Congress does so explicitly and clearly. A small sampling from varied sections of the United States Code will suffice to make the point. *See, e.g.,* Lobbying Disclosure Act of 1995, 2 U.S.C. § 1602(14) ("The term 'person or entity' means any individual, corporation, company, . . . or State or local government."); Weather Modification Reporting Act of 1972,

15 U.S.C. § 330(2) ("The term 'person' means any individual, corporation, company, . . . any State or local government or any agency thereof . . . who is performing weather modification activities."); Marine Mammal Protection Act of 1972, 16 U.S.C. § 1362(10) ("The term 'person' includes (A) any private person or entity, and (B) any officer, employee, agent, department, or instrumentality of the Federal Government, of any State or political subdivision thereof, or of any foreign government."); Pro-Children Act of 1994, 20 U.S.C. § 6082(3) ("The term 'person' means any State or local subdivision thereof, agency of such State or subdivision. . . ."); Resource Conservation and Recovery Act of 1976, 42 U.S.C. § 6903(15) ("The term 'person' means an individual, trust, firm, . . . State, municipality, commission, political subdivision of a State, or any interstate body.").

By contrast to the foregoing statutes, the WARN Act does not define the word "person" to include states. The WARN Act is silent on this crucial issue, a silence that the Court finds telling, since it reinforces the interpretive presumption that when, as here, Congress uses the term "person" without more, Congress does not intend to include within the term sovereign entities such as the State Plaintiffs.

In the teeth of this longstanding interpretive presumption, the State Plaintiffs trot out a multitude of arguments to convince the Court that the Congress deliberately chose the word "person" in § 2104(a)(5) as an expression of its intent to grant the State Plaintiffs standing. As an aside, the Court notes that were it to adopt the State Plaintiffs' expansive interpretation of the word "person" in the WARN Act—which the Court most certainly will not—such a holding would have the potential to initiate more mischief than the State Plaintiffs should truly desire, considering the many instances where the State unquestionably benefits from not being considered to be a "person" under federal law. In any event, the State Plaintiffs' complex—and often convoluted—arguments fail to overcome the high hurdle that the plain language of the statute and the interpretative presumption sets before them.

In their brief in opposition to the motion to dismiss, the State Plaintiffs argue that because Congress has authorized governmental entities to bring representative actions on behalf of employees in other labor laws, the Court should conclude that Congress also intended to give the State Plaintiffs standing to sue to enforce the WARN Act. In support of this argument, the State Plaintiffs cite the following statutes: the Fair Labor Standards Act (FLSA)("The right provided by this subsection to bring an action by or on behalf of any employee, and the right of any employee to become a party plaintiff to any such action, shall terminate upon the filing of a complaint by the Secretary of Labor. . . . The Secretary may bring an action in any court of competent jurisdiction to recover the amount of unpaid minimum wages or overtime compensation and an equal amount as liquidated damages."); the Employee Retirement Income Security Act of 1974 (ERISA), 29 U.S.C. § 1132(a) ("A civil action may be brought . . . by the Secretary . . . by the State . . ."); the Family and Medical Leave Act (FMLA), 29 U.S.C. § 2617(b)(2) ("The Secretary may bring an action in any court of competent jurisdiction to recover . . . damages"); the Employee Polygraph Protection Act, 29 U.S.C. § 2005(b) ("The Secretary may bring an action under this section to restrain violations of this chapter."). . . .

Frankly, the Court finds this argument baffling, for far from supporting the State Plaintiffs' claim of standing, these above-noted statutes undermine it. Each of the statutes cited clearly and unambiguously grants the governmental authorities . . . the right to sue employers on behalf of aggrieved employees. The WARN Act, by contrast, does no such thing, even though—as the State Plaintiffs' argument unwittingly makes clear—Congress apparently knows full well how to draft statutes that explicitly authorize governmental entities to sue on behalf of aggrieved employees. The WARN Act's silence regarding the State Plaintiffs' standing to sue is thus ever more deafening in light of the other labor statutes in which Congress explicitly authorized governmental authorities to sue on behalf of employees.

The State Plaintiffs also make much of the fact that the drafters of the WARN Act could have used the term "employee" instead of "person" in § 2104(a)(5). They point out that the term "person" is not defined in the Act and is only used in § 2104(a)(5), whereas the term "employee" is defined in § 2104(a)(7) and is used throughout the WARN Act. The State Plaintiffs contend that Congress's conscious choice to use the term "person" instead of "employee" in § 2104(a)(5) implies that Congress did not intend to limit standing to sue to aggrieved employees.

This argument does nothing to advance the State Plaintiffs' cause since it does nothing to rebut the presumption that when Congress uses the word "person" in a federal statute, the term does not include states. Of course, Congress did not intend to limit standing to aggrieved employees alone; § 2104(a)(5) expressly recites that the term "person" also includes a "representative of employees or a unit of local government." Therefore, while use of the word "person" in the WARN Act does indeed suggest that Congress had in mind that the Act would be enforced by others beyond aggrieved employees, that does not mean that Congress also contemplated that those "others" would include states. And in light of the long series of cases establishing the presumption that "person" does not include states, this Court may presume that Congress knew that to include states within meaning of the term "person," Congress would have to say so expressly.

In fact, by explicitly *including* unions and local governments within the scope of the term "person," Congress can be deemed to have *excluded* all others not expressly mentioned, such as the State Plaintiffs. That is because "when legislation expressly provides a particular remedy or remedies, courts should not expand the coverage of the statute to subsume other remedies. . . . This principle of statutory construction reflects an ancient maxim—*expressio unius est exclusio alterius.*" Though the *expressio unius* "maxim is not always a reliable guide," in certain circumstances it can be "persuasive evidence" of Congressional intent, or at the very least support other similar evidence of Congressional intent. And while it is certainly true that "not every silence is pregnant," in this case the Court believes that Congress's silence is pregnant because of the long-standing interpretative guide previously discussed.

The State Plaintiffs respond by focusing on Congress's use of the word "including" before the phrase "representative of employees or a unit of local government" in § 2104(a)(5) and by suggesting that unions and local governments are therefore only "illustrative" of those entities entitled to bring suit under the WARN Act. Once again, however, this argument founders when faced with the strong presumption against including sovereigns within the scope of the term "person." For even if union representatives and units of local government are only two examples of a much larger group of parties who fall within the scope of the term "person," to overcome the interpretative principle against including states within the meaning of that term, Congress would have to have done something to make its intention to include states clear. Yet, there is nothing to suggest that Congress intended such a result. Therefore, one can accept *arguendo* that the term "person" may not be limited to aggrieved employees, unions and local governments without also accepting the State Plaintiffs' claim that the term must also include states.

Furthermore, the word "including" need not always be used by Congress in an illustrative manner. The term can also be used and construed as restrictive and definitional. *See, e.g., Adams v. Dole,* 927 F.2d 771, 777 (4th Cir. 1991) (the use of the term "including" to define "employer" in a portion of a broader statute specifically regulating the Nuclear Regulatory Commission (NRC) was "not meant to be illustrative, but rather definitional," thereby restricting the scope of the term "employer" to include the NRC and only those other entities specifically listed after the term "including"); *see also Random House Webster's Unabridged Dictionary* 967 (2d ed. 2001) (the verb "include" defined as "to contain, as a whole does parts or any part or element"). Therefore, it is not unnatural at all to read § 2104(a)(5) and its use of the term "including" as defining the "persons" who have standing to sue under the WARN Act as including only aggrieved employees (the parties most naturally fitting within the scope of the term "person[s]"), unions (who represent those employees) and aggrieved local governmental units (who are entitled to penalties under the Act).

In this regard, the Court notes that the Department of Labor—Congress's designated expert on labor statutes—has also weighed in on the mechanics of WARN Act enforcement. The Department of Labor's regulation on "WARN enforcement" interprets the plain text of the Act in accord with this Court's interpretation, stating in relevant part:

"Enforcement of WARN will be through the courts, as provided in section 5 of the statute. *Employees, their representatives and units of local government may initiate civil actions against employers* believed to be in violation of § 3 of the Act. The Department of Labor has no legal standing in any enforcement action and, therefore, will not be in a position to issue advisory opinions of specific cases."

Thus, the Department of Labor has interpreted the WARN Act as granting only three parties standing to enforce the Act: employees, their union representatives, and local governments. The State Plaintiffs are noticeably absent from the Department of Labor's list.

Finally, the only reported case law on the precise subject raised by the motion to dismiss also is consistent with the Court's decision. In *Blumenthal v. Walker Digital Corp.,* Judge Peter Dorsey of this Court held that the plain text of the statute did not express a clear Congressional intent to confer standing on the State Plaintiffs. This Judge agrees with Judge Dorsey.

In sum, the plain language of the WARN Act does not evidence any intent to include the State Plaintiffs within the meaning of the term "person" in § 2104(a)(5), and long-standing canons of statutory construction weigh heavily against any such interpretation.

2.   The Act's Structure. The structure of a statute as a whole can aid in a court's interpretation of particular statutory language. *See Leocal,* 543 U.S. at ___, 125 S.Ct. at 382 ("[W]e construe language in its context and in light of the terms surrounding it."); *Robinson v. Shell Oil Co.,* 519 U.S. 337, 341, 117 S.Ct. 843, 136 L.Ed.2d 808 (1997) ("The plainness or ambiguity of statutory language is determined by reference to the language itself, the specific context in which that language is used, and the broader context of the statute as a whole."); *Saks v. Franklin Covey Co.,* 316 F.3d 337, 345 (2d Cir. 2003) ("The text's plain meaning can best be understood by looking to the statutory scheme as a whole and placing the particular provision within the context of that statute."); *Auburn Housing Auth. v. Martinez,* 277 F.3d 138, 144 (2d Cir. 2002) ("The meaning of a particular section in a statute can be understood in context with and by reference to the whole statutory scheme, by appreciating how

sections relate to one another. In other words, the preferred meaning of a statutory provision is one that is consonant with the rest of the statute.").

The Court finds that the structure of the WARN Act also supports the Court's reading of the statute's text. The basic structure of the WARN Act creates two exclusive financial remedies—back pay and benefits for former employees under § 2104(a)(1); and a $500 per day penalty for an affected unit of local government under § 2104(a)(3). These remedies run to aggrieved employees, directly or through their union representatives and to local units of government. There are no remedies explicitly directed to states, even though states also receive WARN Act notice. Therefore, a logical and clear reading of the portion of the WARN Act that creates the WARN Act cause of action—§ 2104(a)(5)—is that only those who can recover the exclusive financial remedies provided by the Act have standing to bring suit under the Act.

Units of local government have a direct connection to the $500 per day penalty for failure to provide notice under § 2104(a)(3). Aggrieved employees also have a direct connection to the back pay and benefits owed to employees for failure to provide adequate notice under § 2104(a)(1). Labor unions—the only representatives of the employees recognized by the WARN Act—also have a reasonable connection to or nexus with the back pay and benefits owed to their members, and are explicitly mentioned in the statute's standing provision § 2104(a)(5). States, however, have no clear connection or nexus with the statutory remedies provided by the WARN Act and they are not expressly mentioned in § 2104(a)(5). The Act is thus sensibly structured so that only those with the greatest incentives to bring a lawsuit—i.e., those with clear connections to the exclusive financial remedies provided by the statute— are empowered to enforce its terms.

Indeed, this case demonstrates why it is not necessary to stretch the language of the WARN Act to provide the State Plaintiffs with standing. For, as this lawsuit shows, there are plenty of ready, willing, and able plaintiffs—both the former employees as well as the City Plaintiffs—who have clear financial incentives to enforce the WARN Act and who can recover their attorneys' fees if they are successful in so doing. There appears to be little risk that WARN Act violations will go unremedied if the State Plaintiffs are denied standing.

. . . .

Finally, the State Plaintiffs argue that since the WARN Act is a remedial statute, it should be interpreted liberally to grant standing to the State Plaintiffs. Once again, this argument does not help the State Plaintiffs. Assuming *arguendo* that the WARN Act can properly be characterized as a remedial statute, the overall objective of the Act is to provide financial remedies to aggrieved employees and local governments who are harmed by sudden plant closings or mass layoffs. Therefore, any liberal reading of the statute should be done in furtherance of this specific objective and for the employees' and local governments' benefit, not for the State Plaintiffs who are granted no remedy under the statute.

Therefore, the Court believes that the WARN Act's structure supports the Court's interpretation of its plain language.

3. Legislative History. When authoritative legislative history is available, courts may in appropriate circumstances cautiously look to that history to confirm an interpretation that is otherwise grounded in the text and structure of the act itself. *Murphy ex rel. Estate of Payne v. United States,* 340 F.Supp.2d 160, 171 (D.Conn.2004) ("The Court understands all too well that using legislative history to construe a statute is often akin to chasing a mirage."). As the Second Circuit has stated,

"[r]esort to authoritative legislative history may be justified where there is an open question as to the meaning of a word or phrase in a statute, or where a statute is silent on an issue of fundamental importance to its correct application. As a general matter, we may consider reliable legislative history where ... the statute is susceptible to divergent understandings and, equally important, where there exists authoritative legislative history that assists in discerning what Congress actually meant."

Here, the State Plaintiffs and Defendants agreed at oral argument that the available authoritative legislative history—the Conference Report—did not address the specific issue of whether a State had standing to sue under the WARN Act. Having reviewed the WARN Act's legislative history, the Court agrees. Therefore, the legislative history is, at best, neutral, though some jurists might construe Congress' silence to work against the State Plaintiffs in view of the strong interpretative presumption that the term "person" does not include the state unless indicated otherwise.

In sum, having considered the text, structure, and legislative history of § 2104(a)(5) of the WARN Act, the Court concludes that it does not authorize the State Plaintiffs to sue under the Act. If states like Connecticut wish to be able to sue under the WARN Act, they will need to get that authority from the Congress. Accordingly, the Court grants Defendants' motion to dismiss the State Plaintiffs for lack of standing.

. . . .

EXERCISE V.3

John Yates, a commercial fisherman, caught undersized red grouper in federal waters in the Gulf of Mexico. To prevent federal authorities from confirming that he had harvested undersized fish, Yates ordered a crew member to toss the suspect catch into the sea. For this offense, he was charged with, and convicted of, violating 18 U.S.C. § 1519, which provides:

> Whoever knowingly alters, destroys, mutilates, conceals, covers up, falsifies, or makes a false entry in any record, document, or tangible object with the intent to impede, obstruct, or influence the investigation or proper administration of any matter within the jurisdiction of any department or agency of the United States or any case filed under title 11, or in relation to or contemplation of any such matter or case, shall be fined under this title, imprisoned not more than 20 years, or both.

Yates was also indicted and convicted under § 2232(a), which provides:

> DESTRUCTION OR REMOVAL OF PROPERTY TO PREVENT SEIZURE.—Whoever, before, during, or after any search for or seizure of property by any person authorized to make such search or seizure, knowingly destroys, damages, wastes, disposes of, transfers, or otherwise takes any action, or knowingly attempts to destroy, damage, waste, dispose of, transfer, or otherwise take any action, for the purpose of preventing or impairing the Government's lawful authority to take such property into its custody or control or to continue holding such property under its lawful custody and control, shall be fined under this title or imprisoned not more than 5 years, or both.

Yates does not contest his conviction for violating § 2232(a), but he maintains that fish are not included within the term "tangible object," as that term is used in § 1519.

Section 1519 was enacted as part of the Sarbanes–Oxley Act of 2002, 116 Stat. 745, legislation designed to protect investors and restore trust in financial markets following the collapse of Enron Corporation.

- Identify the textual arguments that the government would make in support of its interpretation of the statute.

- Identify the textual arguments that Yates would make in support of his defense.

- Which view do you find most compelling?

- Which view would a Textualist adopt? What about those who adhere to other theories of interpretation?

YATES V. U.S.

135 S.Ct. 1074 (2015).

As you read this case, consider the following questions:

- What textual moves do each of the opinions make?

- Do the Justices seem to be motivated by their politics?

- What are the central disagreements between the three opinions?

- Which opinion do you most agree with?

- What theory (or theories) of interpretation do the various opinions seem to adopt?

- Are any of the opinions any more or less textual than any of the others?

JUSTICE GINSBURG announced the judgment of the Court and delivered an opinion, in which THE CHIEF JUSTICE, JUSTICE BREYER, and JUSTICE SOTOMAYOR join.

John Yates, a commercial fisherman, caught undersized red grouper in federal waters in the Gulf of Mexico. To prevent federal authorities from confirming that he had harvested undersized fish, Yates ordered a crew member to toss the suspect catch into the sea. For this offense, he was charged with, and convicted of, violating 18 U.S.C. § 1519, which provides:

> Whoever knowingly alters, destroys, mutilates, conceals, covers up, falsifies, or makes a false entry in any record, document, or tangible object with the intent to impede, obstruct, or influence the investigation or proper administration of any matter within the jurisdiction of any department or agency of the United States or any case filed under title 11, or in relation to or contemplation of any such matter or case, shall be fined under this title, imprisoned not more than 20 years, or both.

Yates was also indicted and convicted under § 2232(a), which provides:

> DESTRUCTION OR REMOVAL OF PROPERTY TO PREVENT SEIZURE.—Whoever, before, during, or after any search for or seizure of property by any person authorized to make such search or seizure, knowingly destroys, damages, wastes, disposes of, transfers, or otherwise takes any action, or knowingly attempts to destroy, damage, waste, dispose of, transfer, or otherwise take any action, for the purpose of preventing or impairing the Government's lawful authority to take such property into its custody or control or to continue holding such property under its lawful custody and control, shall be fined under this title or imprisoned not more than 5 years, or both.

Yates does not contest his conviction for violating § 2232(a), but he maintains that fish are not trapped within the term "tangible object," as that term is used in § 1519.

Section 1519 was enacted as part of the Sarbanes–Oxley Act of 2002, 116 Stat. 745, legislation designed to protect investors and restore trust in financial markets following the collapse of Enron Corporation. A fish is no doubt an object that is tangible; fish can be seen, caught, and handled, and a catch, as this case illustrates, is vulnerable to destruction. But it would cut § 1519 loose from its financial-fraud mooring to hold that it encompasses any and all objects, whatever their size or significance, destroyed with obstructive intent. Mindful that in Sarbanes–Oxley, Congress trained its attention on corporate and accounting deception and cover-ups, we conclude that a matching construction of § 1519 is in order:

A tangible object captured by § 1519, we hold, must be one used to record or preserve information.

I

On August 23, 2007, the *Miss Katie,* a commercial fishing boat, was six days into an expedition in the Gulf of Mexico. Officer John Jones of the Florida Fish and Wildlife Conservation Commission decided to board the *Miss Katie* to check on the vessel's compliance with fishing rules.

Suspecting that other undersized fish might be on board, Officer Jones proceeded to inspect the ship's catch, setting aside and measuring only fish that appeared to him to be shorter than 20 inches. Officer Jones ultimately determined that 72 fish fell short of the 20–inch mark; none were less than 18.75 inches. Under questioning, one of the crewmembers admitted that, at Yates's direction, he had thrown overboard the fish Officer Jones had measured at sea, and that he and Yates had replaced the tossed grouper with fish from the rest of the catch. For reasons not disclosed in the record before us, more than 32 months passed before criminal charges were lodged against Yates. By the time of the indictment, the minimum legal length for Gulf red grouper had been lowered from 20 inches to 18 inches. No measured fish in Yates's catch fell below that limit. The record does not reveal what civil penalty, if any, Yates received for his possession of fish undersized under the 2007 regulation.

Yates argued that the section sets forth "a documents offense" and that its reference to "tangible object[s]" subsumes "computer hard drives, logbooks, [and] things of that nature," not fish. Yates acknowledged that the Criminal Code contains "sections that would have been appropriate for the [G]overnment to pursue" if it wished to prosecute him for tampering with evidence.

The Government countered that a "tangible object" within § 1519's compass is "simply something other than a document or record." While recognizing that § 1519 was passed as part of legislation targeting corporate fraud, the Court of Appeals had instructed that "the broad language of § 1519 is not limited to corporate fraud cases, and 'Congress is free to pass laws with language covering areas well beyond the particular crisis *du jour* that initially prompted legislative action.'" the [District C]ourt sentenced Yates to imprisonment for 30 days, followed by supervised release for three years. For life, he will bear the stigma of having a federal felony conviction.

On appeal, the Eleventh Circuit found the text of § 1519 "plain." 733 F.3d 1059, 1064 (2013). Because "tangible object" was "undefined" in the statute, the Court of Appeals gave the term its "ordinary or natural meaning," *i.e.,* its dictionary definition, "[h]aving or possessing physical form." *Ibid.* (quoting Black's Law Dictionary 1592 (9th ed. 2009)).

II

The Sarbanes–Oxley Act, all agree, was prompted by the exposure of Enron's massive accounting fraud and revelations that the company's outside auditor, Arthur Andersen LLP, had systematically destroyed potentially incriminating documents. The Government acknowledges that § 1519 was intended to prohibit, in particular, corporate document-shredding to hide evidence of financial wrongdoing.

In the Government's view, § 1519 extends beyond the principal evil motivating its passage. The words of § 1519, the Government argues, support reading the provision as a general ban on the spoliation of evidence, covering all physical items that might be relevant to any matter under federal investigation.

Yates urges a contextual reading of § 1519, tying "tangible object" to the surrounding words, the placement of the provision within the Sarbanes–Oxley Act, and related provisions enacted at the same time, in particular § 1520 and § 1512(c)(1), he maintains, targets not all manner of evidence, but records, documents, and tangible objects used to preserve them, *e.g.,* computers, servers, and other media on which information is stored.

We agree with Yates and reject the Government's unrestrained reading. "Tangible object" in § 1519, we conclude, is better read to cover only objects one can use to record or preserve information, not all objects in the physical world.

II A

The ordinary meaning of an "object" that is "tangible," as stated in dictionary definitions, is "a discrete . . . thing," Webster's Third New International Dictionary 1555 (2002), that "possess[es] physical form," Black's Law Dictionary 1683 (10th ed. 2014). From this premise, the Government concludes that "tangible object," as that term appears in § 1519, covers the waterfront, including fish from the sea.

Whether a statutory term is unambiguous, however, does not turn solely on dictionary definitions of its component words. Rather, "[t]he plainness or ambiguity of statutory language is determined [not only] by reference to the language itself, [but as well by] the specific context in which that language is used, and the broader context of the statute as a whole." Ordinarily, a word's usage accords with its dictionary definition. In law as in life, however, the same words, placed in different contexts, sometimes mean different things.

"Most words have different shades of meaning and consequently may be variously construed. . . . Where the subject matter to which the words refer is not the same in the several places where [the words] are used, or the conditions are different, or the scope of the legislative power exercised in one case is broader than that exercised in another, the meaning well may vary to meet the purposes of the law, to be arrived at by a consideration of the language in which those purposes are expressed, and of the circumstances under which the language was employed."

In short, although dictionary definitions of the words "tangible" and "object" bear consideration, they are not dispositive of the meaning of "tangible object" in § 1519.

Rule 16 is a discovery rule designed to protect defendants by compelling the prosecution to turn over to the defense evidence material to the charges at issue. In that context, a comprehensive construction of "tangible objects" is fitting. In contrast, § 1519 is a penal provision that refers to "tangible object" not in relation to a request for information relevant to a specific court proceeding, but rather in relation to federal investigations or proceedings of every kind, including those not yet begun.[3]

Just as the context of Rule 16 supports giving "tangible object" a meaning as broad as its dictionary definition, the context of § 1519 tugs strongly in favor of a narrower reading.

II B

Familiar interpretive guides aid our construction of the words "tangible object" as they appear in § 1519. We note first § 1519's caption: "Destruction, alteration, or falsification of records in Federal investigations and bankruptcy." That heading conveys no suggestion that the section prohibits spoliation of any and all physical evidence, however remote from records. Neither does the title of the section of the Sarbanes–Oxley Act in which § 1519 was placed, § 802: "Criminal penalties for altering documents."

Furthermore, § 1520, the only other provision passed as part of § 802, is titled "Destruction of corporate audit records" and addresses only that specific subset of records and documents. While these headings are not commanding, they supply cues that Congress did not intend "tangible object" in § 1519 to sweep within its reach physical objects of every kind, including things no one would describe as records, documents, or devices closely associated with them.

Section 1519's position within Chapter 73 of Title 18 further signals that § 1519 was not intended to serve as a cross-the-board ban on the destruction of physical evidence of every kind. Congress placed § 1519 (and its companion provision § 1520) at the end of the chapter, following immediately after the pre-existing § 1516, § 1517, and § 1518, each of

---

[3] For the same reason, we do not think the meaning of "tangible objects" (or "tangible things," see Fed. Rule Civ. Proc. 26(b)) in other discovery prescriptions cited by the Government leads to the conclusion that "tangible object" in § 1519 encompasses any and all physical evidence existing on land or in the sea.

them prohibiting obstructive acts in specific contexts. See § 1516 (audits of recipients of federal funds); § 1517 (federal examinations of financial institutions); § 1518 (criminal investigations of federal health care offenses). See also S.Rep. No. 107–146, at 7 (observing that § 1517 and § 1518 "apply to obstruction in certain limited types of cases, such as bankruptcy fraud, examinations of financial institutions, and healthcare fraud").

But Congress did not direct codification of the Sarbanes–Oxley Act's other additions to Chapter 73 adjacent to these specialized provisions. Instead, Congress directed placement of those additions within or alongside retained provisions that address obstructive acts relating broadly to official proceedings and criminal trials: Section 806, "Civil Action to protect against retaliation in fraud cases," was codified as § 1514A and inserted between the pre-existing § 1514, which addresses civil actions to restrain harassment of victims and witnesses in criminal cases, and § 1515, which defines terms used in § 1512 and § 1513. Section 1102, "Tampering with a record or otherwise impeding an official proceeding," was codified as § 1512(c) and inserted within the pre-existing § 1512, which addresses tampering with a victim, witness, or informant to impede any official proceeding. Section 1107, "Retaliation against informants," was codified as § 1513(e) and inserted within the pre-existing § 1513, which addresses retaliation against a victim, witness, or informant in any official proceeding. Congress thus ranked § 1519, not among the broad proscriptions, but together with specialized provisions expressly aimed at corporate fraud and financial audits. This placement accords with the view that Congress' conception of § 1519's coverage was considerably more limited than the Government's.

The contemporaneous passage of § 1512(c)(1), which was contained in a section of the Sarbanes–Oxley Act discrete from the section embracing § 1519 and § 1520, is also instructive. Section 1512(c)(1) provides:

> "(c) Whoever corruptly—

> "(1) alters, destroys, mutilates, or conceals a record, document, or other object, or attempts to do so, with the intent to impair the object's integrity or availability for use in an official proceeding

> . . . . .

> "shall be fined under this title or imprisoned not more than 20 years, or both."

The legislative history reveals that § 1512(c)(1) was drafted and proposed after § 1519. See 148 Cong. Rec. 12518, 13088–13089 (2002). The Government argues, and Yates does not dispute, that § 1512(c)(1)'s reference to "other object" includes any and every physical object. But if § 1519's reference to "tangible object" already included all physical objects, as the Government and the dissent contend, then Congress had no reason to enact § 1512(c)(1): Virtually any act that would violate § 1512(c)(1) no doubt would violate § 1519 as well, for § 1519 applies to "the investigation or proper administration of any matter within the jurisdiction of any department or agency of the United States . . . or in relation to or contemplation of any such matter," not just to "an official proceeding."

The Government acknowledges that, under its reading, § 1519 and § 1512(c)(1) "significantly overlap." Nowhere does the Government explain what independent function § 1512(c)(1) would serve if the Government is right about the sweeping scope of § 1519. We resist a reading of § 1519 that would render superfluous an entire provision passed in proximity as part of the same Act. "[T]he canon against surplusage is strongest when an interpretation would render superfluous another part of the same statutory scheme."

The words immediately surrounding "tangible object" in § 1519— "falsifies, or makes a false entry in any record [or] document"—also cabin the contextual meaning of that term. We rely on the principle of *noscitur a sociis*—a word is known by the company it keeps—to "avoid ascribing to one word a meaning so broad that it is inconsistent with its accompanying words, thus giving unintended breadth to the Acts of Congress."

"Tangible object" is the last in a list of terms that begins "any record [or] document." The term is therefore appropriately read to refer, not to any tangible object, but specifically to the subset of tangible objects involving records and documents, *i.e.,* objects used to record or preserve information.

This moderate interpretation of "tangible object" accords with the list of actions § 1519 proscribes. The section applies to anyone who "alters, destroys, mutilates, conceals, covers up, *falsifies,* or *makes a false entry in* any record, document, or tangible object" with the requisite obstructive intent. (Emphasis added.) The last two verbs, "falsif[y]" and "mak[e] a false entry in," typically take as grammatical objects records, documents, or things used to record or preserve information, such as logbooks or hard drives. See, *e.g.,* Black's Law Dictionary 720 (10th ed. 2014) (defining "falsify" as "[t]o make deceptive; to counterfeit, forge, or misrepresent; esp., to tamper with (a document, record, etc.)"). It would be unnatural, for example, to describe a killer's act of wiping his fingerprints from a gun as "falsifying" the murder weapon. But it would not be strange to refer to "falsifying" data stored on a hard drive as simply "falsifying" a hard drive. That contemporaneous omission also suggests that Congress intended "tangible object" in § 1519 to have a narrower scope than "other object" in § 1512(c)(1).7

A canon related to *noscitur a sociis, ejusdem generis,* counsels: "Where general words follow specific words in a statutory enumeration, the general words are [usually] construed to embrace only objects similar in nature to those objects enumerated by the preceding specific words."

In *Begay v. United States,* for example, we relied on this principle to determine what crimes were covered by the statutory phrase "any crime . . . that . . . is burglary, arson, or extortion, involves use of explosives, or otherwise involves conduct that presents a serious potential risk of physical injury to another," 18 U.S.C. § 924(e)(2)(B)(ii). The enumeration of specific crimes, we explained, indicates that the "otherwise involves" provision covers "only *similar* crimes, rather than *every* crime that 'presents a serious potential risk of physical injury to another.'" 554 U.S., at 142. Had Congress intended the latter "all encompassing" meaning, we observed, "it is hard to see why it would have needed to include the examples at all."

Having used traditional tools of statutory interpretation to examine markers of congressional intent within the Sarbanes–Oxley Act and § 1519 itself, we are persuaded that an aggressive interpretation of "tangible object" must be rejected. It is highly improbable that Congress would have buried a general spoliation statute covering objects of any and every kind in a provision targeting fraud in financial record-keeping.

The Government argues, however, that our inquiry would be incomplete if we failed to consider the origins of the phrase "record, document, or tangible object." Congress drew that phrase, the Government says, from a 1962 Model Penal Code (MPC) provision, and reform proposals based on that provision. The MPC provision and proposals prompted by it would have imposed liability on anyone who "alters, destroys, mutilates, conceals, or removes a record, document or thing." See ALI, MPC § 241.7(1), p. 175 (1962). Those proscriptions were understood to refer to all physical evidence. See MPC § 241.7, Comment 3, at 179 (1980) (provision "applies to any physical object"). Accordingly, the Government reasons, and the dissent exuberantly agrees, Congress must have intended § 1519 to apply to the universe of physical evidence.

The inference is unwarranted. True, the 1962 MPC provision prohibited tampering with any kind of physical evidence. But unlike § 1519, the MPC provision did not prohibit actions that specifically relate to records, documents, and objects used to record or preserve information. The MPC provision also ranked the offense as a misdemeanor and limited liability to instances in which the actor "believ[es] that an official proceeding or investigation is pending or about to be instituted." MPC § 241.7(1), at 175. Yates would have had scant reason to anticipate a felony prosecution, and certainly not one instituted at a time when even the smallest of the fish he caught came within the legal limit. A proposed federal offense in line with the MPC provision, advanced by a federal commission in 1971, was similarly qualified.

Section 1519 conspicuously lacks the limits built into the MPC provision and the federal proposal. It describes not a misdemeanor, but a felony punishable by up to 20 years in prison. And the section covers conduct intended to impede any federal investigation or proceeding, including one not even on the verge of commencement. Given these significant differences, the meaning of "record, document, or thing" in the MPC provision and a kindred proposal is not a reliable indicator of the meaning Congress assigned to "record, document, or tangible object" in § 1519. The MPC provision, in short, tells us neither "what Congress wrote [nor] what Congress wanted," concerning Yates's small fish as the subject of a federal felony prosecution.

II C

Finally, if our recourse to traditional tools of statutory construction leaves any doubt about the meaning of "tangible object," as that term is used in § 1519, we would invoke the rule that "ambiguity concerning the ambit of criminal statutes should be resolved in favor of lenity." That interpretative principle is relevant here, where the Government urges a reading of § 1519 that exposes individuals to 20-year prison sentences for tampering with *any* physical object that *might* have evidentiary value in *any* federal investigation into *any* offense, no matter whether the investigation is pending or merely contemplated, or whether the offense subject to investigation is criminal or civil.

Application of the rule of lenity ensures that criminal statutes will provide fair warning concerning conduct rendered illegal and strikes the appropriate balance between the legislature, the prosecutor, and the court in defining criminal liability.

In determining the meaning of "tangible object" in § 1519, "it is appropriate, before we choose the harsher alternative, to require that Congress should have spoken in language that is clear and definite."

For the reasons stated, we resist reading § 1519 expansively to create a coverall spoliation of evidence statute, advisable as such a measure might be. Leaving that important decision to Congress, we hold that a "tangible object" within § 1519's compass is one used to record or preserve information. The judgment of the U.S. Court of Appeals for the Eleventh Circuit is therefore reversed, and the case is remanded for further proceedings.

It is so ordered.

JUSTICE ALITO, concurring in the judgment.

THE PRACTICAL TOOLS OF

This case can and should be resolved on narrow grounds. And though the question is close, traditional tools of statutory construction confirm that John Yates has the better of the argument. Three features of 18 U.S.C. § 1519 stand out to me: the statute's list of nouns, its list of verbs, and its title. Although perhaps none of these features by itself would tip the case in favor of Yates, the three combined do so.

Start with the nouns. Section 1519 refers to "any record, document, or tangible object." The *noscitur a sociis* canon instructs that when a statute contains a list, each word in that list presumptively has a "similar" meaning. A related canon, *ejusdem generis* teaches that general words following a list of specific words should usually be read in light of those specific words to mean something "similar." Applying these canons to § 1519's list of nouns, the term "tangible object" should refer to something similar to records or documents. A fish does not spring to mind—nor does an antelope, a colonial farmhouse, a hydrofoil, or an oil derrick. All are "objects" that are "tangible." But who wouldn't raise an eyebrow if a neighbor, when asked to identify something similar to a "record" or "document," said "crocodile"?

This reading, of course, has its shortcomings. For instance, this is an imperfect *ejusdem generis* case because "record" and "document" are themselves quite general. And there is a risk that "tangible object" may be made superfluous—what is similar to a "record" or "document" but yet is not one? An e-mail, however, could be such a thing. An e-mail, after all, might not be a "document" if, as was "traditionally" so, a document was a "piece of paper with information on it," not "information stored on a computer, electronic storage device, or any other medium." Black's Law Dictionary 587–588 (10th ed. 2014). E-mails might also not be "records" if records are limited to "minutes" or other formal writings "designed to memorialize [past] events." A hard drive, however, is tangible and can contain files that are precisely akin to even these narrow definitions. Both "record" and "document" can be read more expansively, but adding "tangible object" to § 1519 would ensure beyond question that electronic files are included. To be sure, "tangible object" presumably can capture more than just e-mails; Congress enacts "catchall[s]" for "known unknowns." But where *noscitur a sociis* and *ejusdem generis* apply, "known unknowns" should be similar to known knowns, *i.e.,* here, records and documents. This is especially true because reading "tangible object" too broadly could render "record" and "document" superfluous.

Next, consider § 1519's list of verbs: "alters, destroys, mutilates, conceals, covers up, falsifies, or makes a false entry in." . . . But failure to "line up" may suggest that something has gone awry in one's interpretation of a text. Where, as here, each of a statute's verbs applies to a certain category of nouns, there is some reason to think that Congress had that category in mind. Categories, of course, are often underinclusive or overinclusive—

§ 1519, for instance, applies to a bomb-threatening letter but not a bomb. But this does not mean that categories are not useful or that Congress does not enact them. Here, focusing on the verbs, the category of nouns appears to be filekeeping. This observation is not dispositive, but neither is it nothing. The Government also contends that § 1519's verbs cut both ways because it is unnatural to apply "falsifies" to tangible objects, and that is certainly true. One does not falsify the outside casing of a hard drive, but one could falsify or alter data physically recorded on that hard drive.

Finally, my analysis is influenced by § 1519's title: "Destruction, alteration, or falsification of *records* in Federal investigations and bankruptcy." (Emphasis added.) This too points toward filekeeping, not fish. Titles can be useful devices to resolve " 'doubt about the meaning of a statute.'" The title is especially valuable here because it reinforces what the text's nouns and verbs independently suggest—that no matter how other statutes might be read, this particular one does not cover every noun in the universe with tangible form.

Titles, of course, are also not dispositive. Here, if the list of nouns did not already suggest that "tangible object" should mean something similar to records or documents, especially when read in conjunction with § 1519's peculiar list of verbs with their focus on filekeeping, then the title would not be enough on its own. In conjunction with those other two textual features, however, the Government's argument, though colorable, becomes too implausible to accept.

JUSTICE KAGAN, with whom JUSTICE SCALIA, JUSTICE KENNEDY, and JUSTICE THOMAS join, dissenting.

A criminal law, 18 U.S.C. § 1519, prohibits tampering with "any record, document, or tangible object" in an attempt to obstruct a federal investigation. This case raises the question whether the term "tangible object" means the same thing in § 1519 as it means in everyday language—any object capable of being touched. The answer should be easy: Yes. The term "tangible object" is broad, but clear. Throughout the U.S. Code and many States' laws, it invariably covers physical objects of all kinds. And in § 1519, context confirms what bare text says: All the words surrounding "tangible object" show that Congress meant the term to have a wide range. That fits with Congress's evident purpose in enacting § 1519: to punish those who alter or destroy physical evidence— *any* physical evidence—with the intent of thwarting federal law enforcement.

The plurality instead interprets "tangible object" to cover "only objects one can use to record or preserve information." The concurring opinion similarly, if more vaguely, contends that "tangible object" should refer to "something similar to records or documents"—and shouldn't include colonial farmhouses, crocodiles, or fish. In my view, conventional tools of statutory construction all lead to a more conventional result: A "tangible object" is an object that's tangible. I would apply the statute that Congress enacted and affirm the judgment below.

I

While the plurality starts its analysis with § 1519's heading, As the plurality must acknowledge, the ordinary meaning of "tangible object" is "a discrete thing that possesses physical form." A fish is, of course, a discrete thing that possesses physical form. See generally, *Dr. Seuss, One Fish Two Fish Red Fish Blue Fish* (1960). So the ordinary meaning of the term "tangible object" in § 1519, as no one here disputes, covers fish (including too-small red grouper). To my knowledge, no court has ever read any such provision to exclude things that don't record or preserve data; rather, all courts have adhered to the statutory language's ordinary (*i.e.,* expansive) meaning. For example, courts have understood the phrases "tangible objects" and "tangible things" in the Federal Rules of Criminal and Civil Procedure to cover everything from guns to drugs to machinery to . . . animals. No surprise, then, that—until today—courts have uniformly applied the term "tangible object" in § 1519 in the same way.

That is not necessarily the end of the matter; I agree with the plurality (really, who does not?) that context matters in interpreting statutes. We do not "construe the meaning of statutory terms in a vacuum." Rather, we interpret particular words "in their context and with a view to their place in the overall statutory scheme." But this is not such an occasion, for here the text and its context point the same way. Stepping back from the words "tangible object" provides only further evidence that Congress said what it meant and meant what it said. And sometimes that means, as the plurality says, that the dictionary definition of a disputed term cannot control.

Begin with the way the surrounding words in § 1519 reinforce the breadth of the term at issue. Section 1519 refers to "any" tangible object, thus indicating (in line with *that* word's plain meaning) a tangible object "of whatever kind." Webster's Third New International Dictionary 97 (2002). This Court has time and again recognized that "any" has "an expansive meaning," bringing within a statute's reach *all* types of the item (here, "tangible object") to which the law refers. And the adjacent laundry list of verbs in § 1519 ("alters, destroys, mutilates, conceals, covers up, falsifies, or makes a false entry") further shows that Congress wrote a statute with a wide scope. Those words are supposed to ensure— just as "tangible object" is meant to—that § 1519 covers the whole world of evidence-tampering, in all its prodigious variety.

Still more, "tangible object" appears as part of a three-noun phrase (including also "records" and "documents") common to evidence-tampering laws and always understood to embrace things of all kinds. The Model Penal Code's evidence-tampering section, drafted more than 50 years ago, similarly prohibits a person from "alter[ing], destroy[ing], conceal[ing] or remov[ing]" any *record, document or thing*" in an effort to thwart an official investigation or proceeding. ALI, Model Penal Code § 241.7(1), p. 175 (1962) (emphasis added). The Code's commentary emphasizes that the offense described in that provision is "not limited to conduct that [alters] a written instrument." Rather, the language extends to "any physical object." Consistent with that statement—and, of course, with ordinary meaning—courts in the more than 15 States that have laws based on the Model Code's tampering provision apply them to all tangible objects, including drugs, guns, vehicles and . . . yes, animals. Not a one has limited the phrase's scope to objects that record or preserve information.

The words "record, document, or tangible object" in § 1519 also track language in 18 U.S.C. § 1512, the federal witness-tampering law covering (as even the plurality accepts, see *ante,* at 1084) physical evidence in all its forms. Section 1512, both in its original version (preceding § 1519) and today, repeatedly uses the phrase "record, document, or other object"—most notably, in a provision prohibiting the use of force or threat to induce another person to withhold any of those materials from an official proceeding. § 4(a) of the Victim and Witness Protection Act of 1982, 96 Stat. 1249, as amended, 18 U.S.C. § 1512(b)(2). That language, which itself likely derived from the Model Penal Code, encompasses no less the bloody knife than the incriminating letter, as all courts have for decades agreed. And typically "only the most compelling evidence" will persuade this Court that Congress intended "nearly identical language" in provisions dealing with related subjects to bear different meanings.

And legislative history, for those who care about it, puts extra icing on a cake already frosted. Section 1519, as the plurality notes, was enacted after the Enron Corporation's collapse, as part of the Sarbanes–Oxley Act of 2002. But the provision began its life in a separate bill, and the drafters emphasized that Enron was "only a case study exposing the shortcomings in our current laws" relating to both "corporate and criminal" fraud. S.Rep. No. 107–146, pp. 2, 11 (2002). The primary "loophole" Congress identified, arose from limits in the part of § 1512 just described: That provision, as uniformly construed, prohibited a person from inducing another to destroy "record[s], document[s], or other object[s]"—of every type—but not from doing so himself. § 1512(b)(2). Congress (as even the plurality agrees, see *ante,* at 1081) enacted § 1519 to close that yawning gap. But § 1519 could fully achieve that goal only if it covered all the records, documents, and objects § 1512 did, as well as all the means of tampering with them. And so § 1519 was written to do exactly that—"to apply broadly to any acts to destroy or fabricate physical evidence," as long as performed with the requisite intent. S.Rep. No. 107–146, at 14. "When a person destroys evidence," the drafters explained, "overly technical legal distinctions should neither hinder nor prevent prosecution." *Id.,* at 7. Ah well: Congress, meet today's Court, which here invents just such a distinction with just such an effect.

II A

The plurality searches far and wide for anything—*anything*—to support its interpretation of § 1519. But its fishing expedition comes up empty.

The plurality's analysis starts with § 1519's title: "Destruction, alteration, or falsification of records in Federal investigations and bankruptcy."

That's already a sign something is amiss. I know of no other case in which we have *begun* our interpretation of a statute with the title, or relied on a title to override the law's clear terms. Instead, we have followed "the wise rule that the title of a statute and the heading of a section cannot limit the plain meaning of the text."

The reason for that "wise rule" is easy to see: A title is, almost necessarily, an abridgment. Attempting to mention every term in a statute "would often be ungainly as well as useless"; accordingly, "matters in the text . . . are frequently unreflected in the headings.

Just last year, this Court observed that two titles in a nearby section of Sarbanes–Oxley serve as "but a short-hand reference to the general subject matter" of the provision at issue, "not meant to take the place of the detailed provisions of the text." *Lawson v. FMR LLC,* 571 U.S. ——, ——, 134 S.Ct. 1158, 1169, 188 L.Ed.2d 158 (2014). Presumably, the plurality would not refuse to apply § 1519 when a person only conceals evidence rather than destroying, altering, or falsifying it; instead, the plurality would say that a title is just a title, which cannot "undo or limit" more specific statutory text. The same holds true when the evidence in question is not a "record" but something else whose destruction, alteration, etc., is intended to obstruct justice.

The plurality next tries to divine meaning from § 1519's "position within Chapter 73 of Title 18." But that move is yet odder than the last. As far as I can tell, this Court has never once suggested that the section number assigned to a law bears upon its meaning. The plurality next tries to divine meaning from § 1519's "position within Chapter 73 of Title 18." But that move is yet odder than the last. As far as I can tell, this Court has never once suggested that the section number assigned to a law bears upon its meaning. The plurality's third argument, relying on the surplusage canon, at least invokes a known tool of statutory construction—but it too comes to nothing. Says the plurality: If read naturally, § 1519 "would render superfluous" § 1512(c)(1), which Congress passed "as part of the same act." But that is not so: Although the two provisions significantly overlap, each applies to conduct the other does not. The key difference between the two is that § 1519 protects the integrity of "matter [s] within the jurisdiction of any [federal] department or agency" whereas § 1512(c)(1) safeguards "official proceeding[s]" as defined in § 1515(a)(1)(A).

And the legislative history to which the plurality appeals only cuts against it because those materials show that lawmakers knew that § 1519 and § 1512(c)(1) share much common ground. Minority Leader Lott introduced the amendment that included § 1512(c)(1) (along with other criminal and corporate fraud provisions) late in the legislative process, explaining that he did so at the specific request of the President. See 148 Cong. Rec. 12509, 12512 (2002) (remarks of Sen. Lott). Not only Lott but several other Senators noted the overlap between the President's package and provisions already in the bill, most notably § 1519. The presence of both § 1519 and § 1512(c)(1) in the final Act may have reflected belt-and-suspenders caution: If § 1519 contained some flaw, § 1512(c)(1) would serve as a backstop. Or the addition of § 1512(c)(1) may have derived solely from legislators' wish "to satisfy audiences other than courts"—that is, the President and his Justice Department.

And the plurality's invocation of § 1519's verbs does nothing to buttress its canon-based argument. The plurality observes that § 1519 prohibits "falsif[ying]" or "mak[ing] a false entry in" a tangible object, and no one can do those things to, say, a murder weapon (or a fish). But of course someone can alter, destroy, mutilate, conceal, or cover up such a tangible object, and § 1519 prohibits those actions too. The Court has never before suggested that all the verbs in a statute need to match up with all the nouns. And for good reason. It is exactly when Congress sets out to draft a statute broadly—to include every imaginable variation on a theme—that such mismatches will arise. To respond by narrowing the law, as the plurality does, is thus to flout both what Congress wrote and what Congress wanted.

Finally, when all else fails, the plurality invokes the rule of lenity. See *ante,* at 1087. But even in its most robust form, that rule only kicks in when, "after all legitimate tools of interpretation have been exhausted, 'a reasonable doubt persists' regarding whether Congress has made the defendant's conduct a federal crime." No such doubt lingers here. The plurality points to the breadth of § 1519 as though breadth were equivalent to ambiguity. It is not. Section 1519 *is* very broad. It is also very clear. Every traditional tool of statutory interpretation points in the same direction, toward "object" meaning object. Lenity offers no proper refuge from that straightforward (even though capacious) construction.

II B

§ 1519's meaning should not hinge on the odd game of Mad Libs the concurrence proposes. No one reading § 1519 needs to fill in a blank after the words "records" and "documents." That is because Congress, quite helpfully, already did so—adding the term "tangible object." The issue in this case is what that term means. So if the concurrence wishes to ask its neighbor a question, I'd recommend a more pertinent one: Do you think a fish (or, if the concurrence prefers, a crocodile) is a "tangible object"? As to that query, "who wouldn't raise an eyebrow" if the neighbor said "no"?

III

§ 1519 the requirement that a person act "knowingly" and with "the intent to impede, obstruct, or influence" federal law enforcement. And in highlighting § 1519's maximum penalty, the plurality glosses over the absence of any prescribed minimum. (Let's not forget that Yates's sentence was not 20 years, but 30 days.) Congress presumably enacts laws with high maximums and no minimums when it thinks the prohibited conduct may run the gamut from major to minor. That is assuredly true of acts obstructing justice. Compare this case with the following, all of which properly come within, but now fall outside, § 1519Most district judges, as Congress knows, will recognize differences between such cases and prosecutions like this one, and will try to make the punishment fit the crime. Still and all, I tend to think, for the reasons the plurality gives, that § 1519 is a bad law—too broad and undifferentiated, with too-high maximum penalties, which give prosecutors too much leverage and sentencers too much discretion. And I'd go further: In those ways, § 1519 is unfortunately not an outlier, but an emblem of a deeper pathology in the federal criminal code.

I respectfully dissent.

UNITED STATES V. COSTELLO

666 F.3d 1040 (7th Cir. 2012)

As you read this case, consider the following:

- Identify all of the textual and other arguments made by the majority and the dissent.

- Should Google searches be used more often in determining plain meaning?

- What are the major points of disagreement between the majority and the dissent?

- Intuitively, how do you understand the meaning of the word "harbor" in this context? In other words, what do you take to be the plain meaning?

- How does the majority refute the dissent's application of the rule against surplusage (and the rule of meaningful variation, which has the same effect in this case)?

- What theories of interpretation seem to motivate the majority and the dissent?

POSNER, CIRCUIT JUDGE.

The defendant was charged with violating 8 U.S.C. § 1324(a)(1)(A)(iii), which provides that anyone who "knowing or in reckless disregard of the fact that an alien has come to, entered, or remains in the United States in violation of law, conceals, harbors or shields from detection [or attempts to do any of these things], such alien in any place, including any building or any means of transportation," is punishable by a maximum prison term of 5 years and a maximum fine of $250,000. The parties agreed to a bench trial on stipulated facts. The district judge found the defendant guilty and sentenced her to two years' probation and to pay a $200 fine.

The stipulated facts are sparse. The defendant is an American citizen who at the time of the alleged offense lived in a small Illinois town about five miles from St. Louis, named Cahokia. She had a romantic relationship with a Mexican whom she knew to be an illegal alien. He lived with her in Cahokia for about a year, which ended in July 2003 when he was arrested on a federal drug charge. He pleaded guilty, spent several years in prison, and upon completion of his sentence was removed to Mexico. He returned to the United States without authorization, and one day in March 2006 (we don't know how long that was after he'd returned to the United States), the defendant picked him up at the Greyhound bus terminal in St. Louis and drove him to her home in Cahokia, the same home in which they had lived together during his previous sojourn in this country. He lived there more or less continuously until his arrest in October 2006 on drug charges. He was prosecuted, and convicted both of marijuana offenses (conspiracy to distribute marijuana and possession with intent to distribute it), and of having returned to the United States illegally after having been removed, and was given a stiff prison sentence.

The defendant in this case was indicted for all three offenses specified in section 1324(a)(1)(A)(iii)—concealing, harboring, and shielding from detection an alien known to be in this country illegally. . . .

. . . .

[The question is whether she is guilty of] "harboring," which if defined broadly enough describes her action in having permitted the boyfriend to live with her. The government argues that "to harbor" just means to house a person, a meaning that it claims to derive from dictionaries that were in print in 1952 or today; surprisingly the government omits dictionaries that were current in 1917, when concealing and harboring aliens were added to the prohibition of smuggling aliens into this country. . . .

The actual definition of "to harbor" that the government has found in these dictionaries and urges us to adopt is "to shelter," which is not synonymous with "to provide a place to stay." "To shelter" has an aura of protectiveness, as in taking "shelter" from a storm. To shelter is to provide a refuge. "Sheltering" doesn't seem the right word for letting your boyfriend live with you. We have not scoured dictionaries current in 1917 or 1952, but note for what it's worth that the 1910 edition of *Black's Law Dictionary* defines "to harbor" as: "To receive clandestinely and without lawful authority a person for the purpose of so concealing him that another having a right to the lawful custody of such person shall be deprived of the same. A distinction has been taken, in some decisions, between 'harbor' and 'conceal.' A person may be convicted of harboring a slave, although he may not have concealed her."

So the government's reliance on the dictionary definition of "harboring" is mistaken, though a point of greater general importance is that dictionaries must be used as sources of statutory meaning only with great caution. "Of course it is true that the words used, even in their literal sense, are the primary, and ordinarily the most reliable, source of interpreting the meaning of any writing: be it a statute, a contract, or anything else. But it is one of the surest indexes of a mature and developed jurisprudence not to make a fortress out of the dictionary; but to remember that statutes always have some purpose or object to accomplish, whose sympathetic and imaginative discovery is the surest guide to their meaning." "[T]he choice among meanings [of words in statutes] must have a footing more solid than a dictionary—which is a museum of words, an historical catalog rather than a means to decode the work of legislatures." "[I]t makes no sense to declare a unitary meaning that 'the dictionary' assigns to a term. There are a wide variety of dictionaries from which to choose, and all of them usually provide several entries for each word. The selection of a particular dictionary and a particular definition is not obvious and must be defended on some other grounds of suitability. This fact is particularly troubling for those who seek to use dictionaries to determine ordinary meaning. If multiple definitions are available, which one best fits the way an ordinary person would interpret the term?"

Dictionary definitions are acontextual, whereas the meaning of sentences depends critically on context, including all sorts of background understandings. A sign in a park that says "Keep off the grass" is not properly interpreted to forbid the grounds crew to cut the grass. "[O]ne can properly attribute to legislators the reasonable minimum intention 'to say what one would ordinarily be understood as saying, given the circumstances in which it is said.' This principle, it should be noted, does not direct interpreters to follow the literal or dictionary meaning of a word or phrase. To the contrary, it demands careful attention to the nuances and specialized connotations that speakers of the relevant language attach to particular words and phrases in the context in which they are being used." We doubt that the government would argue that a hospital emergency room that takes in a desperately ill person whom the hospital staff knows to be an illegal alien would be guilty of harboring, although it fits the government's definition of the word.

A Google search ... of several terms in which the word "harboring" appears—a search based on the supposition that the number of hits per term is a rough index of the frequency of its use—reveals the following:

"harboring fugitives": 50,800 hits

"harboring enemies": 4,730 hits

"harboring refugees": 4,820 hits

"harboring victims": 114 hits

"harboring flood victims": 0 hits

"harboring victims of disasters": 0 hits

"harboring victims of persecution": 0 hits

"harboring guests": 184 hits

"harboring friends": 256 hits (but some involve harboring Quakers—"Friends," viewed in colonial New England as dangerous heretics)

"harboring Quakers": 3,870 hits

"harboring Jews": 19,100 hits

It is apparent from these results that "harboring," as the word is actually used, has a connotation—which "sheltering," and *a fortiori* "giving a person a place to stay"—does not, of deliberately safeguarding members of a specified group from the authorities, whether through concealment, movement to a safe location, or physical protection. This connotation enables one to see that the emergency staff at the hospital may not be "harboring" an alien when it renders emergency treatment even if he stays in the emergency room overnight, that giving a lift to a gas station to an alien with a flat tire may not be harboring, that driving an alien to the local office of the Department of Homeland Security to apply for an adjustment of status to that of lawful resident may not be harboring, that inviting an alien for a "one night stand" may not be attempted harboring, that placing an illegal alien in a school may not be harboring, and finally that allowing your boyfriend to live with you may not be harboring, even if you know he shouldn't be in the United States.

The prohibition of concealing, shielding from detection, and harboring known illegal aliens grew out of the prohibition of smuggling aliens into the United States. Concealing illegal aliens in the United States and shielding them from detection in the United States are closely related to smuggling; they are active efforts to keep illegal aliens in the United

States. We needn't assume that harboring is redundant; it can be given a meaning that plugs a possible loophole left open by merely forbidding concealing and shielding from detection. Suppose the owner of a Chinese restaurant in New York's or San Francisco's Chinatown employs known illegal aliens as cooks, waiters, and busboys because they are cheap labor, and provides them with housing in order to make the employment, poorly paid though it is, more attractive, and also because they lack documentation that other landlords would require of would-be renters. The owner is harboring these illegal aliens in the sense of taking strong measures to keep them here. Yet there may be no effort at concealment or shielding from detection, simply because the immigration authorities, having very limited investigative resources, may have no interest in rooting out illegal aliens in Chinese restaurants in Chinatowns. It is nonetheless harboring in an appropriate sense because the illegal status of the alien is inseparable from the decision to provide housing—it is a decision to provide a refuge for an illegal alien *because* he's an illegal alien.

The defendant in the present case was not trying to encourage or protect or secrete illegal aliens. There is no suggestion that she prefers illegal aliens as boyfriends to legal aliens or citizens. She had a boyfriend who happened to be (as she knew) an illegal alien, and he lived with her for a time. Had she been aware of section 1324 and fearful of prosecution and hence had told him to move out of her house, he could have found some other place to live in Cahokia, or elsewhere.

It's not as if he was made safer from the feds by living with her. On the contrary, the stipulation of facts—which remember is the only source of the facts upon which she was convicted—states that the boyfriend "had lived with the defendant at 816 LaSalle St. in Cahokia, Illinois, for approximately a year before his arrest in July of 2003 on a federal drug charge. [He] disclosed his cohabitation with the defendant *at this address to federal authorities during a proffer on October 31, 2003. . . .* In March 2006, the defendant picked [the boyfriend] up from a Greyhound Bus Station in St. Louis, Missouri, and transported him to her home *at 816 LaSalle St. in Cahokia, Illinois.*" The stipulation goes on to state that on several occasions while he was living with the defendant after his return to the United States he moved out and stayed with his uncle or his brother, who lived elsewhere in Illinois and whose addresses, as far as we know, were unknown to the authorities. So, had he been living with one of them rather than with her because she refused to take him back when he returned to the United States, he might well have been safer.

. . . .

The restaurant owner in our example provides an inducement to illegal aliens. There is no evidence that the defendant provided an inducement to her boyfriend to remain in or return to the United States. (As we said, she was not charged with inducement.) On the scanty record on which her conviction was based, it is as likely that it was the drug trade that drew and kept him in the United States as it was the girlfriend.

To call this harboring would carry section 1324 far beyond smuggling, and a considerable distance as well from concealing and from shielding from detection. That considerable distance identifies a further problem with the use of dictionaries to determine statutory meaning. Legislative prohibitions are often stated in strings of closely related and overlapping terms, to plug loopholes. They do not have identical dictionary definitions (if they did, the use of multiple terms would have no point), but the overlap means that in many applications they will be redundant, so that to pick out of the dictionary, for each statutory term, a definition remote from that of the other terms may be to misunderstand why the legislature included multiple overlapping terms. We have warned that "the fact that a clause is broadly worded to stop up loopholes doesn't justify a literal interpretation that carries far beyond any purpose that can reasonably be imputed to the drafter. 'When a statute is broadly worded in order to prevent loopholes from being drilled in it by ingenious lawyers, there is a danger of its being applied to situations absurdly remote from the concerns of the statute's framers.' "

The way in which adjacent terms shed light on each other's meaning—a light not to be found in a dictionary—is illustrated by *Begay v. United States*, where the Supreme Court interpreted a statute that defined as a "violent felony" an act or series of acts that is "burglary, arson, or extortion, involves use of explosives, or otherwise involves conduct that presents a serious potential risk of physical injury to another." The Court held that driving under the influence of alcohol, although a dangerous activity, was not within the scope of the subsection's residual clause ("or otherwise involves conduct that presents a serious potential risk of physical injury to another") because it lacked the essential character of the enumerated crimes, all of which involved "purposeful, violent, and aggressive" conduct.

The string of prohibitions in section 1324(a)(1)(A)(iii) is most naturally understood as the following series of loophole-stopping near synonyms: "concealing" is concealing; "shielding from detection" usually is concealing but could involve bribing law enforcement authorities—in other words paying someone else to conceal (yet the shade of difference is tiny—no surprise in a string of near synonyms); and the office left to "harboring" is, then, materially to assist an alien to remain illegally in the United States without publicly advertising his presence but without needing or bothering to conceal it, as in our restaurant example—though harboring *could* involve advertising, for instance if a church publicly offered sanctuary for illegal aliens and committed to resist any effort by the authorities to enter the church's premises to arrest them.

But to make "harboring" sweep so far beyond concealing or shielding from detection as to reach the examples we gave earlier of what we think the word does *not* mean in section 1324 would yield a prohibition that couldn't be understood as just plugging possible loopholes in the first two prohibitions. It would go well beyond the bans on concealing and shielding from detection, and indeed would reach further than any other term in section 1324, which forbids bringing someone one knows to be an illegal alien into the country, transporting a known illegal alien "in furtherance of such violation of law," and "encourag[ing] or induc[ing]" an alien to enter the country illegally.

The number of illegal aliens in the United States was estimated at 10.8 million in 2010. No doubt thousands, perhaps many thousands, of persons are involved in concealing, shielding from detection, or harboring—under unexceptionable understandings of these terms—aliens whom they know to be illegal. The government's lawyer conceded at oral argument that under the government's broader definition of harboring the number of violators of section 1324(a)(1)(A)(iii) might well be two million. Did Congress intend such a leap when it added harboring to the list of offenses in that subsection? Illegal aliens were a smaller fraction of the American population then. But still—is it likely that Congress intended that parents whose child invites an immigrant classmate who, as they know, is illegally in the country to a sleepover might be branded as criminals even if he didn't accept the invitation, since the statute criminalizes attempts?

And notice, among the paradoxes with which the government's position is rife, that although generally it is not a crime to be an illegal alien (though there are important exceptions, as when the alien has eluded examination or inspection by immigration officers, or, as in the case of the defendant's boyfriend, has returned to the United States without authorization after having been removed), an illegal alien becomes a criminal by having a wife, also an illegal alien, living with him in the United States; if they have children, born abroad and hence illegal aliens also, living with them, then each parent has several counts of criminal harboring, on the government's interpretation of the statute. The effect would be a profound change in the legal status of aliens in the United States.

The Justice Department does little to publicize the existence of federal criminal prohibitions, numerous as they are—there are more than 4000 separate federal crimes, as well as countless regulations the violation of which is criminal. There are too few prosecutions for violations of section 1324(a)(1)(A)(iii) to have created widespread public awareness of the law, let alone of its outer reach as conceived by the government. We asked the Department of Justice for statistics, and it informs us that, according to its records (which it tells us may be incomplete), in fiscal year 2011 only 223 cases were filed that included a count under section 1324(a)(1)(A)(iii). We have found a Justice Department press release concerning a prosecution for harboring illegal aliens, but it charges behavior remote from that of the defendant in the present case: "Columbia County Couple Indicted for Harboring Illegal Aliens for Commercial Advantage and Laundering the Proceeds of that Crime."

Courts like to say that knowledge of the law is presumed. But what they mean is that ignorance of the law, though common, is not a defense to a criminal prosecution. There are good practical reasons for this rule, but it results in many injustices, since ignorance of specific legal prohibitions is widespread. The prevalence of such injustices argues for trying to conform criminal prohibitions, by judicial interpretation where that is a permissible option, to prevalent usages. We mustn't forget the rule of lenity in the interpretation of criminal statutes or the words of the great nineteenth-century English jurist of criminal law James Fitzjames Stephen: "Before an act can be treated as a crime, it ought . . . to be of such nature that it is worth while to prevent it at the risk of inflicting great damage, direct and indirect, upon those who commit it."

The government tells us not to worry: we judges can rely on prosecutors to avoid bringing cases at the outer margin of the government's sweeping definition of "harboring." But this case *is* at the outer margin. No doubt it was brought because the Justice Department suspects that the defendant was involved in her boyfriend's drug dealings, but cannot prove it, so the Department reaches into its deep arsenal (the 4000-plus federal crimes) and finds a crime that she doubtless never heard of that it can pin on her. She was sentenced only to probation and to pay a fine but now has a felony record that will dog her for the rest of her life if she loses this appeal.

We've assumed thus far that we have to find a meaning for harboring that will distinguish it sharply from concealing and from shielding from detection. Indulging that assumption may be too generous to the government. Statutory redundancy is common, and also common as we've said is for a statute to string together words of prohibition that are almost synonyms, the better to plug potential loopholes.

Remember that the words "concealing" and "harboring" were added to the smuggling statute in the 1917 act. There is no statutory definition but here is how one court interpreted them: "When taken in connection with the purposes of the act, we conceive the natural meaning of the word 'harbor' to be to clandestinely shelter, succor, and protect improperly admitted aliens, and that the word 'conceal' should be taken in the simple sense of shielding from observation and preventing discovery of such alien persons." So concealment (*"clandestinely* shelter") is an element of harboring. In like vein *United States v. Mack*, an opinion by Learned Hand, states that "the statute is very plainly directed against those who abet evaders of the law against unlawful entry, as the collocation of 'conceal' and 'harbor' shows. Indeed, the word, 'harbor' alone often connotes surreptitious concealment."

A similar statute, entitled "Concealing Person from Arrest," punishes "whoever harbors or conceals any person for whose arrest a warrant or process has been issued under the provisions of any law of the United States, so as to prevent his discovery and arrest, after notice or knowledge of the fact that a warrant or process has been issued for the apprehension of such person." In *United States v. Foy*, we defined to "harbor" in that statute as "to lodge, to care for after secreting the offender." To "harbor" appears in still another federal criminal statute [that] prohibits harboring military deserters, and there the word has been interpreted to mean providing lodging and care "after secreting the deserter."

If as [those previous] opinions suggest, concealment is inherent in harboring, this may seem to make the statutory prohibition of harboring redundant, and that will bother anyone who doubts that statutes ever contain redundancies (is there such an anyone?)—redundant because if harboring always involves concealing, why not just prohibit concealing? But think back to the restaurant example. The owner does not house his illegal employees in order to conceal them, though that is one effect. He is reducing their interactions with citizens, who might report them to the authorities. It is a perfect case of harboring, but might be a weak case of concealing, if the defendant could convince the jury that concealment was not his purpose in housing them.

. . . .

Our rejection of equating harboring to providing a place to stay compels the acquittal of the defendant, for on our understanding of the offense no trier of fact could reasonably find that the defendant had "harbored" her boyfriend based on the stipulated facts, or that she had concealed him or shielded him from detection.

MANION, CIRCUIT JUDGE, dissenting.

The defendant Deanna L. Costello was convicted of "harboring" an illegal alien under 8 U.S.C. § 1324(a)(1)(A)(iii). . . . In this appeal, the court rejects the ordinary definition of the term "harboring" and asserts that the facts cannot support Costello's conviction even when considering a more exacting definition of "harboring"; thus, the court would reverse Costello's conviction. I disagree, and conclude that the plain language of the statute and the stipulated facts support the conviction of harboring. Accordingly, I respectfully dissent.

It is important to recognize the facts of this particular case; we do not need to speculate with hypotheticals. Costello is a legal American resident. When her boyfriend first moved in with her in 2002, he was merely an alien who had entered the United States without being legally admitted. If he had been caught in his undocumented condition by the Department of Homeland Security, charging Costello with harboring, a felony, at that time arguably may have been an unjust application of the law. But that did not happen. Her boyfriend then committed drug crimes, was arrested and convicted of a federal felony, and imprisoned for several years. Following his imprisonment, he was formally deported from the United States, only to reenter the country shortly thereafter in violation of his status and order of deportation. He reunited with Costello when she picked him up at the bus station and then allowed him to live with her in her home for about seven months. His stay with Costello ended after he and his brother crashed when being chased by Drug Enforcement Administration ("DEA") agents. During the chase he contacted Costello, but was taken into custody after the crash.

So Costello was not simply a person who was letting her boyfriend live with her. That may have been the case early in the relationship when all she knew was that he was "a Mexican whom she knew to be an illegal alien." But any naïveté (more likely deliberate ignorance) ceased when her boyfriend was arrested, convicted, imprisoned for a federal drug crime, and then deported. When Costello brought her boyfriend back to her home the second time, she was well aware that he was a convicted felon who had been deported after several years in federal prison, and who had further violated the law by reentering the United States without authorization in violation of his deportation proceedings. What's more, this is not a situation where Costello let her boyfriend stay at her place temporarily; instead, for approximately seven months, she provided him with a place to reside until another altercation with law enforcement ended with his arrest. This is not a case at the "outer margin."

The court appears to find Costello's conviction unfair and worthy of reversal because there are so many potential "harboring" violations that presumably occur throughout the United States but are not prosecuted. But that is not a reason for us to invalidate a federal law that Congress expects the Department of Justice to enforce. Prosecution is not always necessary and proper. "If a person commits a relatively nominal act that is proscribed by § 1324(a)(1)(A)(iii), the executive branch has the discretion to forego prosecution." When interpreting a statute, courts should not overlay the statute with a "veneer" that "appropriates that discretion and also invades the province of Congress." The court's decision both invades congressional province and impermissibly questions the executive's decision to prosecute.

Courts should interpret the statute according to its "plain language," and "assume[ ] that the purpose of the statute is communicated by the ordinary meaning of the words Congress used." In this case, the statute declares that any person who "conceals, harbors, or shields from detection" an illegal alien is criminally liable. Contrary to the court's assertion, the ordinary meaning of "harboring" certainly includes "providing shelter to." This was a common understanding of the term when the term "harbor" was first added to the statute in 1917, and when the statute was amended and the term retained in 1952. As we noted in *Ye*, " 'conceal,' 'harbor,' and 'shield from detection' have independent meanings, and thus a conviction can result from committing (or attempting to commit) any one of the three acts." Perhaps if Costello had shooed her boyfriend out the back door when the police were approaching from the front, she could be accused of shielding. Or if she had hidden him in the basement under a pile of laundry when federal agents showed up with a search warrant, she could also be charged with concealing. But she neither shielded nor concealed; instead, she provided shelter to her boyfriend, and nothing more is required to charge her with harboring under the statute.

The court suggests a more exacting definition of "harboring" than "providing shelter to," namely, "providing . . . a known illegal alien a secure haven, a refuge, a place to stay in which the authorities are unlikely to be seeking him." Certainly Costello qualifies under this more narrow definition. Her home was a refuge and a safe haven because it was protected by the privacy the Fourth Amendment provides her— freedom from unreasonable searches. By allowing her boyfriend to stay with her, it made it much less likely for the authorities to discover that he had reentered the country. Until his criminal conduct exposed him to the police, he lived in a haven secure from any governmental scrutiny. This refuge lasted for approximately seven months until the time her boyfriend was captured with drugs after running from his wrecked car following a high-speed chase.

. . . .

What Costello did—providing her boyfriend with shelter and a safe place to stay—was exactly what Congress intended to prohibit under the statute. . . . Costello was knowingly guilty of harboring under 8 U.S.C. § 1324(a)(1)(A)(iii), and she was properly charged and convicted. Therefore I respectfully dissent.

UNIVERSITY OF TEXAS SOUTHWESTERN MEDICAL CENTER V. NASSAR

Supreme Court of the United States
Decided June 24, 2013
2013 WL 3155234

As you read this case, consider the following questions:

- Can you identify all of the textual and structural arguments made by both sides? What about policy, legislative history, and administrative deference arguments?

- Is there any purposivist or policy-based rationale for the majority's decision?

- Why does the majority decline to defer to the agency?

- If this case had been decided before the 1991 amendments, what would the outcome have been?

- Which opinion makes the larger body of law more coherent and consistent?

- What do you think Congress actually intended?

- Justice Ginsburg's decision is unusually (for her) indignant. Why do you think this is the case?

JUSTICE KENNEDY delivered the opinion of the Court.

When the law grants persons the right to compensation for injury from wrongful conduct, there must be some demonstrated connection, some link, between the injury sustained and the wrong alleged. The requisite relation between prohibited conduct and compensable injury is governed by the principles of causation, a subject most often arising in elaborating the law of torts. This case requires the Court to define those rules in the context of Title VII of the Civil Rights Act of 1964, 42 U.S.C. § 2000e *et seq.,* which provides remedies to employees for injuries related to discriminatory conduct and associated wrongs by employers.

Title VII is central to the federal policy of prohibiting wrongful discrimination in the Nation's workplaces and in all sectors of economic endeavor. This opinion discusses the causation rules for two categories of wrongful employer conduct prohibited by Title VII. The first type is called, for purposes of this opinion, status-based discrimination. The term is used here to refer to basic workplace protection such as prohibitions against employer discrimination on the basis of race, color, religion, sex, or national origin, in hiring, firing, salary structure, promotion and the like. See § 2000e–2(a). The second type of conduct is employer retaliation on account of an employee's having opposed, complained of, or sought remedies for, unlawful workplace discrimination. See § 2000e–3(a).

An employee who alleges status-based discrimination under Title VII need not show that the causal link between injury and wrong is so close that the injury would not have occurred but for the act. So-called but-for causation is not the test. It suffices instead to show that the motive to discriminate was one of the employer's motives, even if the employer also had other, lawful motives that were causative in the employer's decision. This principle is the result of an earlier case from this Court, *Price Waterhouse v. Hopkins*, and an ensuing statutory amendment by Congress that codified in part and abrogated in part the holding in *Price Waterhouse*, see §§ 2000e–2(m), 2000e–5(g)(2)(B). The question the Court must answer here is whether that lessened causation standard is applicable to claims of unlawful employer retaliation under § 2000e–3(a).

Although the Court has not addressed the question of the causation showing required to establish liability for a Title VII retaliation claim, it has addressed the issue of causation in general in a case involving employer discrimination under a separate but related statute, the Age Discrimination in Employment Act of 1967 (ADEA). In *Gross* [*v. FBL Financial Services, Inc.*], the Court concluded that the ADEA requires proof that the prohibited criterion was the but-for cause of the prohibited conduct. The holding and analysis of that decision are instructive here.

I

Petitioner, the University of Texas Southwestern Medical Center (University), is an academic institution within the University of Texas system. The University specializes in medical education for aspiring physicians, health professionals, and scientists. Over the years, the University has affiliated itself with a number of healthcare facilities including, as relevant in this case, Parkland Memorial Hospital (Hospital).

. . . .

Respondent is a medical doctor of Middle Eastern descent who specializes in internal medicine and infectious diseases. In 1995, he was hired to work both as a member of the University's faculty and a staff physician at the Hospital. He left both positions in 1998 for additional medical education and then returned in 2001 as an assistant professor at the University and, once again, as a physician at the Hospital.

In 2004, Dr. Beth Levine was hired as the University's Chief of Infectious Disease Medicine. In that position Levine became respondent's ultimate (though not direct) superior. Respondent alleged that Levine was biased against him on account of his religion and ethnic heritage, a bias manifested by undeserved scrutiny of his billing practices and productivity, as well as comments that " 'Middle Easterners are lazy.' " On different occasions during his employment, respondent met with Dr. Gregory Fitz, the University's Chair of Internal Medicine and Levine's supervisor, to complain about Levine's alleged harassment. Despite obtaining a promotion with Levine's assistance in 2006, respondent continued to believe that she was biased against him. So he tried to arrange to continue working at the Hospital without also being on the University's faculty. After preliminary negotiations with the Hospital suggested this might be possible, respondent resigned his teaching post in July 2006 and sent a letter to Dr. Fitz (among others), in which he stated that the reason for his departure was harassment by Levine. That harassment, he asserted, " 'stems from . . . religious, racial and cultural bias against Arabs and Muslims.' " After reading that letter, Dr. Fitz expressed consternation at respondent's accusations, saying that Levine had been "publicly humiliated by th[e] letter" and that it was "very important that she be publicly exonerated."

Meanwhile, the Hospital had offered respondent a job as a staff physician, as it had indicated it would. On learning of that offer, Dr. Fitz protested to the Hospital, asserting that the offer was inconsistent with the affiliation agreement's requirement that all staff physicians also be members of the University faculty. The Hospital then withdrew its offer.

After exhausting his administrative remedies, respondent filed this Title VII suit in the United States District Court for the Northern District of Texas. He alleged two discrete violations of Title VII. The first was a status-based discrimination claim under § 2000e–2(a). Respondent alleged that Dr. Levine's racially and religiously motivated harassment had resulted in his constructive discharge from the University. Respondent's second claim was that Dr. Fitz's efforts to prevent the Hospital from hiring him were in retaliation for complaining about Dr. Levine's harassment, in violation of § 2000e–3(a). The jury found for respondent on both claims. It awarded him over $400,000 in backpay and more than $3 million in compensatory damages. The District Court later reduced the compensatory damages award to $300,000.

On appeal, the Court of Appeals for the Fifth Circuit affirmed in part and vacated in part. The court first concluded that respondent had submitted insufficient evidence in support of his constructive-discharge claim, so it vacated that portion of the jury's verdict. The court affirmed as to the retaliation finding, however, on the theory that retaliation claims brought under § 2000e–3(a)—like claims of status-based discrimination under § 2000e–2(a)—require only a showing that retaliation was a motivating factor for the adverse employment action, rather than its but-for cause. It further held that the evidence supported a finding that Dr. Fitz was motivated, at least in part, to retaliate against respondent for his complaints against Levine. The Court of Appeals then remanded for a redetermination of damages in light of its decision to vacate the constructive-discharge verdict.

Four judges dissented from the court's decision not to rehear the case en banc, arguing that the Circuit's application of the motivating-factor standard to retaliation cases was "an erroneous interpretation of [Title VII] and controlling caselaw" and should be overruled en banc.

Certiorari was granted.

II

A

This case requires the Court to define the proper standard of causation for Title VII retaliation claims. Causation in fact—*i.e.,* proof that the defendant's conduct did in fact cause the plaintiff's injury—is a standard requirement of any tort claim. This includes federal statutory claims of workplace discrimination.

In the usual course, this standard requires the plaintiff to show "that the harm would not have occurred" in the absence of—that is, but for—the defendant's conduct. It is thus textbook tort law that an action "is not regarded as a cause of an event if the particular event would have occurred without it." This, then, is the background against which

Congress legislated in enacting Title VII, and these are the default rules it is presumed to have incorporated, absent an indication to the contrary in the statute itself.

B

Since the statute's passage in 1964, it has prohibited employers from discriminating against their employees on any of seven specified criteria. Five of them—race, color, religion, sex, and national origin—are personal characteristics and are set forth in § 2000e–2. (As noted at the outset, discrimination based on these five characteristics is called status-based discrimination in this opinion.) And then there is a point of great import for this case: The two remaining categories of wrongful employer conduct—the employee's opposition to employment discrimination, and the employee's submission of or support for a complaint that alleges employment discrimination—are not wrongs based on personal traits but rather types of protected employee conduct. These latter two categories are covered by a separate, subsequent section of Title VII, § 2000e–3(a).

Under the status-based discrimination provision, it is an "unlawful employment practice" for an employer "to discriminate against any individual . . . because of such individual's race, color, religion, sex, or national origin." In its 1989 decision in *Price Waterhouse*, the Court sought to explain the causation standard imposed by this language. It addressed in particular what it means for an action to be taken "because of" an individual's race, religion, or nationality. Although no opinion in that case commanded a majority, six Justices did agree that a plaintiff could prevail on a claim of status-based discrimination if he or she could show that one of the prohibited traits was a "motivating" or "substantial" factor in the employer's decision. If the plaintiff made that showing, the burden of persuasion would shift to the employer, which could escape liability if it could prove that it would have taken the same employment action in the absence of all discriminatory animus. In other words, the employer had to show that a discriminatory motive was not the but-for cause of the adverse employment action.

Two years later, Congress passed the Civil Rights Act of 1991. This statute (which had many other provisions) codified the burden-shifting and lessened-causation framework of *Price Waterhouse* in part but also rejected it to a substantial degree. The legislation first added a new subsection to the end of § 2000e–2, *i.e.*, Title VII's principal ban on status-based discrimination. The new provision, § 2000e–2(m), states:

"[A]n unlawful employment practice is established when the complaining party demonstrates that race, color, religion, sex, or national origin was a motivating factor for any employment practice, even though other factors also motivated the practice."

This, of course, is a lessened causation standard.

The 1991 Act also abrogated a portion of *Price Waterhouse's* framework by removing the employer's ability to defeat liability once a plaintiff proved the existence of an impermissible motivating factor. In its place, Congress enacted § 2000e–5(g)(2), which provides:

"(B) On a claim in which an individual proves a violation under section 2000e–2(m) of this title and [the employer] demonstrates that [it] would have taken the same action in the absence of the impermissible motivating factor, the court—

"(i) may grant declaratory relief, injunctive relief . . . and [limited] attorney's fees and costs . . . ; and

"(ii) shall not award damages or issue an order requiring any admission, reinstatement, hiring, promotion, or payment. . . ."

So, in short, the 1991 Act substituted a new burden-shifting framework for the one endorsed by *Price Waterhouse.* Under that new regime, a plaintiff could obtain declaratory relief, attorney's fees and costs, and some forms of injunctive relief based solely on proof that race, color, religion, sex, or nationality was a motivating factor in the employment action; but the employer's proof that it would still have taken the same employment action would save it from monetary damages and a reinstatement order.

After *Price Waterhouse* and the 1991 Act, considerable time elapsed before the Court returned again to the meaning of "because" and the problem of causation. This time it arose in the context of a different, yet similar statute, the ADEA. Much like the Title VII statute in *Price Waterhouse*, the relevant portion of the ADEA provided that " '[i]t shall be unlawful for an employer . . . to fail or refuse to hire or to discharge any individual or otherwise discriminate against any individual with respect to his compensation, terms, conditions, or privileges of employment, *because of* such individual's age.' "

Concentrating first and foremost on the meaning of the phrase " '*because of* . . . age,' " the Court in *Gross* explained that the ordinary meaning of " 'because of' " is " 'by reason of' " or " 'on account of.' " *Id.,* at 176 (citing 1 Webster's Third New International Dictionary 194 (1966); 1 Oxford English Dictionary 746 (1933); The Random House Dictionary of the English Language 132 (1966); emphasis in original). Thus, the "requirement that an employer took adverse action 'because of' age [meant] that age was the 'reason' that the employer decided to act," or, in other words, that "age was the 'but-for' cause of the employer's adverse decision."

In the course of approving this construction, *Gross* declined to adopt the interpretation endorsed by the plurality and concurring opinions in *Price Waterhouse*. Noting that "the ADEA must be 'read . . . the way Congress wrote it,' " the Court concluded that "the textual differences between Title VII and the ADEA" "prevent[ed] us from applying *Price Waterhouse* . . . to federal age discrimination claims." In particular, the Court stressed the congressional choice not to add a provision like § 2000e–2(m) to the ADEA despite making numerous other changes to the latter statute in the 1991 Act.

Finally, the Court in *Gross* held that it would not be proper to read *Price Waterhouse* as announcing a rule that applied to both statutes, despite their similar wording and near-contemporaneous enactment. This different reading was necessary, the Court concluded, because Congress' 1991 amendments to Title VII, including its "careful tailoring of the 'motivating factor' claim" and the substitution of § 2000e–5(g)(2)(B) for *Price Waterhouse's* full affirmative defense, indicated that the motivating-factor standard was not an organic part of Title VII and thus could not be read into the ADEA.

. . . .

III

A

As noted, Title VII's antiretaliation provision, which is set forth in § 2000e–3(a), appears in a different section from Title VII's ban on status-based discrimination. The antiretaliation provision states, in relevant part:

"It shall be an unlawful employment practice for an employer to discriminate against any of his employees . . . because he has opposed any practice made an unlawful employment practice by this subchapter. . . ."

This enactment, like the statute at issue in *Gross*, makes it unlawful for an employer to take adverse employment action against an employee "because" of certain criteria. Given the lack of any meaningful textual difference between the text in this statute and the one in *Gross,* the proper conclusion here, as in *Gross*, is that Title VII retaliation claims require proof that the desire to retaliate was the but-for cause of the challenged employment action.

The principal counterargument offered by respondent and the United States relies on their different understanding of the motivating-factor section, which—on its face—applies only to status discrimination, discrimination on the basis of race, color, religion, sex, and national origin. In substance, they contend that: (1) retaliation is defined by the statute to be an unlawful employment practice; (2) § 2000e–2(m) allows unlawful employment practices to be proved based on a showing that race, color, religion, sex, or national origin was a motivating factor for— and not necessarily the but-for factor in—the challenged employment action; and (3) the Court has, as a matter of course, held that "retaliation for complaining about race discrimination *is* 'discrimination based on race.'"

There are three main flaws in this reading of § 2000e–2(m). The first is that it is inconsistent with the provision's plain language. It must be acknowledged that because Title VII defines "unlawful employment practice" to include retaliation, the question presented by this case would be different if § 2000e–2(m) extended its coverage to all unlawful employment practices. As actually written, however, the text of the motivating-factor provision, while it begins by referring to "unlawful employment practices," then proceeds to address only five of the seven prohibited discriminatory actions—actions based on the employee's status, *i.e.,* race, color, religion, sex, and national origin. This indicates Congress' intent to confine that provision's coverage to only those types of employment practices. The text of § 2000e–2(m) says nothing about retaliation claims. Given this clear language, it would be improper to conclude that what Congress omitted from the statute is nevertheless within its scope.

The second problem with this reading is its inconsistency with the design and structure of the statute as a whole. Just as Congress' choice of words is presumed to be deliberate, so too are its structural choices. When Congress wrote the motivating-factor provision in 1991, it chose to insert it as a subsection within § 2000e–2, which contains Title VII's ban on status-based discrimination, § 2000e–2(a) to (d), (*l*), and says nothing about retaliation. The title of the section of the 1991 Act that created § 2000e–2(m)—"Clarifying prohibition against impermissible consideration of race, color, religion, sex, or national origin in employment practices"—also indicates that Congress determined to address only claims of status-based discrimination, not retaliation.

What is more, a different portion of the 1991 Act contains an express reference to all unlawful employment actions, thereby reinforcing the conclusion that Congress acted deliberately when it omitted retaliation claims from § 2000e–2(m). The relevant portion of the 1991 Act, § 109(b), allowed certain overseas operations by U.S. employers to engage in "any practice prohibited by section 703 or 704," *i.e.,* § 2000e–2 or § 2000e–3, "if compliance with such section would cause such employer . . . to violate the law of the foreign country in which such workplace is located."

If Congress had desired to make the motivating-factor standard applicable to all Title VII claims, it could have used language similar to that which it invoked in § 109. Or, it could have inserted the motivating-factor provision as part of a section that applies to all such claims, such as § 2000e–5, which establishes the rules and remedies for all Title VII enforcement actions. But in writing § 2000e–2(m), Congress did neither of those things, and "[w]e must give effect to Congress' choice."

The third problem with respondent's and the Government's reading of the motivating-factor standard is in its submission that this Court's decisions interpreting federal antidiscrimination law have, as a general matter, treated bans on status-based discrimination as also prohibiting retaliation. In support of this proposition, both respondent and the United States rely upon decisions in which this Court has "read [a] broadly worded civil rights statute . . . as including an antiretaliation remedy."

. . . .

These decisions are not controlling here. It is true these cases do state the general proposition that Congress' enactment of a broadly phrased antidiscrimination statute may signal a concomitant intent to ban retaliation against individuals who oppose that discrimination, even where the statute does not refer to retaliation in so many words. What those cases do not support, however, is the quite different rule that every reference to race, color, creed, sex, or nationality in an antidiscrimination statute is to be treated as a synonym for "retaliation." For one thing, § 2000e–2(m) is not itself a substantive bar on discrimination. Rather, it is a rule that establishes the causation standard for proving a violation defined elsewhere in Title VII. The cases cited by respondent and the Government do not address rules of this sort, and those precedents are of limited relevance here.

The approach respondent and the Government suggest is inappropriate in the context of a statute as precise, complex, and exhaustive as Title VII. As noted, the laws at issue in [other cases] were broad, general bars on discrimination. In interpreting them the Court concluded that by using capacious language Congress expressed the intent to bar retaliation in addition to status-based discrimination. In other words, when Congress' treatment of the subject of prohibited discrimination was both broad and brief, its omission of any specific discussion of retaliation was unremarkable.

If Title VII had likewise been phrased in broad and general terms, respondent's argument might have more force. But that is not how Title VII was written, which makes it incorrect to infer that Congress meant anything other than what the text does say on the subject of retaliation. Unlike Title IX, § 1981, § 1982, and the federal-sector provisions of the ADEA, Title VII is a detailed statutory scheme. This statute enumerates specific unlawful employment practices. See § 2000e–2(a)(1), (b), (c)(1), (d) (status-based discrimination by employers, employment agencies, labor organizations, and training programs, respectively); § 2000e–2(*l*) (status-based discrimination in employment-related testing); § 2000e–3(a) (retaliation for opposing, or making or supporting a complaint about, unlawful employment actions); § 2000e–3(b) (advertising a preference for applicants of a particular race, color, religion, sex, or national origin). It defines key terms, see § 2000e, and exempts certain types of employers, see § 2000e–1. And it creates an administrative agency with both rulemaking and enforcement authority. See §§ 2000e–5, 2000e–12.

This fundamental difference in statutory structure renders inapposite decisions which treated retaliation as an implicit corollary of status-based discrimination. Text may not be divorced from context. In light of Congress' special care in drawing so precise a statutory scheme, it would be improper to indulge respondent's suggestion that Congress meant to incorporate the default rules that apply only when Congress writes a broad and undifferentiated statute. . . .

Further confirmation of the inapplicability of § 2000e–2(m) to retaliation claims may be found in Congress' approach to the Americans with Disabilities Act of 1990 (ADA). In the ADA Congress provided not just a general prohibition on discrimination "because of [an individual's] disability," but also seven paragraphs of detailed description of the practices that would constitute the prohibited discrimination. And, most pertinent for present purposes, it included an express antiretaliation provision, see § 503(a). That law, which Congress passed only a year before enacting § 2000e–2(m) and which speaks in clear and direct terms to the question of retaliation, rebuts the claim that Congress must have intended to use the phrase "race, color, religion, sex, or national origin" as the textual equivalent of "retaliation." To the contrary, the ADA shows that when Congress elected to address retaliation as part of a detailed statutory scheme, it did so in clear textual terms.

. . . .

B

The proper interpretation and implementation of § 2000e–3(a) and its causation standard have central importance to the fair and responsible allocation of resources in the judicial and litigation systems. This is of particular significance because claims of retaliation are being made with ever-increasing frequency. The number of these claims filed with the Equal Employment Opportunity Commission (EEOC) has nearly doubled in the past 15 years—from just over 16,000 in 1997 to over 31,000 in 2012. Indeed, the number of retaliation claims filed with the EEOC has now outstripped those for every type of status-based discrimination except race.

In addition lessening the causation standard could also contribute to the filing of frivolous claims, which would siphon resources from efforts by employer, administrative agencies, and courts to combat workplace harassment.

. . . .

In sum, Title VII defines the term "unlawful employment practice" as discrimination on the basis of any of seven prohibited criteria: race, color, religion, sex, national origin, opposition to employment discrimination, and submitting or supporting a complaint about employment discrimination. The text of § 2000e–2(m) mentions just the first five of these factors, the status-based ones; and it omits the final two, which deal with retaliation. When it added § 2000e–2(m) to Title VII in 1991, Congress inserted it within the section of the statute that deals only with those same five criteria, not the section that deals with retaliation claims or one of the sections that apply to all claims of unlawful employment practices. And while the Court has inferred a congressional intent to prohibit retaliation when confronted with broadly worded antidiscrimination statutes, Title VII's detailed structure makes that inference inappropriate here. Based on these textual and structural indications, the Court now concludes as follows: Title VII retaliation claims must be proved according to traditional principles of but-for causation, not the lessened causation test stated in § 2000e–2(m). This requires proof that the unlawful retaliation would not have occurred in the absence of the alleged wrongful action or actions of the employer.

IV

Respondent and the Government also argue that applying the motivating-factor provision's lessened causation standard to retaliation claims would be consistent with longstanding agency views, contained in a guidance manual published by the EEOC. It urges that those views are entitled to deference under this Court's decision in *Skidmore v. Swift & Co.* The weight of deference afforded to agency interpretations under *Skidmore* depends upon "the thoroughness evident in its consideration, the validity of its reasoning, its consistency with earlier and later pronouncements, and all those factors which give it power to persuade."

According to the manual in question, the causation element of a retaliation claim is satisfied if "there is credible direct evidence that retaliation was a motive for the challenged action," regardless of whether there is also "[e]vidence as to [a] legitimate motive." After noting a division of authority as to whether motivating-factor or but-for causation should apply to retaliation claims, the manual offers two rationales in support of adopting the former standard. The first is that "[c]ourts have long held that the evidentiary framework for proving [status-based] discrimination . . . also applies to claims of discrimination based on retaliation." Second, the manual states that "an interpretation . . . that permits proven retaliation to go unpunished undermines the purpose of the anti-retaliation provisions of maintaining unfettered access to the statutory remedial mechanism."

These explanations lack the persuasive force that is a necessary precondition to deference under *Skidmore*. As to the first rationale, while the settled judicial construction of a particular statute is of course relevant in ascertaining statutory meaning, the manual's discussion fails to address the particular interplay among the status-based discrimination provision (§ 2000e–2(a)), the antiretaliation provision (§ 2000e–3(a)), and the motivating-factor provision (§ 2000e–2(m)). Other federal antidiscrimination statutes do not have the structure of statutory subsections that control the outcome at issue here. The manual's failure to address the specific provisions of this statutory scheme, coupled with the generic nature of its discussion of the causation standards for status-based discrimination and retaliation claims, call the manual's conclusions into serious question.

The manual's second argument is unpersuasive, too; for its reasoning is circular. It asserts the lessened causation standard is necessary in order to prevent "proven retaliation" from "go[ing] unpunished." Yet this assumes the answer to the central question at issue here, which is what causal relationship must be shown in order to prove retaliation.

. . . .

JUSTICE GINSBURG, with whom JUSTICE BREYER, JUSTICE SOTOMAYOR, and JUSTICE KAGAN join, dissenting.

Title VII of the Civil Rights Act of 1964 makes it an "unlawful employment practice" to "discriminate against any individual . . . *because of* such individual's race, color, religion, sex, or national origin." § 2000e–2(a) (emphasis added). Backing up that core provision, Title VII also makes it an "unlawful employment practice" to discriminate against any individual *"because"* the individual has complained of, opposed, or participated in a proceeding about, prohibited discrimination. § 2000e–3(a) (emphasis added). This form of discrimination is commonly called "retaliation," although Title VII itself does not use that term. The Court has recognized that effective protection against retaliation, the office of § 2000e–3(a), is essential to securing "a workplace where individuals are not discriminated against because of their racial, ethnic, religious, or gender-based status." That is so because "fear of retaliation is the leading reason why people stay silent" about the discrimination they have encountered or observed.

Similarly worded, the ban on discrimination and the ban on retaliation against a discrimination complainant have traveled together: Title VII plaintiffs often raise the two provisions in tandem. Today's decision, however, drives a wedge between the twin safeguards in so-called "mixed-motive" cases. To establish discrimination, all agree, the complaining party need show only that race, color, religion, sex, or national origin was "a motivating factor" in an employer's adverse action; an employer's proof that "other factors also motivated the [action]" will not defeat the discrimination claim. But a retaliation claim, the Court insists, must meet a stricter standard: The claim will fail unless the complainant shows "but-for" causation, *i.e.,* that the employer would not have taken the adverse employment action but for a design to retaliate.

In so reining in retaliation claims, the Court misapprehends what our decisions teach: Retaliation for complaining about discrimination is tightly bonded to the core prohibition and cannot be disassociated from it. Indeed, this Court has explained again and again that "retaliation in response to a complaint about [proscribed] discrimination *is* discrimination" on the basis of the characteristic Congress sought to immunize against adverse employment action.

The Court shows little regard for the trial judges who will be obliged to charge discrete causation standards when a claim of discrimination "because of," *e.g.,* race is coupled with a claim of discrimination "because" the individual has complained of race discrimination. And jurors will puzzle over the rhyme or reason for the dual standards. Of graver concern, the Court has seized on a provision, § 2000e–2(m), adopted by Congress as part of an endeavor to strengthen Title VII, and turned it into a measure reducing the force of the ban on retaliation.

I

. . . .

II

This Court has long acknowledged the symbiotic relationship between proscriptions on discrimination and proscriptions on retaliation. Antidiscrimination provisions, the Court has reasoned, endeavor to create a workplace where individuals are not treated differently on account of race, ethnicity, religion, or sex. Antiretaliation provisions "see[k] to secure that primary objective by preventing an employer from interfering . . . with an employee's efforts to secure or advance enforcement of [antidiscrimination] guarantees." As the Court has comprehended, "Title VII depends for its enforcement upon the cooperation of employees who are willing to file complaints and act as witnesses." " '[E]ffective enforcement,' " therefore, can " 'only be expected if employees . . . [feel] free to approach officials with their grievances.' "

Adverting to the close connection between discrimination and retaliation for complaining about discrimination, this Court has held, in a line of decisions unbroken until today, that a ban on discrimination encompasses retaliation. In *Sullivan v. Little Hunting Park, Inc.,* the Court determined that 42 U.S.C. § 1982, which provides that "[a]ll citizens of the United States shall have the same right . . . as is enjoyed by white citizens . . . to inherit, purchase, lease, sell, hold, and convey real and personal property," protected a white man who suffered retaliation after complaining of discrimination against his black tenant. *Jackson v. Birmingham Board of Education* elaborated on that holding in the context of sex discrimination. "Retaliation against a person because [he] has complained of sex discrimination," the Court found it inescapably evident, "is another form of intentional sex discrimination." As the Court explained:

"Retaliation is, by definition, an intentional act. It is a form of 'discrimination' because the complainant is being subject to differential treatment. Moreover, retaliation is discrimination 'on the basis of sex' because it is an intentional response to the nature of the complaint: an allegation of sex discrimination."

Jackson interpreted Title IX of the Educational Amendments of 1972. Noting that the legislation followed three years after *Sullivan*, the Court found it "not only appropriate but also realistic to presume that Congress was thoroughly familiar with *Sullivan* and . . . expected its enactment of Title IX to be interpreted in conformity with it."

Gómez-Pérez v. Potter was similarly reasoned. The Court there held that the federal-sector provision of the Age Discrimination in Employment Act of 1967 (ADEA), barring discrimination "based on age," also proscribes retaliation. "What *Jackson* said about the relationship between *Sullivan* and the enactment of Title IX," the Court observed, "can be said as well about the relationship between *Sullivan* and the enactment of the ADEA's federal-sector provision." There is no sound reason in this case to stray from the decisions in *Sullivan, Jackson, Gómez-Pérez,* and *CBOCS West.*

III

A

The Title VII provision key here, § 2000e–2(m), states that "an unlawful employment practice is established when the complaining party demonstrates that race, color, religion, sex, or national origin was a motivating factor for any employment practice, even though other factors also motivated the practice." Section 2000e–2(m) was enacted as part of the Civil Rights Act of 1991, which amended Title VII, along with other federal antidiscrimination statutes. The amendments were intended to provide "additional protections against unlawful discrimination in employment," § 2(3), and to "respon[d] to a number of . . . decisions by [this Court] that sharply cut back on the scope and effectiveness" of antidiscrimination laws, H.R.Rep. No. 102–40, pt. II, pp. 2–4 (1991) (hereinafter House Report Part II).

Among the decisions found inadequately protective was *Price Waterhouse.* A plurality of the Court in that case held that the words "because of" in

§ 2000e–2(a) encompass claims challenging an employment decision attributable to "mixed motives," *i.e.*, one motivated by both legitimate and illegitimate factors. A Title VII plaintiff, the plurality concluded, need show only that a prohibited factor contributed to the employment decision—not that it was the but-for or sole cause. An employer would not be liable, however, if it could show by a preponderance of the evidence that it would have taken the same action absent the illegitimate motive.

Congress endorsed the plurality's conclusion that, to be actionable under Title VII, discrimination must be a motivating factor in, but need not be the but-for cause of, an adverse employment action. Congress disagreed with the Court, however, insofar as the *Price Waterhouse* decision allowed an employer to escape liability by showing that the same action would have been taken regardless of improper motive. "If Title VII's ban on discrimination in employment is to be meaningful," the House Report explained, "victims of intentional discrimination must be able to obtain relief, and perpetrators of discrimination must be held liable for their actions."

Superseding *Price Waterhouse* in part, Congress sought to "restore" the rule of decision followed by several Circuits that any discrimination "actually shown to play a role in a contested employment decision may be the subject of liability." To that end, Congress enacted § 2000e–2(m) and § 2000e–5(g)(2)(B). The latter provides that an employer's proof that an adverse employment action would have been taken in any event does not shield the employer from liability; such proof, however, limits the plaintiff's remedies to declaratory or injunctive relief, attorney's fees, and costs.

Critically, the rule Congress intended to "restore" was not limited to substantive discrimination. As the House Report explained, "the Committee endors[ed] . . . the decisional law" in *Bibbs v. Block*, which held that a violation of Title VII is established when the trier of fact determines that "an unlawful motive played some part in the employment decision or decisional process." Prior to the 1991 Civil Rights Act, *Bibbs* had been applied to retaliation claims.

B

There is scant reason to think that, despite Congress' aim to "restore and strengthen . . . laws that ban discrimination in employment," House Report Part II, at 2, Congress meant to exclude retaliation claims from the newly enacted "motivating factor" provision. Section 2000e–2(m) provides that an "unlawful employment practice is established" when the plaintiff shows that a protected characteristic was a factor driving "any employment practice." Title VII, in § 2000e–3(a), explicitly denominates retaliation, like status-based discrimination, an "unlawful employment practice." Because "any employment practice" necessarily encompasses practices prohibited under § 2000e–3(a), § 2000e–2(m), by its plain terms, covers retaliation.

Notably, when it enacted § 2000e–2(m), Congress did not tie the new provision specifically to §§ 2000e–2(a)–(d), which proscribe discrimination "because of" race, color, religion, gender, or national origin. Rather, Congress added an entirely new provision to codify the causation standard, one encompassing "any employment practice."

Also telling, § 2000e–2(m) is not limited to situations in which *the complainant's* race, color, religion, sex, or national origin motivates the employer's action. In contrast, Title VII's substantive antidiscrimination provisions refer to the protected characteristics of the complaining party. See §§ 2000e–2(a)(1)–(2), (c)(2) (referring to "such individual's" protected characteristics); §§ 2000e–2(b), (c)(1), (d) (referring to "his race, color, religion, sex, or national origin"). Congress thus knew how to limit Title VII's coverage to victims of status-based discrimination when it was so minded. It chose, instead, to bring within § 2000e2(m) "any employment practice." To cut out retaliation from § 2000e–2(m)'s scope, one must be blind to that choice.

C

From the inception of § 2000e–2(m), the agency entrusted with interpretation of Title VII and superintendence of the Act's administration, the EEOC, has understood the provision to cover retaliation claims. Shortly after Congress amended Title VII to include the motivating-factor provision, the EEOC issued guidance advising that, "[a]lthough [§ 2000e–2(m)] does not specify retaliation as a basis for finding liability whenever it is a motivating factor for an action, neither does it suggest any basis for deviating from the Commission's long-standing rule that it will find liability . . . whenever retaliation plays any role in an employment decision." As the EEOC's initial guidance explained, "if retaliation were to go unremedied, it would have a chilling effect upon the willingness of individuals to speak out against employment discrimination."

In its compliance manual, the EEOC elaborated on its conclusion that "[§ 2000e–2(m)] applies to retaliation." That reading, the agency observed, tracked the view, widely held by courts, "that the evidentiary framework for proving employment discrimination based on race, sex, or other protected class status also applies to claims of discrimination based on retaliation." "[A]n interpretation of [§ 2000e–2(m)] that permit[ted] proven retaliation to go unpunished," the EEOC noted, would "undermin[e] the purpose of the anti-retaliation provisions of maintaining unfettered access to the statutory remedial mechanism."

The position set out in the EEOC's guidance and compliance manual merits respect. If the breadth of § 2000e–2(m) can be deemed ambiguous (although I believe its meaning is plain), the provision should be construed to accord with the EEOC's well-reasoned and longstanding guidance.

IV

The Court draws the opposite conclusion, ruling that retaliation falls outside the scope of § 2000e–2(m). In so holding, the Court ascribes to Congress the unlikely purpose of separating retaliation claims from discrimination claims, thereby undermining the Legislature's effort to fortify the protections of Title VII. None of the reasons the Court offers in support of its restrictive interpretation of § 2000e–2(m) survives inspection.

A

The Court first asserts that reading § 2000e–2(m) to encompass claims for retaliation "is inconsistent with the provision's plain language." The Court acknowledges, however, that "the text of the motivating-factor provision . . . begins by referring to unlawful employment practices," a term that undeniably includes retaliation. Nevermind that, the Court continues, for § 2000e–2(m) goes on to reference as "motivating factor[s]" only "race, color, religion, sex, or national origin." The Court thus sees retaliation as a protected activity entirely discrete from status-based discrimination.

This vision of retaliation as a separate concept runs up against precedent. Until today, the Court has been clear eyed on just what retaliation is: a manifestation of status-based discrimination. As *Jackson* explained in the context of sex discrimination, "retaliation is discrimination 'on the basis of sex' because it is an intentional response to the nature of the complaint: an allegation of sex discrimination."

The Court does not take issue with *Jackson's* insight. Instead, it distinguishes *Jackson* and like cases on the ground that they concerned laws in which "Congress' treatment of the subject of prohibited discrimination was both broad and brief." Title VII, by contrast, "is a detailed statutory scheme," that "enumerates specific unlawful employment practices," "defines key terms," and "exempts certain types of employers." Accordingly, the Court says, "it would be improper to indulge [the] suggestion that Congress meant to incorporate [in Title VII] the default rules that apply only when Congress writes a broad and undifferentiated statute."

It is strange logic indeed to conclude that when Congress homed in on retaliation and codified the proscription, as it did in Title VII, Congress meant protection against that unlawful employment practice to have *less* force than the protection available when the statute does not mention retaliation. It is hardly surprising, then, that our jurisprudence does not support the Court's conclusion. In *Gómez-Pérez,* the Court construed the federal-sector provision of the ADEA, which proscribes "discrimination based on age," to bar retaliation. The Court did so mindful that another part of the Act, the provision applicable to private-sector employees, explicitly proscribes retaliation and, moreover, "set[s] out a specific list of forbidden employer practices."

The Court suggests that "the la[w] at issue in . . . *Gómez-Pérez* [was a] broad, general ba[r] on discrimination." But, as our opinion in that case observes, some of the ADEA's provisions are brief, broad, and general, while others are extensive, specific, and detailed. It makes little sense to apply a different mode of analysis to Title VII's § 2000e–2(m) and the ADEA's § 633a(a), both brief statements on discrimination in the context of larger statutory schemes.

The Court's reliance on § 109(b) of the Civil Rights Act of 1991, and the Americans with Disabilities Act of 1990 (ADA), is similarly unavailing. According to the Court, Congress' explicit reference to § 2000e–3(a) in § 109(b) "reinforc[es] the conclusion that Congress acted deliberately when it omitted retaliation claims from § 2000e–2(m)." The same is true of the ADA, the Court says, as "Congress provided not just a general prohibition on discrimination 'because of [an individual's] disability,' but also seven paragraphs of detailed description of the practices that would constitute the prohibited discrimination . . . [a]nd . . . an express antiretaliation provision."

This argument is underwhelming. Yes, Congress has sometimes addressed retaliation explicitly in antidiscrimination statutes. When it does so, there is no occasion for interpretation. But when Congress simply targets discrimination "because of" protected characteristics, or, as in § 2000e–2(m), refers to employment practices motivated by race, color, religion, sex, or national origin, how should courts comprehend those phrases? They should read them informed by this Court's consistent holdings that such phrases draw in retaliation, for, in truth, retaliation is a "form of intentional [status-based] discrimination." That is why the Court can point to no prior instance in which an antidiscrimination law was found *not* to cover retaliation. The Court's *volte-face* is particularly imprudent in the context of § 2000e–2(m), a provision added as part of Congress' effort to toughen protections against workplace discrimination.

B

The Court also disassociates retaliation from status-based discrimination by stressing that the bar on the latter appears in § 2000e–2, while the proscription of retaliation appears in a separate provision, § 2000e–3. Section 2000e–2, the Court asserts, "contains Title VII's ban on status-based discrimination . . . and says nothing about retaliation." Retaliation, the Court therefore concludes, should not be read into § 2000e–2(m).

THE PRACTICAL TOOLS OF

The Court's reasoning rests on a false premise. Section 2000e–2 does not deal exclusively with discrimination based on protected characteristics. The provisions stated after §§ 2000e–2(a)–(d) deal with a variety of matters, some of them unquestionably covering retaliation. For example, § 2000e–2(n), enacted in tandem with and located immediately after § 2000e–2(m), limits opportunities to collaterally attack employment practices installed to implement a consent judgment. Section 2000e–2(n) applies beyond the substantive antidiscrimination provisions in § 2000e–2; indeed, it applies beyond Title VII to encompass claims "under the Constitution or [other] Federal civil rights laws." § 2000e–2(n)(1)(A). Thus, if an employee sues for retaliatory discharge in violation of § 2000e–3(a), and a consent judgment orders reinstatement, any person adversely affected by that judgment (e.g., an employee who loses seniority as a result) would generally be barred from attacking the judgment if she was given actual notice of the proposed order and a reasonable opportunity to present objections. That Congress placed the consent-judgment provision in § 2000e–2 and not in § 2000e–3 is of no moment. As the text of the provision plainly conveys, § 2000e–2(n) would reach consent judgments settling complaints about retaliation, just as it would cover consent judgments settling complaints about status-based discrimination.

Section 2000e–2(g) is similarly illustrative. Under that provision, "it shall not be an unlawful employment practice for an employer . . . to discharge [an] individual" if she fails to fulfill any requirement imposed in the interest of national security. Because § 2000e–3(a) renders retaliation an "unlawful employment practice," § 2000e–2(g)'s exemption would no doubt apply to a Title VII retaliatory discharge claim. Given these provisions, Congress' placement of the motivating-factor provision within § 2000e–2 cannot bear the weight the Court places on it.

. . . .

V

A

Having narrowed § 2000e–2(m) to exclude retaliation claims, the Court turns to *Gross* to answer the question presented: Whether a plaintiff must demonstrate but-for causation to establish liability under § 2000e–3(a).

The Court held in *Gross* that, in contrast to Title VII, § 623(a) of the ADEA does not authorize any age discrimination claim asserting mixed motives. Explaining that uniform interpretation of the two statutes is sometimes unwarranted, the Court noted in *Gross* that the phrase "because of . . . age" in § 623(a) has not been read "to bar discrimination against people of all ages, even though the Court had previously interpreted 'because of . . . race [or] sex' in Title VII to bar discrimination against people of all races and both sexes." Yet *Gross*, which took pains to distinguish ADEA claims from Title VII claims, is invoked by the Court today as pathmarking.

The word "because" in Title VII's retaliation provision, the Court tells us, should be interpreted not to accord with the interpretation of that same word in the companion status-based discrimination provision of Title VII. Instead, statutory lines should be crossed: The meaning of "because" in Title VII's retaliation provision should be read to mean just what the Court held "because" means for ADEA-liability purposes. In other words, the employer prevailed in *Gross* because, according to the Court, the ADEA's antidiscrimination prescription is not like Title VII's. But the employer prevails again in Nassar's case, for there is no "meaningful textual difference," between the ADEA's use of "because" and the use of the same word in Title VII's retaliation provision. What sense can one make of this other than "heads the employer wins, tails the employee loses"?

It is a standard principle of statutory interpretation that identical phrases appearing in the same statute—here, Title VII—ordinarily bear a consistent meaning. Following that principle, Title VII's retaliation provision, like its status-based discrimination provision, would permit mixed-motive claims, and the same causation standard would apply to both provisions.

B

The Court's decision to construe § 2000e–3(a) to require but-for causation in line with *Gross* is even more confounding in light of *Price Waterhouse*. Recall that *Price Waterhouse* interpreted "because of" in § 2000e–2(a) to permit mixed-motive claims. The Court today rejects the proposition that, if § 2000e–2(m) does not cover retaliation, such claims are governed by *Price Waterhouse's* burden-shifting framework; *i.e.,* if the plaintiff shows that discrimination was *a* motivating factor in an adverse employment action, the defendant may escape liability only by showing it would have taken the same action had there been no illegitimate motive. It is wrong to revert to *Price Waterhouse*, the Court says, because the 1991 Civil Rights Act's amendments to Title VII abrogated that decision.

This conclusion defies logic. Before the 1991 amendments, several courts had applied *Price Waterhouse's* burden-shifting framework to retaliation claims. In the Court's view, Congress designed § 2000e–2(m)'s motivating-factor standard not only to exclude retaliation claims, but also to override, *sub silentio,* Circuit precedent applying the *Price Waterhouse* framework to such claims. And with what did the 1991 Congress replace the *Price Waterhouse* burden-shifting framework? With a but-for causation requirement *Gross* applied to the ADEA 17 years after the 1991 amendments to Title VII. Shut from the Court's sight is a legislative record replete with statements evincing Congress' intent to strengthen antidiscrimination laws and thereby hold employers accountable for prohibited discrimination. It is an odd mode of statutory interpretation that divines Congress' aim in 1991 by looking to a decision of this Court, *Gross,* made under a different statute in 2008, while ignoring the overarching purpose of the Congress that enacted the 1991 Civil Rights Act.

C

The Court shows little regard for trial judges who must instruct juries in Title VII cases in which plaintiffs allege both status-based discrimination and retaliation. Nor is the Court concerned about the capacity of jurors to follow instructions conforming to today's decision. Causation is a complicated concept to convey to juries in the best of circumstances. Asking jurors to determine liability based on different standards in a single case is virtually certain to sow confusion. That would be tolerable if the governing statute required double standards, but here, for the reasons already stated, it does not.

. . . .

EXERCISE V.4

As we have introduced the textual tools of interpretation, we have reiterated that these rules are not absolute and usually cannot be used in a vacuum. Lawyers may have to thread together several different kinds of textual arguments in order to sway the courts.

Consider the following statutory provision:

The Endangered Species Act of 1973 provides the following protection for endangered species:

> "[W]ith respect to any endangered species of fish or wildlife listed pursuant to section 1533 of this title it is unlawful for any person subject to the jurisdiction of the United States to . . . take any such species within the United States or the territorial sea of the United States." 16 U.S.C. § 1538(a)(1)."

The Act defines the statutory term "take" as follows:

> "The term 'take' means to harass, harm, pursue, hunt, shoot, wound, kill, trap, capture, or collect, or to attempt to engage in any such conduct." 16 U.S.C. § 1532(19).

Finally, the penalty provisions in the Act provide for the forfeiture of "[a]ll guns, traps, nets, and other equipment . . . used to aid the taking" of protected animals. 16 U.S.C. § 1540(e)(4)(B).

The agency charged with implementing the Endangered Species Act issued the following regulation:

> "*Harm* in the definition of 'take' in the Act means an act which actually kills or injures wildlife. Such act may include significant habitat modification or degradation where it actually kills or injures wildlife by significantly impairing essential behavioral patterns, including breeding, feeding, or sheltering." 50 CFR § 17.3 (1994).

A group of small landowners, logging companies, and families dependent on the forest products industries in the Pacific Northwest and in the Southeast argue that the Agency has misinterpreted the Act, and that "habitat modification" cannot constitute a "taking" under the Act.

- Identify the textual arguments that each side would make.

- How you would structure briefs for each side.

- What else would you like to research?

- How would a Textualist rule?

- Who do you think has the better argument?

5. HOW LAWYERS USE THE TEXTUAL TOOLS

Let's now read lawyers' briefs in the case outlined in Exercise x.x to see how lawyers build such a case.The dueling Supreme Court briefs in *Babbitt v. Sweet Home* provide excellent examples of how to structure briefs using the textual tools of interpretation. They can be found at:

1995 WL 89293 (petitioner's brief) and 1995 WL 130541 (respondent's brief)

As you read these briefs, focus on their argument sections. Consider these questions:

- How does each side frame the issue for the Court?

- How does each side use the textual tools of interpretation?

- How are the arguments structured?

- How do the lawyers use their section headings?

- How do the lawyers refer to and use the tools of interpretation?

- Which brief do you think is better written and more persuasive? Why?

BABBITT V. SWEET HOME

515 U.S. 687 (1995)

Now read the opinions in the case. Justices Stevens and Scalia engage in an epic battle using the tools of textual interpretation. Consider the following issues:

- Identify all of the different textual tools employed by the majority and dissent. There are a lot of them.

- Did either Justice come up with any arguments not identified by the attorneys?

- Intuitively, do you think that habitat modification "harms" animals?

- Intuitively, do you think that habitat modification constitutes the "taking" of an animal?

- Who do you think has the better textual argument?

- Because of the *Chevron* doctrine, which we will cover later in the course, the majority must demonstrate only that the Secretary's interpretation of the Act is *a* fairly possible reading, but Justice Scalia must demonstrate that the Act *unambiguously* prohibits the Secretary's reading. In other words, to agree with the majority you need only agree that the statute is ambiguous on this issue, but to agree with the dissent you must agree that the statute is unambiguous. Given that, which do you side with?

- What do you think Congress actually intended?

- Justice Scalia uses legislative history. Why? And do you think his arguments regarding legislative history are persuasive, or do you prefer the majority's?

- Does Justice Scalia reject the whole notion of considering a statute's purpose? Why or why not?

JUSTICE STEVENS delivered the opinion of the Court.

The Endangered Species Act of 1973 contains a variety of protections designed to save from extinction species that the Secretary of the Interior designates as endangered or threatened. Section 9 of the Act makes it unlawful for any person to "take" any endangered or threatened species. The Secretary has promulgated a regulation that defines the statute's prohibition on takings to include "significant habitat modification or degradation where it actually kills or injures wildlife." This case presents the question whether the Secretary exceeded his authority under the Act by promulgating that regulation.

I

Section 9(a)(1) of the Act provides the following protection for endangered species:

"Except as provided in sections 1535(g)(2) and 1539 of this title, with respect to any endangered species of fish or wildlife listed pursuant to section 1533 of this title it is unlawful for any person subject to the jurisdiction of the United States to—

. . . .

"(B) take any such species within the United States or the territorial sea of the United States." 16 U.S.C. § 1538(a)(1)."

Section 3(19) of the Act defines the statutory term "take":

"The term 'take' means to harass, harm, pursue, hunt, shoot, wound, kill, trap, capture, or collect, or to attempt to engage in any such conduct." 16 U.S.C. § 1532(19)."

The Act does not further define the terms it uses to define "take." The Interior Department regulations that implement the statute, however, define the statutory term "harm":

"*Harm* in the definition of 'take' in the Act means an act which actually kills or injures wildlife. Such act may include significant habitat modification or degradation where it actually kills or injures wildlife by significantly impairing essential behavioral patterns, including breeding, feeding, or sheltering." 50 CFR § 17.3 (1994).

This regulation has been in place since 1975.

A limitation on the § 9 "take" prohibition appears in § 10(a)(1)(B) of the Act, which Congress added by amendment in 1982. That section authorizes the Secretary to grant a permit for any taking otherwise prohibited by § 9(a)(1)(B) "if such taking is incidental to, and not the purpose of, the carrying out of an otherwise lawful activity." 16 U.S.C. § 1539(a)(1)(B).

In addition to the prohibition on takings, the Act provides several other protections for endangered species. Section 4, 16 U.S.C. § 1533, commands the Secretary to identify species of fish or wildlife that are in danger of extinction and to publish from time to time lists of all species he determines to be endangered or threatened. Section 5, 16 U.S.C. § 1534, authorizes the Secretary, in cooperation with the States, to acquire land to aid in preserving such species. Section 7 requires federal agencies to ensure that none of their activities, including the granting of licenses and permits, will jeopardize the continued existence of endangered species "or result in the destruction or adverse modification of habitat of such species which is determined by the Secretary . . . to be critical." 16 U.S.C. § 1536(a)(2).

Respondents in this action are small landowners, logging companies, and families dependent on the forest products industries in the Pacific Northwest and in the Southeast, and organizations that represent their interests. They brought this declaratory judgment action against petitioners, the Secretary of the Interior and the Director of the Fish and Wildlife Service, in the United States District Court for the District of Columbia to challenge the statutory validity of the Secretary's regulation defining "harm," particularly the inclusion of habitat modification and degradation in the definition. Respondents challenged the regulation on its face. Their complaint alleged that application of the "harm" regulation to the red-cockaded woodpecker, an endangered species, and the northern spotted owl, a threatened species, had injured them economically.

Respondents advanced three arguments to support their submission that Congress did not intend the word "take" in § 9 to include habitat modification, as the Secretary's "harm" regulation provides. First, they correctly noted that language in the Senate's original version of the ESA would have defined "take" to include "destruction, modification, or curtailment of [the] habitat or range" of fish or wildlife, but the Senate deleted that language from the bill before enacting it. Second, respondents argued that Congress intended the Act's express authorization for the Federal Government to buy private land in order to prevent habitat degradation in § 5 to be the exclusive check against habitat modification on private property. Third, because the Senate added the term "harm" to the definition of "take" in a floor amendment without debate, respondents argued that the court should not interpret the term so expansively as to include habitat modification.

. . . .

II

Because this case was decided on motions for summary judgment, we may appropriately make certain factual assumptions in order to frame the legal issue. First, we assume respondents have no desire to harm either the red-cockaded woodpecker or the spotted owl; they merely wish to continue logging activities that would be entirely proper if not prohibited by the ESA. On the other hand, we must assume, *arguendo,* that those activities will have the effect, even though unintended, of detrimentally changing the natural habitat of both listed species and that, as a consequence, members of those species will be killed or injured. Under respondents' view of the law, the Secretary's only means of forestalling that grave result—even when the actor knows it is certain to occur—is to use his § 5 authority to purchase the lands on which the survival of the species depends. The Secretary, on the other hand, submits that the § 9 prohibition on takings, which Congress defined to include "harm," places on respondents a duty to avoid harm that habitat alteration will cause the birds unless respondents first obtain a permit pursuant to § 10.

The text of the Act provides three reasons for concluding that the Secretary's interpretation is reasonable. First, an ordinary understanding of the word "harm" supports it. The dictionary definition of the verb form of "harm" is "to cause hurt or damage to: injure." Webster's Third New International Dictionary 1034 (1966). In the context of the ESA, that definition naturally encompasses habitat modification that results in actual injury or death to members of an endangered or threatened species.

Respondents argue that the Secretary should have limited the purview of "harm" to direct applications of force against protected species, but the dictionary definition does not include the word "directly" or suggest in any way that only direct or willful action that leads to injury constitutes "harm." Moreover, unless the statutory term "harm" encompasses indirect as well as direct injuries, the word has no meaning that does not duplicate the meaning of other words that § 3 uses to define "take." A reluctance to treat statutory terms as surplusage supports the reasonableness of the Secretary's interpretation.

Second, the broad purpose of the ESA supports the Secretary's decision to extend protection against activities that cause the precise harms Congress enacted the statute to avoid. In *TVA v. Hill,* we described the Act as "the most comprehensive legislation for the preservation of endangered species ever enacted by any nation." Whereas predecessor statutes enacted in 1966 and 1969 had not contained any sweeping prohibition against the taking of endangered species except on federal lands, the 1973 Act applied to all land in the United States and to the Nation's territorial seas. As stated in § 2 of the Act, among its central purposes is "to provide a means whereby the ecosystems upon which endangered species and threatened species depend may be conserved. . . ." 16 U.S.C. § 1531(b).

. . . .

Third, the fact that Congress in 1982 authorized the Secretary to issue permits for takings that § 9(a)(1)(B) would otherwise prohibit, "if such taking is incidental to, and not the purpose of, the carrying out of an otherwise lawful activity," strongly suggests that Congress understood § 9(a)(1)(B) to prohibit indirect as well as deliberate takings. The permit process requires the applicant to prepare a "conservation plan" that specifies how he intends to "minimize and mitigate" the "impact" of his activity on endangered and threatened species, making clear that Congress had in mind foreseeable rather than merely accidental effects on listed species. No one could seriously request an "incidental" take permit to avert § 9 liability for direct, deliberate action against a member of an endangered or threatened species, but respondents would read "harm" so narrowly that the permit procedure would have little more than that absurd purpose. "When Congress acts to amend a statute, we presume it intends its amendment to have real and substantial effect." Congress' addition of the § 10 permit provision supports the Secretary's conclusion that activities not intended to harm an endangered species, such as habitat modification, may constitute unlawful takings under the ESA unless the Secretary permits them.

The Court of Appeals made three errors in asserting that "harm" must refer to a direct application of force because the words around it do. First, the court's premise was flawed. Several of the words that accompany "harm" in the § 3 definition of "take," especially "harass," "pursue," "wound," and "kill," refer to actions or effects that do not require direct applications of force. Second, to the extent the court read a requirement of intent or purpose into the words used to define "take," it ignored § 11's express provision that a "knowin[g]" action is enough to violate the Act. Third, the court employed *noscitur a sociis* to give "harm" essentially the same function as other words in the definition, thereby denying it independent meaning. The canon, to the contrary, counsels that a word "gathers meaning from the words around it." The statutory context of "harm" suggests that Congress meant that term to serve a particular function in the ESA, consistent with, but distinct from, the functions of the other verbs used to define "take." The Secretary's interpretation of "harm" to include indirectly injuring endangered animals through habitat modification permissibly interprets "harm" to have "a character of its own not to be submerged by its association."

Nor does the Act's inclusion of the § 5 land acquisition authority and the § 7 directive to federal agencies to avoid destruction or adverse modification of critical habitat alter our conclusion. Respondents' argument that the Government lacks any incentive to purchase land under § 5 when it can simply prohibit takings under § 9 ignores the practical considerations that attend enforcement of the ESA. Purchasing habitat lands may well cost the Government less in many circumstances than pursuing civil or criminal penalties. In addition, the § 5 procedure allows for protection of habitat before the seller's activity has harmed any endangered animal, whereas the Government cannot enforce the § 9 prohibition until an animal has actually been killed or injured. The Secretary may also find the § 5 authority useful for preventing modification of land that is not yet but may in the future become habitat for an endangered or threatened species. The § 7 directive applies only to the Federal Government, whereas the § 9 prohibition applies to "any person." Section 7 imposes a broad, affirmative duty to avoid adverse habitat modifications that § 9 does not replicate, and § 7 does not limit its admonition to habitat modification that "actually kills or injures wildlife." Conversely, § 7 contains limitations that § 9 does not, applying only to actions "likely to jeopardize the continued existence of any endangered species or threatened species" and to modifications of habitat that has been designated "critical" pursuant to § 4, 16 U.S.C. § 1533(b)(2). Any overlap that § 5 or § 7 may have with § 9 in particular cases is unexceptional and simply reflects the broad purpose of the Act set out in § 2 and acknowledged in *TVA v. Hill*.

We need not decide whether the statutory definition of "take" compels the Secretary's interpretation of "harm," because our conclusions that Congress did not unambiguously manifest its intent to adopt respondents' view and that the Secretary's interpretation is reasonable suffice to decide this case. The latitude the ESA gives the Secretary in enforcing the statute, together with the degree of regulatory expertise necessary to its enforcement, establishes that we owe some degree of deference to the Secretary's reasonable interpretation.

III

Our conclusion that the Secretary's definition of "harm" rests on a permissible construction of the ESA gains further support from the legislative history of the statute. The Committee Reports accompanying the bills that became the ESA do not specifically discuss the meaning of "harm," but they make clear that Congress intended "take" to apply broadly to cover indirect as well as purposeful actions. The Senate Report stressed that " '[t]ake' is defined . . . in the broadest possible manner to include every conceivable way in which a person can 'take' or attempt to 'take' any fish or wildlife." The House Report stated that "the broadest possible terms" were used to define restrictions on takings. The House Report underscored the breadth of the "take" definition by noting that it included "harassment, *whether intentional or not*." The Report explained that the definition "would allow, for example, the Secretary to regulate or prohibit the activities of birdwatchers where the effect of those activities might disturb the birds and make it difficult for them to hatch or raise their young." These comments, ignored in the dissent's welcome but selective foray into legislative history, support the Secretary's interpretation that the term "take" in § 9 reached far more than the deliberate actions of hunters and trappers.

Two endangered species bills, S. 1592 and S. 1983, were introduced in the Senate and referred to the Commerce Committee. Neither bill included the word "harm" in its definition of "take," although the definitions otherwise closely resembled the one that appeared in the bill as ultimately enacted. Senator Tunney, the floor manager of the bill in the Senate, subsequently introduced a floor amendment that added "harm" to the definition, noting that this and accompanying amendments would "help to achieve the purposes of the bill." Respondents argue that the lack of debate about the amendment that added "harm" counsels in favor of a narrow interpretation. We disagree. An obviously broad word that the Senate went out of its way to add to an important statutory definition is precisely the sort of provision that deserves a respectful reading.

The definition of "take" that originally appeared in S. 1983 differed from the definition as ultimately enacted in one other significant respect: It included "the destruction, modification, or curtailment of [the] habitat or range" of fish and wildlife. Respondents make much of the fact that the Commerce Committee removed this phrase from the "take" definition before S. 1983 went to the floor. We do not find that fact especially significant. The legislative materials contain no indication why the habitat protection provision was deleted. That provision differed greatly from the regulation at issue today. Most notably, the habitat protection provision in S. 1983 would have applied far more broadly than the regulation does because it made adverse habitat modification a categorical violation of the "take" prohibition, unbounded by the regulation's limitation to habitat modifications that actually kill or injure wildlife. The S. 1983 language also failed to qualify "modification" with the regulation's limiting adjective "significant." We do not believe the Senate's unelaborated disavowal of the provision in S. 1983 undermines the reasonableness of the more moderate habitat protection in the Secretary's "harm" regulation.

The history of the 1982 amendment that gave the Secretary authority to grant permits for "incidental" takings provides further support for his reading of the Act. The House Report expressly states that "[b]y use of the word 'incidental' the Committee intends to cover situations in which it is known that a taking will occur if the other activity is engaged in but such taking is incidental to, and not the purpose of, the activity." This reference to the foreseeability of incidental takings undermines respondents' argument that the 1982 amendment covered only accidental killings of endangered and threatened animals that might occur in the course of hunting or trapping other animals. Indeed, Congress had habitat modification directly in mind: Both the Senate Report and the House Conference Report identified as the model for the permit process a cooperative state-federal response to a case in California where a development project threatened incidental harm to a species of endangered butterfly by modification of its habitat. Thus, Congress in 1982 focused squarely on the aspect of the "harm" regulation at issue in this litigation. Congress' implementation of a permit program is consistent with the Secretary's interpretation of the term "harm."

. . . .

JUSTICE SCALIA, with whom THE CHIEF JUSTICE and JUSTICE THOMAS join, dissenting.

I think it unmistakably clear that the legislation at issue here (1) forbade the hunting and killing of endangered animals, and (2) provided federal lands and federal funds *for the acquisition of private lands,* to preserve the habitat of endangered animals. The Court's holding that the hunting and killing prohibition incidentally preserves habitat on private lands imposes unfairness to the point of financial ruin—not just upon the rich, but upon the simplest farmer who finds his land conscripted to national zoological use. I respectfully dissent.

I

The Endangered Species Act of 1973 provides that "it is unlawful for any person subject to the jurisdiction of the United States to take—. . . any [protected] species within the United States." The term "take" is defined as "to harass, *harm,* pursue, hunt, shoot, wound, kill, trap, capture, or collect, or to attempt to engage in any such conduct." The challenged regulation defines "harm" thus:

"*Harm* in the definition of 'take' in the Act means an act which actually kills or injures wildlife. Such act may include significant habitat modification or degradation where it actually kills or injures wildlife by significantly impairing essential behavioral patterns, including breeding, feeding or sheltering." 50 CFR § 17.3 (1994).

In my view petitioners must lose—the regulation must fall. . . .

The regulation has three features which, for reasons I shall discuss at length below, do not comport with the statute. First, it interprets the statute to prohibit habitat modification that is no more than the cause-in-fact of death or injury to wildlife. *Any* "significant habitat modification" that in fact produces that result by "impairing essential behavioral patterns" is made unlawful, regardless of whether that result is intended or even foreseeable, and no matter how long the chain of causality between modification and injury.

Second, the regulation does not require an "act": The Secretary's officially stated position is that an *omission* will do. The previous version of the regulation made this explicit. When the regulation was modified in 1981 the phrase "or omission" was taken out, but only because (as the final publication of the rule advised) "the [Fish and Wildlife] Service feels that 'act' is inclusive of either commissions or omissions which would be prohibited by section [1538(a)(1)(B)]."

The third and most important unlawful feature of the regulation is that it encompasses injury inflicted, not only upon individual animals, but upon populations of the protected species. "Injury" in the regulation includes "significantly impairing essential behavioral patterns, including *breeding*[.]" Impairment of breeding does not "injure" living creatures; it prevents them from propagating, thus "injuring" *a population* of animals which would otherwise have maintained or increased its numbers. What the face of the regulation shows, the Secretary's official pronouncements confirm. The Final Redefinition of "Harm" accompanying publication of the regulation said that "harm" is not limited to "direct physical injury to an individual member of the wildlife species," and refers to "injury *to a population*."

None of these three features of the regulation can be found in the statutory provisions supposed to authorize it. The term "harm" . . . has no legal force of its own. An indictment or civil complaint that charged the defendant with "harming" an animal protected under the Act would be dismissed as defective, for the only *operative* term in the statute is to "take." If "take" were not elsewhere defined in the Act, none could dispute what it means, for the term is as old as the law itself. To "take," when applied to wild animals, means to reduce those animals, by killing or capturing, to human control. See, *e.g.,* 11 Oxford English Dictionary (1933) ("Take . . . To catch, capture (a wild beast, bird, fish, etc.)"); Webster's New International Dictionary of the English Language (2d ed. 1949) (take defined as "to catch or capture by trapping, snaring, etc., or as prey"); *Geer v. Connecticut,* 161 U.S. 519, 523, 16 S.Ct. 600, 602, 40 L.Ed.793 (1896) (" '[A]ll the animals which can be taken upon the earth, in the sea, or in the air, that is to say, wild animals, belong to those who take them' ") (quoting the Digest of Justinian); 2 W. Blackstone, Commentaries 411 (1766) ("Every man . . . has an equal right of pursuing and taking to his own use all such creatures as are *ferae naturae*"). This is just the sense in which "take" is used elsewhere in federal legislation and treaty. See, *e.g.,* Migratory Bird Treaty Act, 16 U.S.C. § 703 (1988 ed., Supp. V) (no person may "pursue, hunt, take, capture, kill, [or] attempt to take, capture, or kill" any migratory bird); Agreement on the Conservation of Polar Bears, Nov. 15, 1973, Art. I, 27 U.S.T. 3918, 3921, T.I.A.S. No. 8409 (defining "taking" as "hunting, killing and capturing"). And that meaning fits neatly with the rest of § 1538(a)(1), which makes it unlawful not only to take protected species, but also to import or export them; to possess, sell, deliver, carry, transport, or ship any taken species; and to transport, sell, or offer to sell them in interstate or foreign commerce. The taking prohibition, in other words, is only part of the regulatory plan of § 1538(a)(1), which covers all the stages of the process by which protected wildlife is reduced to man's dominion and made the object of profit. It is obvious that "take" in this sense—a term of art deeply embedded in the statutory and common law concerning wildlife— describes a class of acts (not omissions) done directly and intentionally (not indirectly and by accident) to particular animals (not populations of animals).

The Act's definition of "take" does expand the word slightly (and not unusually), so as to make clear that it includes not just a completed taking, but the process of taking, and all of the acts that are customarily identified with or accompany that process ("to harass, harm, pursue, hunt, shoot, wound, kill, trap, capture, or collect"); and so as to include attempts. The tempting fallacy—which the Court commits with abandon—is to assume that *once defined,* "take" loses any significance, and it is only the definition that matters. The Court treats the statute as though Congress had directly enacted the § 1532(19) definition as a self-executing prohibition, and had not enacted § 1538(a)(1)(B) at all. But § 1538(a)(1)(B) *is* there, and if the terms contained in the definitional section are susceptible of two readings, one of which comports with the standard meaning of "take" as used in application to wildlife, and one of which does not, an agency regulation that adopts the latter reading is necessarily unreasonable, for it reads the defined term "take"—the only operative term—out of the statute altogether.

That is what has occurred here. The verb "harm" has a *range* of meaning: "to cause injury" at its broadest, "to do hurt or damage" in a narrower and more direct sense. See, *e.g.,* 1 N. Webster, An American Dictionary of the English Language (1828) ("Harm, *v.t.* To hurt; to injure; to damage; *to impair soundness of body, either animal* or vegetable") (emphasis added); American College Dictionary 551 (1970) ("harm . . . *n.* injury; damage; hurt: *to do him bodily harm*"). In fact the more directed sense of "harm" is a somewhat more common and preferred usage; "*harm* has in it a little of the idea of specially focused hurt or injury, as if a personal injury has been anticipated and intended." J. Opdycke, Mark My Words: A Guide to Modern Usage and Expression 330 (1949). To define "harm" as an act or omission that, however remotely, "actually kills or injures" a population of wildlife through habitat modification is to choose a meaning that makes nonsense of the word that "harm" defines—requiring us to accept that a farmer who tills his field and causes erosion that makes silt run into a nearby river which depletes oxygen and thereby "impairs [the] breeding" of protected fish has "taken" or "attempted to take" the fish. It should take the strongest evidence to make us believe that Congress has defined a term in a manner repugnant to its ordinary and traditional sense.

Here the evidence shows the opposite. "Harm" is merely one of 10 prohibitory words in § 1532(19), and the other 9 fit the ordinary meaning of "take" perfectly. To "harass, pursue, hunt, shoot, wound, kill, trap, capture, or collect" are all affirmative acts . . . which are directed immediately and intentionally against a particular animal—not acts or omissions that indirectly and accidentally cause injury to a population of animals. The Court points out that several of the words ("harass," "pursue," "wound," and "kill") "refer to actions or effects that do not require direct *applications of force*." That is true enough, but force is not the point. Even "taking" activities in the narrowest sense, activities traditionally engaged in by hunters and trappers, do not all consist of direct applications of force; pursuit and harassment are part of the business of "taking" the prey even before it has been touched. What the nine other words in § 1532(19) have in common—and share with the narrower meaning of "harm" described above, but not with the Secretary's ruthless dilation of the word—is the sense of affirmative conduct intentionally directed against a particular animal or animals.

I am not the first to notice this fact, or to draw the conclusion that it compels. In 1981 the Solicitor of the Fish and Wildlife Service delivered a legal opinion on § 1532(19) that is in complete agreement with my reading:

"The Act's definition of 'take' contains a list of actions that illustrate the intended scope of the term. . . . With the possible exception of 'harm,' these terms all represent forms of conduct that are directed against and likely to injure or kill *individual* wildlife. Under the principle of statutory construction, *ejusdem generis,* . . . the term 'harm' should be interpreted to include only those actions that are directed against, and likely to injure or kill, individual wildlife."

I would call it *noscitur a sociis,* but the principle is much the same: The fact that "several items in a list share an attribute counsels in favor of interpreting the other items as possessing that attribute as well." The Court contends that the canon cannot be applied to deprive a word of all its "independent meaning." That proposition is questionable to begin with, especially as applied to long lawyers' listings such as this. If it were true, we ought to give the word "trap" in the definition its rare meaning of "to clothe" (whence "trappings")—since otherwise it adds nothing to the word "capture." In any event, the Court's contention that "harm" in the narrow sense adds nothing to the other words underestimates the ingenuity of our own species in a way that Congress did not. To feed an animal poison, to spray it with mace, to chop down the very tree in which it is nesting, or even to destroy its entire habitat in order to take it (as by draining a pond to get at a turtle), might neither wound nor kill, but would directly and intentionally harm.

The penalty provisions of the Act counsel this interpretation as well. Any person who "knowingly" violates § 1538(a)(1)(B) is subject to criminal penalties under § 1540(b)(1) and civil penalties under § 1540(a)(1); moreover, under the latter section, any person "who otherwise violates" the taking prohibition (*i.e.,* violates it *un*knowingly) may be assessed a civil penalty of $500 for each violation, with the stricture that "[e]ach such violation shall be a separate offense." This last provision should be clear warning that the regulation is in error, for when combined with the regulation it produces a result that no legislature could reasonably be thought to have intended: A large number of routine private activities— for example, farming, ranching, roadbuilding, construction and logging— are subjected to strict-liability penalties when they fortuitously injure protected wildlife, no matter how remote the chain of causation and no matter how difficult to foresee (or to disprove) the "injury" may be (*e.g.,* an "impairment" of breeding). The Court says that "[the strict-liability provision] is potentially sweeping, but it would be so with or without the Secretary's 'harm' regulation." That is not correct. Without the regulation, the routine "habitat modifying" activities that people conduct to make a daily living would not carry exposure to strict penalties; only acts directed at animals, like those described by the other words in § 1532(19), would risk liability.

The Court says that "[to] read a requirement of intent or purpose into the words used to define 'take' . . . ignore[s] [§ 1540's] express provision that a 'knowin[g]' action is enough to violate the Act." This presumably means that because the reading of § 1532(19) advanced here ascribes an element of purposeful injury to the prohibited acts, it makes superfluous (or inexplicable) the more severe penalties provided for a "knowing" violation. That conclusion does not follow, for it is quite possible to take protected wildlife purposefully without doing so knowingly. A requirement that a violation be "knowing" means that the defendant must "know the facts that make his conduct illegal." The hunter who shoots an elk in the mistaken belief that it is a mule deer has not knowingly violated § 1538(a)(1)(B)—not because he does not know that elk are legally protected (that would be knowledge of the law, which is not a requirement), but because he does not know what sort of animal he is shooting. The hunter has nonetheless committed a purposeful taking of protected wildlife, and would therefore be subject to the (lower) strict-liability penalties for the violation.

So far I have discussed only the immediate statutory text bearing on the regulation. But the definition of "take" in § 1532(19) applies "[f]or the purposes of this chapter," that is, it governs the meaning of the word *as used everywhere in the Act*. Thus, the Secretary's interpretation of "harm" is wrong if it does not fit with the use of "take" throughout the Act. And it does not. In § 1540(e)(4)(B), for example, Congress provided for the forfeiture of "[a]ll guns, traps, nets, and other equipment . . . used to aid the taking, possessing, selling, [etc.]" of protected animals. This listing plainly relates to "taking" in the ordinary sense. If environmental modification were part (and necessarily a major part) of taking, as the Secretary maintains, one would have expected the list to include "plows, bulldozers, and backhoes." As another example, § 1539(e)(1) exempts "the taking of any endangered species" by Alaskan Indians and Eskimos "if such taking is primarily for subsistence purposes"; and provides that "[n]on-edible byproducts of species taken pursuant to this section may be sold . . . when made into authentic native articles of handicrafts and clothing." Surely these provisions apply to taking only in the ordinary sense, and are meaningless as applied to species injured by environmental modification. The Act is full of like examples.

The broader structure of the Act confirms the unreasonableness of the regulation. Section 1536 provides:

"Each Federal agency shall . . . insure that any action authorized, funded, or carried out by such agency . . . is not likely to jeopardize the continued existence of any endangered species or threatened species or *result in the destruction or adverse modification of habitat* of such species which is determined by the Secretary . . . to be critical."

The Act defines "critical habitat" as habitat that is "essential to the conservation of the species," with "conservation" in turn defined as the use of methods necessary to bring listed species "to the point at which the measures provided pursuant to this chapter are no longer necessary."

These provisions have a double significance. Even if §§ 1536(a)(2) and 1538(a)(1)(B) were totally independent prohibitions—the former applying only to federal agencies and their licensees, the latter only to private parties—Congress's explicit prohibition of habitat modification in the one section would bar the inference of an implicit prohibition of habitat modification in the other section. "[W]here Congress includes particular language in one section of a statute but omits it in another . . . , it is generally presumed that Congress acts intentionally and purposely in the disparate inclusion or exclusion." And that presumption against implicit prohibition would be even stronger where the one section which uses the language carefully defines and limits its application. That is to say, it would be passing strange for Congress carefully to define "critical habitat" as used in § 1536(a)(2), but leave it to the Secretary to evaluate, willy-nilly, impermissible "habitat modification" (under the guise of "harm") in § 1538(a)(1)(B).

In fact, however, §§ 1536(a)(2) and 1538(a)(1)(B) do *not* operate in separate realms; federal agencies are subject to *both,* because the "person[s]" forbidden to take protected species under § 1538 include agencies and departments of the Federal Government. See § 1532(13).

This means that the "harm" regulation also contradicts another principle of interpretation: that statutes should be read so far as possible to give independent effect to all their provisions. By defining "harm" in the definition of "take" in § 1538(a)(1)(B) to include significant habitat modification that injures populations of wildlife, the regulation makes the habitat-modification restriction in § 1536(a)(2) almost wholly superfluous. As "critical habitat" is habitat "essential to the conservation of the species," adverse modification of "critical" habitat by a federal agency would also constitute habitat modification that injures a population of wildlife.

Petitioners try to salvage some independent scope for § 1536(a)(2) by the following contortion: Because the definition of critical habitat includes not only "the specific areas within the geographical area occupied by the species [that are] essential to the conservation of the species," but also "specific areas outside the geographical area occupied by the species at the time it is listed [as a protected species] . . . [that are] essential to the conservation of the species," there may be some agency modifications of critical habitat which do *not* injure a population of wildlife. This is dubious to begin with. A principal way to injure wildlife under the Secretary's own regulation is to "significantly impai[r] . . . breeding." To prevent the natural increase of a species by adverse modification of habitat suitable for expansion assuredly impairs breeding. But even if true, the argument only narrows the scope of the superfluity, leaving as so many wasted words the § 1532(5)(A)(i) definition of critical habitat to include currently *occupied* habitat essential to the species' conservation. If the Secretary's definition of "harm" under § 1538(a)(1)(B) is to be upheld, we must believe that Congress enacted § 1536(a)(2) solely because in its absence federal agencies would be able to modify habitat in currently *unoccupied* areas. It is more rational to believe that the Secretary's expansion of § 1538(a)(1)(B) carves out the heart of one of the central provisions of the Act.

II

The Court makes four other arguments. First, "the broad purpose of the [Act] supports the Secretary's decision to extend protection against activities that cause the precise harms Congress enacted the statute to avoid." I thought we had renounced the vice of "simplistically . . . assum[ing] that *whatever* furthers the statute's primary objective must be the law." Deduction from the "broad purpose" of a statute begs the question if it is used to decide by what *means* (and hence to what *length*) Congress pursued that purpose; to get the right answer to that question there is no substitute for the hard job (or, in this case, the quite simple one) of reading the whole text. "The Act must do everything necessary to achieve its broad purpose" is the slogan of the enthusiast, not the analytical tool of the arbiter.

Second, the Court maintains that the legislative history of the 1973 Act supports the Secretary's definition. Even if legislative history were a legitimate and reliable tool of interpretation (which I shall assume in order to rebut the Court's claim); and even if it could appropriately be resorted to when the enacted text is as clear as this; here it shows quite the opposite of what the Court says. I shall not pause to discuss the Court's reliance on such statements in the Committee Reports as " '[t]ake' is defined ... in the broadest possible manner to include every conceivable way in which a person can 'take' or attempt to 'take' any fish or wildlife.' " This sort of empty flourish—to the effect that "this statute means what it means all the way"—counts for little even when enacted into the law itself.

Much of the Court's discussion of legislative history is devoted to two items: first, the Senate floor manager's introduction of an amendment that added the word "harm" to the definition of "take," with the observation that (along with other amendments) it would " 'help to achieve the purposes of the bill' "; second, the relevant Committee's removal from the definition of a provision stating that "take" includes " 'the destruction, modification or curtailment of [the] habitat or range' " of fish and wildlife. The Court inflates the first and belittles the second, even though the second is on its face far more pertinent. But this elaborate inference from various pre-enactment actions and inactions is quite unnecessary, since we have *direct* evidence of what those who brought the legislation to the floor thought it meant—evidence as solid as any ever to be found in legislative history, but which the Court banishes to a footnote.

Both the Senate and House floor managers of the bill explained it in terms which leave no doubt that the problem of habitat destruction on private lands was to be solved principally by the land acquisition program of § 1534, while § 1538 solved a different problem altogether—the problem of takings. Senator Tunney stated:

"Through [the] land acquisition provisions, we will be able to conserve habitats necessary to protect fish and wildlife from further destruction.

"Although most endangered species are threatened primarily by the destruction of their natural habitats, a significant portion of these animals are subject to *predation by man for commercial, sport, consumption, or other purposes.* The provisions of [the bill] would prohibit the commerce in or the importation, exportation, or taking of endangered species. . . ."

The House floor manager, Representative Sullivan, put the same thought in this way:

"[T]he principal threat to animals stems from destruction of their habitat. . . . [*The bill] will meet this problem by providing funds for acquisition of critical habitat.* . . . It will also enable the Department of Agriculture to cooperate with willing landowners who desire to assist in the protection of endangered species, *but who are understandably unwilling to do so at excessive cost to themselves.*

"Another hazard to endangered species arises from those who would *capture or kill them for pleasure or profit.* There is no way that the Congress can make it less pleasurable for a person to take an animal, but we can certainly make it less profitable for them to do so."

Habitat modification and takings, in other words, were viewed as different problems, addressed by different provisions of the Act. The Court really has no explanation for these statements. All it can say is that "[n]either statement even suggested that [the habitat acquisition funding provision in § 1534] would be the Act's exclusive remedy for habitat modification by private landowners or that habitat modification by private landowners stood outside the ambit of [§ 1538]." That is to say, the statements are not as bad as they might have been. Little in life is. They are, however, quite bad enough to destroy the Court's legislative-history case, since they display the clear understanding (1) that habitat modification is separate from "taking," and (2) that habitat destruction on private lands is to be remedied by public acquisition, and *not* by making particular unlucky landowners incur "excessive cost to themselves." The Court points out triumphantly that they do not display the understanding (3) that the land acquisition program is "the [Act's] only response to habitat modification." Of course not, since that is not so (all *public* lands are subject to habitat-modification restrictions); but (1) and (2) are quite enough to exclude the Court's interpretation. They identify the land acquisition program as the Act's only response to habitat modification *by private landowners,* and thus do not in the least "contradic[t]," the fact that § 1536 prohibits habitat modification *by federal agencies.*

Third, the Court seeks support from a provision that was added to the Act in 1982, the year after the Secretary promulgated the current regulation. The provision states:

"[T]he Secretary may permit, under such terms and conditions as he shall prescribe—

. . . .

"any taking otherwise prohibited by section 1538(a)(1)(B) . . . if such taking is incidental to, and not the purpose of, the carrying out of an otherwise lawful activity."

This provision does not, of course, implicate our doctrine that reenactment of a statutory provision ratifies an extant judicial or administrative interpretation, for neither the taking prohibition in § 1538(a)(1)(B) nor the definition in § 1532(19) was reenacted. The Court claims, however, that the provision "strongly suggests that Congress understood [§ 1538(a)(1)(B)] to prohibit indirect as well as deliberate takings." That would be a valid inference if habitat modification were the only substantial "otherwise lawful activity" that might incidentally and nonpurposefully cause a prohibited "taking." Of course it is not. This provision applies to the many otherwise lawful takings that incidentally take a protected species—as when fishing for unprotected salmon also takes an endangered species of salmon. Congress has referred to such "incidental takings" in other statutes as well—for example, a statute referring to "the incidental taking of . . . sea turtles in the course of . . . harvesting [shrimp]" and to the "rate of incidental taking of sea turtles by United States vessels in the course of such harvesting"; and a statute referring to "the incidental taking of marine mammals in the course of commercial fishing operations." The Court shows that it misunderstands the question when it says that "[n]o one could seriously request an 'incidental' take permit to avert . . . liability for direct, deliberate action *against a member of an endangered or threatened species.*" That is not an *incidental* take at all.

This is enough to show, in my view, that the 1982 permit provision does not support the regulation. I must acknowledge that the Senate Committee Report on this provision, and the House Conference Committee Report, clearly contemplate that it will enable the Secretary to permit environmental modification. But the *text* of the amendment cannot possibly bear that asserted meaning, when placed within the context of an Act that must be interpreted (as we have seen) not to prohibit private environmental modification. The neutral language of the amendment cannot possibly alter that interpretation, nor can its legislative history be summoned forth to contradict, rather than clarify, what is in its totality an unambiguous statutory text. There is little fear, of course, that giving no effect to the relevant portions of the Committee Reports will frustrate the real-life expectations of a majority of the Members of Congress. If they read and relied on such tedious detail on such an obscure point (it was not, after all, presented as a revision of the statute's prohibitory scope, but as a discretionary-waiver provision) the Republic would be in grave peril.

. . . .

The Endangered Species Act is a carefully considered piece of legislation that forbids all persons to hunt or harm endangered animals, but places upon the public at large, rather than upon fortuitously accountable individual landowners, the cost of preserving the habitat of endangered species. There is neither textual support for, nor even evidence of congressional consideration of, the radically different disposition contained in the regulation that the Court sustains. For these reasons, I respectfully dissent.

6. EXERCISE: BUILDING A CASE WITH THE TEXTUAL TOOLS

Now, having studied the textual tools and having seen how judges apply them and lawyers build a case around them, it is your turn to put these rules into action.

Using the tools of statutory interpretation that we have studied thus far, consider the following question:

Is home schooling by a parent who does not have teaching credentials lawful as a form of private schooling under California's Education Code section 4200? Assume that the parent does not assert a religious reason for wishing to home school the child. What other sources would you want to consult prior to deciding this case, if any?

Relevant Statute

In 1920, California amended its compulsory education statute to state as follows (Ed. Code § 4200):

(a) Each person between the ages of 6 and 18 years who is not exempted under subsection (b) of this section is subject to compulsory full-time education. Each person subject to compulsory full-time education shall attend the public full-time day school for the full time designated as the length of the school day by the governing board of the school district in which the residency of the legal guardian is located.

(b) Compulsory public school education shall not apply to persons between the ages of 6 and 18 years who

(1) are being instructed in a private full-time day school by persons capable of teaching. Such school shall be taught in the English language and shall offer instruction in the several branches of study required to be taught in the public schools of the state; or

(2) are being instructed in study and recitation by a tutor or other person for at least three hours per day for 175 days each calendar year in the several branches of study required to be taught in the public schools of this state. The tutor or other person must hold a valid state credential for the grade taught. The instruction shall be offered between the hours of 8 o'clock a.m. and 4 o'clock p.m.

Historical Context

In 1903, California enacted its first compulsory education statute, the predecessor statute to the current statute. As you know, at the time, statutes were not highly detailed. The statute provided that parents had to send their children to public school. However, a child was exempt from attending public school "upon proof that such child is being taught in a private school, or by a private tutor, or at home by any person capable of teaching."

Recent Developments

Since the 1980s, California has experienced a boom in home schooling. Today, roughly 250,000 children are home schooled.

The California Department of Education has not prosecuted any home schooling parent for failing to comply with the education code, at least since 1968. Although the Department of Education has not issued any regulations concerning home schools, it has instructed parents who have inquired that it considers home schools to be a form of private schools. Every other state in the country has a statute on the books that permits home schooling.

Over the past two decades, other provisions of the education code have undergone changes. Of particular interest in this case is the following. The education code, as originally enacted, required that private schools provide affidavits to the Department of Education containing their teaching materials. In 1991, the legislature amended the affidavit requirement for private schools (§ 4310) to state that "private schools with five or fewer students need not comply with the affidavit requirement." The committee report to this section states that "private schools with five or fewer children are typically those where the parents have declared the home to be a school where parents teach their own children, and the purpose of this section is to relieve parents who home school of this requirement."

Further, in 1995, the legislature enacted provisions in the health and safety code prohibiting certain hazardous air emissions within 1000 feet of a school, but exempted from the definition of "school" as "any private school in which education is primarily conducted in private homes."

C. JUDGE-MADE RULES OF INTERPRETATION: THE SUBSTANTIVE CANONS

Sometimes the textual tools of interpretation are not dispositive and terms remain ambiguous. In such cases, interpreters will resort to additional, non-textual considerations to determine the meaning and proper application of a statute. One set of non-textual considerations is the substantive canons of interpretation. These canons, sometimes referred to as presumptions, are generated by judges and are not moored to statutory text. Some of the canons are invoked quite frequently, while others are controversial among some judges or of limited use because of their narrow application.

You might think that textualists, intentionalists, and purposivists would reject the substantive canons. After all, the substantive canons give little evidence as to the likely understanding of the legislatures at the time of passage, their intent, or their overall purposes. Nevertheless, even textualists like Justice Scalia use many of the canons of interpretation. As you learn about the substantive canons, ask yourself why evens these judges have adopted them.

It might be helpful to think of *stare decisis*, with which you are familiar from this and other classes, as a kind of template for the substantive canons of interpretation. After all, judges made up this rule. It does not come from any statute or directly from the Constitution. It sheds no light on legislative intent or meaning. Yet judges recognize that it protects important values in our legal system, and therefore, they will ordinarily defer to precedent unless there is a compelling reason not to do so. Still, as we have already seen, some judges are more deferential to precedent than others, and *stare decisis* is not absolute. Much the same can be said about all of the substantive canons of interpretation that we will study.

In this section, we will consider in depth four of the substantive canons, namely the rules of constitutional avoidance, lenity, consistency with common law, and against preemption. You should be aware that there are several other substantive canons of interpretation, but these are typically limited to narrow contexts or have limited force.

1. CONSTITUTIONAL AVOIDANCE

(A) Understanding the Rule

The constitutional avoidance canon applies differently in different contexts—and according to different judges. In its least controversial form, the constitutional avoidance canon states that where possible, statutes will be interpreted in a manner that does not violate the Constitution. In other words, when there are two possible interpretations of a statute, the interpretation that does not render the statute unconstitutional is adopted. Some judges would rephrase the rule as follows: when there are two *plausible*—or, according to some, *equally plausible* or *fairly possible*—interpretations of a statute, the interpretation that does not render the statute unconstitutional is adopted.

In other contexts, judges may adopt a version of the rule that states that if one possible (or fairly possible, plausible, or equally plausible) interpretation avoids raising constitutional doubts about a statute, that interpretation is preferred.

Finally, in some cases the rule is stated as, whenever one interpretation of the statute allows the court to avoid resolving difficult constitutional questions, that interpretation will be adopted.

Can you articulate the differences among these different versions of the rule? How do you think they play out in practice?

However this rule is framed, why do you think that judges have adopted it? Why is there a preference in favor of constitutionality?

Consider the following two cases in which the Supreme Court recently addressed the constitutional avoidance doctrine. Bear in mind that these two cases are among the most politically controversial and consequential in recent years.

CITIZENS UNITED V. FEDERAL ELECTION COMMISSION
558 U.S. 310 (2010)

As you read the following case, focus on the following:

- How many constitutional avoidance arguments does the majority reject? Why?

- Likewise, the majority rejects the argument that it should defer to precedent. Why? Recall our earlier discussions concerning the value of precedent.

- Do you find any of the avoidance arguments or the *stare decisis* argument of the dissent compelling? Why or why not?

- How do the majority and dissent differ as to the proper framing of the constitutional avoidance doctrine?

- What values would applying the constitutional avoidance doctrine, as the dissent wishes, serve in this case?

- How powerful do you think the constitutional avoidance argument is in practice?

JUSTICE KENNEDY delivered the opinion of the Court.

Federal law prohibits corporations and unions from using their general treasury funds to make independent expenditures for speech defined as an "electioneering communication" or for speech expressly advocating the election or defeat of a candidate. 2 U.S.C. § 441b. Limits on electioneering communications were upheld in *McConnell v. Federal Election Comm'n* (2003). The holding of *McConnell* rested to a large extent on an earlier case, *Austin v. Michigan Chamber of Commerce* (1990). *Austin* had held that political speech may be banned based on the speaker's corporate identity.

In this case we are asked to reconsider *Austin* and, in effect, *McConnell*. It has been noted that "*Austin* was a significant departure from ancient First Amendment principles," *Federal Election Comm'n v. Wisconsin Right to Life, Inc. (WRTL),* (SCALIA, J., concurring in part and concurring in judgment). We agree with that conclusion and hold that *stare decisis* does not compel the continued acceptance of *Austin*. The Government may regulate corporate political speech through disclaimer and disclosure requirements, but it may not suppress that speech altogether. We turn to the case now before us.

I

A

Citizens United is a nonprofit corporation. It brought this action in the United States District Court for the District of Columbia. A three-judge court later convened to hear the cause. The resulting judgment gives rise to this appeal.

Citizens United has an annual budget of about $12 million. Most of its funds are from donations by individuals; but, in addition, it accepts a small portion of its funds from for-profit corporations.

In January 2008, Citizens United released a film entitled *Hillary: The Movie*. We refer to the film as *Hillary*. It is a 90-minute documentary about then-Senator Hillary Clinton, who was a candidate in the Democratic Party's 2008 Presidential primary elections. *Hillary* mentions Senator Clinton by name and depicts interviews with political commentators and other persons, most of them quite critical of Senator Clinton. *Hillary* was released in theaters and on DVD, but Citizens United wanted to increase distribution by making it available through video-on-demand.

Video-on-demand allows digital cable subscribers to select programming from various menus, including movies, television shows, sports, news, and music. The viewer can watch the program at any time and can elect to rewind or pause the program. In December 2007, a cable company offered, for a payment of $1.2 million, to make *Hillary* available on a video-on-demand channel called "Elections '08." Some video-on-demand services require viewers to pay a small fee to view a selected program, but here the proposal was to make *Hillary* available to viewers free of charge.

To implement the proposal, Citizens United was prepared to pay for the video-on-demand; and to promote the film, it produced two 10-second ads and one 30-second ad for *Hillary*. Each ad includes a short (and, in our view, pejorative) statement about Senator Clinton, followed by the name of the movie and the movie's Website address. Citizens United desired to promote the video-on-demand offering by running advertisements on broadcast and cable television.

B

Before the Bipartisan Campaign Reform Act of 2002 (BCRA), federal law prohibited—and still does prohibit—corporations and unions from using general treasury funds to make direct contributions to candidates or independent expenditures that expressly advocate the election or defeat of a candidate, through any form of media, in connection with certain qualified federal elections. An electioneering communication is defined as "any broadcast, cable, or satellite communication" that "refers to a clearly identified candidate for Federal office" and is made within 30 days of a primary or 60 days of a general election. § 434(f)(3)(A). . . . Corporations and unions are barred from using their general treasury funds for express advocacy or electioneering communications. . . .

C

Citizens United wanted to make *Hillary* available through video-on-demand within 30 days of the 2008 primary elections. It feared, however, that both the film and the ads would be covered by § 441b's ban on corporate-funded independent expenditures, thus subjecting the corporation to civil and criminal penalties. . . . In December 2007, Citizens United sought declaratory and injunctive relief against the FEC. It argued that (1) § 441b is unconstitutional as applied to *Hillary;* and (2) BCRA's disclaimer and disclosure requirements, BCRA §§ 201 and 311, are unconstitutional as applied to *Hillary* and to the three ads for the movie.

. . . .

II

Before considering whether *Austin* should be overruled, we first address whether Citizens United's claim that § 441b cannot be applied to *Hillary* may be resolved on other, narrower grounds.

A

Citizens United contends that § 441b does not cover *Hillary,* as a matter of statutory interpretation, because the film does not qualify as an "electioneering communication." . . . . Under the definition of electioneering communication, the video-on-demand showing of *Hillary* on cable television would have been a "cable . . . communication" that "refer[red] to a clearly identified candidate for Federal office" and that was made within 30 days of a primary election. Citizens United, however, argues that *Hillary* was not "publicly distributed," because a single video-on-demand transmission is sent only to a requesting cable converter box and each separate transmission, in most instances, will be seen by just one household—not 50,000 or more persons.

This argument ignores the regulation's instruction on how to determine whether a cable transmission "[c]an be received by 50,000 or more persons." The regulation provides that the number of people who can receive a cable transmission is determined by the number of cable subscribers in the relevant area. Here, Citizens United wanted to use a cable video-on-demand system that had 34.5 million subscribers nationwide. Thus, *Hillary* could have been received by 50,000 persons or more.

One *amici* brief asks us, alternatively, to construe the condition that the communication "[c]an be received by 50,000 or more persons" to require "a plausible likelihood that the communication will be viewed by 50,000 or more potential voters"—as opposed to requiring only that the communication is "technologically capable" of being seen by that many people. Whether the population and demographic statistics in a proposed viewing area consisted of 50,000 registered voters—but not "infants, pre-teens, or otherwise electorally ineligible recipients"—would be a required determination, subject to judicial challenge and review, in any case where the issue was in doubt.

In our view the statute cannot be saved by limiting the reach of 2 U.S.C. § 441b through this suggested interpretation. In addition to the costs and burdens of litigation, this result would require a calculation as to the number of people a particular communication is likely to reach, with an inaccurate estimate potentially subjecting the speaker to criminal sanctions. The First Amendment does not permit laws that force speakers to retain a campaign finance attorney, conduct demographic marketing research, or seek declaratory rulings before discussing the most salient political issues of our day. Prolix laws chill speech for the same reason that vague laws chill speech: People "of common intelligence must necessarily guess at [the law's] meaning and differ as to its application." The Government may not render a ban on political speech constitutional by carving out a limited exemption through an amorphous regulatory interpretation. We must reject the approach suggested by the *amici.* Section 441b covers *Hillary.*

B

Citizens United next argues that § 441b may not be applied to *Hillary* under the approach taken in [our precedents]. . . . As explained by [the] controlling opinion in [an earlier case], the functional-equivalent test is objective: "a court should find that [a communication] is the functional equivalent of express advocacy only if [it] is susceptible of no reasonable interpretation other than as an appeal to vote for or against a specific candidate."

Under this test, *Hillary* is equivalent to express advocacy. The movie, in essence, is a feature-length negative advertisement that urges viewers to vote against Senator Clinton for President. In light of historical footage, interviews with persons critical of her, and voiceover narration, the film would be understood by most viewers as an extended criticism of Senator Clinton's character and her fitness for the office of the Presidency. The narrative may contain more suggestions and arguments than facts, but there is little doubt that the thesis of the film is that she is unfit for the Presidency. The movie concentrates on alleged wrongdoing during the Clinton administration, Senator Clinton's qualifications and fitness for office, and policies the commentators predict she would pursue if elected President. It calls Senator Clinton "Machiavellian" and asks whether she is "the most qualified to hit the ground running if elected President." The narrator reminds viewers that "Americans have never been keen on dynasties" and that "a vote for Hillary is a vote to continue 20 years of a Bush or a Clinton in the White House."

Citizens United argues that *Hillary* is just "a documentary film that examines certain historical events." We disagree. The movie's consistent emphasis is on the relevance of these events to Senator Clinton's candidacy for President. The narrator begins by asking "could [Senator Clinton] become the first female President in the history of the United States?" And the narrator reiterates the movie's message in his closing line: "Finally, before America decides on our next president, voters should need no reminders of . . . what's at stake—the well being and prosperity of our nation."

As the District Court found, there is no reasonable interpretation of *Hillary* other than as an appeal to vote against Senator Clinton. . . . [T]he film qualifies as the functional equivalent of express advocacy.

C

Citizens United further contends that § 441b should be invalidated as applied to movies shown through video-on-demand, arguing that this delivery system has a lower risk of distorting the political process than do television ads. On what we might call conventional television, advertising spots reach viewers who have chosen a channel or a program for reasons unrelated to the advertising. With video-on-demand, by contrast, the viewer selects a program after taking "a series of affirmative steps": subscribing to cable; navigating through various menus; and selecting the program.

While some means of communication may be less effective than others at influencing the public in different contexts, any effort by the Judiciary to decide which means of communications are to be preferred for the particular type of message and speaker would raise questions as to the courts' own lawful authority. Substantial questions would arise if courts were to begin saying what means of speech should be preferred or disfavored. And in all events, those differentiations might soon prove to be irrelevant or outdated by technologies that are in rapid flux.

Courts, too, are bound by the First Amendment. We must decline to draw, and then redraw, constitutional lines based on the particular media or technology used to disseminate political speech from a particular speaker. It must be noted, moreover, that this undertaking would require substantial litigation over an extended time, all to interpret a law that beyond doubt discloses serious First Amendment flaws. The interpretive process itself would create an inevitable, pervasive, and serious risk of chilling protected speech pending the drawing of fine distinctions that, in the end, would themselves be questionable. First Amendment standards, however, "must give the benefit of any doubt to protecting rather than stifling speech."

D

Citizens United also asks us to carve out an exception to § 441b's expenditure ban for nonprofit corporate political speech funded overwhelmingly by individuals. As an alternative to reconsidering *Austin,* the Government also seems to prefer this approach. This line of analysis, however, would be unavailing.

. . . .

[T]o hold for Citizens United on this argument, the Court would be required to revise the text of *MCFL* [*Federal Election Comm'n v. Massachusetts Citizens for Life, Inc.*], sever BCRA's Wellstone Amendment, § 441b(c)(6), and ignore the plain text of BCRA's Snowe-Jeffords Amendment, § 441b(c)(2). If the Court decided to create a *de minimis* exception to *MCFL* or the Snowe-Jeffords Amendment, the result would be to allow for-profit corporate general treasury funds to be spent for independent expenditures that support candidates. There is no principled basis for doing this without rewriting *Austin*'s holding that the Government can restrict corporate independent expenditures for political speech.

Though it is true that the Court should construe statutes as necessary to avoid constitutional questions, the series of steps suggested would be difficult to take in view of the language of the statute. . . .

E

As the foregoing analysis confirms, the Court cannot resolve this case on a narrower ground without chilling political speech, speech that is central to the meaning and purpose of the First Amendment. It is not judicial restraint to accept an unsound, narrow argument just so the Court can avoid another argument with broader implications. Indeed, a court would be remiss in performing its duties were it to accept an unsound principle merely to avoid the necessity of making a broader ruling. Here, the lack of a valid basis for an alternative ruling requires full consideration of the continuing effect of the speech suppression upheld in *Austin*.

. . . .

III

[Having determined that it could not avoid the constitutional question, the majority proceeded to strike down the statute as unconstitutional.]

CHIEF JUSTICE ROBERTS, with whom JUSTICE ALITO joins, concurring.

. . . .

The majority's step-by-step analysis accords with our standard practice of avoiding broad constitutional questions except when necessary to decide the case before us. The majority begins by addressing—and quite properly rejecting—Citizens United's statutory claim that 2 U.S.C. § 441b does not actually cover its production and distribution of *Hillary: The Movie* (hereinafter *Hillary*). If there were a valid basis for deciding this statutory claim in Citizens United's favor (and thereby avoiding constitutional adjudication), it would be proper to do so. Indeed, that is precisely the approach the Court took just last Term in *Northwest Austin Municipal Util. Dist. No. One v. Holder,* when eight Members of the Court agreed to decide the case on statutory grounds instead of reaching the appellant's broader argument that the Voting Rights Act is unconstitutional.

It is only because the majority rejects Citizens United's statutory claim that it proceeds to consider the group's various constitutional arguments, beginning with its narrowest claim (that *Hillary* is not the functional equivalent of express advocacy) and proceeding to its broadest claim (that *Austin v. Michigan Chamber of Commerce* should be overruled). . . .

The dissent advocates an approach to addressing Citizens United's claims that I find quite perplexing. It presumably agrees with the majority that Citizens United's narrower statutory and constitutional arguments lack merit—otherwise its conclusion that the group should lose this case would make no sense. Despite agreeing that these narrower arguments fail, however, the dissent argues that the majority should nonetheless latch on to one of them in order to avoid reaching the broader constitutional question of whether *Austin* remains good law. It even suggests that the Court's failure to adopt one of these concededly meritless arguments is a sign that the majority is not "serious about judicial restraint."

This approach is based on a false premise: that our practice of avoiding unnecessary (and unnecessarily broad) constitutional holdings somehow trumps our obligation faithfully to interpret the law. It should go without saying, however, that we cannot embrace a narrow ground of decision simply because it is narrow; it must also be right. Thus while it is true that "[i]f it is not necessary to decide more, it is necessary not to decide more," sometimes it *is* necessary to decide more. There is a difference between judicial restraint and judicial abdication. When constitutional questions are "indispensably necessary" to resolving the case at hand, "the court must meet and decide them."

. . . .

JUSTICE STEVENS, with whom JUSTICE GINSBURG, JUSTICE BREYER, and JUSTICE SOTOMAYOR join, concurring in part and dissenting in part.

. . . .

In his landmark concurrence in *Ashwander v. TVA,* 297 U.S. 288, 346, 56 S.Ct. 466, 80 L.Ed.688 (1936), Justice Brandeis stressed the importance of adhering to rules the Court has "developed . . . for its own governance" when deciding constitutional questions. . . . I emphatically dissent from [the majority's] principal holding.

I

The Court's ruling threatens to undermine the integrity of elected institutions across the Nation. The path it has taken to reach its outcome will, I fear, do damage to this institution. Before turning to the question whether to overrule *Austin* and part of *McConnell,* it is important to explain why the Court should not be deciding that question.

Scope of the Case

The first reason is that the question was not properly brought before us. In declaring § 203 of BCRA facially unconstitutional on the ground that corporations' electoral expenditures may not be regulated any more stringently than those of individuals, the majority decides this case on a basis relinquished below, not included in the questions presented to us by the litigants, and argued here only in response to the Court's invitation. This procedure is unusual and inadvisable for a court. Our colleagues' suggestion that "we are asked to reconsider *Austin* and, in effect,

McConnell" would be more accurate if rephrased to state that "we have asked ourselves" to reconsider those cases.

In the District Court, Citizens United initially raised a facial challenge to the constitutionality of § 203. In its motion for summary judgment, however, Citizens United expressly abandoned its facial challenge, and the parties stipulated to the dismissal of that claim. The District Court therefore resolved the case on alternative grounds, and in its jurisdictional statement to this Court, Citizens United properly advised us that it was raising only "an as-applied challenge to the constitutionality of . . . BCRA § 203." The jurisdictional statement never so much as cited *Austin,* the key case the majority today overrules. And not one of the questions presented suggested that Citizens United was surreptitiously raising the facial challenge to § 203 that it previously agreed to dismiss. In fact, not one of those questions raised an issue based on Citizens United's corporate status. Moreover, even in its merits briefing, when Citizens United injected its request to overrule *Austin,* it never sought a declaration that § 203 was facially unconstitutional as to all corporations and unions; instead it argued only that the statute could not be applied to it because it was "funded overwhelmingly by individuals."

" 'It is only in exceptional cases coming here from the federal courts that questions not pressed or passed upon below are reviewed," and it is "only in the most exceptional cases" that we will consider issues outside the questions presented. The appellant in this case did not so much as assert an exceptional circumstance, and one searches the majority opinion in vain for the mention of any. That is unsurprising, for none exists.

. . . .

Narrower Grounds

[T]he parties have advanced numerous ways to resolve the case that would facilitate electioneering by nonprofit advocacy corporations such as Citizens United, without toppling statutes and precedents. Which is to say, the majority has transgressed yet another "cardinal" principle of the judicial process: "[I]f it is not necessary to decide more, it is necessary not to decide more."

Consider just three of the narrower grounds of decision that the majority has bypassed. First, the Court could have ruled, on statutory grounds, that a feature-length film distributed through video-on-demand does not qualify as an "electioneering communication" under § 203 of BCRA, 2 U.S.C. § 441b. BCRA defines that term to encompass certain communications transmitted by "broadcast, cable, or satellite." When Congress was developing BCRA, the video-on-demand medium was still in its infancy, and legislators were focused on a very different sort of programming: short advertisements run on television or radio. The sponsors of BCRA acknowledge that the FEC's implementing regulations do not clearly apply to video-on-demand transmissions. In light of this ambiguity, the distinctive characteristics of video-on-demand, and "[t]he elementary rule . . . that every reasonable construction must be resorted to, in order to save a statute from unconstitutionality," the Court could have reasonably ruled that § 203 does not apply to *Hillary*.

Second, the Court could have expanded the *MCFL* exemption to cover § 501(c)(4) nonprofits that accept only a *de minimis* amount of money from for-profit corporations. Citizens United professes to be such a group: Its brief says it "is funded predominantly by donations from individuals who support [its] ideological message." Numerous Courts of Appeal have held that *de minimis* business support does not, in itself, remove an otherwise qualifying organization from the ambit of *MCFL*. This court could have simply followed their lead.

Finally, let us not forget Citizens United's as-applied constitutional challenge. Precisely because Citizens United looks so much like the *MCFL* organizations we have exempted from regulation, while a feature-length video-on-demand film looks so unlike the types of electoral advocacy Congress has found deserving of regulation, this challenge is a substantial one. As the appellant's own arguments show, the Court could have easily limited the breadth of its constitutional holding had it declined to adopt the novel notion that speakers and speech acts must always be treated identically—and always spared expenditures restrictions—in the political realm. Yet the Court nonetheless turns its back on the as-applied review process that has been a staple of campaign finance litigation since *Buckley v. Valeo* (1976), and that was affirmed and expanded just two Terms ago. . . .

This brief tour of alternative grounds on which the case could have been decided is not meant to show that any of these grounds is ideal, though each is perfectly "valid." It is meant to show that there were principled, narrower paths that a Court that was serious about judicial restraint could have taken. . . .

II

The final principle of judicial process that the majority violates is the most transparent: *stare decisis.* I am not an absolutist when it comes to *stare decisis,* in the campaign finance area or in any other. No one is. But if this principle is to do any meaningful work in supporting the rule of law, it must at least demand a significant justification, beyond the preferences of five Justices, for overturning settled doctrine. "[A] decision to overrule should rest on some special reason over and above the belief that a prior case was wrongly decided." No such justification exists in this case, and to the contrary there are powerful prudential reasons to keep faith with our precedents.

The Court's central argument for why *stare decisis* ought to be trumped is that it does not like *Austin*. The opinion "was not well reasoned," our colleagues assert, and it conflicts with First Amendment principles. This, of course, is the Court's merits argument, the many defects in which we will soon consider. I am perfectly willing to concede that if one of our precedents were dead wrong in its reasoning or irreconcilable with the rest of our doctrine, there would be a compelling basis for revisiting it. But neither is true of *Austin,* as I explain at length . . . and restating a merits argument with additional vigor does not give it extra weight in the *stare decisis* calculus.

Perhaps in recognition of this point, the Court supplements its merits case with a smattering of assertions. The Court proclaims that "*Austin* is undermined by experience since its announcement." This is a curious claim to make in a case that lacks a developed record. The majority has no empirical evidence with which to substantiate the claim; we just have its *ipse dixit* that the real world has not been kind to *Austin*. Nor does the majority bother to specify in what sense *Austin* has been "undermined."

. . . .

Although the majority opinion spends several pages making these surprising arguments, it says almost nothing about the standard considerations we have used to determine *stare decisis* value, such as the antiquity of the precedent, the workability of its legal rule, and the reliance interests at stake. . . .

We have recognized that "*[s]tare decisis* has special force when legislators or citizens 'have acted in reliance on a previous decision, for in this instance overruling the decision would dislodge settled rights and expectations or require an extensive legislative response.'" *Stare decisis* protects not only personal rights involving property or contract but also the ability of the elected branches to shape their laws in an effective and coherent fashion. Today's decision takes away a power that we have long permitted these branches to exercise. State legislatures have relied on their authority to regulate corporate electioneering, confirmed in *Austin,* for more than a century. The Federal Congress has relied on this authority for a comparable stretch of time, and it specifically relied on *Austin* throughout the years it spent developing and debating BCRA. The total record it compiled was *100,000 pages* long. Pulling out the rug beneath Congress after affirming the constitutionality of § 203 six years ago shows great disrespect for a coequal branch.

. . . .

Beyond the reliance interests at stake, the other *stare decisis* factors also cut against the Court. Considerations of antiquity are significant for similar reasons. *McConnell* is only six years old, but *Austin* has been on the books for two decades, and many of the statutes called into question by today's opinion have been on the books for a half-century or more. The Court points to no intervening change in circumstances that warrants revisiting *Austin*. Certainly nothing relevant has changed since we decided *WRTL* two Terms ago. And the Court gives no reason to think that *Austin* and *McConnell* are unworkable.

In fact, no one has argued to us that *Austin*'s rule has proved impracticable, and not a single for-profit corporation, union, or State has asked us to overrule it. Quite to the contrary, leading groups representing the business community, organized labor, and the nonprofit sector, together with more than half of the States, urge that we preserve *Austin*. As for *McConnell,* the portions of BCRA it upheld may be prolix, but all three branches of Government have worked to make § 203 as user-friendly as possible. . . .

In the end, the Court's rejection of *Austin* and *McConnell* comes down to nothing more than its disagreement with their results. Virtually every one of its arguments was made and rejected in those cases, and the majority opinion is essentially an amalgamation of resuscitated dissents. The only relevant thing that has changed since *Austin* and *McConnell* is the composition of this Court. Today's ruling thus strikes at the vitals of *stare decisis,* "the means by which we ensure that the law will not merely change erratically, but will develop in a principled and intelligible fashion" that "permits society to presume that bedrock principles are founded in the law rather than in the proclivities of individuals."

III

[JUSTICE STEVENS goes on to respond to the majority's constitutional arguments.]

NATIONAL FEDERATION OF INDEPENDENT
BUSINESS V. SEBELIUS
132 S. Ct. 2566 (2012)

Now consider the so-called ObamaCare case, another momentous decision of the Roberts court with substantial political stakes. Consider the following questions:

- Whose interpretation of the statutory language is more persuasive, Justice Roberts' or Justice Scalia's?

- How does Justice Roberts use the constitutional avoidance argument here?

- Is Justice Roberts' constitutional avoidance argument consistent with his position in *Citizens United*? Can you reconcile them?

- Why does Justice Roberts bother addressing the Commerce Clause argument given that he found the statutory provision constitutional as a tax? By doing so, has he actually avoided the constitutional question?

- Based on this case and *Citizens United*, can you come up with any reason that courts *should* practice constitutional avoidance? In other words, why have judges adopted this rule?

- Why does Justice Roberts begin his opinion with a long preamble before getting to the facts and the basis of his decision?

- On what basis does Justice Scalia reject the constitutional avoidance argument?

- Justice Scalia generally claims not to pay any attention to legislative history. See if you can catch where he deviates from that practice in his dissent. Can you offer any defense of his apparent departure from his judicial philosophy?

- Note that during the passage of the Act, President Obama and allied Democrats repeatedly insisted that the penalty did not amount to a tax. Was it duplicitous for the administration to then defend the constitutionality of the Act by arguing that the penalty was, in fact, a tax? Should the Court have paid more attention to the administration's characterization of the penalty in deciding whether it is a tax? Why or why not?

- Note Justice Roberts' reference to the vehicle in the parks hypothetical. Be assured that statutory interpretation nerds all across the country rejoiced and fondly recalled their statutory interpretation classes.

CHIEF JUSTICE ROBERTS announced the judgment of the Court and delivered the opinion of the Court. . . .

Today we resolve [a] constitutional challenge[ ] to [a] provision[ ] of the Patient Protection and Affordable Care Act of 2010: the individual mandate, which requires individuals to purchase a health insurance policy providing a minimum level of coverage. . . . We do not consider whether the Act embodies sound policies. That judgment is entrusted to the Nation's elected leaders. We ask only whether Congress has the power under the Constitution to enact the challenged provisions.

In our federal system, the National Government possesses only limited powers; the States and the people retain the remainder. . . . In this case we must again determine whether the Constitution grants Congress powers it now asserts, but which many States and individuals believe it does not possess. Resolving this controversy requires us to examine both the limits of the Government's power, and our own limited role in policing those boundaries.

The Federal Government "is acknowledged by all to be one of enumerated powers." That is, rather than granting general authority to perform all the conceivable functions of government, the Constitution lists, or enumerates, the Federal Government's powers. Congress may, for example, "coin Money," "establish Post Offices," and "raise and support Armies." The enumeration of powers is also a limitation of powers, because "[t]he enumeration presupposes something not enumerated." The Constitution's express conferral of some powers makes clear that it does not grant others. And the Federal Government "can exercise only the powers granted to it."

. . . .

This case concerns two powers that the Constitution does grant the Federal Government, but which must be read carefully to avoid creating a general federal authority akin to the police power [held by individual states]. The Constitution authorizes Congress to "regulate Commerce with foreign Nations, and among the several States, and with the Indian Tribes." Our precedents read that to mean that Congress may regulate "the channels of interstate commerce," "persons or things in interstate commerce," and "those activities that substantially affect interstate commerce." The power over activities that substantially affect interstate commerce can be expansive. That power has been held to authorize federal regulation of such seemingly local matters as a farmer's decision to grow wheat for himself and his livestock, and a loan shark's extortionate collections from a neighborhood butcher shop.

Congress may also "lay and collect Taxes, Duties, Imposts and Excises, to pay the Debts and provide for the common Defence and general Welfare of the United States." Put simply, Congress may tax and spend. This grant gives the Federal Government considerable influence even in areas where it cannot directly regulate. The Federal Government may enact a tax on an activity that it cannot authorize, forbid, or otherwise control. And in exercising its spending power, Congress may offer funds to the States, and may condition those offers on compliance with specified conditions. These offers may well induce the States to adopt policies that the Federal Government itself could not impose.

. . . .

Our permissive reading of these powers is explained in part by a general reticence to invalidate the acts of the Nation's elected leaders. "Proper respect for a coordinate branch of the government" requires that we strike down an Act of Congress only if "the lack of constitutional authority to pass [the] act in question is clearly demonstrated." Members of this Court are vested with the authority to interpret the law; we possess neither the expertise nor the prerogative to make policy judgments. Those decisions are entrusted to our Nation's elected leaders, who can be thrown out of office if the people disagree with them. It is not our job to protect the people from the consequences of their political choices.

Our deference in matters of policy cannot, however, become abdication in matters of law. "The powers of the legislature are defined and limited; and that those limits may not be mistaken, or forgotten, the constitution is written." Our respect for Congress's policy judgments thus can never extend so far as to disavow restraints on federal power that the Constitution carefully constructed. "The peculiar circumstances of the moment may render a measure more or less wise, but cannot render it more or less constitutional." And there can be no question that it is the responsibility of this Court to enforce the limits on federal power by striking down acts of Congress that transgress those limits.

The questions before us must be considered against the background of these basic principles.

I

In 2010, Congress enacted the Patient Protection and Affordable Care Act. The Act aims to increase the number of Americans covered by health insurance and decrease the cost of health care. . . .

The individual mandate requires most Americans to maintain "minimum essential" health insurance coverage. . . . [For] individuals who are not exempt [from the mandate] and do not receive health insurance through a third party, the means of satisfying the requirement is to purchase insurance from a private company.

Beginning in 2014, those who do not comply with the mandate must make a "[s]hared responsibility payment" to the Federal Government. That payment, which the Act describes as a "penalty," is calculated as a percentage of household income, subject to a floor based on a specified dollar amount and a ceiling based on the average annual premium the individual would have to pay for qualifying private health insurance. . . . The Act provides that the penalty will be paid to the Internal Revenue Service with an individual's taxes, and "shall be assessed and collected in the same manner" as tax penalties, such as the penalty for claiming too large an income tax refund. The Act, however, bars the IRS from using several of its normal enforcement tools, such as criminal prosecutions and levies. And some individuals who are subject to the mandate are nonetheless exempt from the penalty—for example, those with income below a certain threshold and members of Indian tribes.

. . . .

The plaintiffs alleged, among other things, that the individual mandate provisions of the Act exceeded Congress's powers under Article I of the Constitution. . . .

. . . .

II

[In this Part, the Court considered and rejected the argument that it did not have jurisdiction to decide this case.]

III

The Government advances two theories for the proposition that Congress had constitutional authority to enact the individual mandate. First, the Government argues that Congress had the power to enact the mandate under the Commerce Clause. Under that theory, Congress may order individuals to buy health insurance because the failure to do so affects interstate commerce, and could undercut the Affordable Care Act's other reforms. Second, the Government argues that if the commerce power does not support the mandate, we should nonetheless uphold it as an exercise of Congress's power to tax. According to the Government, even if Congress lacks the power to direct individuals to buy insurance, the only effect of the individual mandate is to raise taxes on those who do not do so, and thus the law may be upheld as a tax.

A

[In this Section, the Court held that the individual mandate fails constitutional muster under the Commerce Clause.]

B

. . . Because the Commerce Clause does not support the individual mandate, it is necessary to turn to the Government's second argument:

that the mandate may be upheld as within Congress's enumerated power to "lay and collect Taxes."

. . . .

[T]he Government asks us to read the mandate not as ordering individuals to buy insurance, but rather as imposing a tax on those who do not buy that product.

The text of a statute can sometimes have more than one possible meaning. To take a familiar example, a law that reads "no vehicles in the park" might, or might not, ban bicycles in the park. And it is well established that if a statute has two possible meanings, one of which violates the Constitution, courts should adopt the meaning that does not do so. Justice Story said that 180 years ago: "No court ought, unless the terms of an act rendered it unavoidable, to give a construction to it which should involve a violation, however unintentional, of the constitution." Justice Holmes made the same point a century later: "[T]he rule is settled that as between two possible interpretations of a statute, by one of which it would be unconstitutional and by the other valid, our plain duty is to adopt that which will save the Act."

The most straightforward reading of the mandate is that it commands individuals to purchase insurance. After all, it states that individuals "shall" maintain health insurance. Congress thought it could enact such a command under the Commerce Clause, and the Government primarily defended the law on that basis. But, for the reasons explained above, the Commerce Clause does not give Congress that power. Under our precedent, it is therefore necessary to ask whether the Government's alternative reading of the statute—that it only imposes a tax on those without insurance—is a reasonable one.

Under the mandate, if an individual does not maintain health insurance, the only consequence is that he must make an additional payment to the IRS when he pays his taxes. That, according to the Government, means the mandate can be regarded as establishing a condition—not owning health insurance—that triggers a tax—the required payment to the IRS. Under that theory, the mandate is not a legal command to buy insurance. Rather, it makes going without insurance just another thing the Government taxes, like buying gasoline or earning income. And if the mandate is in effect just a tax hike on certain taxpayers who do not have health insurance, it may be within Congress's constitutional power to tax.

The question is not whether that is the most natural interpretation of the mandate, but only whether it is a "fairly possible" one. As we have explained, "every reasonable construction must be resorted to, in order to save a statute from unconstitutionality." The Government asks us to interpret the mandate as imposing a tax, if it would otherwise violate the

Constitution. Granting the Act the full measure of deference owed to federal statutes, it can be so read, for the reasons set forth below.

C

The exaction the Affordable Care Act imposes on those without health insurance looks like a tax in many respects. The "[s]hared responsibility payment," as the statute entitles it, is paid into the Treasury by "taxpayer[s]" when they file their tax returns. It does not apply to individuals who do not pay federal income taxes because their household income is less than the filing threshold in the Internal Revenue Code. For taxpayers who do owe the payment, its amount is determined by such familiar factors as taxable income, number of dependents, and joint filing status. The requirement to pay is found in the Internal Revenue Code and enforced by the IRS, which—as we previously explained—must assess and collect it "in the same manner as taxes." This process yields the essential feature of any tax: it produces at least some revenue for the Government. Indeed, the payment is expected to raise about $4 billion per year by 2017.

It is of course true that the Act describes the payment as a "penalty," not a "tax." But . . . [that label] does not determine whether the payment may be viewed as an exercise of Congress's taxing power. It is up to Congress whether to apply the Anti-Injunction Act to any particular statute, so it makes sense to be guided by Congress's choice of label on that question. That choice does not, however, control whether an exaction is within Congress's constitutional power to tax.

Our precedent reflects this: In 1922, we decided two challenges to the "Child Labor Tax" on the same day. In the first, we held that a suit to enjoin collection of the so-called tax was barred by the Anti-Injunction Act. Congress knew that suits to obstruct taxes had to await payment under the Anti-Injunction Act; Congress called the child labor tax a tax; Congress therefore intended the Anti-Injunction Act to apply. In the second case, however, we held that the same exaction, although labeled a tax, was not in fact authorized by Congress's taxing power. That constitutional question was not controlled by Congress's choice of label.

We have similarly held that exactions not labeled taxes nonetheless were authorized by Congress's power to tax. In the *License Tax Cases,* for example, we held that federal licenses to sell liquor and lottery tickets— for which the licensee had to pay a fee—could be sustained as exercises of the taxing power. And in *New York v. United States* we upheld as a tax a "surcharge" on out-of-state nuclear waste shipments, a portion of which was paid to the Federal Treasury. We thus ask whether the shared responsibility payment falls within Congress's taxing power, "[d]isregarding the designation of the exaction, and viewing its substance and application."

Our cases confirm this functional approach. For example, in *Drexel Furniture,* we focused on three practical characteristics of the so-called tax on employing child laborers that convinced us the "tax" was actually a penalty. First, the tax imposed an exceedingly heavy burden—10 percent of a company's net income—on those who employed children, no matter how small their infraction. Second, it imposed that exaction only on those who knowingly employed underage laborers. Such scienter requirements are typical of punitive statutes, because Congress often wishes to punish only those who intentionally break the law. Third, this "tax" was enforced in part by the Department of Labor, an agency responsible for punishing violations of labor laws, not collecting revenue.

The same analysis here suggests that the shared responsibility payment may for constitutional purposes be considered a tax, not a penalty: First, for most Americans the amount due will be far less than the price of insurance, and, by statute, it can never be more. It may often be a reasonable financial decision to make the payment rather than purchase insurance, unlike the "prohibitory" financial punishment in *Drexel Furniture.* Second, the individual mandate contains no scienter requirement. Third, the payment is collected solely by the IRS through the normal means of taxation—except that the Service is *not* allowed to use those means most suggestive of a punitive sanction, such as criminal prosecution. The reasons the Court in *Drexel Furniture* held that what was called a "tax" there was a penalty support the conclusion that what is called a "penalty" here may be viewed as a tax.

None of this is to say that the payment is not intended to affect individual conduct. Although the payment will raise considerable revenue, it is plainly designed to expand health insurance coverage. But taxes that seek to influence conduct are nothing new. Some of our earliest federal taxes sought to deter the purchase of imported manufactured goods in order to foster the growth of domestic industry. Today, federal and state taxes can compose more than half the retail price of cigarettes, not just to raise more money, but to encourage people to quit smoking. And we have upheld such obviously regulatory measures as taxes on selling marijuana and sawed-off shotguns. Indeed, "[e]very tax is in some measure regulatory. To some extent it interposes an economic impediment to the activity taxed as compared with others not taxed." That § 5000A seeks to shape decisions about whether to buy health insurance does not mean that it cannot be a valid exercise of the taxing power.

In distinguishing penalties from taxes, this Court has explained that "if the concept of penalty means anything, it means punishment for an unlawful act or omission." While the individual mandate clearly aims to induce the purchase of health insurance, it need not be read to declare that failing to do so is unlawful. Neither the Act nor any other law attaches negative legal consequences to not buying health insurance, beyond requiring a payment to the IRS. The Government agrees with that reading, confirming that if someone chooses to pay rather than obtain health insurance, they have fully complied with the law.

Indeed, it is estimated that four million people each year will choose to pay the IRS rather than buy insurance. We would expect Congress to be troubled by that prospect if such conduct were unlawful. That Congress apparently regards such extensive failure to comply with the mandate as tolerable suggests that Congress did not think it was creating four million outlaws. It suggests instead that the shared responsibility payment merely imposes a tax citizens may lawfully choose to pay in lieu of buying health insurance.

The plaintiffs contend that Congress's choice of language—stating that individuals "shall" obtain insurance or pay a "penalty"—requires reading § 5000A as punishing unlawful conduct, even if that interpretation would render the law unconstitutional. We have rejected a similar argument before. In *New York v. United States* we examined a statute providing that " '[e]ach State shall be responsible for providing . . . for the disposal of . . . low-level radioactive waste.' " A State that shipped its waste to another State was exposed to surcharges by the receiving State, a portion of which would be paid over to the Federal Government. And a State that did not adhere to the statutory scheme faced "[p]enalties for failure to comply," including increases in the surcharge. New York urged us to read the statute as a federal command that the state legislature enact legislation to dispose of its waste, which would have violated the Constitution. To avoid that outcome, we interpreted the statute to impose only "a series of incentives" for the State to take responsibility for its waste. We then sustained the charge paid to the Federal Government as an exercise of the taxing power. We see no insurmountable obstacle to a similar approach here.

The joint dissenters argue that we cannot uphold § 5000A as a tax because Congress did not "frame" it as such. In effect, they contend that even if the Constitution permits Congress to do exactly what we interpret this statute to do, the law must be struck down because Congress used the wrong labels. An example may help illustrate why labels should not control here. Suppose Congress enacted a statute providing that every taxpayer who owns a house without energy efficient windows must pay $50 to the IRS. The amount due is adjusted based on factors such as taxable income and joint filing status, and is paid along with the taxpayer's income tax return. Those whose income is below the filing threshold need not pay. The required payment is not called a "tax," a "penalty," or anything else. No one would doubt that this law imposed a tax, and was within Congress's power to tax. That conclusion should not change simply because Congress used the word "penalty" to describe the payment. Interpreting such a law to be a tax would hardly "[i]mpos[e] a tax through judicial legislation." Rather, it would give practical effect to the Legislature's enactment.

Our precedent demonstrates that Congress had the power to impose the exaction in § 5000A under the taxing power, and that § 5000A need not be read to do more than impose a tax. That is sufficient to sustain it. The "question of the constitutionality of action taken by Congress does not depend on recitals of the power which it undertakes to exercise."

. . . .

The Affordable Care Act's requirement that certain individuals pay a financial penalty for not obtaining health insurance may reasonably be characterized as a tax. Because the Constitution permits such a tax, it is not our role to forbid it, or to pass upon its wisdom or fairness.

. . . .

JUSTICE SCALIA, JUSTICE KENNEDY, JUSTICE THOMAS, and JUSTICE ALITO, dissenting.

Congress has set out to remedy the problem that the best health care is beyond the reach of many Americans who cannot afford it. It can assuredly do that, by exercising the powers accorded to it under the Constitution. The question in this case, however, is whether the complex structures and provisions of the Patient Protection and Affordable Care Act go beyond those powers. We conclude that they do.

. . . .

II

The Taxing Power

. . . .

Of course in many cases what was a regulatory mandate enforced by a penalty *could have been* imposed as a tax upon permissible action; or what was imposed as a tax upon permissible action *could have been* a regulatory mandate enforced by a penalty. But we know of no case, and the Government cites none, in which the imposition was, for constitutional purposes, both. The two are mutually exclusive. . . . It is important to bear this in mind in evaluating the tax argument of the Government and of those who support it: The issue is not whether Congress had the *power* to frame the minimum-coverage provision as a tax, but whether it *did* so.

In answering that question we must, if "fairly possible," construe the provision to be a tax rather than a mandate-with-penalty, since that would render it constitutional rather than unconstitutional. But we cannot rewrite the statute to be what it is not. " ' "[A]lthough this Court will often strain to construe legislation so as to save it against constitutional attack, it must not and will not carry this to the point of perverting the purpose of a statute . . ." or judicially rewriting it.'" In this case, there is simply no way, "without doing violence to the fair meaning of the words used," to escape what Congress enacted: a mandate that individuals maintain minimum essential coverage, enforced by a penalty.

Our cases establish a clear line between a tax and a penalty: " '[A] tax is an enforced contribution to provide for the support of government; a penalty . . . is an exaction imposed by statute as punishment for an unlawful act.'" In a few cases, this Court has held that a "tax" imposed upon private conduct was so onerous as to be in effect a penalty. But we have never held—*never*—that a penalty imposed for violation of the law was so trivial as to be in effect a tax. We have never held that *any* exaction imposed for violation of the law is an exercise of Congress' taxing power—even when the statute *calls* it a tax, much less when (as here) the statute repeatedly calls it a penalty. When an act "adopt[s] the criteria of wrongdoing" and then imposes a monetary penalty as the "principal consequence on those who transgress its standard," it creates a regulatory penalty, not a tax.

So the question is, quite simply, whether the exaction here is imposed for violation of the law. It unquestionably is. The minimum-coverage provision is found in 26 U.S.C. § 5000A, entitled *"Requirement* to maintain minimum essential coverage." It commands that every "applicable individual *shall* . . . ensure that the individual . . . is covered under minimum essential coverage." And the immediately following provision states that, "[i]f . . . an applicable individual . . . fails to meet the *requirement* of subsection (a) . . . there is hereby imposed . . . a *penalty*." § 5000A(b). And several of Congress' legislative "findings" with regard to § 5000A confirm that it sets forth a legal requirement and constitutes the assertion of regulatory power, not mere taxing power.

The Government and those who support its view on the tax point rely on *New York v. United States* to justify reading "shall" to mean "may." The "shall" in that case was contained in an introductory provision—a recital that provided for no legal consequences—which said that "[e]ach State shall be responsible for providing . . . for the disposal of . . . low-level radioactive waste." The Court did not hold that "shall" could be construed to mean "may," but rather that this preliminary provision could not impose upon the operative provisions of the Act a mandate that they did not contain: "We . . . decline petitioners' invitation to construe § 2021c(a)(1)(A), alone and in isolation, as a command to the States independent of the remainder of the Act." Our opinion then proceeded to "consider each [of the three operative provisions] in turn." Here the mandate—the "shall"—is contained not in an inoperative preliminary recital, but in the dispositive operative provision itself. *New York* provides no support for reading it to be permissive.

Quite separately, the fact that Congress (in its own words) "imposed . . . a penalty" for failure to buy insurance is alone sufficient to render that failure unlawful. It is one of the canons of interpretation that a statute that penalizes an act makes it unlawful: "[W]here the statute inflicts a penalty for doing an act, although the act itself is not expressly prohibited, yet to do the act is unlawful, because it cannot be supposed that the Legislature intended that a penalty should be inflicted for a lawful act." Or in the words of Chancellor Kent: "If a statute inflicts a penalty for doing an act, the penalty implies a prohibition, and the thing is unlawful, though there be no prohibitory words in the statute."

We never have classified as a tax an exaction imposed for violation of the law, and so too, we never have classified as a tax an exaction described in the legislation itself as a penalty. To be sure, we have sometimes treated as a tax a statutory exaction (imposed for something other than a violation of law) which bore an agnostic label that does not entail the significant constitutional consequences of a penalty—such as "license" or "surcharge." But we have never—*never*—treated as a tax an exaction which faces up to the critical difference between a tax and a penalty, and explicitly denominates the exaction a "penalty." Eighteen times in § 5000A itself and elsewhere throughout the Act, Congress called the exaction in § 5000A(b) a "penalty."

That § 5000A imposes not a simple tax but a mandate to which a penalty is attached is demonstrated by the fact that some are exempt from the tax who are not exempt from the mandate—a distinction that would make no sense if the mandate were not a mandate. Section 5000A(d) exempts three classes of people from the definition of "applicable individual" subject to the minimum coverage requirement: Those with religious objections or who participate in a "health care sharing ministry," those who are "not lawfully present" in the United States, and those who are incarcerated. Section 5000A(e) then creates a separate set of exemptions, excusing from liability for the penalty certain individuals who are subject to the minimum coverage requirement: Those who cannot afford coverage, who earn too little income to require filing a tax return, who are members of an Indian tribe, who experience only short gaps in coverage, and who, in the judgment of the Secretary of Health and Human Services, "have suffered a hardship with respect to the capability to obtain coverage." If § 5000A were a tax, these two classes of exemption would make no sense; there being no requirement, *all* the exemptions would attach to the penalty (renamed tax) alone.

In the face of all these indications of a regulatory requirement accompanied by a penalty, the Solicitor General assures us that "neither the Treasury Department nor the Department of Health and Human Services interprets Section 5000A as imposing a legal obligation," and that "[i]f [those subject to the Act] pay the tax penalty, they're in compliance with the law." These self-serving litigating positions are entitled to no weight. What counts is what the statute says, and that is entirely clear. It is worth noting, moreover, that these assurances contradict the Government's position in related litigation. Shortly before the Affordable Care Act was passed, the Commonwealth of Virginia enacted Va. Code Ann. § 38.2–3430.1:1, which states, "No resident of [the] Commonwealth . . . shall be required to obtain or maintain a policy of individual insurance coverage except as required by a court or the Department of Social Services. . . ." In opposing Virginia's assertion of standing to challenge § 5000A based on this statute, the Government said that "if the minimum coverage provision is unconstitutional, the [Virginia] statute is unnecessary, and if the minimum coverage provision is upheld, the state statute is void under the Supremacy Clause." But it would be void under the Supremacy Clause only if it was contradicted by a federal "require[ment] to obtain or maintain a policy of individual insurance coverage."

Against the mountain of evidence that the minimum coverage requirement is what the statute calls it—a requirement—and that the penalty for its violation is what the statute calls it—a penalty—the Government brings forward the flimsiest of indications to the contrary. It notes that "[t]he minimum coverage provision amends the Internal Revenue Code to provide that a non-exempted individual . . . will owe a monetary penalty, in addition to the income tax itself," and that "[t]he [Internal Revenue Service (IRS)] will assess and collect the penalty in the same manner as assessable penalties under the Internal Revenue Code." The manner of collection could perhaps suggest a tax if IRS penalty-collection were unheard-of or rare. It is not. In *Reorganized CF & I Fabricators of Utah, Inc.*, we held that an exaction not only *enforced* by the Commissioner of Internal Revenue but even *called* a "tax" was in fact a penalty. "[I]f the concept of penalty means anything," we said, "it means punishment for an unlawful act or omission." Moreover, while the penalty is assessed and collected by the IRS, § 5000A is administered both by that agency and by the Department of Health and Human Services (and also the Secretary of Veteran Affairs), which is responsible for defining its substantive scope—a feature that would be quite extraordinary for taxes.

The Government points out that "[t]he amount of the penalty will be calculated as a percentage of household income for federal income tax purposes, subject to a floor and [a] ca[p]," and that individuals who earn so little money that they "are not required to file income tax returns for the taxable year are not subject to the penalty" (though they are, as we discussed earlier, subject to the mandate). But varying a penalty according to ability to pay is an utterly familiar practice.

The last of the feeble arguments in favor of petitioners ... is the contention that what this statute repeatedly calls a penalty is in fact a tax because it contains no scienter requirement. The *presence* of such a requirement suggests a penalty—though one can imagine a tax imposed only on willful action; but the *absence* of such a requirement does not suggest a tax. Penalties for absolute-liability offenses are commonplace. And where a statute is silent as to scienter, we traditionally presume a *mens rea* requirement if the statute imposes a "severe penalty." Since we have an entire jurisprudence addressing when it is that a scienter requirement should be inferred from a penalty, it is quite illogical to suggest that a penalty is not a penalty for want of an express scienter requirement.

And the nail in the coffin is that the mandate and penalty are located in Title I of the Act, its operative core, rather than where a tax would be found—in Title IX, containing the Act's "Revenue Provisions." In sum, "the terms of [the] act rende[r] it unavoidable" that Congress imposed a regulatory penalty, not a tax.

For all these reasons, to say that the Individual Mandate merely imposes a tax is not to interpret the statute but to rewrite it. Judicial tax-writing is particularly troubling. Taxes have never been popular, and in part for that reason, the Constitution requires tax increases to originate in the House of Representatives. That is to say, they must originate in the legislative body most accountable to the people, where legislators must weigh the need for the tax against the terrible price they might pay at their next election, which is never more than two years off. The Federalist No. 58 "defend[ed] the decision to give the origination power to the House on the ground that the Chamber that is more accountable to the people should have the primary role in raising revenue." We have no doubt that Congress knew precisely what it was doing when it rejected an earlier version of this legislation that imposed a tax instead of a requirement-with-penalty. See Affordable Health Care for America Act. Imposing a tax through judicial legislation inverts the constitutional scheme, and places the power to tax in the branch of government least accountable to the citizenry. . . .

(B) Exercise: The Homeschool Case Redux

Consider again the exercise regarding the legality of home schooling under California statutory law. Read *Pierce v. Society of Sisters*, 268 U.S. 510 (1925), and *Wisconsin v. Yoder*, 406 U.S. 205 (1972). Can you use these cases to construct a constitutional avoidance argument on behalf of parents wishing to home school their children? How would you respond if you represented the state?

2.   THE RULE OF LENITY

(A) Understanding the Rule

The rule of lenity states that in criminal cases ambiguous statutes should be interpreted in favor of defendants. One common justification for this rule is that criminal penalties should not be imposed on defendants without clear warning. Consequently, courts sometimes distinguish between criminal statutes that prohibit behavior that is *malum in se* (inherently or obviously wrong), in which case the rule of lenity should not apply because the defendant should have known what she was doing was wrong, and behavior that is *malum prohibitum* (wrong only because it has been prohibited by the legislature).

According to some judges and commentators, the rule of lenity may be understood as a subset of the constitutional avoidance canon: it would violate the Due Process Clauses of the United States Constitution to criminally punish a defendant when she had no reason to believe that her conduct was unlawful. Therefore, where possible, judges should prefer narrow interpretations of criminal statutes.

As a practical matter, some judges reject the rule of lenity. That is, although judges typically acknowledge the rule of lenity, they often find enough reasons to declare that a statute unambiguously favors the government. Judges may merely pay lip service to the rule of lenity. This is not to say that the rule of lenity is useless for lawyer; only that its persuasive value depends heavily on the judge and the degree of statutory ambiguity.

Interestingly, and perhaps contrary to your intuition, Justice Scalia is among the staunchest defenders of the rule of lenity.

MUSCARELLO V. UNITED STATES
524 U.S. 125 (1998)

As you read this case, consider the following:

- Are you surprised by who is in the majority and who dissents? How might you account for this?

- What do you think the plain meaning of "carry" is in this context?

- What do you think of the majority's use of dictionaries, newspaper accounts, and literature?

- Can you articulate the various textual and structural arguments made by each side?

- What do you think of the majority's purposivist argument?

- How do the majority and dissent differ as to the correct application of the rule of lenity? In your opinion, does it make sense to apply the rule of lenity in this case? Why or why not?

- Justice Ginsburg quotes Justice Breyer from a different case. Why?

JUSTICE BREYER delivered the opinion of the Court.

A provision in the firearms chapter of the federal criminal code imposes a 5-year mandatory prison term upon a person who "uses or carries a firearm" "during and in relation to" a "drug trafficking crime." 18 U.S.C. § 924(c)(1). The question before us is whether the phrase "carries a firearm" is limited to the carrying of firearms on the person. We hold that it is not so limited. Rather, it also applies to a person who knowingly possesses and conveys firearms in a vehicle, including in the locked glove compartment or trunk of a car, which the person accompanies.

I

The question arises in two cases, which we have consolidated for argument. Petitioner in the first case, Frank J. Muscarello, unlawfully sold marijuana, which he carried in his truck to the place of sale. Police officers found a handgun locked in the truck's glove compartment. During plea proceedings, Muscarello admitted that he had "carried" the gun "for protection in relation" to the drug offense, though he later claimed to the contrary, and added that, in any event, his "carr[ying]" of the gun in the glove compartment did not fall within the scope of the statutory word "carries."

Petitioners in the second case, Donald Cleveland and Enrique Gray-Santana, placed several guns in a bag, put the bag in the trunk of a car, and then traveled by car to a proposed drug-sale point, where they intended to steal drugs from the sellers. Federal agents at the scene stopped them, searched the cars, found the guns and drugs, and arrested them.

In both cases the Courts of Appeals found that petitioners had "carrie[d]" the guns during and in relation to a drug trafficking offense. We granted certiorari to determine whether the fact that the guns were found in the locked glove compartment, or the trunk, of a car precludes application of § 924(c)(1). We conclude that it does not.

II

A

We begin with the statute's language. The parties vigorously contest the ordinary English meaning of the phrase "carries a firearm." Because they essentially agree that Congress intended the phrase to convey its ordinary, and not some special legal, meaning, and because they argue the linguistic point at length, we too have looked into the matter in more than usual depth. Although the word "carry" has many different meanings, only two are relevant here. When one uses the word in the first, or primary, meaning, one can, as a matter of ordinary English, "carry firearms" in a wagon, car, truck, or other vehicle that one accompanies. When one uses the word in a different, rather special, way, to mean, for example, "bearing" or (in slang) "packing" (as in "packing a gun"), the matter is less clear. But, for reasons we shall set out below, we believe Congress intended to use the word in its primary sense and not in this latter, special way.

Consider first the word's primary meaning. The Oxford English Dictionary gives as its *first* definition "convey, originally by cart or wagon, hence in any vehicle, by ship, on horseback, etc." 2 Oxford English Dictionary 919 (2d ed. 1989); see also Webster's Third New International Dictionary 343 (1986) (*first* definition: "move while supporting (*as in a vehicle* or in one's hands or arms)"); Random House Dictionary of the English Language Unabridged 319 (2d ed. 1987) (*first* definition: "to take or support from one place to another; convey; transport").

The origin of the word "carries" explains why the first, or basic, meaning of the word "carry" includes conveyance in a vehicle. See Barnhart Dictionary of Etymology 146 (1988) (tracing the word from Latin "carum," which means "car" or "cart"); 2 Oxford English Dictionary, *supra,* at 919 (tracing the word from Old French "carier" and the late Latin "carricare," which meant to "convey in a car"); Oxford Dictionary of English Etymology 148 (C. Onions ed. 1966) (same); Barnhart Dictionary of Etymology, *supra,* at 143 (explaining that the term "car" has been used to refer to the automobile since 1896).

The greatest of writers have used the word with this meaning. See, *e.g.,* The King James Bible, 2 Kings 9:28 ("[H]is servants carried him in a chariot to Jerusalem"); *id.,* Isaiah 30:6 ("[T]hey will carry their riches upon the shoulders of young asses"). Robinson Crusoe says, "[w]ith my boat, I carry'd away every Thing." D. Defoe, Robinson Crusoe 174 (J. Crowley ed. 1972). And the owners of Queequeg's ship, Melville writes, "had lent him a [wheelbarrow], in which to carry his heavy chest to his boarding-house." H. Melville, Moby Dick 43 (U. Chicago 1952). This Court, too, has spoken of the "carrying" of drugs in a car or in its "trunk." *California v. Acevedo,* 500 U.S. 565, 572–573 (1991); *Florida v. Jimeno,* 500 U.S. 248, 249 (1991).

These examples do not speak directly about carrying guns. But there is nothing linguistically special about the fact that weapons, rather than drugs, are being carried. Robinson Crusoe might have carried a gun in his boat; Queequeg might have borrowed a wheelbarrow in which to carry not a chest, but a harpoon. And, to make certain that there is no special ordinary English restriction (unmentioned in dictionaries) upon the use of "carry" in respect to guns, we have surveyed modern press usage, albeit crudely, by searching computerized newspaper databases—both the New York Times database in Lexis/Nexis, and the "US News" database in Westlaw. We looked for sentences in which the words "carry," "vehicle," and "weapon" (or variations thereof) all appear. We found thousands of such sentences, and random sampling suggests that many, perhaps more than one-third, are sentences used to convey the meaning at issue here, *i.e.,* the carrying of guns in a car.

The New York Times, for example, writes about "an ex-con" who "arrives home driving a stolen car and carrying a load of handguns," Mar. 21, 1992, section 1, p. 18, col. 1, and an "official peace officer who carries a shotgun in his boat," June 19, 1988, section 12WC, p. 2, col. 1; cf. The New York Times Manual of Style and Usage, a Desk Book of Guidelines for Writers and Editors, foreword (L. Jordan rev. ed. 1976) (restricting Times journalists and editors to the use of proper English). The Boston Globe refers to the arrest of a professional baseball player "for carrying a semiloaded automatic weapon in his car." Dec. 10, 1994, p. 75, col. 5. The Colorado Springs Gazette Telegraph speaks of one "Russell" who "carries a gun hidden in his car." May 2, 1993, p. B1, col. 2. The Arkansas Gazette refers to a "house" that was "searched" in an effort to find "items that could be carried in a car, such as . . . guns." Mar. 10, 1991, p. A1, col. 2. The San Diego Union-Tribune asks, "What, do they carry guns aboard these boats now?" Feb. 18, 1992, p. D2, col. 5.

Now consider a different, somewhat special meaning of the word "carry"— a meaning upon which the linguistic arguments of petitioners and the dissent must rest. The Oxford English Dictionary's *twenty-sixth* definition of "carry" is "bear, wear, hold up, or sustain, as one moves about; habitually to bear about with one." Webster's defines "carry" as "to move while supporting," not just in a vehicle, but also "in one's hands or arms." And Black's Law Dictionary defines the entire phrase "carry arms or weapons" as

"To wear, bear or carry them upon the person or in the clothing or in a pocket, for the purpose of use, or for the purpose of being armed and ready for offensive or defensive action in case of a conflict with another person." Black's Law Dictionary 214 (6th ed. 1990).

These special definitions, however, do not purport to *limit* the "carrying of arms" to the circumstances they describe. No one doubts that one who bears arms on his person "carries a weapon." But to say that is not to deny that one may *also* "carry a weapon" tied to the saddle of a horse or placed in a bag in a car.

Nor is there any linguistic reason to think that Congress intended to limit the word "carries" in the statute to any of these special definitions. To the contrary, all these special definitions embody a form of an important, but secondary, meaning of "carry," a meaning that suggests support rather than movement or transportation, as when, for example, a column "carries" the weight of an arch. In this sense a gangster might "carry" a gun (in colloquial language, he might "pack a gun") even though he does not move from his chair. It is difficult to believe, however, that Congress intended to limit the statutory word to this definition—imposing special punishment upon the comatose gangster while ignoring drug lords who drive to a sale carrying an arsenal of weapons in their van.

We recognize, as the dissent emphasizes, that the word "carry" has other meanings as well. But those other meanings, (*e.g.,* "carry all he knew," "carries no colours"), are not relevant here. And the fact that speakers often do *not* add to the phrase "carry a gun" the words "in a car" is of no greater relevance here than the fact that millions of Americans did *not* see Muscarello carry a gun in his truck. The relevant linguistic facts are that the word "carry" in its ordinary sense includes carrying in a car and that the word, used in its ordinary sense, keeps the same meaning whether one carries a gun, a suitcase, or a banana.

Given the ordinary meaning of the word "carry," it is not surprising to find that the Federal Courts of Appeals have unanimously concluded that "carry" is not limited to the carrying of weapons directly on the person but can include their carriage in a car.

B

We now explore more deeply the purely legal question of whether Congress intended to use the word "carry" in its ordinary sense, or whether it intended to limit the scope of the phrase to instances in which a gun is carried "on the person." We conclude that neither the statute's basic purpose nor its legislative history support circumscribing the scope of the word "carry" by applying an "on the person" limitation.

This Court has described the statute's basic purpose broadly, as an effort to combat the "dangerous combination" of "drugs and guns." And the provision's chief legislative sponsor has said that the provision seeks "to persuade the man who is tempted to commit a Federal felony to leave his gun at home."

From the perspective of any such purpose (persuading a criminal "to leave his gun at home"), what sense would it make for this statute to penalize one who walks with a gun in a bag to the site of a drug sale, but to ignore a similar individual who, like defendant Gray-Santana, travels to a similar site with a similar gun in a similar bag, but instead of walking, drives there with the gun in his car? How persuasive is a punishment that is without effect until a drug dealer who has brought his gun to a sale (indeed has it available for use) actually takes it from the trunk (or unlocks the glove compartment) of his car? It is difficult to say that, considered as a class, those who prepare, say, to sell drugs by placing guns in their cars are less dangerous, or less deserving of punishment, than those who carry handguns on their person.

We have found no significant indication elsewhere in the legislative history of any more narrowly focused relevant purpose. We have found an instance in which a legislator referred to the statute as applicable when an individual "has a firearm on his person," an instance in which a legislator speaks of "a criminal who takes a gun in his hand," and a reference in the Senate Report to a "gun carried in a pocket." But in these instances no one purports to define the scope of the term "carries"; and the examples of guns carried on the person are not used to illustrate the reach of the term "carries" but to illustrate, or to criticize, a different aspect of the statute.

Regardless, in other instances, legislators suggest that the word "carries" has a broader scope. One legislator indicates that the statute responds in part to the concerns of law enforcement personnel, who had urged that "carrying short firearms in motor vehicles be classified as carrying such weapons concealed." Another criticizes a version of the proposed statute by suggesting it might apply to drunken driving, and gives as an example a drunken driver who has a "gun in his car." Others describe the statute as criminalizing gun "possession"—a term that could stretch beyond both the "use" of a gun and the carrying of a gun on the person.

C

We are not convinced by petitioners' remaining arguments to the contrary. First, they say that our definition of "carry" makes it the equivalent of "transport." Yet, Congress elsewhere in related statutes used the word "transport" deliberately to signify a different, and broader, statutory coverage. The immediately preceding statutory subsection, for example, imposes a different set of penalties on one who, with an intent to commit a crime, "ships, transports, or receives a firearm" in interstate commerce. Moreover, § 926A specifically "entitle[s]" a person "not otherwise prohibited . . . from transporting, shipping, or receiving a firearm" to "transport a firearm . . . from any place where he may lawfully possess and carry" it to "any other place" where he may do so. Why, petitioners ask, would Congress have used the word "transport," or used both "carry" and "transport" in the same provision, if it had intended to obliterate the distinction between the two?

The short answer is that our definition does not equate "carry" and "transport." "Carry" implies personal agency and some degree of possession, whereas "transport" does not have such a limited connotation and, in addition, implies the movement of goods in bulk over great distances. If Smith, for example, calls a parcel delivery service, which sends a truck to Smith's house to pick up Smith's package and take it to Los Angeles, one might say that Smith has shipped the package and the parcel delivery service has transported the package. But only the truck driver has "carried" the package in the sense of "carry" that we believe Congress intended. Therefore, "transport" is a broader category that includes "carry" but also encompasses other activity.

. . . .

And, if Congress intended "carry" to have the limited definition the dissent contends, it would have been quite unnecessary to add the proviso in § 926A requiring a person, to be exempt from penalties, to store her firearm in a locked container not immediately accessible. See § 926A (exempting from criminal penalties one who transports a firearm from a place where "he may lawfully possess and carry such firearm" but not exempting the "transportation" of a firearm if it is "readily accessible or is directly accessible from the passenger compartment of such transporting vehicle"). The statute simply could have said that such a person may not "carry" a firearm. But, of course, Congress did not say this because that is not what "carry" means.

As we interpret the statutory scheme, it makes sense. Congress has imposed a variable penalty with no mandatory minimum sentence upon a person who "transports" (or "ships" or "receives") a firearm knowing it will be used to commit any "offense punishable by imprisonment for [more than] one year," § 924(b), and it has imposed a 5-year mandatory minimum sentence upon one who "carries" a firearm "during and in relation to" a "drug trafficking crime," § 924(c). The first subsection imposes a less strict sentencing regime upon one who, say, ships firearms by mail for use in a crime elsewhere; the latter subsection imposes a mandatory sentence upon one who, say, brings a weapon with him (on his person or in his car) to the site of a drug sale.

Second, petitioners point out that, in *Bailey v. United States,* 516 U.S. 137 (1995), we considered the related phrase "uses . . . a firearm" found in the same statutory provision now before us. We construed the term "use" narrowly, limiting its application to the "active employment" of a firearm. Petitioners argue that it would be anomalous to construe broadly the word "carries," its statutory next-door neighbor.

In *Bailey,* however, we limited "use" of a firearm to "active employment" in part because we assumed "that Congress . . . intended each term to have a particular, nonsuperfluous meaning." A broader interpretation of "use," we said, would have swallowed up the term "carry." But "carry" as we interpret that word does not swallow up the term "use." "Use" retains the same independent meaning we found for it in *Bailey,* where we provided examples involving the displaying or the bartering of a gun. "Carry" also retains an independent meaning, for, under *Bailey,* carrying a gun in a car does not necessarily involve the gun's "active employment." More importantly, having construed "use" narrowly in *Bailey,* we cannot also construe "carry" narrowly without undercutting the statute's basic objective. For the narrow interpretation would remove the act of carrying a gun in a car entirely from the statute's reach, leaving a gap in coverage that we do not believe Congress intended.

Third, petitioners say that our reading of the statute would extend its coverage to passengers on buses, trains, or ships, who have placed a firearm, say, in checked luggage. To extend this statute so far, they argue, is unfair, going well beyond what Congress likely would have thought possible. They add that some lower courts, thinking approximately the same, have limited the scope of "carries" to instances where a gun in a car is immediately accessible, thereby most likely excluding from coverage a gun carried in a car's trunk or locked glove compartment.

In our view, this argument does not take adequate account of other limiting words in the statute—words that make the statute applicable only where a defendant "carries" a gun *both* "during *and* in relation to" a drug crime. § 924(c)(1) (emphasis added). Congress added these words in part to prevent prosecution where guns "played" no part in the crime.

Once one takes account of the words "during" and "in relation to," it no longer seems beyond Congress' likely intent, or otherwise unfair, to interpret the statute as we have done. If one carries a gun in a car "during" and "in relation to" a drug sale, for example, the fact that the gun is carried in the car's trunk or locked glove compartment seems not only logically difficult to distinguish from the immediately accessible gun, but also beside the point.

At the same time, the narrow interpretation creates its own anomalies. The statute, for example, defines "firearm" to include a "bomb," "grenade," "rocket having a propellant charge of more than four ounces," or "missile having an explosive or incendiary charge of more than one-quarter ounce," where such device is "explosive," "incendiary," or delivers "poison gas." 18 U.S.C. § 921(a)(4)(A). On petitioners' reading, the "carry" provision would not apply to instances where drug lords, engaged in a major transaction, took with them "firearms" such as these, which most likely could not be carried on the person.

Fourth, petitioners argue that we should construe the word "carry" to mean "immediately accessible." And, as we have said, they point out that several Courts of Appeals have limited the statute's scope in this way. That interpretation, however, is difficult to square with the statute's language, for one "carries" a gun in the glove compartment whether or not that glove compartment is locked. Nothing in the statute's history suggests that Congress intended that limitation. And, for reasons pointed out above, we believe that the words "during" and "in relation to" will limit the statute's application to the harms that Congress foresaw.

Finally, petitioners and the dissent invoke the "rule of lenity." The simple existence of some statutory ambiguity, however, is not sufficient to warrant application of that rule, for most statutes are ambiguous to some degree. To invoke the rule, we must conclude that there is a "grievous ambiguity or uncertainty in the statute." Certainly, our decision today is based on much more than a "guess as to what Congress intended," and there is no "grievous ambiguity" here. The problem of statutory interpretation in these cases is indeed no different from that in many of the criminal cases that confront us. Yet, this Court has never held that the rule of lenity automatically permits a defendant to win.

In sum, the "generally accepted contemporary meaning" of the word "carry" includes the carrying of a firearm in a vehicle. The purpose of this statute warrants its application in such circumstances. The limiting phrase "during and in relation to" should prevent misuse of the statute to penalize those whose conduct does not create the risks of harm at which the statute aims.

For these reasons, we conclude that petitioners' conduct falls within the scope of the phrase "carries a firearm." The judgments of the Courts of Appeals are affirmed.

It is so ordered.

JUSTICE GINSBURG, with whom THE CHIEF JUSTICE, JUSTICE SCALIA, and JUSTICE SOUTER join, dissenting.

Section 924(c)(1) of Title 18, United States Code, is a punishment-enhancing provision; it imposes a mandatory five-year prison term when the defendant "during and in relation to any crime of violence or drug trafficking . . . uses or carries a firearm." In *Bailey*, this Court held that the term "uses," in the context of § 924(c)(1), means "active employment" of the firearm. In today's cases we confront a related question: What does the term "carries" mean in the context of § 924(c)(1), the enhanced punishment prescription again at issue.

It is uncontested that § 924(c)(1) applies when the defendant bears a firearm, *i.e.,* carries the weapon on or about his person "for the purpose of being armed and ready for offensive or defensive action in case of a conflict." Black's Law Dictionary 214 (6th ed. 1990) (defining the phrase "carry arms or weapons"). The Court holds that, in addition, "carries a firearm," in the context of § 924(c)(1), means personally transporting, possessing, or keeping a firearm in a vehicle, anyplace in a vehicle.

Without doubt, "carries" is a word of many meanings, definable to mean or include carting about in a vehicle. But that encompassing definition is not a ubiquitously necessary one. Nor, in my judgment, is it a proper construction of "carries" as the term appears in § 924(c)(1). In line with *Bailey* and the principle of lenity the Court has long followed, I would confine "carries a firearm," for § 924(c)(1) purposes, to the undoubted meaning of that expression in the relevant context. I would read the words to indicate not merely keeping arms on one's premises or in one's vehicle, but bearing them in such manner as to be ready for use as a weapon.

I

A

I note first what is at stake for petitioners. The question before the Court "is not *whether* possession of a gun [on the drug offender's premises or in his car, during and in relation to commission of the offense,] means a longer sentence for a convicted drug dealer. It most certainly does.... Rather, the question concerns *which sentencing statute* governs the precise length of the extra term of punishment," § 924(c)(1)'s "blunt 'mandatory minimum'" five-year sentence, or the more finely tuned "sentencing guideline statutes, under which extra punishment for drug-related gun possession varies with the seriousness of the drug crime."

Accordingly, there would be no "gap," no relevant conduct "ignore[d]," were the Court to reject the Government's broad reading of § 924(c)(1). To be more specific, as cogently explained on another day by today's opinion writer:

"The special 'mandatory minimum' sentencing statute says that anyone who '*uses or carries*' a gun 'during and in relation to any ... drug trafficking crime' must receive a mandatory five-year prison term added on to his drug crime sentence. 18 U.S.C. § 924(c). At the same time, the Sentencing Guidelines, promulgated under the authority of a different statute, 28 U.S.C. § 994, provide for a two-level (i.e., a 30% to 40%) sentence enhancement where a 'firearm ... was possessed' by a drug offender, U.S.S.G. § 2D1.1(b)(1), unless the possession clearly was not 'connected with the [drug] offense.'" *United States v. McFadden*, 13 F.3d 463, 467 (C.A.1 1994) (Breyer, C.J., dissenting).

In Muscarello's case, for example, the underlying drug crimes involved the distribution of 3.6 kilograms of marijuana, and therefore carried a base offense level of 12. After adjusting for Muscarello's acceptance of responsibility, his final offense level was 10, placing him in the 6-to-12 month sentencing range. The two-level enhancement for possessing a firearm would have increased his final offense level to 12 (a sentencing range of 10 to 16 months). In other words, the less rigid (tailored to "the seriousness of the drug crime") Guidelines regime would have added four months to Muscarello's prison time, in contrast to the five-year minimum addition the Court's reading of § 924(c)(1) mandates.

In sum, drug traffickers will receive significantly longer sentences if they are caught traveling in vehicles in which they have placed firearms. The question that divides the Court concerns the proper reference for enhancement in the cases at hand, the Guidelines or § 924(c)(1).

B

Unlike the Court, I do not think dictionaries, surveys of press reports, or the Bible tell us, dispositively, what "carries" means embedded in

§ 924(c)(1). On definitions, "carry" in legal formulations could mean, *inter alia,* transport, possess, have in stock, prolong (carry over), be infectious, or wear or bear on one's person. At issue here is not "carries" at large but "carries a firearm." The Court's computer search of newspapers is revealing in this light. Carrying guns in a car showed up as the meaning "perhaps more than one-third" of the time. One is left to wonder what meaning showed up some two-thirds of the time. Surely a most familiar meaning is, as the Constitution's Second Amendment ("keep and *bear* Arms") (emphasis added) and Black's Law Dictionary, at 214, indicate: "wear, bear, or carry . . . upon the person or in the clothing or in a pocket, for the purpose . . . of being armed and ready for offensive or defensive action in a case of conflict with another person."

On lessons from literature, a scan of Bartlett's and other quotation collections shows how highly selective the Court's choices are. If "[t]he greatest of writers" have used "carry" to mean convey or transport in a vehicle, so have they used the hydra-headed word to mean, *inter alia,* carry in one's hand, arms, head, heart, or soul, sans vehicle. Consider, among countless examples:

> "[H]e shall gather the lambs with his arm, and carry them in his bosom." The King James Bible, Isaiah 40:11.
> "And still they gaz'd, and still the wonder grew,
> That one small head could carry all he knew."

> O. Goldsmith, The Deserted Village, ll. 215–216, in The Poetical Works of Oliver Goldsmith 30 (A. Dobson ed. 1949).
> "There's a Legion that never was 'listed,
> That carries no colours or crest."

> R. Kipling, The Lost Legion, st. 1, in Rudyard Kipling's Verse, 1885–1918, p. 222 (1920).
> "There is a homely adage which runs, 'Speak softly and carry a big stick; you will go far.' " T. Roosevelt, Speech at Minnesota State Fair, Sept. 2, 1901, in J. Bartlett, Familiar Quotations 575:16 (J. Kaplan ed. 1992).

These and the Court's lexicological sources demonstrate vividly that "carry" is a word commonly used to convey various messages. Such references, given their variety, are not reliable indicators of what Congress meant, in § 924(c)(1), by "carries a firearm."

C

Noting the paradoxical statement, " 'I *use* a gun to protect my house, but I've never had to *use* it,' " the Court in *Bailey* emphasized the importance of context—the statutory context. Just as "uses" was read to mean not simply "possession," but "active employment," so "carries," correspondingly, is properly read to signal the most dangerous cases—the gun at hand, ready for use as a weapon. It is reasonable to comprehend Congress as having provided mandatory minimums for the most life-jeopardizing gun-connection cases (guns in or at the defendant's hand when committing an offense), leaving other, less imminently threatening, situations for the more flexible Guidelines regime. As the Ninth Circuit suggested, it is not apparent why possession of a gun in a drug dealer's moving vehicle would be thought more dangerous than gun possession on premises where drugs are sold: "A drug dealer who packs heat is more likely to hurt someone or provoke someone else to violence. A gun in a bag under a tarp in a truck bed [or in a bedroom closet] poses substantially less risk."

For indicators from Congress itself, it is appropriate to consider word usage in other provisions of Title 18's chapter on "Firearms." The Court, however, does not derive from the statutory complex at issue its thesis that " '[c]arry' implies personal agency and some degree of possession, whereas 'transport' does not have such a limited connotation and, in addition, implies the movement of goods in bulk over great distances." Looking to provisions Congress enacted, one finds that the Legislature did not acknowledge or routinely adhere to the distinction the Court advances today; instead, Congress sometimes employed "transports" when, according to the Court, "carries" was the right word to use.

Section 925(a)(2)(B), for example, provides that no criminal sanction shall attend "the transportation of [a] firearm or ammunition carried out to enable a person, who lawfully received such firearm or ammunition from the Secretary of the Army, to engage in military training or in competitions." The full text of § 926A, rather than the truncated version the Court presents, is also telling:

"Notwithstanding any other provision of any law or any rule or regulation of a State or any political subdivision thereof, any person who is not otherwise prohibited by this chapter from transporting, shipping, or receiving a firearm shall be entitled to transport a firearm for any lawful purpose from any place where he may lawfully possess and carry such firearm to any other place where he may lawfully possess and carry such firearm if, during such transportation the firearm is unloaded, and neither the firearm nor any ammunition being transported is readily accessible or is directly accessible from the passenger compartment of such transporting vehicle: *Provided,* That in the case of a vehicle without a compartment separate from the driver's compartment the firearm or ammunition shall be contained in a locked container other than the glove compartment or console."

In describing when and how a person may travel in a vehicle that contains his firearm without violating the law, §§ 925(a)(2)(B) and 926A use "transport," not "carry," to "impl[y] personal agency and some degree of possession."

Reading "carries" in § 924(c)(1) to mean "on or about [one's] person" is fully compatible with these and other "Firearms" statutes. For example, under § 925(a)(2)(B), one could carry his gun to a car, transport it to the shooting competition, and use it to shoot targets. Under the conditions of § 926A, one could transport her gun in a car, but under no circumstances could the gun be readily accessible while she travels in the car. "[C]ourts normally try to read language in different, but related, statutes, so as best to reconcile those statutes, in light of their purposes and of common sense." So reading the "Firearms" statutes, I would not extend the word "carries" in § 924(c)(1) to mean transports out of hand's reach in a vehicle.

II

Section 924(c)(1), as the foregoing discussion details, is not decisively clear one way or another. The sharp division in the Court on the proper reading of the measure confirms, "[a]t the very least, . . . that the issue is subject to some doubt. Under these circumstances, we adhere to the familiar rule that, 'where there is ambiguity in a criminal statute, doubts are resolved in favor of the defendant.'" . . . "Carry" bears many meanings, as the Court and the "Firearms" statutes demonstrate. The narrower "on or about [one's] person" interpretation is hardly implausible nor at odds with an accepted meaning of "carries a firearm."

Overlooking that there will be an enhanced sentence for the gun-possessing drug dealer in any event, the Court asks rhetorically: "How persuasive is a punishment that is without effect until a drug dealer who has brought his gun to a sale (indeed has it available for use) actually takes it from the trunk (or unlocks the glove compartment) of his car?" Correspondingly, the Court defines "carries a firearm" to cover "a person who knowingly possesses and conveys firearms [anyplace] in a vehicle . . . which the person accompanies." Congress, however, hardly lacks competence to select the words "possesses" or "conveys" when that is what the Legislature means. Notably in view of the Legislature's capacity to speak plainly, and of overriding concern, the Court's inquiry pays scant attention to a core reason for the rule of lenity: "[B]ecause of the seriousness of criminal penalties, and because criminal punishment usually represents the moral condemnation of the community, legislatures and not courts should define criminal activity. This policy embodies 'the instinctive distaste against men languishing in prison unless the lawmaker has clearly said they should.'"

* * *

The narrower "on or about [one's] person" construction of "carries a firearm" is consistent with the Court's construction of "uses" in *Bailey* to entail an immediacy element. It respects the Guidelines system by resisting overbroad readings of statutes that deviate from that system. It fits plausibly with other provisions of the "Firearms" chapter, and it adheres to the principle that, given two readings of a penal provision, both consistent with the statutory text, we do not choose the harsher construction. The Court, in my view, should leave it to Congress to speak " 'in language that is clear and definite' " if the Legislature wishes to impose the sterner penalty. Accordingly, I would reverse the judgments of the First and Fifth Circuits.

3. STATUTES IN DEROGATION OF COMMON LAW SHALL BE NARROWLY CONSTRUED

(A) Understanding the Rule

According to this rule, ambiguous statutes are to be construed as being consistent with the common law. In other words, if a statute does not manifestly change the law from the preexisting common law, courts should not interpret it to effect a change in the law. In effect, where a statute is unclear, the common law is presumed to fill any gaps. Stated differently, there is a presumption of continuity between the common law and related statutory law.

You should note the close relationship between this rule and the rule against implied repeals, the rule that common law terms may supply definitions to statutory terms, and other rules we have covered. Indeed, not everyone would categorize this as a substantive canon of interpretation, preferring instead to lump it together with these other tools of interpretation. In any case, all of these rules seek to impose coherence and stability on the larger *corpus* of the law. Which theories of interpretation justify that principle?

In truth, this particular canon of interpretation is in decline. More and more of our law is governed by statute rather than by common law. Consequently, the baseline against which new statutes are enacted is often older statutes rather than the common law, and the common law may not be a particularly useful source of interpretation in such cases. Nevertheless, this canon of interpretation continues to be useful in some cases.

ROBBINS V. PEOPLE

107 P.3d 384 (Colo. 2005)

As you read this case, consider these issues:

- Identify all of the arguments made by each side.

- How does each side respond to the other's arguments?

- The dissent claims that the statute is unambiguous, and therefore that common law has no bearing. Do you agree? How does the majority respond to this?

- With whom do you agree?

- Why doesn't the rule of lenity apply?

- What does the majority assert the effect of the statute was?

- What does the dissent assert the effect of the statute was?

- How does the majority frame the task of the court in interpreting statutes? Does the dissent adopt the same framework? How would Justice Scalia frame the task? How would he rule?

KOURLIS, JUSTICE.

The defendant, Richard D. Robbins, filed a motion . . . to vacate a judgment of conviction entered against him in 1958 for felony first degree murder. The trial court dismissed the motion after a hearing on the grounds that it was barred by laches. The court of appeals affirmed . . . and we accepted certiorari to consider the question of whether section 16–5–402, C.R.S. (2004), which sets forth no time limit on the filing of postconviction motions as to first degree felony convictions, precludes the court from considering whether the motion should nonetheless be barred by laches. We now hold that section 16–5–402 does not explicitly abrogate the common law defense of laches, and that such doctrine is consistent with the general legislative intent of the statute. Therefore, it was not error for the trial court to consider and apply the doctrine in this case. Accordingly, we affirm the decision of the court of appeals.

I.   Facts

At age nineteen, Robbins, together with an accomplice, Gregory Warner, attempted to rob a pedestrian. On the evening of May 18, 1958, Warner and Robbins accosted the victim and informed him it was a "stickup." The defendant stood behind the victim with a pistol while Warner stood in front of the victim with a knife. After Warner had "poked" the victim a few times with his knife, Robbins struck the victim in the head with the butt of the pistol. The gun discharged and the bullet struck Warner, killing him.

Criminal charges, including one count of first degree murder, were filed against Robbins in Denver District Court. Robbins entered a plea of not guilty.

. . . .

At the conclusion of the trial, the jury returned a verdict of guilty to the first degree murder charge. Robbins was sentenced to life imprisonment.

. . . .

In 1994 he arrived at the Limon Correctional Facility where a fellow inmate allegedly assisted him in formulating the postconviction challenge which the court now addresses.

II.   Procedural History

Robbins, represented by Mr. Zarlengo, first challenged his conviction in 1960 on [other grounds]. . . . This court found no error in the trial and affirmed the conviction.

The case lay dormant until April 21, 1995, when Robbins brought a pro se motion . . . alleging ineffective assistance of counsel. As grounds for his motion, Robbins alleged that Zarlengo had conducted an inadequate investigation into possible affirmative defenses and that Zarlengo denied Robbins the right to testify at trial.

. . . .

[T]he district court held an evidentiary hearing on Robbins' . . . Motion. Following the hearing, the district court found that . . . Robbins' claim was barred by [laches, due to an] unconscionable delay that resulted in irreparable prejudice to the People. . . .

This time, the court of appeals affirmed the trial court's order. . . . It is from this decision that Robbins now appeals. We granted certiorari to determine whether the equitable doctrine of laches can be applied, as a time bar, to avoid postconviction review of a class one felony conviction.

III. Analysis

Crim. P. 35(c) affords every person convicted of a crime the right to seek postconviction review upon the grounds that the conviction was obtained in violation of the Constitution or laws of the United States or the constitution or laws of this state. Since 1984, motions under Rule 35(c) have been constrained by section 16–5–402, which imposes a time limitation for commencing collateral attacks on judgments of conviction. Today, we consider whether the absence of a limitation period for class one felonies in section 16–5–402 signifies the general assembly's intent to abrogate the [common law] doctrine of laches where a defendant seeks delayed postconviction relief from a class one felony.

A.   Statutory Limitations on Postconviction Relief

In construing a statute, it is our primary purpose to ascertain and give effect to the intent of the legislature. To that end, we look first to the language of the statute itself. Words and phrases are given effect according to their plain and ordinary meaning. This plain meaning rule informs our principle that a statute may not be construed to abrogate the common law unless such abrogation was clearly the intent of the general assembly. Absent such clear intent, statutes must be deemed subject to the common law. Finally, statutes in derogation of the common law must be strictly construed in favor of the person against whom the provisions are intended to apply.

As relevant in this case, the statute of limitations for collateral attack upon convictions provides:

"Except as otherwise provided in subsection (2) of this section, no person who has been convicted as an adult or who has been adjudicated as a juvenile under a criminal statute of this or any other state of the United States shall collaterally attack the validity of that conviction or adjudication unless such attack is commenced within the applicable time period, as provided in subsection (1), following the date of said conviction . . . :

All class 1 felonies:	No limit
All other felonies:	Three years

§ 16–5–402(1). This statute was adopted in 1981 to address the inherent difficulties of defending against stale claims. The objective of the general assembly in enacting section 16–5–402 was to reduce the availability of postconviction review to the extent constitutionally permissible. The goals of section 16–5–402 are two-fold. First, the statute seeks to alleviate "the difficulties attending the litigation of stale claims." Second, section 16–5–402 gives finality to judgments of conviction so that other provisions directed at repeat offenders, former offenders and habitual offenders will not be undermined. Within the reach of these two principles we must decided whether the common law defense of laches survives the enactment of section 16–5–402.

Presumably because of the severity of sentences imposed for class one felonies, the legislature determined that attacks on judgment of convictions for such offenses should not be subject to absolute statutory limits. *Id.* at 428. However, the statute is silent as to whether laches may still bar such an attack. First, we consider the nature and application of the doctrine of laches.

B.   Equitable Doctrine of Laches

Laches is an equitable doctrine that may be asserted to deny relief to a party whose unconscionable delay in enforcing his rights has prejudiced the party against whom relief is sought. We have held that where extensive delay has resulted in the death of witnesses, or where their memories have dimmed, equity should bar relief. However, the application of laches cannot be predicated upon delay alone. Rather, the record must show lack of diligence in the face of actual knowledge of the conditions giving rise to the claim. Finally, the party asserting laches as an affirmative defense has the burden of demonstrating prejudice. If the court invokes the doctrine *sua sponte,* the party against whom laches is asserted must be given an opportunity to explain the delay and rebut the claim of prejudice.

Although courts have primarily applied laches in a civil context, it has also been used as a time bar against stale postconviction attacks in a number of jurisdictions.

Prior to the enactment of section 16–5–402, this court applied laches as a time bar against defendants who delayed in asserting their claims. Even where the court did not explicitly mention the defense of laches, we have denied postconviction relief to defendants who failed to bring their claim in a timely manner.

It is clear that before the enactment of section 16–5–402, Colorado courts had the power to apply laches as a bar to postconviction relief. In interpreting statutes, the court presumes the legislation was passed with deliberate and full knowledge of all existing law dealing with the same subject. We therefore presume the general assembly was aware that laches worked as a time bar against criminal postconviction challenges to any conviction. Thus, we must consider whether the legislature abrogated that doctrine by imposing no time limit on challenges to first degree murder convictions.

C.   Application of Laches Within Statutory Limits

Although the statute provides no limitation on the time in which a postconviction challenge to a class one felony may be brought, the mere existence of a statute of limitations does not preclude the application of laches. Rather, laches and statutory limits can be co-extensive. Where this is the case we have held that the statute will be followed but "within this limit the peculiar doctrine of courts of equity should prevail." Hence, laches may be invoked against a stale claim where there is otherwise no time limitation to collateral attack—unless it has been clearly abrogated by statute. Because we find the statute's silence with respect to the doctrine of laches or other common law defenses ambiguous, we look to the legislative history of section 16–5–402 and our case law to determine whether the abrogation of laches is here within the intent of the general assembly.

Before the statute was enacted into law, both the Senate and the House Committee on Judiciary received testimony from various witnesses. Whether section 16–5–402 would preclude the application of laches was not discussed in either hearing. Rather, the bill was characterized as codifying a time limit for attacks on convictions such that if the defendant did not file within the time limit, he would be presumed to have waived his rights. Such a presumption was justified "because of laches and sleeping on your rights." Testifying before the House, [Assistant District Attorney] Moore again stated that the purpose of the proposed legislation was to "provide a statute of limitations beyond which no collateral attack could be made on a judgment of conviction of a crime." He did state that "there is no statute of limitations against a class one felony." In response to Representative Scherling's concern that without a limit to class one felonies, the statute would not eliminate the problem of delay, Moore responded that while the legislature could not bar collateral attacks, the intent was to establish a time frame in which "a person should come in [sic] and realize the fact that he'd been unjustly convicted." While this exchange does not conclusively resolve the issue before this court, we do not discern a clear intent to abrogate laches as to class one felonies. To the contrary, the proponents of the bill appear to have been motivated primarily by a strong desire to curb stale collateral attacks.

D. Case Law Considering Limitations on Collateral Attack

Our case law has also acknowledged the importance of curbing delayed postconviction motions. We have recognized section 16–5–402 as "one means" of precluding stale or repetitive attacks on criminal convictions. The majority of Colorado cases applying section 16–5–402 have done so without comment on the alternative doctrine of laches. At least two modern cases have considered laches as a time bar to postconviction relief.

In *Bravo,* the court of appeals applied laches as a bar to the defendant's challenge to his 1955 robbery conviction. In *Bravo,* the defendant filed a motion for a new trial in 1981. The trial court denied his motion holding that his request was time barred under the doctrine of laches. The court of appeals affirmed, concluding that since a motion for relief under Crim. P. 35 was governed by equitable principles, laches was applicable.

Following *Bravo,* a trial court again considered laches as a possible bar to postconviction relief.

Finally, we note that when the general assembly wishes to abrogate the common law in other areas of criminal law, it has done so explicitly. We have found no such statement here with regard to equitable defenses such as laches. Moreover, our courts have relied on common law for amplification of the criminal code where necessary.

Our legislature and courts have evinced a strong desire to curb stale postconviction claims in order to ensure finality of convictions in our criminal justice system, give force to repeat offender statutes, and alleviate the difficulties of litigating stale claims. The preservation of laches as a time bar against stale claims comports with that intent. We now hold there is no express implication that the equitable doctrine of laches was abrogated by the enactment of section 16–5–402. Crim. P. 35(c) is a postconviction remedy grounded in equitable principles, and under certain circumstances, laches may work to bar the defendant's claim for relief where section 16–5–402 otherwise would not.

. . . .

V. Conclusion

We now hold that while section 16–5–402 does not impose an absolute statutory limitation on the period in which a defendant may bring a collateral attack against a class one felony, time bars may arise out of the application of the doctrine of laches under certain circumstances. Trial courts have the flexibility to assess cases individually and to decide whether equitable considerations should preclude postconviction relief.

In this case, the record supports the trial court's finding that the defendant filed his Rule 35(c) Motion after unconscionable delay, which resulted in irreparable prejudice to the People. Because we have found no indication that section 16–5–402 was intended to abrogate the equitable doctrine of laches, we affirm the trial court's denial of Robbins' Rule 35(c) Motion, and accordingly affirm the court of appeals as well.

JUSTICE RICE dissents, and CHIEF JUSTICE MULLARKEY and JUSTICE BENDER join in the dissent.

RICE, J., dissenting.

The majority essentially concludes that the common law doctrine of laches survives the General Assembly's enactment of time limitations for collateral attacks upon trial judgments in section 16–5–402. Thus, even though the statute expressly provides that there is "[n]o limit" on when a felon may collaterally attack a class one conviction, the majority holds that the defendant is time-barred by operation of laches. Since I conclude that the express, unambiguous, plain language of section 16–5–402 evidences the General Assembly's intent to abrogate the common law doctrine of laches as applied to collateral attacks on class one felony convictions, I respectfully dissent.

In construing statutes, this Court does not make policy decisions, but must give effect to the intent of the General Assembly, looking first to the plain language of the statute at issue. Even "[i]n the face of statutory silence, questions of interpretation are governed by legislative intent." Ambiguity generally exists only when at least one of the statute's terms is susceptible to multiple meanings.

When the statute is unambiguous on its face, this Court need not look beyond the plain language because " 'if courts can give effect to the ordinary meaning of the words adopted by a legislative body, the statute should be construed as written since it may be presumed that the General Assembly meant what it clearly said.' " Also, "[i]f . . . a statute can be construed and applied as written, the legislature's silence on collateral matters is not this [C]ourt's concern. . . ."

When it acts, the General Assembly is presumed to be aware of existing, applicable case law. Of course, the General Assembly may modify or abrogate the common law, but " 'it must manifest its intent either expressly or by clear implication.' " Vigil, 103 P.3d at 327 (quoting Vaughan v. McMinn, 945 P.2d 404, 408 (Colo.1997)), because " '[a] statute, general in its terms, is always to be taken as subject to . . . the common law.' " Thus, although subject to strict construction, a statute need not expressly abrogate or modify the common law to affect a change;

the General Assembly must provide only a " 'clear expression of intent' " to do so.

Section 16–5–402 enumerates time limitations for collateral attacks upon trial judgments. However, relevant here, "class 1 felonies" have "[n]o limit." Thus, following the plain meaning of the statute's express language as written, a defendant convicted of a class one felony is not limited to a specific time period within which to raise a collateral attack upon his conviction; necessarily, a convicted class one felon may raise such a collateral attack at any time.

Despite the statute's plain meaning, the majority concludes that the phrase "[n]o limit" actually means no limit in addition to that already imposed by common law laches because "there is no express implication that the equitable doctrine of laches was abrogated by the enactment of section 16–5–402." I have difficulty imagining a more obvious instance of the General Assembly clearly expressing its intent to abrogate the common law. With presumed knowledge of this Court's established laches case law, the General Assembly spoke with exactitude, unequivocally saying that upon enactment of section 16–5–402, class one felons are not time-barred, that is they face no time limit when collaterally attacking their convictions. By doing so, the General Assembly evidenced by clear implication its intent to abrogate the common law doctrine of laches as a time limitation on a class one felon's ability to collaterally attack his conviction.

Despite the fundamental rule of statutory construction that the General Assembly may abrogate or modify the common law either expressly or by clear implication, the majority requires the General Assembly to abrogate laches "explicitly" because it has done so with the common law elsewhere in criminal statutes. Yet, such a requirement imposes upon the General Assembly an affirmative duty in drafting and enacting criminal statutes that this Court has never before required.

Had the General Assembly intended to time-bar collateral attacks by class one felons, it easily could have imposed a limitations period, as it did for petty offenses, misdemeanors, and all non-class one felonies. Moreover, had it so intended, the General Assembly certainly could have adopted a more flexible limitation for class one felonies modeled after the common law doctrine of laches. Based upon the plain language of the statute, however, the General Assembly clearly intended neither limitation. By section 16–5–402(1)'s express terms, class one felons face "[n]o limit" on when they may raise a collateral attack on their convictions. Thus, the majority, in my view, replaces the General Assembly's reasoned policy decision with that of its own.

I further find it improper to consult the statute's legislative history, as the statute is clear and unambiguous. Nevertheless, since the statute does not expressly negate application of laches, the majority finds it necessary to examine the legislative history to determine the General Assembly's intent. To my knowledge, however, this Court has never before gone so far as to find an ambiguity from nothing more than mere statutory silence. Such restraint was prudent: a statute's silence on a particular issue easily could be used to manufacture ambiguity where none exists in practically any case involving statutory construction.

Even with reference to the statute's legislative history, I fail to understand how the majority can disregard the plain language of section 16–5–402(1). Indeed, the majority quotes a hearing witness stating that " 'there is no statute of limitations against a class one felony,' " prompting one lawmaker to express his concern that "the problem of delay" would persist. The legislative history demonstrates that the General Assembly ultimately made a policy decision that while some crimes should trigger a statutory time limitation on collateral attacks, class one felonies should not.

In conclusion, finding the statutory language clear and unambiguous, I would apply section 16–5–402 as written, and hold that the General Assembly clearly intended no time limit on a class one felon's ability to collaterally attack his conviction, thereby abrogating the common law doctrine of laches. If it agrees with the majority that class one felons are limited by how long they can collaterally attack trial judgments, then the General Assembly and not this Court should amend section 16–5–402 to add a statute of limitations.

4. PRESUMPTION AGAINST FEDERAL PREEMPTION

(A) Understanding the Rule

According to this canon of interpretation, statutes will not be held to preempt state law unless they do so clearly. Of course, under the Supremacy Clause, if a state statute directly conflicts with a federal statute, the federal statute controls. However, where state law merely *supplements* federal law—for example, by prohibiting something that federal law permits—the presumption against preemption applies.

That said, even strong adherents of this canon concede that a statute need not explicitly provide for preemption in order for state law to be preempted. Rather, if a federal statute manifests a clear legislative intent to "occupy the field," then courts will deem the state law to be preempted. As you might imagine, what constitutes clear intent to occupy the field is the subject of intense debate among judges.

Example. In *Arizona v. United States*, 132 S. Ct. 2492 (2012), the Supreme Court held that Arizona could not enact certain immigration laws because immigration law is the province of the federal government. Although the federal immigration statutes did not expressly preempt state laws, their comprehensiveness and the federal government's overriding interest in immigration law occupied the field. Even state laws that complemented federal immigration laws were preempted.

Why do you think courts have adopted this canon of interpretation? There is also a presumption against statutory waivers of sovereign immunity that may share a similar justification. Can you articulate it?

5. OTHER CANONS AND ISSUES TO CONSIDER

There are many other canons or presumptions that judges sometimes invoke. Based on our discussions concerning the canons we have covered in depth, can you articulate possible justifications for the following examples? What values do they protect?

- Presumption against diminishment of American Indian rights;

- Presumption of Indian tribal immunity from state regulation;

- Presumptions that statutes are consistent with international law and treaties;

- Presumption against retroactivity;

- Presumption in favor of judicial review;

- Presumption against derogation of judicial powers.

Always remember that the substantive canons of interpretation or presumptions can be defeated by clear statutory language. Of course, as we have seen, what one judge considers clear another may consider ambiguous.

How much thought do you think legislative drafters give to these substantive canons when they draft statutes? If the courts are sufficiently clear as to what the presumptions are, then shouldn't legislatures be able to draft around them easily with clear statements? Note that some of these canons and presumptions are sometimes framed as clear statement rules for this very reason.

D.   EXTERNAL SOURCES OF STATUTORY MEANING

The final piece of the statutory interpretation puzzle is the external sources of meaning and application. When we say external sources, we mean those that provide evidence and guidance as to the particular statute's meaning and application but that are not found in statutory texts. We consider three such sources in this section: the context in which the statute was enacted; the statute's legislative history; and the interpretations of the statute by administrative agencies.

In examining these sources we will consider why they provide meaning, how persuasive they are to judges, and how lawyers can use them in advising clients and making arguments to courts.

1.   LEGISLATIVE CONTEXT

The context in which a statute was enacted can provide useful evidence as to the legislature's intention and purposes, as well as to legislators' likely understanding of the statute's effects. Was the statute enacted in response to a particular problem or incident? If so, perhaps its legal effect ought to be limited to the problem it was meant to address even if it could be read more broadly. For instance, if a sign says "no shirt, no shoes, no service," we probably understand *expressio unius* does not apply to permit entry and service to anyone who is wearing a shirt and shoes but no clothing below the waist.

Similarly, context can provide evidence as to the statute's purpose, again helping to resolve ambiguities. Thus, if a school imposes a rule that shoelaces must be tied at all times, should we conclude that shoes secured with Velcro are prohibited? If the context at the time of the rule's adoption was that students were constantly tripping on untied shoelaces, we would probably understand the rule to mean, "if a student wears shoes with shoelaces, the shoelaces must be tied" rather than "all students must wear shoes with shoelaces that are tied."[1] Can you think of any context that would lead to the latter conclusion?

---

[1]   This example is based on a real event. When the author of this casebook was in sixth grade it became fashionable among the boys to wear large, high-top sneakers with garishly colored laces left untied. The school administration deemed this style both unsafe and unisghtly, and consequently announced that shoes must be tied. A classmate of the author wore sneakers secured with Velcro and was sent to the office by an overzealous teacher for violating the rule.

LEO SHEEP CO. V. UNITED STATES
440 U.S. 668 (1979)

As you read this case, focus on the following issues:

- Construct the strongest argument possible for the United States.

- Why does the opinion include all of the background and contextual information? That is, what use is the history lesson? Where is the practical payoff?

- What do you think Congress actually intended?

- Why does the Court decline to apply the Unlawful Inclosures of Public Lands Act in the manner suggested the United States?

MR. JUSTICE REHNQUIST delivered the opinion of the Court.

This is one of those rare cases evoking episodes in this country's history that, if not forgotten, are remembered as dry facts and not as adventure. Admittedly the issue is mundane: Whether the Government has an implied easement to build a road across land that was originally granted to the Union Pacific Railroad under the Union Pacific Act of 1862—a grant that was part of a governmental scheme to subsidize the construction of the transcontinental railroad. But that issue is posed against the backdrop of a fascinating chapter in our history. As this Court noted in another case involving the Union Pacific Railroad, "courts, in construing a statute, may with propriety recur to the history of the times when it was passed; and this is frequently necessary, in order to ascertain the reason as well as the meaning of particular provisions in it." In this spirit we relate the events underlying passage of the Union Pacific Act of 1862.

I

The early 19th century—from the Louisiana Purchase in 1803 to the Gadsden Purchase in 1853—saw the acquisition of the territory we now regard as the American West. During those years, however, the area remained a largely untapped resource, for the settlers on the eastern seaboard of the United States did not keep pace with the rapidly expanding western frontier. A vaguely delineated area forbiddingly referred to as the "Great American Desert" can be found on more than one map published before 1850, embracing much of the United States' territory west of the Missouri River. As late as 1860, for example, the entire population of the State of Nebraska was less than 30,000 persons, which represented one person for every five square miles of land area within the State.

With the discovery of gold at Sutter's Mill in California in 1848, the California gold rush began and with it a sharp increase in settlement of the West. Those in the East with visions of instant wealth, however, confronted the unenviable choice among an arduous 4-month overland trek, risking yellow fever on a 35-day voyage via the Isthmus of Panama, and a better than 4-month voyage around Cape Horn. They obviously yearned for another alternative, and interest focused on the transcontinental railroad.

The idea of a transcontinental railroad predated the California gold rush. From the time that Asa Whitney had proposed a relatively practical plan for its construction in 1844, it had, in the words of one of this century's leading historians of the era, "engaged the eager attention of promoters and politicians until dozens of schemes were in the air." The building of the railroad was not to be the unalloyed product of the free-enterprise system. There was indeed the inspiration of men like Thomas Durant and

Leland Stanford and the perspiration of a generation of immigrants, but animating it all was the desire of the Federal Government that the West be settled. This desire was intensified by the need to provide a logistical link with California in the heat of the Civil War. That the venture was much too risky and much too expensive for private capital alone was evident in the years of fruitless exhortation; private investors would not move without tangible governmental inducement.

In the mid-19th century there was serious disagreement as to the forms that inducement could take. Mr. Justice Story, in his Commentaries on the Constitution, described one extant school of thought which argued that "internal improvements," such as railroads, were not within the enumerated constitutional powers of Congress. Under such a theory, the direct subsidy of a transcontinental railroad was constitutionally suspect—an uneasiness aggravated by President Andrew Jackson's 1830 veto of a bill appropriating funds to construct a road from Maysville to Lexington within the State of Kentucky.

The response to this constitutional "gray" area, and source of political controversy, was the "checkerboard" land-grant scheme. The Union Pacific Act of 1862 granted public land to the Union Pacific Railroad for each mile of track that it laid. Land surrounding the railway right-of-way was divided into "checkerboard" blocks. Odd-numbered lots were granted to the Union Pacific; even-numbered lots were reserved by the Government. As a result, Union Pacific land in the area of the right-of-way was usually surrounded by public land, and vice versa. The historical explanation for this peculiar disposition is that it was apparently an attempt to disarm the "internal improvement" opponents by establishing a grant scheme with "demonstrable" benefits. As one historian notes in describing an 1827 federal land grant intended to facilitate private construction of a road between Columbus and Sandusky, Ohio:

"Though awkwardly stated, and not fully developed in the Act of 1827, this was the beginning of a practice to be followed in most future instances of granting land for the construction of specific internal improvements: donating alternate sections or one half of the land within a strip along the line of the project and reserving the other half for sale. . . . In later donations the price of the reserved sections was doubled so that it could be argued, as the *Congressional Globe* shows *ad infinitum*, that by giving half the land away and thereby making possible construction of the road, canal, or railroad, the government would recover from the reserved sections as much as it would have received from the whole."

In 1850 this technique was first explicitly employed for the subsidization of a railroad when the Illinois delegation in Congress, which included Stephen A. Douglas, secured the enactment of a bill that granted public lands to aid the construction of the Illinois Central Railroad. The Illinois

Central and proposed connecting lines to the south were granted nearly three million acres along rights-of-way through Illinois, Mississippi, and Alabama, and by the end of 1854 the main line of the Illinois Central from Chicago to Cairo, Ill., had been put into operation. Before this line was constructed, public lands had gone begging at the Government's minimum price; within a few years after its completion, the railroad had disposed of more than one million acres and was rapidly selling more at prices far above those at which land had been originally offered by the Government.

The "internal improvements" theory was not the only obstacle to a transcontinental railroad. In 1853 Congress had appropriated moneys and authorized Secretary of War Jefferson Davis to undertake surveys of various proposed routes for a transcontinental railroad. Congress was badly split along sectional lines on the appropriate location of the route—so badly split that Stephen A. Douglas, now a Senator from Illinois, in 1854 suggested the construction of a northern, central, and southern route, each with connecting branches in the East. That proposal, however, did not break the impasse.

The necessary impetus was provided by the Civil War. Senators and Representatives from those States which seceded from the Union were no longer present in Congress, and therefore the sectional overtones of the dispute as to routes largely disappeared. Although there were no major engagements during the Civil War in the area between the Missouri River and the west coast which would be covered by any transcontinental railroad, there were two minor engagements which doubtless made some impression upon Congress of the necessity for being able to transport readily men and materials into that area for military purposes.

Accounts of the major engagements of the Civil War do not generally include the Battle of Picacho Pass, because in the words of Edwin Corle, author of The Gila, "[i]t could be called nothing more than a minor skirmish today." It was fought 42 miles northwest of Tucson, Ariz., on April 15, 1862, between a small contingent of Confederate cavalry commanded by Captain Sherod Hunter and Union troops under Colonel James H. Carleton consisting of infantry, cavalry, and artillery components known as the "California Volunteers." The battle was a draw, with the Union forces losing three men and the badly outnumbered Confederates apparently suffering two men killed and two captured. Following the battle, the Confederate forces abandoned Tucson, which they had previously occupied, and Carleton's Union forces entered that city on May 20, 1862.

The Battle of Glorieta Pass has similarly endured anonymity. Also described as La Glorieta Pass or Apache Canyon, Glorieta Pass lies in the upper valley of the Pecos River, in the southern foothills of the Sangre de Cristo range of the Rocky Mountains near Sante Fe, N. M. Here in the early spring of 1862 a regiment of Colorado volunteers, having moved by forced marches from Denver to Ft. Union, turned back Confederate forces led by Brigadier General Henry Sibley which, until this encounter, had marched triumphantly northward up the Rio Grande Valley from Ft. Bliss. As a result of the Battle of Glorieta Pass, New Mexico was saved for the Union, and Sibley's forces fell back in an easterly direction through Texas before the advance of Carleton's column of Californians.

These engagements gave some immediacy to the comments of Congressman Edwards of New Hampshire during the debate on the Pacific Railroad bill:

"If this Union is to be preserved, if we are successfully to combat the difficulties around us, if we are to crush out this rebellion against the lawful authority of the Government, and are to have an entire restoration, it becomes us, with statesmanlike prudence and sagacity, to look carefully into the future, and to guard in advance against all possible considerations which may threaten the dismemberment of the country hereafter."

As is often the case, war spurs technological development, and Congress enacted the Union Pacific Act in May 1862. Perhaps not coincidentally, the Homestead Act was passed the same month.

The Union Pacific Act specified a route west from the 100th meridian, between a site in the Platte River Valley near the cities of Kearney and North Platte, Neb., to California. The original plan was for five eastern terminals located at various points on or near the Missouri River; but in fact Omaha was the only terminal built according to the plan.

The land grants made by the Union Pacific Act included all the odd-numbered lots within 10 miles on either side of the track. When the Union Pacific's original subscription drive for private investment proved a failure, the land grant was doubled by extending the checkerboard grants to 20 miles on either side of the track. Private investment was still sluggish, and construction did not begin until July 1865, three months after the cessation of Civil War hostilities. Thus began a race with the Central Pacific Railroad, which was laying track eastward from Sacramento, for the Government land grants which went with each mile of track laid. The race culminated in the driving of the golden spike at Promontory, Utah, on May 10, 1869.

II

This case is the modern legacy of these early grants. Petitioners, the Leo Sheep Co. and the Palm Livestock Co., are the Union Pacific Railroad's successors in fee to specific odd-numbered sections of land in Carbon County, Wyo. These sections lie to the east and south of the Seminoe Reservoir, an area that is used by the public for fishing and hunting. Because of the checkerboard configuration, it is physically impossible to enter the Seminoe Reservoir sector from this direction without some minimum physical intrusion upon private land. In the years immediately preceding this litigation, the Government had received complaints that private owners were denying access over their lands to the reservoir area or requiring the payment of access fees. After negotiation with these owners failed, the Government cleared a dirt road extending from a local county road to the reservoir across both public domain lands and fee lands of the Leo Sheep Co. It also erected signs inviting the public to use the road as a route to the reservoir.

Petitioners initiated this action pursuant to 28 U.S.C. § 2409a to quiet title against the United States. The District Court granted petitioners' motion for summary judgment, but was reversed on appeal by the Court of Appeals for the Tenth Circuit. The latter court concluded that when Congress granted land to the Union Pacific Railroad, it implicitly reserved an easement to pass over the odd-numbered sections in order to reach the even-numbered sections that were held by the Government. Because this holding affects property rights in 150 million acres of land in the Western United States, we granted certiorari and now reverse.

The Government does not claim that there is any express reservation of an easement in the Union Pacific Act that would authorize the construction of a public road on the Leo Sheep Co.'s property. Section 3 of the 1862 Act sets out a few specific reservations to the "checkerboard" grant. The grant was not to include land "sold, reserved, or otherwise disposed of by the United States," such as land to which there were homestead claims. Mineral lands were also excepted from the operation of the Act. Given the existence of such explicit exceptions, this Court has in the past refused to add to this list by divining some "implicit" congressional intent. In *Missouri, K. & T. R. Co. v. Kansas Pacific R. Co.*, for example, this Court in an opinion by Mr. Justice Field noted that the intent of Congress in making the Union Pacific grants was clear: "It was to aid in the construction of the road by a gift of lands along its route, without reservation of rights, except such as were specifically mentioned. . . ." The Court held that, although a railroad right-of-way under the grant may not have been located until years after 1862, by the clear terms of the Act only claims established prior to 1862 overrode the railroad grant; conflicting claims arising after that time could not be given effect. To overcome the lack of support in the Act itself, the Government here argues that the implicit reservation of the asserted easement is established by "settled rules of property law" and by the Unlawful Inclosures of Public Lands Act of 1885.

Where a private landowner conveys to another individual a portion of his lands in a certain area and retains the rest, it is presumed at common law that the grantor has reserved an easement to pass over the granted property if such passage is necessary to reach the retained property.

These rights-of-way are referred to as "easements by necessity." There are two problems with the Government's reliance on that notion in this case. First of all, whatever right of passage a private landowner might have, it is not at all clear that it would include the right to construct a road for public access to a recreational area. More importantly, the easement is not actually a matter of necessity in this case because the Government has the power of eminent domain. Jurisdictions have generally seen eminent domain and easements by necessity as alternative ways to effect the same result. For example, the State of Wyoming no longer recognizes the common-law easement by necessity in cases involving landlocked estates. It provides instead for a procedure whereby the landlocked owner can have an access route condemned on his behalf upon payment of the necessary compensation to the owner of the servient estate. For similar reasons other state courts have held that the "easement by necessity" doctrine is not available to the sovereign.

The applicability of the doctrine of easement by necessity in this case is, therefore, somewhat strained, and ultimately of little significance. The pertinent inquiry in this case is the intent of Congress when it granted land to the Union Pacific in 1862. The 1862 Act specifically listed reservations to the grant, and we do not find the tenuous relevance of the common-law doctrine of ways of necessity sufficient to overcome the inference prompted by the omission of any reference to the reserved right asserted by the Government in this case. It is possible that Congress gave the problem of access little thought; but it is at least as likely that the thought which was given focused on negotiation, reciprocity considerations, and the power of eminent domain as obvious devices for ameliorating disputes. So both as matter of common-law doctrine and as a matter of construing congressional intent, we are unwilling to imply rights-of-way, with the substantial impact that such implication would have on property rights granted over 100 years ago, in the absence of a stronger case for their implication than the Government makes here.

The Government would have us decide this case on the basis of the familiar canon of construction that, when grants to federal lands are at issue, any doubts "are resolved for the Government not against it." *Andrus v. Charlestone Stone Products Co.* But this Court long ago declined to apply this canon in its full vigor to grants under the railroad Acts. In 1885 this Court observed:

"The solution of [ownership] questions [involving the railroad grants] depends, of course, upon the construction given to the acts making the grants; and they are to receive such a construction as will carry out the intent of Congress, however difficult it might be to give full effect to the language used if the grants were by instruments of private conveyance. To ascertain that intent we must look to the condition of the country when the acts were passed, as well as to the purpose declared on their face, and read all parts of them together."

The Court harmonized the longstanding rule enunciated most recently . . . when it said:

"It is undoubtedly, as urged by the plaintiffs in error, the well-settled rule of this court that public grants are construed strictly against the grantees, but they are not to be so construed as to defeat the intent of the legislature, or to withhold what is given either expressly or by necessary or fair implication. . . .

" . . . When an act, operating as a general law, and manifesting clearly the intention of Congress to secure public advantages, or to subserve the public interests and welfare by means of benefits more or less valuable, offers to individuals or to corporations as an inducement to undertake and accomplish great and expensive enterprises or works of a *quasi* public character in or through an immense and undeveloped public domain, such legislation stands upon a somewhat different footing from merely a private grant, and should receive at the hands of the court a more liberal construction in favor of the purposes for which it was enacted."

Thus, invocation of the canon reiterated in *Andrus* does little to advance the Government's position in this case.

Nor do we find the Unlawful Inclosures of Public Lands Act of 1885 of any significance in this controversy. That Act was a response to the "range wars," the legendary struggle between cattlemen and farmers during the last half of the 19th century. Cattlemen had entered Kansas, Nebraska, and the Dakota Territory before other settlers, and they grazed their herds freely on public lands with the Federal Government's acquiescence. To maintain their dominion over the ranges, cattlemen used homestead and pre-emption laws to gain control of water sources in the range lands. With monopoly control of such sources, the cattlemen found that ownership over a relatively small area might yield effective control of thousands of acres of grassland. Another exclusionary technique was the illegal fencing of public lands which was often the product of the checkerboard pattern of railroad grants. By placing fences near the borders of their parts of the checkerboard, cattlemen could fence in thousands of acres of public lands. Reports of the Secretary of the Interior indicated that vast areas of public grazing land had been pre-empted by such fencing patterns. In response Congress passed the Unlawful Inclosures Act of 1885.

Section 1 of the Unlawful Inclosures Act states that "[a]ll inclosures of any public lands . . . constructed by any person . . . to any of which land included within the inclosure the person . . . had no claim or color of title made or acquired in good faith . . . are declared to be unlawful." Section 3 further provides:

"No person, by force, threats, intimidation, or by any fencing or inclosing, or any other unlawful means, shall prevent or obstruct, or shall combine and confederate with others to prevent or obstruct, any person from peaceably entering upon or establishing a settlement or residence on any tract of public land subject to settlement or entry under the public land laws of the United States, or shall prevent or obstruct free passage or transit over or through the public lands: *Provided*, This section shall not be held to affect the right or title of persons, who have gone upon, improved, or occupied said lands under the land laws of the United States, claiming title thereto, in good faith."

The Government argues that the prohibitions of this Act should somehow be read to include the Leo Sheep Co.'s refusal to acquiesce in a public road over its property. . . . We [reject this argument].

. . . .

[W]e cannot see how the Leo Sheep Co.'s unwillingness to entertain a public road without compensation can be a violation of that Act. It is certainly true that the problem we confront today was not a matter of great concern during the time the 1862 railroad grants were made. The order of the day was the open range—barbed wire had not made its presence felt—and the type of incursions on private property necessary to reach public land was not such an interference that litigation would serve any motive other than spite. Congress obviously believed that when development came, it would occur in a parallel fashion on adjoining public and private lands and that the process of subdivision, organization of a polity, and the ordinary pressures of commercial and social intercourse would work itself into a pattern of access roads. . . . It is some testament to common sense that the present case is virtually unprecedented, and that in the 117 years since the grants were made, litigation over access questions generally has been rare.

Nonetheless, the present times are litigious ones and the 37th Congress did not anticipate our plight. Generations of land patents have issued without any express reservation of the right now claimed by the Government. Nor has a similar right been asserted before. When the Secretary of the Interior has discussed access rights, his discussion has been colored by the assumption that those rights had to be purchased. This Court has traditionally recognized the special need for certainty and predictability where land titles are concerned, and we are unwilling to upset settled expectations to accommodate some ill-defined power to construct public thoroughfares without compensation. The judgment of the Court of Appeals for the Tenth Circuit is accordingly

Reversed.

2. LEGISLATIVE HISTORY

The use of legislative history in interpreting and applying statutes is controversial among judges. For reasons that should already be clear, intentionalists, purposivists, and pragmatists support the use of legislative history (albeit for somewhat different reasons and to different ends), whereas textualists typically reject it. However, some textualists will allow the use of legislative history if it is used for the limited purpose of assisting the court in understanding how the legislature used and understood ambiguous language. How do you think this differs from how intentionalists and others might use legislative history?

Judges universally agree that legislative history cannot trump the plain text of the statute. They typically maintain that legislative history should be consulted only if the statute itself is ambiguous. As we have seen, though, ambiguity is often in the eye of the beholder.

Further, many judges—especially lower court judges—will incorporate legislative history into their opinions even when they find a statute unambiguous. Textualists lament this practice, arguing that it just encourages the legislature to produce more and more legislative history, but the practice persists. It can probably best be understood as a "belt and suspenders" approach to opinion-writing or as a way of demonstrating to litigants and appellate court judges that the district judge carefully considered all arguments.

Legislative history includes the following:

• Committee reports;

• Statements of legislative sponsors and drafters;

• Deliberations in the legislature. This includes discussions among legislators, rejected proposals, and the "dog that didn't bark" rule, under which there is a presumption that a previous law applies unless someone in the legislature discussed changes imposed by a new law;

• Post-enactment legislative history; and

• Legislative inaction.

Recall the *Weber* and *Johnson* cases from the very beginning of the course. What sources of legislative history from this list did Justices Brennan and Rehnquist refer to?

The hierarchical order in which these sources are listed is significant: the higher something is listed, the more persuasive power it has. The lower down on the list it is, the easier it is for a court to simply ignore or reject. Thus, committee reports are the gold standard of legislative history. In contrast, post-enactment legislative history (that is, statements by legislators made *after* the passage of legislation) is considered relatively weak evidence of the statute's meaning. Can you articulate why this hierarchy exists? That is, why are some kinds of legislative history more decisive than others?

You have already read several cases that reference legislative history, and you will read several more at the conclusion of this chapter. Here, however, are three cases in which legislative history proved unusually dispositive or the judges engaged in forceful debate concerning its proper use.

KOSAK V. UNITED STATES
465 U.S. 848 (1984)

As you read this case, consider the following:

- Who has the more plausible textual argument?

- Who has the better purposivist argument?

- Who has the better argument based on the substantive canons?

- What kind of legislative history does Justice Marshall use? Why does Justice Stevens reject it so forcefully?

JUSTICE MARSHALL delivered the opinion of the Court.

The question presented in this case is whether 28 U.S.C. § 2680(c), which exempts from the coverage of the Federal Tort Claims Act "[a]ny claim arising in respect of . . . the detention of any goods or merchandise by any officer of customs," precludes recovery against the United States for injury to private property sustained during a temporary detention of the property by the Customs Service.

I

While a serviceman stationed in Guam, petitioner assembled a large collection of oriental art. When he was transferred from Guam to Philadelphia, petitioner brought his art collection with him. In his customs declaration, petitioner stated that he intended to keep the contents of the collection for himself. Subsequently, acting upon information that, contrary to his representations, petitioner planned to resell portions of his collection, agents of the United States Customs Service obtained a valid warrant to search petitioner's house. In executing that warrant, the agents seized various antiques and other objects of art.

Petitioner was charged with smuggling his art collection into the country, in violation of 18 U.S.C. § 545. After a jury trial, he was acquitted. The Customs Service then notified petitioner that the seized objects were subject to civil forfeiture under 19 U.S.C. § 1592 (1976), which at the time permitted confiscation of goods brought into the United States "by means of any false statement." Relying on 19 U.S.C. § 1618, petitioner filed a petition for relief from the forfeiture. The Customs Service granted the petition and returned the goods.

Alleging that some of the objects returned to him had been injured while in the custody of the Customs Service, petitioner filed an administrative complaint with the Service requesting compensation for the damage. The Customs Service denied relief. Relying on the Federal Tort Claims Act, 28 U.S.C. §§ 1346(b), 2671–2680, petitioner then filed suit in the United States District Court for the Eastern District of Pennsylvania, seeking approximately $12,000 in damages for the alleged injury to his property. . . .

II

A

The Federal Tort Claims Act, enacted in 1946, provides generally that the United States shall be liable, to the same extent as a private party, "for injury or loss of property, or personal injury or death caused by the negligent or wrongful act or omission of any employee of the Government while acting within the scope of his office or employment." 28 U.S.C. § 1346(b). The Act's broad waiver of sovereign immunity is, however, subject to 13 enumerated exceptions. One of those exceptions, § 2680(c), exempts from the coverage of the statute "[a]ny claim arising in respect of . . . the detention of any goods or merchandise by any officer of customs. . . ." Petitioner asks us to construe the foregoing language to cover only claims "for damage caused by the detention itself and not for the negligent . . . destruction of property while it is in the possession of the customs service." By "damage caused by the detention itself," petitioner appears to mean harms attributable to an illegal detention, such as a decline in the economic value of detained goods (either because of depreciation or because of a drop in the price the goods will fetch), injury resulting from deprivation of the ability to make use of the goods during the period of detention, or consequential damages resulting from lack of access to the goods. The Government asks us to read the exception to cover all injuries to property sustained during its detention by customs officials.

The starting point of our analysis of these competing interpretations must, of course, be the language of § 2680(c). . . . At first blush, the statutory language certainly appears expansive enough to support the Government's construction; the encompassing phrase, "arising in respect of," seems to sweep within the exception all injuries associated in any way with the "detention" of goods. It must be admitted that this initial reading is not ineluctable; as Judge Weis, dissenting in the Court of Appeals, pointed out, it is possible (with some effort) to read the phrase, "in respect of" as the equivalent of "as regards" and thereby to infer that "the statutory exception is directed to the fact of detention itself, and that alone." But we think that the fairest interpretation of the crucial portion of the provision is the one that first springs to mind: "any claim arising in respect of" the detention of goods means any claim "arising out of" the detention of goods, and includes a claim resulting from negligent handling or storage of detained property.

. . . [P]etitioner argues that the foregoing reading of the plain language of § 2680(c) is undercut by the context in which the provision appears.

> "That the exception does not and was not intended to bar actions based on the negligent destruction, injury or loss of goods in the possession or control of the customs authorities is best illustrated by the fact that the exception immediately preceding it expressly bars actions 'arising out of the loss, miscarriage, or negligent transmission' of mail. 28 U.S.C. § 2680(b). If Congress had similarly wished to bar actions based on the negligent loss of goods which governmental agencies other than the postal system undertook to handle, the exception in 28 U.S.C. § 2680(b) shows that it would have been equal to the task. The conclusion is inescapable that it did not choose to bestow upon all such agencies general absolution from carelessness in handling property belonging to others."

We find [this conclusion] far from "inescapable." The specificity of
§ 2680(b), in contrast with the generality of § 2680(c), suggests, if
anything, that Congress intended the former to be *less* encompassing
than the latter. The motivation for such an intent is not hard to find. One
of the principal purposes of the Federal Tort Claims Act was to waive the
Government's immunity from liability for injuries resulting from auto
accidents in which employees of the Postal System were at fault. In order
to ensure that § 2680(b), which governs torts committed by mailmen, did
not have the effect of barring precisely the sort of suit that Congress was
most concerned to authorize, the draftsmen of the provision carefully
delineated the types of misconduct for which the Government was not
assuming financial responsibility—namely, "the loss, miscarriage, or
negligent transmission of letters or postal matter"—thereby excluding, by
implication, negligent handling of motor vehicles. The absence of any
analogous desire to limit the reach of the statutory exception pertaining
to the detention of property by customs officials explains the lack of
comparable nicety in the phraseology of § 2680(c).

B

The legislative history of § 2680(c), though meager, supports the
interpretation of the provision that we have derived from its language
and context. Two specific aspects of the evolution of the provision are
telling. First, the person who almost certainly drafted the language under
consideration clearly thought that it covered injury to detained property
caused by the negligence of customs officials. It appears that the portion
of § 2680(c) pertaining to the detention of goods was first written by
Judge Alexander Holtzoff, one of the major figures in the development of
the Tort Claims Act. In his Report explicating his proposals, Judge
Holtzoff explained:

"[The proposed provision would exempt from the coverage of the Act]
[c]laims arising in respect of the assessment or collection of any tax or
customs duty. This exception appears in all previous drafts. It is
expanded, however, so as to include immunity from liability in respect of
loss in connection with the detention of goods or merchandise by any
officer of customs or excise. The additional proviso has special reference to
the detention of imported goods in appraisers' warehouses or customs
houses, as well as seizures by law enforcement officials, internal revenue
officers, and the like." A. Holtzoff, Report on Proposed Federal Tort
Claims Bill 16 (1931) (Holtzoff Report).

Though it cannot be definitively established that Congress relied upon
Judge Holtzoff's report, it is significant that the apparent draftsman of
the crucial portion of § 2680(c) believed that it would bar a suit of the sort
brought by petitioner.

Second, the Congressional committees that submitted reports on the
various bills that ultimately became the Tort Claims Act suggested that

the provision that was to become § 2680(c), like the other exceptions from the waiver of sovereign immunity, covered claims "arising out of" the designated conduct. Thus, for example, the House Judiciary Committee described the proposed exceptions as follows:

"These exemptions cover claims arising out of the loss or miscarriage of postal matter; the assessment or collection of taxes or assessments; the detention of goods by customs officers; admiralty and maritime torts; deliberate torts such as assault and battery; and others."

The Committees' casual use of the words, "arising out of," with reference to the exemption of claims pertaining to the detention of goods substantially undermines petitioner's contention that the phrase, "in respect of," was designed to limit the sorts of suits covered by the provision.

Of perhaps greater importance than these two clues as to the meaning of the prepositional phrase contained in § 2680(c) is the fact that our interpretation of the plain language of the provision accords with what we know of Congress' general purposes in creating exceptions to the Tort Claims Act. The three objectives most often mentioned in the legislative history as rationales for the enumerated exceptions are: ensuring that "certain governmental activities" not be disrupted by the threat of damage suits; avoiding exposure of the United States to liability for excessive or fraudulent claims; and not extending the coverage of the Act to suits for which adequate remedies were already available.

The exemption of claims for damage to goods in the custody of customs officials is certainly consistent with the first two of these purposes. One of the most important sanctions available to the Customs Service in ensuring compliance with the customs laws is its power to detain goods owned by suspected violators of those laws. Congress may well have wished not to dampen the enforcement efforts of the Service by exposing the Government to private damage suits by disgruntled owners of detained property.

Congress may also have been concerned that a waiver of immunity from suits alleging damage to detained property would expose the United States to liability for fraudulent claims. The Customs Service does not have the staff or resources it would need to inspect goods at the time it seizes them. Lacking a record of the condition of a piece of property when the Service took custody of it, the Government would be in a poor position to defend a suit in which the owner alleged that the item was returned in damaged condition. Congress may have reasoned that the frequency with which the Government would be obliged to pay undeserving claimants if it waived immunity from such suits offset the inequity, resulting from retention of immunity, to persons with legitimate grievances.

To a lesser extent, our reading of § 2680(c) is consistent with the third articulated purpose of the exceptions to the Tort Claims Act. At common law, a property owner had (and retains) a right to bring suit against an individual customs official who negligently damaged his goods. 28 U.S.C. § 2006 provides that judgments in such suits shall be paid out of the federal Treasury if a court certifies that there existed probable cause for the detention of the goods and that the official was acting under the directions of an appropriate supervisor. Congress in 1946 may have concluded that this mode of obtaining recompense from the United States (or from an individual officer) was "adequate." To be sure, there are significant limitations to the common-law remedy, the most important of which is the apparent requirement that the plaintiff prove negligence on the part of a particular customs official. Such proof will often be difficult to come by. But Congress may well have concluded that exposing the United States to liability for injury to property in the custody of the Customs Service under circumstances in which the owner is not able to demonstrate such specific negligence would open the door to an excessive number of fraudulent suits.

III

Petitioner and some commentators argue that § 2680(c) should not be construed in a fashion that denies an effectual remedy to many persons whose property is damaged through the tortious conduct of customs officials. That contention has force, but it is properly addressed to Congress, not to this Court. The language of the statute as it was written leaves us no choice but to affirm the judgment of the Court of Appeals that the Tort Claims Act does not cover suits alleging that customs officials injured property that had been detained by the Customs Service.

It is so ordered.

JUSTICE STEVENS, dissenting.

The Government's construction of 28 U.S.C. § 2680(c) is not the one that "first springs" to my mind. Rather, I read the exception for claims arising "in respect of . . . the detention of goods" as expressing Congress's intent to preclude liability attributable to the temporary interference with the owner's possession of his goods, as opposed to liability for physical damage to his goods. That seems to me to be the normal reading of the statutory language that Congress employed, and the one that most Members of Congress voting on the proposal would have given it. Moreover, my reading, unlike the Court's, is supported by an examination of the language used in other exceptions. Congress did not use the words "arising out of" in § 2680(c) but did use those words in three other subsections of the same section of the Act. See § 2680(b), (e) and (h). Absent persuasive evidence to the contrary, we should assume that when Congress uses different language in a series of similar provisions, it intends to express a different intention.

The language of the statute itself is thus clear enough to persuade me that Congress did not intend to exempt this property damage claim from the broad coverage of the Act. I would, of course, agree that if there were legislative history plainly identifying a contrary congressional intent, that history should be given effect. I do not believe, however, that it is proper for the Court to attach any weight at all to the kind of "clues" to legislative intent that it discusses, or to its concept of the "general purposes" that motivated various exceptions to the statute. Because the Court has done so, however, I shall respond to both parts of its rather creative approach to statutory construction.

I

In the entire 15 year history preceding the enactment of the Tort Claims Act in 1946, the Court finds only two "clues" that it believes shed any light on the meaning of § 2680(c). The first—the so-called "Holtzoff Report"—is nothing but an internal Justice Department working paper prepared in 1931 and never even mentioned in the legislative history of the 1946 Act. There is no indication that any Congressman ever heard of the document or knew that it even existed. The position of the majority— that it is "significant" that the "apparent draftsman" of the relevant language himself "believed that it would bar a suit of the sort brought by petitioner"—is manifestly ill-advised. The intent of a lobbyist—no matter how public spirited he may have been—should not be attributed to the Congress without positive evidence that elected legislators were aware of and shared the lobbyist's intent.

Unless we know more about the collective legislative purpose than can be gleaned from an internal document prepared by a person who was seeking legislative action, we should be guided by the sensible statement that "in construing a statute . . . the worst person to construe it is the person who is responsible for its drafting. He is very much disposed to confuse what he intended to do with the effect of the language which in fact has been employed." If the draftsman of the language in question intended it to cover such cases as this one, he failed.

The second "clue" relied upon by the majority consists of a brief summary in the House Committee Report which casually uses the prepositional phrase "arising out of" to introduce a truncated list of the exceptions. But the "casual" use of the latter phrase in the committee report is as understandable as it is insignificant. It is nothing more than an introduction. In such an introduction, precision of meaning is naturally and knowingly sacrificed in the interest of brevity.

II

The Court's reliance on the "general purposes" for creating exceptions does nothing more than explain why Congress might reasonably have decided to create this exception. Those purposes are no more persuasive than the general purposes motivating the enactment of the broad waiver of sovereign immunity effected by the statute itself.

The hypothetical rationales attributed to Congress by the majority are also internally inconsistent. If Congress, as a matter of public policy, determined that these claims should not be entertained because of the possibility for fraud, the majority's suggestion that petitioner may have a remedy under the Tucker Act is quite inexplicable. Similarly, if Congress "may well have wished not to dampen the enforcement efforts of the Service by exposing the *Government* to private damages suits by disgruntled owners of detained property," its failure to abrogate the common law remedy against the individual customs officer is inexplicable. For I would assume that customs officers' enforcement efforts would be dampened far more by a threat of personal liability than by a threat of governmental liability. Reliance on an assumed reluctance to waive immunity regarding claims for which "adequate" remedies were already available simply begs the question. A basic reason for the Tort Claims Act was, of course, the inadequacy of the existing remedies, and there is no indication in the legislative history that Congress considered the previous remedies in this specific area adequate.

A discussion of the general reasons for drafting exceptions to the Act is no more enlightening regarding the specific exception at issue here than a consideration of the principal purpose that Congress sought to achieve by enacting this important reform legislation.

Tort claims bills had floundered on legislative shoals for nearly two decades. A general waiver of sovereign immunity for torts was finally propelled into law by the legislative reform movement which culminated in the Legislative Reorganization Act of 1946. The "overwhelming purpose" of the Congress which enacted the Tort Claims Act was to remove the burden of dealing with tort claims from Congress which had adjudicated these claims in the form of passing private bills, and the "reports at that session omitted previous discussions which tended to restrict the scope of the Tort Claims bill." Hence, the Joint Committee on the Organization of Congress recommended that "Congress delegate authority to the Federal Courts and to the Court of Claims to hear and settle claims against the Federal Government," explaining its recommendation, and the shortcomings of resolving such claims through consideration of private bills, as follows:

"Congress is poorly equipped to serve as a judicial tribunal for the settlement of private claims against the Government of the United States. This method of handling individual claims does not work well either for the Government or for the individual claimant, while the cost of legislating the settlement in many cases far exceeds the total amounts involved.

"Long delays in consideration of claims against the Government, time consumed by the Claims Committees in the House and Senate, and crowded private calendars combine to make this an inefficient method of procedure.

"The United States courts are well able and equipped to hear these claims and to decide them with justice and equity both to the Government and to the claimants."

If our construction of the narrow provision before us is to be determined by reference to broad purposes, in the context of the 1946 Act the exceptions are best rationalized by reference to Congress's central purpose. Absent specific legislative history pertaining to the sort of claims involved in this case, the general bases for exceptions relied upon by the majority are surely less persuasive than the overwhelming purpose of the statute. Courts of law have been up to the task of discovering fraud for centuries; it is completely unrealistic to suggest that Congress did not think the judiciary up to this task, or that it wanted to reserve such cases for its own adjudication because it is better equipped to weed out fraudulent claims.

In the final analysis, one must conclude that the legislative history provides only the most general guidance on resolving the issue in this case. For any basic policy argument in favor of making an exception will support a broad construction of the provision in question, just as any basic policy argument in favor of the Act's waiver of sovereign immunity will support a narrow construction of this or any other exception. The government's policy arguments respecting the administrative burden on the Customs Service and the potential for fraudulent claims, like petitioner's policy arguments, "are properly addressed to Congress, not to this Court."

III

Therefore, this is "a case for applying the canon of construction of the wag who said, when the legislative history is doubtful, go to the statute." I would acknowledge—indeed I do acknowledge—that the Court's reading of the statutory language is entirely plausible. I would, however, tilt the scales in favor of recovery by attaching some weight to the particular language used in § 2680(c). And I must disagree with the Court's reliance on the general purposes underlying exceptions when no consideration is given to the general purpose of the statute itself. But most importantly, I would eschew any reliance on the intent of the lobbyist whose opinion on the question before us was not on the public record.

I therefore respectfully dissent.

MONTANA WILDERNESS ASSOC. v.
UNITED STATES FOREST SERVICE

655 F.2d 951 (9th Cir. 1981)

As you read this case, consider the following questions:

- What are the textual arguments for each side?

- What do you think the strongest argument is for each side?

- In the absence of the subsequent legislative history discovered by the court, how would you have voted? Why? How close a case do you think this is?

- Does the subsequent legislative history cause you to change your mind or reinforce your initial position?

- In general, how much weight do you think should be given to such subsequent legislative history? Might it depend on the circumstances? If so, how?

NORRIS, CIRCUIT JUDGE:

Environmentalists and a neighboring property owner seek to block construction by Burlington Northern of roads over parts of the Gallatin National Forest. They appeal from a partial summary judgment in the district court granting Burlington Northern a right of access to its totally enclosed timberlands. The district court held that Burlington Northern has an easement by necessity or, alternatively, an implied easement under the Northern Pacific Land Grant of 1864. The defendants argue that the Alaska National Interest Lands Act of 1980, passed subsequent to the district court's decision, also grants Burlington Northern assured access to its land. The appellants contend that the doctrine of easement by necessity does not apply to the sovereign, that there was no implied easement conveyed by the 1864 land grant, and that the access provisions of the Alaska Lands Act do not apply to land outside the state of Alaska. We conclude that the Alaska Lands Act does grant access to Burlington Northern. We therefore affirm the partial summary judgment and remand the case for further proceedings.

I.

Defendant-Appellee Burlington Northern, Inc. owns timberland located within the Gallatin National Forest southwest of Bozeman, Montana. This land was originally acquired by its predecessor, the Northern Pacific Railroad, under the Northern Pacific Land Grant Act of 1864. The Act granted odd-numbered square sections of land to the railroad, which, with the even-number sections retained by the United States, formed a checkerboard pattern.

To harvest its timber, Burlington Northern in 1979 acquired a permit from defendant-appellee United States Forest Service, allowing it to construct an access road across national forest land. The proposed roads would cross the Buck Creek and Yellow Mules drainages, which are protected by the Montana Wilderness Study Act of 1977 as potential wilderness areas. The proposed logging and road-building will arguably disqualify the areas as wilderness under the Act.

The plaintiffs, Montana Wilderness Association, The Wilderness Society, and Nine Quarter Circle Ranch, having contested the granting of the permit, filed suit after it was granted, seeking declaratory and injunctive relief. . . .

II.

The sole issue on appeal is whether Burlington Northern has a right of access across federal land to its inholdings of timberland. Appellees contend that the recently enacted Alaska National Interest Lands Conservation Act (Alaska Lands Act) establishes an independent basis for affirming the judgment of the district court. They argue that s[ection]

1323(a) of the Act requires that the Secretary of Agriculture provide access to Burlington Northern for its enclosed land.

Section 1323 is a part of the administrative provisions, Title XIII, of the Alaska Lands Act. Appellees argue that it is the only section of the Act which applies to the entire country; appellants argue that, like the rest of the Act, it applies only to Alaska. Section 1323 reads as follows:

"Sec. 1323. (a) Notwithstanding any other provision of law, and subject to such terms and conditions as the Secretary of Agriculture may prescribe, the Secretary shall provide such access to nonfederally owned land within the boundaries of the National Forest System as the Secretary deems adequate to secure to the owner the reasonable use and enjoyment thereof: Provided, That such owner comply with rules and regulations applicable to ingress and egress to or from the National Forest System.

"(b) Notwithstanding any other provision of law, and subject to such terms and conditions as the Secretary of the Interior may prescribe, the Secretary shall provide such access to nonfederally owned land surrounded by public lands managed by the Secretary under the Federal Land Policy and Management Act of 1976 as the Secretary deems adequate to secure to the owner the responsible use and enjoyment thereof: Provided, That such owner comply with rules and regulations applicable to access across public lands."

This section provides for access to nonfederally owned lands surrounded by certain kinds of federal lands. Subsection (b) deals with access to nonfederal lands "surrounded by public lands managed by the Secretary (of the Interior)." Section 102(3) of the Act defines "public lands" as certain lands "situated in Alaska." Subsection (b), therefore, is arguably limited by its terms to Alaska, though we do not find it necessary to settle that issue here. Our consideration of the scope of s[ection] 1323(a) proceeds under the assumption that s[ection] 1323(b) is limited to Alaska.

Subsection (a) deals with access to nonfederally owned lands "within the boundaries of the National Forest System." The term "National Forest System" is not specifically defined in the Act.

The question before the court is whether the term "National Forest System" as used in s[ection] 1323(a) is to be interpreted as being limited to national forests in Alaska or as including the entire United States. We note at the outset that the bare language of s[ection] 1323(a) does not, when considered by itself, limit the provision of access to Alaskan land. We must look, however, to the context of the section to determine its meaning.

Elsewhere in the Act, Congress used the term "National Forest System" in a context which refers to and deals with national forests in Alaska. Title V of the Act is entitled "National Forest System." Section 501(a) states: "The following units of the National Forest System are hereby expanded. . . ." It is not unreasonable to read section 1323(a) as referring to the "National Forest System" in the context in which it is used in Title V of the Act, rather than to all national forests in the United States.

Congress did, however, supply us with a general definition of the term in another statute. 16 U.S.C. s[ection] 1609(a) states *inter alia* that:

"Congress declares that the National Forest System consists of units of federally owned forest, range, and related lands throughout the United States and its territories, united into a nationally significant system dedicated to the long-term benefit for present and future generations, and that it is the purpose of this section to include all such areas into one integral system. The 'National Forest System' shall include all national forest lands reserved or withdrawn from the public domain of the United States,. . . ."

Application of this definition to s[ection] 1323(a) would necessarily yield the conclusion that the section was intended to have nation-wide effect. This seems especially so when Congress uses the term "National Forest System" in s[ection] 1323(a) without limitation or qualification.

As the parties agreed at oral argument, however, s[ection] 1323(b) is *in pari materia* with s[ection] 1323(a). The two subsections are placed together in the same section, and use not only a parallel structure but many of the same words and phrases. The natural interpretation is that they were meant to have the same effect, one on lands controlled by the Secretary of Agriculture, the other on lands controlled by the Secretary of the Interior. Since we assume that s[ection] 1323(b), by definition of public lands in s[ection] 102(3), applies only to Alaskan land, we face a presumption that s[ection] 1323(a) was meant to apply to Alaska as well.

That interpretation is supported by a review of the entire Act which discloses no other provision having nation-wide application. We therefore conclude that the language of the Act provides tentative support for the view that s[ection] 1323(a) applies only to national forests in Alaska. Bearing in mind that "(a)bsent a clearly expressed legislative intent to the contrary, (the statutory) language must ordinarily be regarded as conclusive," we turn to the legislative history.

The legislative history concerning s[ection] 1323 is surprisingly sparse. The report of the Senate committee which drafted the section is ambiguous. At times when the Senate could have been expected to comment on its intention to make a major change in current law, it did not. The only expression of intent that s[ection] 1323 apply nation-wide came from a single senator eight days after the Alaska Lands Act was passed by Congress. In the House debates, three representatives suggested that s[ection] 1323 did apply nation-wide, but the chairman of one of the responsible committees said it did not. Two chairmen of House subcommittees responsible for the bill did state in a letter to the Attorney General that they believed that s[ection] 1323 applied nation-wide, but there is no indication that the contents of this letter were generally known by members of the House, and so the letter carries little weight in our analysis. All this gives only slight support at best to the appellees' interpretation that s[ection] 1323 applies nation-wide.

The appellees, however, have uncovered subsequent legislative history that, given the closeness of the issue, is decisive. Three weeks after Congress passed the Alaska Lands Act, a House-Senate Conference Committee considering the Colorado Wilderness Act interpreted s[ection] 1323 of the Alaska Lands Act as applying nation-wide:

"Section 7 of the Senate amendment contains a provision pertaining to access to non-Federally owned lands within national forest wilderness areas in Colorado. The House bill has no such provision.

"The conferees agreed to delete the section because similar language has already passed Congress in Section 1323 of the Alaska National Interest Lands Conservation Act."

H.R.Rep.No.1521, 96th Cong., 2d Sess., 126 Cong.Rec.

This action was explained to both Houses during discussion of the Conference Report. Both houses then passed the Colorado Wilderness bill as it was reported by the Conference Committee.

Although a subsequent conference report is not entitled to the great weight given subsequent legislation, it is still entitled to significant weight, particularly where it is clear that the conferees had carefully considered the issue. The conferees, including Representatives Udall and Sieberling and Senator Melcher, had an intimate knowledge of the Alaska Lands Act. Moreover, the Conference Committee's interpretation of s[ection] 1323 was the basis for their decision to leave out an access provision passed by one house. In these circumstances, the Conference Committee's interpretation is very persuasive. We conclude that it tips the balance decidedly in favor of the broader interpretation of s[ection] 1323. We therefore hold that Burlington Northern has an assured right of access to its land pursuant to the nation-wide grant of access in s[ection] 1323.

. . . .

BOB JONES UNIVERSITY V. UNITED STATES
461 U.S. 574 (1983)

As you read this case, consider the following:

- Who has the stronger textual argument? Why?

- The majority relies on the presumption in favor of consistency with the common law. The dissent rejects that presumption in this case. Why? Who has the better argument?

- The majority finds support in the enactment of section 501(i). The dissent also finds support in the enactment of section 501(i)—but for exactly the opposite proposition. Why? Who has the better argument?

- According to the majority, under what circumstances should legislative inaction serve as evidence as to the legislature's intent? On what basis does the dissent dispute this? Who has the better argument?

- The debate concerning legislative inaction seems to mirror the debate between Justices Brennan and Scalia in *Johnson* concerning the legislative acquiescence argument in favor of deferring to precedent. Do you see how?

- The dissent also finds support in the legislative history. How?

- What theories of interpretation are represented by these opinions?

- Would you have voted with the majority or the dissent? Why?

- Can you think of any constitutional avoidance arguments that might support one side or the other?

CHIEF JUSTICE BURGER delivered the opinion of the Court.

We granted certiorari to decide whether petitioners, nonprofit private schools that prescribe and enforce racially discriminatory admissions standards on the basis of religious doctrine, qualify as tax-exempt organizations under § 501(c)(3) of the Internal Revenue Code of 1954.

I

A

Until 1970, the Internal Revenue Service granted tax-exempt status to private schools, without regard to their racial admissions policies, under § 501(c)(3) of the Internal Revenue Code, 26 U.S.C. § 501(c)(3), and granted charitable deductions for contributions to such schools under § 170 of the Code.

On January 12, 1970, a three-judge District Court for the District of Columbia issued a preliminary injunction prohibiting the IRS from according tax-exempt status to private schools in Mississippi that discriminated as to admissions on the basis of race. Thereafter, in July 1970, the IRS concluded that it could "no longer legally justify allowing tax-exempt status [under § 501(c)(3)] to private schools which practice racial discrimination." At the same time, the IRS announced that it could not "treat gifts to such schools as charitable deductions for income tax purposes [under § 170]." By letter dated November 30, 1970, the IRS formally notified private schools, including those involved in this case, of this change in policy, "applicable to all private schools in the United States at all levels of education."

On June 30, 1971, the three-judge District Court issued its opinion on the merits of the Mississippi challenge. That court approved the IRS' amended construction of the Tax Code. The court also held that racially discriminatory private schools were not entitled to exemption under § 501(c)(3) and that donors were not entitled to deductions for contributions to such schools under § 170. The court permanently enjoined the Commissioner of Internal Revenue from approving tax-exempt status for any school in Mississippi that did not publicly maintain a policy of nondiscrimination.

The revised policy on discrimination was formalized in Revenue Ruling 71–447:

"Both the courts and the Internal Revenue Service have long recognized that the statutory requirement of being 'organized and operated exclusively for religious, charitable, . . . or educational purposes' was intended to express the basic common law concept [of 'charity']. . . . All charitable trusts, educational or otherwise, are subject to the requirement that the purpose of the trust may not be illegal or contrary to public policy."

Based on the "national policy to discourage racial discrimination in education," the IRS ruled that "a private school not having a racially nondiscriminatory policy as to students is not 'charitable' within the common law concepts reflected in sections 170 and 501(c)(3) of the Code."

The application of the IRS construction of these provisions to petitioners, two private schools with racially discriminatory admissions policies, is now before us.

B

No. 81–3, Bob Jones University v. United States

Bob Jones University is a nonprofit corporation located in Greenville, South Carolina. Its purpose is "to conduct an institution of learning . . . , giving special emphasis to the Christian religion and the ethics revealed in the Holy Scriptures." The corporation operates a school with an enrollment of approximately 5,000 students, from kindergarten through college and graduate school. Bob Jones University is not affiliated with any religious denomination, but is dedicated to the teaching and propagation of its fundamentalist Christian religious beliefs. It is both a religious and educational institution. Its teachers are required to be devout Christians, and all courses at the University are taught according to the Bible. Entering students are screened as to their religious beliefs, and their public and private conduct is strictly regulated by standards promulgated by University authorities.

The sponsors of the University genuinely believe that the Bible forbids interracial dating and marriage. To effectuate these views, Negroes were completely excluded until 1971. From 1971 to May 1975, the University accepted no applications from unmarried Negroes, but did accept applications from Negroes married within their race.

Following the decision of the United States Court of Appeals for the Fourth Circuit . . . prohibiting racial exclusion from private schools, the University revised its policy. Since May 29, 1975, the University has permitted unmarried Negroes to enroll; but a disciplinary rule prohibits interracial dating and marriage. That rule reads:

"*There is to be no interracial dating.*

"1. Students who are partners in an interracial marriage will be expelled.

"2. Students who are members of or affiliated with any group or organization which holds as one of its goals or advocates interracial marriage will be expelled.

"3. Students who date outside their own race will be expelled.

"4. Students who espouse, promote, or encourage others to violate the University's dating rules and regulations will be expelled."

The University continues to deny admission to applicants engaged in an interracial marriage or known to advocate interracial marriage or dating.

Until 1970, the IRS extended tax-exempt status to Bob Jones University under § 501(c)(3). By the letter of November 30, 1970, that followed the injunction issued in *Green v. Kennedy,* the IRS formally notified the University of the change in IRS policy, and announced its intention to challenge the tax-exempt status of private schools practicing racial discrimination in their admissions policies.

. . . .

II

A

In Revenue Ruling 71–447, the IRS formalized the policy first announced in 1970, that § 170 and § 501(c)(3) embrace the common law "charity" concept. Under that view, to qualify for a tax exemption pursuant to § 501(c)(3), an institution must show, first, that it falls within one of the eight categories expressly set forth in that section, and second, that its activity is not contrary to settled public policy.

Section 501(c)(3) provides that "[c]orporations . . . organized and operated exclusively for religious, charitable . . . or educational purposes" are entitled to tax exemption. Petitioners argue that the plain language of the statute guarantees them tax-exempt status. They emphasize the absence of any language in the statute expressly requiring all exempt organizations to be "charitable" in the common law sense, and they contend that the disjunctive "or" separating the categories in § 501(c)(3) precludes such a reading. Instead, they argue that if an institution falls within one or more of the specified categories it is automatically entitled to exemption, without regard to whether it also qualifies as "charitable." The Court of Appeals rejected that contention and concluded that petitioners' interpretation of the statute "tears section 501(c)(3) from its roots."

It is a well-established canon of statutory construction that a court should go beyond the literal language of a statute if reliance on that language would defeat the plain purpose of the statute:

"The general words used in the clause . . . , taken by themselves, and literally construed, without regard to the object in view, would seem to sanction the claim of the plaintiff. But this mode of expounding a statute has never been adopted by any enlightened tribunal—because it is evident that in many cases it would defeat the object which the Legislature intended to accomplish. And it is well settled that, in interpreting a statute, the court will not look merely to a particular clause in which general words may be used, *but will take in connection with it the whole statute . . . and the objects and policy of the law. . . ."*

Section 501(c)(3) therefore must be analyzed and construed within the framework of the Internal Revenue Code and against the background of the Congressional purposes. Such an examination reveals unmistakable evidence that, underlying all relevant parts of the Code, is the intent that entitlement to tax exemption depends on meeting certain common law standards of charity—namely, that an institution seeking tax-exempt status must serve a public purpose and not be contrary to established public policy.

This "charitable" concept appears explicitly in § 170 of the Code. That section contains a list of organizations virtually identical to that contained in § 501(c)(3). It is apparent that Congress intended that list to have the same meaning in both sections. In § 170, Congress used the list of organizations in defining the term "charitable contributions." On its face, therefore, § 170 reveals that Congress' intention was to provide tax benefits to organizations serving charitable purposes. The form of § 170 simply makes plain what common sense and history tell us: in enacting both § 170 and § 501(c)(3), Congress sought to provide tax benefits to charitable organizations, to encourage the development of private institutions that serve a useful public purpose or supplement or take the place of public institutions of the same kind.

Tax exemptions for certain institutions thought beneficial to the social order of the country as a whole, or to a particular community, are deeply rooted in our history, as in that of England. The origins of such exemptions lie in the special privileges that have long been extended to charitable trusts.

More than a century ago, this Court announced the caveat that is critical in this case:

"[I]t has now become an established principle of American law, that courts of chancery will sustain and protect . . . a gift . . . to public charitable uses, *provided the same is consistent with local laws and public policy. . . .*"

Soon after that, in 1878, the Court commented:

"A charitable use, *where neither law nor public policy forbids,* may be applied to almost any thing *that tends to promote the well-doing and well-being of social man.*"

In 1891, in a restatement of the English law of charity which has long been recognized as a leading authority in this country, Lord MacNaghten stated:

" 'Charity' in its legal sense comprises four principal divisions: trusts for the relief of poverty; *trusts for the advancement of education;* trusts for the advancement of religion; and trusts for *other purposes beneficial to the community,* not falling under any of the preceding heads."

These statements clearly reveal the legal background against which Congress enacted the first charitable exemption statute in 1894: charities were to be given preferential treatment because they provide a benefit to society.

What little floor debate occurred on the charitable exemption provision of the 1894 Act and similar sections of later statutes leaves no doubt that Congress deemed the specified organizations entitled to tax benefits because they served desirable public purposes. In floor debate on a similar provision in 1917, for example, Senator Hollis articulated the rationale:

"For every dollar that a man contributes to these public charities, educational, scientific, or otherwise, the public gets 100 percent."

In 1924, this Court restated the common understanding of the charitable exemption provision:

"Evidently the exemption is made in recognition of the benefit which the public derives from corporate activities of the class named, and is intended to aid them when not conducted for private gain."

In enacting the Revenue Act of 1938, Congress expressly reconfirmed this view with respect to the charitable deduction provision:

"The exemption from taxation of money and property devoted to charitable and other purposes is based on the theory that the Government is compensated for the loss of revenue by its relief from financial burdens which would otherwise have to be met by appropriations from other public funds, and by the benefits resulting from the promotion of the general welfare."

A corollary to the public benefit principle is the requirement, long recognized in the law of trusts, that the purpose of a charitable trust may not be illegal or violate established public policy. In 1861, this Court stated that a public charitable use must be "consistent with local laws and public policy." Modern commentators and courts have echoed that view.

When the Government grants exemptions or allows deductions all taxpayers are affected; the very fact of the exemption or deduction for the donor means that other taxpayers can be said to be indirect and vicarious "donors." Charitable exemptions are justified on the basis that the exempt entity confers a public benefit—a benefit which the society or the community may not itself choose or be able to provide, or which supplements and advances the work of public institutions already supported by tax revenues. History buttresses logic to make clear that, to warrant exemption under § 501(c)(3), an institution must fall within a category specified in that section and must demonstrably serve and be in harmony with the public interest. The institution's purpose must not be so at odds with the common community conscience as to undermine any public benefit that might otherwise be conferred.

B

We are bound to approach these questions with full awareness that determinations of public benefit and public policy are sensitive matters with serious implications for the institutions affected; a declaration that a given institution is not "charitable" should be made only where there can be no doubt that the activity involved is contrary to a fundamental public policy. But there can no longer be any doubt that racial discrimination in education violates deeply and widely accepted views of elementary justice. Prior to 1954, public education in many places still was conducted under the pall of *Plessy v. Ferguson*; racial segregation in primary and secondary education prevailed in many parts of the country. This Court's decision in *Brown v. Board of Education,* signalled an end to that era. Over the past quarter of a century, every pronouncement of this Court and myriad Acts of Congress and Executive Orders attest a firm national policy to prohibit racial segregation and discrimination in public education.

An unbroken line of cases following *Brown v. Board of Education* establishes beyond doubt this Court's view that racial discrimination in education violates a most fundamental national public policy, as well as rights of individuals.

. . . .

Congress, in Titles IV and VI of the Civil Rights Act of 1964 clearly expressed its agreement that racial discrimination in education violates a fundamental public policy. Other sections of that Act, and numerous enactments since then, testify to the public policy against racial discrimination.

The Executive Branch has consistently placed its support behind eradication of racial discrimination. Several years before this Court's decision in *Brown v. Board of Education, supra,* President Truman issued Executive Orders prohibiting racial discrimination in federal employment decisions and in classifications for the Selective Service. In 1957, President Eisenhower employed military forces to ensure compliance with federal standards in school desegregation programs. And in 1962, President Kennedy announced:

"[T]he granting of federal assistance for . . . housing and related facilities from which Americans are excluded because of their race, color, creed, or national origin is unfair, unjust, and inconsistent with the public policy of the United States as manifested in its Constitution and laws."

These are but a few of numerous Executive Orders over the past three decades demonstrating the commitment of the Executive Branch to the fundamental policy of eliminating racial discrimination.

Few social or political issues in our history have been more vigorously debated and more extensively ventilated than the issue of racial discrimination, particularly in education. Given the stress and anguish of the history of efforts to escape from the shackles of the "separate but equal" doctrine of *Plessy v. Ferguson,* it cannot be said that educational institutions that, for whatever reasons, practice racial discrimination, are institutions exercising "beneficial and stabilizing influences in community life," or should be encouraged by having all taxpayers share in their support by way of special tax status.

There can thus be no question that the interpretation of § 170 and § 501(c)(3) announced by the IRS in 1970 was correct. That it may be seen as belated does not undermine its soundness. It would be wholly incompatible with the concepts underlying tax exemption to grant the benefit of tax-exempt status to racially discriminatory educational entities, which "exer[t] a pervasive influence on the entire educational process." Whatever may be the rationale for such private schools' policies, and however sincere the rationale may be, racial discrimination in education is contrary to public policy. Racially discriminatory educational institutions cannot be viewed as conferring a public benefit within the "charitable" concept discussed earlier, or within the Congressional intent underlying § 170 and § 501(c)(3).

C

. . . .

D

The actions of Congress since 1970 leave no doubt that the IRS reached the correct conclusion in exercising its authority. It is, of course, not unknown for independent agencies or the Executive Branch to misconstrue the intent of a statute; Congress can and often does correct such misconceptions, if the courts have not done so. Yet for a dozen years Congress has been made aware—acutely aware—of the IRS rulings of 1970 and 1971. As we noted earlier, few issues have been the subject of more vigorous and widespread debate and discussion in and out of Congress than those related to racial segregation in education. Sincere adherents advocating contrary views have ventilated the subject for well over three decades. Failure of Congress to modify the IRS rulings of 1970 and 1971, of which Congress was, by its own studies and by public discourse, constantly reminded, and Congress' awareness of the denial of tax-exempt status for racially discriminatory schools when enacting other and related legislation make out an unusually strong case of legislative acquiescence in and ratification by implication of the 1970 and 1971 rulings.

Ordinarily, and quite appropriately, courts are slow to attribute significance to the failure of Congress to act on particular legislation. We have observed that "unsuccessful attempts at legislation are not the best of guides to legislative intent." Here, however, we do not have an ordinary claim of legislative acquiescence. Only one month after the IRS announced its position in 1970, Congress held its first hearings on this precise issue. Exhaustive hearings have been held on the issue at various times since then. These include hearings in February 1982, after we granted review in this case.

Non-action by Congress is not often a useful guide, but the non-action here is significant. During the past 12 years there have been no fewer than 13 bills introduced to overturn the IRS interpretation of § 501(c)(3). Not one of these bills has emerged from any committee, although Congress has enacted numerous other amendments to § 501 during this same period, including an amendment to § 501(c)(3) itself. It is hardly conceivable that Congress—and in this setting, any Member of Congress—was not abundantly aware of what was going on. In view of its prolonged and acute awareness of so important an issue, Congress' failure to act on the bills proposed on this subject provides added support for concluding that Congress acquiesced in the IRS rulings of 1970 and 1971.

The evidence of Congressional approval of the policy embodied in Revenue Ruling 71–447 goes well beyond the failure of Congress to act on legislative proposals. Congress affirmatively manifested its acquiescence in the IRS policy when it enacted the present § 501(i) of the Code [in 1976]. That provision denies tax-exempt status to social clubs whose charters or policy statements provide for "discrimination against any person on the basis of race, color, or religion." Both the House and Senate committee reports on that bill articulated the national policy against granting tax exemptions to racially discriminatory private clubs.

Even more significant is the fact that both reports focus on this Court's affirmance of *Green v. Connally,* as having established that "discrimination on account of race is inconsistent with an *educational institution's* tax exempt status." These references in Congressional committee reports on an enactment denying tax exemptions to racially discriminatory private social clubs cannot be read other than as indicating approval of the standards applied to racially discriminatory private schools by the IRS subsequent to 1970, and specifically of Revenue Ruling 71–447.

JUSTICE REHNQUIST, dissenting.

The Court points out that there is a strong national policy in this country against racial discrimination. To the extent that the Court states that

Congress in furtherance of this policy could deny tax-exempt status to educational institutions that promote racial discrimination, I readily agree. But, unlike the Court, I am convinced that Congress simply has failed to take this action and, as this Court has said over and over again, regardless of our view on the propriety of Congress' failure to legislate we are not constitutionally empowered to act for them.

In approaching this statutory construction question the Court quite adeptly avoids the statute it is construing. This I am sure is no accident, for there is nothing in the language of § 501(c)(3) that supports the result obtained by the Court. Section 501(c)(3) provides tax-exempt status for:

"Corporations, and any community chest, fund, or foundation, organized and operated exclusively for religious, charitable, scientific, testing for public safety, literary, or educational purposes, or to foster national or international amateur sports competition (but only if no part of its activities involve the provision of athletic facilities or equipment), or for the prevention of cruelty to children or animals, no part of the net earnings of which inures to the benefit of any private shareholder or individual, no substantial part of the activities of which is carrying on propaganda, or otherwise attempting, to influence legislation (except as otherwise provided in subsection (h)), and which does not participate in, or intervene in (including the publishing or distributing of statements), any political campaign on behalf of any candidate for public office." 26 U.S.C. § 501(c)(3).

With undeniable clarity, Congress has explicitly defined the requirements for § 501(c)(3) status. An entity must be (1) a corporation, or community chest, fund, or foundation, (2) organized for one of the eight enumerated purposes, (3) operated on a nonprofit basis, and (4) free from involvement in lobbying activities and political campaigns. Nowhere is there to be found some additional, undefined public policy requirement.

The Court first seeks refuge from the obvious reading of § 501(c)(3) by turning to § 170 of the Internal Revenue Code which provides a tax deduction for contributions made to § 501(c)(3) organizations. In setting forth the general rule, § 170 states:

"There shall be allowed as a deduction any charitable contribution (as defined in subsection (c)) payment of which is made within the taxable year. A charitable contribution shall be allowable as a deduction only if verified under regulations prescribed by the Secretary." 26 U.S.C. § 170(a)(1).

The Court seizes the words "charitable contribution" and with little discussion concludes that "[o]n its face, therefore, § 170 reveals that Congress' intention was to provide tax benefits to organizations serving charitable purposes," intimating that this implies some unspecified common law charitable trust requirement.

The Court would have been well advised to look to subsection (c) where, as § 170(a)(1) indicates, Congress has defined a "charitable contribution":

"For purposes of this section, the term 'charitable contribution' means a contribution or gift to or for the use of . . . [a] corporation, trust, or community chest, fund, or foundation . . . organized and operated exclusively for religious, charitable, scientific, literary, or educational purposes, or to foster national or international amateur sports competition (but only if no part of its activities involve the provision of athletic facilities or equipment), or for the prevention of cruelty to children or animals; . . . no part of the net earnings of which inures to the benefit of any private shareholder or individual; and . . . which is not disqualified for tax exemption under section 501(c)(3) by reason of attempting to influence legislation, and which does not participate in, or intervene in (including the publishing or distributing of statements), any political campaign on behalf of any candidate for public office." 26 U.S.C. § 170(c).

Plainly, § 170(c) simply tracks the requirements set forth in § 501(c)(3). Since § 170 is no more than a mirror of § 501(c)(3) and, as the Court points out, § 170 followed § 501(c)(3) by more than two decades, it is at best of little usefulness in finding the meaning of § 501(c)(3).

Making a more fruitful inquiry, the Court next turns to the legislative history of § 501(c)(3) and finds that Congress intended in that statute to offer a tax benefit to organizations that Congress believed were providing a public benefit. I certainly agree. But then the Court leaps to the conclusion that this history is proof Congress intended that an organization seeking § 501(c)(3) status "must fall within a category specified in that section *and must demonstrably serve and be in harmony with the public interest.*" To the contrary, I think that the legislative history of § 501(c)(3) unmistakably makes clear that *Congress has decided* what organizations are serving a public purpose and providing a public benefit within the meaning of § 501(c)(3) and has clearly set forth in § 501(c)(3) the characteristics of such organizations. In fact, there are few examples which better illustrate Congress' effort to define and redefine the requirements of a legislative act.

The first general income tax law was passed by Congress in the form of the Tariff Act of 1894. A provision of that Act provided an exemption for "corporations, companies, or associations organized and conducted solely for charitable, religious, or educational purposes." The income tax portion of the 1894 Act was held unconstitutional by this Court, but a similar exemption appeared in the Tariff Act of 1909 which imposed a tax on corporate income. The 1909 Act provided an exemption for "any corporation or association organized and operated exclusively for religious, charitable, or educational purposes, no part of the net income of which inures to the benefit of any private stockholder or individual."

With the ratification of the Sixteenth Amendment, Congress again turned its attention to an individual income tax with the Tariff Act of 1913. And again, in the direct predecessor of § 501(c)(3), a tax exemption was provided for "any corporation or association organized and operated exclusively for religious, charitable, scientific, or educational purposes, no part of the net income of which inures to the benefit of any private stockholder or individual." In subsequent acts Congress continued to broaden the list of exempt purposes. The Revenue Act of 1918 added an exemption for corporations or associations organized "for the prevention of cruelty to children or animals." The Revenue Act of 1921 expanded the groups to which the exemption applied to include "any community chest, fund, or foundation" and added "literary" endeavors to the list of exempt purposes. The exemption remained unchanged in the Revenue Acts of 1924, 1926, 1928, and 1932. In the Revenue Act of 1934 Congress added the requirement that no substantial part of the activities of any exempt organization can involve the carrying on of "propaganda" or "attempting to influence legislation." Again, the exemption was left unchanged by the Revenue Acts of 1936 and 1938.

The tax laws were overhauled by the Internal Revenue Code of 1939, but this exemption was left unchanged. When the 1939 Code was replaced with the Internal Revenue Code of 1954, the exemption was adopted in full in the present § 501(c)(3) with the addition of "testing for public safety" as an exempt purpose and an additional restriction that tax-exempt organizations could not "participate in, or intervene in (including the publishing or distributing of statements), any political campaign on behalf of any candidate for public office." Then in 1976 the statute was again amended adding to the purposes for which an exemption would be authorized, "to foster national or international amateur sports competition," provided the activities did not involve the provision of athletic facilities or equipment.

One way to read the opinion handed down by the Court today leads to the conclusion that this long and arduous refining process of § 501(c)(3) was certainly a waste of time, for when enacting the original 1894 statute Congress intended to adopt a common law term of art, and intended that this term of art carry with it all of the common law baggage which defines it. Such a view, however, leads also to the unsupportable idea that Congress has spent almost a century adding illustrations simply to clarify an already defined common law term.

Another way to read the Court's opinion leads to the conclusion that even though Congress has set forth *some* of the requirements of a § 501(c)(3) organization, it intended that the IRS additionally require that organizations meet a higher standard of public interest, not stated by Congress, but to be determined and defined by the IRS and the courts. This view I find equally unsupportable. Almost a century of statutory history proves that Congress itself intended to decide what § 501(c)(3) requires. Congress has expressed its decision in the plainest of terms in § 501(c)(3) by providing that tax-exempt status is to be given to any corporation, or community chest, fund, or foundation that is organized for one of the eight enumerated purposes, operated on a nonprofit basis, and uninvolved in lobbying activities or political campaigns. The IRS certainly is empowered to adopt regulations for the enforcement of these specified requirements, and the courts have authority to resolve challenges to the IRS's exercise of this power, but Congress has left it to neither the IRS nor the courts to select or add to the requirements of § 501(c)(3).

The Court suggests that unless its new requirement be added to § 501(c)(3), nonprofit organizations formed to teach pickpockets and terrorists would necessarily acquire tax exempt status. Since the Court does not challenge the characterization of *petitioners* as "educational" institutions within the meaning of § 501(c)(3), and in fact states several times in the course of its opinion that petitioners *are* educational institutions, it is difficult to see how this argument advances the Court's reasoning for disposing of petitioners' cases.

. . . .

Prior to 1970, when the charted course was abruptly changed, the IRS had continuously interpreted § 501(c)(3) and its predecessors in accordance with the view I have expressed above. This, of course, is of considerable significance in determining the intended meaning of the statute.

In 1970 the IRS was sued by parents of black public school children seeking to enjoin the IRS from according tax-exempt status under § 501(c)(3) to private schools in Mississippi that discriminated against blacks. The IRS answered, consistent with its long standing position, by maintaining a lack of authority to deny the tax-exemption if the schools met the specified requirements of § 501(c)(3). Then "[i]n the midst of this litigation," and in the face of a preliminary injunction, the IRS changed its position and adopted the view of the plaintiffs.

Following the close of the litigation, the IRS published its new position in Revenue Ruling 71–447, stating that "a school asserting a right to the benefits provided for in section 501(c)(3) of the Code as being organized and operated exclusively for educational purposes must be a common law charity in order to be exempt under that section." The IRS then concluded that a school that promotes racial discrimination violates public policy and therefore cannot qualify as a common law charity. The circumstances under which this change in interpretation was made suggest that it is entitled to very little deference. But even if the circumstances were different, the latter-day wisdom of the IRS has no basis in § 501(c)(3).

Perhaps recognizing the lack of support in the statute itself, or in its history, for the 1970 IRS change in interpretation, the Court finds that "[t]he actions of Congress since 1970 leave no doubt that the IRS reached the correct conclusion in exercising its authority," concluding that there is "an unusually strong case of legislative acquiescence in and ratification by implication of the 1970 and 1971 rulings." The Court relies first on several bills introduced to overturn the IRS interpretation of § 501(c)(3). But we have said before, and it is equally applicable here, that this type of congressional inaction is of virtually no weight in determining legislative intent. These bills and related hearings indicate little more than that a vigorous debate has existed in Congress concerning the new IRS position.

The Court next asserts that "Congress affirmatively manifested its acquiescence in the IRS policy when it enacted the present § 501(i) of the Code," a provision that "denies tax-exempt status to social clubs whose charters or policy statements provide for" racial discrimination. Quite to the contrary, it seems to me that in § 501(i) Congress showed that when it wants to add a requirement prohibiting racial discrimination to one of the tax-benefit provisions, it is fully aware of how to do it.

. . . .

This Court continuously has been hesitant to find ratification through inaction. This is especially true where such a finding "would result in a construction of the statute which not only is at odds with the language of the section in question and the pattern of the statute taken as a whole, but also is extremely far reaching in terms of the virtually untrammeled and unreviewable power it would vest in a regulatory agency." Few cases would call for more caution in finding ratification by acquiescence than the present one. The new IRS interpretation is not only far less than a long standing administrative policy, it is at odds with a position maintained by the IRS, and unquestioned by Congress, for several decades prior to 1970. The interpretation is unsupported by the statutory language, it is unsupported by legislative history, the interpretation has lead to considerable controversy in and out of Congress, and the interpretation gives to the IRS a broad power which until now Congress had kept for itself. Where in addition to these circumstances Congress has shown time and time again that it is ready to enact positive legislation to change the tax code when it desires, this Court has no business finding that Congress has adopted the new IRS position by failing to enact legislation to reverse it.

I have no disagreement with the Court's finding that there is a strong national policy in this country opposed to racial discrimination. I agree with the Court that Congress has the power to further this policy by denying § 501(c)(3) status to organizations that practice racial discrimination. But as of yet Congress has failed to do so. Whatever the reasons for the failure, this Court should not legislate for Congress.

. . . .

3. ADMINISTRATIVE AGENCY INTERPRETATIONS

In many cases, the courts are not the first governmental bodies called upon to authoritatively interpret and apply statutes. Often, these tasks first fall upon the agencies that are given the responsibility to implement a statutory scheme. We have already seen some examples of administrative agencies interpreting statutes. Think back to the *Babbitt* case, in which the agency interpreted the word "harm" to include habitat modification. Can you identify any other cases we have studied in which an agency has interpreted a statute in order to implement it?

Indeed, administrative agencies wield enormous lawmaking and policymaking power in our modern legal system. Nearly any complex statutory scheme you can think of is administered by an administrative agency: tax law, labor law, environmental law, immigration, broadcasting, transportation; the list goes on. It is worth your while to take an administrative law course, which focuses on the myriad ways that agencies make law and policy and the degree to which courts and legislatures impose constraints on agencies.

Why do you think that Congress delegates so much power to agencies? For example, why didn't Congress define "harm" itself? For that matter, why does an agency, rather than Congress, decide what must be included in school lunches? Can you think of some potential problems with delegating so much authority to agencies?

Because administrative agencies must often interpret laws in order to implement them, by the time a case gets to a court, the question is often whether the administrative agency properly interpreted the statute.

In this section, we consider what deference, if any, courts should give to administrative agency interpretations. The leading cases, which are included below, are the *Skidmore*, *Chevron*, and *Mead* cases. They establish the basic framework for answering this question and are among the most-cited cases in judicial and scholarly literature. You should be aware, however, that there are many other cases that tweak this framework for specific contexts.

Before reading these cases, see if you can come up with reasons that the courts should or should not defer to agency interpretations.

SKIDMORE V. SWIFT & CO.
323 U.S. 134 (1944)

As you read this case, consider these questions:

- What statutory term did the agency interpret?

- What interpretation did the agency give the statute?

- What reasons does the Court give for deferring to the agency?

- How much deference does the Court give to the agency? In other words, what is the *Skidmore* test?

- Why doesn't the Court give more deference to the agency?

- If you want to challenge an agency interpretation, what should you argue under the *Skidmore* test?

MR. JUSTICE JACKSON delivered the opinion of the Court.

Seven employees of the Swift and Company packing plant at Fort Worth, Texas, brought an action under the Fair Labor Standards Act to recover overtime, liquidated damages, and attorneys' fees, totalling approximately $77,000. The District Court rendered judgment denying this claim wholly, and the Circuit Court of Appeals for the Fifth Circuit affirmed.

It is not denied that the daytime employment of these persons was working time within the Act. Two were engaged in general fire hall duties and maintenance of fire-fighting equipment of the Swift plant. The others operated elevators or acted as relief men in fire duties. They worked from 7:00 a.m. to 3:30 p.m., with a half-hour lunch period, five days a week. They were paid weekly salaries.

Under their oral agreement of employment, however, petitioners undertook to stay in the fire hall on the Company premises, or within hailing distance, three and a half to four nights a week. This involved no task except to answer alarms, either because of fire or because the sprinkler was set off for some other reason. No fires occurred during the period in issue, the alarms were rare, and the time required for their answer rarely exceeded an hour. For each alarm answered the employees were paid in addition to their fixed compensation an agreed amount, fifty cents at first, and later sixty-four cents. The Company provided a brick fire hall equipped with steam heat and air-conditioned rooms. It provided sleeping quarters, a pool table, a domino table, and a radio. The men used their time in sleep or amusement as they saw fit, except that they were required to stay in or close by the fire hall and be ready to respond to alarms. It is stipulated that 'they agreed to remain in the fire hall and stay in it or within hailing distance, subject to call, in event of fire or other casualty, but were not required to perform any specific tasks during these periods of time, except in answering alarms.' . . . It said, however, as a 'conclusion of law' that 'the time plaintiffs spent in the fire hall subject to call to answer fire alarms does not constitute hours worked, for which overtime compensation is due them under the Fair Labor Standards Act, as interpreted by the Administrator and the Courts,' and in its opinion observed, 'of course we know pursuing such pleasurable occupations or performing such personal chores does not constitute work.' The Circuit Court of Appeals affirmed.

. . . . [W]e hold that no principle of law found either in the statute or in Court decisions precludes waiting time from also being working time. We have not attempted to, and we cannot, lay down a legal formula to resolve cases so varied in their facts as are the many situations in which employment involves waiting time. Whether in a concrete case such time falls within or without the Act is a question of fact to be resolved by appropriate findings of the trial court. This involves scrutiny and construction of the agreements between the particular parties, appraisal of their practical construction of the working agreement by conduct, consideration of the nature of the service, and its relation to the waiting time, and all of the surrounding circumstances. Facts may show that the employee was engaged to wait, or they may show that he waited to be engaged. His compensation may cover both waiting and task, or only performance of the task itself. Living quarters may in some situations be furnished as a facility of the task and in another as a part of its compensation. The law does not impose an arrangement upon the parties. It imposes upon the courts the task of finding what the arrangement was.

We do not minimize the difficulty of such an inquiry where the arrangements of the parties have not contemplated the problem posed by the statute. But it does not differ in nature or in the standards to guide judgment from that which frequently confronts courts where they must find retrospectively the effect of contracts as to matters which the parties failed to anticipate or explicitly to provide for.

Congress did not utilize the services of an administrative agency to find facts and to determine in the first instance whether particular cases fall within or without the Act. Instead, it put this responsibility on the courts. But it did create the office of Administrator, impose upon him a variety of duties, endow him with powers to inform himself of conditions in industries and employments subject to the Act, and put on him the duties of bringing injunction actions to restrain violations. Pursuit of his duties has accumulated a considerable experience in the problems of ascertaining working time in employments involving periods of inactivity and a knowledge of the customs prevailing in reference to their solution. From these he is obliged to reach conclusions as to conduct without the law, so that he should seek injunctions to stop it, and that within the law, so that he has no call to interfere. He has set forth his views of the application of the Act under different circumstances in an interpretative bulletin and in informal rulings. They provide a practical guide to employers and employees as to how the office representing the public interest in its enforcement will seek to apply it.

The Administrator thinks the problems presented by inactive duty require a flexible solution, rather than the all-in or all-out rules respectively urged by the parties in this case, and his Bulletin endeavors to suggest standards and examples to guide in particular situations. In some occupations, it says, periods of inactivity are not properly counted as working time even though the employee is subject to call. Examples are an operator of a small telephone exchange where the switchboard is in her home and she ordinarily gets several hours of uninterrupted sleep each night; or a pumper of a stripper well or watchman of a lumber camp during the off season, who may be on duty twenty-four hours a day but ordinarily 'has a normal night's sleep, has ample time in which to eat his meals, and has a certain amount of time for relaxation and entirely private pursuits.' Exclusion of all such hours the Administrator thinks may be justified. In general, the answer depends 'upon the degree to which the employee is free to engage in personal activities during periods of idleness when he is subject to call and the number of consecutive hours that the employee is subject to call without being required to perform active work.' 'Hours worked are not limited to the time spent in active labor but include time given by the employee to the employer.'

The facts of this case do not fall within any of the specific examples given, but the conclusion of the Administrator, as expressed in the brief amicus curiae, is that the general tests which he has suggested point to the exclusion of sleeping and eating time of these employees from the work-week and the inclusion of all other on-call time: although the employees were required to remain on the premises during the entire time, the evidence shows that they were very rarely interrupted in their normal sleeping and eating time, and these are pursuits of a purely private nature which would presumably occupy the employees' time whether they were on duty or not and which apparently could be pursued adequately and comfortably in the required circumstances; the rest of the time is different because there is nothing in the record to suggest that, even though pleasurably spent, it was spent in the ways the men would have chosen had they been free to do so.

There is no statutory provision as to what, if any, deference courts should pay to the Administrator's conclusions. And, while we have given them notice, we have had no occasion to try to prescribe their influence. The rulings of this Administrator are not reached as a result of hearing adversary proceedings in which he finds facts from evidence and reaches conclusions of law from findings of fact. They are not, of course, conclusive, even in the cases with which they directly deal, much less in those to which they apply only by analogy. They do not constitute an interpretation of the Act or a standard for judging factual situations which binds a district court's processes, as an authoritative pronouncement of a higher court might do. But the Administrator's policies are made in pursuance of official duty, based upon more specialized experience and broader investigations and information than is likely to come to a judge in a particular case. They do determine the policy which will guide applications for enforcement by injunction on behalf of the Government. Good administration of the Act and good judicial administration alike require that the standards of public enforcement and those for determining private rights shall be at variance only where justified by very good reasons. The fact that the Administrator's policies and standards are not reached by trial in adversary form does not mean that they are not entitled to respect. This

Court has long given considerable and in some cases decisive weight to Treasury Decisions and to interpretative regulations of the Treasury and of other bodies that were not of adversary origin.

We consider that the rulings, interpretations and opinions of the Administrator under this Act, while not controlling upon the courts by reason of their authority, do constitute a body of experience and informed judgment to which courts and litigants may properly resort for guidance. The weight of such a judgment in a particular case will depend upon the thoroughness evident in its consideration, the validity of its reasoning, its consistency with earlier and later pronouncements, and all those factors which give it power to persuade, if lacking power to control.

.... [I]n this case, although the District Court referred to the Administrator's Bulletin, its evaluation and inquiry were apparently restricted by its notion that waiting time may not be work, an understanding of the law which we hold to be erroneous. Accordingly, the judgment is reversed and the cause remanded for further proceedings consistent herewith.

CHEVRON U.S.A. INC. V. NATURAL RESOURCES DEFENSE COUNCIL, INC.

467 U.S. 837 (1984)

As you read this case, consider these questions:

- What is the "bubble" concept under review in the case?

- What is the *Chevron* two-step analysis? How does it differ from *Skidmore*?

- Why didn't the Court follow *Skidmore*?

- Is *Skidmore* dead law?

- In determining whether a statute is clear, what sources should a court consider? How is this different from any other case of statutory interpretation?

- Under what circumstances does *Chevron* apply?

- What reasons does the Court give for deferring to agency interpretations? Can you think of any other reasons?

- If you want to challenge an agency interpretation, what do you need to do in light of *Chevron*?

- Do you think that the *Chevron* test binds judges or limits their traditional powers? If so, how? If not, why not?

JUSTICE STEVENS delivered the opinion of the Court.

In the Clean Air Act Amendments of 1977 Congress enacted certain requirements applicable to States that had not achieved the national air quality standards established by the Environmental Protection Agency (EPA) pursuant to earlier legislation. The amended Clean Air Act required these "nonattainment" States to establish a permit program regulating "new or modified major stationary sources" of air pollution. Generally, a permit may not be issued for a new or modified major stationary source unless several stringent conditions are met. The EPA regulation promulgated to implement this permit requirement allows a State to adopt a plantwide definition of the term "stationary source." Under this definition, an existing plant that contains several pollution-emitting devices may install or modify one piece of equipment without meeting the permit conditions if the alteration will not increase the total emissions from the plant. The question presented by these cases is whether EPA's decision to allow States to treat all of the pollution-emitting devices within the same industrial grouping as though they were encased within a single "bubble" is based on a reasonable construction of the statutory term "stationary source."

. . . .

II

When a court reviews an agency's construction of the statute which it administers, it is confronted with two questions. First, always, is the question whether Congress has directly spoken to the precise question at issue. If the intent of Congress is clear, that is the end of the matter; for the court, as well as the agency, must give effect to the unambiguously expressed intent of Congress. If, however, the court determines Congress has not directly addressed the precise question at issue, the court does not simply impose its own construction on the statute, as would be necessary in the absence of an administrative interpretation. Rather, if the statute is silent or ambiguous with respect to the specific issue, the question for the court is whether the agency's answer is based on a permissible construction of the statute.

"The power of an administrative agency to administer a congressionally created . . . program necessarily requires the formulation of policy and the making of rules to fill any gap left, implicitly or explicitly, by Congress." If Congress has explicitly left a gap for the agency to fill, there is an express delegation of authority to the agency to elucidate a specific provision of the statute by regulation. Such legislative regulations are given controlling weight unless they are arbitrary, capricious, or manifestly contrary to the statute. Sometimes the legislative delegation to an agency on a particular question is implicit rather than explicit. In such a case, a court may not substitute its own construction of a statutory provision for a reasonable interpretation made by the administrator of an agency.

We have long recognized that considerable weight should be accorded to an executive department's construction of a statutory scheme it is entrusted to administer, and the principle of deference to administrative interpretations "has been consistently followed by this Court whenever decision as to the meaning or reach of a statute has involved reconciling conflicting policies, and a full understanding of the force of the statutory policy in the given situation has depended upon more than ordinary knowledge respecting the matters subjected to agency regulations." . . . If this choice represents a reasonable accommodation of conflicting policies that were committed to the agency's care by the statute, we should not disturb it unless it appears from the statute or its legislative history that the accommodation is not one that Congress would have sanctioned."

In light of these well-settled principles it is clear that the Court of Appeals misconceived the nature of its role in reviewing the regulations at issue. Once it determined, after its own examination of the legislation, that Congress did not actually have an intent regarding the applicability of the bubble concept to the permit program, the question before it was not whether in its view the concept is "inappropriate" in the general context of a program designed to improve air quality, but whether the Administrator's view that it is appropriate in the context of this particular program is a reasonable one. Based on the examination of the legislation and its history which follows, we agree with the Court of Appeals that Congress did not have a specific intention on the applicability of the bubble concept in these cases, and conclude that the EPA's use of that concept here is a reasonable policy choice for the agency to make.

III

In the 1950's and the 1960's Congress enacted a series of statutes designed to encourage and to assist the States in curtailing air pollution. The Clean Air Amendments of 1970 "sharply increased federal authority and responsibility in the continuing effort to combat air pollution," but continued to assign "primary responsibility for assuring air quality" to the several States. Section 109 of the 1970 Amendments directed the EPA to promulgate National Ambient Air Quality Standards (NAAQS's) and § 110 directed the States to develop plans (SIP's) to implement the standards within specified deadlines. In addition, § 111 provided that major new sources of pollution would be required to conform to technology-based performance standards; the EPA was directed to publish a list of categories of sources of pollution and to establish new source performance standards (NSPS) for each. Section 111(e) prohibited the operation of any new source in violation of a performance standard.

Section 111(a) defined the terms that are to be used in setting and enforcing standards of performance for new stationary sources. It provided:

"For purposes of this section:

. . . .

"(3) The term 'stationary source' means any building, structure, facility, or installation which emits or may emit any air pollutant."

. . . .

Statutory Language

The definition of the term "stationary source" in § 111(a)(3) refers to "any building, structure, facility, or installation" which emits air pollution. This definition is applicable only to the NSPS program by the express terms of the statute; the text of the statute does not make this definition applicable to the permit program. Petitioners therefore maintain that there is no statutory language even relevant to ascertaining the meaning of stationary source in the permit program aside from § 302(j), which defines the term "major stationary source." We disagree with petitioners on this point.

The definition in § 302(j) tells us what the word "major" means—a source must emit at least 100 tons of pollution to qualify—but it sheds virtually no light on the meaning of the term "stationary source." It does equate a source with a facility—a "major emitting facility" and a "major stationary source" are synonymous under § 302(j). The ordinary meaning of the term "facility" is some collection of integrated elements which has been designed and constructed to achieve some purpose. Moreover, it is certainly no affront to common English usage to take a reference to a major facility or a major source to connote an entire plant as opposed to its constituent parts. Basically, however, the language of § 302(j) simply does not compel any given interpretation of the term "source."

Respondents recognize that, and hence point to § 111(a)(3). Although the definition in that section is not literally applicable to the permit program, it sheds as much light on the meaning of the word "source" as anything in the statute. As respondents point out, use of the words "building, structure, facility, or installation," as the definition of source, could be read to impose the permit conditions on an individual building that is a part of a plant. A "word may have a character of its own not to be submerged by its association." On the other hand, the meaning of a word must be ascertained in the context of achieving particular objectives, and the words associated with it may indicate that the true meaning of the series is to convey a common idea. The language may reasonably be interpreted to impose the requirement on any discrete, but integrated, operation which pollutes. This gives meaning to all of the terms—a single building, not part of a larger operation, would be covered if it emits more than 100 tons of pollution, as would any facility, structure, or installation. Indeed, the language itself implies a "bubble concept" of sorts: each enumerated item would seem to be treated as if it were encased in a bubble. While respondents insist that each of these terms must be given a discrete meaning, they also argue that § 111(a)(3) defines "source" as that term is used in § 302(j). The latter section, however, equates a source with a facility, whereas the former defines "source" as a facility, among other items.

We are not persuaded that parsing of general terms in the text of the statute will reveal an actual intent of Congress. We know full well that this language is not dispositive; the terms are overlapping and the language is not precisely directed to the question of the applicability of a given term in the context of a larger operation. To the extent any congressional "intent" can be discerned from this language, it would appear that the listing of overlapping, illustrative terms was intended to enlarge, rather than to confine, the scope of the agency's power to regulate particular sources in order to effectuate the policies of the Act.

Legislative History

In addition, respondents argue that the legislative history and policies of the Act foreclose the plantwide definition, and that the EPA's interpretation is not entitled to deference because it represents a sharp break with prior interpretations of the Act.

Based on our examination of the legislative history, we agree with the Court of Appeals that it is unilluminating. The general remarks pointed to by respondents "were obviously not made with this narrow issue in mind and they cannot be said to demonstrate a Congressional desire. . . ." Respondents' argument based on the legislative history relies heavily on Senator Muskie's observation that a new source is subject to the LAER [lowest achievable emission rate] requirement. But the full statement is ambiguous and like the text of § 173 itself, this comment does not tell us what a new source is, much less that it is to have an inflexible definition. We find that the legislative history as a whole is silent on the precise issue before us. It is, however, consistent with the view that the EPA should have broad discretion in implementing the policies of the 1977 Amendments.

More importantly, that history plainly identifies the policy concerns that motivated the enactment; the plantwide definition is fully consistent with one of those concerns—the allowance of reasonable economic growth— and, whether or not we believe it most effectively implements the other, we must recognize that the EPA has advanced a reasonable explanation for its conclusion that the regulations serve the environmental objectives as well. Indeed, its reasoning is supported by the public record developed in the rulemaking process, as well as by certain private studies.

Our review of the EPA's varying interpretations of the word "source"—both before and after the 1977 Amendments—convinces us that the agency primarily responsible for administering this important legislation has consistently interpreted it flexibly—not in a sterile textual vacuum, but in the context of implementing policy decisions in a technical and complex arena. The fact that the agency has from time to time changed its interpretation of the term "source" does not, as respondents argue, lead us to conclude that no deference should be accorded the agency's interpretation of the statute. An initial agency interpretation is not instantly carved in stone. On the contrary, the agency, to engage in informed rulemaking, must consider varying interpretations and the wisdom of its policy on a continuing basis. Moreover, the fact that the agency has adopted different definitions in different contexts adds force to the argument that the definition itself is flexible, particularly since Congress has never indicated any disapproval of a flexible reading of the statute. . . .

Policy

The arguments over policy that are advanced in the parties' briefs create the impression that respondents are now waging in a judicial forum a specific policy battle which they ultimately lost in the agency and in the 32 jurisdictions opting for the "bubble concept," but one which was never waged in the Congress. Such policy arguments are more properly addressed to legislators or administrators, not to judges.

In these cases, the Administrator's interpretation represents a reasonable accommodation of manifestly competing interests and is entitled to deference: the regulatory scheme is technical and complex, the agency considered the matter in a detailed and reasoned fashion, and the decision involves reconciling conflicting policies. Congress intended to accommodate both interests, but did not do so itself on the level of specificity presented by these cases. Perhaps that body consciously desired the Administrator to strike the balance at this level, thinking that those with great expertise and charged with responsibility for administering the provision would be in a better position to do so; perhaps it simply did not consider the question at this level; and perhaps Congress was unable to forge a coalition on either side of the question, and those on each side decided to take their chances with the scheme devised by the agency. For judicial purposes, it matters not which of these things occurred.

Judges are not experts in the field, and are not part of either political branch of the Government. Courts must, in some cases, reconcile competing political interests, but not on the basis of the judges' personal policy preferences. In contrast, an agency to which Congress has delegated policy-making responsibilities may, within the limits of that delegation, properly rely upon the incumbent administration's views of wise policy to inform its judgments. While agencies are not directly accountable to the people, the Chief Executive is, and it is entirely appropriate for this political branch of the Government to make such policy choices—resolving the competing interests which Congress itself either inadvertently did not resolve, or intentionally left to be resolved by the agency charged with the administration of the statute in light of everyday realities.

When a challenge to an agency construction of a statutory provision, fairly conceptualized, really centers on the wisdom of the agency's policy, rather than whether it is a reasonable choice within a gap left open by Congress, the challenge must fail. In such a case, federal judges—who have no constituency—have a duty to respect legitimate policy choices made by those who do. The responsibilities for assessing the wisdom of such policy choices and resolving the struggle between competing views of the public interest are not judicial ones: "Our Constitution vests such responsibilities in the political branches."

We hold that the EPA's definition of the term "source" is a permissible construction of the statute which seeks to accommodate progress in reducing air pollution with economic growth. "The Regulations which the Administrator has adopted provide what the agency could allowably view as . . . [an] effective reconciliation of these twofold ends. . . ."

UNITED STATES V. MEAD CORP.
533 U.S. 218 (2001)

In the wake of *Chevron*, courts had to figure out when *Chevron* applies. Does it apply to *all* agency interpretations? Only some? If only some interpretations, which ones? This came to be known in the scholarly literature and in some judicial opinions as the "*Chevron* Step-0" issue.

The Supreme Court and the appellate courts gave conflicting signals over the years, and this was a heavily debated question. In the following case, the Supreme Court gave its most definitive ruling concerning when *Chevron* applies. As you read it, consider the following questions:

- In what circumstances will *Chevron* apply to an agency interpretation?

- Why does it not apply in this case?

- What level of deference applies instead? How should a court determine how to apply this lower level of deference?

- Does the agency have special expertise as to whether a day planner is a diary under the statute?

- If you were a lawyer faced with an unfavorable agency interpretation, how would the application *Mead*, *Chevron*, or *Skidmore* influence your advice to your client? How would argue to the courts that the agency interpretation should be rejected under each of these cases?

JUSTICE SOUTER delivered the opinion of the Court.

The question is whether a tariff classification ruling by the United States Customs Service deserves judicial deference. The Federal Circuit rejected Customs's invocation of *Chevron U.S.A. Inc. v. Natural Resources Defense Council, Inc.*, in support of such a ruling, to which it gave no deference. We agree that a tariff classification has no claim to judicial deference under *Chevron,* there being no indication that Congress intended such a ruling to carry the force of law, but we hold that under *Skidmore v. Swift & Co.,* the ruling is eligible to claim respect according to its persuasiveness.

I

A

Imports are taxed under the Harmonized Tariff Schedule of the United States (HTSUS). Title 19 U.S.C. § 1500(b) provides that Customs "shall, under rules and regulations prescribed by the Secretary [of the Treasury,] ... fix the final classification and rate of duty applicable to ... merchandise" under the HTSUS. Section 1502(a) provides that

"[t]he Secretary of the Treasury shall establish and promulgate such rules and regulations not inconsistent with the law (including regulations establishing procedures for the issuance of binding rulings prior to the entry of the merchandise concerned), and may disseminate such information as may be necessary to secure a just, impartial, and uniform appraisement of imported merchandise and the classification and assessment of duties thereon at the various ports of entry."

The Secretary provides for tariff rulings before the entry of goods by regulations authorizing "ruling letters" setting tariff classifications for particular imports. A ruling letter

"represents the official position of the Customs Service with respect to the particular transaction or issue described therein and is binding on all Customs Service personnel in accordance with the provisions of this section until modified or revoked. In the absence of a change of practice or other modification or revocation which affects the principle of the ruling set forth in the ruling letter, that principle may be cited as authority in the disposition of transactions involving the same circumstances."

After the transaction that gives it birth, a ruling letter is to "be applied only with respect to transactions involving articles identical to the sample submitted with the ruling request or to articles whose description is identical to the description set forth in the ruling letter." As a general matter, such a letter is "subject to modification or revocation without notice to any person, except the person to whom the letter was addressed," and the regulations consequently provide that "no other person should rely on the ruling letter or assume that the principles of that ruling will be applied in connection with any transaction other than the one described in the letter." Since ruling letters respond to transactions of the moment, they are not subject to notice and comment before being issued, may be published but need only be made "available for public inspection," and, at the time this action arose, could be modified without notice and comment under most circumstances. A broader notice-and-comment requirement for modification of prior rulings was added by statute in 1993, and took effect after this case arose.

Any of the 46 port-of-entry Customs offices may issue ruling letters, and so may the Customs Headquarters Office, in providing "[a]dvice or guidance as to the interpretation or proper application of the Customs and related laws with respect to a specific Customs transaction [which] may be requested by Customs Service field offices . . . at any time, whether the transaction is prospective, current, or completed." Most ruling letters contain little or no reasoning, but simply describe goods and state the appropriate category and tariff. A few letters, like the Headquarters ruling at issue here, set out a rationale in some detail.

B

Respondent, the Mead Corporation, imports "day planners," three-ring binders with pages having room for notes of daily schedules and phone numbers and addresses, together with a calendar and suchlike. The tariff schedule on point falls under the HTSUS heading for "[r]egisters, account books, notebooks, order books, receipt books, letter pads, memorandum pads, diaries and similar articles," which comprises two subcategories. Items in the first, "[d]iaries, notebooks and address books, bound; memorandum pads, letter pads and similar articles," were subject to a tariff of 4.0% at the time in controversy. Objects in the second, covering "[o]ther" items, were free of duty.

Between 1989 and 1993, Customs repeatedly treated day planners under the "other" HTSUS subheading. In January 1993, however, Customs changed its position, and issued a Headquarters ruling letter classifying Mead's day planners as "Diaries, . . . bound" subject to tariff under subheading 4820.10.20. That letter was short on explanation, but after Mead's protest, Customs Headquarters issued a new letter, carefully reasoned but never published, reaching the same conclusion. This letter considered two definitions of "diary" from the Oxford English Dictionary, the first covering a daily journal of the past day's events, the second a book including " 'printed dates for daily memoranda and jottings; also . . . calendars. . . .' " Customs concluded that "diary" was not confined to the first, in part because the broader definition reflects commercial usage and hence the "commercial identity of these items in the marketplace." As for the definition of "bound," Customs concluded that HTSUS was not referring to "bookbinding," but to a less exact sort of fastening described in the Harmonized Commodity Description and Coding System Explanatory Notes to Heading 4820, which spoke of binding by " 'reinforcements or fittings of metal, plastics, etc.' "

. . . .

We granted certiorari in order to consider the limits of *Chevron* deference owed to administrative practice in applying a statute. We hold that administrative implementation of a particular statutory provision qualifies for *Chevron* deference when it appears that Congress delegated authority to the agency generally to make rules carrying the force of law, and that the agency interpretation claiming deference was promulgated in the exercise of that authority. Delegation of such authority may be shown in a variety of ways, as by an agency's power to engage in adjudication or notice-and-comment rulemaking, or by some other indication of a comparable congressional intent. The Customs ruling at issue here fails to qualify, although the possibility that it deserves some deference under *Skidmore* leads us to vacate and remand.

II

A

When Congress has "explicitly left a gap for an agency to fill, there is an express delegation of authority to the agency to elucidate a specific provision of the statute by regulation," and any ensuing regulation is binding in the courts unless procedurally defective, arbitrary or capricious in substance, or manifestly contrary to the statute. But whether or not they enjoy any express delegation of authority on a particular question, agencies charged with applying a statute necessarily make all sorts of interpretive choices, and while not all of those choices bind judges to follow them, they certainly may influence courts facing questions the agencies have already answered. "[T]he well-reasoned views of the agencies implementing a statute 'constitute a body of experience and informed judgment to which courts and litigants may properly resort for guidance.' " The fair measure of deference to an agency administering its own statute has been understood to vary with circumstances, and courts have looked to the degree of the agency's care, its consistency, formality, and relative expertness, and to the persuasiveness of the agency's position. The approach has produced a spectrum of judicial responses, from great respect at one end to near indifference at the other. Justice Jackson summed things up in *Skidmore v. Swift & Co.*:

"The weight [accorded to an administrative] judgment in a particular case will depend upon the thoroughness evident in its consideration, the validity of its reasoning, its consistency with earlier and later pronouncements, and all those factors which give it power to persuade, if lacking power to control."

Since 1984, we have identified a category of interpretive choices distinguished by an additional reason for judicial deference. This Court in *Chevron* recognized that Congress not only engages in express delegation of specific interpretive authority, but that "[s]ometimes the legislative delegation to an agency on a particular question is implicit." Congress, that is, may not have expressly delegated authority or responsibility to implement a particular provision or fill a particular gap. Yet it can still be apparent from the agency's generally conferred authority and other statutory circumstances that Congress would expect the agency to be able to speak with the force of law when it addresses ambiguity in the statute or fills a space in the enacted law, even one about which "Congress did not actually have an intent" as to a particular result. When circumstances implying such an expectation exist, a reviewing court has no business rejecting an agency's exercise of its generally conferred authority to resolve a particular statutory ambiguity simply because the agency's chosen resolution seems unwise, but is obliged to accept the agency's position if Congress has not previously spoken to the point at issue and the agency's interpretation is reasonable.

We have recognized a very good indicator of delegation meriting *Chevron* treatment in express congressional authorizations to engage in the process of rulemaking or adjudication that produces regulations or rulings for which deference is claimed. It is fair to assume generally that Congress contemplates administrative action with the effect of law when it provides for a relatively formal administrative procedure tending to foster the fairness and deliberation that should underlie a pronouncement of such force. Thus, the overwhelming number of our cases applying *Chevron* deference have reviewed the fruits of notice-and-comment rulemaking or formal adjudication. That said, and as significant as notice-and-comment is in pointing to *Chevron* authority, the want of that procedure here does not decide the case, for we have sometimes found reasons for *Chevron* deference even when no such administrative formality was required and none was afforded. The fact that the tariff classification here was not a product of such formal process does not alone, therefore, bar the application of *Chevron*.

There are, nonetheless, ample reasons to deny *Chevron* deference here. The authorization for classification rulings, and Customs's practice in making them, present a case far removed not only from notice-and-comment process, but from any other circumstances reasonably suggesting that Congress ever thought of classification rulings as deserving the deference claimed for them here.

B

No matter which angle we choose for viewing the Customs ruling letter in this case, it fails to qualify under *Chevron*. On the face of the statute, to begin with, the terms of the congressional delegation give no indication that Congress meant to delegate authority to Customs to issue classification rulings with the force of law. We are not, of course, here making any global statement about Customs's authority, for it is true that the general rulemaking power conferred on Customs authorizes some regulation with the force of law, or "legal norms," as we put it [elsewhere]. It is true as well that Congress had classification rulings in mind when it explicitly authorized, in a parenthetical, the issuance of "regulations establishing procedures for the issuance of binding rulings prior to the entry of the merchandise concerned." The reference to binding classifications does not, however, bespeak the legislative type of activity that would naturally bind more than the parties to the ruling, once the goods classified are admitted into this country. And though the statute's direction to disseminate "information" necessary to "secure" uniformity seems to assume that a ruling may be precedent in later transactions, precedential value alone does not add up to *Chevron* entitlement; interpretive rules may sometimes function as precedents, and they enjoy no *Chevron* status as a class. In any event, any precedential claim of a classification ruling is counterbalanced by the provision for independent review of Customs classifications by the [Court of International Trade]; the scheme for CIT review includes a provision that treats classification rulings on par with the Secretary's rulings on "valuation, rate of duty, marking, restricted merchandise, entry requirements, drawbacks, vessel repairs, or similar matters." It is hard to imagine a congressional understanding more at odds with the *Chevron* regime.

It is difficult, in fact, to see in the agency practice itself any indication that Customs ever set out with a lawmaking pretense in mind when it undertook to make classifications like these. Customs does not generally engage in notice-and-comment practice when issuing them, and their treatment by the agency makes it clear that a letter's binding character as a ruling stops short of third parties; Customs has regarded a classification as conclusive only as between itself and the importer to whom it was issued, and even then only until Customs has given advance notice of intended change. Other importers are in fact warned against assuming any right of detrimental reliance.

Indeed, to claim that classifications have legal force is to ignore the reality that 46 different Customs offices issue 10,000 to 15,000 of them each year. Any suggestion that rulings intended to have the force of law are being churned out at a rate of 10,000 a year at an agency's 46 scattered offices is simply self-refuting. Although the circumstances are less startling here, with a Headquarters letter in issue, none of the relevant statutes recognizes this category of rulings as separate or different from others; there is thus no indication that a more potent delegation might have been understood as going to Headquarters even when Headquarters provides developed reasoning, as it did in this instance.

Nor do the amendments to the statute made effective after this case arose disturb our conclusion. The new law requires Customs to provide notice-and-comment procedures only when modifying or revoking a prior classification ruling or modifying the treatment accorded to substantially identical transactions; and under its regulations, Customs sees itself obliged to provide notice-and-comment procedures only when "changing a practice" so as to produce a tariff increase, or in the imposition of a restriction or prohibition, or when Customs Headquarters determines that "the matter is of sufficient importance to involve the interests of domestic industry." The statutory changes reveal no new congressional objective of treating classification decisions generally as rulemaking with force of law, nor do they suggest any intent to create a *Chevron* patchwork of classification rulings, some with force of law, some without.

In sum, classification rulings are best treated like "interpretations contained in policy statements, agency manuals, and enforcement guidelines." They are beyond the *Chevron* pale.

C

To agree with the Court of Appeals that Customs ruling letters do not fall within *Chevron* is not, however, to place them outside the pale of any deference whatever. *Chevron* did nothing to eliminate *Skidmore*'s holding that an agency's interpretation may merit some deference whatever its form, given the "specialized experience and broader investigations and information" available to the agency, and given the value of uniformity in its administrative and judicial understandings of what a national law requires.

There is room at least to raise a *Skidmore* claim here, where the regulatory scheme is highly detailed, and Customs can bring the benefit of specialized experience to bear on the subtle questions in this case: whether the daily planner with room for brief daily entries falls under "diaries," when diaries are grouped with "notebooks and address books, bound; memorandum pads, letter pads and similar articles," and whether a planner with a ring binding should qualify as "bound," when a binding may be typified by a book, but also may have "reinforcements or fittings of metal, plastics, etc." A classification ruling in this situation may therefore at least seek a respect proportional to its "power to persuade." Such a ruling may surely claim the merit of its writer's thoroughness, logic, and expertness, its fit with prior interpretations, and any other sources of weight.

. . . .

[Justice Scalia's lengthy dissent is omitted. Justice Scalia would apply *Chevron* deference much more broadly.]

KING V. BURWELL
135 S.Ct. 2480

In 2015 the Supreme Court heard a second challenge centered on the Affordable Care Act (a.k.a. Obamacare). The plaintiffs challenged an administrative agency regulation that interpreted a provision of the statute.

As you read the opinions in the case, consider these questions:

- What is the interpretive question in this case?

- If you were to apply *Chevron*, how would you think the Court should consider the question?

- Why does Justice Roberts say *Chevron* does not apply?

- What practical difference would it make in this case if Justice Roberts had applied *Chevron*?

- What theory of interpretation does Justice Roberts seem to adopt?

- What textual, contextual, and legislative history arguments does Justice Roberts make?

- Are you surprised by Justice Scalia's dissent? Are you persuaded?

- Nearly all observers would agree that what really happened here is that the legislature made a mistake of sloppy drafting. Why might that have happened? Should it matter to the Justices? Why doesn't either opinion candidly admit that sloppy drafting was the cause of problem?

CHIEF JUSTICE ROBERTS delivered the opinion of the Court.

The Patient Protection and Affordable Care Act adopts a series of interlocking reforms designed to expand coverage in the individual health insurance market. First, the Act bars insurers from taking a person's health into account when deciding whether to sell health insurance or how much to charge. Second, the Act generally requires each person to maintain insurance coverage or make a payment to the Internal Revenue Service. And third, the Act gives tax credits to certain people to make insurance more affordable.

In addition to those reforms, the Act requires the creation of an "Exchange" in each State—basically, a marketplace that allows people to compare and purchase insurance plans. The Act gives each State the opportunity to establish its own Exchange, but provides that the Federal Government will establish the Exchange if the State does not.

This case is about whether the Act's interlocking reforms apply equally in each State no matter who establishes the State's Exchange. Specifically, the question presented is whether the Act's tax credits are available in States that have a Federal Exchange.

* * *

I. B.

First, the Act adopts the guaranteed issue and community rating requirements. The Act provides that "each health insurance issuer that offers health insurance coverage in the individual . . . market in a State must accept every . . . individual in the State that applies for such coverage." 42 U.S.C. § 300gg–1(a). The Act also bars insurers from charging higher premiums on the basis of a person's health. § 300gg.

Second, the Act generally requires individuals to maintain health insurance coverage or make a payment to the IRS. 26 U.S.C. § 5000A. Congress recognized that, without an incentive, "many individuals would wait to purchase health insurance until they needed care." 42 U.S.C. § 18091(2)(I). So Congress adopted a coverage requirement to "minimize this adverse selection and broaden the health insurance risk pool to include healthy individuals, which will lower health insurance premiums." In Congress's view, that coverage requirement was "essential to creating effective health insurance markets." Congress also provided an exemption from the coverage requirement for anyone who has to spend more than eight percent of his income on health insurance.

Third, the Act seeks to make insurance more affordable by giving refundable tax credits to individuals with household incomes between 100 percent and 400 percent of the federal poverty line. § 36B. Individuals who meet the Act's requirements may purchase insurance with the tax credits, which are provided in advance directly to the individual's insurer.

These three reforms are closely intertwined. As noted, Congress found that the guaranteed issue and community rating requirements would not work without the coverage requirement. And the coverage requirement would not work without the tax credits. The reason is that, without the tax credits, the cost of buying insurance would exceed eight percent of income for a large number of individuals, which would exempt them from the coverage requirement.

I. C.

In addition to those three reforms, the Act requires the creation of an "Exchange" in each State where people can shop for insurance, usually online. 42 U.S.C. § 18031(b)(1). An Exchange may be created in one of two ways. First, the Act provides that "[e]ach State shall . . . establish an American Health Benefit Exchange . . . for the State." *Ibid.* Second, if a State nonetheless chooses not to establish its own Exchange, the Act provides that the Secretary of Health and Human Services "shall . . . establish and operate such Exchange within the State." § 18041(c)(1).

The issue in this case is whether the Act's tax credits are available in States that have a Federal Exchange rather than a State Exchange. The Act initially provides that tax credits "shall be allowed" for any "applicable taxpayer." 26 U.S.C. § 36B(a). The Act then provides that the amount of the tax credit depends in part on whether the taxpayer has enrolled in an insurance plan through "an Exchange *established by the State* under section 1311 of the Patient Protection and Affordable Care Act 26 U.S.C. §§ 36B(b)-(c) (emphasis added).

The IRS addressed the availability of tax credits by promulgating a rule that made them available on both State and Federal Exchanges.

As relevant here, the IRS Rule provides that a taxpayer is eligible for a tax credit if he enrolled in an insurance plan through "an Exchange," 26 CFR § 1.36B–2 (2013), which is defined as "an Exchange serving the individual market . . . regardless of whether the Exchange is established and operated by a State . . . or by HHS," 45 CFR § 155.20 (2014). At this point, 16 States and the District of Columbia have established their own Exchanges; the other 34 States have elected to have HHS do so.

I. D.

Petitioners are four individuals who live in Virginia, which has a Federal Exchange. They do not wish to purchase health insurance. In their view, Virginia's Exchange does not qualify as "an Exchange established by the State under [42 U.S.C. § 18031]," so they should not receive any tax credits. That would make the cost of buying insurance more than eight percent of their income, which would exempt them from the Act's coverage requirement.

Under the IRS Rule, however, Virginia's Exchange *would* qualify as "an Exchange established by the State under [42 U.S.C. § 18031]," so petitioners would receive tax credits. That would make the cost of buying insurance *less* than eight percent of petitioners' income, which would subject them to the Act's coverage requirement. The IRS Rule therefore requires petitioners to either buy health insurance they do not want, or make a payment to the IRS.

Petitioners challenged the IRS Rule in Federal District Court. The District Court dismissed the suit, holding that the Act unambiguously made tax credits available to individuals enrolled through a Federal Exchange. The Court of Appeals for the Fourth Circuit affirmed. The Fourth Circuit viewed the Act as "ambiguous and subject to at least two different interpretations." The court therefore deferred to the IRS's interpretation under *Chevron*.

II.

The Affordable Care Act addresses tax credits in what is now Section 36B of the Internal Revenue Code. Section 36B goes on to define the two italicized terms—"premium assistance amount" and "coverage month"— in part by referring to an insurance plan that is enrolled in through "an Exchange established by the State under 42 U.S.C. § 18031.

The parties dispute whether Section 36B authorizes tax credits for individuals who enroll in an insurance plan through a Federal Exchange. Petitioners argue that a Federal Exchange is not "an Exchange established by the State under 42 U.S.C. § 18031," and that the IRS Rule therefore contradicts Section 36B The Government responds that the IRS Rule is lawful because the phrase "an Exchange established by the State under 42 U.S.C. § 18031" should be read to include Federal Exchanges.

When analyzing an agency's interpretation of a statute, we often apply the two-step framework announced in *Chevron*. Under that framework, we ask whether the statute is ambiguous and, if so, whether the agency's interpretation is reasonable. This approach "is premised on the theory that a statute's ambiguity constitutes an implicit delegation from Congress to the agency to fill in the statutory gaps." "In extraordinary cases, however, there may be reason to hesitate before concluding that Congress has intended such an implicit delegation."

This is one of those cases. The tax credits are among the Act's key reforms, involving billions of dollars in spending each year and affecting the price of health insurance for millions of people. Whether those credits are available on Federal Exchanges is thus a question of deep "economic and political significance" that is central to this statutory scheme; had Congress wished to assign that question to an agency, it surely would have done so expressly. It is especially unlikely that Congress would have delegated this decision to the *IRS,* which has no expertise in crafting health insurance policy of this sort.

It is instead our task to determine the correct reading of Section 36B. If the statutory language is plain, we must enforce it according to its terms. But oftentimes the "meaning—or ambiguity—of certain words or phrases may only become evident when placed in context." So when deciding whether the language is plain, we must read the words "in their context and with a view to their place in the overall statutory scheme." Our duty, after all, is "to construe statutes, not isolated provisions."

II. A.

We begin with the text of Section 36B. As relevant here, Section 36B allows an individual to receive tax credits only if the individual enrolls in an insurance plan through "an Exchange established by the State under 42 U.S.C. § 18031." In other words, three things must be true: First, the individual must enroll in an insurance plan through "an Exchange." Second, that Exchange must be "established by the State." And third, that Exchange must be established "under 42 U.S.C. § 18031." We address each requirement in turn.

By using the phrase "such Exchange," Section 18041 instructs the Secretary to establish and operate the *same* Exchange that the State was directed to establish under Section 18031. See Black's Law Dictionary 1661 (10th ed. 2014) (defining "such" as "That or those; having just been mentioned"). In other words, State Exchanges and Federal Exchanges are equivalent—they must meet the same requirements, perform the same functions, and serve the same purposes. Although State and Federal Exchanges are established by different sovereigns, Sections 18031 and 18041 do not suggest that they differ in any meaningful way. A Federal Exchange therefore counts as "an Exchange" under Section 36B.

Second, we must determine whether a Federal Exchange is "established by the State" for purposes of Section 36B. At the outset, it might seem that a Federal Exchange cannot fulfill this requirement. After all, the Act defines "State" to mean "each of the 50 States and the District of Columbia"—a definition that does not include the Federal Government. 42 U.S.C. § 18024(d). But when read in context, "with a view to [its] place in the overall statutory scheme," the meaning of the phrase "established by the State" is not so clear.

After telling each State to establish an Exchange, Section 18031 provides that all Exchanges "shall make available qualified health plans to qualified individuals." 42 U.S.C. § 18031(d)(2)(A). Section 18032 then defines the term "qualified individual" in part as an individual who "resides in the State that established the Exchange. And that's a problem: If we give the phrase "the State that established the Exchange" its most natural meaning, there would be *no* "qualified individuals" on Federal

Exchanges. But the Act clearly contemplates that there will be qualified individuals on *every* Exchange. As we just mentioned, the Act requires all Exchanges to "make available qualified health plans to qualified individuals"—something an Exchange could not do if there were no such individuals.

This problem arises repeatedly throughout the Act. See, *e.g.,* § 18031(b)(2) (allowing a State to create "one Exchange . . . for providing . . . services to both qualified individuals and qualified small employers," rather than creating separate Exchanges for those two groups).

These provisions suggest that the Act may not always use the phrase "established by the State" in its most natural sense. Thus, the meaning of that phrase may not be as clear as it appears when read out of context.

Third, we must determine whether a Federal Exchange is established "under [42 U.S.C. § 18031]." This too might seem a requirement that a Federal Exchange cannot fulfill, because it is Section 18041 that tells the Secretary when to "establish and operate such Exchange." But here again, the way different provisions in the statute interact suggests otherwise.

The Act defines the term "Exchange" to mean "an American Health Benefit Exchange established under section 18031." If we import that definition into Section 18041, the Act tells the Secretary to "establish and operate such 'American Health Benefit Exchange established under section 18031.'" That suggests that Section 18041 authorizes the Secretary to establish an Exchange under Section 18031, not (or not only) under Section 18041. Otherwise, the Federal Exchange, by definition, would not be an "Exchange" at all.

This interpretation of "under 42 U.S.C. § 18031" fits best with the statutory context. All of the requirements that an Exchange must meet are in Section 18031, so it is sensible to regard all Exchanges as established under that provision. In addition, every time the Act uses the word "Exchange," the definitional provision requires that we substitute the phrase "Exchange established under section 18031." If Federal Exchanges were not established under Section 18031, therefore, literally none of the Act's requirements would apply to them.

The upshot of all this is that the phrase "an Exchange established by the State under [42 U.S.C. § 18031]" is properly viewed as ambiguous. The phrase may be limited in its reach to State Exchanges. But it is also possible that the phrase refers to *all* Exchanges—both State and Federal—at least for purposes of the tax credits. If a State chooses not to follow the directive in Section 18031 that it establish an Exchange, the Act tells the Secretary to establish "such Exchange." § 18041. And by using the words "such Exchange," the Act indicates that State and Federal Exchanges should be the same. But State and Federal Exchanges would differ in a fundamental way if tax credits were available only on State Exchanges—one type of Exchange would help make insurance more affordable by providing billions of dollars to the States' citizens; the other type of Exchange would not.

The conclusion that Section 36B is ambiguous is further supported by several provisions that assume tax credits will be available on both State and Federal Exchanges. For example, the Act requires all Exchanges to create outreach programs that must "distribute fair and impartial information concerning . . . the availability of premium tax credits under section 36B." The Act also requires all Exchanges to "establish and make available by electronic means a calculator to determine the actual cost of coverage after the application of any premium tax credit under section 36B." And the Act requires all Exchanges to report to the Treasury Secretary information about each health plan they sell, including the "aggregate amount of any advance payment of such credit," "[a]ny information . . . necessary to determine eligibility for, and the amount of, such credit," and any "[i]nformation necessary to determine whether a taxpayer has received excess advance payments." If tax credits were not available on Federal Exchanges, these provisions would make little sense.

Petitioners and the dissent respond that the words "established by the State" would be unnecessary if Congress meant to extend tax credits to both State and Federal Exchanges. The canon against surplusage is not an absolute rule. And specifically with respect to this Act, rigorous application of the canon does not seem a particularly useful guide to a fair construction of the statute.

The Affordable Care Act contains more than a few examples of inartful drafting. Congress wrote key parts of the Act behind closed doors, rather than through "the traditional legislative process." And Congress passed much of the Act using a complicated budgetary procedure known as "reconciliation," which limited opportunities for debate and amendment, and bypassed the Senate's normal 60-vote filibuster requirement. As a result, the Act does not reflect the type of care and deliberation that one might expect of such significant legislation.

Anyway, we "must do our best, bearing in mind the fundamental canon of statutory construction that the words of a statute must be read in their context and with a view to their place in the overall statutory scheme." After reading Section 36B along with other related provisions in the Act, we cannot conclude that the phrase "an Exchange established by the State under Section 18031" is unambiguous.

Given that the text is ambiguous, we must turn to the broader structure of the Act to determine the meaning of Section 36B. "A provision that may seem ambiguous in isolation is often clarified by the remainder of the statutory scheme . . . because only one of the permissible meanings produces a substantive effect that is compatible with the rest of the law." Here, the statutory scheme compels us to reject petitioners' interpretation because it would destabilize the individual insurance market in any State with a Federal Exchange, and likely create the very "death spirals" that Congress designed the Act to avoid. "We cannot interpret federal statutes to negate their own stated purposes."

Congress made the guaranteed issue and community rating requirements applicable in every State in the Nation. But those requirements only work when combined with the coverage requirement and the tax credits. So it stands to reason that Congress meant for those provisions to apply in every State as well.

Petitioners respond that Congress was not worried about the effects of withholding tax credits from States with Federal Exchanges because "Congress evidently believed it was offering states a deal they would not refuse." Congress may have been wrong about the States' willingness to establish their own Exchanges, petitioners continue, but that does not allow this Court to rewrite the Act to fix that problem.

The whole point of that provision is to create a federal fallback in case a State chooses not to establish its own Exchange. Contrary to petitioners' argument, Congress did not believe it was offering States a deal they would not refuse—it expressly addressed what would happen if a State *did* refuse the deal.

I. D.

Petitioners' arguments about the plain meaning of Section 36B are strong. But while the meaning of the phrase "an Exchange established by the State under 42 U.S.C. § 18031" may seem plain "when viewed in isolation," such a reading turns out to be "untenable in light of [the statute] as a whole. In this instance, the context and structure of the Act compel us to depart from what would otherwise be the most natural reading of the pertinent statutory phrase.

Reliance on context and structure in statutory interpretation is a "subtle business, calling for great wariness lest what professes to be mere rendering becomes creation and attempted interpretation of legislation becomes legislation itself." For the reasons we have given, however, such reliance is appropriate in this case, and leads us to conclude that Section 36B allows tax credits for insurance purchased on any Exchange created under the Act. Those credits are necessary for the Federal Exchanges to function like their State Exchange counterparts, and to avoid the type of calamitous result that Congress plainly meant to avoid.

The judgment of the United States Court of Appeals for the Fourth Circuit is

Affirmed.

JUSTICE SCALIA, with whom JUSTICE THOMAS and JUSTICE ALITO join, dissenting.

The Court holds that when the Patient Protection and Affordable Care Act says "Exchange established by the State" it means "Exchange established by the State or the Federal Government." That is of course quite absurd, and the Court's 21 pages of explanation make it no less so.

I

The Patient Protection and Affordable Care Act makes major reforms to the American health-insurance market. It provides, among other things, that every State "shall . . . establish an American Health Benefit Exchange"—a marketplace where people can shop for health-insurance plans. And it provides that if a State does not comply with this instruction, the Secretary of Health and Human Services must "establish and operate such Exchange within the State."

An individual has a coverage month only when he is covered by an insurance plan "that was enrolled in through an Exchange established by the State under [§ 18031]." And the law ties the size of the premium assistance amount to the premiums for health plans which cover the individual "and which were enrolled in through an Exchange established by the State under § 18031."

This case requires us to decide whether someone who buys insurance on an Exchange established by the Secretary gets tax credits. You would think the answer would be obvious—so obvious there would hardly be a need for the Supreme Court to hear a case about it. In order to receive any money under § 36B, an individual must enroll in an insurance plan through an "Exchange established by the State." The Secretary of Health and Human Services is not a State. So an Exchange established by the Secretary is not an Exchange established by the State—which means people who buy health insurance through such an Exchange get no money under § 36B.

Words no longer have meaning if an Exchange that is *not* established by a State is "established by the State." It is hard to come up with a clearer way to limit tax credits to state Exchanges than to use the words "established by the State." And it is hard to come up with a reason to include the words "by the State" other than the purpose of limiting credits to state Exchanges. "[T]he plain, obvious, and rational meaning of a statute is always to be preferred to any curious, narrow, hidden sense that nothing but the exigency of a hard case and the ingenuity and study of an acute and powerful intellect would discover." all the usual rules of interpretation, in short, the Government should lose this case. But normal rules of interpretation seem always to yield to the overriding principle of the present Court: The Affordable Care Act must be saved.

I wholeheartedly agree with the Court that sound interpretation requires paying attention to the whole law, not homing in on isolated words or even isolated sections. Context always matters. Let us not forget, however, *why* context matters: It is a tool for understanding the terms of the law, not an excuse for rewriting them.

Any effort to understand rather than to rewrite a law must accept and apply the presumption that lawmakers use words in "their natural and ordinary signification." Ordinary connotation does not always prevail, but the more unnatural the proposed interpretation of a law, the more compelling the contextual evidence must be to show that it is correct. Today's interpretation is not merely unnatural; it is unheard of. Who would ever have dreamt that "Exchange established by the State" means "Exchange established by the State *or the Federal Government*"? Little short of an express statutory definition could justify adopting this singular reading. Yet the only pertinent definition here provides that "State" means "each of the 50 States and the District of Columbia." Because the Secretary is neither one of the 50 States nor the District of Columbia, that definition positively contradicts the eccentric theory that an Exchange established by the Secretary has been established by the State.

Far from offering the overwhelming evidence of meaning needed to justify the Court's interpretation, other contextual clues undermine it at every turn. To begin with, other parts of the Act sharply distinguish between the establishment of an Exchange by a State and the establishment of an Exchange by the Federal Government. The States' authority to set up Exchanges comes from one provision; the Secretary's authority comes from an entirely different provision. Funding for States to establish Exchanges comes from one part of the law; funding for the Secretary to establish Exchanges comes from an entirely different part of the law. States generally run state-created Exchanges; the Secretary generally runs federally created Exchanges. And the Secretary's authority to set up an Exchange in a State depends upon the State's "*[f]ailure* to establish [an] Exchange." § 18041(c) (emphasis added). Provisions such as these destroy any pretense that a federal Exchange is in some sense also established by a State.

Reading the rest of the Act also confirms that, as relevant here, there are *only* two ways to set up an Exchange in a State: establishment by a State and establishment by the Secretary. So saying that an Exchange established by the Federal Government is "established by the State" goes beyond giving words bizarre meanings; it leaves the limiting phrase "by the State" with no operative effect at all. That is a stark violation of the elementary principle that requires an interpreter "to give effect, if possible, to every clause and word of a statute."

Making matters worse, the reader of the whole Act will come across a number of provisions beyond § 36B that refer to the establishment of Exchanges by States. Adopting the Court's interpretation means nullifying the term "by the State" not just once, but again and again throughout the Act. Consider for the moment only those parts of the Act that mention an "Exchange established by the State" in connection with tax credits:

- The formula for calculating the amount of the tax credit, as already explained, twice mentions "an Exchange established by the State." 26 U.S.C. § 36B(b)(2)(A), (c)(2)(A)(i).

- The Act directs States to screen children for eligibility for "[tax credits] under section 36B" and for "any other assistance or subsidies available for coverage obtained through" an "Exchange established by the State." 42 U.S.C. § 1396w–3(b)(1)(B)–(C).

- The Act requires "an Exchange established by the State" to use a "secure electronic interface" to determine eligibility for (among other things) tax credits.

- The Act authorizes "an Exchange established by the State" to make arrangements under which other state agencies "determine whether a State resident is eligible for [tax credits] under section 36B."

- The Act directs States to operate Web sites that allow anyone "who is eligible to receive [tax credits] under section 36B" to compare insurance plans offered through "an Exchange established by the State."

- One of the Act's provisions addresses the enrollment of certain children in health plans "offered through an Exchange established by the State" and then discusses the eligibility of these children for tax credits.

It is bad enough for a court to cross out "by the State" once. But seven times?

Congress did not, by the way, repeat "Exchange established by the State under § 18031" by rote throughout the Act. Quite the contrary, clause after clause of the law uses a more general term such as "Exchange" or "Exchange established under § 18031." It is common sense that any speaker who says "Exchange" some of the time, but "Exchange established by the State" the rest of the time, probably means something by the contrast.

The Court emphasizes that if a State does not set up an Exchange, the Secretary must establish "such Exchange." It claims that the word "such" implies that federal and state Exchanges are "the same." To see the error in this reasoning, one need only consider a parallel provision from our Constitution: "The Times, Places and Manner of holding Elections for Senators and Representatives, shall be prescribed in each State by the Legislature thereof; but the Congress may at any time by Law make or alter *such Regulations*." Art. I, § 4, cl. 1 Just as the Affordable Care Act directs States to establish Exchanges while allowing the Secretary to establish "such Exchange" as a fallback, the Elections Clause directs state legislatures to prescribe election regulations while allowing Congress to make "such Regulations" as a fallback. Would anybody refer to an election regulation made by Congress as a "regulation prescribed by the state legislature"? Would anybody say that a federal election law and a state election law are in all respects equivalent? Of course not. The word "such" does not help the Court one whit. The Court's argument also overlooks the rudimentary principle that a specific provision governs a general one. Even if it were true that the term "such Exchange" in § 18041(c) implies that federal and state Exchanges are the same in general, the term "established by the State" in § 36B makes plain that they differ when it comes to tax credits in particular.

Roaming even farther afield from § 36B, the Court turns to the Act's provisions about "qualified individuals." individuals receive favored treatment on Exchanges, although customers who are not qualified individuals may also shop there. The Court claims that the Act must equate federal and state establishment of Exchanges when it defines a qualified individual as someone who (among other things) lives in the "State that established the Exchange." Otherwise, the Court says, there would be no qualified individuals on federal Exchanges, contradicting (for example) the provision requiring every Exchange to take the " 'interests of qualified individuals' " into account when selecting health plans. Pure applesauce. Imagine that a university sends around a bulletin reminding every professor to take the "interests of graduate students" into account when setting office hours, but that some professors teach only undergraduates. Would anybody reason that the bulletin implicitly presupposes that every professor has "graduate students," so that "graduate students" must really mean "graduate or undergraduate students"? Surely not. Just as one naturally reads instructions about graduate students to be inapplicable to the extent a particular professor has no such students, so too would one naturally read instructions about qualified individuals to be inapplicable to the extent a particular Exchange has no such individuals. There is no need to rewrite the term "State that established the Exchange" in the definition of "qualified individual," much less a need to rewrite the separate term "Exchange established by the State" in a separate part of the Act.

Compounding its errors, the Court forgets that it is no more appropriate to consider one of a statute's purposes in isolation than it is to consider one of its words that way. No law pursues just one purpose at all costs, and no statutory scheme encompasses just one element. Most relevant here, the Affordable Care Act displays a congressional preference for state participation in the establishment of Exchanges: Each State gets the first opportunity to set up its Exchange; States that take up the opportunity receive federal funding for "activities . . . related to establishing" an Exchange, and the Secretary may establish an Exchange in a State only as a fallback, But setting up and running an Exchange involve significant burdens—meeting strict deadlines, implementing requirements related to the offering of insurance plans, setting up outreach programs, § 18031(i), and ensuring that the Exchange is self-sustaining by 2015. A State would have much less reason to take on these burdens if its citizens could receive tax credits no matter who establishes its Exchange. Even if making credits available on all Exchanges advances the goal of improving healthcare markets, it frustrates the goal of encouraging state involvement in the implementation of the Act. *This* is what justifies going out of our way to read "established by the State" to mean "established by the State or not established by the State"?

Worst of all for the repute of today's decision, the Court's reasoning is largely self-defeating. The Court predicts that making tax credits unavailable in States that do not set up their own Exchanges would cause disastrous economic consequences there. If that is so, however, wouldn't one expect States to react by setting up their own Exchanges? And wouldn't that outcome satisfy two of the Act's goals rather than just one: enabling the Act's reforms to work *and* promoting state involvement in the Act's implementation? The Court protests that the very existence of a federal fallback shows that Congress expected that some States might fail to set up their own Exchanges. So it does. It does not show, however, that Congress expected the number of recalcitrant States to be particularly large. The more accurate the Court's dire economic predictions, the smaller that number is likely to be. That reality destroys the Court's pretense that applying the law as written would imperil "the viability of the entire Affordable Care Act." All in all, the Court's arguments about the law's purpose and design are no more convincing than its arguments about context.

I dissent.

E. REVIEW EXERCISE

Now let's help to solidify your understanding of the rules and sources of statutory interpretation with an exercise.

The following article initially appeared in 12 Green Bag 2d 337 (2009). As you read it, footnote all of the arguments made by the "judges" by referencing the rules and sources you studied above. Which case would you cite for each proposition? In addition, assess the strength of the opinions. Which do you agree with? Which are wrong and why? What theories of interpretation are represented in the different opinions?

THE FOOD STAYS IN THE KITCHEN: EVERYTHING I NEEDED TO KNOW ABOUT STATUTORY INTERPRETATION I LEARNED BY THE TIME I WAS NINE

Hillel Y. Levin

On March 23, 1986, the following proclamation, henceforth known as Ordinance 7.3, was made by the Supreme Lawmaker, Mother:

I am tired of finding popcorn kernels, pretzel crumbs, and pieces of cereal all over the family room. From now on, no food may be eaten outside the kitchen.

Thereupon, litigation arose.

FATHER, C.J., issued the following ruling on March 30, 1986:

Defendant Anne, age 14, was seen carrying a glass of water into the family room. She was charged with violating Ordinance 7.3 ("the Rule"). We hold that drinking water outside of the kitchen does not violate the Rule.

The Rule prohibits "food" from being eaten outside of the kitchen. This prohibition does not extend to water, which is a beverage rather than food. Our interpretation is confirmed by Webster's Dictionary, which defines food to mean, in relevant part, a "material consisting essentially of protein, carbohydrate, and fat used in the body of an organism to sustain growth, repair, and vital processes and to furnish energy" and "nutriment in solid form." Plainly, water, which contains no protein, carbohydrate, or fat, and which is not in solid form, is not a food.

Customary usage further substantiates our distinction between "food" and water. Ordinance 6.2, authored by the very same Supreme Lawmaker, declares: "[a]fter you get home from school, have some food and something to drink, and then do your homework." This demonstrates that the Supreme Lawmaker speaks of food and drink separately and is fully capable of identifying one or both as appropriate. After all, if "food," as used in the Family Code, included beverages, then the word "drink" in Ordinance 6.2 would be redundant and mere surplusage. Thus, had the

Supreme Lawmaker wished to prohibit beverages from being taken out of the kitchen, she could easily have done so by declaring that "no food or drink is permitted outside the kitchen."

Our understanding of the word "food" to exclude water is further buttressed by the evident purpose of the Rule. The Supreme Lawmaker enacted the Rule as a response to the mess produced by solid foods. Water, even when spilled, does not produce a similar kind of mess.

Some may argue that the cup from which the Defendant was drinking water may, if left in the family room, itself be a mess. But we are not persuaded. The language of the Rule speaks to the Supreme Lawmaker's concern with small particles of food rather than to a more generalized concern with the containers in which food is held. A cup or other container bears a greater resemblance to other bric-a-brac, such as toys and backpacks, to which the Rule does not speak, than it does to the food spoken of in the Rule. Although we need not divine the Supreme Lawmaker's reasons for such a distinction, there are at least two plausible explanations. First, it could be that small particles of food left around the house are more problematic than the stray cup or bowl because they find their way into hard-to-reach places and may lead to rodent infestation. Second, it is possible that the Supreme Lawmaker was unconcerned with containers being left in the family room because citizens of this jurisdiction have been meticulous about removing such containers.

BABYSITTER SUE, J., issued the following ruling on April 12, 1986:

Defendant Beatrice, age 12, is charged with violating Ordinance 7.3 by drinking a beverage, to wit: orange juice, in the family room.

The Defendant relies on our ruling of March 30, 1986, which "h[e]ld that drinking water outside of the kitchen does not violate the [Ordinance]," and urges us to conclude that all beverages are permitted in the family room under Ordinance 7.3. While we believe this is a difficult case, we agree. As we have previously explained, the term "food" does not extend to beverages.

Our hesitation stems not from the literal meaning of the Ordinance, which strongly supports the Defendant's claim, but rather from an understanding of its purpose. As we have previously stated, and as evidenced by the language of the Ordinance itself, the Ordinance was enacted as a result of the Supreme Lawmaker's concern with mess. Unlike the case with water, if the Defendant were to spill orange juice on the couch or rug in the family room, the mess would be problematic— perhaps even more so than the mess produced by crumbs of food. It is thus difficult to infer why the Supreme Lawmaker would choose to prohibit solid foods outside of the kitchen but to permit orange juice.

Nevertheless, we are bound the plain language of the Ordinance and by precedent. We are confident that if the Supreme Lawmaker disagrees with the outcome in this case, she can change or clarify the law accordingly.

GRANDMA, SENIOR J., issued the following ruling on May 3, 1986:

Defendant Charlie, age 10, is charged with violating Ordinance 7.3 by eating popcorn in the family room. The Defendant contends, and we agree, that the Ordinance does not apply in this case.

Ordinance 7.3 was enacted to prevent messes outside of the kitchen. This purpose is demonstrated by the language of the Ordinance itself, which refers to food being left "all over the family room" as the immediate cause of its adoption.

Such messes are produced only when one transfers food from a container to his or her mouth outside of the kitchen. During that process—what the Ordinance refers to as "eat[ing]"—crumbs and other food particles often fall out of the eater's hand and onto the floor or sofa.

As the record shows, the Defendant placed all of the popcorn into his mouth prior to leaving the kitchen. He merely masticated and swallowed while in the family room. At no time was there any danger that a mess would be produced.

We are certain that there was no intent to prohibit merely the chewing or swallowing of food outside of the kitchen. After all, the Supreme Lawmaker has expressly permitted the chewing of gum in the family room. It would be senseless and absurd to treat gum differently from popcorn that has been ingested prior to leaving the kitchen.

If textual support is necessary to support this obvious and commonsensical interpretation, abundant support is available. First, the Ordinance prohibits food from being "eaten" outside of the kitchen. The term "eat" is defined to mean "to take in through the mouth as food: ingest, chew, and swallow in turn." The Defendant, having only chewed and swallowed, did not "eat." Further, the Ordinance prohibits the "eat[ing]" rather than the "bringing" of food outside of the kitchen; and indeed, food is often brought out of the kitchen and through the family room, as when school lunches are delivered to the front door for carpool pickup. There is no reason to treat food enclosed in a brown bag any differently from food enclosed within the Defendant's mouth.

Finally, if any doubt remains as to the meaning of this Ordinance as it pertains to the chewing and swallowing of food, we cannot punish the Defendant for acting reasonably and in good faith reliance upon the text of the Ordinance and our past pronouncements as to its meaning and intent.

UNCLE RICK, J., issued the following ruling on May 20, 1986:

Defendant Charlie, age 10, is charged with violating Ordinance 7.3 ("the Rule") by bringing a double thick mint chocolate chip milkshake into the family room.

Were I writing on a clean slate, I would surely conclude that the Defendant has violated the Rule. A double thick milkshake is "food" because it contains protein, carbohydrate, and/or fat. Further, the purpose of the Rule—to prevent messes—would be undermined by permitting a double thick milkshake to be brought into the family room. Indeed, it makes little sense to treat a milkshake differently from a pretzel or a scoop of ice cream.

However, I am not writing on a clean slate. Our precedents have now established that all beverages are permitted outside of the kitchen under the Rule. The Defendant relied on those precedents in good faith. Further, the Supreme Lawmaker has had ample opportunity to clarify or change the law to prohibit any or all beverages from being brought out of the kitchen, and she has elected not to exercise that authority. I can only conclude that she is satisfied with the status quo.

GRANDMA, SENIOR J., issued the following ruling on July 2, 1986:

Defendant Anne, age 14, is charged with violating Ordinance 7.3 by eating apple slices in the family room.

As we have repeatedly held, the Ordinance pertains only to messy foods. Moreover, the Ordinance explicitly refers to "popcorn kernels, pretzel crumbs, and pieces of cereal." Sliced apples, not being messy (and certainly being no worse than orange juice and milkshakes, which have been permitted by our prior decisions), and being wholly dissimilar from the crumbly foods listed in the Ordinance, do not come within the meaning of the Ordinance.

We also find it significant that the consumption of healthy foods such as sliced apples is a behavior that this jurisdiction supports and encourages. It would be odd to read the Ordinance in a way that would discourage such healthy behaviors by limiting them to the kitchen.

AUNT SARAH, J., issued the following ruling on August 12, 1986:

Defendant Beatrice, age 13, is charged with violating Ordinance 7.3 by eating pretzels, popcorn, cereal, and birthday cake in the family room. Under ordinary circumstances, the Defendant would clearly be subject to the Ordinance. However, the circumstances giving rise to the Defendant's action in this case are far from ordinary.

The Defendant celebrated her thirteenth birthday on August 10, 1986. For the celebration, she invited four of her closest friends to sleep over. During the evening, and as part of the festivities, the celebrants watched a movie in the family room. Chief Justice Father provided those present with drinks and snacks, including the aforesaid pretzels, popcorn, and cereal, for consumption during the movie-watching. Father admonished the Defendant to clean up after the movie, and there is no evidence in the record suggesting that the Defendant failed to do so.

We frankly concede that the Defendant's action were violative of the plain meaning of the Ordinance. However, given the special and unique nature of the occasion, the fact that Father, a representative of the Supreme Lawmaker—as well as of this Court—implicitly approved of the Defendant's actions, and the apparent efforts of the Defendant in upholding the spirit of the Ordinance by cleaning up after her friends, we believe that the best course of action is to release the Defendant.

In light of the growing confusion in the interpretation of this ambiguous Ordinance, we urge the Supreme Lawmaker to exercise her authority to clarify and/or change the law if and as she deems it appropriate.

FATHER, C.J., issued the following ruling on September 17, 1986:

Defendant Derek, age 9, was charged with violating Ordinance 7.3 ("the Rule") by eating pretzels, potato chips, popcorn, a bagel with cream cheese, cottage cheese, and a chocolate bar in the family room.

The Defendant argues that our precedents have clearly established a pattern permitting food to be eaten in the family room so long as the eater cleans up any mess. He further maintains that it would be unjust for this Court to punish him after having permitted past actions such as drinking water, orange juice, and a milkshake, as well as swallowing popcorn, eating apple slices, and eating pretzels, popcorn, and cereal on a special occasion. The Defendant avers that there is no rational distinction between his sister's eating foods in the family room during a movie on a special occasion and his eating foods in the family room during a weekly television show.

We agree. The citizens of this jurisdiction look to the rulings of this Court, as well as to general practice, to understand their rights and obligations as citizens. In the many months since the Rule was originally announced, the cumulative rulings of this Court on the subject would signify to any citizen that, whatever the technical language of the Rule, the real Rule is that they must clean up after eating any food outside of the kitchen. To draw and enforce any other line now would be arbitrary and, as such, unjust.

On November 4, 1986, the following proclamation, henceforth known as The New Ordinance 7.3, was made by the Supreme Lawmaker, Mother:

Over the past few months, I have found empty cups, orange juice stains, milkshake spills, slimy spots of unknown origin, all manner of crumbs, melted chocolate, and icing from cake in the family room. I thought I was clear the first time! And you've all had a chance to show me that you could use your common sense and clean up after yourselves. So now let me be clearer: No food, gum, or drink of any kind, on any occasion or in any form, is permitted in the family room. Ever. Seriously. I mean it.

F. CASES THAT PUT IT ALL TOGETHER

Now let's consider some real cases involving multiple sources of interpretation.

EXERCISE V.5

Consider this statutory provision:

"Whoever [is convicted of possessing child pornography] shall be fined under this title or imprisoned not more than 10 years, or both, but if such person has a prior conviction relating to aggravated sexual abuse, sexual abuse, or abusive sexual conduct involving a minor or ward, such person shall be fined under this title and imprisoned for not less than 10 years nor more than 20 years."

Your client was convicted of possessing child pornography. He had previously been convicted of sexual abuse of an adult. The prosecutor argues that your client is subject to imprisonment for 10 to 20 years. Do you agree? Identify all the arguments that you and the prosecutor are likely to make.

LOCKHART V. UNITED STATES
Decided March 1, 2016.

SOTOMAYOR, J., delivered the opinion of the Court, in which ROBERTS, C.J., and KENNEDY, THOMAS, GINSBURG, and ALITO, JJ., joined. KAGAN, J., filed a dissenting opinion, in which BREYER, J., joined.

Now consider how the Court resolved that issue. As you read the following case, consider these questions:

- What theory or theories of interpretation to the majority and dissent follow?

- Which opinion do you think Justice Scalia would have joined, if any? Had he written an opinion, what would it have said?

- Compare this opinion to the Court's opinion in *Holy Trinity Church*. Has the Court's approach to statutory changed? If so, how?

- Identify all of the different kinds of moves each side makes.

- Is there any principled way to choose between the last antecedent rule and the series qualifier rule?

- Is there a clearly better Textualist argument here?

- Who has the better argument, in your opinion? Which specific argument convinces you?

- Which reading tracks the natural use of the English language better? Should that determine the outcome?

- What does the outcome in this case suggest about the use and viability of the rule of lenity?

- Which do you think the legislature intended?

- Which reading, if any, is likely to cause the legislature to weigh in to "correct" the Court's interpretation?

JUSTICE SOTOMAYOR delivered the opinion of the Court.

Defendants convicted of possessing child pornography in violation of 18 U.S.C. § 2252(a)(4) are subject to a 10-year mandatory minimum sentence and an increased maximum sentence if they have "a prior conviction . . . under the laws of any State relating to aggravated sexual abuse, sexual abuse, or abusive sexual conduct involving a minor or ward." § 2252(b)(2).

The question before us is whether the phrase "involving a minor or ward" modifies all items in the list of predicate crimes ("aggravated sexual abuse," "sexual abuse," and "abusive sexual conduct") or only the one item that immediately precedes it ("abusive sexual conduct"). Below, the Court of Appeals for the Second Circuit joined several other Courts of Appeals in holding that it modifies only "abusive sexual conduct." The Eighth Circuit has reached the contrary result. We granted certiorari to resolve that split. We affirm the Second Circuit's holding that the phrase "involving a minor or ward" in § 2252(b)(2) modifies only "abusive sexual conduct."

I

In April 2000, Avondale Lockhart was convicted of sexual abuse in the first degree. . . . The crime involved his then-53-year-old girlfriend. Eleven years later, Lockhart was indicted in the Eastern District of New York for attempting to receive child pornography in violation of 18 U.S.C. § 2252(a)(2) and for possessing child pornography in violation of § 2252(a)(4)(b). Lockhart pleaded guilty to the possession offense and the Government dismissed the receipt offense.

Lockhart's presentence report calculated a guidelines range of 78 to 97 months for the possession offense. But the report also concluded that Lockhart was subject to § 2252(b)(2)'s mandatory minimum because his prior New York abuse conviction related "to aggravated sexual abuse, sexual abuse, or abusive sexual conduct involving a minor or ward."

Lockhart objected, arguing that the statutory phrase "involving a minor or ward" applies to all three listed crimes: "aggravated sexual abuse," "sexual abuse," *and* "abusive sexual conduct." He therefore contended that his prior conviction for sexual abuse involving an *adult* fell outside the enhancement's ambit. The District Court rejected Lockhart's argument and applied the mandatory minimum. The Second Circuit affirmed his sentence.

II

Section 2252(b)(2) reads in full:

> "Whoever violates, or attempts or conspires to violate [18 U.S.C. § 2252(a)(4)] shall be fined under this title or imprisoned not more than 10 years, or both, but . . . if such person has a prior

> conviction . . . relating to aggravated sexual abuse, sexual abuse, or abusive sexual conduct involving a minor or ward, or the production, possession, receipt, mailing, sale, distribution, shipment, or transportation of child pornography, such person shall be fined under this title and imprisoned for not less than 10 years nor more than 20 years."

This case concerns that provision's list of state sexual-abuse offenses. The issue before us is whether the limiting phrase that appears at the end of that list—"involving a minor or ward"—applies to all three predicate crimes preceding it in the list or only the final predicate crime. We hold that "involving a minor or ward" modifies only "abusive sexual conduct," the antecedent immediately preceding it. Although § 2252(b)(2)'s list of state predicates is awkwardly phrased (to put it charitably), the provision's text and context together reveal a straightforward reading. A timeworn textual canon is confirmed by the structure and internal logic of the statutory scheme.

A

Consider the text. When this Court has interpreted statutes that include a list of terms or phrases followed by a limiting clause, we have typically applied an interpretive strategy called the "rule of the last antecedent." The rule provides that "a limiting clause or phrase . . . should ordinarily be read as modifying only the noun or phrase that it immediately follows."

This Court has applied the rule from our earliest decisions to our more recent. The rule reflects the basic intuition that when a modifier appears at the end of a list, it is easier to apply that modifier only to the item directly before it. That is particularly true where it takes more than a little mental energy to process the individual entries in the list, making it a heavy lift to carry the modifier across them all. For example, imagine you are the general manager of the Yankees and you are rounding out your 2016 roster. You tell your scouts to find a defensive catcher, a quick-footed shortstop, or a pitcher from last year's World Champion Kansas City Royals. It would be natural for your scouts to confine their search for a pitcher to last year's championship team, but to look more broadly for catchers and shortstops.

Applied here, the last antecedent principle suggests that the phrase "involving a minor or ward" modifies only the phrase that it immediately follows: "abusive sexual conduct." As a corollary, it also suggests that the phrases "aggravated sexual abuse" and "sexual abuse" are not so constrained.

Of course, as with any canon of statutory interpretation, the rule of the last antecedent "is not an absolute and can assuredly be overcome by other indicia of meaning." For instance, take " 'the laws, the treaties, and the constitution of the United States.' " A reader intuitively applies "of the United States" to "the laws," "the treaties" and "the constitution" because (among other things) laws, treaties, and the constitution are often cited together, because readers are used to seeing "of the United States" modify each of them, and because the listed items are simple and parallel without unexpected internal modifiers or structure. Section 2252(b)(2), by contrast, does not contain items that readers are used to seeing listed together or a concluding modifier that readers are accustomed to applying to each of them. And the varied syntax of each item in the list makes it hard for the reader to carry the final modifying clause across all three.

More importantly, here the interpretation urged by the rule of the last antecedent is not overcome by other indicia of meaning. To the contrary, § 2252(b)(2)'s context fortifies the meaning that principle commands.

B

Our inquiry into § 2252(b)(2)'s context begins with the internal logic of that provision. Section 2252(b)(2) establishes sentencing minimums and maximums for three categories of offenders. The first third of the section imposes a 10-year maximum sentence on offenders with no prior convictions. The second third imposes a 10-year minimum and 20-year maximum on offenders who have previously violated a federal offense listed within various chapters of the Federal Criminal Code. And the last third imposes the same minimum and maximum on offenders who have previously committed state "sexual abuse, aggravated sexual abuse, or abusive sexual conduct involving a minor or ward" as well as a number of state crimes related to the possession and distribution of child pornography.

Among the chapters of the Federal Criminal Code that can trigger § 2252(b)(2)'s recidivist enhancement are crimes "under ... chapter 109A." Chapter 109A criminalizes a range of sexual-abuse offenses involving adults *or* minors and wards. And it places those federal sexual-abuse crimes under headings that use language nearly identical to the language § 2252(b)(2) uses to enumerate the three categories of state sexual-abuse predicates. The first section in Chapter 109A is titled "Aggravated sexual abuse." 18 U.S.C. § 2241. The second is titled "Sexual abuse." § 2242. And the third is titled "Sexual abuse of a minor or ward." § 2243. Applying the rule of the last antecedent, those sections mirror precisely the order, precisely the divisions, and nearly precisely the words used to describe the three state sexual-abuse predicate crimes in § 2252(b)(2): "aggravated sexual abuse," "sexual abuse," and "abusive sexual conduct involving a minor or ward."

This similarity appears to be more than a coincidence. We cannot state with certainty that Congress used Chapter 109A as a template for the list of state predicates set out in § 2252(b)(2), but we cannot ignore the parallel, particularly because the headings in Chapter 109A were in place when Congress amended the statute to add § 2252(b)(2)'s state sexual-abuse predicates.

If Congress had intended to limit each of the state predicates to conduct "involving a minor or ward," we doubt it would have followed, or thought it needed to follow, so closely the structure and language of Chapter 109A. The conclusion that Congress followed the federal template is supported by the fact that Congress did nothing to indicate that offenders with prior federal sexual-abuse convictions are more culpable, harmful, or worthy of enhanced punishment than offenders with nearly identical state priors. We therefore see no reason to interpret § 2252(b)(2) so that "[s]exual abuse" that occurs in the Second Circuit courthouse triggers the sentence enhancement, but "sexual abuse" that occurs next door in the Manhattan municipal building does not.

III

A

Lockhart argues, to the contrary, that the phrase "involving a minor or ward" should be interpreted to modify all three state sexual-abuse predicates. He first contends, as does our dissenting colleague, that the so-called series-qualifier principle supports his reading. This principle, Lockhart says, requires a modifier to apply to all items in a series when such an application would represent a natural construction.

This Court has long acknowledged that structural or contextual evidence may "rebut the last antecedent inference." For instance, in *Porto Rico Railway, Light & Power Co. v. Mor,* 253 U.S. 345, (1920), on which Lockhart relies, this Court declined to apply the rule of the last antecedent where "[n]o reason appears why" a modifying clause is not "applicable as much to the first and other words as to the last" and where "special reasons exist for so construing the clause in question." . . .

But in none of those cases did the Court describe, much less apply, a countervailing grammatical mandate that could bear the weight that either Lockhart or the dissent places on the series qualifier principle. Instead, the Court simply observed that sometimes context weighs against the application of the rule of the last antecedent. Whether a modifier is "applicable as much to the first . . . as to the last" words in a list, whether a set of items form a "single, integrated list," and whether the application of the rule would require acceptance of an "unlikely premise" are fundamentally contextual questions.

Lockhart attempts to identify contextual indicia that he says rebut the rule of the last antecedent, but those indicia hurt rather than help his prospects. He points out that the final two state predicates, "sexual abuse" and "abusive sexual conduct," are "nearly synonymous as a matter of everyday speech." And, of course, anyone who commits "aggravated sexual abuse" has also necessarily committed "sexual abuse." So, he posits, the items in the list are sufficiently similar that a limiting phrase could apply equally to all three of them.

But Lockhart's effort to demonstrate some similarity among the items in the list of state predicates reveals far too much similarity. The three state predicate crimes are not just related on Lockhart's reading; they are hopelessly redundant. Any conduct that would qualify as "aggravated sexual abuse . . . involving a minor or ward" or "sexual abuse . . . involving a minor or ward" would also qualify as "abusive sexual conduct involving a minor or ward." We take no position today on the meaning of the terms "aggravated sexual abuse," "sexual abuse," and "abusive sexual conduct," including their similarities and differences. But it is clear that applying the limiting phrase to all three items would risk running headlong into the rule against superfluity by transforming a list of separate predicates into a set of synonyms describing the same predicate.

Applying the limiting phrase "involving a minor or ward" more sparingly, by contrast, preserves some distinction between the categories of state predicates by limiting only the third category to conduct "involving a minor or ward." We recognize that this interpretation does not eliminate all superfluity between "aggravated sexual abuse" and "sexual abuse." But there is a ready explanation for the redundancy that remains: It follows the categories in Chapter 109A's federal template. We see no similar explanation for Lockhart's complete collapse of the list.

The dissent offers a suggestion rooted in its impressions about how people ordinarily speak and write. The problem is that, as even the dissent acknowledges, § 2252(b)(2)'s list of state predicates is hardly intuitive. No one would mistake its odd repetition and inelegant phrasing for a reflection of the accumulated wisdom of everyday speech patterns. It would be as if a friend asked you to get her tart lemons, sour lemons, or sour fruit from Mexico. If you brought back lemons from California, but your friend insisted that she was using customary speech and obviously asked for Mexican fruit only, you would be forgiven for disagreeing on both counts.

Faced with § 2252(b)(2)'s inartful drafting, then, do we interpret the provision by viewing it as a clear, commonsense list best construed as if conversational English? Or do we look around to see if there might be some provenance to its peculiarity? With Chapter 109A so readily at hand, we are unpersuaded by our dissenting colleague's invocation of basic examples from day-to-day life. Whatever the validity of the dissent's broader point, this simply is not a case in which colloquial practice is of much use. Section 2252(b)(2)'s list is hardly the way an average person, or

even an average lawyer, would set about to describe the relevant conduct
if they had started from scratch.

. . . .

C

Lockhart, joined by the dissent, next says that the provision's legislative
history supports the view that Congress deliberately structured
§ 2252(b)(2) to treat state and federal predicates differently. They rely on
two sources. The first is a reference in a Report from the Senate Judiciary
Committee on the Child Pornography Prevention Act of 1996. That Act
was the first to add the language at issue here—"aggravated sexual
abuse, sexual abuse, or abusive sexual conduct involving a minor or
ward"—to the U.S. Code.

The Report noted that the enhancement applies to persons with prior
convictions "under any State child abuse law or law relating to the
production, receipt or distribution of child pornography." But that
reference incompletely describes the state pornography production and
distribution predicates, which cover not only "production, receipt, or
distributing of child pornography," as the Report indicates, but also
"production, possession, receipt, mailing, sale, distribution, shipment, or
transportation of child pornography," § 2252(b)(2). For the reasons
discussed, we have no trouble concluding that the Report also
incompletely describes the state sexual-abuse predicates.

Lockhart and the dissent also rely on a letter sent from the Department
of Justice (DOJ) to the House of Representative's Committee on the
Judiciary commenting on the proposed "Child Protection and Sexual
Predator Punishment Act of 1998." the letter, DOJ provides commentary
on the then-present state of §§ 2252(b)(1) and 2252(b)(2), noting that
although there is a "5-year mandatory minimum sentence for individuals
charged with receipt or distribution of child pornography and who have
prior state convictions for child molestation" pursuant to § 2252(b)(1),
there is "no enhanced provision for those individuals charged with
possession of child pornography who have prior convictions for child
abuse" pursuant to § 2252(b)(2). That letter, they say, demonstrates that
DOJ understood the language at issue here to impose a sentencing
enhancement only for prior state convictions involving children.

We doubt that DOJ was trying to describe the full reach of the language
in § 2252(b)(1), as the dissent suggests. To the contrary, there are several
clues that the letter was relaying on just one of the provision's many
salient features. For instance, the letter's references to "child
molestation" and "child abuse" do not encompass a large number of state
crimes that are unambiguously covered by "abusive sexual conduct
involving a minor or ward"—namely, crimes involving "wards." Wards
can be minors, but they can also be adults. See, *e.g.,* § 2243(b) (defining

"wards" as persons who are "in official detention" and "under . . . custodial, supervisory, or disciplinary authority"). Moreover, we doubt that DOJ intended to express a belief that the potentially broad scope of serious crimes encompassed by "aggravated sexual abuse, sexual abuse, and abusive sexual conduct" reaches no further than state crimes that would traditionally be characterized as "child molestation" or "child abuse."

Thus, Congress' amendment to the provision did give "DOJ just what it wanted." But the amendment also did more than that. We therefore think it unnecessary to restrict our interpretation of the provision to the parts of it that DOJ chose to highlight in its letter. Just as importantly, the terse descriptions of the provision in the Senate Report and DOJ letter do nothing to explain *why* Congress would have wanted to apply the mandatory minimum to individuals convicted in federal court of sexual abuse or aggravated sexual abuse involving an adult, but not to individuals convicted in state court of the same. The legislative history, in short, "hardly speaks with [a] clarity of purpose" through which we can discern Congress' statutory objective.

The best explanation Lockhart can muster is a basic administrability concern: Congress "knew what conduct it was capturing under federal law and could be confident that all covered federal offenses were proper predicates. But Congress did not have the same familiarity with the varied and mutable sexual-abuse laws of all fifty states." Perhaps Congress worried that state laws punishing relatively minor offenses like public lewdness or indecent exposure involving an adult would be swept into § 2252(b)(2). But the risk Lockhart identifies is minimal. Whether the terms in § 2252(b)(2) are given their "generic" meaning, or are defined in light of their federal counterparts—which we do not decide—they are unlikely to sweep in the bizarre or unexpected state offenses that worry Lockhart.

D

Finally, Lockhart asks us to apply the rule of lenity. We have used the lenity principle to resolve ambiguity in favor of the defendant only "at the end of the process of construing what Congress has expressed" when the ordinary canons of statutory construction have revealed no satisfactory construction. That is not the case here. To be sure, Lockhart contends that if we applied a different principle of statutory construction—namely, his "series-qualifier principle"—we would arrive at an alternative construction of § 2252(b)(2). But the arguable availability of multiple, divergent principles of statutory construction cannot automatically trigger the rule of lenity. Here, the rule of the last antecedent is well supported by context and Lockhart's alternative is not. We will not apply the rule of lenity to override a sensible grammatical principle buttressed by the statute's text and structure.

We conclude that the text and structure of § 2252(b)(2) confirm that the provision applies to prior state convictions for "sexual abuse" and "aggravated sexual abuse," whether or not the convictions involved a minor or ward. We therefore hold that Lockhart's prior conviction for sexual abuse of an adult is encompassed by § 2252(b)(2). The judgment of the Court of Appeals, accordingly, is affirmed.

So ordered.

JUSTICE KAGAN, with whom JUSTICE BREYER joins, dissenting.

Imagine a friend told you that she hoped to meet "an actor, director, or producer involved with the new Star Wars movie." You would know immediately that she wanted to meet an actor from the Star Wars cast—not an actor in, for example, the latest Zoolander. Suppose a real estate agent promised to find a client "a house, condo, or apartment in New York." Wouldn't the potential buyer be annoyed if the agent sent him information about condos in Maryland or California? And consider a law imposing a penalty for the "violation of any statute, rule, or regulation relating to insider trading." Surely a person would have cause to protest if punished under that provision for violating a traffic statute. The reason in all three cases is the same: Everyone understands that the modifying phrase—"involved with the new Star Wars movie," "in New York," "relating to insider trading"—applies to each term in the preceding list, not just the last.

That ordinary understanding of how English works, in speech and writing alike, should decide this case. Avondale Lockhart is subject to a 10–year mandatory minimum sentence for possessing child pornography if, but only if, he has a prior state-law conviction for "aggravated sexual abuse, sexual abuse, or abusive sexual conduct involving a minor or ward." 18 U.S.C. § 2252(b)(2). The Court today, relying on what is called the "rule of the last antecedent," reads the phrase "involving a minor or ward" as modifying only the final term in that three-item list. But properly read, the modifier applies to each of the terms—just as in the examples above. That normal construction finds support in uncommonly clear-cut legislative history, which states in so many words that the three predicate crimes all involve abuse of children. And if any doubt remained, the rule of lenity would command the same result: Lockhart's prior conviction for sexual abuse *of an adult* does not trigger § 2252(b)(2)'s mandatory minimum penalty. I respectfully dissent.

I

Begin where the majority does—with the rule of the last antecedent. This Court most fully discussed that principle in *Barnhart v. Thomas,* 540 U.S.

20 (2003), which considered a statute providing that an individual qualifies as disabled if "he is not only unable to do his previous work but cannot, considering his age, education, and work experience, engage in any other kind of substantial gainful work *which exists in the national economy*." The Court held, invoking the last-antecedent rule, that the italicized phrase modifies only the term "substantial gainful work," and not the term "previous work" occurring earlier in the sentence. Two points are of especial note. First, *Barnhart* contained a significant caveat: The last-antecedent rule "can assuredly be overcome by other indicia of meaning." Second, the grammatical structure of the provision in *Barnhart* is nothing like that of the statute in this case: The modifying phrase does not, as here, immediately follow a list of multiple, parallel terms. That is true as well in the other instances in which this Court has followed the rule.

Indeed, this Court has made clear that the last-antecedent rule does not generally apply to the grammatical construction present here: when "[t]he modifying clause appear[s] . . . at the end of a single, integrated list." Then, the exact opposite is usually true: As in the examples beginning this opinion, the modifying phrase refers alike to each of the list's terms. A leading treatise puts the point as follows: "When there is a straightforward, parallel construction that involves all nouns or verbs in a series," a modifier at the end of the list "normally applies to the entire series." That interpretive practice of applying the modifier to the whole list boasts a fancy name—the "series-qualifier canon," see Black's Law Dictionary 1574 (10th ed. 2014)—but, as my opening examples show, it reflects the completely ordinary way that people speak and listen, write and read.

Even the exception to the series-qualifier principle is intuitive, emphasizing both its common-sensical basis and its customary usage. When the nouns in a list are so disparate that the modifying clause does not make sense when applied to them all, then the last-antecedent rule takes over. Suppose your friend told you not that she wants to meet "an actor, director, or producer involved with Star Wars," but instead that she hopes someday to meet "a President, Supreme Court Justice, or actor involved with Star Wars." Presumably, you would know that she wants to meet a President or Justice even if that person has no connection to the famed film franchise. But so long as the modifying clause "is applicable as much to the first and other words as to the last," this Court has stated, "the natural construction of the language demands that the clause be read as applicable to all." In other words, the modifier then qualifies not just the last antecedent but the whole series.

. . . .

That analysis holds equally for § 2252(b)(2), the sentencing provision at issue here. The relevant language—"aggravated sexual abuse, sexual abuse, or abusive sexual conduct involving a minor or ward"—contains a "single, integrated list" of parallel terms (*i.e.,* sex crimes) followed by a modifying clause. Given the close relation among the terms in the series, the modifier makes sense "as much to the first and other words as to the last." In other words, the reference to a minor or ward applies as well to sexual abuse and aggravated sexual abuse as to abusive sexual conduct. (The case would be different if, for example, the statute established a mandatory minimum for any person previously convicted of "arson, receipt of stolen property, or abusive sexual conduct involving a minor or ward.") So interpreting the modifier "as applicable to all" the preceding terms is what "the natural construction of the language" requires.

The majority responds to all this by claiming that the "inelegant phrasing" of § 2252(b)(2) renders it somehow exempt from a grammatical rule reflecting "how people ordinarily" use the English language. But to begin with, the majority is wrong to suggest that the series-qualifier canon is only about "colloquial" or "conversational" English. In fact, it applies to both speech and writing, in both their informal and their formal varieties. Here is a way to test my point: Pick up a journal, or a book, or for that matter a Supreme Court opinion—most of which keep "everyday" colloquialisms at a far distance. You'll come across many sentences having the structure of the statutory provision at issue here: a few nouns followed by a modifying clause. And you'll discover, again and yet again, that the clause modifies every noun in the series, not just the last—in other words, that even (especially?) in formal writing, the series-qualifier principle works. And the majority is wrong too in suggesting that the "odd repetition" in § 2252(b)(2)'s list of state predicates causes the series-qualifier principle to lose its force. *Ibid.* The majority's own made-up sentence proves that much. If a friend asked you "to get her tart lemons, sour lemons, or sour fruit from Mexico," you might well think her list of terms perplexing: You might puzzle over the difference between tart and sour lemons, and wonder why she had specifically mentioned lemons when she apparently would be happy with sour fruit of any kind. But of one thing, you would have no doubt: Your friend wants some produce *from Mexico*; it would not do to get her, say, sour lemons from Vietnam. However weird the way she listed fruits—or the way § 2252(b)(2) lists offenses—the modifying clause still refers to them all.

The majority as well seeks refuge in the idea that applying the series-qualifier canon to § 2252(b)(2) would violate the rule against superfluity. Says the majority: "Any conduct that would qualify as 'aggravated sexual abuse . . . involving a minor or ward' or 'sexual abuse . . . involving a minor or ward' would also qualify as 'abusive sexual conduct involving a minor or ward.'" But that rejoinder doesn't work. "[T]he canon against superfluity," this Court has often stated, "assists only where a competing interpretation gives effect to every clause and word of a statute." And the majority's approach produces superfluity too—and in equal measure. Now (to rearrange the majority's sentence) any conduct that would qualify as "abusive sexual conduct involving a minor or ward" or "aggravated sexual abuse" would also qualify as "sexual abuse." In other words, on the majority's reading as well, two listed crimes become subsets of a third, so that the three could have been written as one. And indeed, the majority's superfluity has an especially odd quality, because it relates to the modifying clause itself: The majority, that is, makes the term "involving a minor or ward" wholly unnecessary. Remember the old adage about the pot and the kettle? That is why the rule against superfluity cannot excuse the majority from reading § 2252(b)(2)'s modifier, as ordinary usage demands, to pertain to all the terms in the preceding series.

II

Legislative history confirms what the natural construction of language shows: Each of the three predicate offenses at issue here must involve a minor. The list of those crimes appears in two places in § 2252(b)—both in § 2252(b)(1), which contains a sentencing enhancement for those convicted of distributing or receiving child pornography, and in § 2252(b)(2), which includes a similar enhancement for those (like Lockhart) convicted of possessing such material. Descriptions of that list of offenses, made at the time Congress added it to those provisions, belie the majority's position.

The relevant language—again, providing for a mandatory minimum sentence if a person has a prior state-law conviction for "aggravated sexual abuse, sexual abuse, or abusive sexual conduct involving a minor or ward"—first made its appearance in 1996, when Congress inserted it into § 2252(b)(1). At that time, the Senate Report on the legislation explained what the new language meant: The mandatory minimum would apply to an "offender with a prior conviction under . . . any *State child abuse law*." It is hard to imagine saying any more directly that the just-added state sexual-abuse predicates all involve minors, and minors only.

Two years later, in urging Congress to include the same predicate offenses in § 2252(b)(2), the Department of Justice (DOJ) itself read the list that way. In a formal bill comment, DOJ noted that proposed legislation on child pornography failed to fix a statutory oddity: Only § 2252(b)(1), and not § 2252(b)(2), then contained the state predicates at issue here. DOJ described that discrepancy as follows: Whereas § 2252(b)(1) provided a penalty enhancement for "individuals charged with receipt or distribution of child pornography *and who have prior state convictions for child molestation,* " the adjacent § 2252(b)(2) contained no such enhancement for those "charged with possession of child pornography *who have prior convictions for child abuse.*" That should change, DOJ wrote: A possessor of child pornography should also be subject to a 2-year mandatory minimum if he had "*a prior conviction for sexual abuse of a minor.*" DOJ thus made clear that the predicate offenses it recommended adding to § 2252(b)(2)—like those already in § 2252(b)(1)—related not to all sexual abuse but only to sexual abuse of children. And Congress gave DOJ just what it wanted: Soon after receiving the letter, Congress added the language at issue to § 2252(b)(2), resulting in the requested 2-year minimum sentence. So every indication, in 1998 no less than in 1996, was that all the predicate crimes relate to children alone.

. . . .

Further, the majority objects that the Senate Report's (and DOJ letter's) drafters did "nothing to explain *why* " Congress would have limited § 2252(b)'s state sexual-abuse predicates to those involving children when the provision's federal sexual-abuse predicates (as all agree) are not so confined. But Congress is under no obligation to this Court to justify its choices. (Nor is DOJ obliged to explain them to Congress itself.) Rather, the duty is on this Court to carry out those decisions, regardless of whether it understands all that lay behind them. The Senate Report (and DOJ letter too) says what it says about § 2252(b)'s meaning, confirming in no uncertain terms the most natural reading of the statutory language. Explanation or no, that is more than sufficient.

. . . .

IV

Suppose, for a moment, that this case is not as clear as I've suggested. Assume there is no way to know whether to apply the last-antecedent or the series-qualifier rule. Imagine, too, that the legislative history is not quite so compelling and the majority's "template" argument not quite so strained. Who, then, should prevail?

This Court has a rule for how to resolve genuine ambiguity in criminal statutes: in favor of the criminal defendant. As the majority puts the point, the rule of lenity insists that courts side with the defendant "when the ordinary canons of statutory construction have revealed no satisfactory construction." At the very least, that principle should tip the scales in Lockhart's favor, because nothing the majority has said shows that the modifying clause in § 2252(b)(2) *unambiguously* applies to only the last term in the preceding series.

But in fact, Lockhart's case is stronger. Consider the following sentence, summarizing various points made above: "The series-qualifier principle, the legislative history, and the rule of lenity discussed in this opinion all point in the same direction." Now answer the following question: Has only the rule of lenity been discussed in this opinion, or have the series-qualifier principle and the legislative history been discussed as well? Even had you not read the preceding 16-plus pages, you would know the right answer—because of the ordinary way all of us use language. That, in the end, is why Lockhart should win.

UNITED STATES V. NOSAL

676 F.3d 854 (9th Cir. 2012)

As you read this case, focus on the following:

- Identify all of the arguments made by both sides. Notice how the majority weaves together textual arguments, legislative history, and the substantive rules of interpretation. Which argument(s) do you think the majority considered the most persuasive?

- Which side do you think has the better plain meaning argument?

- Which opinion would you join?

- How does the dissent respond to the majority's lenity argument? Is the behavior charged in the indictment *malum in se* or *malum prohibitum*?

- Which theories of interpretation do the majority and the dissent seem to adopt?

- Why does the majority seem so concerned with the problems that a broad reading of the statute would pose? How does the dissent respond to the majority's concerns?

KOZINSKI, CHIEF JUDGE:

Computers have become an indispensable part of our daily lives. We use them for work; we use them for play. Sometimes we use them for play at work. Many employers have adopted policies prohibiting the use of work computers for nonbusiness purposes. Does an employee who violates such a policy commit a federal crime? How about someone who violates the terms of service of a social networking website? This depends on how broadly we read the Computer Fraud and Abuse Act (CFAA), 18 U.S.C. § 1030.

FACTS

David Nosal used to work for Korn/Ferry, an executive search firm. Shortly after he left the company, he convinced some of his former colleagues who were still working for Korn/Ferry to help him start a competing business. The employees used their log-in credentials to download source lists, names and contact information from a confidential database on the company's computer, and then transferred that information to Nosal. The employees were authorized to access the database, but Korn/Ferry had a policy that forbade disclosing confidential information. The government indicted Nosal on twenty counts, including trade secret theft, mail fraud, conspiracy and violations of the CFAA. The CFAA counts charged Nosal with violations of 18 U.S.C. § 1030(a)(4), for aiding and abetting the Korn/Ferry employees in "exceed[ing their] authorized access" with intent to defraud.

Nosal filed a motion to dismiss the CFAA counts, arguing that the statute targets only hackers, not individuals who access a computer with authorization but then misuse information they obtain by means of such access. . . .

The district court . . . dismissed counts 2 and 4–7 for failure to state an offense. The government appeals. . . .

DISCUSSION

The CFAA defines "exceeds authorized access" as "to access a computer with authorization and to use such access to obtain or alter information in the computer that the accesser is not entitled so to obtain or alter." This language can be read either of two ways: First, as Nosal suggests and the district court held, it could refer to someone who's authorized to access only certain data or files but accesses unauthorized data or files—what is colloquially known as "hacking." For example, assume an employee is permitted to access only product information on the company's computer but accesses customer data: He would "exceed[ ] authorized access" if he looks at the customer lists. Second, as the government proposes, the language could refer to someone who has unrestricted physical access to a computer, but is limited in the use to which he can put the information.

For example, an employee may be authorized to access customer lists in order to do his job but not to send them to a competitor.

The government argues that the statutory text can support only the latter interpretation of "exceeds authorized access." In its opening brief, it focuses on the word "entitled" in the phrase an "accesser is not *entitled* so to obtain or alter." Pointing to one dictionary definition of "entitle" as "to furnish with a right," *Webster's New Riverside University Dictionary* 435, the government argues that Korn/Ferry's computer-use policy gives employees certain rights, and when the employees violated that policy, they "exceed[ed] authorized access." But "entitled" in the statutory text refers to how an accesser "obtain[s] or alter[s]" the information, whereas the computer-use policy uses "entitled" to limit how the information is used after it is obtained. This is a poor fit with the statutory language. An equally or more sensible reading of "entitled" is as a synonym for "authorized." So read, "exceeds authorized access" would refer to data or files on a computer that one is not authorized to access.

In its reply brief and at oral argument, the government focuses on the word "so" in the same phrase. *See* 18 U.S.C. § 1030(e)(6) ("accesser is not entitled *so* to obtain or alter" (emphasis added)). The government reads "so" to mean "in that manner," which it claims must refer to use restrictions. In the government's view, reading the definition narrowly would render "so" superfluous.

The government's interpretation would transform the CFAA from an anti-hacking statute into an expansive misappropriation statute. This places a great deal of weight on a two-letter word that is essentially a conjunction. If Congress meant to expand the scope of criminal liability to everyone who uses a computer in violation of computer-use restrictions—which may well include everyone who uses a computer—we would expect it to use language better suited to that purpose. Under the presumption that Congress acts interstitially, we construe a statute as displacing a substantial portion of the common law only where Congress has clearly indicated its intent to do so.

In any event, the government's "so" argument doesn't work because the word has meaning even if it doesn't refer to use restrictions. Suppose an employer keeps certain information in a separate database that can be viewed on a computer screen, but not copied or downloaded. If an employee circumvents the security measures, copies the information to a thumb drive and walks out of the building with it in his pocket, he would then have obtained access to information in the computer that he is not "entitled *so* to obtain." Or, let's say an employee is given full access to the information, provided he logs in with his username and password. In an effort to cover his tracks, he uses another employee's login to copy information from the database. Once again, this would be an employee who is authorized to access the information but does so in a manner he was not authorized "so to obtain." Of course, this all assumes that "so" must have a substantive meaning to make sense of the statute. But Congress could just as well have included "so" as a connector or for emphasis.

While the CFAA is susceptible to the government's broad interpretation, we find Nosal's narrower one more plausible. Congress enacted the CFAA in 1984 primarily to address the growing problem of computer hacking, recognizing that, "[i]n intentionally trespassing into someone else's computer files, the offender obtains at the very least information as to how to break into that computer system." S. Rep. No. 99–432, at 9 (1986), 1986 U.S.C.C.A.N. 2479, 2487 (Conf. Rep.). The government agrees that the CFAA was concerned with hacking, which is why it also prohibits accessing a computer "without authorization." According to the government, *that* prohibition applies to hackers, so the "exceeds authorized access" prohibition must apply to people who are authorized to use the computer, but do so for an unauthorized purpose. But it is possible to read both prohibitions as applying to hackers: "[W]ithout authorization" would apply to *outside* hackers (individuals who have no authorized access to the computer at all) and "exceeds authorized access" would apply to *inside* hackers (individuals whose initial access to a computer is authorized but who access unauthorized information or files). This is a perfectly plausible construction of the statutory language that maintains the CFAA's focus on hacking rather than turning it into a sweeping Internet-policing mandate.

The government's construction of the statute would expand its scope far beyond computer hacking to criminalize any unauthorized use of information obtained from a computer. This would make criminals of large groups of people who would have little reason to suspect they are committing a federal crime. While ignorance of the law is no excuse, we can properly be skeptical as to whether Congress, in 1984, meant to criminalize conduct beyond that which is inherently wrongful, such as breaking into a computer.

The government argues that defendants here did have notice that their conduct was wrongful by the fraud and materiality requirements in subsection 1030(a)(4), which punishes whoever:

"knowingly and with intent to defraud, accesses a protected computer without authorization, or exceeds authorized access, and by means of such conduct furthers the intended fraud and obtains anything of value, unless the object of the fraud and the thing obtained consists only of the use of the computer and the value of such use is not more than $5,000 in any 1-year period."

But "exceeds authorized access" is used elsewhere in the CFAA as a basis for criminal culpability without intent to defraud. Subsection 1030(a)(2)(C) requires only that the person who "exceeds authorized access" have "obtain[ed] . . . information from any protected computer." Because "protected computer" is defined as a computer affected by or involved in interstate commerce—effectively all computers with Internet access—the government's interpretation of "exceeds authorized access" makes every violation of a private computer-use policy a federal crime.

The government argues that our ruling today would construe "exceeds authorized access" only in subsection 1030(a)(4), and we could give the phrase a narrower meaning when we construe other subsections. This is just not so: Once we define the phrase for the purpose of subsection 1030(a)(4), that definition must apply equally to the rest of the statute pursuant to the "standard principle of statutory construction . . . that identical words and phrases within the same statute should normally be given the same meaning." The phrase appears five times in the first seven subsections of the statute, including subsection 1030(a)(2)(C). Giving a different interpretation to each is impossible because Congress provided a *single* definition of "exceeds authorized access" for all iterations of the statutory phrase. Congress obviously meant "exceeds authorized access" to have the same meaning throughout section 1030. We must therefore consider how the interpretation we adopt will operate wherever in that section the phrase appears.

In the case of the CFAA, the broadest provision is subsection 1030(a)(2)(C), which makes it a crime to exceed authorized access of a computer connected to the Internet *without* any culpable intent. Were we to adopt the government's proposed interpretation, millions of unsuspecting individuals would find that they are engaging in criminal conduct.

Minds have wandered since the beginning of time and the computer gives employees new ways to procrastinate, by G-chatting with friends, playing games, shopping or watching sports highlights. Such activities are routinely prohibited by many computer-use policies, although employees are seldom disciplined for occasional use of work computers for personal purposes. Nevertheless, under the broad interpretation of the CFAA, such minor dalliances would become federal crimes. While it's unlikely that you'll be prosecuted for watching Reason.TV on your work computer, you *could* be. Employers wanting to rid themselves of troublesome employees without following proper procedures could threaten to report them to the FBI unless they quit. Ubiquitous, seldom-prosecuted crimes invite arbitrary and discriminatory enforcement.

Employer-employee and company-consumer relationships are traditionally governed by tort and contract law; the government's proposed interpretation of the CFAA allows private parties to manipulate their computer-use and personnel policies so as to turn these relationships into ones policed by the criminal law. Significant notice problems arise if we allow criminal liability to turn on the vagaries of private policies that are lengthy, opaque, subject to change and seldom read. Consider the typical corporate policy that computers can be used only for business purposes. What exactly is a "nonbusiness purpose"? If you use the computer to check the weather report for a business trip? For the company softball game? For your vacation to Hawaii? And if minor personal uses are tolerated, how can an employee be on notice of what constitutes a violation sufficient to trigger criminal liability?

Basing criminal liability on violations of private computer-use policies can transform whole categories of otherwise innocuous behavior into federal crimes simply because a computer is involved. Employees who call family members from their work phones will become criminals if they send an email instead. Employees can sneak in the sports section of the *New York Times* to read at work, but they'd better not visit ESPN.com. And sudoku enthusiasts should stick to the printed puzzles, because visiting www.dailysudoku.com from their work computers might give them more than enough time to hone their sudoku skills behind bars.

The effect this broad construction of the CFAA has on workplace conduct pales by comparison with its effect on everyone else who uses a computer, smart-phone, iPad, Kindle, Nook, X-box, Blu-Ray player or any other Internet-enabled device. The Internet is a means for communicating via computers: Whenever we access a web page, commence a download, post a message on somebody's Facebook wall, shop on Amazon, bid on eBay, publish a blog, rate a movie on IMDb, read www.NYT.com, watch YouTube and do the thousands of other things we routinely do online, we are using one computer to send commands to other computers at remote locations. Our access to those remote computers is governed by a series of private agreements and policies that most people are only dimly aware of and virtually no one reads or understands.

For example, it's not widely known that, up until very recently, Google forbade minors from using its services. *See* Google Terms of Service, effective April 16, 2007—March 1, 2012, § 2.3 . . . ("You may not use the Services and may not accept the Terms if . . . you are not of legal age to form a binding contract with Google. . . ."). Adopting the government's interpretation would turn vast numbers of teens and pre-teens into juvenile delinquents—and their parents and teachers into delinquency contributors. Similarly, Facebook makes it a violation of the terms of service to let anyone log into your account. *See* Facebook Statement of Rights and Responsibilities § 4.8 http://www.facebook.com/legal/terms ("You will not share your password . . . let anyone else access your account, or do anything else that might jeopardize the security of your account."). Yet it's very common for people to let close friends and relatives check their email or access their online accounts. Some may be aware that, if discovered, they may suffer a rebuke from the ISP or a loss of access, but few imagine they might be marched off to federal prison for doing so.

Or consider the numerous dating websites whose terms of use prohibit inaccurate or misleading information. *See, e.g.,* eHarmony Terms of Service § 2(I), http://www.eharmony.com/about/terms ("You will not provide inaccurate, misleading or false information to eHarmony or to any other user."). Or eBay and Craigslist, where it's a violation of the terms of use to post items in an inappropriate category. *See, e.g.,* eBay User Agreement, http://pages.ebay.com/help/policies/user-agreement.html ("While using eBay sites, services and tools, you will not: post content or items in an inappropriate category or areas on our sites and services. . . ."). Under the government's proposed interpretation of the CFAA, posting for sale an item prohibited by Craigslist's policy, or describing yourself as "tall, dark and handsome," when you're actually short and homely, will earn you a handsome orange jumpsuit.

Not only are the terms of service vague and generally unknown—unless you look real hard at the small print at the bottom of a webpage—but website owners retain the right to change the terms at any time and without notice. . . . Accordingly, behavior that wasn't criminal yesterday can become criminal today without an act of Congress, and without any notice whatsoever.

The government assures us that, whatever the scope of the CFAA, it won't prosecute minor violations. But we shouldn't have to live at the mercy of our local prosecutor. . . . And it's not clear we *can* trust the government when a tempting target comes along. Take the case of the mom who posed as a 17-year-old boy and cyber-bullied her daughter's classmate. The Justice Department prosecuted her under 18 U.S.C. § 1030(a)(2)(C) for violating MySpace's terms of service, which prohibited lying about identifying information, including age. *See United States v. Drew.* . . . By giving that much power to prosecutors, we're inviting discriminatory and arbitrary enforcement.

. . . .

CONCLUSION

We need not decide today whether Congress *could* base criminal liability on violations of a company or website's computer-use restrictions. Instead, we hold that the phrase "exceeds authorized access" in the CFAA does not extend to violations of use restrictions. If Congress wants to incorporate misappropriation liability into the CFAA, it must speak more clearly. The rule of lenity requires "penal laws ... to be construed strictly."

. . . .

The rule of lenity not only ensures that citizens will have fair notice of the criminal laws, but also that Congress will have fair notice of what conduct its laws criminalize. We construe criminal statutes narrowly so that Congress will not unintentionally turn ordinary citizens into criminals. . . .

This narrower interpretation is also a more sensible reading of the text and legislative history of a statute whose general purpose is to punish hacking—the circumvention of technological access barriers—not misappropriation of trade secrets—a subject Congress has dealt with elsewhere.

. . . .

SILVERMAN, CIRCUIT JUDGE, with whom TALLMAN, CIRCUIT JUDGE concurs, dissenting:

This case has nothing to do with playing sudoku, checking email, fibbing on dating sites, or any of the other activities that the majority rightly values. It has everything to do with stealing an employer's valuable information to set up a competing business with the purloined data, siphoned away from the victim, knowing such access and use were prohibited in the defendants' employment contracts. The indictment here charged that Nosal and his co-conspirators knowingly exceeded the access to a protected company computer they were given by an executive search firm that employed them; that they did so with the intent to defraud; and further, that they stole the victim's valuable proprietary information by means of that fraudulent conduct in order to profit from using it. In ridiculing scenarios not remotely presented by *this* case, the majority does a good job of knocking down straw men—far-fetched hypotheticals involving neither theft nor intentional fraudulent conduct, but innocuous violations of office policy.

The majority also takes a plainly written statute and parses it in a hyper-complicated way that distorts the obvious intent of Congress. No other circuit that has considered this statute finds the problems that the majority does.

18 U.S.C. § 1030(a)(4) is quite clear. It states, in relevant part:

"(a) Whoever—

"(4) knowingly and with intent to defraud, accesses a protected computer without authorization, or exceeds authorized access, and by means of such conduct furthers the intended fraud and obtains anything of value

. . .

shall be punished. . . ."

Thus, it is perfectly clear that a person with *both* the requisite mens rea *and* the specific intent to defraud—but *only* such persons—can violate this subsection in one of two ways: first, by accessing a computer without authorization, or second, by exceeding authorized access. 18 U.S.C. § 1030(e)(6) defines "exceeds authorized access" as "to access a computer with authorization and to use such access to obtain or alter information in the computer that the accesser is not entitled so to obtain or alter."

"As this definition makes clear, an individual who is authorized to use a computer for certain purposes but goes beyond those limitations is considered by the CFAA as someone who has 'exceed[ed] authorized access.' "

"[T]he definition of the term 'exceeds authorized access' from § 1030(e)(6) implies that an employee can violate employer-placed limits on accessing information stored on the computer and still have authorization to access that computer. . . ."

. . . .

This is not an esoteric concept. A bank teller is entitled to access a bank's money for legitimate banking purposes, but not to take the bank's money for himself. A new car buyer may be entitled to take a vehicle around the block on a test drive. But the buyer would not be entitled—he would "exceed his authority"—to take the vehicle to Mexico on a drug run. A person of ordinary intelligence understands that he may be totally prohibited from doing something *altogether*, or authorized to do something but prohibited from going *beyond* what is authorized. This is no doubt why the statute covers not only "unauthorized access," but also "exceed[ing] authorized access." The statute contemplates both means of committing the theft.

The majority holds that a person "exceeds authorized access" only when that person has permission to access a computer generally, but is *completely* prohibited from accessing a different portion of the computer (or different information on the computer). The majority's interpretation conflicts with the plain language of the statute.

. . . .

At the very least, when an employee "knows that the purpose for which she is accessing information in a computer is both in violation of an employer's policies and is part of [a criminally fraudulent] scheme, it would be 'proper' to conclude that such conduct 'exceeds authorized access.' "

. . . .

[I]t does not advance the ball to consider, as the majority does, the parade of horribles that might occur under *different* subsections of the CFAA, such as subsection (a)(2)(C), which does not have the scienter or specific intent to defraud requirements that subsection (a)(4) has. . . . Other sections of the CFAA may or may not be unconstitutionally vague or pose other problems. We need to wait for an actual case or controversy to frame these issues, rather than posit a laundry list of wacky hypotheticals. I express no opinion on the validity or application of other subsections of 18 U.S.C. § 1030, other than § 1030(a)(4), and with all due respect, neither should the majority.

. . . .

18 U.S.C. § 1030(a)(4) clearly is aimed at, and limited to, knowing and intentional fraud. Because the indictment adequately states the elements of a valid crime, the district court erred in dismissing the charges.

I respectfully dissent.

SEKHAR V. UNITED STATES
133 S.Ct. 2720 (2013)

As you read this case, consider these questions:

- Why does Justice Scalia begin with the common law rather than the plain text of the statute? Does this surprise you?

- Do you think the defendant extorted?

- Does Justice Scalia use legislative history in tracing the development of the Hobbs Act?

- Do you agree with Justice Scalia that the government's case is exceedingly weak?

- The Hobbs Act was originally enacted to combat racketeering in labor relations. Does this fact help the government or the defendant? Do you think it would have been worth addressing in the opinion?

- Why doesn't the majority opinion—written by Justice Scalia, one of the Court's strongest proponents of the rule of lenity—use the rule of lenity to buttress its position?

- How do the majority and concurring opinions differ from one another?

JUSTICE SCALIA delivered the opinion of the Court.

We consider whether attempting to compel a person to recommend that his employer approve an investment constitutes "the obtaining of property from another" under 18 U.S.C. § 1951(b)(2).

I

New York's Common Retirement Fund is an employee pension fund for the State of New York and its local governments. As sole trustee of the Fund, the State Comptroller chooses Fund investments. When the Comptroller decides to approve an investment he issues a "Commitment." A Commitment, however, does not actually bind the Fund. For that to happen, the Fund and the recipient of the investment must enter into a limited partnership agreement.

Petitioner Giridhar Sekhar was a managing partner of FA Technology Ventures. In October 2009, the Comptroller's office was considering whether to invest in a fund managed by that firm. The office's general counsel made a written recommendation to the Comptroller not to invest in the fund, after learning that the Office of the New York Attorney General was investigating another fund managed by the firm. The Comptroller decided not to issue a Commitment and notified a partner of FA Technology Ventures. That partner had previously heard rumors that the general counsel was having an extramarital affair.

The general counsel then received a series of anonymous e-mails demanding that he recommend moving forward with the investment and threatening, if he did not, to disclose information about his alleged affair to his wife, government officials, and the media. The general counsel contacted law enforcement, which traced some of the e-mails to petitioner's home computer and other e-mails to offices of FA Technology Ventures.

Petitioner was indicted for, and a jury convicted him of, attempted extortion, in violation of the Hobbs Act, 18 U.S.C. § 1951(a). That Act subjects a person to criminal liability if he "in any way or degree obstructs, delays, or affects commerce or the movement of any article or commodity in commerce, by robbery or extortion or attempts or conspires so to do." The Act defines "extortion" to mean "the obtaining of property from another, with his consent, induced by wrongful use of actual or threatened force, violence, or fear, or under color of official right." § 1951(b)(2). On the verdict form, the jury was asked to specify the property that petitioner attempted to extort: (1) "the Commitment"; (2) "the Comptroller's approval of the Commitment"; or (3) "the General Counsel's recommendation to approve the Commitment." The jury chose only the third option. [The Second Circuit affirmed.]

. . . .

II

A

Whether viewed from the standpoint of the common law, the text and genesis of the statute at issue here, or the jurisprudence of this Court's prior cases, what was charged in this case was not extortion.

It is a settled principle of interpretation that, absent other indication, "Congress intends to incorporate the well-settled meaning of the common-law terms it uses."

"[W]here Congress borrows terms of art in which are accumulated the legal tradition and meaning of centuries of practice, it presumably knows and adopts the cluster of ideas that were attached to each borrowed word in the body of learning from which it was taken and the meaning its use will convey to the judicial mind unless otherwise instructed."

Or as Justice Frankfurter colorfully put it, "if a word is obviously transplanted from another legal source, whether the common law or other legislation, it brings the old soil with it."

The Hobbs Act punishes "extortion," one of the oldest crimes in our legal tradition. The crime originally applied only to extortionate action by public officials, but was later extended by statute to private extortion. As far as is known, no case predating the Hobbs Act—English, federal, or state—ever identified conduct such as that charged here as extortionate. Extortion required the obtaining of items of value, typically cash, from the victim. . . . It did not cover mere coercion to act, or to refrain from acting.

The text of the statute at issue confirms that the alleged property here cannot be extorted. Enacted in 1946, the Hobbs Act defines its crime of "extortion" as "the *obtaining of property from another,* with his consent, induced by wrongful use of actual or threatened force, violence, or fear, or under color of official right." Obtaining property requires "not only the deprivation but also the acquisition of property." That is, it requires that the victim "part with" his property, and that the extortionist "gain possession" of it. The property extorted must therefore be *transferable*— that is, capable of passing from one person to another. The alleged property here lacks that defining feature.

[margin annotation: victim must part with and extortion must gain ↓ here it lacks]

The genesis of the Hobbs Act reinforces that conclusion. The Act was modeled after § 850 of the New York Penal Law (1909), which was derived from the famous Field Code, a 19th-century model penal code. Congress borrowed, nearly verbatim, the New York statute's definition of extortion. The New York statute contained, in addition to the felony crime of extortion, a new (that is to say, nonexistent at common law) misdemeanor crime of coercion. Whereas the former required, as we have said, "'the criminal acquisition of . . . property,'" the latter required merely the use of threats "to compel another person to do or to abstain from doing an act which such other person has a legal right to do or to abstain from doing." Congress did not copy the coercion provision. The omission must have been deliberate, since it was perfectly clear that extortion did not include coercion. At the time of the borrowing (1946), New York courts had consistently held that the sort of *interference* with rights that occurred here was coercion.

. . . .

B

The Government's shifting and imprecise characterization of the alleged property at issue betrays the weakness of its case. According to the jury's verdict form, the "property" that petitioner attempted to extort was "the General Counsel's recommendation to approve the Commitment." But the Government expends minuscule effort in defending that theory of conviction. And for good reason—to wit, our decision in *Cleveland v. United States*, 531 U.S. 12 (2000), which reversed a business owner's mail-fraud conviction for "obtaining money or property" through misrepresentations made in an application for a video-poker license issued by the State. We held that a "license" is not "property" while in the State's hands and so cannot be "obtained" from the State. Even less so can an employee's yet-to-be-issued recommendation be called obtainable property, and less so still a yet-to-be-issued recommendation that would merely approve (but not effect) a particular investment.

Hence the Government's reliance on an alternative, more sophisticated (and sophistic) description of the property. Instead of defending the jury's description, the Government hinges its case on the general counsel's "intangible property right to give his disinterested legal opinion to his client free of improper outside interference." But *what,* exactly, would the petitioner have obtained for himself? A right to give *his own* disinterested legal opinion to *his own* client free of improper interference? Or perhaps, a right to give *the general counsel's* disinterested legal opinion to *the general counsel's* client?

Either formulation sounds absurd, because it is. Clearly, petitioner's goal was not to acquire the general counsel's "intangible property right to give disinterested legal advice." It was to force the general counsel to offer advice that accorded with petitioner's wishes. But again, that is coercion, not extortion. No fluent speaker of English would say that "petitioner *obtained and exercised* the general counsel's right to make a recommendation," any more than he would say that a person "*obtained and exercised* another's right to free speech." He would say that "petitioner *forced* the general counsel to make a particular recommendation," just as he would say that a person "*forced* another to make a statement." Adopting the Government's theory here would not only make nonsense of words; it would collapse the longstanding distinction between extortion and coercion and ignore Congress's choice to penalize one but not the other. That we cannot do.

The judgment of the Court of Appeals for the Second Circuit is reversed.

It is so ordered.

JUSTICE ALITO, with whom JUSTICE KENNEDY and JUSTICE SOTOMAYOR join, concurring in the judgment.

The question that we must decide in this case is whether "the General Counsel's recommendation to approve the Commitment,"—or his right to make that recommendation—is property that is capable of being extorted under the Hobbs Act. In my view, they are not.

I

The jury in this case returned a special verdict form and stated that the property that petitioner attempted to extort was "the General Counsel's recommendation to approve the Commitment." What the jury obviously meant by this was the general counsel's internal suggestion to his superior that the state government issue a nonbinding commitment to invest in a fund managed by FA Technology Ventures. We must therefore decide whether this nonbinding internal recommendation by a salaried state employee constitutes "property" within the meaning of the Hobbs Act, which defines "extortion" as "the obtaining of property from another, with his consent, induced by wrongful use of actual or threatened force, violence, or fear, or under color of official right."

The Hobbs Act does not define the term "property," but even at common law the offense of extortion was understood to include the obtaining of any thing of value. 2 E. Coke, The First Part of the Institutes of the Laws of England 368b (18th English ed. 1823) ("Extortion . . . is a great misprison, by wresting or unlawfully taking by any officer, by colour of his office, any money or valuable thing of or from any man"); 4 W. Blackstone, Commentaries (extortion is "an abuse of public, justice which consists in any officer's unlawfully taking, by colour of his office, from any man, any money or thing of value"). See also 2 J. Bishop, Criminal Law § 401, pp. 331–332 (9th ed. 1923) ("In most cases, the thing obtained is money. . . . But probably anything of value will suffice"); 3 F. Wharton, A Treatise on Criminal Law § 1898, p. 2095 (11th ed. 1912) ("[I]t is enough if any valuable thing is received").

At the time Congress enacted the Hobbs Act, the contemporary edition of Black's Law Dictionary included an expansive definition of the term. See Black's Law Dictionary 1446 (3d ed. 1933). It stated that "[t]he term is said to extend to every species of valuable right and interest. . . . The word is also commonly used to denote everything which is the subject of ownership, corporeal or incorporeal, tangible or intangible, visible or invisible, real or personal; everything that has an exchangeable value or which goes to make up wealth or estate." And the lower courts have long given the term a similarly expansive construction. See, *e.g., United States v. Tropiano*, 418 F.2d 1069, 1075 (C.A.2 1969) ("The concept of property under the Hobbs Act . . . includes, in a broad sense, any valuable right considered as a source or element of wealth").

Despite the breadth of some of these formulations, however, the term "property" plainly does not reach everything that a person may hold dear; nor does it extend to everything that might in some indirect way portend the possibility of future economic gain. I do not suggest that the current lower court case law is necessarily correct, but it seems clear that the case now before us is an outlier and that the jury's verdict stretches the concept of property beyond the breaking point.

It is not customary to refer to an internal recommendation to make a government decision as a form of property. It would seem strange to say that the government or its employees have a property interest in their internal recommendations regarding such things as the issuance of a building permit, the content of an environmental impact statement, the approval of a new drug, or the indictment of an individual or a corporation. And it would be even stranger to say that a private party who might be affected by the government's decision can obtain a property interest in a recommendation to make the decision.

Our decision in *Cleveland v. United States* supports the conclusion that internal recommendations regarding government decisions are not property. In *Cleveland*, we vacated a business owner's conviction under the federal mail fraud statute for "obtaining money or property" through misrepresentations made in an application for a video poker license issued by the State. We held that a video poker license is not property in the hands of the State. I do not suggest that the concepts of property under the mail fraud statute and the Hobbs Act are necessarily the same. But surely a video poker license has a stronger claim to be classified as property than a mere internal recommendation that a state government take an initial step that might lead eventually to an investment that would be beneficial to private parties.

The Government has not cited any Hobbs Act case holding that an internal recommendation regarding a government decision constitutes property. Nor has the Government cited any other example of the use of the term "property" in this sense.

The Second Circuit recharacterized the property that petitioner attempted to obtain as the general counsel's "right to make a recommendation consistent with his legal judgment." And the Government also presses that theory in this Court. According to the Government, the general counsel's property interest in his recommendation encompasses the right to make the recommendation.

But this argument assumes that the recommendation itself is property. If an internal recommendation regarding a government decision does not constitute property, then surely a government employee's right to make such a recommendation is not property either (nor could it be deemed a *property* right).

II

The Government argues that the recommendation was the general counsel's *personal* property because it was inextricably related to his right to pursue his profession as an attorney. But that argument is clearly wrong: If the general counsel had left the State's employ before submitting the recommendation, he could not have taken the recommendation with him, and he certainly could not have given it or sold it to someone else. Therefore, it is obvious that the recommendation (and the right to make it) were inextricably related to the general counsel's position with the government, and not to his broader personal right to pursue the practice of law.

The general counsel's job surely had economic value to him, as did his labor as a lawyer, his law license, and his reputation as an attorney. But the indictment did not allege, and the jury did not find, that petitioner attempted to obtain those things. Nor would such a theory make sense in the context of this case. Petitioner did not, for example, seek the general counsel's legal advice or demand that the general counsel represent him in a legal proceeding. Nor did petitioner attempt to enhance his own ability to compete with the general counsel for legal work by threatening to do something that would, say, tarnish the general counsel's reputation or cause his law license to be revoked.

The Court holds that petitioner's conduct does not amount to attempted extortion, but for a different reason: According to the Court, the alleged property that petitioner pursued was not transferrable and therefore is not capable of being "obtained." Because I do not believe that the item in question constitutes property, it is unnecessary for me to determine whether or not petitioner sought to obtain it.

If Congress had wanted to classify internal recommendations pertaining to government decisions as property, I think it would have spoken more clearly than it did in the Hobbs Act. But even if the Hobbs Act were ambiguous on this point, the rule of lenity would counsel in favor of an interpretation of the statute that does not reach so broadly. This is not to say that the Government could not have prosecuted petitioner for extortion on these same facts under some other theory. The question before us is whether the general counsel's recommendation—or the right to make it—constitutes property under the Hobbs Act. In my view, they do not.

For these reasons, I concur in the Court's judgment.

TENNESSEE VALLEY AUTHORITY V. HILL
437 U.S. 153 (1978)

This case offers a first-rate example of Supreme Court Justices debating a thorny issue of interpretation. All of the different categories of interpretative doctrines and tools are amply represented. As you read the case, focus on these issues:

- What is the ambiguous language? In other words, what is the source of the disagreement as to how to interpret the statute?

- How would you characterize each of the opinions in terms of the theories of statutory interpretation?

- Identify all of the different kinds of arguments the Justices make. Which ones do you think are decisive for the majority? For the dissent?

- How would a textualist like Justice Scalia have voted? How would an opinion by Justice Scalia read?

- Which opinion do you agree with, if any, and why?

CHIEF JUSTICE BURGER delivered the opinion of the Court.

The questions presented in this case are (a) whether the Endangered Species Act of 1973 requires a court to enjoin the operation of a virtually completed federal dam—which had been authorized prior to 1973—when, pursuant to authority vested in him by Congress, the Secretary of the Interior has determined that operation of the dam would eradicate an endangered species; and (b) whether continued congressional appropriations for the dam after 1973 constituted an implied repeal of the Endangered Species Act, at least as to the particular dam.

I

The Little Tennessee River originates in the mountains of northern Georgia and flows through the national forest lands of North Carolina into Tennessee, where it converges with the Big Tennessee River near Knoxville. The lower 33 miles of the Little Tennessee takes the river's clear, free-flowing waters through an area of great natural beauty. . . .

In this area of the Little Tennessee River the Tennessee Valley Authority, a wholly owned public corporation of the United States, began constructing the Tellico Dam and Reservoir Project in 1967, shortly after Congress appropriated initial funds for its development. Tellico is a multipurpose regional development project designed principally to stimulate shoreline development, generate sufficient electric current to heat 20,000 homes, and provide flatwater recreation and flood control, as well as improve economic conditions in "an area characterized by underutilization of human resources and outmigration of young people." Of particular relevance to this case is one aspect of the project, a dam which TVA determined to place on the Little Tennessee, a short distance from where the river's waters meet with the Big Tennessee. When fully operational, the dam would impound water covering some 16,500 acres— much of which represents valuable and productive farmland—thereby converting the river's shallow, fast-flowing waters into a deep reservoir over 30 miles in length.

The Tellico Dam has never opened, however, despite the fact that construction has been virtually completed and the dam is essentially ready for operation. Although Congress has appropriated monies for Tellico every year since 1967, progress was delayed, and ultimately stopped, by a tangle of lawsuits and administrative proceedings. After unsuccessfully urging TVA to consider alternatives to damming the Little Tennessee, local citizens and national conservation groups brought suit in the District Court, claiming that the project did not conform to the requirements of the National Environmental Policy Act of 1969 (NEPA). After finding TVA to be in violation of NEPA, the District Court enjoined the dam's completion pending the filing of an appropriate environmental impact statement. The injunction remained in effect until late 1973, when the District Court concluded that TVA's final environmental impact statement for Tellico was in compliance with the law.

A few months prior to the District Court's decision dissolving the NEPA injunction, a discovery was made in the waters of the Little Tennessee which would profoundly affect the Tellico Project. Exploring the area around Coytee Springs, which is about seven miles from the mouth of the river, a University of Tennessee ichthyologist, Dr. David A. Etnier, found a previously unknown species of perch, the snail darter, or *Percina (Imostoma) tanasi*. This three-inch, tannish-colored fish, whose numbers are estimated to be in the range of 10,000 to 15,000, would soon engage the attention of environmentalists, the TVA, the Department of the Interior, the Congress of the United States, and ultimately the federal courts, as a new and additional basis to halt construction of the dam.

Until recently the finding of a new species of animal life would hardly generate a cause célèbre. This is particularly so in the case of darters, of which there are approximately 130 known species, 8 to 10 of these having been identified only in the last five years. The moving force behind the snail darter's sudden fame came some four months after its discovery, when the Congress passed the Endangered Species Act of 1973 (Act). This legislation, among other things, authorizes the Secretary of the Interior to declare species of animal life "endangered" and to identify the "critical habitat" of these creatures. When a species or its habitat is so listed, the following portion of the Act—relevant here—becomes effective:

"The Secretary [of the Interior] shall review other programs administered by him and utilize such programs in furtherance of the purposes of this chapter. All other Federal departments and agencies shall, in consultation with and with the assistance of the Secretary, utilize their authorities in furtherance of the purposes of this chapter by carrying out programs for the conservation of endangered species and threatened species listed pursuant to section 1533 of this title and *by taking such action necessary to insure that actions authorized, funded, or carried out by them do not jeopardize the continued existence of such endangered species and threatened species or result in the destruction or modification of habitat of such species* which is determined by the Secretary, after consultation as appropriate with the affected States, to be critical."

In January 1975, the respondents in this case and others petitioned the Secretary of the Interior to list the snail darter as an endangered species. After receiving comments from various interested parties, including TVA and the State of Tennessee, the Secretary formally listed the snail darter as an endangered species on October 8, 1975. In so acting, it was noted that "the snail darter is a living entity which is genetically distinct and reproductively isolated from other fishes." More important for the purposes of this case, the Secretary determined that the snail darter apparently lives only in that portion of the Little Tennessee River which would be completely inundated by the reservoir created as a consequence of the Tellico Dam's completion. The Secretary went on to explain the significance of the dam to the habitat of the snail darter:

"[T]he snail darter occurs only in the swifter portions of shoals over clean gravel substrate in cool, low-turbidity water. Food of the snail darter is almost exclusively snails which require a clean gravel substrate for their survival. *The proposed impoundment of water behind the proposed Tellico Dam would result in total destruction of the snail darter's habitat.*"

Subsequent to this determination, the Secretary declared the area of the Little Tennessee which would be affected by the Tellico Dam to be the "critical habitat" of the snail darter. Using these determinations as a predicate, and notwithstanding the near completion of the dam, the Secretary declared that pursuant to § 7 of the Act, "all Federal agencies must take such action as is necessary to insure that actions authorized, funded, or carried out by them do not result in the destruction or modification of this critical habitat area." This notice, of course, was pointedly directed at TVA and clearly aimed at halting completion or operation of the dam.

During the pendency of these administrative actions, other developments of relevance to the snail darter issue were transpiring. Communication was occurring between the Department of the Interior's Fish and Wildlife Service and TVA with a view toward settling the issue informally. These negotiations were to no avail, however, since TVA consistently took the position that the only available alternative was to attempt relocating the snail darter population to another suitable location. To this end, TVA conducted a search of alternative sites which might sustain the fish, culminating in the experimental transplantation of a number of snail darters to the nearby Hiwassee River. However, the Secretary of the Interior was not satisfied with the results of these efforts, finding that TVA had presented "little evidence that they have carefully studied the Hiwassee to determine whether or not" there were "biological and other factors in this river that [would] negate a successful transplant."

Meanwhile, Congress had also become involved in the fate of the snail darter. Appearing before a Subcommittee of the House Committee on Appropriations in April 1975—some seven months before the snail darter was listed as endangered—TVA representatives described the discovery of the fish and the relevance of the Endangered Species Act to the Tellico Project. At that time TVA presented a position which it would advance in successive forums thereafter, namely, that the Act did not prohibit the completion of a project authorized, funded, and substantially constructed before the Act was passed. TVA also described its efforts to transplant the snail darter, but contended that the dam should be finished regardless of the experiment's success. Thereafter, the House Committee on Appropriations, in its June 20, 1975, Report, stated the following in the course of recommending that an additional $29 million be appropriated for Tellico:

"The *Committee* directs that the project, for which an environmental impact statement has been completed and provided the Committee, should be completed as promptly as possible. . . ."

Congress then approved the TVA general budget, which contained funds for continued construction of the Tellico Project. In December 1975, one month after the snail darter was declared an endangered species, the President signed the bill into law.

In February 1976, pursuant to § 11(g) of the Endangered Species Act, respondents filed the case now under review, seeking to enjoin completion of the dam and impoundment of the reservoir on the ground that those actions would violate the Act by directly causing the extinction of the species *Percina (Imostoma) tanasi*. The District Court denied respondents' request for a preliminary injunction and set the matter for trial. Shortly thereafter the House and Senate held appropriations hearings which would include discussions of the Tellico budget.

At these hearings, TVA Chairman Wagner reiterated the agency's position that the Act did not apply to a project which was over 50% finished by the time the Act became effective and some 70% to 80% complete when the snail darter was officially listed as endangered. It also notified the Committees of the recently filed lawsuit's status and reported that TVA's efforts to transplant the snail darter had "been very encouraging."

Trial was held in the District Court on April 29 and 30, 1976, and on May 25, 1976, the court entered its memorandum opinion and order denying respondents their requested relief and dismissing the complaint. The District Court found that closure of the dam and the consequent impoundment of the reservoir would "result in the adverse modification, if not complete destruction, of the snail darter's critical habitat," making it "highly probable" that "the continued existence of the snail darter" would be "jeopardize[d]." Despite these findings, the District Court declined to embrace the plaintiffs' position on the merits: that once a federal project was shown to jeopardize an endangered species, a court of equity is compelled to issue an injunction restraining violation of the Endangered Species Act.

In reaching this result, the District Court stressed that the entire project was then about 80% complete and, based on available evidence, "there [were] no alternatives to impoundment of the reservoir, short of scrapping the entire project." The District Court also found that if the Tellico Project was permanently enjoined, "[s]ome $53 million would be lost in nonrecoverable obligations," meaning that a large portion of the $78 million already expended would be wasted. The court also noted that the Endangered Species Act of 1973 was passed some seven years after construction on the dam commenced and that Congress had continued appropriations for Tellico, with full awareness of the snail darter problem. Assessing these various factors, the District Court concluded:

"At some point in time a federal project becomes so near completion and so incapable of modification that a court of equity should not apply a statute enacted long after inception of the project to produce an unreasonable result. . . . Where there has been an irreversible and irretrievable commitment of resources by Congress to a project over a span of almost a decade, the Court should proceed with a great deal of circumspection."

To accept the plaintiffs' position, the District Court argued, would inexorably lead to what it characterized as the absurd result of requiring "a court to halt impoundment of water behind a fully completed dam if an endangered species were discovered in the river on the day before such impoundment was scheduled to take place. We cannot conceive that Congress intended such a result." Less than a month after the District Court decision, the Senate and House Appropriations Committees recommended the full budget request of $9 million for continued work on Tellico. In its Report accompanying the appropriations bill, the Senate Committee stated:

"During subcommittee hearings, TVA was questioned about the relationship between the Tellico project's completion and the November 1975 listing of the snail darter (a small 3-inch fish which was discovered in 1973) as an endangered species under the Endangered Species Act. TVA informed the Committee that it was continuing its efforts to preserve the darter, while working towards the scheduled 1977 completion date. TVA repeated its view that the Endangered Species Act did not prevent the completion of the Tellico project, which has been under construction for nearly a decade. The subcommittee brought this matter, as well as the recent U. S. District Court's decision upholding TVA's decision to complete the project, to the attention of the full Committee. *The Committee does not view* the Endangered Species Act as prohibiting the completion of the Tellico project at its advanced stage and directs that this project be completed as promptly as possible in the public interest."

On June 29, 1976, both Houses of Congress passed TVA's general budget, which included funds for Tellico; the President signed the bill on July 12, 1976.

Thereafter, in the Court of Appeals, respondents argued that the District Court had abused its discretion by not issuing an injunction in the face of "a blatant statutory violation." The Court of Appeals agreed, and on January 31, 1977, it reversed, remanding "with instructions that a permanent injunction issue halting all activities incident to the Tellico Project which may destroy or modify the critical habitat of the snail darter." The Court of Appeals directed that the injunction "remain in effect until Congress, by appropriate legislation, exempts Tellico from compliance with the Act or the snail darter has been deleted from the list of endangered species or its critical habitat materially redefined."

The Court of Appeals accepted the District Court's finding that closure of the dam would result in the known population of snail darters being "significantly reduced if not completely extirpated." TVA, in fact, had conceded as much in the Court of Appeals, but argued that "closure of the Tellico Dam, as the last stage of a ten-year project, falls outside the legitimate purview of the Act if it is rationally construed." Disagreeing, the Court of Appeals held that the record revealed a prima facie violation of § 7 of the Act, namely that TVA had failed to take "such action . . . necessary to insure" that its "actions" did not jeopardize the snail darter or its critical habitat.

The reviewing court thus rejected TVA's contention that the word "actions" in § 7 of the Act was not intended by Congress to encompass the terminal phases of ongoing projects. Not only could the court find no "positive reinforcement" for TVA's argument in the Act's legislative history, but also such an interpretation was seen as being "inimical to . . . its objectives." By way of illustration, that court pointed out that "the detrimental impact of a project upon an endangered species may not always be clearly perceived before construction is well underway." Given such a likelihood, the Court of Appeals was of the opinion that TVA's position would require the District Court, sitting as a chancellor, to balance the worth of an endangered species against the value of an ongoing public works measure, a result which the appellate court was not willing to accept. Emphasizing the limits on judicial power in this setting, the court stated:

"Current project status cannot be translated into a workable standard of judicial review. Whether a dam is 50% or 90% completed is irrelevant in calculating the social and scientific costs attributable to the disappearance of a unique form of life. Courts are ill-equipped to calculate how many dollars must be invested before the value of a dam exceeds that of the endangered species. Our responsibility under § 1540(g)(1)(A) is merely to preserve the status quo where endangered species are threatened, thereby guaranteeing the legislative or executive branches sufficient opportunity to grapple with the alternatives."

As far as the Court of Appeals was concerned, it made no difference that Congress had repeatedly approved appropriations for Tellico, referring to such legislative approval as an "advisory opinio[n]" concerning the proper application of an existing statute. In that court's view, the only relevant legislation was the Act itself, "[t]he meaning and spirit" of which was "clear on its face."

Turning to the question of an appropriate remedy, the Court of Appeals ruled that the District Court had erred by not issuing an injunction. While recognizing the irretrievable loss of millions of dollars of public funds which would accompany injunctive relief, the court nonetheless decided that the Act explicitly commanded precisely that result:

"It is conceivable that the welfare of an endangered species may weigh more heavily upon the public conscience, as expressed by the final will of Congress, than the writeoff of those millions of dollars already expended for Tellico in excess of its present salvageable value."

Following the issuance of the permanent injunction, members of TVA's Board of Directors appeared before Subcommittees of the House and Senate Appropriations Committees to testify in support of continued appropriations for Tellico. The Subcommittees were apprised of all aspects of Tellico's status, including the Court of Appeals' decision. TVA reported that the dam stood "ready for the gates to be closed and the reservoir filled," and requested funds for completion of certain ancillary parts of the project, such as public use areas, roads, and bridges. As to the snail darter itself, TVA commented optimistically on its transplantation efforts, expressing the opinion that the relocated fish were "doing well and ha[d] reproduced."

Both Appropriations Committees subsequently recommended the full amount requested for completion of the Tellico Project. In its June 2, 1977, Report, the House Appropriations Committee stated:

"It is *the Committee's view* that the Endangered Species Act was not intended to halt projects such as these in their advanced stage of completion, and [the Committee] strongly recommends that these projects not be stopped because of misuse of the Act."

As a solution to the problem, the House Committee advised that TVA should cooperate with the Department of the Interior "to relocate the endangered species to another suitable habitat so as to permit the project to proceed as rapidly as possible." Toward this end, the Committee recommended a special appropriation of $2 million to facilitate relocation of the snail darter and other endangered species which threatened to delay or stop TVA projects. Much the same occurred on the Senate side, with its Appropriations Committee recommending both the amount requested to complete Tellico and the special appropriation for transplantation of endangered species. Reporting to the Senate on these measures, the Appropriations Committee took a particularly strong stand on the snail darter issue:

"This *committee has not viewed* the Endangered Species Act as preventing the completion and use of these projects which were well under way at the time the affected species were listed as endangered. If the act has such an effect which is contrary to *the Committee's understanding* of the intent of Congress in enacting the Endangered Species Act, funds should be appropriated to allow these projects to be completed and their benefits realized in the public interest, the Endangered Species Act notwithstanding."

TVA's budget, including funds for completion of Tellico and relocation of the snail darter, passed both Houses of Congress and was signed into law on August 7, 1977.

We granted certiorari to review the judgment of the Court of Appeals.

II

We begin with the premise that operation of the Tellico Dam will either eradicate the known population of snail darters or destroy their critical habitat. Petitioner does not now seriously dispute this fact. In any event, under § 4(a)(1) of the Act, the Secretary of the Interior is vested with exclusive authority to determine whether a species such as the snail darter is "endangered" or "threatened" and to ascertain the factors which have led to such a precarious existence. By § 4(d) Congress has authorized—indeed commanded—the Secretary to "issue such regulations as he deems necessary and advisable to provide for the conservation of such species." As we have seen, the Secretary promulgated regulations which declared the snail darter an endangered species whose critical habitat would be destroyed by creation of the Tellico Dam. Doubtless petitioner would prefer not to have these regulations on the books, but there is no suggestion that the Secretary exceeded his authority or abused his discretion in issuing the regulations. Indeed, no judicial review of the Secretary's determinations has ever been sought and hence the validity of his actions are not open to review in this Court.

Starting from the above premise, two questions are presented: (a) Would TVA be in violation of the Act if it completed and operated the Tellico Dam as planned? (b) If TVA's actions would offend the Act, is an injunction the appropriate remedy for the violation? For the reasons stated hereinafter, we hold that both questions must be answered in the affirmative.

(A)

It may seem curious to some that the survival of a relatively small number of three-inch fish among all the countless millions of species extant would require the permanent halting of a virtually completed dam for which Congress has expended more than $100 million. The paradox is not minimized by the fact that Congress continued to appropriate large sums of public money for the project, even after congressional Appropriations Committees were apprised of its apparent impact upon the survival of the snail darter. We conclude, however, that the explicit provisions of the Endangered Species Act require precisely that result.

One would be hard pressed to find a statutory provision whose terms were any plainer than those in § 7 of the Endangered Species Act. Its very words affirmatively command all federal agencies "to *insure* that actions *authorized, funded,* or *carried out* by them do not *jeopardize* the continued existence" of an endangered species or "*result* in the destruction or modification of habitat of such species. . . ." This language admits of no exception. Nonetheless, petitioner urges, as do the dissenters, that the Act cannot reasonably be interpreted as applying to a federal project which was well under way when Congress passed the Endangered Species Act of 1973. To sustain that position, however, we would be forced to ignore the ordinary meaning of plain language. It has not been shown, for example, how TVA can close the gates of the Tellico Dam without "carrying out" an action that has been "authorized" and "funded" by a federal agency. Nor can we understand how such action will "*insure*" that the snail darter's habitat is not disrupted. Accepting the Secretary's determinations, as we must, it is clear that TVA's proposed operation of the dam will have precisely the opposite effect, namely the *eradication* of an endangered species.

Concededly, this view of the Act will produce results requiring the sacrifice of the anticipated benefits of the project and of many millions of dollars in public funds. But examination of the language, history, and structure of the legislation under review here indicates beyond doubt that Congress intended endangered species to be afforded the highest of priorities.

When Congress passed the Act in 1973, it was not legislating on a clean slate. The first major congressional concern for the preservation of the endangered species had come with passage of the Endangered Species Act of 1966. In that legislation Congress gave the Secretary power to identify "the names of the species of native fish and wildlife found to be threatened with extinction," as well as authorization to purchase land for the conservation, protection, restoration, and propagation of "selected species" of "native fish and wildlife" threatened with extinction. Declaring the preservation of endangered species a national policy, the 1966 Act directed all federal agencies both to protect these species and "*insofar as is practicable and consistent with the[ir] primary purposes,*" "preserve the habitats of such threatened species on lands under their jurisdiction." The 1966 statute was not a sweeping prohibition on the taking of endangered species, however, except on federal lands, and even in those federal areas the Secretary was authorized to allow the hunting and fishing of endangered species.

In 1969 Congress enacted the Endangered Species Conservation Act, which continued the provisions of the 1966 Act while at the same time broadening federal involvement in the preservation of endangered species. Under the 1969 legislation, the Secretary was empowered to list species "threatened with worldwide extinction"; in addition, the importation of any species so recognized into the United States was prohibited. An indirect approach to the taking of endangered species was also adopted in the Conservation Act by way of a ban on the transportation and sale of wildlife taken in violation of any federal, state, or foreign law.

Despite the fact that the 1966 and 1969 legislation represented "the most comprehensive of its type to be enacted by any nation" up to that time, Congress was soon persuaded that a more expansive approach was needed if the newly declared national policy of preserving endangered species was to be realized. By 1973, when Congress held hearings on what would later become the Endangered Species Act of 1973, it was informed that species were still being lost at the rate of about one per year, and "the pace of disappearance of species" appeared to be "accelerating." Moreover, Congress was also told that the primary cause of this trend was something other than the normal process of natural selection:

"[M]an and his technology has [*sic*] continued at any ever-increasing rate to disrupt the natural ecosystem. This has resulted in a dramatic rise in the number and severity of the threats faced by the world's wildlife. The truth in this is apparent when one realizes that half of the recorded extinctions of mammals over the past 2,000 years have occurred in the most recent 50-year period."

. . . .

The legislative proceedings in 1973 are, in fact, replete with expressions of concern over the risk that might lie in the loss of *any* endangered species. Typifying these sentiments is the Report of the House Committee on Merchant Marine and Fisheries on H.R. 37, a bill which contained the essential features of the subsequently enacted Act of 1973; in explaining the need for the legislation, the Report stated:

"As we homogenize the habitats in which these plants and animals evolved, and as we increase the pressure for products that they are in a position to supply (usually unwillingly) we threaten their—and our own— genetic heritage. The value of this genetic heritage is, quite literally, incalculable.

. . . .

"From the most narrow possible point of view, *it is in the best interests of mankind to minimize the losses of genetic variations*. The reason is simple: they are potential resources. They are keys to puzzles which we cannot solve, and may provide answers to questions which we have not yet learned to ask.

"To take a homely, but apt, example: one of the critical chemicals in the regulation of ovulations in humans was found in a common plant. Once discovered, and analyzed, humans could duplicate it synthetically, but had it never existed—or had it been driven out of existence before we knew its potentialities—we would never have tried to synthesize it in the first place.

"Who knows, or can say, what potential cures for cancer or other scourges, present or future, may lie locked up in the structures of plants which may yet be undiscovered, much less analyzed? . . . Sheer self-interest impels us to be cautious.

"*The institutionalization of that caution* lies at the heart of H.R. 37. . . ."

As the examples cited here demonstrate, Congress was concerned about the *unknown* uses that endangered species might have and about the *unforeseeable* place such creatures may have in the chain of life on this planet.

In shaping legislation to deal with the problem thus presented, Congress started from the finding that "[t]he two major causes of extinction are hunting and destruction of natural habitat." Of these twin threats, Congress was informed that the greatest was destruction of natural habitats. . . .

Virtually every bill introduced in Congress during the 1973 session responded to this concern by incorporating language similar, if not identical, to that found in the present § 7 of the Act. These provisions were designed, in the words of an administration witness, "for the first time [to] *prohibit* [a] federal agency from taking action which does jeopardize the status of endangered species. . . ."

As it was finally passed, the Endangered Species Act of 1973 represented the most comprehensive legislation for the preservation of endangered species ever enacted by any nation. Its stated purposes were "to provide a means whereby the ecosystems upon which endangered species and threatened species depend may be conserved," and "to provide a program for the conservation of such . . . species. . . ." In furtherance of these goals, Congress expressly stated in § 2(c) that "all Federal departments and agencies *shall* seek *to conserve endangered species* and threatened species. . . ." Lest there be any ambiguity as to the meaning of this statutory directive, the Act specifically defined "conserve" as meaning "to use and the use of *all methods and procedures which are necessary* to bring *any endangered species or threatened species* to the point at which the measures provided pursuant to this chapter are no longer necessary."

Aside from § 7, other provisions indicated the seriousness with which Congress viewed this issue. . . .

Section 7 of the Act, which of course is relied upon by respondents in this case, provides a particularly good gauge of congressional intent. As we have seen, this provision had its genesis in the Endangered Species Act of 1966, but that legislation qualified the obligation of federal agencies by stating that they should seek to preserve endangered species only *"insofar as is practicable and consistent with the[ir] primary purposes. . . ."* Likewise, every bill introduced in 1973 contained a qualification similar to that found in the earlier statutes. Exemplary of these was the administration bill, H.R. 4758, which in § 2(b) would direct federal agencies to use their authorities to further the ends of the Act *"insofar as is practicable and consistent with the[ir] primary purposes. . . ."* Explaining the idea behind this language, an administration spokesman told Congress that it "would further signal to all . . . agencies of the Government that this is the *first priority, consistent with their primary objectives.*" This type of language did not go unnoticed by those advocating strong endangered species legislation. A representative of the Sierra Club, for example, attacked the use of the phrase "consistent with the primary purpose" in proposed H.R. 4758, cautioning that the qualification "could be construed to be a declaration of congressional policy that other agency purposes are necessarily more important than protection of endangered species and would always prevail if conflict were to occur."

What is very significant in this sequence is that the final version of the 1973 Act carefully omitted all of the reservations described above. In the bill which the Senate initially approved (S. 1983), however, the version of the current § 7 merely required federal agencies to "carry out such programs *as are practicable* for the protection of species listed. . . ." S. 1983, § 7(a). By way of contrast, the bill that originally passed the House, H.R. 37, contained a provision which was essentially a mirror image of the subsequently passed § 7—indeed all phrases which might have qualified an agency's responsibilities had been omitted from the bill. In explaining the expected impact of this provision in H.R. 37 on federal agencies, the House Committee's Report states:

"This subsection *requires* the Secretary and the heads of all other Federal departments and agencies to use their authorities in order to carry out programs for the protection of endangered species, and it further *requires* that those agencies take *the necessary action* that will *not jeopardize* the continuing existence of endangered species or result in the destruction of critical habitat of those species." H.R.Rep.No.93–412, p. 14 (1973).

Resolution of this difference in statutory language, as well as other variations between the House and Senate bills, was the task of a

Conference Committee. The Conference Report basically adopted the Senate bill, S. 1983; but the conferees rejected the Senate version of § 7 and adopted the stringent, mandatory language in H.R. 37. While the Conference Report made no specific reference to this choice of provisions, the House manager of the bill, Representative Dingell, provided an interpretation of what the Conference bill would require, making it clear that the mandatory provisions of § 7 were not casually or inadvertently included:

"[Section 7] substantially amplifie[s] the obligation of [federal agencies] to take steps within their power to carry out the purposes of this act. A recent article . . . illustrates the problem which might occur absent this new language in the bill. It appears that the whooping cranes of this country, perhaps the best known of our endangered species, are being threatened by Air Force bombing activities along the gulf coast of Texas. Under existing law, the Secretary of Defense has some discretion as to whether or not he will take the necessary action to see that this threat disappears. . . . [O]nce the bill is enacted, [the Secretary of Defense] *would be required to take the proper steps.* . . .

"Another example . . . [has] to do with the continental population of grizzly bears which may or may not be endangered, but which is surely threatened. . . . Once this bill is enacted, the appropriate Secretary, whether of Interior, Agriculture or whatever, *will have to take action* to see that this situation is not permitted to worsen, and that these bears are not driven to extinction. The purposes of the bill included the conservation of the species and of the ecosystems upon which they depend, and *every agency of government is committed* to see that those purposes are carried out. . . . [T]he agencies of Government can no longer plead that they can do nothing about it. *They can, and they must. The law is clear.*"

It is against this legislative background that we must measure TVA's claim that the Act was not intended to stop operation of a project which, like Tellico Dam, was near completion when an endangered species was discovered in its path. While there is no discussion in the legislative history of precisely this problem, the totality of congressional action makes it abundantly clear that the result we reach today is wholly in accord with both the words of the statute and the intent of Congress. The plain intent of Congress in enacting this statute was to halt and reverse the trend toward species extinction, whatever the cost. This is reflected not only in the stated policies of the Act, but in literally every section of the statute. All persons, including federal agencies, are specifically instructed not to "take" endangered species, meaning that no one is "to harass, harm, pursue, hunt, shoot, wound, kill, trap, capture, or collect" such life forms. Agencies in particular are directed by §§ 2(c) and 3(2) of the Act to "use . . . *all methods* and procedures which are necessary" to preserve endangered species. In addition, the legislative history undergirding § 7 reveals an explicit congressional decision to require agencies to afford first priority to the declared national policy of saving endangered species. The pointed omission of the type of qualifying language previously included in endangered species legislation reveals a conscious decision by Congress to give endangered species priority over the "primary missions" of federal agencies.

It is not for us to speculate, much less act, on whether Congress would have altered its stance had the specific events of this case been anticipated. In any event, we discern no hint in the deliberations of Congress relating to the 1973 Act that would compel a different result than we reach here. Indeed, the repeated expressions of congressional concern over what it saw as the potentially enormous danger presented by the eradication of *any* endangered species suggest how the balance would have been struck had the issue been presented to Congress in 1973.

Furthermore, it is clear Congress foresaw that § 7 would, on occasion, require agencies to alter ongoing projects in order to fulfill the goals of the Act. Congressman Dingell's discussion of Air Force practice bombing, for instance, obviously pinpoints a particular activity—intimately related to the national defense—which a major federal department would be obliged to alter in deference to the strictures of § 7. A similar example is provided by the House Committee Report:

"Under the authority of [§ 7], the Director of the Park Service would be required *to conform the practices of his agency* to the need for protecting the rapidly dwindling stock of grizzly bears within Yellowstone Park. These bears, which may be endangered, and are undeniably threatened, should at least be protected by supplying them with carcasses from excess elk within the park, *by curtailing the destruction of habitat by clearcutting National Forests surrounding the Park*, and by preventing hunting until their numbers have recovered sufficiently to withstand these pressures."

One might dispute the applicability of these examples to the Tellico Dam by saying that in this case the burden on the public through the loss of millions of unrecoverable dollars would greatly outweigh the loss of the snail darter. But neither the Endangered Species Act nor Art. III of the Constitution provides federal courts with authority to make such fine utilitarian calculations. On the contrary, the plain language of the Act, buttressed by its legislative history, shows clearly that Congress viewed the value of endangered species as "incalculable." Quite obviously, it would be difficult for a court to balance the loss of a sum certain—even $100 million—against a congressionally declared "incalculable" value, even assuming we had the power to engage in such a weighing process, which we emphatically do not.

In passing the Endangered Species Act of 1973, Congress was also aware of certain instances in which exceptions to the statute's broad sweep would be necessary. Thus, § 10 creates a number of limited "hardship exemptions," none of which would even remotely apply to the Tellico Project. In fact, there are no exemptions in the Endangered Species Act for federal agencies, meaning that under the maxim *expressio unius est exclusio alterius*, we must presume that these were the only "hardship cases" Congress intended to exempt.

Notwithstanding Congress' expression of intent in 1973, we are urged to find that the continuing appropriations for Tellico Dam constitute an implied repeal of the 1973 Act, at least insofar as it applies to the Tellico Project. In support of this view, TVA points to the statements found in various House and Senate Appropriations Committees' Reports; as described in Part I, *supra*, those Reports generally reflected the attitude of the *Committees* either that the Act did not apply to Tellico or that the dam should be completed regardless of the provisions of the Act. Since we are unwilling to assume that these latter Committee statements constituted advice to ignore the provisions of a duly enacted law, we assume that these Committees believed that the Act simply was not applicable in this situation. But even under this interpretation of the Committees' actions, we are unable to conclude that the Act has been in any respect amended or repealed.

There is nothing in the appropriations measures, as passed, which states that the Tellico Project was to be completed irrespective of the requirements of the Endangered Species Act. These appropriations, in fact, represented relatively minor components of the lump-sum amounts for the *entire* TVA budget. To find a repeal of the Endangered Species Act under these circumstances would surely do violence to the " 'cardinal rule . . . that repeals by implication are not favored.' " In *Posadas* [*v. National City Bank*] this Court held, in no uncertain terms, that "the intention of the legislature to repeal must be clear and manifest." In practical terms, this "cardinal rule" means that "[i]n the absence of some affirmative showing of an intention to repeal, the only permissible justification for a repeal by implication is when the earlier and later statutes are irreconcilable."

The doctrine disfavoring repeals by implication "applies with full vigor when . . . the subsequent legislation is an *appropriations* measure." This is perhaps an understatement since it would be more accurate to say that the policy applies with even *greater* force when the claimed repeal rests solely on an Appropriations Act. We recognize that both substantive enactments and appropriations measures are "Acts of Congress," but the latter have the limited and specific purpose of providing funds for authorized programs. When voting on appropriations measures, legislators are entitled to operate under the assumption that the funds will be devoted to purposes which are lawful and not for any purpose forbidden. Without such an assurance, every appropriations measure would be pregnant with prospects of altering substantive legislation, repealing by implication any prior statute which might prohibit the expenditure. Not only would this lead to the absurd result of requiring Members to review exhaustively the background of every authorization before voting on an appropriation, but it would flout the very rules the Congress carefully adopted to avoid this need. House Rule XXI(2), for instance, specifically provides:

"No appropriation shall be reported in any general appropriation bill, or be in order as an amendment thereto, for any expenditure not previously authorized by law, unless in continuation of appropriations for such public works as are already in progress. *Nor shall any provision in any such bill or amendment thereto changing existing law be in order.*"

Thus, to sustain petitioner's position, we would be obliged to assume that Congress meant to repeal *pro tanto* § 7 of the Act by means of a procedure expressly prohibited under the rules of Congress.

Perhaps mindful of the fact that it is "swimming upstream" against a strong current of well-established precedent, TVA argues for an exception to the rule against implied repealers in a circumstance where, as here, Appropriations Committees have expressly stated their "understanding" that the earlier legislation would not prohibit the proposed expenditure. We cannot accept such a proposition. Expressions of committees dealing with requests for appropriations cannot be equated with statutes enacted by Congress, particularly not in the circumstances presented by this case. First, the Appropriations Committees had no jurisdiction over the subject of endangered species, much less did they conduct the type of extensive hearings which preceded passage of the earlier Endangered Species Acts, especially the 1973 Act. We venture to suggest that the House Committee on Merchant Marine and Fisheries and the Senate Committee on Commerce would be somewhat surprised to learn that their careful work on the substantive legislation had been undone by the simple—and brief—insertion of some inconsistent language in Appropriations Committees' Reports.

Second, there is no indication that Congress as a whole was aware of TVA's position, although the Appropriations Committees apparently agreed with petitioner's views. Only recently in *SEC v. Sloan,* we declined to presume general congressional acquiescence in a 34-year-old practice of the Securities and Exchange Commission, despite the fact that the Senate Committee *having jurisdiction over the Commission's activities* had long expressed approval of the practice. Mr. Justice REHNQUIST, speaking for the Court, observed that we should be "extremely hesitant to presume general congressional awareness of the Commission's construction based only upon a few isolated statements in the thousands of pages of legislative documents." *A fortiori,* we should not assume that petitioner's views—and the Appropriations Committees' acceptance of them—were any better known, especially when the TVA is not the agency with primary responsibility for administering the Endangered Species Act.

Quite apart from the foregoing factors, we would still be unable to find that in this case "the earlier and later statutes are irreconcilable"; here it is entirely possible "to regard each as effective." The starting point in this analysis must be the legislative proceedings leading to the 1977 appropriations since the earlier funding of the dam occurred prior to the listing of the snail darter as an endangered species. In all successive years, TVA confidently reported to the Appropriations Committees that efforts to transplant the snail darter appeared to be successful; this surely gave those Committees some basis for the impression that there was no direct conflict between the Tellico Project and the Endangered Species Act. Indeed, the special appropriation for 1978 of $2 million for transplantation of endangered species supports the view that the Committees saw such relocation as the means whereby collision between Tellico and the Endangered Species Act could be avoided. It should also be noted that the Reports issued by the Senate and House Appropriations Committees in 1976 came within a month of the District Court's decision in this case, which hardly could have given the Members cause for concern over the possible applicability of the Act. This leaves only the 1978 appropriations, the Reports for which issued after the Court of Appeals' decision now before us. At that point very little remained to be accomplished on the project; the Committees understandably advised TVA to cooperate with the Department of the Interior "to relocate the endangered species to another suitable habitat so as to permit the project to proceed as rapidly as possible." It is true that the *Committees* repeated their earlier expressed "view" that the Act did not prevent completion of the Tellico Project. Considering these statements in context, however, it is evident that they " 'represent only the personal views of these legislators,' " and "however explicit, [they] cannot serve to change the legislative intent of Congress expressed before the Act's passage."

. . . .

MR. JUSTICE POWELL, with whom MR. JUSTICE BLACKMUN joins, dissenting.

The Court today holds that § 7 of the Endangered Species Act requires a federal court, for the purpose of protecting an endangered species or its habitat, to enjoin permanently the operation of any federal project, whether completed or substantially completed. This decision casts a long shadow over the operation of even the most important projects, serving vital needs of society and national defense, whenever it is determined that continued operation would threaten extinction of an endangered species or its habitat. This result is said to be required by the "plain intent of Congress" as well as by the language of the statute.

In my view § 7 cannot reasonably be interpreted as applying to a project that is completed or substantially completed when its threat to an endangered species is discovered. Nor can I believe that Congress could have intended this Act to produce the "absurd result"—in the words of the District Court—of this case. If it were clear from the language of the Act and its legislative history that Congress intended to authorize this result, this Court would be compelled to enforce it. It is not our province to rectify policy or political judgments by the Legislative Branch, however egregiously they may disserve the public interest. But where the statutory language and legislative history, as in this case, need not be construed to reach such a result, I view it as the duty of this Court to adopt a permissible construction that accords with some modicum of common sense and the public weal.

. . . .

I

In 1975, 1976, and 1977, Congress, with full knowledge of the Tellico Project's effect on the snail darter and the alleged violation of the Endangered Species Act, continued to appropriate money for the completion of the Project. In doing so, the Appropriations Committees expressly stated that the Act did not prohibit the Project's completion, a view that Congress presumably accepted in approving the appropriations each year. For example, in June 1976, the Senate Committee on Appropriations released a report noting the District Court decision and recommending approval of TVA's full budget request for the Tellico Project. The Committee observed further that it did "not view the Endangered Species Act as prohibiting the completion of the Tellico project at its advanced stage," and it directed "that this project be completed as promptly as possible in the public interest." The appropriations bill was passed by Congress and approved by the President.

. . . .

In June 1977, and after being informed of the decision of the Court of Appeals, the Appropriations Committees in both Houses of Congress again recommended approval of TVA's full budget request for the Tellico Project. Both Committees again stated unequivocally that the

Endangered Species Act was not intended to halt projects at an advanced stage of completion:

"[The Senate] Committee has not viewed the Endangered Species Act as preventing the completion and use of these projects which were well under way at the time the affected species were listed as endangered. If the act has such an effect, which is contrary to the Committee's understanding of the intent of Congress in enacting the Endangered Species Act, funds should be appropriated to allow these projects to be completed and their benefits realized in the public interest, the Endangered Species Act notwithstanding."

"It is the [House] Committee's view that the Endangered Species Act was not intended to halt projects such as these in their advanced stage of completion, and [the Committee] strongly recommends that these projects not be stopped because of misuse of the Act."

Once again, the appropriations bill was passed by both Houses and signed into law.

II

Today the Court, like the Court of Appeals below, adopts a reading of § 7 of the Act that gives it a retroactive effect and disregards 12 years of consistently expressed congressional intent to complete the Tellico Project. With all due respect, I view this result as an extreme example of a literalist construction, not required by the language of the Act and adopted without regard to its manifest purpose. Moreover, it ignores established canons of statutory construction.

A

The starting point in statutory construction is, of course, the language of § 7 itself. I agree that it can be viewed as a textbook example of fuzzy language, which can be read according to the "eye of the beholder." The critical words direct all federal agencies to take "such action [as may be] necessary to insure that actions authorized, funded, or carried out by them do not jeopardize the continued existence of . . . endangered species . . . or result in the destruction or modification of [a critical] habitat of such species. . . ." Respondents—as did the Sixth Circuit—read these words as sweepingly as possible to include all "actions" that any federal agency ever may take with respect to any federal project, whether completed or not.

The Court today embraces this sweeping construction. Under the Court's reasoning, the Act covers every existing federal installation, including great hydroelectric projects and reservoirs, every river and harbor project, and every national defense installation—however essential to the Nation's economic health and safety. The "actions" that an agency would be prohibited from "carrying out" would include the continued operation of such projects or any change necessary to preserve their continued usefulness. The only precondition, according to respondents, to thus destroying the usefulness of even the most important federal project in our country would be a finding by the Secretary of the Interior that a continuation of the project would threaten the survival or critical habitat of a newly discovered species of water spider or amoeba.

"[F]requently words of general meaning are used in a statute, words broad enough to include an act in question, and yet a consideration of the whole legislation, or of the circumstances surrounding its enactment, or of the absurd results which follow from giving such broad meaning to the words, makes it unreasonable to believe that the legislator intended to include the particular act." The result that will follow in this case by virtue of the Court's reading of § 7 makes it unreasonable to believe that Congress intended that reading. Moreover, § 7 may be construed in a way that avoids an "absurd result" without doing violence to its language.

holy trinity "absurdity"

The critical word in § 7 is "actions" and its meaning is far from "plain." It is part of the phrase: "actions authorized, funded or carried out." In terms of planning and executing various activities, it seems evident that the "actions" referred to are not all actions that an agency can ever take, but rather actions that the agency is *deciding whether* to authorize, to fund, or to carry out. In short, these words reasonably may be read as applying only to *prospective actions, i. e.,* actions with respect to which the agency has reasonable decisionmaking alternatives still available, actions *not yet* carried out. At the time respondents brought this lawsuit, the Tellico Project was 80% complete at a cost of more than $78 million. The Court concedes that as of this time and for the purpose of deciding this case, the Tellico Dam Project is "completed" or "virtually completed and the dam is essentially ready for operation[.]" Thus, under a prospective reading of § 7, the action already had been "carried out" in terms of any remaining reasonable decisionmaking power. This is a reasonable construction of the language and also is supported by the presumption against construing statutes to give them a retroactive effect. As this Court stated in *United States Fidelity & Guaranty Co. v. United States ex rel. Struthers Wells Co.,* the "presumption is very strong that a statute was not meant to act retrospectively, and it ought never to receive such a construction if it is susceptible of any other." This is particularly true where a statute enacts a new regime of regulation. For example, the presumption has been recognized in cases under the National Environmental Policy Act, holding that the requirement of filing an environmental impact statement cannot reasonably be applied to projects substantially completed. The Court of Appeals for the Fourth Circuit explained these holdings.

critical word is "actions" ↓ should only apply to prospective actions

Similarly under § 7 of the Endangered Species Act, at some stage of a federal project, and certainly where a project has been completed, the agency no longer has a reasonable choice simply to abandon it. When that point is reached, as it was in this case, the presumption against retrospective interpretation is at its strongest. The Court today gives no weight to that presumption.

B

The Court recognizes that the first purpose of statutory construction is to ascertain the intent of the legislature. The Court's opinion reviews at length the legislative history, with quotations from Committee Reports and statements by Members of Congress. The Court then ends this discussion with curiously conflicting conclusions.

It finds that the "totality of congressional action makes it abundantly clear that the result we reach today [justifying the termination or abandonment of any federal project] is wholly in accord with both the words of the statute and the intent of Congress." Yet, in the same paragraph, the Court acknowledges that "there is no discussion in the legislative history of precisely this problem." The opinion nowhere makes clear how the result it reaches can be "abundantly" self-evident from the legislative history when the result was never discussed. While the Court's review of the legislative history establishes that Congress intended to require governmental agencies to take endangered species into account in the planning and execution of their programs, there is not even a hint in the legislative history that Congress intended to compel the undoing or abandonment of any project or program later found to threaten a newly discovered species.

If the relevant Committees that considered the Act, and the Members of Congress who voted on it, had been aware that the Act could be used to terminate major federal projects authorized years earlier and nearly completed, or to require the abandonment of essential and long-completed federal installations and edifices, we can be certain that there would have been hearings, testimony, and debate concerning consequences so wasteful, so inimical to purposes previously deemed important, and so likely to arouse public outrage. The absence of any such consideration by the Committees or in the floor debates indicates quite clearly that no one participating in the legislative process considered these consequences as within the intendment of the Act.

As indicated above, this view of legislative intent at the time of enactment is abundantly confirmed by the subsequent congressional actions and expressions. We have held, properly, that post-enactment statements by individual Members of Congress as to the meaning of a statute are entitled to little or no weight. The Court also has recognized that subsequent Appropriations Acts themselves are not necessarily entitled to significant weight in determining whether a prior statute has been superseded. But these precedents are inapposite. There was no effort here to "bootstrap" a post-enactment view of prior legislation by isolated statements of individual Congressmen. Nor is this a case where Congress, without explanation or comment upon the statute in question, merely has voted apparently inconsistent financial support in subsequent Appropriations Acts. Testimony on this precise issue was presented before congressional committees, and the Committee Reports for three consecutive years addressed the problem and affirmed their understanding of the original congressional intent. We cannot assume— as the Court suggests—that Congress, when it continued each year to approve the recommended appropriations, was unaware of the contents of the supporting Committee Reports. All this amounts to strong corroborative evidence that the interpretation of § 7 as not applying to completed or substantially completed projects reflects the initial legislative intent.

III

I have little doubt that Congress will amend the Endangered Species Act to prevent the grave consequences made possible by today's decision. Few, if any, Members of that body will wish to defend an interpretation of the Act that requires the waste of at least $53 million, and denies the people of the Tennessee Valley area the benefits of the reservoir that Congress intended to confer. There will be little sentiment to leave this dam standing before an empty reservoir, serving no purpose other than a conversation piece for incredulous tourists.

But more far reaching than the adverse effect on the people of this economically depressed area is the continuing threat to the operation of every federal project, no matter how important to the Nation. If Congress acts expeditiously, as may be anticipated, the Court's decision probably will have no lasting adverse consequences. But I had not thought it to be the province of this Court to force Congress into otherwise unnecessary action by interpreting a statute to produce a result no one intended.

CHAPTER VI

PUTTING IT ALL TOGETHER: PRACTICAL LAWYERING WITH STATUTORY INTERPRETATION

■ ■ ■

By now you should have a sophisticated understanding of the theories and practical tools of statutory interpretation. In addition, you have done several small exercises designed to put you in the position of an attorney drafting or interpreting legislation. You have also seen the work product of real attorneys who have had to generate interpretive arguments, recognize and respond to counterarguments, and organize, construct, and draft persuasive briefs.

In this chapter we will bring all of these elements together by putting you in the position of a lawyer dealing with complicated questions of statutory interpretation. In contrast to your typical law school task of reading cases, where your job is to understand and evaluate arguments and doctrine articulated by judges, your task as a lawyer—and in the exercises in this chapter—is to take the doctrine you have learned and to apply it to new sets of facts, statutes, and other materials by reading legislative materials and generating, evaluating, organizing, and developing arguments in order to assist your client.

Your professor will give you detailed instructions for each assignment.

EXERCISE VI.1

Statutory Interpretation Case File 1

Facts

Veggie Heaven is a popular restaurant in College Town, East Dakota. The College Town location of the national Veggie Heaven chain is a franchise owned and operated by Carlos "Big Joe" Jordan. In January of 2009, Big Joe received a letter from corporate headquarters informing him that at the end of the term of his current franchise agreement, he would have to shut down his Veggie Heaven location. The letter explained that the national Veggie Heaven chain would be withdrawing from East Dakota and surrounding states' markets due to economic circumstances.

Big Joe sued Veggie Heaven for violating the East Dakota Franchise Act. According to Big Joe, the Act prohibits the franchisor from terminating, cancelling, or failing to renew a franchise except for good cause, and further that "market withdrawal" does not constitute good cause.

You are an associate in the law firm Bernard Dervin Wilcox LLP, which represents the franchisor (the defendant), namely the national Veggie Heaven company.

According to the owners of the national Veggie Heaven company, the company has no choice but to close down some of its franchises. They admit that the local franchisees have done nothing wrong per se, but they maintain that the company expanded too rapidly during the economic boom period. Now, as a result of the recent economic decline, the company must consolidate and focus on its core markets. Indeed, if the company does not withdraw from some underperforming markets, the entire company will likely go bankrupt.

Your supervising attorney tells you that the statute is clear that a franchise can be terminated only for good cause, but that Veggie Heaven's defense against Big Joe's lawsuit is that market withdrawal constitutes good cause. She has asked you to draft the argument section of the brief to that effect. Based on your research, you have put together the following case file. Note that Big Joe secured the lease for his Veggie Heaven franchise location by himself. Your client has no interest at stake regarding the real estate.

The Statute

Section 38–422 of the East Dakota Code provides, in relevant part:

(a) This Section shall be known as the East Dakota Franchise Act. The purpose of this Act is to protect local franchisees from abusive business conduct by franchisors and to encourage and protect the development of franchises, which serve an important business and economic function in this State.

(b) No franchisor shall, directly, or through any officer, agent or employee, terminate, cancel or fail to renew a franchise, except for good cause. Good cause shall include the franchisee's refusal or failure to comply substantially with any material and reasonable obligation of the franchise agreement or for the reasons stated in subsection (e) of this section.

. . . .

(e)   A franchisor may elect not to renew a franchise which involves the lease by the franchisor to the franchisee of real property and improvement, in the event the franchisor (1) sells or leases such real property and improvements to other than a subsidiary or affiliate of the franchisor for any use; or (2) sells or leases such real property to a subsidiary or affiliate of the franchisor, except such subsidiary or affiliate shall not use such real property for the operation of the same business of the franchisee.

Background Information

The franchise form of business became popular in the 1950s. A franchise relationship is created by contract. The franchisor allows the franchisee to sell trademarked goods, and the franchisee agrees to do so under certain conditions and to not damage or destroy the franchisor's trademark. Historically, franchise agreements were terminable at will.

Beginning in the mid-1950s, as the franchise form became more popular, policymakers identified certain abuses of this relationship by franchisors. Specifically, after franchisees developed a local market, the franchisor would cancel, terminate, or elect not to renew the franchise and begin selling goods directly to the consumer, cutting out the franchisee. This was harmful to franchisees because they had put the effort and costs into developing the market, only to have the national franchise come in and take over the market just when it was becoming profitable.

A majority of states around the country responded to this perceived abuse by enacting protections for franchisees. Among the most important provisions of such laws are those that prohibit termination, cancellation, or nonrenewal of franchisees without good cause. The East Dakota Franchise Act is typical in this regard (and in most others).

East Dakota courts are not the first in the nation to face the question of whether market withdrawal constitutes good cause in this sort of statute. The highest courts in three other states have declared that it does, while two high courts in other states have held that it does not.

State Franchise Board

The East Dakota Franchise Board has been charged by the legislature with implementing and overseeing the Franchise Act. The Franchise Board has stated in an opinion letter that market withdrawal does not constitute good cause under the statute for terminating, cancelling, or failing to renew a franchise agreement.

EXERCISE VI.2

Statutory Interpretation Case File 2

Facts

Mayble Bodine purchased a used car from the Graco Auto Group. When she purchased the car, she received an accurate odometer statement from Graco. However, Graco did not provide her with a copy of the vehicle's title. The vehicle's title would have shown that the vehicle had been branded "restored salvage" and that it had been severely damaged in an earlier collision. Bodine would not have purchased the vehicle if she had seen the title. Bodine discovered this information when she subsequently received a copy of the vehicle's registration. She also discovered that the car had mechanical problems rendering it dangerous to drive. Graco refused to take the car back, even though it knew of the vehicle's history and status.

The question in this case is whether Bodine is entitled to triple damages in a private cause of action due to Graco's failure to provide her with the vehicle's title. The circuit courts are split on this issue.

You must draft a brief on behalf of Graco. Based on your research, you have compiled the following case file.

The Odometer Act

The Odometer Act begins with a list of Congress's findings and purposes, 49 U.S.C. § 32701:

(a) Congress finds that—

(1) buyers of motor vehicles rely heavily on the odometer reading as an index of the condition and value of a vehicle;

(2) buyers are entitled to rely on the odometer reading as an accurate indication of the mileage of the vehicle;

(3) an accurate indication of the mileage assists a buyer in deciding on the safety and reliability of the vehicle; and

(4) motor vehicles move in, or affect, interstate and foreign commerce.

(b) The Act's purposes are—

(1) to prohibit tampering with motor vehicle odometers; and

(2) to provide safeguards to protect purchasers in the sale of motor vehicles with altered or reset odometers.

The Act provides a two-part scheme for effectuating these purposes. First, the Act regulates and prohibits odometer "tampering" (taking actions that would cause discrepancies between a vehicle's actual mileage and its odometer reading). Specifically, the Act prohibits odometer tampering with intent "to change the mileage registered by the odometer." § 32703(2). It also forbids advertising for sale, selling, using, installing, or having installed "a device that makes an odometer of a motor vehicle register a mileage different from the mileage the vehicle was driven, as registered by the odometer within the designed tolerance of the manufacturer of the odometer." § 32703(1). It is also unlawful to, "with intent to defraud, operate a motor vehicle on a street, road, or highway if the person knows that the odometer of the vehicle is disconnected or not operating." § 32703(3).

Second, the Act seeks to empower consumers by providing them with accurate information at the time of vehicle transfer. Thus, section 32705(a) provides, in part:

(1) Disclosure requirements.—Under regulations prescribed by the Secretary of Transportation [of the National Highway Traffic Safety Administration] that include the way in which information is disclosed and retained under this section, a person transferring ownership of a motor vehicle shall give the transferee the following written disclosure:

(A) Disclosure of the cumulative mileage registered on the odometer.

(B) Disclosure that the actual mileage is unknown, if the transferor knows that the odometer reading is different from the number of miles the vehicle has actually traveled.

(2) A person transferring ownership of a motor vehicle may not violate a regulation prescribed under this section or give a false statement to the transferee in making the disclosure required by such a regulation.

(3) A person acquiring a motor vehicle for resale may not accept a written disclosure under this section unless it is complete.

Further, section 32705(a)(1) of the Act provides that the Secretary of Transportation of the National Highway Traffic Safety Administration must "prescribe . . . the way in which information is disclosed and retained" under the Act.

Finally, the Act provides for a private cause of action as a means for enforcement of the Act. Section 37210(a) provides for the following damages in a private enforcement action: "A person that violates this chapter or a regulation prescribed or order issued under this chapter, with intent to defraud, is liable for 3 times the actual damages or $1,500, whichever is greater."

The Relevant Regulation

As provided in the state, the Secretary of Transportation of the National Highway Traffic Safety Administration issued the following regulation as the means for disclosing mileage information:

"In connection with the transfer of ownership of a motor vehicle, each transferor shall disclose the mileage to the transferee in writing on the title."

EXERCISE VI.3

Statutory Interpretation Case File 3

Facts

David Figueroa is a citizen of Mexico. In January 2006, Figueroa illegally entered the United States with the help of a "coyote" (an individual who brings people across the border in exchange for payment).

In March 2006, Figueroa applied for a job as a line cook at a fast food restaurant in Burbank, California. On his application, Figueroa falsely claimed to be a United States citizen. Citizenship or other lawful status (which Figueroa did not possess) was a precondition for the job. He was offered the job but was told that he would have to show evidence of citizenship on the first day of work.

Figueroa immediately contacted a friend who was known to provide false papers. In exchange for $400, Figueroa got a Social Security card bearing his name and the number 097–99–5525. He provided a copy of this card to his new employer and began work.

Two months later, after having been tipped off that the fast food restaurant employed undocumented immigrants, the Department of Homeland Security ("DHS") conducted a sweep of the premises. The DHS determined that Figueroa was not a United States citizen and that the Social Security number he held rightfully belonged to Rafer Mannick, a United States citizen residing in Madison, Wisconsin.

Figueroa was charged with the crime of falsely claiming to be a United States citizen, to which he pled guilty. The prosecutor seeks an enhancement to the normal sentence associated with falsely claiming to be a citizen, pursuant to 18 U.S.C. § 1028A(a)(1). Draft a brief arguing that 18 U.S.C. § 1028A(a)(1) does or does not apply in this case.

The Statute

18 U.S.C. § 1028A(a) imposes a mandatory consecutive two-year sentence enhancement on anyone who, during and in relation to certain crimes (including falsely claiming to be a United States citizen):

(1) knowingly transfers, possesses, or uses, without lawful authority, a means of identification of another person, or

(2) [if the underlying crime relates to terrorism,] knowingly transfers, possesses, or uses, without lawful authority, a means of identification of another person or a false identification document, or

(3) [if the underlying crime involves or relates to a gun,] knowingly transfers, possesses, or uses, without lawful authority, a concealed carry license belonging to another person. . . .

Relevant Legislative History

Congress initially passed 18 U.S.C. § 1028A in 1993. At that time, only subsection (3) of the statute, pertaining to gun crimes, was enacted. In 1999, Congress amended the statute to include subsection (2), pertaining to terrorism-related offenses.

In 2004, Congress passed the Identity Theft Prevention Act ("ITPA"), designed to combat the growing problem of identity theft. Dozens and dozens of pages long, the ITPA amended many already existing criminal statutes. Among these statutes was 18 U.S.C. § 1028A, with the ITPA enhancing the criminal penalties for certain crimes when the person committing the crimes commits identity theft in order to do so.

The House Committee Report explains that the ITPA was designed to prevent identity theft and explains that identity theft encompasses "all types of crimes in which someone wrongfully obtains or uses another person's personal data in some way that involves fraud or deception."

The Senate Committee Report contains a brief discussion of the section of ITPA that amended 18 U.S.C. § 1028A. In it, the Report gives two examples of people who would be subject to the sentencing enhancement: a person who dives in dumpsters to retrieve Social Security numbers and other sensitive personal information, and a person "who collects such information for authorized purposes, but then uses it for unauthorized purposes." The Report gives examples such as "database hacking" and "illicit employee access to confidential information" to illustrate how this second category of identity theft occurs.

EXERCISE VI.4

Statutory Interpretation Case File 4

Facts

Last year, Symeon Park ("Park"), who is blind, tried to use URent.com, an online-only apartment rental company, to search for and secure a new apartment. Blind individuals can use the many websites that are programmed to be compatible with screen reader technology, which "reads" the written text of a website aloud. However, URent.com does not use screen reader technology and, as a result, Park was unable to use the website.

Procedural History and Legal Issue

Park filed suit here in the District of Newstate, seeking damages and an order requiring URent.com to make its website accessible to the blind, pursuant to the Americans with Disabilities Act ("the ADA," "the Act," or "the statute").

Under the ADA, a business that operates a "place of public accommodation" must make its goods and services accessible to the disabled. The ADA recognizes blindness as a disability. The question is whether the website is a place of public accommodation.

It is an open question here in the 14th Circuit as to whether a website can be a place of public accommodation under the ADA, or whether only physical places can be places of public accommodation. The U.S. Supreme Court has never spoken on the issue, and the courts that have spoken on the issue are split, with the majority of circuit and district courts limiting the statute's application to physical places.

Note that the statute provides that if making accommodations for the disabled would be "unduly burdensome," the entity need not make them. However, at this stage of the case, you are not asked to determine whether the accommodation for Park would be unduly burdensome, but only whether the statute applies to URent.com in the first place—that is, whether a website can be considered a place of public accommodation.

The Statute

What follows are relevant excerpts from the Americans with Disabilities Act. Section 12101 is the opening section of the Act, stating the purpose. Section 12182 is the section that requires businesses that operate places of public accommodation to accommodate the disabled. Section 12182 also provides relevant statutory definitions.

Section 12101. Purpose

(a) Purpose: It is the purpose of this Act—

(1) to provide a clear and comprehensive national mandate for the elimination of discrimination against individuals with disabilities;

(2) to provide clear, strong, consistent, enforceable standards addressing discrimination against individuals with disabilities;

(3) to balance the interests and needs of the disabled with those of businesses affected by the Act.

. . . .

Sec. 12182. Prohibition of discrimination by public accommodations

(a) General rule

No individual shall be discriminated against on the basis of disability in the full and equal enjoyment of the goods, services, facilities, privileges, advantages, or accommodations of any place of public accommodation by any person who owns, leases (or leases to), or operates a place of public accommodation.

(b) Definitions

. . . .

(7) Place of public accommodation

The following private entities are considered places of public accommodation for purposes of this subchapter, if the operations of such entities affect commerce:

(A) an inn, hotel, motel, or other place of lodging;

(B) a restaurant, bar, or other establishment serving food or drink;

(C) a motion picture house, theater, concert hall, stadium, or other place of exhibition entertainment;

(D) an auditorium, convention center, lecture hall, or other place of public gathering;

(E) a bakery, grocery store, clothing store, hardware store, shopping center, or other sales or rental establishment;

(F) a laundromat, dry-cleaner, bank, barber shop, beauty shop, travel service, shoe repair service, funeral parlor, professional office, hospital, or other service establishment;

(G) a museum, library, gallery, or other place of public display or collection;

(H) a park, zoo, amusement park, or other place of recreation;

(I) a gymnasium, health spa, bowling alley, golf course, or other place of exercise or recreation.

Relevant Background and Pre-Passage History of the ADA

The ADA, enacted in 1990, was a landmark piece of legislation. Its goal was to equalize opportunity for disabled Americans. It has many different components. One notable component is that it requires businesses that operate places of public accommodation to accommodate disabled customers.

Thus, a store with steps in it might be required to install a ramp, escalator, and/or elevator to accommodate a wheelchair.

Not surprisingly, nothing in the legislative history of the ADA specifically mentions its applicability to commercial websites, which, after all, did not really exist at the time.

However, the legislative history is rife with general comments about the importance and purpose of the ADA. For example, the conference committee report states that:

"The ADA requires all places of public accommodation to accommodate disabled people. The purpose of this requirement is that disabled individuals must have access to all of the goods and services that are available to those without disabilities. The prototypical case includes requiring a grocery store to widen its aisles to permit a wheelchair to pass through, or requiring a restaurant to permit a seeing eye dog on its premises. Although these requirements will impose costs on businesses, the evidence shows that in most cases, such costs will not be unduly burdensome to businesses."

At the presidential signing ceremony, President George H. W. Bush issued a statement extolling the virtues of the ADA. He called the ADA "comprehensive" and a "historic achievement" because "[i]t promises to open up all aspects of American life to individuals with disabilities—employment opportunities, government services, public accommodations, transportation, and telecommunications."

He also sought to allay fears that it would impose too many costs on business. For example, he stated that "[t]he Administration and the Congress have carefully crafted the ADA to give the business community the flexibility to meet the requirements of the Act without incurring undue costs."

He then went on to cite to a dozen or more different ways in which the Act balances the needs and interests of the disabled and the needs and interests of businesses and employers.

Relevant Post-Passage History of the ADA

In 2000, after the issuance of dueling court opinions from the circuit courts on the question of whether a website can be a place of public accommodation, a congressional committee held hearings to determine whether to amend the ADA to explicitly require some or all websites to comply with the ADA. The committee took testimony from:

- Amy Barclay, the President of the American Chamber of Commerce, which represents many large, mid-size, and small businesses. Barclay testified that screen reader technology is still in its infancy, but that online businesses have market-based incentives to adopt it, where feasible, in order to serve blind customers. She urged the committee to refrain from amending the statute. She expressed concern for the ability of blind Americans to use the Internet, but argued that a one-size-fits-all solution might stunt the development of the optimal technology and prove too expensive for some businesses to implement.

- Mark Belchuk, the Executive Director of the American Association for the Blind. Belchuk testified that vision-impaired Americans are currently unable to fully enjoy the services of most commercial websites because the websites are not compatible with screen reader technology. He urged the committee to take action to update the ADA to explicitly require commercial websites to comply with the statute. He argued that it is senseless to treat online merchants differently from bricks-and-mortar merchants. He said: "For example, it makes no sense to treat a corner bookstore differently from Amazon.com. Under the current state of the law, however, the corner bookstore must serve the blind by providing clerks to assist blind people in locating books; but according to some courts, the same law does not require Amazon.com to assist the blind in any way."

- Deval Patrick, then the Deputy Director of the Department of Justice (the agency charged with implementing the statute). Patrick testified that "an Internet website may be a place of public accommodation under the ADA if it falls within one of the statutory categories or definitions. Thus, a travel service that operates online would be a place of public accommodation and would be required to comply with the statute." Accordingly, he saw no need to amend the statute.

After deliberating, the committee decided not to recommend amending the statute. The committee chair, Maxine Wine, closed the proceedings with the following statement:

"The committee unanimously recommends that Congress take no action at this time. The ADA tasks the Department of Justice with implementing the statute, and the Department has taken the position a commercial website may be a place of public accommodation and must therefore comply with the statute. The committee defers to the Department and agrees that this is the *(chevron?)* best interpretation of the statute. Amending the statute at this time is therefore unnecessary."

Information About the Statute upon Which the ADA Was Modeled

The ADA was modeled on a statute called the Fair Housing Amendments Act ("FHAA"). The FHAA was enacted prior to the ADA and applied only to government entities. It defined "place of public accommodation" in precisely the same way that the ADA did. However, in 2001, Congress amended the FHAA's definition of "place of public accommodation" in drastic ways. In particular, Congress added a section in the FHAA that clearly classified government websites as places of public accommodation that had to accommodate disabled people.

Relevant Agency Materials

In 1991, shortly after the passage of the ADA, the Department of Justice adopted the following regulations to interpret and implement the statute:

"The phrase 'place of public accommodation' is defined in the regulations as a facility, operated by a private entity, whose operations affect commerce and fall within at least one of the categories listed in § 12182(b)(7).

"The term 'facility' is defined in the regulations as all or any portion of buildings, structures, site improvements, complexes, equipment, roads, walks, passageways, parking lots, or other real or personal property located on a site."

As noted previously, in 2000, after the issuance of dueling circuit court opinions, a congressional committee called upon the Deputy Director of the Department of Justice to testify as to the agency's interpretation of the statute. The Deputy Director testified that "the agency has determined that an Internet website may be a 'place of public accommodation' under the ADA if it falls within one of the statutory categories or definitions. Thus, a travel service that operates online would be a place of public accommodation and would be required to comply with the statute."

EXERCISE VI.5

Statutory Interpretation Case File 5

Facts

Dr. Michelle Mansanto is a researcher at Harvard Medical School. Her research focuses on adult stem cells. Such stem cells are obtained harmlessly from within the human body or from umbilical cord tissue that is discarded after birth. Medical researchers like Dr. Mansanto hope that such adult stem cell ("ASC") research may lead to breakthroughs in treating a variety of diseases and injuries, including Alzheimer's, nerve damage, cancer, Parkinson's, and many others. In addition, because ASC research does not harm anyone, it is uncontroversial among ethicists.

The National Institutes of Health, a federal institute that provides federal funding grants for medical research, has begun to allocate less funding for ASC research, and instead has chosen to direct more funding to embryonic stem cell ("ESC") research. Research on ESCs requires doctors to obtain stem cells from a human embryo and then perform research on those cells or on their clones. In the process of obtaining stem cells from a human embryo, the embryo is necessarily destroyed. As a result, those who believe that human life begins at conception consider this research immoral. Most medical professionals and researchers believe that ESC research is much more likely to lead to a broad range of treatments than is ASC research.

As a result of the NIH's new funding priorities, Dr. Mansanto has found it difficult to fund her research. She sued the administrator of the NIH, claiming that its funding of ESC research violates a federal statute, the Human Embryonic Stem Cell Research Funding Act ("HESCRFA" or "the Act"). The federal district court judge assigned to the case agreed with Dr. Mansanto's claim and ordered that all funding of ESC research must cease immediately. That order has been stayed on appeal.

You represent the government (the defendant). The government has appealed the district judge's ruling because it wishes to continue to fund ESC research. You must draft the argument section of the appellate brief.

The Statute

The HESCRFA provides, in relevant part: "Federal funds may not be used for research in which a human embryo or human embryos are destroyed, discarded, or knowingly subjected to risk of injury or death."

Background Information

The HESCRFA was passed in 1995 by large majorities in both Houses of Congress. At that time, ESC research could be performed only on the actual stem cells derived from a human embryo. In 1998, privately funded scientists succeeded for the first time in cloning human embryonic stem cells. There was a great deal of excitement in the scientific and medical research community about the potential for medical breakthroughs as a result of ESC research, and particularly on such research using cloned ESCs, because this would allow scientists to have an unending supply of identical cells upon which to conduct research. Researchers across the country began to apply to the NIH for funding of their ESC research.

Federal administrators in the Clinton administration were keenly aware of the controversy surrounding the use of ESCs and concerned about the application of the HESCRFA. After much consideration, the Secretary of the Health and Human Services Agency (the Agency that controls the NIH) adopted a regulation interpreting the HESCRFA to provide that federal funds could not be directed (1) to costs associated with the destruction of a human embryo for the purpose of obtaining ESCs or (2) to research on those ESCs actual obtained directly from a human embryo. However, they concluded that federal funds could be directed towards research on the clones of such ESCs, generally referred to as "stem cell lines." As a result of this regulation, privately funded scientists began to extract ESCs from human embryos and to clone stem cell lines. They then made the stem cell lines available to other researchers, who could then obtain federal funding from the NIH.

In 2001, soon after President Bush took office, he issued an Executive Order substantially narrowing the availability of funds for ESC research. In particular, he ordered that federal funds could be used to fund ESC research only on the limited number of stem lines that had already been developed when he came into office and not on any newly created stem cell lines. By this time, there were only 18 stem cell lines available, and as a result, scientists could do only limited kinds of research on them. Consequently, most federal funding shifted back toward ASC research.

Many in the medical research community were angry about this change. At the same time, some conservative activists and religious leaders believed that President Bush's order did not go far enough, because it still allowed federal funding of some ESC research to continue despite the fact that these stem cell lines were the product of the destruction of a human embryo. Congress held many hearings and considered many bills on this issue. Twice during President Bush's terms in office, he was presented with congressional bills that would overturn his Executive Order and revert to the approach adopted by the Clinton administration. Both times, President Bush vetoed the bills. At no point was there a significant movement in Congress to overturn President Bush's Executive Order in a way that would prohibit all funding of ESC research.

Soon after President Obama took office, he rescinded President Bush's Executive Order. The agency re-adopted the Clinton-era regulation and policy. Specifically, federal funding could not be provided for any process that involved the actual destruction of human embryos or for research on ESCs directly obtained from human embryos, but funding would be made available for the stem cell lines created by cloning such ESCs.

As a result, privately funded scientists rushed to create hundreds of new lines of ESCs and to make these available to other researchers. These researchers obtained funding from the NIH, and, consequently, most funding for ASC research dried up.

The Administrative Regulation

The regulation provides, in relevant part, as follows:

(a)   NIH funding of the derivation of stem cells from human embryos is prohibited by the Human Embryonic Stem Cell Research Funding Act ("HESCRFA").

(b)   Although ESCs are derived from human embryos, such stem cells are not themselves human embryos. Consequently, stem cell lines developed from ESCs that were derived from human embryos in a process that resulted in the destruction a human embryo are eligible for funding, provided that:

1.   in keeping with the HESCRFA, the initial ESCs were derived and developed into stem cell lines by researchers not receiving federal funding; and

2.   [several other qualifications not relevant to the present lawsuit or your analysis are met].